Writing Memphis

Edited by
Katherine Fredlund

hayden-mcneil
Macmillan Learning

Macmillan Learning Curriculum Solutions
14903 Pilot Drive
Plymouth, MI 48170
www.macmillanlearning.com

Fredlund 2428-5 F20

Sustainability

Hayden-McNeil/Macmillan Learning Curriculum Solutions is proud to be a part of the larger sustainability initiative of Macmillan, our parent company. Macmillan has a goal to reduce its carbon emissions by 65% by 2020 from our 2010 baseline. Additionally, paper purchased must adhere to the Macmillan USA Paper Sourcing and Use Policy.

Hayden-McNeil partners with printers that use paper that is consistent with the environmental goals and values of Macmillan USA. This includes using paper certified by the Forest Stewardship Council (FSC), Sustainable Forestry Initiative (SFI), and/or the Programme for the Endorsement of Forest Certification (PEFC). We also offer paper with varying percentages of post-consumer waste as well as a 100% recycled stock. Additionally, Hayden-McNeil Custom Digital provides authors with the opportunity to convert print products to a digital format to use no paper at all. Visit http://sustainability.macmillan.com to learn more.

TABLE OF CONTENTS

ACKNOWLEDGEMENTS

This textbook would not be possible without the help and contributions of a number of current and former members of the Department of English at the University of Memphis. Thank you to Jessica Swan, Luke Brake, Rhonda Powers, Andrea Bishop, Vincent Kenny-Cincotta, Marisa Manuel, Kendra Vanderlip, Bess Myers, Shima Faresh, and Angela Morris for their help providing invaluable feedback and ideas for *Writing Memphis*. I also want to thank all of the instructors who responded to surveys about the previous editions and all the first-year writing students who participated in focus groups and provided feedback on the first and second edition.

A NOTE FOR INSTRUCTORS

English 1020 aims to reinforce and further develop the academic writing and reading practices—inquiry, critical analysis, synthesis, argumentation, research, and documentation—students encounter in English 1010. By the conclusion of the course, students should meet the following learning outcomes:

- Demonstrate **rhetorical knowledge** by writing effectively for different contexts, audiences, genres, and purposes.

- Illustrate an awareness of **composing processes**, particularly when it comes to invention, drafting, revision, and delivery.

- Demonstrate an ability to conduct **research-based inquiries** by posing research questions, conducting academic research, evaluating secondary sources, integrating sources to support claims, and citing sources appropriately.

- Indicate an ability to thoughtfully use **digital writing technologies** when appropriate to the rhetorical situation.

- Demonstrate **knowledge of conventions** by producing organized, stylistically appropriate, and carefully proofread writing.

The updates to the third edition of *Writing Memphis* respond to emerging research in the field of composition that argues for the importance of student exposure to cultural rhetorics and emphasizes a need for explicitly anti-racist writing pedagogy; instructor responses to a survey about the textbook; and the necessity of providing a digital textbook option for students. Since we live in the majority Black city of Memphis and this course asks students to write and research a topic related to or located within our city, this edition includes a new chapter on African American Rhetorical Traditions and also includes new readings that use these traditions. In an effort to further diversify the reading selection, this edition planned to include readings by immigrants written in multiple languages, but the publisher was unable to reach the author and receive permission to include these readings. Instead, a report on the economic impact of immigration in Memphis has been added, and instructors are encouraged to add supplemental readings written by L2 writers. Providing a digital option for students became a necessity as a consequence of the growth of UofM Global and the move to online teaching as a result of the 2020 pandemic. However, this option dramatically increased the permissions costs for many of the readings from the second edition, and as a result, some of those readings do not appear in this edition.

You should feel free to bring other readings, ideas, guest speakers, and topics from the Memphis community into your classroom and syllabus. I hope doing so will allow you to make the course your own. If you have materials or assignments that you think work particularly well, then please share them with Dr. Fredlund and Dr. Myers, and we will add them to the English 1020 ecourseware shell. This shell is within the English Department Resources page, and if you do not have access, then you should contact the front office to get access. If you have any questions about the textbook or the course more generally, please feel free to contact me via email or stop by my office.

PREFACE

Katherine Fredlund, PhD
Director of First-Year Writing
University of Memphis

As the city of #gritandgrind, Memphis is made beautiful by its resilience—by a history of invention, contradiction, and even tragedy. Like dry-rub ribs, the Bluff City seems to be something you either get or you don't. Some people think writing is the same way: that it is something you either get or you don't...that you can be born a good or a bad writer. While this idea that people are born with innate writing talent is quite common, the reality is that successful writers read a lot and work hard to improve their writing skills. Anyone can become an effective writer, but effective writing requires hard work. Effective writing requires *grit* and *grind*.

This textbook and course are designed to help students as they put in the hard work to become successful academic writers. As the editor of this textbook and director of the first-year writing program, I worked with instructors and graduate students to develop this textbook, which includes chapters about writing and researching written specifically for students enrolled in English 1020 as well as anthologized readings about Memphis. These readings were selected to help you develop research topics, move from the kind of writing you did in high school and English 1010 to the kind of writing you will do in English 1020, and think about the discourse conventions of different writing genres. Because writing research tells us that one or two classes can't teach you to write for every writing situation you will face in college and beyond, this course doesn't pretend there is a one size fits all approach to writing. Instead, this textbook and course were designed to help you continue to discover and develop your writing process, to increase your ability to discern and respond to rhetorical situations, and to learn revision strategies that will improve the products of your writing.

Writing Memphis also aims to help you understand how rhetoric works and how arguments are presented. While the media often refers to rhetoric negatively, the reality is that rhetoric is ubiquitous (always present) and necessary in any democratic society. Rhetoric is also inescapable. While it is most commonly thought of in the political sense, you encounter rhetoric everywhere you go (in advertisements, in the news, in everyday conversations, and even in television shows and movies). Ancient Greek philosopher Aristotle defined rhetoric as "the faculty of observing in any given case the available means of persuasion" (Book 1 Chapter 2). More recently, literary theorist and rhetorician Kenneth Burke defined rhetoric as "the use of words by human agents to form attitudes or induce actions in other human agents" (41). Put more simply, rhetoric has been historically understood as the art of persuasion, but as humans moved from oral to literate to digital cultures, rhetoric has been defined in a number of different ways. In the introduction to *The Rhetorical Tradition*, Patricia Bizzell and Bruce Herzberg offer a list of definitions rhetoric has accumulated:

- The practice of oratory
- The study of the strategies of effective oratory

- The use of language, written or spoken, to inform or persuade
- The study of the persuasive effects of language
- The study of the relation between language and knowledge
- The classification and use of tropes and figures
- The use of empty promises and half-truths as a form of propaganda (1)

Thus, while rhetoric has many definitions, most if not all of these definitions include language use and persuasion, and these are the definitions of rhetoric we will rely on in this course. Rhetorical situations require a writer or speaker to consider their audience, cultural moment, and even their own abilities in order to determine the best way to present an argument. When writers or speakers do this well, they are more likely to persuade their audience. Indeed, understanding how rhetoric works is essential to your ability to convey information via both the written and spoken word, especially if your goal is to persuade.

In order to help you develop your rhetorical skills, English 1020 starts with a rhetorical analysis assignment that asks you to consider and evaluate how someone else presented an argument. The remainder of the semester will be spent doing research in order to compose an academic argument. Because developing researched arguments takes time, multiple drafts, and a lot of academic research, you will produce three drafts of this argument: a first draft, a new media draft, and, finally, a revised draft. In order to help you focus your argument, your research will need to somehow connect to Memphis, but luckily, you can bring your interests to Memphis, whether you are from here or not. In fact, whether you are originally from Memphis or you just moved here a week ago, many students find that they enjoy the opportunity to learn more about Memphis.

The rest of this preface provides research from the field of Rhetoric and Writing Studies to help you understand why the course and textbook are designed as they are. It also concludes with an overview that should help you read the different sections in this book and get the most out of the readings. As the director of the program and editor of this textbook, I hope that knowing why you are being asked to do certain kinds of research or write certain kinds of texts will help you see the value in and get the most out of this course.

FROM WRITING ABOUT WRITING TO RHETORIC

If you took English 1010, then you spent time reading, learning, and writing about writing. You likely learned that writing is a process and that everyone's writing processes are different. You probably reflected on your own literacy acquisition and recognized how your hometown as well as your educational experiences, family, economic status, gender, and race impacted your feelings about reading and writing. Hopefully, you learned that a discourse community is a group of people who communicate via genres and have their own lexis (jargon specific to a community and required for communication within that community). You might have conducted primary research about how writing works, interviewed a professional writer about their practices, or revised a traditional assignment into something creative or digital. Additionally, you probably learned that successful writers spend a lot of time revising—often even more time than they spend drafting.

You might also remember that threshold concepts are ideas about writing that you need to grasp before you can really understand how writing is produced and how writing functions in the world. In *Naming What We Know*, writing scholars Linda Adler-Kassner and Elizabeth Wardle explain that threshold concepts

> are ideas, ways of seeing, ways of understanding that change a learner's stance. They help that learner see things differently and make connections across sites and ideas that previously might have seemed unconnected. In other words, learning threshold concepts doesn't just change *what* people know; they change *how* people know because they lead to different ways of approaching ideas by thinking through and with these concepts. (x)

For writing scholars, such concepts include "writing is a social and rhetorical activity"; "writing speaks to situations through recognizable forms"; "writing enacts and creates identities and ideologies"; "writing is (also always) a cognitive activity"; and "all writers have more to learn" (Adler-Kassner and Wardle 29–31).

Since this course moves from English 1010's writing about writing approach to a rhetorical approach, this textbook won't explicitly discuss these threshold concepts as frequently as your English 1010 textbook did. You should know, however, that this course and textbook were created with these threshold concepts in mind.

- **"Writing is a social and rhetorical activity."** This course asks you to consider audience when analyzing and then responding to rhetorical situations, and this textbook emphasizes that by incorporating sources into your arguments you are joining a scholarly conversation and a discourse community.

- **"Writing speaks to situations through recognizable forms."** This textbook encourages you to consider how different genres of writing serve different rhetorical purposes and have different rhetorical effects while the course emphasizes analysis so that you can recognize writing forms (genres) in the future.

- **"Writing enacts and creates identities and ideologies."** This course asks you to consciously consider how you craft your writerly voice, and the readings challenge you to think about how writing functions in the Memphis community. Your teacher might also ask you to write reflections throughout the semester that ask you to consider how other aspects of your life (a busy work schedule, making new friends in college, caring for kids while also taking courses, etc.) might impact your work in this course and vice versa.

- **"Writing is (also always) a cognitive activity."** This textbook includes "Questions for Discussion and Journaling" after the readings about Memphis in the four anthology sections and "Writing Prompts and Activities" after the chapters in the first section. These questions, prompts, and activities are not the dreaded and (understandably) hated busy work. Since writing is a mode of learning and actually allows you to think in ways that you otherwise might not, these prompts are included to help you write to learn as well as to process your thoughts about what you have just read.

- **"Writing is a process, and all writers have more to learn."** Finally, since you will likely learn as you write your researched argument (the focus of this course), time for revision is built into the course. You may end up with conclusions or ideas that your original introduction didn't expect, let alone introduce, and that will make revision all the more necessary.

While all of these threshold concepts are important, "all writers have more to learn" is the only one you have to really accept and understand from this moment forward. Since "all writers have more to learn," both the textbook and the course assume that you accept 1. that writing is something you can learn (not a talent you either are born with or lack forever) and 2. that you have something to learn about writing. Even if you always get good grades in writing classes, you can still learn more and improve your writing in this course. Despite my PhD in Rhetoric and Writing, my job as director of a writing program, and my published writing, I still want to be a better writer, and I am constantly working in order to get better. All I ask is that you, too, want to become a better writer and that you use this course as an opportunity to do just that. You may hate writing, you may love writing, or you may be indifferent to writing, but the reality is that writing will help you succeed in college and beyond, and you should take advantage of this opportunity to learn about and improve your writing.

While the writing about writing approach asked you to learn about how writing works and how writers write, a rhetorical approach encourages you to understand the social nature of writing and rhetoric and to consider how you can best persuade an audience. Now that you better understand writing theories and processes, this course will ask you to take what you know about writing and put it into practice in an academic setting. Rather than read about theories of writing, you will practice the theories of writing you learned in English 1010 while doing research on a topic of your choice. Now that you know about discourse communities, writing processes, and more, this course asks you to use that knowledge in order to intentionally develop and improve your own writing practices.

You should keep in mind, however, that your work will not be done when you complete this course. Each time you are asked to compose, you will have to do the hard work that writing requires—evaluating the genre, audience, and goals for that piece of writing (particularly if you are writing within an unfamiliar discourse community and genre). Every time you sit down to write, you should ask yourself about your audience's expectations, about the genre and disciplinary requirements for writing, and about your goals for that specific piece of writing. More simply put, whenever you start the writing process, you should consider the rhetorical situation, and this class aims to give you the tools to evaluate each rhetorical situation you encounter. So while this course may not be able to prepare you to write for each and every class you take or for every job you have in the future (because that is impossible), we can prepare you to evaluate rhetorical situations and help you practice responding to those situations.

English 1020 also emphasizes revision. Writing researchers have found that revision practices are one of the major differences between novice writers and expert writers (Sommers 51–2). Novice writers often compose a single draft, spend a little time editing and proofreading, and then consider the writing done. Expert writers, on the other hand, understand revision as an essential part of the writing process. Sometimes they even discard most of their first draft because they recognize that writing is a mode of learning, and as such, drafts are often messy because we process our thoughts as we write (Emig 7). Consider the following quotes about revision from famous authors:

> "Almost all good writing begins with terrible first efforts. You need to start somewhere. Start by getting something—anything—down on paper. A friend of mine says that the first draft is the down draft—you just get it down. The second draft is the up draft—you fix it up. You try to say what you have to say more accurately. And the third draft is the dental draft, where you check every tooth, to see if it's loose or cramped or decayed, or even, God help us, healthy." — Anne Lamott

> "I have rewritten—often several times—every word I have ever published. My pencils outlast their erasers." — Vladimir Nabokov

> "I don't write easily or rapidly. My first draft usually has only a few elements worth keeping. I have to find what those are and build from them and throw out what doesn't work, or what simply is not alive." — Susan Sontag

> "Put down everything that comes into your head and then you're a writer. But an author is one who can judge his own stuff's worth, without pity, and destroy most of it." — Sidonie Gabrielle Colette

> "By the time I am nearing the end of a story, the first part will have been reread and altered and corrected at least one hundred and fifty times. I am suspicious of both facility and speed. Good writing is essentially rewriting. I am positive of this." — Roald Dahl

> "The best advice I can give on this is, once it's done, to put it away until you can read it with new eyes. Finish the short story, print it out, then put it in a drawer and write other things. When you're ready, pick it up and read it, as if you've never read it before. If there are things you aren't satisfied with as a reader, go in and fix them as a writer: that's revision." — Neil Gaiman

As evidenced by these quotes, these authors think of revision as an essential aspect of good writing and as a necessary part of their writing process. While their revision processes are likely very different from one another, they all recognize that their writing would not be as successful if they did not spend a great deal of time drafting and revising.

One of the goals of this course is to get you to think of revision that way, too. Consequently, time for revision is built into the semester. You will compose a draft of your research paper before switching genres and taking that argument online. Revising your argument from a text-based paper to a digital genre such as an infographic, animation, or YouTube video will help you think about how to recognize and respond to the demands of the rhetorical situation, as your audience for the academic research paper will likely be very different from your audience for a digital version of the same argument. Recognizing the changing nature of writing in the twenty-first century, this digital project will also help prepare you to write in a digital world. Since you will encounter new writing technologies throughout your life, this digital project gives you an opportunity to learn about digital composing tools, design, and multimodality, recognizing that you will have to keep learning how to use new writing technologies long after you leave this course. After you complete your digital project, you will return to academic writing and revise your draft of the researched argument. The space between your first draft and your revision (along with the formative feedback you receive from your instructor and peers) will allow you to look at your own writing with a more critical eye and increase the likelihood of substantial (and successful) revision.

Rhetoric really is all around you. Whether you recognize it or not, people, companies, and religious and political groups are constantly trying to convince you to do something, to buy something, or to believe something. This textbook aims to help you understand how rhetoric works with a focus on Memphis so that you can not only successfully navigate the rhetorical situation in your own writing but also recognize when an argument is using facts or research selectively or dishonestly. Your ability to analyze arguments and respond to them thoughtfully will impact your ability to succeed in your college courses and to respond to rhetoric effectively in your daily life. Rhetoric is everywhere, and if you want to be able to use it for your own purposes, then you need to understand how it works.

WHY WRITE ABOUT MEMPHIS?

This textbook considers Memphis as a subject of study and a place where writing is an essential part of community and society. The anthologized readings in this book will show you how people write about Memphis and how writing functions to change the Memphis community. Writing scholar Nedra Reynolds explains that the where of writing is not only about "the places where writing occurs, but the sense of place and space that readers and writers bring with them to [the] intellectual work of writing, to navigating, arranging, remembering, and composing. Writing can be studied or understood only in cultural context—and only through the thin smudged layers of a palimpsest, without the sharp focus of a digital camera" (176).[1] As students at the University of Memphis, you reside in a city with a unique and complicated history, an exciting yet problematic present, and a promising yet unwritten future. The city of Memphis, consequently, provides a variety of avenues for academic research and writing. Writing about the place where you live and study will allow you to immerse yourself in your writing and in Memphis culture while also allowing for primary research (such as interviews and trips to the archives) that would not be possible with a broader course focus. Whether you grew up in or near Memphis or not, focusing your research project within Memphis will help you think about research and writing differently and may even let you discover new things about the city that your university calls home.

While you will be reading about Memphis, it is important to remember that the subject of this course is still writing and rhetoric. The readings about Memphis should help you consider how argument works in different genres and responds to different rhetorical

---

1 A palimpsest is "the imprint of marks on a tablet, overwritten by other marks" (Reynolds 139). Thinking of writing as a palimpsest allows us to recognize that all writing relies on the writing that came before it.

situations. They should also help you think about different possibilities for your own research. Students in first-year writing classes often want to tackle the big topics (abortion, the death penalty, gun control, etc.), but these topics cannot be sufficiently introduced in an 8–10 page paper, let alone fully fleshed out and developed. Such topics are too broad (and in some ways too tired) for a research paper that has to be completed in a semester or less. Focusing on Memphis will help you narrow your topic. This focus doesn't mean you can't pursue your interests or use sources that don't mention or focus on Memphis. It just means that you will need to locate those interests in Memphis. The "Choosing a Topic" chapter of this textbook discusses how you can locate your own interests in Memphis in further detail. Since Memphis is a city with all the benefits and problems that come with a metropolitan area, there are endless topics to pursue, and you can write about just about anything. You can focus on music, education, food, business, economics, religion, politics, tourism, social justice, sports, health, the environment, medicine, and much, much more. The focus on Memphis will ultimately help you choose a topic that can be sufficiently researched and understood in a single semester, and this narrow focus will help you focus your argument and produce better writing.

HOW TO READ THIS BOOK

The first section of this book was written to help you learn about rhetoric, academic research, and writing processes. Instructors and graduate students who have taught English 1020 at the University of Memphis wrote these chapters specifically for UofM students. Since these chapters were written for students enrolled in this course, they all focus on writing and researching about Memphis in the context of English 1020. They will help you understand what rhetoric is and does, think about how rhetoric changes when it shifts from a Word document to a video or infographic, and develop your writing process. The section begins with an introduction to argument and rhetoric and continues with a chapter about African American rhetorical strategies before turning to a chapter on rhetorical analysis. The next two chapters will help you choose a topic and conduct academic research. Then, there is a chapter to help you think about how to craft your own voice and avoid plagiarism followed by a chapter that will help you do academic research about Memphis. The following chapter will help you and your classmates collaborate, a skill that will be particularly helpful as you navigate the group presentation. The next two chapters will help you think about your writing process, particularly when it comes to revision and self-critique, and the final two chapters consider composing in digital spaces. The last two chapters in this section follow two students as they progress through the course. These chapters include reflections, rhetorical analyses, research paper drafts, and research paper revisions as well as a brief narrative that explains how each student successfully moved from one assignment to the next. These should not be read as perfect examples but rather as model papers that do a lot well and yet still reflect student writing.

The next four sections of this book anthologize texts about Memphis. In these sections, each text is accompanied by a brief introduction to the text and author and followed by "Questions for Discussion and Journaling." These introductions provide necessary background information (when and where the text was published, who the author is, etc.) and draw attention to the author's use of rhetorical strategies. These text introductions are not exhaustive, however, so as you read, you should think about how rhetorical appeals and strategies are being used throughout the reading. In class, you should spend time not only discussing the content of the readings but also considering how the author has crafted an argument. As you read each selection, remember that while the content is important, it is more important (for the purposes of this course) to consider how that content is presented in order to persuade an audience. In fact, each time you read you should ask yourself, "What is this author's purpose?" If you think the author's purpose is simply to educate you or explain something, then ask yourself why they want you to be educated about that subject.[2] Often, argument is hidden under explanation or analysis, and asking yourself what the author's purpose is can help you understand the underlying argument (if there is one). The questions that follow each reading will help you process and think about what you have read. These questions may be assigned as homework or incorporated into class activities. Even if your instructor does not assign these questions and activities, they should guide your reading of the text.

The Memphis readings are separated by genre, beginning with "Narratives and Testimonies." We begin here because rhetoric is complicated, and it is helpful to look at the rhetoric contained in these shorter pieces of writing first. These selections may also inspire (or persuade) you to see Memphis in a new light. While the argument in these selections is sometimes implicit (not stated outright), the authors are still trying to convince you of something. Remember, when we talk about an argument within a piece of writing, we aren't referring to an angry and combative person yelling about their ideas. Instead, we are referring to rhetoric—an attempt to persuade. As you read these selections, ask yourself what the author might be trying to convince you of, even if they don't come out and say it explicitly. Such arguments are especially important to recognize and understand, as even if we don't recognize something as an argument, it can still persuade or even change us.

The next section, "Writing about Culture," includes interviews, biographies, and newspaper columns. These readings range in focus, discussing everything from music, to activism, to criminal justice reform, to tourism. In many of these readings, the arguments are still implicit, but they are more actively attempting to persuade you than the readings in the first section. For instance, in "The Resistance: Memphis Activism Sprouts Everywhere" members of the Flyer Staff summarize and describe a number of different activist organizations in Memphis. While this may not seem argumentative, they end with a quote that says "it's never too late for someone to get involved." With this concluding quote, they are trying to convince readers to get involved with the organizations they described. In contrast, some of the rhetoric in this section is explicit. For example, the reading about "Calvin Newborn" explicitly argues that Calvin is "one of the greatest unsung heroes of blues and jazz."

---

2   In January of 2016, the American Dialect Society voted to make the singular they (a gender-neutral pronoun that recognizes genders beyond the male / female binary) the 2015 word of the year. The singular they is used in this sentence (and elsewhere in this textbook). Traditional grammar rules would mark this as incorrect, but changing conceptions of gender have forced grammar to change with it and now the singular they is acceptable to some (though some of your teachers may still mark this as incorrect).

Like the previous section, the third section, "Investigative Journalism," includes readings published by newspapers or non-profit institutions, but the readings in this section rely more heavily on statistics, investigation, and research. In these readings, you should pay attention to how the authors use sources to support their arguments. The first reading, Selections from *Southern Horrors* by Ida B. Wells, presents an explicit argument (and one that challenged how the North and South understood lynch law at the end of the nineteenth century). The rest of the readings were written more recently and use a variety of research to present arguments about the past, present, and future.

The final section of Memphis readings, "Academic Writing," includes texts written for an academic audience. These selections should help you consider how research is used in different academic disciplines, how tone and style depend on the discipline and genre of writing, and how academic writing differs from the other kinds of writing you read daily and have read in this class. Because each academic discipline has different genre conventions and expectations, it is impossible for a class or textbook to consider all the potential rhetorical situations you will encounter in your college career. However, reading and analyzing the texts in this section can help you develop tools to approach unfamiliar academic genres in the future.

UNDERSTANDING ACADEMIC WRITING AND RESEARCH

Unfortunately, the term academic writing is misleading, as it implies that "academic writing" is one genre of writing with set conventions. The reality is that academic writing is generally serious and objective in tone and almost always relies on research, but beyond that, academic writing varies by discipline, style guide, publication venue, and even goal. As you can imagine, the writing done by biologists differs a great deal from the writing done by philosophers in intent, presentation, and tone. The rhetorical approach in this course will help you learn how to evaluate rhetorical situations and react to those situations within your writing, and this will benefit your writing no matter what courses you take later in your college career.

This class and textbook also ask you to learn how to conduct academic research. While academic writing and research differs by field, academic research is required in the humanities, the social and natural sciences, the medical fields, and all academic disciplines. Thus, when you choose your research topic for this course, it will benefit you in the long-term if you choose something related to your major. This will allow you to read sources from your field of study and begin to use the conventions of your discipline in your writing. If you choose not to focus your project within your major, then just keep in mind that when you do begin to write for your major you will need to evaluate the rhetorical situation and adjust your writing in response to that situation and discourse community.

Shifting from writing narratives and reports (like many of you did in English 1010) to writing an academic research paper is not going to be easy. This textbook was designed to make that transition easier by beginning with readings in genres that you are more familiar with and ending with academic texts from a variety of fields that should help you understand how writing is molded by the rhetorical situation. Writing scholar David Bartholomae explains:

> Every time a student sits down to write for us, he has to invent the university for the occasion—invent the university, that is, or a branch of it, like history or anthropology or economics or English. The student has to learn to speak our language, to speak as we do, to try on the peculiar ways of knowing, selecting, evaluating, reporting, concluding, and arguing that define the discourse of our community. (623)

In the same article, Bartholomae argues that a student's writing success depends on the student's ability to imagine the audience and pretend to be a part of a discourse community the student doesn't yet belong to. Essentially (and perhaps unfortunately), student success in academic writing courses depends on the student's ability to imitate academic discourse (632). In order to imitate, however, you have to analyze, and so that is where this course begins.

Bartholomae ends his article with the claim that, "It may very well be that some students will need to learn to crudely mimic the 'distinctive register' of academic discourse before they are prepared to actually and legitimately do the work of the discourse, and before they are sophisticated enough with refinements of tone and gesture to do it with grace or elegance. To say this, however, is to say that our students must be students" (650). Ultimately, this means that transitioning from your previous writing experiences to the writing expected of you in college is going to be messy, frustrating, and even ugly. Your prose might be confusing and your organization may struggle to present your argument cohesively. Yet this also means that such hurdles shouldn't feel insurmountable because most students struggle with this transition. You should expect to encounter hurdles in this course and still feel proud of your writing, even if it isn't perfect. Perfection isn't the goal of this course (or of writing in general). The goal is for you become a better communicator with the ability to analyze and imitate unfamiliar genres of writing, a stronger reviser with the capacity for self-critique, a thoughtful researcher who can discern the difference between reliable and unreliable texts, a self-reflective writer who is aware of the writing process that works best for you, and a savvy rhetor with the ability to analyze and respond to a variety of rhetorical situations. As the length of this list implies, this is going to take some of that Memphis grit and grind our city is known for, and we can't think of anyone more prepared for this challenge than Memphians, new and old.[3] Go Tigers!

---

3   In his picture anthology of famous Memphians, editor Richard Murff defines a Memphian as "someone who was born in the city, went to school here, has made the city home, or spent a significant portion of their life here" (5). Thus, even those of you who have recently moved to Memphis in order to attend UofM are considered Memphians.

WORKS CITED

Adler-Kassner, Linda and Elizabeth Wardle, editors. *Naming What We Know: Threshold Concepts of Writing Studies Classroom Edition*. Utah State UP, 2016.

Aristotle. "Rhetoric." Translated by W. Rhys Roberts, *The Complete Works of Aristotle Vol. II*, Edited by Jonathan Barnes, Princeton UP, 1984.

Bartholomae, David. "Inventing the University." *Cross-Talk in Comp Theory: A Reader*, 2nd ed., edited by Victor Villanueva, National Council of Teachers of English, 2003, 623–654.

Bizzell, Patricia and Bruce Herzberg. *The Rhetorical Tradition: Readings from Classical Times to the Present*, 2nd ed. Boston: Bedford/St. Martins, 2000.

Burke, Kenneth. *A Rhetoric of Motives*. U of California P, 1969.

Emig, Janet. "Writing as a Mode of Learning." *Cross-Talk in Comp Theory: A Reader*, 2nd ed., edited by Victor Villanueva, National Council of Teachers of English, 2003, 7–15.

Murff, Richard. *Memphians*. Nautilus P, 2011.

Sommers, Nancy. "Revision Strategies of Student Writers and Experienced Adult Writers." *Cross-Talk in Comp Theory: A Reader*, 2nd ed., edited by Victor Villanueva, National Council of Teachers of English, 2003, 43–54.

WRITING ABOUT MEMPHIS

WHAT IS ARGUMENT?

Gilbert Verbist

Gilbert Verbist has an MA in English Literature from the University of Georgia and is working toward a PhD in Composition Studies here at the University of Memphis. He has been teaching first-year writing at UofM since 2012, and he has loved every minute of it. He has also been a tutor at the University's Center for Writing and Communication and, while his schedule no longer allows him to work there, one-on-one revision sessions with students remain a highlight of his job. Gilbert's favorite things about Memphis are dry-rub ribs from the Bar-B-Q Shop, walking his dog in Overton Park, and Muddy's Grindhouse iced coffees.

When you hear the word "argument," what comes to mind? You most likely imagine a shouting match. You might think of raised voices, angry gestures, or maybe even a few insults flying back and forth. It's perfectly reasonable if that is what pops into your head because that's how we tend to use the word "argument" in our day-to-day lives: as a term for a heated or emotional disagreement. At the University of Memphis (and at other institutes of higher education), however, that word means something different. In college, we use **argument** to denote any type of communication—spoken, written, visual, or otherwise—that is meant to convince or persuade an audience. There are many different types of arguments, and they serve many different purposes. Some arguments are meant to talk you into believing something (such as, "Memphis's infrastructure is outdated and in need of serious renewal efforts.") Some arguments are meant to elicit an emotional response from you (such as, "It's just *ridiculous* that we have so many potholes on Poplar!") Some arguments are meant to prod you into taking a particular course of action (such as, "Vote Jane Doe for Memphis mayor—she'll bring our roads into the 21st century!") But all arguments are meant to persuade—to win people over through discourse.

When you think about argument in these terms, you can see how common, even ubiquitous, arguments are. Human beings are social creatures, and we navigate a lot of the complexities of our shared lives together by talking through our wants, needs, expectations, frustrations, and disagreements. (Some of us, admittedly, do this more calmly and effectively than others!) All around us—whether on podcasts, television screens, social media platforms, or in newspapers, classrooms, and conversations with friends—we encounter attempts to change our minds, to solicit agreement, to make us feel certain ways.

Arguments in our personal lives can be trivial, like if you and your parents disagree on what you should order from Garibaldi's, or they can be serious, like if you and your parents disagree on what your major should be. Arguments in our public lives run the same spectrum—from debates about where Memphis should install speedbumps to debates about whether Memphis is failing to provide a quality public education for children. You can see arguments no matter what scale of society you're looking at, too. They range from local controversies over parking (see the insert below) to giant, nationwide disputes about civil rights, immigration, abortion, foreign policy, global warming, terrorism, state surveillance, and the like.

Once you start to look for it, you'll notice argument is an integral and unavoidable part of our lives.

The Greensward Controversy

Memphis provides us with plenty of examples of the type of arguments that are carried out in our public lives. One that stands out in the past few years is the controversy over the greensward at Overton Park. The controversy began in the winter of 2016 when the Memphis Zoo removed some trees from public property in order to expand zoo parking. Shortly thereafter, they announced that they would be paving a portion of Overton Park's greensward (a large grassy field that Memphians often use for walking dogs, playing frisbee, picnicking, and similar activities) in order to accommodate the increased number of visitors that they expected their new hippo exhibit to attract to the zoo.

The reaction to the zoo's announcement from the Memphis community was immediate and vociferous (not to mention unexpected). The citizens of Memphis, especially residents of Midtown, entered into a lively—even angry at times—public debate over the move. On the one side was the Memphis Zoo and its supporters who saw the move as necessary for accommodating the growth of the zoo. They argued that the zoo was a major attraction for Memphis. They explained the zoo provides jobs, tourism dollars, and tax revenue for the city. Thus, in their minds, the expanded parking would benefit the entire city. The Overton Park Conservancy and its supporters, on the other side, strenuously objected to what they saw as an unethical and unilateral annexation of public space. They pointed out how valuable the greensward was to Memphians—especially to less privileged Memphians who, without a resource like the greensward, might struggle to find a safe place to have a picnic or let their children play outside. They also presented solutions to the zoo's parking problems that didn't include expanding their parking lots into Overton's fields.

The ensuing argument went on for months and took many different forms. Citizens of Memphis distributed petitions, launched protests, called their local politicians, and contracted lawyers to make their opinions on the matter heard. The debate raged in the pages of periodicals like *The Commercial Appeal* and *The Memphis Flyer*. Memphians exchanged their opinions in person, on social media, in public zoning meetings, and elsewhere. All over the city, yard signs and banners featuring the slogan "Save The Greensward" popped up. Homeowners in the neighborhood adjacent to the zoo even organized a campaign to direct overflow parking from the zoo onto the streets in front of their homes. The greensward controversy had ballooned into a huge civic debate, involving thousands of Memphis residents and showcasing dozens of different strategies of persuasion on both sides.

Currently, the Overton Park Conservancy and its supporters seem to have won the debate, having successfully swung public opinion against the zoo's proposal. But only time will tell whether supporters of the annexation can manage to reverse Memphis's collective attitude on the matter. Controversies like the so-called "Battle of the Greensward" illustrate the role that argument has in our public lives and the real effects that our communities experience based on the outcomes of our arguments. Because the Overton Park Conservancy and its allies were so successful in putting forth their argument (that the park space of the greensward should remain available for all Memphians), the field remains open for anyone to use and enjoy. Had the Memphis Zoo and its allies been successful in putting forth *their* argument (that the growth of their institution was a more important public good), then it would be easier to find a parking spot at the zoo but Overton Park would be a little smaller and more cramped. The conflict between these two groups was waged entirely in the realm of discourse—signs, speeches, phone calls, letters—but it had an observable impact on our shared lives as citizens of Memphis.

Think about other public debates going on in Memphis, such as whether the city is taking the right steps to address violent crime or whether the Tennessee Valley Authority should be allowed to drill wells into the sand aquifer from which MLGW provides Memphians with their drinking water. The stakes of these arguments involve very different sets of concerns than the potential misappropriation of park property, but their outcomes will also have serious ramifications for the lives of people in our city, as well as the *quality* of those lives. Those outcomes will, to a large extent, also be determined by which side can produce the most effective and influential arguments.

RHETORIC

Certain aspects of the world are so important to our lives that, since ancient times, countless men and women have dedicated their lives to studying them and contributing to bodies of knowledge about them. Natural phenomena (like weather and the laws of physics) play such determinative roles in our day to day existence that humankind has developed entire fields of science to better understand them. The same could be said for illnesses, disease, and injury. They touch everyone at some point in our lives, and so the discipline of medicine was created and improved upon century after century in order to try to prevent, or at least limit, the sometimes-terrible effects they have on us. Agriculture was developed because everyone needs food to eat. Architecture and engineering were developed because everyone needs safe and comfortable places to live. In each of these instances, we can see that people are determined to understand and control, as much as they can, the aspects of their lives that affect them the most.

It shouldn't surprise you, then, that something as central to the human experience as argument also has an entire field of study dedicated to it. Nor should it surprise you that this study goes back thousands of years. This field of study is known as **rhetoric**. It is the study of writing and speaking as a means of persuasion: the study of argument and discourse.[1] Different cultures throughout history have developed their own approaches to rhetoric, but in the English-speaking world at least, the origins of many of our ideas about rhetoric can be traced back to the Classical World, to the civilizations of Rome and Greece. They can be traced back to Greek thinkers like Plato, Isocrates, and Aristotle and Romans like Cicero and Quintilian.

The concepts and terminology that we have inherited from the Classical world (and from countless other thinkers in the intervening two millennia) are not the *only* way to think about argument and persuasion, but they have endured in part because they are *very useful and insightful* ways to think about argument and persuasion.

With that in mind, we'll turn our attention to learning some of these concepts and terms, hopefully laying a solid foundation for the many readings on and discussions about argument that your semester in English 1020 will involve.

THE RHETORICAL TRIANGLE

Rhetoric, as we just mentioned, includes the study of writing and speaking persuasively. In the literature on rhetoric, the term for the individual *doing* the persuasion is **rhetor**. One reason why rhetor is a useful word is that—unlike the term "speaker" or "writer"—it doesn't specify the particular medium that the rhetor is using to get his or her message out, which is good because persuasion comes in many different forms. Our head football coach trying to rally the Tigers with a rousing halftime speech is a rhetor. A mathematics professor submitting a *Daily Helmsman* column on how to raise graduation rates is a rhetor. An art major pinning consciousness-raising photographs to a bulletin board in the UC is a rhetor. They all qualify as rhetors because they're all attempting to persuade an audience, even if their methods of persuasion differ dramatically.

That brings us to our second important term from rhetorical theory: **audience**. If a rhetor is the one doing the persuading, then the audience is the person or group of people the rhetor hopes to persuade. Normally, we think of an audience as a crowd of people sitting in an auditorium and watching a play or maybe a movie. But that's not the only type of audience. Audiences, like persuasion, come in many forms. If you're writing a letter or an e-mail, then your audience is the people you send it to. If you're posting on social media, then your audience is your followers. If you're installing a PSA on a billboard, then your audience is

---

1   It is important to note here that the study of rhetoric is larger than just the study of persuasion. As Patricia Bizzell and Bruce Herzberg argue in their introduction to *The Rhetorical Tradition*, "Rhetoric has a number of overlapping meanings: the practice of oratory; the study of the strategies of effective oratory; the use of language, written or spoken, to inform or persuade; the study of the persuasive effects of language; the study of the relation between language and knowledge; [and] the classification and use of tropes and figures" (1). Since ENGL 1020 revolves around argument, however, we will be paying especial attention to the persuasive aspects of rhetoric.

anyone who happens to see it as they drive or walk past. Audiences can be in close proximity to the rhetor or they can—especially in this digital, internet age—be wildly distant. They can even be separated by time, as is the case with a lot of written and visual arguments that continue to attract attention long after the rhetor publishes them.

However the audience is comprised, a rhetor *has* to have one. There are certain types of communication that are not intended to be heard by others—diaries, self-pep talks, prayers, etc.—but an argument is always intended for an audience. An argument without an audience is like a phone call to no one—it's hard to imagine!

So now we have a term for any person making an argument: rhetor. And we have a term for any person or group of people that the argument is intended to persuade: audience. There's one more term that traditional rhetorical theory suggests we associate with these two terms: **subject**. Subject is simple enough to define. The subject of an argument is the topic that the rhetor is communicating with his or her audience about. As we mentioned in the opening section of this book, humans are social creatures and we get into arguments about all sorts of things. We argue about bike lanes and seatbelt laws, diet and nutrition, truth, justice, quantum mechanics, our favorites sports teams and TV shows, climate change, foreign military interventions, minimum wage laws, and even who makes the best BBQ in Memphis. These topics (and more) are the *subjects* of our arguments. They are what the rhetor is attempting to change the mind of the audience about.

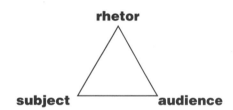

Figure 1-1. Rhetorical Triangle

With these three terms in mind, we can construct a model for argument and persuasion known as the **rhetorical triangle** (see FIGURE 1-1). On one vertex of the triangle, we have the rhetor. On another, we have the audience. And on the last, we have the subject. The rhetorical triangle is another tool for thinking about communication that has survived for a very long time because of its usefulness. The three vertices of the triangle remind us that the three elements of persuasion: rhetor, audience, and subject interact with each other during the course of an argument and thus have to be considered as three parts of a greater whole. They remind us that effective arguments are ones in which these three elements are in harmony with one another, that persuasion is neither one-size-fits-all nor a simple linear process, and that it must be understood as an exchange with many moving parts and changing variables.

The rhetor, for instance, must consider his or her purpose in putting forth an argument, as well as whether he or she will be taken as a credible authority on the subject. The rhetor must also consider the makeup of their audience in order to make educated guesses about what kinds of arguments will be most persuasive for that audience. A rhetor might ask: what is the level of my intended audience's education? What is their cultural background? Average age? What is their pre-existing attitude towards me and my subject? Questions like these have to be considered if the rhetor hopes to connect with the people they are addressing. Lastly, the subject itself has to be examined. Is it a highly technical, specialized subject (like biomedical engineering), or is it something that pretty much everyone is already familiar with (like school zones)? Is it a relatively new controversy (like gene editing) or one that has been a bone of contention for decades (like abortion)? Is it a polarizing topic that is likely to evoke strong emotions or a relatively mundane matter? A smart rhetor will mull over questions like these and tailor their approach accordingly.

In other words, the rhetorical triangle helps us visualize and understand how many different factors must be taken into account when planning an argument (or analyzing someone else's). It helps to understand that it's not possible to learn "the best way" to write or speak persuasively and then apply that to every rhetorical situation. Instead, we must approach each argument with a keen awareness of how the interplay of rhetor, audience, and subject determine what sort of communication will be appropriate and effective in that particular moment.

RHETORICAL APPEALS

The rhetorical triangle also helps us explore the **rhetorical appeals**. Appeals can be thought of as the individual components that, when added together, make up an argument. If you think of an argument as a drive in football, where the overall goal is to reach the end zone, then appeals are the plays that the team runs to get there. Or, to use another analogy, if you think of an argument as a haunted house, where the overall goal is to spook visitors, then appeals are the individual shocks and scares that the rooms foist on the people walking through them.

For example, let's say that I am your (responsible, wise, and caring) roommate, and I am trying to convince you to study for a test tomorrow rather than binge watch Netflix all night. My overall *argument* is that you'll be better off if you study, but I might make any number of *appeals* in order to convince you that I'm right. I might tell you that you'll sleep more soundly tonight and be less stressed in the morning if you hit the books. I might point out that you can watch Netflix any time but that tomorrow's chemistry exam will only happen once. I might insist that there's nothing good to watch on Netflix anyway—it's all boring! All of these statements are appeals. They're the individual strategies that I deploy to try to bring you around to my way of thinking.

If we take a closer look at appeals, we see that we can place them in three main categories and that each of these categories corresponds to a different vertex of the rhetorical triangle. **Logical appeals** correspond to the subject vertex of the triangle; **pathetic appeals** correspond to the audience vertex; and **ethical appeals** correspond to the rhetor vertex.[2]

---

2   Vocabulary note: don't let the usual definitions of "pathetic" or "ethical" confuse you. Just like how we're using the word "argument" in a different way than you're used to hearing, we're using the terms pathetic and ethical in a different way as well. Pay close attention so you can see what those two terms mean in the context of this class!

LOGICAL APPEALS

A logical appeal is, obviously enough, an appeal to logic. It is an attempt to communicate with the audience in a rational and reasonable way. Logical appeals correspond to the subject vertex because they concern the topic at hand and the "facts of the matter." If you try to convince your uncle to stop smoking by showing him medical literature about how it causes lung cancer, then that's a logical appeal. If you defend Tennessee's mandatory seatbelt laws by citing the statistics that they led to a sharp reduction in traffic fatalities, then that's a logical appeal as well. Whenever you appeal to data, facts, historical analogies, empirical observations, and/or other such objective points of reference, you're relying on logic. When you are constructing an academic research paper, your essay should rely primarily on these kinds of appeals.

> ### Additional examples of logical appeals:
>
> If you're feeling down, then you should exercise! When we exercise, our brains release endorphins, which make us feel happier and more optimistic.
>
> Economic data suggests that legalizing marijuana has improved Colorado's economy. Maybe we should consider that in Tennessee?
>
> The lessons of the British Empire are clear: if an empire stretches itself too far it will inevitably collapse.
>
> The dangers of caffeine are overstated. Statistics show that there is no correlation between regular coffee intake and increased mortality and that, if anything, caffeine actually promotes more positive health outcomes.

PATHETIC APPEALS

The Greek word for emotion is "pathos," which is the root of the English word "pathetic." Pathetic appeals, then, are appeals that target the emotions of the audience. Unlike the logical appeal, a pathetic appeal does not *have* to involve facts or reasoning at all. It doesn't have to be rational. It's simply an attempt to make the audience *feel* a certain way. Commercials for the Humane Society often rely on pathetic appeals, featuring sad but adorable looking puppies in the hopes that you will feel pity and donate to society. Billboards around Memphis that read "Drive Sober or Get Pulled Over" constitute pathetic appeals, intended to make people fearful enough about getting a DUI that they arrange for a designated driver or call an Uber. It's not necessarily true that you *will* be pulled over if you drive drunk, but a pathetic appeal doesn't have to be one-hundred-percent true to work.[3] All it has to do is elicit the right mix of emotions to make the intended audience act in the manner the rhetor wants them to. That is the essence of the pathetic appeal.

---

3   Because pathetic appeals do not necessarily have to be true, you'll want to avoid relying on these when you're writing your research paper for this class.

Additional examples of pathetic appeals:

You're quitting? What kind of person walks away from a job just because of a little overtime?

The University of Memphis community has given so much to us. It's time that we give it a little something in return.

It seems like every day I hear about someone getting victimized downtown. We shouldn't go out there tonight!

If we don't take this little stray kitten in, who else will? We can't just leave her out here!

ETHICAL APPEALS

Last but not least, we have the ethical appeal. Sometimes ethical appeals can be a little confusing to students, but it helps to remember that ethical appeals are associated with the rhetor vertex of the rhetorical triangle. When using an ethical appeal, therefore, the rhetor is attempting to convince the audience that they are credible, trustworthy, and qualified to talk about the subject at hand. It is sometimes referred to as an "appeal to authority" because the rhetor, in making an ethical appeal, is declaring that they are an *authority* on the matter. When your dentist tells you that you need to start flossing, she is making an ethical appeal, and you're likely to trust her based on her educational and work experience. When your friend tells you to take a certain professor for English 2201 because he enjoyed taking the class with that professor, that's also an ethical appeal: he's saying that his past experience makes him competent to judge whether you'll also enjoy the class.

There are more subtle versions of the ethical appeals, too. If you're writing a letter to the mayor, for instance, taking pains to make sure all of your grammar, spelling, and punctuation is correct is a type of ethical appeal. You're ensuring that you come across as an educated, thoughtful person—someone who should be taken seriously. Orators who can project a sense of calm and confidence through their tone are also making an ethical appeal, implicitly suggesting to their audience that they know what they're doing and what they're talking about. The fundamental goal of the ethical appeal is to raise the rhetor's stature in the eyes of the audience, and there are many different ways to accomplish that.

Additional examples of ethical appeals:

I have taught at this university since 2003, and I can tell you that once a student misses more than three or four classes in a row, they hardly ever come back.

I have a degree in art history. Trust me when I say that's a famous Rembrandt painting.

Have I ever, in the ten years that you've known me, lied to you before? I'm telling you, I left the keys right there!

As your dentist, I recommend that you invest in an electronic toothbrush. The results are well worth the money!

GENRES OF ARGUMENT

1

If you think back to your English 1010 class, you'll remember that your *Writing About Writing* textbook spent a lot of time exploring the concept of **genre**. It was one of the "threshold concepts" of writing that the textbook authors Elizabeth Wardle and Doug Downs discussed in their introductory chapter. One of the key insights they emphasized was that certain types of writing "recur, happening over and over again because they facilitate certain functions in life" (17). These recurring types of writing are called genres, and they evolve over time because they are sensible ways to respond to situations that people frequently encounter.

Let's look at an example: the "thank you" note is a textual genre. People often find themselves on the receiving end of kindnesses from family and friends, whether it's in the form of a birthday present or a Christmas gift or just some help moving into a dorm room. The idea of a thank you note has emerged, therefore, as a standard response to this situation, allowing us to acknowledge the thoughtfulness of our loved ones. Cover letters and resumes are another textual genre, one that evolved out of, on the one hand, businesses needing to quickly find out more about the qualifications of the people they're looking to hire and, on the other, job applicants needing to highlight all the past work and educational experiences that would make them ideal for an advertised position.

There are genres of argument as well, and these genres—just like textual genres or genres in film and music—arose because of rhetors encountering similar rhetorical situations day after day and year after year. Each genre of argument has a unique set of conventions and expectations that make it particularly suited for the rhetorical situation it evolved to address.

Many genres of argument are commercial. Prints ads in magazines and newspapers function as visual arguments trying to convince you to buy a product or a service. TV commercials are a genre of argument, as are the ads that auto-play before your YouTube videos or between your songs on Pandora radio. That big Central Barbecue sign by the side of the road with the impossibly delicious looking ribs and the impossibly crispy looking fries— that's an example of a commercial genre of argument as well. Very few commercial arguments are rational ones. They often eschew logical appeals and rely on pathetic and ethical (think celebrity endorsements) appeals, but they're nevertheless a type of argument with recognizable genre features that has been adapted to the constant need of corporations and businesses to make money and move their inventories.

Politics provides us with many different genres as well. Some of these, such as campaign advertisements, are very similar to commercial arguments. But there are plenty of genres of political argument that are fairly unique: rally speeches, live debates, and carefully scripted and rehearsed addresses on national TV. There are genres of political argument that private citizens like you and I participate in as well: canvassing from door to door to promote a particular candidate, protests and demonstrations, and phone calls and letters sent to our elected representatives. It's important to know the characteristics of each of these genres of political argument if you want to be successful when performing them.

The genres of argument that you'll become most familiar with in this class, however, are neither commercial nor political but academic.

ACADEMIC ARGUMENT AND DISCOURSE COMMUNITIES

Another concept that you may recall from English 1010 is the idea of a **discourse community**. If you were assigned a discourse community analysis, then you almost certainly remember the six criteria that linguist Jon Swales posited a community must fulfill in order to be considered a *discourse community*.[4] But we won't revisit the concept in that level of detail! For our purposes here, it's sufficient to remember that a discourse community is a community tightly knit enough to produce its own unique language practices. Many of the genre conventions of academic argument are best understood through this lens.

In "Discourse Communities and Communities of Practice" (another article from *Writing About Writing*), Ann M. Johns describes some of the characteristics of the "general, shared academic language" (505) that many scholars in academia have in common. One aspect of this shared academic language is a particular style of argument known as **formal argument**, a specialized genre that is marked, among other things, by high standards of intellectual rigor. Since you will encounter some version of formal argument whether you are studying English, Philosophy, Cellular Biology, Criminology, or whatever else, it is expected that you will become familiar with its conventions.

You're probably already somewhat familiar with formal argument from your prior school experiences. Formal argument revolves around a **thesis**, which is a term that you no doubt remember from all those five-paragraph essays you had to write in high school. A thesis is the central claim that the rhetor is trying to prove or gain support for. It is expected that this thesis will be supported or proven by drawing on **evidence** from accurate and reliable sources. (It's also expected that this evidence will be thoroughly and correctly cited.) Furthermore, as Johns describes, academic argument also demands a certain degree of restraint. Objectivity is valued, and heated or emotional language is generally avoided. Academic rhetors are expected to be fair to the opposing side, too, and to engage with the ideas of others without misrepresenting, mocking, or maligning them.

That said, we can, and should, complicate the picture a little more than this. As Johns concedes in her article, treating all of academia as one discourse community "presents major problems for scholars and literacy practitioners" who can identify not one but *many* different discourse communities on any given college campus. For example, although sociologists and electrical engineers have some language practices in common, they also have language practices unique to the discourse community that their discipline constitutes. Scholarly arguments in sociology and scholarly arguments in engineering have significant differences in the types of evidence they employ, the authorial voices they prefer, and even in the structure of their papers. The same is true for all the other fields of study that higher education encompasses.

One of the major undertakings of English 1020 is to prepare you to identify and adopt the genre conventions of the type of argument that *your* major field of study prefers, and the readings included in this textbook will help illustrate the different forms that academic arguments can take. We'll preview some of those articles now and try to point out the sub-genres of formal argument that they represent.

---

4   These six criteria can be found on page 500 of *Writing About Writing* 3rd edition.

When you read, "Entrepreneurship and Crime: The Case of New Restaurant Location Decisions," for instance, you will be reading an argument that comes from the discourse community of economics. You will probably be struck by how much of the paper sounds like a statistics lecture. You'll hear words like "variables," "level of confidence," "model," and "collinearity," and you'll hear this mathematical terminology because mathematical models and statistics are how economists *make* their arguments. It's the sort of evidence that the discourse community of academic economics has decided is meaningful and persuasive. That community prizes hard numbers and statistical analysis.

Contrast that very quantitative style of argument to the qualitative one you'll encounter in "Culture and Resistance: Civil Rights Photography: Memphis, 1968," which hails from the African American Studies discourse community. While this article is certainly not devoid of numbers, statistics, or data, you'll notice that the strength of its persuasiveness comes from the photographs that it includes and its explanation of the powerful narratives those photographs contain. The rhetor who wrote "Culture and Resistance" leverages photographic imagery, rather than facts and figures, to challenge our understandings and correct our misunderstandings of the Civil Rights movement in Memphis. This type of analysis would be out of place in a journal of economics, but it's perfectly appropriate in journals of cultural studies. That's the kind of evidence that the author and her academic peers value.

Different from both the number crunching of "Entrepreneurship and Crime" and visual analysis of "Culture and Resistance" is the archival research approach adopted by the geographer who wrote "Form, Function, and the Making of Music-themed Entertainment Districts in Nashville and Memphis."

Formal, academic argument is a demanding genre. It requires that we familiarize ourselves with a topic through careful and well-documented research. It requires that we create compelling and coherent reasons for why we believe what we believe. It requires that we express disagreement without resorting to name-calling or cheap shots. Academic argument probably seems even *more* demanding when you realize that, in addition to all of these overall conventions, you must also adopt the particularities of whichever disciplinary discourse community you hope to join in your time at University of Memphis. But maybe that's why learning how to argue like the scholars you read in the pursuit of your degree is such a rewarding achievement—because it's a difficult one.

This chapter has provided you with a conceptual framework that you can use to start working toward that achievement, however difficult it may be. The three vertices of the rhetorical triangle and their associated appeals will help you think about argument in general—how to analyze the arguments of others and how to plan arguments of your own. The concept of genre takes you a step further, encouraging you to think about the types of arguments we commonly encounter and the expectations we have internalized about how those arguments look or sound. And, last but not least, the idea of discourse communities brings you further still, asking you to pay special attention to what types of evidence scholars in your intended field of study value and the unique ways in which they interpret what it means to make a formal, academic argument. Taken together, these are the concepts of argument that will prepare you to succeed as a rhetor in this class as well as in the rest of your academic career at UofM and whatever follows.

Writing Prompts and Activities

1. Think about a time when you tried to persuade someone but failed. It doesn't matter whether the argument was trivial or serious, in-person or online, recent or from quite a while back—just think of an argument that went wrong. Using some of the concepts and terminology from this chapter, can you analyze *where* it went wrong?

    Did you, for instance, misread your audience? Did you misunderstand the subject? Did you make an ineffective appeal or violate a genre convention that you weren't aware of at the time?

    Describe why you think your attempt at persuasion failed and how you would approach the argument differently if you had it to do over again.

2. In a small group, choose one of the academic readings from your *Writing Memphis* textbook that was not analyzed above. Using what you have learned in this chapter, answer the following questions:

    *   What academic discourse community does the author of your reading belong to?

    *   What types of evidence does that discourse community seem to value?

    *   What genre conventions (relating to voice, style, or argument) can you identify? Why does the discourse community value those genre conventions?

    Prepare a short, informal presentation that explains your findings to the rest of the class. Be sure to point out specific parts of the reading that support your claims.

WORKS CITED

Bizzell, Patricia and Bruce Herzberg. Introduction. *The Rhetorical Tradition*, 5th ed., by Patricia Bizzell and Bruce Herzberg, Bedford/St. Martin's, 2000, pp. 1–16.

Johns, Ann M. "Discourse Communities and Communities of Practice: Membership, Conflict, and Diversity." *Writing About Writing*, 3rd ed., edited by Elizabeth Wardle and Douglas Downs, Bedford/St. Martin's, 2016, pp. 319–342.

Wardle, Elizabeth and Douglas Downs. "Threshold Concepts of Writing." *Writing About Writing*, 3rd ed., by Elizabeth Wardle and Douglas Downs, Bedford/St. Martin's, 2016, pp. 6–20.

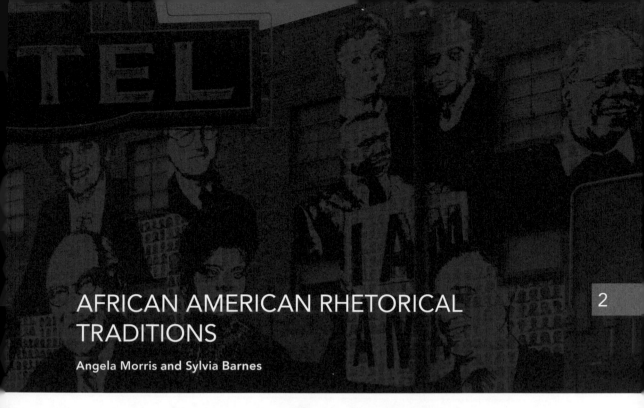

AFRICAN AMERICAN RHETORICAL TRADITIONS

Angela Morris and Sylvia Barnes

Angela Morris has an MFA in Creative Writing from the University of Central Oklahoma and is currently working on her PhD in Writing, Rhetoric, and Technical Communication at the University of Memphis. She has taught First-Year Writing and Literary Heritage at UofM since 2017, works as a consultant for the Center for Writing and Communication, and was a grant writer for seven years. You can catch her most Sundays enjoying brunch at Midtown Crossing. She's also known to frequent local punk shows, get lost in the woods of Shelby Forest, or take her bicycle for a spin on one of Memphis's many bike trails.

Sylvia Barnes is pursuing a PhD in Literary and Cultural Studies at the University of Memphis, focusing on nineteenth-century African American Literature. From Murfreesboro, Tennessee, she has taught First-Year Writing courses as well as African American Literary Heritage courses at the University of Memphis. She enjoys working out at the Rec Center, reliving her undergraduate basketball career, as well as playing intramural sports at the University of Memphis. She likes that living in Memphis allows her to visit her grandparents often.

So... where to begin? Should I start by telling y'all the numerous stories of me being called an "oreo" throughout my K-12 experience, or should I tell y'all the numerous stories of my parents telling me to speak properly? Growing up Black in Murfreesboro, TN was an interesting experience that really shaped and molded me into the person I am today. My parents wanted me to have the best education, so they tested me for admission to a magnet school.[1] The smart child I was, I got accepted into the school and spent the remainder of my elementary and middle school years there. This was a pivotal move by my parents because it

---

1   A magnet school is a choice public school that is geared towards gifted students. In order to gain admittance to a magnet school, a student has to take a test and an interview and pass both of those assessments in order to attend.

prepared me for high school and college, BUT I was not prepared to be the only Black girl in my grade from first to eighth grade.

During these formative years of my life, I was often called an "oreo." Just like the oreo cookie, my classmates said that I was Black on the outside and white on the inside. Now, what could this mean? Well, although I was wearing my Baby Phat tennis-shoes and South Pole jackets, the way that I talked was "proper" or white. I was not aware that the way that I talked was "proper" or white; what I did know was that I did not want to sound like what my classmates called "ghetto."

Now, let's be real, I did not know what "ghetto" really meant, but I assumed that "ghetto" signified uneducated, poor, and just overall bad. Growing up the way I grew up, you wanted to be the complete opposite of "ghetto" because "ghetto" meant unsuccessful. The only place where I was safe enough to talk "ghetto" or to not be "proper" was with my family. My family was my haven where I could truly be myself, but anywhere outside of my familiar setting, I was always told to annunciate my words, a.k.a. don't use any slang. For example, whenever I was around my family at home I was able to use words like "ain't" and "finna," but whenever my parents and I were in public, I was reminded, either by certain glances or with different phrases, not to speak like that.

Even today, as a PhD student in English and a writing instructor, I still get accused of sounding white. Whenever I answer the phone for work or whenever I meet someone new who had previously only heard my voice, the first comment is often "oh, I thought that you were white." *Insert eyeroll emoji here.* Constantly hearing assumptions like this is beyond annoying, but it just reiterates the concept of what is acceptable and what is not. From those first impressions that people make of me, which could be aided by my name, Sylvia, which also "sounds white," it goes to show that speaking in a particular dialect is preferred and valued over others. In other words, the closer to white a person sounds, especially if they are a Black person, the better or more successful that person may become in society. This particular mindset is limiting because it eliminates the numerous possibilities that one can have if only their language or dialect is treated synonymously to the dominant language, a turn which academia is slowly beginning to address. Furthermore, if one's language is understandable and successfully communicates and persuades, why should it be deemed less valuable? By devaluing someone's language and rhetorical traditions aren't we in a sense devaluing that person as well? This chapter is here to discuss just this issue!

This chapter focuses on how African American language and rhetorical practices are used to persuade. In fact, scholar and linguist Geneva Smitherman conducted a study in the early 1990s that revealed that high school students who utilized African American rhetorical traditions in essays scored by the National Assessment of Educational Progress received higher scores than those who did not rely on African American rhetorical tactics. Therefore, this chapter presents these rhetorical traditions not only to discuss the language of a culture often overlooked and undervalued, but also as a means to improve your writing. By learning how to both identify and use the rhetorical styles and techniques we introduce in this chapter, styles you likely have encountered in everyday life, the writing process can also become more personal and relatable.

A BRIEF HISTORY OF AFRICAN AMERICAN RHETORICAL TRADITIONS

2

The first academic inquiry into African American rhetorical traditions and vernacular Englishes began in the 1970s with queen of talkin' and testifyin' Geneva Smitherman. Smitherman earned her Ph.D. in Linguistics and began researching African American Englishes and rhetorical traditions shortly after the first Black Studies program was founded at San Francisco State University. However, the origins of African American rhetorical traditions and Englishes date back several hundreds of years to 1619 when the *White Lion*, an English privateer commanded by John Jope, brought 20 stolen Africans to Jamestown, an act often considered the origins of slavery in America. That's right, African slavery in the United States is as old as the first British settlement of the New World, meaning Africans have worked and lived on American soil for the same amount of time as the early European colonists. Thus, African American rhetorical traditions are as important as any other rhetorical practice in the United States.

By now, you've read "What Is Argument?" and have learned that different cultures build their own approaches to rhetoric and successful persuasion. English speaking countries have long focused on the rhetorical traditions of Ancient Greece and Rome and the works of "Greek thinkers like Plato, Isocrates, and Aristotle and Romans like Cicero and Quintilian" (6). Colonized by the British Empire, the United States inherited both the English language as well as several traditions of study that accompany English-speaking heritage, such as ethos, pathos, and logos. While these tools can be helpful when presenting an argument, they aren't the only tools that can help you persuade an audience.

Smitherman, as well as other scholars, began studying Slave Narratives, Spirituals, and Abolitionist speeches in the 1970s in order to identify African American rhetorical tactics. In order to understand this tradition, it helps to understand how the origins of African American rhetorical traditions differ from those of the Romans and Greeks.

Within Plato's school of thought, clear discussion and debate provided the avenue for individuals to access an ultimate truth and enlightenment. This individualistic pursuit, however, was only granted to upper-class, Anglo men who could afford education. A student of Plato's, Aristotle was adamant that such an intellectual endeavor remained out of reach for those who had to work for a living. Women and people of color were barred from scholarly pursuits in the Anglo-patriarchal societies of Ancient Rome and Greece. Furthermore, the Greeks believed poetics (aesthetic value in an argument) clouded this pursuit towards enlightenment, distracting the rhetor and audience from what really mattered: ultimate truth. Thus, while classical rhetorical traditions valued an individualistic, non-poetic pursuit for an ultimate truth by upper-class, white men, African American rhetorical traditions were born out of a very different reality.

Stolen from their African lands and forced on a treacherous transatlantic crossing only to be met by further harrowing conditions upon arrival to North America, slaves were often shackled to people from other tribes who spoke different languages. Yet despite these language barriers, communication and community amongst slaves was key to survival, not only on the ships but also during the hundreds of years of slavery that followed the transatlantic slave trade. But what could the first slaves do when none of them spoke the same language and educating slaves was banned in most colonies-turned-states? In order to survive, slaves had to develop a common language. Listening to those running the slave ship and then their masters once on the plantation, the only language all slaves were consistently exposed to was English. In order to communicate with one another, slaves took Afrocentric elements—such as verb usage—from their African languages and adapted the usage to the English words they heard in day-to-day life. This combination allowed them to communicate with one another in familiar languages patterns but with new English words, and this allowed them to communicate and share vital information that helped keep them alive and potentially sheltered them from worse harm.

While slaves in the United States learned to speak a common language that was necessary to build communities and support survival, reading and writing was still commonly forbidden of slaves. Slave owners were aware of literacy's power and couldn't risk slaves gaining that edge. Thus, several African American rhetorical traditions were established through an oral culture and then passed down from generation to generation through folklore, spirituals, and songs. The slaves who had the opportunity to break the law and learned to read and write and escape to freedom sometimes documented their feats via slave narratives and often went on to join and speak for the abolitionist movement, building communities in the North whose sole purpose was to help slaves in the South survive.

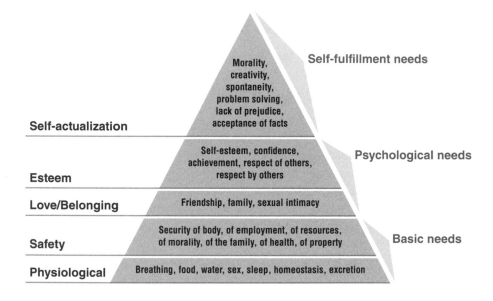

Figure 2-1. Maslow's Hierarchy of Needs

Thus, unlike the Roman and Greek traditions which primarily sought ultimate truth for its privileged citizens, African American rhetorical traditions began with a more basic need: survival. Maslow's Hierarchy of Needs (see FIGURE 2-1) is a widely endorsed psychology

2

theory that contends an individual's needs are built in the following order: physiological needs, safety needs, love and belonging, esteem, and self-actualization. This means that if someone does not have access to food, shelter, and safety, then they are less likely to be concerned with the other matters found above basic needs in the hierarchy. Since slaves often lacked adequate meals and shelter, were subjected to frequent beatings, rapings, and killings, and were also often separated from family members through slave trades, their top priority for all communication became surviving and ensuring their basic needs. Slaves also relied on song and dance to keep their downtrodden spirits alive, making poetic aspects of language and communication not a distraction from the ultimate truth, as Plato believed, but a necessity for survival.

With these realities in mind, this chapter now introduces and examines four African American rhetorical traditions discovered by scholars: testifying or narrative sequencing, call and response, rhythm and cadence, and signifying. Just as the Greek rhetorical practices are used to analyze and build argumentation, African American rhetorical traditions function in the same manner. They just originated with a primary concern for survival that relied on community and collaboration, and these practices were eventually used to persuade white America of the basic rights of African Americans.

TESTIFYING AND NARRATIVE SEQUENCING

To open this chapter, Sylvia shared a short narrative about what it was like growing up as the only Black girl for her first eight years of schooling—being told her own English wasn't proper enough and only being able to talk like herself around close family and friends. What did you think and feel reading her narrative? Could you relate? Could you empathize? Did it grab your attention? Did it make you wonder why certain people's languages are valued and others are not?

Narrative sequencing, or one way to tell a story, has long been important to African Americans and can be a very persuasive tool. In *Talkin' and Testifyin'*, Smitherman explains that "Black English speakers will render their general, abstract observations about life, love, people in the form a concrete narrative... The relating of events (real or hypothetical) becomes a black rhetorical strategy to explain a point, to persuade holders of opposing views to one's own point of view..." (147–148). We often see politicians use narrative sequencing to the same effect. They often tell stories they've heard on the campaign trail. They'll talk about veterans affected by war, children affected by gun violence, or young adults affected by student loans. They do this because stories carry weight with people and can often influence thoughts.

While narrative sequencing includes storytelling, testifying refers to sharing a personal experience in order to provide an audience with evidence of some larger truth. Sylvia didn't just tell you a story, she testified on her own experience. Her testimony included some of the instances where she felt the most vulnerable, but it also included a moment of hope or the chance for a breakthrough. While it may seem odd that you can include such rhetorical strategies in a research-based paper, narrative sequencing and testifying can be just as effective rhetorically as presenting statistics. Several slave narratives and abolitionist speeches built their anti-slavery arguments on personal narratives, testifying to the horrors of slavery in order to contend that slavery should be outlawed.

In our textbook, you can find narrative sequencing and testifying in Ida B. Wells-Barnett's Selections from *Southern Horrors: Lynch Law in All Its Phases*. Early in the essay she states, "The Afro-American is not a bestial race. If this work can contribute in any way towards proving this, and at the same time arouse the conscience of the American people to a demand for justice to every citizen, and punishment by law for the lawless, I shall feel I have done my race a service" (298). To do all this, she provides narrative sequences regarding lynches. She shares the false narratives of African Americans included by the white press, and she then combats these narratives with a narrative sequence that illustrates how the law-abiding owners of the People's Grocery were murdered in Memphis. She testifies of her own experiences when her press was burned downed for reporting on the facts of lynching in the South. She shares stories and testifies on her own personal experience to argue that "the Afro-American is not a bestial race" and call for justice.

A rhetorical analysis of Ida B. Wells-Barnett's *Southern Horrors* could consider how she used the African American tradition of narrative sequencing and testifying successfully. Furthermore, you can also use narratives or your own personal testimony when composing an argument. You can interview people regarding your paper topic and collect primary research and include other people's stories in your argument, just like Wells-Barnett. You can use anecdotes to begin your paper or, if appropriate, begin by connecting your own experiences to your research topic, just like this chapter began with Sylvia's narrative. If you want to argue that Memphis music helped break down racial barriers in the city and you have a narrative that strengthens that argument, then use it. If you want to argue about healthcare in Memphis and you or a loved one have an experience being ill and navigating the system, then sharing those testimonies can strengthen your argument.

CALL AND RESPONSE

Have you ever heard a pastor cry: Can I get an amen? Only for the congregation to reply with a boisterous: Amen! Call and response rhetoric requires audience engagement and participation. Call and response found its roots in spirituals and was a technique often used in abolitionist speeches. Rather than simply viewing audience members as empty vessels for a rhetor to provide information and present an argument, call and response rhetoric requires active participation from the audience. It requires community. The audience has the opportunity to actively participate throughout the argument, the speech, or the text. Can we get a hallelujah?

While this tradition began within enslaved African American communities, it is now used globally. Beyoncé is an artist who loves to utilize the call and response method. In her self-titled album, Beyoncé can be heard telling her audience to say "Hey Mrs. Carter" repeatedly in "Partition." She is providing a call and asking the audience to respond. If you go to a sporting event and someone proclaims, "When I say Memphis, you say Tigers!" don't you respond with "Tigers" to the call of "Memphis"? See, call and response has become a common phenomenon. But how can you use call and response when analyzing an argument or building one of your own?

Writers often include calls in their arguments, and when done successfully, such calls elicit a response. For example, in "Letter to My City" Troy Wiggins argues that Memphis doesn't love its black citizens, frequently repeating the words, "I love Memphis. Memphis doesn't love me" (213). He says these words throughout the last page. So, when he ends the essay with the single sentence, "I love Memphis," he doesn't need to include the response, "But Memphis doesn't love me," because the audience will respond automatically. He has set up a call throughout his article that ends with an expected response from the audience: Memphis doesn't love black people. Revisit "Letter to My City" and see if you notice any other places where Wiggins is calling for a response from the article's audience.

Call and response can also be helpful when writing a researched argument. As you are writing an argument for your audience, think about how you want your audience to respond. Maybe you want them to yell, "Hallelujah," to make some noise, to cry that change is needed, to cheer in excitement for the great things happening in our city. How can you craft your call in order to garner the reponse your argument seeks?

RHYTHM AND CADENCE

Ike Turner. B.B. King. Memphis Minnie. If there is one thing our city in the Southwest corner of Tennessee has its rhythm and cadence. Rhythm (the pattern of sound) and cadence (the inflection of voice) has long pumped through the veins of African Americans, dating back to spirituals (inspirational songs sung by slaves working in the field) and the black church (the only place slaves were allowed to gather without being watched).

Spirituals centered around Blackness and the Black experience and were inspired by the drums of Africa. Spirituals were the first form of home-grown American music and eventually inspired both the blues and jazz. Its this same drumbeat rhythm that birthed rock and roll and continues to be the foundation of modern music genres such as hip hop, rap, R&B, and pop. But the rhythm doesn't stop when the music goes quiet. It's worked its way into the speeches of abolitionists and into the narratives of former slaves. It's become a part of several people's daily speech and can be found in the writing of Jesse Jackson, MLK, Malcolm X, Obama, and other skilled rhetoricians.

In Geneva Smitherman's *Talkin' and Testifyin'*, she notes the rhythm and cadence in one of Reverend Jesse Jackson's speeches: "Africa would if Africa could. America could if America would. But African cain't and American ain't" (3). Here Jackson set a rhythm, a beat similar to that found in spirituals and blues, in order to build a lyrical element with the repetition of would and could and cain't and ain't.

Martin Luther King Jr. also used rhythm and cadence to build his now famous "I Have a Dream" speech:

> I have a dream that one day this nation will rise up, live out the true meaning of its creed "We hold these truths to be self-evident, that all men are created equal." I have a dream that one day on the red hill of George sons of former slaves and former slave-owners will be able to sit down together at the table of brotherhood. I have a dream that one day even the state of Mississippi, a state sweltering with the heat of injustice, sweltering

with the heat of oppression, will be transformed into an oasis of freedom and justice. I have a dream that my four little children will one day live in a nation where they will not be judged by the color of their skin but by the content of their character. (104)

Here, MLK uses the repetition of "I have a dream," like a spiritual would use a drum. These words are the beat to his message—a beat that allows him to build a rhythm that better presents his ideas about civil rights, moral character, and equality for all. This rhythm builds on the same sermonic traditions of those in the black church who came before him. He closes his speech with nods to a well-known spiritual and inflicts emphasis via repetition and parallelism: "When we allow freedom to ring—when we let it ring from every city and every hamlet, from every state and every city, we will be able to speed up that day when all of God's children, black men and white men, Jews and Gentiles, Protestants and Catholics, will be able to join hands and sing in the words of the old Negro spiritual 'Free at last, Free at last, Great God Almighty, we are free at last'" (105–106). By repeating "every" in the beginning of the sentence, he foreshadows the repetition in the spiritual "free at last, free at last." Furthermore, he builds on this rhythm with the repeated coupling of seeming opposites: "black and whites, Jews and Gentiles, Protestants and Catholics." While we can see the rhythm in the written words, how many of you heard the inflection of MLK's speech in your head while reading? How many of you heard his voice clearly through the text? You likely would not have heard either his words or his voice if he hadn't so effectively relied on the African American rhetorical tradition of rhythm and cadence. This use of rhythm and cadence has arguably made this speech his most famous. The rhythm and inflection make the words permeate human consciousness. They stick in our heads just like the catchy beat of a song. His rhetorical use of rhythm and cadence wielded tremendous power that permanently seared his argument into the American consciousness.

While not all texts use rhythm and cadence as obviously or effectively as Martin Luther King Jr.'s "I Have a Dream" speech, there are other less obvious ways for writers and rhetors to utilize this rhetorical tactic. As you complete your rhetorical analysis assignment, examine the words and the sentence structures that the author chose to present the argument. Think about how short sentences read differently than longer sentences. Short paragraphs differently than long paragraphs. Think about the rhythm Troy Wiggins establishes in "Letter to My City" by opening the essay with a single sentence paragraph: "There are dead and dying black people everywhere" (211). He then builds on that rhythm by repeating the sentence throughout the essay. Consider his two short succinct sentences on the bottom of page 212: "Do what you gotta do. Fear for your life if you need to." The horrifying question of police brutality becomes slightly more palpable within the rhythm Wiggins establishes with these sentences.

Other writing choices can also build rhythm and cadence. Commas, question marks, and exclamation points all create a different rhetorical effect for the reader. The use of rhythm and cadence in writing can help grab audiences, keep audiences, and enable one's words and arguments to resonate with audiences. When writing an argumentative paper, think about the ways you can build your own rhythm using sentence length, punctuation, and repetition.

SIGNIFYING

So we definitely saved the hardest African American rhetorical tradition for last, but bear with us. Before we can discuss just how rhetorically effectively signifying can be, we need to explain what signifying is. If I write the word "dog," what is the first thing that comes to your mind? What is the image in your head when you read the word dog? Do you have an image? Is the dog big or small? Old or young? Black, brown, white, or brindle? Long haired or short haired? Did you think about the animal at all? Or did you think about a homie, friend, or someone who has your back? Did anyone think about the kind of dog Big Mama Thorton was referencing in the song Elvis Presley famously covered: "you ain't nothing but a hound dog, snooping around my door." The word DOG is a sign, but what it is referencing, or signifying, is infinite. The textual sign DOG might be signifying a fluffy corgi with one eye; a stocky blue pit bull; a massive great dane; a pocket-sized chihuahua; a goofy dalmation; the sad puppy you saw on the animal shelter commercial; a friend who has had your back; or even an uninvited suitor who tries to flirt with everyone. Language is layered like that. One word or a single phrase can have multiple meanings. Words can have several denotative meanings (the meanings of a word easily found in a dictionary) and they have several connotative meanings (the meaning of words more likely to be found in Urban Dictionary than Websters). If someone says "that song slaps," they do not literally mean the song hit someone with the palm of its hand, they mean that song is really good. If someone says "sick shirt," you wouldn't assume your shirt looked unhealthy, but rather that your shirt looked cool.

During slavery, signifying was a means of survival. Slaves relied on the layered meanings of various words and phrases in order to communicate with other slaves while ensuring the master could not understand what they were really talking about. Have you ever heard the spiritual song "Wade in the Water"? If not, go listen to it on YouTube. The opening lines of the song are: "Wade in the water/ Wade in the water children/ Wade in the water/ God's gon' trouble the water." The slave owners would hear the slaves sing this song and think the slaves were just talking about working in the rain or cleaning themselves, when really they were providing one another with routes for escape. The word "wade" is not the same as "swim"; to slaves, this word meant that a route to freedom is through water that one could walk through or "wade" in instead of swimming. With that knowledge communicated, certain lakes and rivers referenced in the song would signify the direction the slave would need to take in order to successfully escape to freedom, and through the rhetorical tactic of signifying, this path to freedom could be communicated right in front of those keeping the slaves in chains.

Signifying is a way to communicate in code. When you see a mobster on television tell the boss, "I'll take care of it," you know he really means he is going to kill someone, but in order to give the boss plausible deniability if the law ever gets involved, the mobster signifies. Often, people might purposely misunderstand what is being signified for a humorous or witty effect. If someone says "screw you" and you respond with "you have to kiss me first," then you are purposefully misidentifying what the initial speaker was signifying with the words "screw you."

Geneva Smitherman defines signifying as something that "can be indirect yet directed at a person present in a situational context... signifying can be humorous, ironic, teachy but not preachy, punning, a play on words" (121). Keith Gilyard and Elaine Richardson define it as the "use of indirection to make points. May employ oppositional logic, overstatement, understatement, and/or reliance on the reader's knowledge of implicit assumption that is taken to be common knowledge" (221). In "Letter to My City," Troy Wiggins discusses the brutal deaths of African Americans caught in 4k resolution on cell phone cameras, and he asks, "aren't these new phones amazing? Look at that quality; you can see each individual shudder in that death rattle" (211). Here, he is not only engaging in call and response, he is also layering the meaning of his writing. Does he really want us to think about how wonderful the high definition of cell phone cameras are when someone's painful last breaths are being captured, or does he want us to think about what we choose to value in life? He purposely references the consumer demand for a high-quality cell phone camera in juxtaposition to the lack of demand for the quality of life for African Americans, several of whom live in fear of an unjust shudder of death's rattle brought on by an inane traffic stop. By overstating "aren't these new phones amazing," he isn't asking you to say "Yes!" He is asking you to think about what we hold dear in this country, why, and if a change is needed. What about when Wiggins uses signifying when discussing the "blue eyes in the sky"? Why does Wiggins not just call them the police cameras that line several streets in Memphis? Why would he layer the meaning? Maybe he is further playing on the "blue eye" / "blue lives matter" movement. Maybe he's making a reference to an Orwellian Big Brother who is constantly watching you, eyeing you, invading privacy to suppress civil rights. Maybe the blue eye signifies on Toni Morrison's debut novel *The Bluest Eye,* which resists the perceived inferiority of Black life and Black beauty. What point do you think he makes with this layering?

When you compose your researched argument or when you revise that argument for a new media genre, you may need to use certain words or phrases that have different meanings or signify different things for different audiences. For the new media argument, you may want to pair certain words with images or songs that will layer the meaning of your words. Think back to the different discourse communities you and your classmates studied in ENGL 1010. Do you want your argument to signify on the lexi, phrasing, images, or music of a particular discourse community? Think about how a discourse community's lexis might mean different things to outsiders. If your audience changes from one project to the next, then your use of those terms may need to change, or you may not change those terms and instead decide to signify and intentionally present different meanings to different audiences. If you pick a controversial topic, then you may decide to use signification to make your argument more palatable to one audience while driving your argument home to a second audience. Being witty, ironic, and/or sarcastic and layering meanings can create a particular desired rhetorical effect, and the rhetorical tactic of signifying can let you present different messages to different audiences simultaneously.

CONCLUSION

Understanding African American rhetorical traditions can improve the ways you use language and present arguments. These traditions can also help you craft more artistic prose that can better drive arguments home by resonating and interacting with your audience. Learning about the four traditions included in this chapter—testifying and narrative sequencing, call and response, rhythm and cadence, and signifying—can also further enhance your linguistic understanding of Memphis culture. But learning about these traditions can do even more on a personal level. We started out this article with a testimonial from one of the chapter's authors, Sylvia, and we thought that to keep with the rhythm of the piece, we should end this chapter with a testimonial from the other chapter author, Angela.

I'm gonna be completely honest with you. I'm white. And I have borne all the privileges of whiteness throughout my educational career. I never had my language suppressed and the rhetorical traditions of my heritage have been taught to me for as long as I can remember. During my very first week of teaching years ago, I was made aware that this was not the experience of several of my students. Like Sylvia, their experiences and their cultures have often been underrepresented in their educational journey, whether because of their race, class, gender, nationality, sexual orientation, etc. They shared with me the sorta double-consciousness thrust upon them by being told their Englishes, their rhetorical traditions, weren't good enough—that their language wasn't as valid as those typically associated with academia. Therefore, they must acculturate to a second type of consciousness and language, the one expected of them in school. How unfair. How untrue. I then learned that throughout the last few decades, several scholars, such as Geneva Smitherman, have worked tirelessly to correct this wrong and to resist this cultural oppression. I have personally benefited from learning these realities as it has helped raise awareness within myself as well as sprung a deep appreciation for the rhetorical tools of other cultures. American culture has been so influenced by African American heritage to the point that the use of rhythm, the use of testimonials, the use of call and response and signification had, unbeknownst to me, become so enmeshed in my daily rhetorical practices that it was eye-opening and important for me to learn about where these traditions came, to learn of the hardships that birthed these successful forms of argumentation.

Memphis is enriched by our African American community which currently makes up more than sixty percent of the population. Several members of our community are the descendants of the slaves who used the rhetorical practices we outlined here (as well as others) in order to survive and preserve their communities. To write Memphis is to write using the language and historical rhetorical practices of those who played a vital and important role in building this community and creating the beauty that makes us all love Memphis even when Memphis doesn't quite love us. Learning these rhetorical traditions, sharing them with the Memphis community, and using them in our own practices has the power to make Memphis a more accepting place for all—a place that both receives love and returns it.

Writing Prompts and Activities

1. This chapter is meant to represent some of the rhetorical practices used in Memphis, but by no means does this chapter present a comprehensive look at all rhetorical traditions in the city and beyond. Take a moment to think of your own heritage and cultural influences. Then identify one of those heritages, groups, identity markers, or communities with which you identify, and research its rhetorical practices.

2. Think of a simple argument you could make in a few paragraphs. It could be something as simple as convincing a friend where you two should go eat, which movie you should watch, why your favorite sports team is awesome, or why a new song slaps hard. Now that you've come up with a short argument, write a few paragraphs using at least one of the four rhetorical traditions we've discussed in this chapter in order to make that argument.

3. We've used Troy Wiggins's "Letter to My City" as one of the examples for how these rhetorical tools can be used. However, Wiggins's article provides many more examples of testifying and narrative sequences, call and response, rhythm and cadence, and signifying than we were able to mention in this article. Go through the text and see just how many examples you can find. Which one of your classmates can find the most uses of African American rhetorical traditions?

4. In small groups, choose one of the other readings from the textbook. Then see if you can locate uses of any of the rhetorical traditions discussed in this chapter. Craft a short presentation on that reading's use of African American rhetorical traditions that you can share with the class.

5. In this chapter we've discussed four tools of African American rhetoric, however, there are several more that we did not cover, including: reference to color-race-ethnicity; use of proverbs, aphorisms, biblical verses; direct address-conversational tone; cultural references; ethnolinguistic idioms; verbal inventiveness, unique nomenclature; cultural values-community consciousness; field dependency; topic association. Choose one of these practices and research its origins and use, and write a short report on what you find.

WORKS CITED

Gilyard, Keith and Elaine Richardson. "Students' Right to Possibility: Basic Writing and African American Rhetoric." *Students' Right to Their Own Language: A Critical Sourcebook*, edited by Staci Perryman Clark, David E. Kirkland, and Austin Jackson, Bedford /St. Martins, 2015, pp. 217–228.

King, Martin Luther Jr. "I Have a Dream." *I Have a Dream: Writings and Speeches that Changed the World*, edited by James Melvin Washington. Harper One, 1992, pp. 101–106.

Smitherman, Geneva. "African American Student Writers in the NAEP, 1969-88/89" and "The Blacker the Beery, the Sweeter the Juice." *Students' Right to Their Own Language: A Critical Sourcebook*, edited by Staci Perryman Clark, David E. Kirkland, and Austin Jackson, Bedford /St. Martins, 2015, pp. 191–216.

___.*Talkin' and Testifyin': The Language of Black America*. Wayne State University Press, 1977.

Verbist, Gilbert. "What Is Argument?" *Writing Memphis*, 3rd ed., edited by Katherine Fredlund. Macmillan Curriculum Solutions, 2020. pp. 1–14.

Wells-Barnett, Ida B. "Selections from *Southern Horrors: Lynch Laws in All Its Phases*." *Writing Memphis*, 3rd ed., edited by Katherine Fredlund. Macmillan Curriculum Solutions, 2020. pp. 297–306.

Wiggins, Troy. "Letter to My City." *Writing Memphis*, 3rd ed., edited by Katherine Fredlund. Macmillan Curriculum Solutions, 2020. pp. 211–213.

2

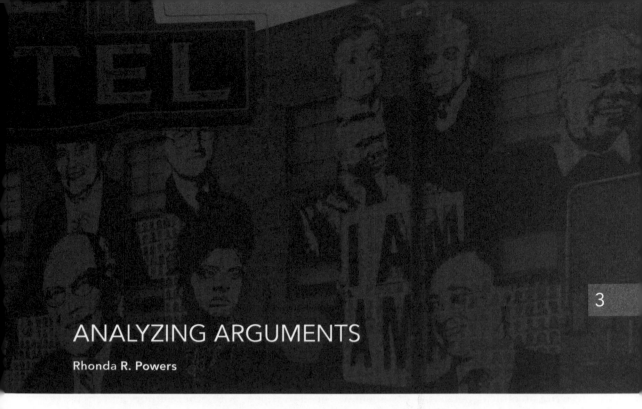

ANALYZING ARGUMENTS

Rhonda R. Powers

Rhonda R. Powers joined the faculty at the University of Memphis as an instructor in 2010, and served as the Assistant Director of First Year Writing from 2013 to 2018. She has previously taught at Auburn University, Georgia Military College, and Missouri State University. She enjoys the theater district and the live music that Memphis has to offer, especially the concert series at the Levitt Shell. She currently volunteers with Literacy Mid-South and Tennessee Shakespeare.

"She's saccharine and extremely banal" (Palisades Princess).

"LOL! You sure are da smart one, aren't ya? *wink!" (Mina Lasta).

"Try not being a sanctimonious twit, DARLING" (Palisades Princess).

Read the comments under any online article and you might conclude that our public discourse is broken. However, this doesn't necessarily suggest that we are all mean-spirited trolls. Instead, comments such as those above point to the communication failures caused by our 24/7 digital lifestyle and multitasking distractions. We don't read carefully, and we respond emotionally to a piece of writing in the moment, not stopping to think rationally. Unfortunately, these bad communication habits are infecting our ability to engage in academic arguments and, therefore, to solve major problems.

Reading critically is different than reading for information. When we are looking for the requirements for a Marketing and Communications degree, we open the *Undergraduate Catalog* and quickly skim through what is written in order to determine whether we are interested in the necessary classes. We are reading quickly for information, and we are making assumptions—that the author is credible and is ethically representing the facts correctly. However, when we are considering trips for spring break, we are conducting research, and we must critically assess the marketing materials we are being inundated with online: "*Happiness is calling—San Diego*" (YouListener). Happiness may be calling, but is a trip to San Diego going to make our bank account happy? Is it more expensive to fly or drive? If we drive to San Diego and back won't we spend our entire break driving? Isn't New Orleans or Panama City closer and less expensive? Won't that make us happier? When we read critically, we are interrogating or questioning the text and the strategies the writer uses to persuade us.

Like advertising, academic argument utilizes rhetoric, the art of persuasion. We can't assume that articles are unbiased. If Yellow Dog Records is trying to sell CDs by Calvin Newborn, shouldn't we question their credibility in arguing that Newborn is an "unsung guitar hero"? The skill of critical or analytical reading is necessary for researching and writing our own arguments. Too often we equate research with gathering data: getting on the computer, logging into the library databases, collecting scholarly articles, and reporting information. We forget the vital and time-consuming process of analyzing the articles.

To write an ethical, persuasive argument, we need to engage with other authors and their views on the same subject. We must read and re-read our data, analyzing the way in which facts are presented to persuade us. Our own ethos depends upon our use of these sources. If we misunderstand or misrepresent evidence, we lose credibility and, ultimately, lose our ability to present a persuasive argument.

THE PROCESS OF ANALYSIS

To read critically is to read analytically. We hear the word analysis or evaluation in every class, but it can be confusing because it seems to mean something different in each academic discipline. However, while analyzing a disease process in nursing may *appear* different from evaluating a conductor circuit in electrical engineering, the *process* of analysis is the same: we develop criteria and then evaluate the subject under analysis using the criteria we have developed.

In fact, we practice this process unconsciously as consumers. When we head to Verizon or T-Mobile to buy a new cell phone, we generally have evaluative questions with which we will make our final purchasing decision: What does the phone cost? What operating system does it use? How large is the screen? What's the pixelation on the camera? What are the data plans available? We apply our criteria (cost, ios, size, quality, coverage) to each phone and make the best choice for our needs. The *process* we use when buying a car is the same; it is only the *criteria* that changes. We will visit CarMax or Wolfchase Auto Sales and look at several vehicles, but we will make our selection after evaluating the cars using criteria (cost, make and model, safety, maintenance costs, mpg, insurance costs, etc.) appropriate to this task.

Thus, when we are conducting a rhetorical analysis, we know that we are evaluating a text using the rhetorical criteria that we were introduced to in the "What Is Argument?" chapter. Our criteria for evaluating a text is based upon the rhetorical triangle that we discussed in the previous chapter.

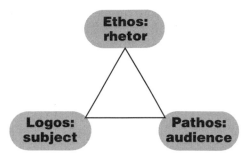

Figure 3-1. The Rhetorical Triangle

Looking at this conceptualization of communication, we can identify three categories for analysis: the rhetor, the audience, and the subject. Each category will have its own criteria, making rhetorical analysis multilayered, which accounts for the need for multiple readings and adequate time spent engaging in analysis to thoroughly evaluate a piece of writing.

ETHOS: ANALYZING THE WRITER OR RHETOR

If **Ethos** represents the writer or rhetor, then we must evaluate the expertise and purposes that motivate them. A failure to adequately research another author may, again, cause us to misrepresent facts, and damage our persuasive success:

- **Who is the author?** What is their expertise? This data is necessary to judge the quality of the information being presented and means that we must research the writer unless the expertise is given to us in a biographical section. Would you take medical advice from a mechanic? Probably not.

- **What is their purpose for writing?** Many arguments in our public discourse are engaged in trying to solve problems such as global warming. A geophysicist might write an argument proposing the use of alternative fuels to alleviate the problems created by global warming, such as famine. On the other hand, the owner of a solar panel company might make the same argument to sell more of their product.

  Determining purpose can help us identify unconscious or unethical bias. Bias, in and of itself, is not an issue unless it is hidden to manipulate the reader. Mothers Against Drunk Driving (MADD) has a declared bias—the organization is biased against drunk driving; just as the National Rifle Association (NRA) is biased toward gun ownership; both organizations ethically present their bias.

- **What is the occasion, or, as we learned in English 1010, the Kairos?** Is the author responding to a previous argument? Academic arguments are part of the larger discourse, and articles are often in conversation, responding to previous arguments. If a writer proposes a solution for fighting poverty by reducing crime in Memphis, then another author may evaluate that proposal and argue for further educational programs instead.

  Is the writer responding to a recent event? Note the number of articles and arguments in our current public discourse about topics such as the Black Lives Matter movement in response to police actions. Is the author responding to an historical event? Consider the number of arguments that have been written in response to the assassination of Martin Luther King Jr.

- **Where or in what context does the article appear?** *The New York Times* and *USA Today* are both newspapers, but they have vastly different reputations. *The New York Times* is respected worldwide for its journalistic integrity and ethos. *USA Today* employs far fewer actual writers, getting its news from wire services instead. This means that *USA Today's* information is second hand and may be less reliable.

The validity of information can often be equated with the source of information.

Scholarly Journals print articles written by scholars who are not paid for their work and that are reviewed by experts in the field. Because scholarly journals are published by research institutions and accept no advertising, this is considered the most reliable information.

Trade Publications print articles for a specific trade. *Behind the Chair* is the trade publication for cosmetologists, for example. Because such publications accept advertising and offer reviews of new products and techniques by these same advertisers, such publications are often deemed biased.

Popular Magazines often print articles by anonymous, freelance writers, and therefore reliability is often much more difficult to discern. It must be noted that there are a vast number of popular magazines, both in print and on the web; this makes it difficult to make sweeping judgments and makes careful analysis imperative.

Internet Sources often demand much more attention as we must be vigilant against fake and satirical sources whose purpose is to confuse or strictly entertain. For example, Sean Spicer, former White House Press Secretary experienced an ethos failure when he responded to an article in the *Onion*, a well-known satirical news outlet.

When using web sources, we use the same rhetorical analysis process outlined in this chapter. However, there is additional information that can aid our analysis. First, examining the **URL** can often help us understand purpose:

- **.gov** refers to government websites, which are often very reliable.

- **.net** or **.com** are general commercial sites that must be thoroughly vetted. These websites often operate to generate revenue and can be suspect for this reason.

- **.org** denotes a non-profit organizational site that often displays their bias prominently. As we discussed above, Mothers Against Drunk Driving (MADD) portrays their purpose in the title of the organization. Some organizations are not so forthcoming and need further examination.

3

- **.edu** are educational websites that must still be examined as anyone associated with the institution may be able to post information at the .edu. Posted student papers are not considered as reliable as scholarly essays.

If the URL doesn't provide enough information, then **the "About" Button** will generally take us to a page that will outline information about the author/organization, purpose or "mission," funding, etc. You can also look up a source's Wikipedia page to learn things they may not share intentionally, such as sources of funding, previous scandals or mistakes, or political affiliations.

Library databases are costly subscriptions to repositories of articles. The articles are initially screened for validity before being uploaded. While this does not negate the need for our further analysis, it is generally understood that these essays present valid information. By contrast, Google articles appear in an order generated by algorithms that are driven by advertising revenue, and this makes the information more suspect.

For academic arguments, in which we are often trying to argue and solve problems in the public discourse, it is crucial that we use the most reliable and ethical information available. For this reason, and because we are learning the foundational skills of research, our research draft will contain many scholarly sources generally found in the library databases or in government publications.

PATHOS: ANALYZING THE AUDIENCE

When evaluating the audience, we ask similar questions as we did during our analysis of the author. In many ways analysis replicates the scientific method. When we make assertions, we become more credible if we can offer multiple pieces of evidence. So, we ask many of the same questions about the audience that we ask of the writer. Being able to replicate and make connections between the answers adds validity to our analysis and leads to a deeper analysis of the text.

For example, if we misinterpret the selections from Ida B. Wells-Barnett's *Southern Horrors: Lynch Law in All Its Phases* because we don't recognize that her audience is Caucasian-Americans who lived in the late nineteenth century, then we may also incorrectly identify her purpose: to refute the assumption that the press, owned largely by Caucasian-Americans, is unbiased. Her argument intends to make the press bias against African-Americans visible, and she does so by presenting evidence. We may notice, however, that she uses language that we would not use today, and as we conduct our analysis, we should recognize that the terms she uses were acceptable and appropriate given the time period. Not considering context in this way will devalue our analysis, and we might lose our credibility because we are not the intended audience of this piece of writing.

While the context in which the article appears is examined under ethos, and may tell us a lot about our audience, further analysis is often necessary, especially when we use Internet sources. It may be helpful to ask demographic questions to correctly identify the readers of a text.

- **What is the target age of the audience?** Age is often associated with subject, as we are often interested in different topics throughout our lives. We might make an argument about the necessity of registering to vote and target it toward a younger audience, assuming that most voters register when they reach eligibility at eighteen. An argument on the necessity for retirement reforms will likely be aimed at older readers. We need to consider what assumptions the author makes about the age of the audience, either consciously or unconsciously.

- **Is there a targeted gender?** While most arguments are not gendered, as they affect all equally, there are cases in which we are writing to a gendered audience. We might aim an argument on the necessity for prenatal healthcare checkups towards expecting mothers, while we attempt to persuade men that self-examinations are necessary to prevent testicular cancer. Consider whether there are gender assumptions that undermine the argument.

- **Is there a targeted ethnic group, or are there racial implications?** We have recently seen a number of arguments in the public domain that have ethnic and racial implications: for example, the current argument over the looming 2020 Census and how we use only six racial/ethnic categories to identify citizens. Many believe that this will misrepresent the true make-up of the country, which could have implications on public policy (Wagner). Consider whether the writer of an argument unconsciously shows ethnic or race bias.

- **What assumptions are made about the religious affiliations of the audience?** In the recent controversy over using "Merry Christmas" versus "Happy Holidays" as a greeting, there are religious implications. "Merry Christmas" automatically assumes a Christian audience, while "Happy Holidays" acknowledges the diverse religions that celebrate holidays in December/January: Christmas, Kwanzaa, Hanukkah, Mawlid el-Nabi, Bodhi Day, and the Solstice. Consider whether there are unconscious religious biases the author does not acknowledge. Do these undermine or negate the argument? How/why?

- **Is the targeted audience politically identified?** The political division in our public discourse is apparent and often riddled with misrepresentation. Note how arguments of Internet privacy, birth control, and even science have been politicized in our public policy discourse. Consider how politicization of an argument effects the reader. Does it oversimplify the issues? How or why?

- **What socioeconomic status is presumed?** Much like age, the socio-economic status of an audience may be discovered by subject or the stance on that subject. A persuasive article in favor of payday loans may be targeted to the socioeconomically advantaged as a great return on investment. The same subject may be targeted toward lower socioeconomic readers by arguing against payday loans as predatory and detrimental to repayment. Consider whether there are assumptions made about the income of the reader or the concerns that a reader will have about a given class status. How does this affect the argument?

- **What is the education level of the reader?** The presumed education of the audience is often indicated by the vocabulary and the simplicity of sentence structures. Look at a *New York Times* newspaper that is offered for free to Memphis students and can be found in the lobby of Patterson Hall. Note the depth of articles, and the lexis used. What is the level of education presumed? Consider how the writer's presumption of reader education impacts their structural or linguistic choices.

- **Are there geographic cultural markers?** In Memphis, barbeque generally means dry rub, but in Kansas City it means sauce. Geography may impact the subject, the stance, and/or the language used to persuade. Consider the impact the geographical location of the audience has on the choices that the writer is making in vocabulary and rhetorical appeals.

A demographic analysis of the audience should help us determine the logical strategies a writer makes in shaping their argument and may help uncover errors within the author's reasoning.

When writing our own argument, a demographic audience analysis will help us determine whether our audience will initially agree or resist our argument. For example, if we argue for a ban on assault weapons for a broad Tennessee audience, then we should recognize that our politically conservative readers will generally resist our argument, which will help us shape the structure and the way in which we utilize the rhetorical appeals.

Many of the analytical questions noted here will be repeated in the Logos section that follows. As we discussed earlier, because analysis is a multilayered process, the process will overlap and create replication or corroboration of our evidence.

LOGOS: ANALYZING THE TEXT

The greatest portion of our analysis will be in examining the linguistic choices that an author makes. The words on the page are the best direct evidence for our analytical assertions, and our examination must be thorough and multifaceted. Reading critically works best when we break our reading down into smaller tasks. First, we read the article through for understanding. The second, third, and perhaps, fourth time we read, we analyze the text in sections, not the essay in its entirety. Taking a section at a time allows us to focus on how the writing is constructed to persuade.

When reading for the actual argument of the text, we read the introduction followed immediately by the conclusion. Experienced writers don't merely restate their thesis in the conclusion, but we will see a repetition of the argument that will corroborate the argument from the introduction.

In the body of the essay, we study the evidence. What rhetorical devices has the author used? Where is the writer using ethical appeals, appeals to pathos, and logical appeals? Where has the author erred? Does the author address the oppositional argument? Again, we are interrogating the text. We must read and re-read the essay to answer each of these questions, which, as stated previously, makes analyzing a text a time-consuming endeavor.

Thus, to persuade an audience, a writer shapes the message of the argument by making choices in how to structure the text and utilizing rhetorical devices and rhetorical appeals, all while trying to avoid errors known as fallacies. These choices and strategies become the criteria we will use to analyze the Logos: Structure, Rhetorical Devices, Rhetorical Appeals, and Rhetorical Fallacies.

STRUCTURE AND ORGANIZATION

Academic arguments generally follow a four-part structure that you are already familiar with as a student of academic writing:

- an introduction that contains a thesis statement;
- the body of the essay, which presents the evidence that supports the thesis;
- a refutation that counters the oppositional argument;
- and a conclusion that summarizes key points and helps the reader know how to utilize the information presented.

The **thesis** statement of an academic argument is often made up of two parts: part one—the **claim**, which is followed by part two—the **reason(s)** for the claim or a **how** to make the claim possible. At the end of the introduction to her research draft, "The Income Gap in Memphis: Higher Education and Closing the Gap," we get Davis's thesis: "Higher education is the key to lessening the income gap between races in Memphis" (479).

> **Claim**: we can lessen the income gap between races in Memphis
>
> **Implied Reason**: equality is ethical and necessary to a democracy
>
> **How to make the claim possible**: using education

As student writers, we are often encouraged to use the formal argument thesis structure, explicitly stating our claim and reason at the end of our introduction. However, the thesis statement in an academic article may be more than one sentence long and may come within any of the paragraphs on the first few pages. This convention, as well as others, is dictated by the discourse community we are writing for and the genre conventions agreed upon by the community. Some authors never explicitly state a thesis at all but imply their argument. They may imply the thesis to engage the audience, relying on our analytical reading skills, or to avoid immediately offending readers if they think their audience will resist their argument.

If we are struggling to identify the thesis of an article, we might first attempt to determine the genre of the argument to help us determine the purpose; this can lead us to the claim. Once we have identified the claim, it is generally easier to identify the reason(s) for the claim. The most common argument genres are:

Definition Arguments attempt to define terms or concepts. Our public discourse has been engaged in a definition argument over marriage for at least the past decade with one side arguing that marriage is defined as a union between two consenting adults and the oppositional view arguing that marriage is a union between a man and a woman.

Causal Arguments attempt to persuade us of the causes of a problem. In "Memphis Burning," Peter Lauterbach argues that Memphis is the poorest city in the nation because of historical racial segregation in housing.

Proposal Arguments attempt to persuade us to follow a certain solution(s) to solve a specific problem. As we noted previously, Amoriana Davis's researched essay argues that education is the solution to economic inequality in Memphis.

Problem/Solution Arguments are generally longer arguments that combine both the Causal and Proposal Arguments. We have already noted such an argument in this chapter: the problem of global warming with suggested solutions of alternative fuel sources over fossil fuels. Another major problem/solution argument in our current public discourse is the number of gun deaths in the country, and the proposed solution of introducing gun control legislation.

Evaluative Arguments may evaluate products and/or services, comparing different options. This is exactly what *Consumer Reports* does. They evaluate the best cell phones, evaluating each phone using the same criteria to make a recommendation. The second, more complex evaluation argument evaluates or critiques a system. "The Education of Dasmine Cathey" is a good example of an evaluative argument, as the article essentially evaluates the ways in which student athletes are exploited and often denied education.

Refutation Arguments are necessary when the oppositional view is invisible. Drawing upon Ida B. Wells-Barnett again, we noted earlier that the white press was unaware of its own biased representations of blacks. Her argument refuted the then assumed belief that the white press was impartial and unbiased.

RHETORICAL DEVICES

Authors can also organize the body of the argument by utilizing creative devices that help to persuade us. We erroneously presume that academic writing is formal, straightforward, and lacking in creativity. To engage with readers, academic authors must be creative, relying on rhetorical devices that students often associate only with literature and poetry. "The Soul of Memphis" is an effective title because it uses personification and allusion. The title gives Memphis a soul, equating the city with a person, while at the same time alluding to the musical styles (gospel, rhythm and blues, and rock 'n' roll) that make Memphis unique. One way that we can analyze an essay is to examine the devices (presented below) an author uses that make an argument subtly persuasive.

Allusion makes a reference to something else to unconsciously help us connect concepts. The title of Preston Lauterbach's article, "Memphis Burning," is an allusion to the 1988 film, *Mississippi Burning*, which takes up similar themes of racially motivated crime.

Analogy shows similarity between two things. We have a perfect example here in Memphis. The Mississippi River has been seen as analogous, or similar, to the Nile River, and thus our city was named after the capital of ancient Egypt, Memphis. We often make analogous arguments. We might argue that the health policy of a specific state has been so successful that it should become national policy. This argument rests upon the analogy between the state government and the federal government.

Alliteration uses the repetition of letters at the beginning of words in adjacent proximity in a title or sentence. This acts as a mnemonic device, making a title or sentence memorable. Note the alliteration in the title of this chapter, "Analyzing Arguments."

Hyperbole is extreme exaggeration. When some Memphians claim, "It is hotter than Hades," they are using hyperbole. We expect Hades to be hotter than even the worst July day in Memphis.

Imagery is when the author uses language that invokes our senses (sight, hearing, touch, taste, smell, and memory) to bring us into the moment. "The Soul of Memphis" opens by painting a picture of white birdhouses, "a chalet here, a pagoda there" (19) creating images in our minds.

Metaphors and **Similes** make comparisons between two seemingly dissimilar ideas or objects. However, upon reflection, the metaphor or simile helps us to see the comparative object or idea more deeply. The main difference between metaphor and simile is that similes use the word "like" or "as" to make the comparison, and metaphors do not. In "The Alien Has Landed" we see an effective simile; "But when Mongo sleeps, he does it on a little mat in the living room, like a poverty-stricken college student" (42).

Only the most common of rhetorical devices are discussed here, however, a simple Internet search of "rhetorical devices" will lead you to any number of great resources to expand your knowledge.

THE RHETORICAL APPEALS AND FALLACIES

As we learned in "What Is Argument?," rhetors/writers use the Rhetorical Appeals to persuade, utilizing ethos, logos, and pathos to prove their thesis. However, authors often make errors when they use these appeals. When we analyze the use of appeals, we are often looking for these errors, which we call **fallacies**. A discussion of each appeal, and the most common fallacies made, follows.

THE APPEAL TO ETHOS

The appeal to ethos is the writer's attempt to persuade us that they are fairly representing their evidence and are worthy of our trust. We have analyzed the author extensively in the ethos section, but we now examine the text to see that the writer continues to present information ethically. We need to evaluate the sources of information that the author presents. Is the author citing their sources of information so that we can evaluate the reliability of those sources? Are facts and statistics presented from unbiased sources?

In analyzing ethos, we focus on the "appeal to authority." Who does the author recognize and quote as an expert? Brad Wolverton, in evaluating athletes and education, quotes Dr. Joseph Jones as the then Director of First Year Writing, and Joseph P. Luckey as the Director of Athletic Academic Services. Because an "expert" and their credentials can be questionable, we must evaluate for fallacies or errors.

FALLACIES OF ETHOS

False Authority asks us to agree with an assertion based simply on the authority of the arguer, even though they may be unqualified. Example: In an interview with Matt Lauer, Tom Cruise famously stated, "And I know that psychology is a pseudoscience." As an actor, Tom Cruise is no authority on psychology, which has been accepted as a human science for two-hundred years (YouTube).

Ad Hominem arguments attack a writer's character rather than their reasoning or may reject an argument based on the author's character. *Example*: Rather than addressing James Comey's information in the book *A Higher Loyalty: Truth, Lies, and Leadership*, President Trump attacks Comey's character: "Slippery James Comey, a man who always ends up badly and out of whack (he is not smart!), will go down as the WORST FBI Director in history, by far!" (Stewart).

Straw man arguments set up and dismantle easily refutable arguments to misrepresent an opponent's argument to defeat them. Example: When responding to the argument that medical marijuana should be available to patients in need, the straw man reply would be, "if we just make drugs available to everyone, the crime will increase exponentially!" ("Straw Man").

Moral Equivalence compares minor problems with much more serious crimes. Example: In a banned German ad, PETA argued, "To animals, all people are Nazis," egregiously equating the Holocaust deaths of the Jews with our animal food production (Bashion Image 3).

THE APPEAL TO PATHOS

While we have already addressed the audience evaluation under pathos, when looking at the "appeal to pathos" we are examining the way in which an author appeals to our emotion or experiences. "The Resistance: Memphis Activism Sprouts Everywhere" utilizes the appeal to pathos effectively, connecting to the lived experience of Memphians by referencing and describing the De Soto Bridge closure by the Black Lives Matter movement, as one example. The article further uses photographs of Memphians to humanize the issues described, thereby invoking an emotional response from us as we identify with the individuals protesting oppression. This appeal can be used to manipulate our emotions, thus the need to analyze for fallacies.

FALLACIES OF PATHOS

Red Herrings use misleading or unrelated evidence to support a conclusion. The term originates from the practice of using a smoked herring in fox hunting to throw the dogs off the foxes' scent. The fallacy refers to throwing the audience off the trail of an initial claim to raise (or solve) another. Example: During an interview, Chuck Todd was trying to extract answers from President Trump's "Counselor," Kellyanne Conway.

Todd: '...the facts he uttered were just not true. Look, alternative facts are not facts; they're falsehoods.'

Conway: 'Chuck do you think it's a fact or not that millions of people have lost their plans and health insurance and their doctors under President Obama?'

Healthcare was not the subject of the conversation. Todd's argument was essentially: 'lies were told, they undermine credibility, the White House shouldn't have sanctioned this.' Confronted with that argument, Conway's rebuttal was basically: 'How dare you bring up facts!? We do a bad job at helping sick people!' (Peters par. 7).

Appeals to Fear, or Scare Tactics try to frighten us into agreeing with the writer by threatening us or predicting unrealistically dire consequences. Example: In the last recession, it was argued that if we didn't bail out the big banks, then the US economy would fail.

Slippery Slope arguments suggest that one thing will lead to another negative thing, or that one thing will spark a chain of negative events. Example: If we ban AR15 assault weapons, then soon we will be banning hunting rifles, until Americans are finally stripped of gun ownership altogether.

Either-or and False Dilemma reduce complicated issues to only two choices. Either-or suggests there are only two sides, two choices, two possibilities; false dilemma insists that the only options are limited to those stated. Example: We can fund healthcare, or we can make our country safe by funding the military.

THE APPEAL TO LOGOS

The "Appeal to Logos" is the use of facts and statistics to be persuasive. Students often believe that facts and statistics are the best evidence because they are irrefutable. However, a deeper examination reveals that facts must be interpreted, and statistics can skew the reality of information. That the Earth is warming is a scientifically proven fact. However, while this fact has been interpreted as a major human survival issue by most, there are those who interpret this warming as part of a natural weather cycle of the planet demanding no environmental action on our part.

Statistics can also be very persuasive if we don't stop to ask how those statistics were derived. An ad stating that 90% of dentists prefer that patients chew sugarless bubblegum might make us switch from our favorite brand. 90% appears to be an overwhelming majority. However, on further examination we find that the sugarless bubblegum company using this statistic only polled twenty dentists. The 90% referenced literally represents eighteen dentists. Not so impressive. It is important to try to determine the parameters of how statistics are derived to be valid. For these reasons, fallacies of logos must be examined.

FALLACIES OF LOGOS

Hasty Generalizations draw conclusions from scanty evidence. Many stereotypes are based on hasty generalizations. Example: My friend was attacked by her Uber driver; taking Uber is dangerous and should be avoided.

Equivocation fallacy occurs when a partially synonymous or unclear—equivocal—word or phrase makes an unsound argument appear sound. It might be a half-truth, or a statement that is partially correct but that purposefully obscures the entire truth. Example: I am not free to yell "fire" in a crowded theater, thus I do not have freedom of speech!

Shifting the Burden of Proof occurs when we don't provide support for our claim but require proof from our opponent. The burden of proof in support of a claim is always on whoever advances the claim. Example: You can't prove the existence of aliens, thus there are no aliens.

Faulty Causality or **Post Hoc Ergo Propter Hoc** arguments confuse chronology with causation: one event can occur after another without being caused by the first event. These fallacies are often the root of superstitions. Example: My child was diagnosed with Autism after receiving childhood vaccinations. Vaccinations obviously cause Autism.

A **Non-Sequitur** is a statement that does not logically relate to what comes before it. Example: In a presidential debate, Mitt Romney was asked about his philosophical inconsistency as a candidate. His reply is a now famous non-sequitur fallacy, "I'm a man of steadiness and constancy. I don't think you are going to find somebody who has more of those attributes than I do. I have been married to the same woman for 25—excuse me, I will get in trouble, for 42 years. […] I have been in the same church my entire life. I worked at one company, Bain, for 25 years. And I left that to go off and help save the Olympic Games" (Lewis).

Faulty Analogies are inaccurate, inappropriate, or misleading comparisons between two things. Example: Just like dogs, students respond to discipline.

FINAL THOUGHTS

Rhetorical analysis is a practice, just as learning to play a sport or an instrument is a practice. We must learn the steps, just like we learn to first dribble a ball, swing a bat, or play the musical scales before we can drill a three-point shot, hit a double, or play a famous Memphis horn chart. Just as we use the rules of the game and the proficiency of the skills to evaluate a basketball player, we know to use the tools of rhetoric to evaluate communication. And just like playing the game or the piano, we know we must use these skills consistently if we are going to improve.

It will help to remember that the analytical process is always the same—we evaluate using criteria. It is only the context that changes those criteria. We practice rhetorical analysis by taking every opportunity that presents itself. In fact, it should be the process by which we read for every class. As we educate ourselves, we are not merely reading for information, we are reading to interrogate what knowledge is and how it is produced.

Beyond the written text, rhetorical analysis is a life skill. Rhetoric is the act of persuasion, and we must learn to listen as analytically as we read. To succeed in our careers, we will need to persuasively communicate with our employers, colleagues, and clients. To have healthy and happy relationships, we will need to analyze communication with our parents, partners, and children. Most importantly, to solve the very real and pressing problems of climate change, racial and gender inequality, gun violence, education funding, and health care funding, we must be able to put aside emotional responses to logically analyze the information available to us to make better decisions for the good of the country. Rhetorical analysis is the foundation of education, and education is imperative to a functioning democracy.

Writing Prompts and Activities

1. Do you generally find yourself reading for information or reading analytically? Why? How does reading analytically benefit you in most cases?

2. What was the last major purchase you or your family made? How did you evaluate your options? What criteria did you establish? How/why? Did this make the decision-making process easier? How?

3. Watch the national evening news. What arguments can you identify in our public discourse? What genre are most of our public arguments in? Can you find any fallacies in these arguments?

4. Find several ads and analyze them for audience and persuasive techniques. Look for rhetorical devices and fallacies. Advertisements often contain fallacies, and analyzing ads is a good way to familiarize yourself with spotting fallacies.

5. As a group or class, use what you learned in this chapter to construct an analysis worksheet that can then be utilized for analyzing articles as you write the Rhetorical Analysis Essay and as you analyze articles while conducting your research later in the course.

WORKS CITED

Bashion, Kim. "13 Most Offensive PETA Advertisements." *Business Insider*. October 12, 2011. http://www.businessinsider.com/peta-shocking-controversial-ads-2011-10#a-scantily-clad-pamela-anderson-starred-in-this-ad-which-was-banned-in-montreal-because-it-was-sexist-2

Davis, Amoriana. "The Income Gap in Memphis: Higher Education and Closing the Gap," *Writing Memphis*, 2nd ed., edited by Katherine Fredlund. Macmillan Curriculum Solutions, 2018. pp. 479–487.

Flyer Staff. "The Resistance: Memphis Activism Sprouts Everywhere." *Memphis Flyer*. February 23, 2017. https://www.memphisflyer.com/memphis/the-resistance-memphis-activism-sprouts-everywhere/Content?oid=5369230

Katz, Jamie. "The Soul of Memphis." *Writing Memphis*, 2nd ed., edited by Katherine Fredlund. Macmillan Curriculum Solutions, 2018. pp. 19–39.

Lauterbach, Preston. "Memphis Burning." *Writing Memphis*, 2nd ed., edited by Katherine Fredlund. Macmillan Curriculum Solutions, 2018. pp. 183–201.

Lewis, Matt. "Mitt Romney's brilliantly devious non sequitur." *The Daily Caller*. November 10, 2011. http://dailycaller.com/2011/11/10/mitt-romneys-brilliantly-devious-non-sequitur/

Mina Lasta. Comment on "The Reinvention of Taylor Swift." *Rolling Stone*, September 8, 2014. https://www.rollingstone.com/music/features/taylor-swift-1989-cover-story-20140908

Norman, Bob. "The Alien Has Landed." *Writing Memphis*, 2nd ed., edited by Katherine Fredlund. Macmillan Curriculum Solutions, 2018. pp. 41–44.

Palisades Princess. Comment on "The Reinvention of Taylor Swift." *Rolling Stone*, September 8, 2014. https://www.rollingstone.com/music/features/taylor-swift-1989-cover-story-20140908

Peters, Jared. "Red herring logical fallacies are flopping around in way too many arguments." *Scienceosaurus*. May 7, 2017. https://scienceosaurus.com/red-herring-logical-fallacies-are-flopping-around-in-way-too-many-arguments/

Stewart, Emily. "Donald Trump is losing it on Twitter over James Comey." *Vox*. April 15, 2018. https://www.vox.com/policy-and-politics/2018/4/15/17239688/james-comey-book-interview-donald-trump

"Straw Man Arguments: What They Are and How to Counter Them." *Effectiviology*. 2016–18 https://effectiviology.com/straw-man-arguments-recognize-counter-use/

Wagner, Alex. "The Americans Our Government Won't Count." *New York Times*, March 30, 2018. https://www.nytimes.com/2018/03/30/opinion/sunday/united-states-census.html?rref=collection%2Ftimestopic%2FRace%20and%2Ethnicity&action=click&contentCollection=timestopics&region=stream&module=stream_unit&version=latest&contentPlacement=6&pgtype=collection

Wells-Barnett, Ida B. "Selections from *Southern Horrors: Lynch Law in All Its Phases*." *Writing Memphis*, 2nd ed., edited by Katherine Fredlund. Macmillan Curriculum Solutions, 2018. pp. 119–128.

Wolverton, Brad. "The Education of Dasmine Cathey." *Writing Memphis*, 2nd ed., edited by Katherine Fredlund. Macmillan Curriculum Solutions, 2018. pp. 143–162.

Yellow Dog Records, "Calvin Newborn." *Writing Memphis*, 2nd ed., edited by Katherine Fredlund. Macmillan Curriculum Solutions, 2018. pp. 75–78.

YouListener. "Happiness is calling—San Diego." *YouTube*. January 24, 2015. https://www.youtube.com/playlist?list=PLB9E36EE25510E2A4

YouTube. "Tom Cruise's Heated Interview with Matt Lauer." *Today*. June 2, 2014. https://www.youtube.com/watch?v=tFgF1JPNR5E

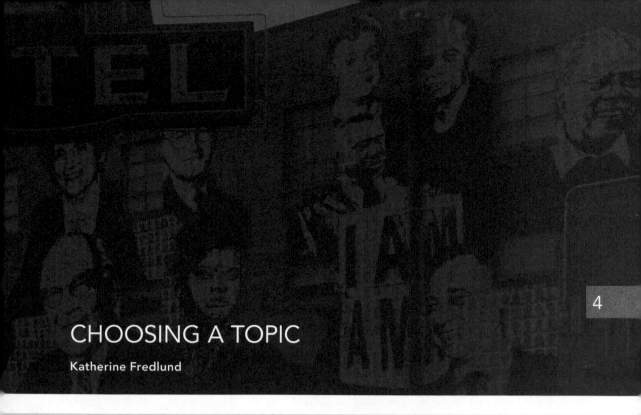

CHOOSING A TOPIC

Katherine Fredlund

Katherine Fredlund has her PhD in Rhetoric and Writing and is the Director of the First-Year Writing program at UofM. She loves to write, and she loves to teach writing. Her research has appeared in a number of journals and edited collections. Originally from Rochester, NY, she taught writing courses at St. Bonaventure University, Bowling Green State University, and Indiana State University before moving to Memphis in 2016. While she loves all things Memphis, her favorite part of Memphis is the soccer community.

All too often, writing courses ask students to begin the writing and research process with a thesis. (As you likely already know, in writing courses a thesis refers to the main idea or argument presented by a paper.) This, however, is not how researchers or academics do research. In the sciences, a researcher may have a hypothesis that needs to be tested, but the researcher doesn't even form a hypothesis without some evidence or research. Researchers may even change their methods and do multiple experiments in order to test one hypothesis. In the humanities, researchers often begin new projects by reading about a subject they are interested in and looking for gaps in that research or noticing a trend that occurs in multiple texts or places but has yet to be investigated. Indeed, researchers in all fields may even find new avenues for research by mistake.

Choosing a topic for your researched argument can seem overwhelming, especially if you think you need to know your conclusions before you have started your research. Being flexible about your argument will make the process of choosing a topic less daunting and may even lead you to a better argument. For example, when I began working on my dissertation, I planned to write about how nineteenth-century women used anti-woman rhetoric to establish their ethos with a male audience. To look for evidence of this claim, I went to the Oberlin College Archives where I found something quite different. I found the records of the Ladies Literary Society, a group formed by the first women attending a coeducational college in the United States. These records illustrated how women worked together and organized to educate themselves. As a result of this discovery, I changed my dissertation topic and instead of focusing on individual women rhetors, I focused on how women collaborated to educate themselves about writing and rhetoric in the nineteenth century. Thus, my general research topic (nineteenth-century women) remained the same, but the focus of that research shifted as a result of my findings. This rather lengthy example is all to say that you shouldn't feel like you need to know where you are going or what you are arguing when you choose your topic. Instead, you should pick a topic that you are interested in and that meets the criteria outlined below. Then you should treat the research process as a process of discovery. Your thesis should be a result of the research you find.

One of the main reasons this course is focused around Memphis is to help you narrow your topic to something that can be successfully researched in a semester and written about in a paper of less than ten pages. All too often, students want to tackle the big topics in their papers (gun control, abortion, legalizing marijuana, underage drinking, etc.). Unfortunately, these topics have been written about so often that it is hard for a novice writer and researcher to say something new or unique about these topics. Often, papers about these topics become simple retellings of arguments other people have made, and while rewording other people's arguments is useful when assigned a summary, the goal of this course is to get you to think and write critically. If your teacher allows it and you really want to focus on one of these topics, then you will still need to locate that topic within Memphis specifically. For instance, if you are interested in legalizing marijuana, then you could do research on the 2016 Memphis law that allowed police officers to lessen penalties for possession of small amounts of marijuana and the resulting state law that repealed this law (ending its existence after just seven months). The trick to successful topic selection is choosing something that will allow you to complete academic research without requiring you to sift through thousands and thousands of articles or books.

While it may seem like the Memphis focus of this course is limiting (and it is, but intentionally so), you can still write about just about anything you are interested in as long as it meets the following requirements. Thus, as you consider a topic, you may want to begin with a broader topic and then do research in order to find a way to locate this topic in Memphis. For instance, if you are concerned about water scarcity and cleanliness, then you may want to do some research on the Memphis Aquifer. There are a number of research avenues you can take here, from arguing that we are using up too much of the aquifer water too quickly, to arguing against businesses using the aquifer's water for cooling purposes, to proposing a plan to keep the aquifer safe from contaminants. In order to decide which is the best avenue, you would need to do research to see what argument the data supports. If the data supports more than one argument, then you can use the following questions to help you decide which avenue you want to follow. As you work to narrow your topic with your instructor, consider the following questions.

CAN YOU READ AND WRITE ABOUT THIS TOPIC FOR THE REST OF THE SEMESTER?

Choosing your research topic for this course is especially important because you will spend most of the semester researching and writing about that topic. The final three projects in this course ask you to focus on your chosen topic. First, you will do academic research and compose a draft of your research paper. Next you will compose that same argument in a digital genre for a different audience. Then you will use the feedback you received on both your first written draft and your digital composition to compose a revised draft of your research paper. Keeping this in mind, you should pick a topic that interests you and won't bore you after ten weeks of reading and writing.

IS THERE ACADEMIC RESEARCH ABOUT THIS TOPIC?

The research paper assignment requires a number of your sources to be "academic sources." This means that the sources you use need to be books published by an academic press, data or reports published by the government (such as the US Census), peer-reviewed journal articles, or other sources published by objective research institutes, universities, or governmental agencies. While some things about Memphis may excite you, the reality may be that it will be hard to do academic research about certain topics. For instance, if you love the Grizzlies, you may want to write about the players and culture of the team. Unfortunately, that likely won't facilitate academic research and, therefore, would not be a successful topic choice. However, if you want to write about the economic impact of the Grizzlies on downtown Memphis, then you likely will be able to find sources about major league sports teams and their economic impact on metropolitan areas. You could even find data from the Memphis Chamber of Commerce about the amount of people the Grizzlies employ and the amount of money that goes into local businesses on game nights.

Paranormal activity in Memphis might be another topic that appeals to you. This topic will be especially hard to find academic research about, unless you want to argue that the stories of paranormal activity in Memphis help create a cultural memory for the city. In this case, you wouldn't do academic research about paranormal activity. You would do academic research about cultural memory and folklore. As you can see, it is possible to find ways to write about almost anything, but it will be a great deal harder to find research that facilitates a paper about cultural memory and paranormal activity than to write about a lot of other topics.

CAN YOU BE OBJECTIVE ABOUT THIS TOPIC?

As you likely noticed in the academic readings section of the textbook, academic writing generally strives to be objective (though it doesn't always succeed at this). This means that authors, while they certainly have opinions, should always be able to consider all sides of the argument. If you are too passionate about a subject, then you may need to steer clear of it for this assignment. While a little bit of passion is a good thing since you will need to spend a lot of time with your topic, too much passion can mean that you will not accept research that disproves or challenges your opinions on the topic and not being able to objectively read and respond to research will ultimately hurt your ability to write a successful argument.

Choosing your topic for this course is important. You will spend a great deal of time with this topic, and once you write your first draft, you are stuck with this topic for the rest of the semester. *Take your time.* Do some research before you make a final decision on your topic. Talk to your instructor or peers and bounce ideas off of other people. Begin with a list of three general topics that interest you. Ask yourself the above three questions. If you answer no to any of the questions, then cross that topic off the list and move on to a new topic. Once you find yourself with a topic that you can be objective about, that you are excited about, and that will allow for academic research, then you can rest assured that you have selected well.

Writing Prompts and Activities

1. Think about the readings you have done for this class. Which reading did you find to be the most interesting or enjoyable? How come? Go back to the reading and briefly skim it to refresh your memory. Are you left with any questions about the author's argument? Do they make any claims that need more research to support them? What could your own research add to the discussion?

2. Develop a list of three topics you are interested in researching and writing about for this course. Don't be too general (Memphis music) and don't be too specific (Memphis grunge music in 1997). Instead, try to consider broad topics that interest you but that you don't quite know what you want to say about yet (the connection between tourism and music in Memphis in the 21st century). Now ask yourself the three questions from this chapter about each topic on your list. Can you read and write about this topic for the rest of the semester? Will you be able to find academic research on this topic? Can you be objective about this topic? After you answer these questions, you should have a better idea of which topic will be the best option for you, but if you still aren't excited about your topic, don't commit. Meet with your instructor, make an appointment at the Center for Writing and Communication, or ask your friends to help you come up with ideas.

CONDUCTING ACADEMIC RESEARCH

Katherine Fredlund

Katherine Fredlund has her PhD in Rhetoric and Writing and is the Director of the First-Year Writing program at UofM. She loves to write, and she loves to teach writing. Her research has appeared in a number of journals and edited collections. Originally from Rochester, NY, she taught writing courses at St. Bonaventure University, Bowling Green State University, and Indiana State University before moving to Memphis in 2016. While she loves all things Memphis, her favorite part of Memphis is the soccer community.

The first challenge of conducting academic research is learning what counts as an academic source. Academic sources range from print books, to e-books, to journal articles, to research reports. Government documents are also considered acceptable for use in academic writing. The texts you read online or even in print are generally not academic sources, and, as a result, they go through a less rigorous process from conception to publication. If, for example, a writer employed by the *Memphis Flyer* decides to pitch a story about Memphis BBQ, then the writer will likely pitch the idea to an editor or a team that works for that publication. If it gets approved, then the writer will go do research and write the story. After it is written, the story will need to be approved by an editor or an editorial team and get copyedited before publication.

Academic research follows a very different trajectory. Academic authors do research and write articles or even books without a guarantee that the research will be published. Once an article or book is completed, it is submitted to a journal or an academic publisher in order to go through the peer review process. The peer review process is blind; this means that the identity of the researcher is not shared with the people reviewing the research and deciding whether or not it should be published. Publishers generally use double-blind peer review, which means that the author also doesn't know the identity of the reviewers. For journal articles, an article is often sent to two reviewers, and they might decide the research has promise but ask the writer to revise before it will be accepted. Research can still be rejected even after it is revised. As you might imagine, this is a time-consuming process, and articles can take anywhere from a few months to a few years to move through the peer review process. Books take even longer. This blind peer review process ensures a level of quality, and that is why this course requires academic research. The quality of the research is verified through the peer review process.

So how can you tell if a source qualifies as "academic"? The first thing to consider is the publisher and the audience. If the publication is intended for a general audience or for the general public, then it is likely not an academic source. Academic sources are written for specialists and scholars. If a book is published by a University Press, then it is probably academic. That said, there are academic publishers that are not affiliated with specific universities, so you should Google the publication and read about them. Academic publishers generally identify themselves as either academic or scholarly. If you are looking at an article from a journal, then you will check to see if that journal is academic. Again, if you Google the journal name, it will tell you if it is "academic" (or "scholarly"). Academic research is important because it requires multiple experts from a field to agree that the research is worth publication. This means that research that lacks rigor, has fundamental methodological problems, or is poorly written will not get published.

ACCESSING LIBRARY SEARCH ENGINES

As students at the University of Memphis, you have access to a number of search engines through the library website. While you may do some research on Google or Bing, most of your research for this class should be done through the library website because public search engines do not provide access to academic sources. If you aren't using the library website, then you will not find academic sources, as most of these sources are not available to the public and are only available to you because the library pays hefty fees in order to make them available to University of Memphis students and faculty. The search engines provided by the library work in much the same way as the search engines you use everyday, but they aren't quite as intuitive. (If you spell a word wrong, for instance, they won't return results for the correct spelling of the word.) That said, don't let the fact that you have to access these search engines through the library intimidate you; you likely search for information on the internet multiple times a day. Looking for academic research simply requires you to build upon knowledge you already have.

The most popular of these search engines are JSTOR and EBSCOhost. To get to these search engines, go to the UofM Library website (http://www.memphis.edu/libraries/). You will notice a search bar on the homepage, and you can use this search bar to look for books and articles, but it will be much easier to find articles if you use one of the academic search engines. To access these search engines, click the "Databases" tab directly above the search bar. You can then use the same search bar to search for a database if you know which one you want to use. (For the sake of brevity, this chapter discusses using JSTOR, but using EBSCOhost and other search engines will follow similar steps.) If you type in JSTOR, then the database will be the only search result. Click on "Database" below the result, and JSTOR will open. If you are off campus, then you will be asked to enter your username and password. Use your MyMemphis username and password to sign in.

LIMITING YOUR RESULTS

Once in JSTOR, select "Advanced Search." This option allows you to limit the results and use multiple search terms. Below the search bars, there is a section called "Narrow By." This allows you to select the kind of document you need. You will definitely want to search for articles, but you may also want to look for books, pamphlets, or research reports. Reviews summarize and analyze academic books, so if you want to see if a book is useful by reading a summary of that book before requesting the book itself, then you can search for reviews, but reviews likely won't be something you will cite in your research paper.

Next you will need to consider date range. This will depend on your subject of study. In scientific, technological, and medical fields, research becomes dated quickly. If your topic falls under any of these (very broad) classifications, then you will likely want to limit your research to the last 5–10 years, depending on the topic. Research in the humanities (philosophy, literary studies, writing studies, history) does not become dated as quickly, so such date limits will be less important if you are doing research in these fields.

Finally, you can narrow by discipline. If you aren't quite sure which discipline your research falls under, you can either select multiple options or none at all. This limitation will only search within the journals that have been classified within the selected disciplines. So if you select "Economics," then rather than search all of the journals within JSTOR, your search will only look within the 175 journals classified as economics journals. This limiting option weeds out unnecessary results that may include your search terms but are not actually within the field of study you are researching.

SELECTING SEARCH TERMS

Now that you have limited your results, it is time for the hard part: selecting your search terms. Your first inclination is going to be to include the search term "Memphis," and for a first search, this makes good sense. However, you are likely going to find that there is not enough research specifically on Memphis and your topic. Consequently, you are going to need to use broader search terms in order to find academic research that supports your argument. The goal of academic research is not to find sources that say exactly what you want to say. Instead, the goal is to find research that helps support your claims without doing exactly what you are doing in your own writing. Because this is a challenging task, you should seek help from librarians and your instructor.

One way to develop search terms is to write down your research question. Try to make this research question as specific as possible. After you have a question that you are happy with, cross out all the prepositions (as, about, in, of, etc.) and conjunctions (and, or, but, etc.).

The remaining words can function as your search terms. Try searching for them in different combinations and using different Boolean terms. Boolean terms direct the search engine to conduct the search in a specific way. If you use "and," then the search engine will only look for results that include *all* of your search terms. If you use "or," then the search engine will return results that use *any* of the search terms you selected. If you get stuck at any point, then ask your instructor or a librarian for help.

ACADEMIC RESEARCH EXAMPLE

Reading about the intricacies of academic research may provide some useful information, but going through a process of trial and error is unavoidable as you learn how to conduct research using academic search engines. Returning to the aquifer example from the "Choosing a Topic" chapter, this section summarizes the process I went through with one of my students after the student struggled to find academic research on her own. This student, like many others, was not ready to draft a research question when she began her research. As a result, this example starts with general search terms rather than a research question. This example will be most useful if you open JSTOR and follow along. Keep in mind that this chapter lists the results found in Spring 2017, but since sources are added to search engines all the time, you may see slightly different results within your own search.

We began our research by limiting the results and searching for only articles and books. We also selected the following disciplines: biological sciences, environmental science, environmental studies, geology, public health, public policy and administration, and urban studies. With these limitations, we used two search terms: "Memphis" and "aquifer." Our search returned 21 results. Some of these results were more useful than others. The first two sources are from the same journal: *American Water Works Association*. They will both be useful in learning about Memphis's aquifer. The first, "Aeration Experiments at Memphis, Tenn." by R.L. Brown, was published in 1950. While this source will not provide current information on how the aquifer works, it does present a useful history that will help the student (and perhaps her audience too) understand the history of the Memphis water supply. The next source, "The Water Supply of Memphis, Tennessee" by J.N. Chester and D.E. Davis, is even older (published in 1921). This article provides an even more detailed history, discussing the discovery of the "artesian sands" (another term for aquifer). While these two sources will be useful for understanding the history of the Memphis Aquifer, they will not help us understand how the aquifer works today, and they are too dated to consider contemporary threats to Memphis's water supply.

The next few sources in the search results are about aquifers in other states and, at least for now, do not appear helpful. As we click on the remaining sources and quickly read through their abstracts or introductions, we notice that many of them are either too dated to be useful or too descriptive in nature. One does include a map that the student could insert into her research paper in order to illustrate where the aquifer is under the city and surrounding areas, but this research is not helping the student develop a concrete understanding of the aquifer or the challenges such a water supply faces.

We need to do another search, but both of us are frustrated and decide to try to find government sources via Google. We start simple and search for "Memphis Aquifer." Most of the sources that come back are from news outlets, but we know those won't work because they aren't considered scholarly, so we scroll down and see that the 6th result is a government study published in 1990 ("Geology and Ground-Water Resources of the Memphis Sand in Western Tennessee"). As we look at the table of contents, we decide this source will be quite useful because the student doesn't know much about aquifers in general, and this source will provide her with some specific information about Memphis's aquifer (ranging from information about the size of the sands to the average daily use in 1990).

As we continue to read the government report, the student realizes she needs a source that explains what an aquifer is and provides more general information about her topic. This will be essential information for the paper's introduction. Knowing that articles are short and thus generally directed toward a specialist audience that wouldn't need simple definitions and explanations, we decide that a book is more likely to provide this information. Rather than return to JSTOR, we decide to use the search engine on the library homepage. We type in a single search term ("aquifer"), and the first result is an ebook (*Aquifers: Properties, Roles, and Research*) that was published in 2017 (finally a contemporary source!). Unfortunately, our library doesn't own this ebook, so we have to request access via interlibrary loan (ILLiad) and wait for an email granting access. Since this source seems to be exactly what the student needs to better understand her research topic, she is going to have to wait for this source to come through ILLiad. This is one benefit of avoiding procrastination: she has the time to wait for a source that she knows she needs. Had she been doing her research at the last minute, she would have had to write her entire argument draft without a source that she knows will make her paper better.

At this point, we have found four academic sources that the student plans to use in her paper, but she still needs a few more sources. We return to the goal of developing a research question because doing so will allow us to look for more specific sources. The student notes that she was interested in the news stories that popped up on Google, particularly those about the Tennessee Valley Authority (TVA) pumping millions of gallons of water from the aquifer each day in order to cool a power plant. In those readings, she learned that environmentalist groups are concerned that pumping this much water daily could lead to ground water contamination. She decides on "Does increased water pumping pose a contamination risk to the Memphis Aquifer and ground-water supply?" as her research question. We return to JSTOR with these new search terms and type in "water supply," "ground-water," and "contamination." The first search result, "Ground-Water Contamination in the United States" by Veronica I. Pye and Ruth Patrick, provides useful definitions of both ground-water and aquifer, and the student decides to use these definitions in her introduction, but as we keep reading, we don't see any indication that over-pumping can lead to contamination, though it is clear that this article does not discuss all of the ways ground-water can be contaminated.

We return to our search results and notice a source titled "Human Interactions with Ground-Water." Since over-pumping would qualify as a human interaction, we decide to check this source out. The abstract begins:

Ground-Water could be considered as an immense reservoir, from which only a certain amount of water can be withdrawn without affecting the quantity and quality of water. This amount is determined by the characteristics of the environment in which ground-water occurs and by the interactions of ground-water with precipitation, surface water, and people. It should be recognized that quantity and quality of ground-water are intimately related and should be considered accordingly. Quantity refers to usable water and water is usable for any specific purpose only so long as its quality has not deteriorated beyond acceptable limits. (Zaporozec 427)

This source has (finally!) given the student what she needs to move from a research question to an argument, and she decides to argue that the amount of water TVA plans to pump from the well on a daily basis poses a significant contamination risk to Memphis's water supply. She still feels she needs a few more sources, however, so we scroll down to the references page at the bottom of the same article and find 2–4 citations of additional sources that she plans to read. At this point, the student feels confident that she has found enough academic research. While she may find she needs to search for additional research as her argument develops, she has plenty of sources to help her develop a concrete understanding of aquifers and ground-water as well as to establish a connection between over-pumping and ground-water contamination.

As this example illustrates, doing research is a time-consuming and difficult process, especially when search engines and search terms are new to the researcher. While this section has focused on finding academic sources, it is important to note that this student decided to use the news stories she found in her Google search to help her introduce the problem (TVA pumping) and to locate her argument in Memphis. When you begin your own research, you may also find that you need to use a variety of sources. Just be sure that you meet the academic source requirements. Non-academic sources should only be used when they are absolutely necessary. For instance, because the issue of TVA pumping was relatively new when this student started her research, academic sources on the topic had not yet been published. This made using news sources necessary and acceptable. If you aren't sure when to use news sources or other non-academic sources, then you should talk to your teacher and make sure your use of such sources is appropriate for your purposes.

RESEARCH TIPS

Read the Abstracts: A lot of journal articles include abstracts. When an article title indicates the article might be useful (but you aren't sure based on the title alone), read the abstract. The abstract should include the equivalent of a thesis statement. This statement will let you know what the article is arguing, presenting, or explaining. This should provide you with enough information to determine whether or not you should keep reading.

Read Introductions and Conclusions: Sometimes, articles lack abstracts or appear useful based on their title but don't end up providing the information you are looking for. While they won't be labeled as such, you should start by reading the introduction, generally the first few pages of an article (for some articles, this will mean reading until you reach a methods section), and the conclusion, found on the last few pages of the article (this may be labeled discussion or findings or any number of other things). Doing this will, once again, help you determine if the article is going to be useful for your purposes. Further, reading the conclusion will help you better understand the rest of the article if you decide reading an entire article is necessary (i.e., if you decide to use the article in your paper). Beginning with the introduction and conclusion will save you a lot of time; there is no reason to read an article in full until you know it is directly relevant to your research.

Utilize Bibliographies: Works cited pages and bibliographies exist for a reason, and you should take advantage of them. Once you have found a source that is useful, scroll to the end and look at the sources the author cited. Use the titles and journal names to determine which sources might be useful and then search for those sources within the library website. If the library doesn't have the source or provide access to it, then you should request it via interlibrary loan. Even if your first draft is due in a few days, you should request the source, as while you may not be able to use it in the first draft, it will definitely arrive in time for the revision. Journals also publish similar work, so if the bibliography doesn't help you, then search for the journal that the article was published in and then search for articles related to your topic within that journal.

Use the Library Services: The University of Memphis librarians are expert researchers, and you should take advantage of the many services they provide. As a student, you can schedule a research consultation with a librarian. This consultation can be scheduled online on the "Ask-a-Librarian" page. In this consultation, a librarian will help you do research on your topic, and since they are experts, they will be aware of the best places to look for research on your subject. They are also quite skilled at selecting search terms, so if you are struggling with this aspect of the research process, then scheduling a consultation might be productive. You can also always stop at the reference desk and get immediate help if you are struggling to locate a specific book or need general help doing research. If you have a simple question or are not able to come to campus, then try the Chat feature. Located on both the library's homepage and the "Ask-a-Librarian" page, you can click the link in order to chat with a librarian. Finally, there are a number of additional resources provided by the library. If you open the resources page, then you will notice that they provide database tutorials, citation help, and even a research guide designed specifically for students in English 1020. While you may think you don't need the library because a lot of articles and books are now available online, failing to take advantage of the many services the library provides for students is a missed opportunity.

KEEP CALM AND RESEARCH ON

Doing research can be frustrating, but it can also be rewarding. When you finally find the sources you need, the struggle will feel worth it, but it can, admittedly, take much longer to get to that point than any student may like or expect. When frustration hits, you should feel free to walk away from the computer. Take a break. Go for a run, play video games, treat yourself to a nice meal, or spend time with friends. These breaks are a necessary part of the writing and research process.

You should also not be scared to seek help. Whether you ask a friend to help you come up with search terms, schedule a research consultation with a librarian, or go to your instructor's office hours to ask for help, you will benefit from talking to someone else about your research (and your writing). Many people hate writing because they think of it as a solitary process, but most people who spend a lot of time writing constantly discuss their ideas and writing struggles, share their drafts with friends or colleagues, and even ask other people for source recommendations. Since everyone in your class will be doing research about Memphis, you may even be able to use some of the same sources as your classmates.

As you do research for this course, you will undoubtedly experience moments of exasperation, but in those moments, you should remind yourself that solid research is the foundation of a successful academic argument. Without the right research, you will not be able to successfully persuade your audience. So while it may be tempting to just give up and start writing without the research you need, this will only make composing your argument more difficult. If you spend time doing research and keep searching until you find what you need, then not only will your argument be stronger, but it will also be easier and more enjoyable to write.

Writing Prompts and Activities

1. When writing academic papers, you will often need to define key terms. While it may be tempting to simply look up a dictionary definition, academic genres often require you to define terms using academic sources. In the aquifer example discussed above, it is best to use academic sources to explain ground water and aquifers because they will provide more details. If I search Google for aquifer definitions, I get this definition from dictionary.com: "a body of permeable rock that can contain or transmit groundwater." If I use the source I mentioned above to educate my audience about my key terms, then I might introduce the terms like this:

   Pye and Patrick explain that ground water "that is used by humans consists of subsurface water which occurs in fully saturated soils and geological formations. Nearly half the population of the United States use ground water from wells or springs as their primary source of drinking water; 36 percent of the municipal public drinking supply comes from ground water; and 75 percent of major U.S. Cities depend on ground water for most of their supply" (713). Like most major cities, Memphis relies on ground water. Our supply comes from an aquifer. Pye and Patrick explain that, "Aquifers may be composed of permeable or porous geological materials, either unconsolidated sand or gravel or consolidated material such as carbonate rocks, volcanic rocks, or fractured igneous, metamorphic, or sedimentary rocks. Unconfined aquifers are the most susceptible to contamination. They are not overlain by impermeable material and are recharged by water seeping through the soil" (713–4).

   Why is the second example more useful for both the writer and the audience? Using the two quotations, rewrite the above as an introductory paragraph that introduces an argument about the problem of TVA's water pumping and Memphis's aquifer. Then write a brief explanation of your rhetorical decisions. What did you add? Delete? Why? Why would a dictionary definition be less effective than the above definitions?

2. Write your research question down on a piece of paper. Cross out all the prepositions (as, about, in, of, etc.) and conjunctions (and, or, but, etc.). Open a library search engine and search using your terms. Now delete Memphis from your search terms, and try searching again. What kind of sources do you need that you haven't been able to find? How can you change your search terms to find those sources? (For example, if you search for "ground water" instead of "aquifer," then you will find more results.)

WORKS CITED

Aquifer. (n.d.). In Dictionary.com. Retrieved from https://www.google.com/search?q=Dictionary#dobs=aquifer

Bailey, Heather. *Aquifers: Properties, Roles and Research*. Nova Science P Inc., 2017.

Brown, R.L. "Aeration Experiments at Memphis, Tenn." *American Water Works Association*, vol. 44, no. 4, 1952, pp. 336–44.

Chester, J.N., and D.E. Davis. "The Water Supply of Memphis, Tennessee. *American Water Works Association*, vol. 8, no. 4, 1921, pp. 377–96.

Parks, W.S., and J.K. Carmichael. "Geology and Ground-Water Resources of the Memphis Sand in Western Tennessee." Department of the Interior. U.S. Geological Survey. Water-Resources Investigations Report 88-4182, 1990.

Pye, Veronica, and Ruth Patrick. "Ground Water Contamination in the United States." *Science*, vol, 221, no. 4621, 1983, pp. 713–18.

Zaporozec, A. "Human Interactions with Ground-Water." *GeoJournal*, vol. 7, no. 5, 1983, pp. 427–33.

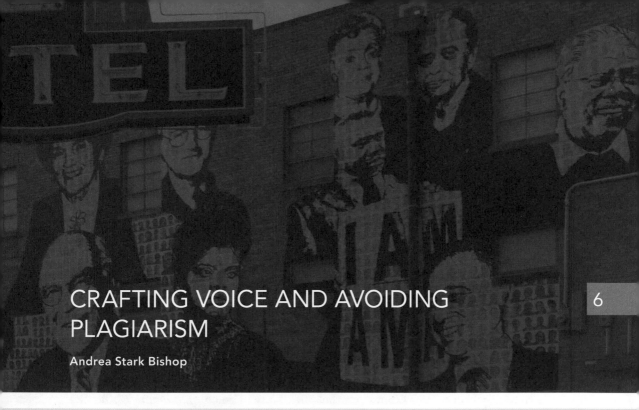

CRAFTING VOICE AND AVOIDING PLAGIARISM

Andrea Stark Bishop

Andrea Stark Bishop is completing her PhD in Composition Studies at the University of Memphis. Originally from a small town in Oklahoma, she married into the Navy and spent many years moving from state to state. She taught writing courses and academic success courses at Olympic College in Washington and Southwest Tennessee Community College before teaching at UofM. She has also worked in the Center for Writing and Communication and has served as its Graduate Assistant Director. Her favorite Memphis things to do with her husband and two sons include enjoying the Memphis Zoo, dining out in Overton Square, and sipping old fashioned soda fountain drinks at A. Schwab's in the heart of downtown Memphis.

Yeah, I know. You hate citing sources. You hate reading about plagiarism. You hate me right now for even writing this chapter. People read or hear the word *plagiarism* and either immediately stop reading/listening or have a mild panic attack because they aren't sure what might get them locked up in Plagiarism Prison, but don't worry! I'm approaching this topic from a different perspective. Instead of hitting you with a bunch of rules and warnings, I'll explain how understanding writerly voice can help you avoid plagiarism.

MAINTAINING YOUR VOICE WHILE INCORPORATING SOURCES

My voice is a product of the people who raised me—and of the people I'm now raising. It is born of the places where I've lived, of the life that I've chosen. It is also a result of the texts I've read and the things that spark an interest in me. I'm a total word nerd. Words and how they work, how they can be put together in different and exciting ways, how one word can completely change the meaning of an entire argument—these things excite me. I know that's probably not your story though. For you, maybe a sport is your obsession. Maybe you love fashion or travel or cooking or Star Wars. Regardless of what your thing is, it helps shape you and helps create your voice. Your writerly voice is a product of who you are. It is distinctive. It is the *you* that is written into your work. Good writers are able to make their voices enticing, interesting, captivating, and very real. Good writers also realize that to borrow someone else's work is to borrow someone else's voice. Like all instances of borrowing, there are acceptable and unacceptable ways to go about it. Borrowing in an unacceptable way is…well…basically stealing (which is bad). Borrowing in acceptable ways, with permission and respect, is often very good, especially when you are writing an argument.

When I teach students how to use outside sources in their researched arguments, I like to begin with voice. Each writer, each and every one of us, has this inner spark that enables us to write in a way that no one else writes—to sound like no one else sounds. Just as you'd be able to recognize your mom's voice even if you couldn't see her face, your writerly voice can be recognized by your readers. Dr. Peter Elbow, Professor Emeritus at the University of Massachusetts Amherst, writes, "We have selves that are individual and to some degree unique (though not simple, unitary, or unchanging), and it helps our writing to honor our self and voice" (*Everyone Can Write* xiv). In other words, he suggests that our writing is strengthened when we recognize the value of our voice and allow that part of ourselves to enter the writing.

Peter Elbow is the preeminent scholar on voice in writing. He has been writing about voice for more than fifty years. Peter Elbow says that "flexibility of voice" (*Landmark Essays* xlv) is basically a range of voices that are all still mine. I like to think of my writerly voice as a sort of slide ruler or a continuum with the many different versions of me situated along the line. When I write for myself, in personal writing or in freewriting, I use one *me*, and when I write for another audience, I use another *me*. In other words, there are many different voices within my writerly voice.

Just think about how you might talk to your grandmother and consider how that voice is different from the voice you use when you talk to a puppy or a friend or a coworker. All of those voices are you; they are just variations of you for a specific audience and a specific context. The same is true of writing. You can remain true to yourself—true to your voice— and still write appropriately for various audiences.

HOW TO CONSTRUCT *YOUR* VOICE

As I stated earlier, your writerly voice is a product of who you are. It is distinctive. It is the *you* that is written into your work. Voice is awesome, but your writerly voice does not just magically appear. **You must create it**.

Strong writers use specific strategies to construct a voice that is appropriate for the context and audience, while remaining very much a reflection of the author. Below are five specific strategies to help you construct your writerly voice. While this list is not exhaustive, utilizing some of these strategies in your writing will certainly improve both your voice and your argument.

The following stylistic elements of voice—**diction**, **details**, **imagery**, **syntax**, and **tone**— offer an effective, engaging approach for achieving a strong voice.

6

DICTION

Diction refers to the word choices you make when you write. Word choice matters. However, please keep in mind that using a word you don't fully understand because you think the word might make you sound "smart" is actually NOT the best idea. If you use words that aren't familiar to you, then you are likely using them incorrectly—which means your word choice is certainly not reflecting any part of who you are. Also keep this in mind: strong diction does not come from randomly selecting a synonym by using the synonym function in Microsoft Word. Careless or haphazard synonym-selecting ends up creating a disjointed written product, one that often lacks any semblance of writerly voice.

Since word choice matters, BE THOUGHTFUL when you write. Consider the differences between using the word *courageous* rather than *bold*. They may be synonyms, but *courageous* and *bold* are not interchangeable. Why might you want to replace the word *tenacious* with the word *gritty*? What are the denotations (dictionary type definitions) and the connotations (underlying meaning or associations) of the words? Thoughtfully choosing specific words helps you make your voice appropriate for the rhetorical situation.

Think of it this way: sometimes I call my mom "mother" and sometimes I say "mama." Both are correct, but I use "mother" when I want her to take me seriously, and I use "mama" when I want her to take care of me. Word choice matters. Be thoughtful about the choices you make, and consider what sounds most like you and is also most appropriate for the context and audience. Diction means word choice, and word choice matters.

DETAILS

When you want to improve your writing, including appropriate and helpful details always helps. The details you choose to include also help you construct your writerly voice. For example, in a literacy narrative, a writer might say that her older brother always read her children's books at bedtime. However, if that writer wanted to construct a strong voice, she would include details that make her narrative much more interesting. She might write something like this: "When I was fresh from my bath, dressed in soft footie pajamas with my damp hair tied up in a bun, my brother, Derek, would let me choose two books from my bookcase. I often chose books with animals because Derek did all of the animal sounds for me. One of my favorite books was called *Bear Wants More*. It had a bear, a rabbit, a wren, and a mole who were all friends. Derek made each character sound different and funny; he added in roars and tweeting noises. I would snuggle into my fleece blanket while he sat on the floor by my bed and read." The details add layers to the account, but they also show the parts of the story that are important to the writer. This helps create voice.

For academic arguments, you can (and should) use details in your writing. Such details might include statistics, but you can also include anecdotes or descriptive information when appropriate. If you are writing an argument about graffiti as an art form in Memphis, then you need to describe the buildings, the neighborhoods, the colors, the styles, the meanings, and the actual graffiti. Details matter.

IMAGERY

Like details, using imagery builds additional layers of context into your writing. Imagery is also a fantastic way to craft voice because the imagery you choose to use is often somewhat unique to you. Imagery can be crafted by painting word pictures for your reader using the five senses (see, touch, smell, hear, taste), but imagery also includes writing in metaphors or making allusions to other things. The things you choose to allude to will be of interest to you, so they will obviously reflect some part of yourself. I grew up in a tiny Oklahoma town and was raised on farming, fishing, and football, so I often allude to such ideas in my writing. Your own interests can and should make their way into your writing.

SYNTAX

Syntax refers to the ways you put together your sentences. It is the order of your words and the use of punctuation within the framework of the sentence. Perhaps you've been told that your sentences should have variety—that you don't want all short sentences or all long sentences—because sameness in your syntax creates a sort of monotony in writing. This is very true. Changing up sentence construction is one way to craft your voice. Following up a long, complex sentence structure with a short two-word sentence is one way to make a statement in your writing. It also creates a rhythm that helps reflect voice.

Syntax. Keep in mind that audience and context should always determine syntax. If you are tasked with writing an instruction manual or a lab report, a monotonous syntax structure would be entirely appropriate if not necessary. However, this book is intended to help you write in a way to effectively argue or persuade; therefore, your syntax should *not* be dry and monotonous.

Consider the following example, which comes from a reflective letter written at the end of English 1010. The reflective letter was the final writing assignment of the semester and was included in the student's end-of-term portfolio of work. The purpose of the letter was to allow the student to essentially prove his or her growth throughout the academic term. You will see that this student writer has a syntax structure that is quite tedious in its sameness. The only part of the paragraph that isn't monotonous is one three word sentence and the concluding sentence. While the author of this paragraph could have used some additional work on syntax, you cannot deny that a certain voice becomes apparent as you read this work. (It just might not be the best voice for the context and audience.)

> The research paper was my most challenging paper. I chose to research how texting has affected our way of writing. I have written research papers before but not like this one. We had to interview people and do surveys and stuff. I'd never thought about how to write a survey so that was tricky. I think my survey questions ended up being pretty lame. My results weren't' too exciting. I basically just discovered what I already knew. My generation texts so much that almost everyone I surveyed had accidentally included text-type in their schoolwork. We used the IMRaD format for this paper. I liked the structure of that okay. IMRaD helped me understand how to organize my paper. The writing sucked. But I think I'll use IMRaD when I have to write again, so I guess that's helpful.

TONE

Tone expresses your attitude toward the subject or audience of the paper. Tone is often considered a synonym for voice in writing. While tone is not the same thing as voice, it is certainly part of voice. Crafting an intentional tone goes hand-in-hand with crafting your voice. In the previous example, the tone is apathetic. This student writer obviously does NOT care about the assignment, which is made quite clear for his audience.

Do you want your readers to see you as confident or questioning? Passionate or violent? Enthusiastic or critical? The tone you weave into your argument will help you establish both *ethos* and *pathos* for your audience, and the tone will also help you voice what is most important to your argument.

Strategies for creating tone in your writing include using **boldface type**, *italics*, and punctuation—such as an emdash or parentheses. The emdash (looks like this—and is three times longer than a normal hyphen) can be used in place of commas or colons. This emdash punctuation—one that sets off something important—has an almost exclamatory tone. It practically shouts to the reader, "You need to *see* this information." In contrast, the use of parentheses tends to evoke a more intimate tone (one in which you might be *whispering* something to the reader). Using **boldface type** is generally used for highlighting key terms, such as terms you might need to define, while the use of italics can be used *sparingly* for emphasis. If you look back over this chapter, you'll see that I've used these strategies to create the tone I wanted for this publication. Keep in mind that each of these strategies should be used intentionally and minimally. In other words, don't go crazy with the emdash, or your reader will be exhausted from all of the excitement. Additionally, in academic writing, the use of the exclamation point (!) is not appropriate.

When you can control your **diction**, **syntax**, and **tone**, when you provide **details** and **imagery** that show rather than tell, you are presenting polished writing in an authoritative voice. Knowing the different connotations of a single word or crafting syntax that is sophisticated or surprising can help you claim ownership over your own writing while you assert a voice that is yours and yours alone.

USING VOICE TO UNDERSTAND SOURCE INCORPORATION

So how does voice help you incorporate sources? When we incorporate information from other sources, the temptation is to let the other writers do the work. I mean, these other writers have been published somewhere. They are the experts. They seem to know what they're talking about, right? In many ways, it makes sense to let them take the lead; so when we find a good quote—something that seems to have some power or punch behind the words—we drop that quote into our writing and keep on moving. However, this method of incorporating sources is NOT a good one. I call this **dropping quote bombs** and, like most bombs, the results can be destructive. Dropping quote bombs means that you are leaving your reader with unexplained, and often, unhelpful information in some other person's voice. It's confusing. It's disjointed. Frankly, it's lazy writing, and it's completely counterproductive to the entire reason that you are expected to incorporate sources in the first place.

WHY DO YOU NEED TO USE MATERIAL FROM OTHER SOURCES WHEN YOU ARE WRITING A PAPER?

Seriously, what's the point of using other sources? The answer is pretty simple; we use other sources to *support our arguments*.

I'll say that again. **You use other sources, other writers' work, to support your arguments.** This does not mean that you should use other sources to **state** your argument. It does not mean you should use other sources to **create** your argument. I hate to be the bearer of bad news, but creating and stating your argument are 100% your job. You are responsible for determining the topic, for figuring out the possible sides of the argument, for choosing your stance, for finding the right research, and for figuring out any steps that need to be taken or supporting points that need to be made. YOU are the writer, so these are your tasks. In order for readers to believe you and trust you as the author since you are most likely not an expert on the topic, you need to find sources that back you up and provide you with some credibility. The other sources you use should help you create a trustworthy **ethos**.

EXAMPLES OF INCORPORATING SOURCES TO SUPPORT AN ARGUMENT

Example 1. A few years ago I needed to persuade the University of Memphis that a class I'd taken at Harding University should transfer to UofM and meet one of my degree requirements. My basic argument is as follows and should be read as general grumbling:

> I've taken a course called Quantitative Research Methods worth three credit hours at Harding University. That ridiculously hard class should satisfy the requirement for a research methods class at this university. Please, for all that is good and holy, *please* don't make me take another quantitative research methods class *here* since I already took one *there*. Plus, I got a freakin' A, and it was a really hard class involving a lot of math. I hate math. I hated that class. I don't want to endure it again.

That was my argument, but since I knew it had to be approved by The Important People in the Graduate Studies office, I needed to back up my argument with sources that lent some credibility to my words. I also needed to slide across my voice scale and use the appropriate voice for this context and this audience. I used the course catalogue from my previous university and quoted the description of the class to prove how its description was closely aligned with the one I was supposed to take at the other university. I also quoted the Graduate Studies Handbook that stated, "course requirements may be satisfied by courses taken at previous institutions if students can prove a close affiliation between the two classes." My new argument looked something like this:

> In 2012, I successfully completed a course called Quantitative Research Methods for three credit hours at Harding University. The course was described in the course catalog as one which "covers the fundamental principles of quantitative research methods in the social sciences with a strong focus on research integrity and ethics. Covers various research designs, measurement, and sampling" (Catalog 332). As you can see on my attached transcript, I earned an A in this course. Since the Graduate Studies Handbook indicates that I can transfer credit under certain conditions when it states

that "course requirements may be satisfied by courses taken at previous institutions if students can prove a close affiliation between the two classes" (Graduate Handbook 117), I respectfully ask that you grant me transfer credit for the required Quantitative Research Methods course at this university.

You will be happy to know (though probably not as happy I was) that credit was granted, and I didn't have to take another math-heavy research methods class. Hopefully, you can also see that the sources I used improved my credibility while my voice was intentionally crafted to be respectful toward my specific audience. The voice I used for that situation was just one of my many voices, but it was the voice most appropriate for the task at hand.

Example 2. I need a new car. My husband and I are trying to agree on what kind of car to get. He's much more knowledgeable about cars in general—in other words, he knows engines, understands what words like "torque" mean, and he has firmly-held opinions on what we should get. He wants to buy a truck...a big truck. However, I do NOT want a truck. I have two active children, two even more active dogs, and one adorable nephew. I am often the chauffeur of those little hooligans. I'm also somewhat "vertically challenged," with short legs and short arms, and I know how difficult it is to buckle kids into car seats when I can barely reach them. I also don't especially want to carry around a stepladder just to get into my vehicle. I want a minivan. Yes, darn it, I *know* minivans aren't cool—and that a minivan completely offends my husband's sense of manliness and car knowledge—but I also know that a minivan would make my life easier.

My job is to convince my husband that my choice of vehicle makes more sense than his choice. I know that if I go to him with only my opinion, then he will see himself as the expert and my opinion will be just that...*opinion*. So I do research. I educate myself on the worth of minivans, of the miles per gallon, of the types of engines available, and of the resale value. Only then do I go to him using information from other sources to solidify my argument. Rather than simply telling him that a minivan is easier for me to get the kids buckled safely into their seats, I make that statement and then follow it up with examples from the sources I've gathered.

Both my college credit and car anecdotes are simplistic examples of how we use sources to solidify our arguments. We determine our primary and secondary points and then back them up with another strong voice. That other voice is one that lends authority to our argument, but it only works if we introduce the voice as *someone else's voice*. If we try to claim those words as our own, then not only are we plagiarizing, but we are also derailing our argument **because the argument needs more than just my voice**.

For academic arguments, the importance of incorporating strong secondary sources cannot be overstated. When we interweave the words and ideas of academic scholars into our own academic writing, we are engaging in a scholarly conversation. We are participating in the work of the university. We are becoming scholars.

Rather than thinking about using academic sources as a punishment concocted by your professor, think of these sources as a way for you to prove to yourself and to the university community that **you belong here** (because you do). Your voice and the voices of published scholars should work together. Your words and ideas, partnered with those from academic sources, enter into a conversation or a discourse that should be interesting to you and to others in your class. Incorporating academic sources is one way for you to show that you too are a scholar and that you too have something to add to the conversation.

TIME TO TALK THE P-WORD (PLAGIARISM)

Let's talk for a minute about the most dreaded word in all writing courses: **Plagiarism**. It's not a fun topic, but it is a necessary topic. I'll do my best to make it better than any other thing you've ever read about plagiarism; you do your best to finish reading the chapter.

One of my favorite composition studies scholars, Rebecca Moore Howard, breaks plagiarism into four distinct forms that I find much more useful than the catch-all term *plagiarism*. Her terms for those distinct forms are *fraud*, *insufficient citation*, *patchwriting*, and *excessive repetition* (Howard 1207).

Fraud is when an entire paper is ghostwritten, which basically means it was purchased or possibly borrowed from a friend. Fraud is when the intended author (you) gets someone else to do the authoring. This is fraudulent behavior. Thievery. *Wrong*. Howard says, "Handing in a paper that somebody else wrote is as bad as falsifying a transcript or hiring a test-taker: It thwarts two of the academy's most basic functions—to teach and to certify intellectual accomplishment" (1219). Therefore, if you commit fraud, you are a cheater and deserve to be punished. Fraud also shows intent to deceive. Fraud is bad, and in my class, it gets you a failing grade for the course.

Insufficient citation is when you borrow without giving credit. You drop a quote without explaining who originally wrote it and why. You find a great idea somewhere, but you fail to give voice to the one who originally came up with the idea. In an academic argument, your voice should be supported by the voices of experts, and this insufficient citation means that you aren't doing your job. You are not supporting your ideas with the voices of others. Insufficient citation is bad, but it's certainly not fraud. Many professors will assume that insufficient citation is intentional on your part, that you were perhaps too lazy to cite, or that you were trying to use someone else's ideas as your own. Insufficient citation can definitely get you into trouble with most professors, though some will allow you to revise so you can fix the problems.

Patchwriting is when you take brief strings of another person's discourse—perhaps part of a sentence, perhaps just a word or two—and patch them into your own sentences. Patchwriting often ends up sounding disjointed and somehow wrong because your voice is not really yours any longer. Suddenly your voice is being stabbed with the words of another's voice. The result is sloppy writing. This sort of writing happens a lot when students are trying to write something at the very last minute and haven't allowed themselves enough time to work with their sources properly. Instead of paraphrasing or quoting correctly, they do a rush job that is neither paraphrase nor quote and is, instead, basically writing that needs to be revised. Paraphrasing can be tricky for some writers, so I'll come back to this later in the chapter.

Excessive repetition is just annoying writing. It happens when you try to take a chunk of information from a text and condense it down to some overly obvious and uninteresting idea rather than pick out the bits that would be most useful. It's lazy writing, and again, it does not help you write an effective argument. Excessive repetition also occurs when you have more words from someone else in your writing than you have from your own head. In other words, if every other sentence in a paragraph is from a source rather than from you, then you aren't doing your job properly.

In any instructor's classroom, fraud will end up with a zero on a project if not a failing grade for the entire course and can even lead to expulsion from the university. For those of you who are student athletes, members of the ROTC, Honors College students, or active in sororities or fraternities, fraud can have serious consequences on your continued participation in such programs—you could lose your scholarship or your membership. In many instructors' classes, insufficient citation will result in a failing grade unless you do some serious revision to correct the problem. Patchwriting and excessive repetition will result in a paper that is weak and not yours in the sense that your voice can't shine through it, and rarely are such papers rewarded with good scores.

What's the lesson to be learned about the P-word? **Be true to your voice**. Be you. Write your argument and use those outside sources to firm up what you want to say by giving those voices credit. Don't let the other voices speak in your place because fraud is wrong and lazy writing is annoying and ineffective.

QUOTING, PARAPHRASING, AND SUMMARIZING

There are three primary strategies for borrowing the words and ideas of other scholars to support your argument: quoting, paraphrasing, and summarizing. Each strategy has its own defining characteristics and uses, which will be explained below. Regardless of whether you are quoting, paraphrasing, or summarizing, you should tell your reader whose voice you are borrowing. It does not matter whether the borrowed part is short or long or in quotation marks (or not): you must give credit to the one who gave you the words and ideas. *Always*.

QUOTE
When you quote from a source, you are providing a passage of writing—sometimes a few words, sometimes a few sentences—in the author's exact wording, and you are placing quotation marks around those words. There should always be a good reason why you choose to quote an author rather than simply paraphrasing the ideas into your own words.

Some good reasons for directly quoting:

- Quote when the original language is in some way powerful—if you changed the words, then you would lose that power.

- Quote when the author is a respected authority on the topic and his or her words would lend support to your idea.

- Quote when the author's opinion is either different from your own or is different from what most people think about the topic.

- Quote when your purpose is to analyze the text.

Practical Application for Directly Quoting

As I mentioned before, Peter Elbow is THE scholar on voice, which means he is a respected authority on the topics of voice and writing. He also is a brilliant weaver of words. This means there are many times when it just makes more sense to quote him rather than to paraphrase him. When his words are more powerful than my own would be, I quote him. If I were writing about using metaphors, I would need to quote this passage from Elbow's book *Writing Without Teachers* because his word choice is both powerful and humorous, and I would lose that power and humor in a paraphrase.

"A mixed metaphor is never bad because it's mixed, only because it's badly mixed. Anyone who is against mixed metaphors because they are mixed is like someone who is against kissing twice: he probably doesn't really like kissing once. He's entitled to his taste but he mustn't be taken as a judge of kisses" (54).

Keep in mind that when you quote, you are allowing another voice to take charge, and when you allow too many other voices into your argument, there is a possibility that you'll lose control of the writing. Quote because you believe the author's words are powerful and helpful. Don't quote because you need more words to reach a word count or because it's easier to quote than to paraphrase. Also keep this general rule of thumb in mind: having more than one or two quotes in a paragraph is like having too many cooks in the kitchen— too much confusion, too much noise, too much conflict. And... not enough of you.

A Quick Word about *Leading In* and *Leading Out* of a Quote

Introduce a quote by using a **signal phrase**. A signal phrase (also referred to as an attribution phrase) gives credit to the original author and also lets readers know that someone else's voice is coming. A good signal phrase not only gives the name of the author but also situates him or her by explaining why the author is worthy of being quoted. Is the author a scientist? A photographer? A mail carrier? A scholar? A dog washer? Tell your audience the name and their significance in your signal phrase.

If I were to quote a line from a book I'm currently reading about antiracism in the writing class by Asao Inoue, I might use the following signal phrase (noted in italics): *Writing scholar Asao Inoue points out,* "The influence of the concept of race is in the coded ways we talk about each other, the words we use for race and to avoid its reference. It is in the way we behave and perform our identities" (25).

But even if I used that signal phrase and provided the proper page number in parentheses after the quote, I would not yet be finished incorporating that quote. I will have led my reader into the quote, but I will not yet have led her out. To properly incorporate a quote into my paragraph, I must lead in *and* lead out. **My signal phrase is my lead in. My explanation of the quote is the lead out**. Here's an example of what a good lead in/lead out looks like:

6

Writing scholar Asao Inoue points out, "The influence of the concept of race is in the coded ways we talk about each other, the words we use for race and to avoid its reference. It is in the way we behave and perform our identities" (25). Inoue is arguing that even if we believe we live a life that is not informed by racism, we are deceiving ourselves because racism, like race itself, is in how we talk and interact with our world.

Keep in mind that each time you use a quotation, you need to lead in and lead out of that quote. Use your signal phrase, give the page number or source information, and then explain the purpose of that particular quote. *Explain what it means and why it is useful for your argument.* A solid lead in and lead out allows you to quote another author while maintaining *your voice* as the primary voice in the paragraph.

You can Google "signal phrases" to get some ideas to spice up your writing and help you incorporate quotations.

PARAPHRASE

When you paraphrase from a source, you are borrowing an idea from another author and using your own language to express that idea. Because the idea belongs to someone else, you still *always cite* the source. However, because you are using your own words, a paraphrase often flows more naturally within your writing. A paraphrase rewords the original passage but does not necessarily shorten the passage. In fact, sometimes a paraphrase will actually be longer than the original quotation.

Some good reasons for paraphrasing:

- Paraphrase when the details are important, but the way the author wrote those details isn't really memorable.

- Paraphrase when the author's words are really technical or wordy or somehow difficult to wade through. If you have a hard time understanding what the author was saying, then don't make your audience suffer through the same hardship. Make it easier for your audience to understand by paraphrasing.

- Paraphrase if you have other quotations in a paragraph and yet need to include the ideas from this other source.

Okay, but how do I paraphrase? Honestly, it takes some practice to get really good at paraphrasing. Paraphrasing is best accomplished when you *listen* to the passage you want to incorporate into your writing. Listening requires that you have a helper or a recording device. Ask someone to read a particular passage to you while you listen. You might need to hear the passage a couple of times. After you've heard it, write what you heard. When you aren't looking at the exact words on the page or on the screen, it is a lot easier to write the ideas in your own natural language. When no one is around to read a passage to you, use your phone and record yourself reading it. Then listen once or twice before writing the paraphrase down.

If you thought that paraphrasing was actually easier than quoting, then you'd be mistaken. Successful paraphrasing requires more time and attention than quoting, but a good paraphrase is often the best way to maintain control over the writing and keep your voice at the center of your essay. Additionally, there are many academic disciplines that require paraphrasing instead of direct quotes. If you will be going into a social science field or a medical field, then you need to know how to paraphrase because it's the only way you'll be allowed to incorporate sources into your researched papers.

SUMMARIZE

Summarizing is the least common strategy you might use to help make your argument. When you summarize, you are taking a very long section of a source, or perhaps the entire source itself, and stating the main idea quite succinctly. You might summarize an eight-page article in two to three sentences, while an entire book might require a paragraph summary. In any case, a summary is significantly more general and less lengthy than the original source material. A summary is useful if you need to step back from the details and give an overview or provide some context. For example, if you were writing an argument about recycling in Memphis, you might first summarize an article about recycling in Tennessee or in the United States before getting into the meat of your own argument about Memphis.

NONE-OR-IZE

Okay, yes, this is a made up word. *None-or-ize* is my own word for when you don't actually need to acknowledge or cite a source. There may be a time when you are providing information in your argument and you're not quite sure if you have to cite it. My general rule of thumb is that if you had to look it up or you needed to do research to learn it, then you need to cite it. But let's say you are writing about the history of terrorism in America and you mention in your paper that Osama Bin Laden was one of the men behind the terrorist attack on September 11, 2001, do you actually have to cite a source for this information? The answer here is no. Knowing that Bin Laden was responsible for 9/11 is a *none-or-ize* situation.

These are the types of information that don't need citations in your argument:

- Common knowledge (such as Bin Laden as a member of Al Qaeda)
- Facts found basically everywhere (America declared war on Japan in 1941, the number of oceans on Earth, the number of teeth in the human body)
- Your own **unpublished research** (if you did a survey of your classmates about how often they recycle each week, you would not cite yourself)

Take Note:

Self-plagiarism is a real thing. Self-plagiarism is essentially using your own previously written work in a different context than when you originally wrote it. For example, if you wrote a paper for an anthropology class last semester, and you submit that paper in full for your English class, then you would be self-plagiarizing. If you want to use ideas from previous work, then the safest bet is to consult your professor for advice on how to proceed. Self-plagiarism can come with harsh consequences, so avoid this practice.

6

Maintaining your voice while you incorporate sources into your argument is how you write a solid paper that shows your ownership of the topic and your acknowledgment of other scholars who helped support your points. If you remember to simply write in your flexible voice for the appropriate audience and context and to provide credit where credit is due, then your paper will be stronger, more readable, and more persuasive.

VOICE AS AMPLIFICATION

The beauty of voice in writing is that voice functions like a megaphone. It amplifies the content of the paper. It demands attention. It convinces a reader to listen. Voice can help pull the reader through your paper because voice engages with them. It holds passion and power. Voice can also cover a multitude of sins. When voice is present in a paper, the little surface mistakes seem less important because the content of the paper is engaging and worth reading.

Your voice is tied to your personality, to your preferences, to your style. Your voice reflects who you are. If you can't locate any of yourself in your writing, then there is no voice there. And where there is no voice, there is often nothing meaningful to you, which might mean there will be nothing meaningful for your reader either.

When you read your own writing, can you hear *your own* ideas? Can you see where you are passionate or interested in the topic? Can you identify passages that show your opinion or attitude on the topic? Can you picture yourself talking to friends or family about the topic in a way that shows your conviction? If so, you've found your voice. If not, you might need to rethink your topic. If you can't invest any of your passion or heart into the topic, then it's almost impossible to write well.

FINAL THOUGHTS

The best advice I can give you for writing your academic argument is to allow yourself time to work with your sources. It's hard (if not impossible) to use sources well when you don't know what they really say. It's also hard (impossible) to write a solid argument supported by solid sources when you don't really know what **you want to say**. Your job is to think, freewrite, consider, freewrite, think, read, read, read, and freewrite before you'll be ready to write this argument. Then, of course, you will need to revise, rethink, and rewrite to polish the paper for submission. Writing is a constant process of thinking and rethinking, so give your brain time to do the work.

Good luck and happy writing.

Writing Prompts and Activities

1. Voiced Tweets

   Consider the following tweets found on Twitter about the topic of rape culture. Even though each tweet is short, these authors manage to infuse their texts with voice through diction, details, imagery, syntax, and tone. Which of the following voices do you find most persuasive? Why?

   > **@OhNoSheTwitnt**
   > A perfect example of rape culture is allowing predatory men to profit off their stories while attempting to discredit their victims. And people still have the audacity to ask why women hesitate to come forward.

   > **@PeachesAndHam_23h**
   > I wish men talked about rape culture and misogyny when not trying to be funny. That'd be neat.

   > **@WarrenIsDead**
   > there are plenty of dudes who have gotten laid who nevertheless hold a similar resentment over not getting laid as much as they think they deserve and guess where that goes!!!! it's **rape culture**, folks!!!! it's cosby and ck and lauer and weinstein

   > **@AlexSchar**
   > i'm tired of surprise dick pics
   > "i make gay girls str8"
   > women will never be = to men
   > aggressive authority and entitlement
   > rape culture being accepted and encouraged
   > cheating being justified bc MEN JUST CHEAT
   > i'm tired

2. Funky Aliens

   You've probably noticed that this textbook was written by a number of different authors. This means there are many different voices at work in this book. Two authors who have very distinctive voices are Dan Conaway and Bob Norman. These authors have crafted their voices through intentional use of diction, details, imagery, syntax, and tone. Read Conaway's "All Funked Up" (under the *I'm a Memphian* Readings) and Norman's "The Alien Has Landed." As you read, attempt to identify examples of word choice (diction) that help craft voice for each author. Then use the chart below to identify specific details, imagery, syntax, and tone used by each author. Be very specific with your analysis so that you can compare your findings with classmates.

6

	"All Funked Up"	"The Alien Has Landed"
Diction		
Details		
Imagery		
Syntax		
Tone		

Now, write a reflection in which you compare and contrast the voices of Conaway and Norman using the specific examples of diction, details, imagery, syntax, and tone you found. What might change about the voices of these authors if they had used different words, different punctuation, or different details? Consider how you can apply these strategies to your own writing.

WORKS CITED

Elbow, Peter. "About Voice and Writing." *Landmark Essays on Voice and Writing*. Ed. Peter Elbow. Hermagoras Press, 1994. pp. xi–xlvii.

___."Introduction." *Everyone Can Write: Essays Toward a Hopeful Theory of Writing and Teaching Writing*. Ed. Peter Elbow. Oxford, 2000. pp. xiii–xxiv.

___.*Writing Without Teachers*, 2nd Edition. Oxford, 1973, 1998.

Howard, Rebecca Moore. "Sexuality, Textuality: The Cultural Work of Plagiarism." *The Norton Book of Composition Studies*. Ed. Susan Miller. Norton, 2009, pp. 1205–1222.

Inoue, Asao B. *Antiracist Writing Assessment Ecologies: Teaching and Assessing Writing for a Socially Just Future*. WAC Clearinghouse and Parlor Press, 2015.

RESEARCHING MEMPHIS: DRAFTING AND WRITING A RESEARCH PAPER

7

Errol Rivers

Errol Rivers Jr. is pursuing a PhD in Technical Writing at the University of Memphis. He writes every single day and enjoys talking to others about their own creative processes, strategies, and interests when it comes to putting their thoughts on the page *or electronic screen*. When teaching first-year writing, he is especially interested in helping students rhetorically analyze the messages they receive and create through the media. A native Memphian, Errol enjoys exploring the more active side of the Bluff City, which includes the RiverFit fitness trail at Tom Lee Park, Overton Park, and many other sites.

Imagine this: You've been assigned the New Media project and placed in a group of your peers. Two weeks before the assignment is due, you all agree to work collaboratively in the UC's Tech Hub to complete it. However, one of your group members appears distracted: he takes personal phone calls, scrolls down his various social media timelines, and looks off into the distance. Oh! And when he actually recognizes that the group exists, he either complains or talks only about subjects that are off-topic. You (very politely, of course) ask, "Don't you care about the assignment?" He chuckles and says, "Oh, I'll do it the night before." Another member of the group responds, "But this is a big project, so we shouldn't blow it off." He says, "But I've always done it this way, and it works just fine!" You and your other partners look at each other, and a silence takes over the room. Yelling erupts, and your group is banned from the Tech Hub *for life*.

Many of us are guilty of committing this crime against good logic. In our attempts to defend our choices, ultimately, we communicate ideas such as "I like it because I like it" and "it should be done this way because that's how it has always been done." We often stand by our ideas, even if logic and goodwill defy our stances. Sound familiar?

Let's face it: the **research paper** isn't the most well-liked **genre** of writing that students encounter in their academic careers. The research paper requires us to avoid **logical fallacies**, use clunky academic search engines, and read lots of academic research. Yet, this genre is invaluable in that research helps us avoid making hasty and half-baked decisions, requires us to plan and organize our writing, and empowers us to make well-informed and persuasive arguments. Unlike other writing assignments you may have had to complete, such as the literacy narrative, the research paper requires you to choose a topic and *explicitly* take a stance on that issue.

If you completed English 1010, then you may remember doing **primary research**, which may include piloting a limited experiment, conducting an interview, writing on a case study, creating and disseminating a survey, or combining some of these things. Rather than primarily relying on primary research, as a student in English 1020, you will be required to scour the internet (particularly via academic search engines), books, newspapers, and other sources of information to find **secondary research**, other people's published works, to support your claims. In order to reasonably articulate and defend the stance you are taking, these assignments are usually lengthier and require more citation than you're used to. Finally, for the purpose of this course, you have the added responsibility of localizing your topic to the city of Memphis.

For these reasons, the research paper can seem overwhelming and downright scary. However, researched writing helps academic disciplines function, as it provides a way for readers to trace the knowledge that contributes to a particular stance, opinion, or course of action in an organized and systematic way. This manner of organizing our thoughts and thoroughly supporting them can seem challenging because it is very different from the ways in which we converse in casual conversation, but engaging in this process is certainly worthwhile, especially when you're faced with an individual who only does things because they "say so." Research is persuasive.

WHY CONDUCT RESEARCH?

Regardless of our major or discipline, we conduct research to make sense of our world and establish order in a systematic manner. We turn to studies that have been thoroughly **peer-reviewed** (a process through which scientific, academic, or professional work is evaluated by others working in the same field) and conduct our own studies to ensure that the things we say, believe, and do are in accordance with the reality we and our peers accept.

Preparing to critically analyze, closely engage with, and knowingly commit an entire semester to a research topic can be intimidating; however, it is for these reasons that the information you learn and the skills you gain through this process can be incredibly eye-opening, mind-boggling, and easily **transferable** to your other courses. That is to say, the skills you will acquire through this process should help you to conduct research and write research papers in other courses and professional contexts. However, as you will learn, research is formed, tested, and written about in vastly different ways across disciplines. While this chapter will discuss research at length, this discussion will be considered primarily from the vantage point of English 1020 and its research paper component. When you are asked to write research papers in other courses, you will need to evaluate the discourse community and its genres of writing *before* you write.

RECOGNIZING CONVENTIONS AND FOLLOWING THE "RIGID RULES" OF RESEARCH PAPERS

Writers beware! Not all research papers are written the same! While this genre of writing is typically more formulaic than others you may encounter, there is no one-size-fits-all framework for completing research papers. In fact, the **conventions** of a research paper, or the stylistic and architectural ways in which this genre is usually written and constructed, will differ based on the discipline or field for which you are writing, your chosen topic, your intentions, the style guide you are using, and your (and your professors') personal preferences.

You may be wondering how, why, and to what extent these factors contribute to the composition of a research paper. These would be valid questions since all research papers include a lot of the same types of information: an introduction, primary or secondary research, sources, a form of a closing, and a citation page. Why does it matter whether you're writing a research paper in English or in biology? This question, first, leads us to the importance of understanding audience as more than simply a single body of related people.

KNOWING YOUR AUDIENCE: DISCIPLINARY DISCOURSE COMMUNITIES

Research papers, and, generally, any genre of writing, have an intended audience that is implied through the features and historical expectations of that genre. Think about handwritten letters and online messages. Sometimes, people expect handwritten letters to be used for more formal correspondences while social media messages are typically reserved for more casual exchanges. Research papers also have their own implicitly associated meaning affixed to them. Think about it: as you have read, research papers tackle very specific issues; thus, they may feature specialized *lexis, concepts, data,* and *references to associated information* that the general public might not know. With these characteristics in mind, it wouldn't be too far-fetched to assume that most research papers are usually written for academic and other professional **discourse communities** that are formed around an interest in a particular **discipline**, branch of knowledge, or field.

These groups of specialists are then separated by their interests or the discipline and field that is most related to their chosen career paths. In each discipline, many scholars have made choices (both in the ways they conduct their research and the ways they present them in writing) that have helped to define their collective goals, values, practices, and principles. In many cases, decades (or even centuries) of scholarship have reinforced those choices. Essentially, the things that are important to instructors of biology courses differ from those deemed important by instructors of English courses. As such, not only do the things we research reflect those disciplinary differences but *the ways we write about the things we research* reflect our value differences, too.

COSTS OF BREAKING THE RULES

You may have learned in your English 1010 course that many of what Mike Rose referred to as the "rigid rules" of writing can and should be broken once they begin to stifle your writing. Yet, breaking the rules of your discipline, especially when writing a research paper, can be a costly act of rebellion. Deviating from your discipline's rules (such as not including particular headings that most other articles in your field seem to include) holds the potential to distract, confuse, or upset readers who are accustomed to and believe in the conventions of your discipline. Even more, breaking these rules may affect your ethos, bringing your credibility as a knowledgeable writer into question.

Think of it this way: you know Muddy's Bake Shop cupcakes are delicious. We can all agree that cupcakes are, more or less, comprised of cake and frosting, right? But if you were to bite into a bright pink Muddy's cupcake, and your mouth filled with the rancid tang of expired fish, you would probably feel more than a little confused. You might feel too distracted to notice that the bottom half of the cupcake was baked to perfection. You might just feel angry! Similarly, people who are part of a disciplinary discourse community have their expectations for what research papers should feature and look like. They certainly do not want to read a research paper that overwhelms them with the sense that something is *fishy* with your work.

Throughout your college career, it will be paramount that you identify who your audience is and in which disciplinary contexts you are writing in order to avoid violating the genre's conventions. Surely, across fields and disciplines, these conventions will conflict. For example, in this course, you will be allowed to use some personal knowledge and experiences to help support your claims in your research paper. Even more, you will be allowed to use a wide-range of pathetic, ethical, and logical appeals to better represent your claims and impact your audience. However, in an argumentative essay for a history course, using first-person pronouns or your personal experiences would be highly inappropriate. Each time you write, it is your responsibility to figure out the genre conventions and respond to them accordingly.

PARTICIPATING IN A DISCOURSE: REVISITING JOHN SWALES'S C.A.R.S. MODEL

You may be familiar with John Swales's piece titled "Create a Research Space," in which he describes his Creating a Research Space (C.A.R.S.) model for writing research. In this piece, he provides several "moves" that can be used to **situate**, or place, the writer's thoughts into the large genre of academic research writing. In the first move, he states writers must stress three things: 1. They must assert that whatever they have to say is part of a larger discourse; 2. they must make statements about current knowledge or practices; and 3. they must review previous items of research (Swales). Through these methods, writers can bolster the rhetorical power they wield, which, in turn, can make their arguments more persuasive.

How might you place your issue within the larger discourse? Think about how others are writing about an issue. You will want to search the library for books, look online for articles, and check out documentaries to understand the thoughts top scholars have about your topic. For instance, a stance on mass incarceration does not simply come out of *nowhere*;

rather, your thoughts should be informed by the ideas of those who have personal experience, have conducted research, and are experts on the topic. Even more, you may turn to debates between news pundits captured on television or posts on social media about current events related to mass incarceration. Knowing how others talk about your issue can equip you with the **discursive knowledge** to participate in an ongoing conversation. This will not only build your ethos but it will also help others to understand how you **conceptualize** and define the issue you are discussing.

IDENTIFYING DISCIPLINARY CONVENTIONS FOR RESEARCH PAPERS

In most cases, you will be expected to learn the conventions of the discipline you are writing for on your own. Because you may only be taking a course for a semester and know very little about the field, this can be a daunting task. However, there are several ways you can begin to understand how to write for a discipline when you are not yet familiar with that discipline's genre conventions:

- **Read other texts within the discipline**—Many instructors, especially those who do not teach writing, expose students to published articles in hopes that, by way of reading them, students will become **enculturated**, or gradually familiarized, with the style of writing that is expected of them. Through this process, you can learn who important figures in the field are, what kinds of formatting are acceptable, and how people within your discipline usually frame an issue (do they say "global warming" or "climate change"). You can speed up the process of familiarization by looking for common features across two or more pieces of writing. If you notice more than one author using similar section headings, providing similar content, or using similar transitions, then you can assume those aspects of the text are expected by the genre and discourse community.

- **Refer to your style guide or Tiger Handbook**—Using an in-hand or online (Purdue OWL) style guide can help you to understand what may be expected of you as you write research for other classes.

Recognizing the conventions of your discipline will not be a simple task, but it will certainly help your work to fit into larger discourses that are occurring within a field. This will serve to assert your legitimacy as a researcher and communicate to others that you have a clear understanding of the context of the issue you are writing about.

ARGUMENT TYPES AND PURPOSES

Maybe you are not sold on the idea of writing a research paper just yet. It sounds like a lot of hard—maybe even boring—work with very little pay-off, doesn't it? That is the reality of researching and writing papers on topics *you have little interest or stake in*. It is for this reason that you should find a topic that both satisfies the requirements of the assignment and piques your interest. There are various topics research papers can be written about and different ways those arguments can be written. Whatever your topic is, for the purpose of this course, you will be asked to choose a local issue or to choose another issue to localize to the city of Memphis. Whether you are originally from the Bluff City or have recently relocated to the city, finding things to write about in Memphis is far easier than you would expect.

With so much potential for research, whittling down your options might seem impossible at first, but there are a few easily identifiable types of arguments that can be used for this paper:

- **Polarizing (Political) Arguments**—These arguments tackle hot-button issues, such as the death penalty or minimum wage, in a manner that is directly tied to how the issue impacts the city of Memphis.

- **Historical Arguments**—These arguments rely on archival and historical sources to argue for or against the importance of a historical site or figure in Memphis, such as the Civil Rights Museum in downtown Memphis or Elvis's Graceland.

- **Arguments for Change**—Change arguments aim to change the audience's beliefs about something. For instance, you may choose to address why Memphians should be concerned about a particular law in Memphis. Even more, change arguments may also aim to influence Memphians to *take action* to change something about the Memphis area, such as cleaning up the River Walk in downtown Memphis.

- **Logistic Arguments**—Logistic arguments ask the intended audience to adopt a *specific* plan and apply it to a current issue in the Memphis area. This may be an attempt to convince the University of Memphis to add soundproof technology to the Patterson building to help diminish the noise pollution caused by the sounds of the passing trains. Using the terms "train," "noise-pollution," and "noise-canceling," you may research how noise pollution hinders learning or even people's health before considering types of windows, conducting interviews with students and instructors who have classes in Patterson, and presenting a way funds may be able to be raised for the project.

Of course, you can certainly make arguments that do not seem to fit into one of the above categories. These are simply in place to help you think more about how good, in-depth, and locally relevant research papers can emerge from various purposes of research.

ON PURPOSE

As a rhetor, or someone who is a public speaker or writer, it is incredibly important for you to know your reasons for communicating. If you don't know why your ideas matter, then your audience won't know either. As you narrow your topic, you need to articulate your purpose. Do you want your audience to change their beliefs? Their actions? To do or not to do something? Answering these questions matters because your answers will inform the research you do and the rhetorical decisions you make as you build your argument. If you want people to follow a particular plan-of-action, then it will be important to tell them which steps you want them to follow and to show them why following those steps will positively benefit them and the Memphis community. Likewise, if you hope to simply inform Memphians about a particular issue, then you will need to explain why the information you present to them is important *for them* to know.

CONSIDERING SCOPE

When you hear "research paper," you probably think of buzz-worthy topics that are featured on national news platforms, such as gun laws, prison reform, immigration law, and freedom of speech. If you completed English 1010, then you may think of the writing research paper or discourse community analysis, wherein you wrote a paper about an interview or a study you conducted. While these are all very important and interesting topics, the **scopes**, or the extent of influence, of these topics are either too wide (the national issues) or too narrow (your writing research project) to satisfy the requirements of your research paper in this course.

However, while there are many ways to arrive at the research topic you will commit to, **inductive** or **deductive reasoning** will allow you to either focus your research paper on issues tied to the experiences that affect you or to zero-in on the national issues you care about in a local context. These methods of organizing your thoughts and establishing what you believe to be true are logics you already use to think about the things you see in your everyday life and will be beneficial to you if you feel overwhelmed by the idea of finding a topic.

- **Inductive Reasoning and Localizing Individual Observations**: **Inductive reasoning** is the logical method of considering specific instances and forming a generalized conclusion from those instances. If you're walking in downtown Memphis and you notice that a church is located on each block you pass, then you may begin to generalize that there are many churches located in Memphis and that religion has a special place in the fabric of the city. From there, you may consider the role of religion in Memphis, and a research topic may spring from your line of questioning.

- **Deductive Reasoning and Localizing National Issues**: **Deductive reasoning** is a logical method of considering ideas that are known to be true and attempting to form a specific conclusion about those ideas. For example, perhaps your general idea is that, across the country, the minimum wage is too low for workers to afford reasonably comfortable lives. This is an issue that has been discussed on a large scale because it affects Americans everywhere; therefore, it is a general idea or issue. However, if you were to consider what a specific local business pays their workers and compared those figures to standards of living in Memphis, then you could certainly take a position on whether that organization should increase the salaries of their lowest-paid workers.

HELPFUL TIPS FOR LOCALIZING ISSUES

In your attempts to localize a national issue, you may be inclined to simply connect an issue that is occurring nationwide to a particular instance of that issue in Memphis. However, doing so would be insufficient for this paper. Instead, your topic must engage with specific concerns, histories, and other elements of the Memphis area. With this in mind, there are a couple of methods you may consider using to do this successfully:

- **Extrapolate External Interventions**—Argue for the **extrapolation** of solutions from other contexts to issues that are present in the city of Memphis. To **extrapolate** is to extend the application of a method or conclusion to an unknown situation by assuming that existing trends will continue and similar methods will be applicable. More simply, you apply methods that have been used in other contexts to a new context. For instance, if a K–12 school system in Louisville, Kentucky, was able to mediate an issue that the Memphis City school system is currently facing, then you may argue for the ***extrapolation*** of their solution to the context of Memphis. To do this responsibly, you would choose a setting that has a similar demographic and socioeconomic composition to those of Memphis. Otherwise, your comparison and research would be *deeply* flawed.

- **Investigate Local Organizations**—Investigate to find local organizations that help to support your stance on an issue or serve communities related to your issue. If you are interested in topics related to the LGBTQIA+ community, then you might search local journals or search the internet for resource centers that specifically serve this community, such as OutMemphis or CHOICES. Then, you might ask representatives from those organizations for information about your area of interest as it pertains to people in Memphis.

REVISITING INTRODUCTIONS

As you begin to draft your paper, you may want to write it from start to finish, introduction-down. While this method helps some writers to organize their thoughts, the process of writing is rarely this cut-and-dried. Instead, you should always revisit sections of your paper that you worked on before your ideas were fully developed. Frequently, it is students' introductions that need a hard second and third look. Remember: your introduction is the first impression you will make on your audience (there is a reason this chapter began with a relatable story about group projects!). If it is not a stellar one, then some readers may not continue to read beyond it. To help intrigue readers, there are many **draw-ins** you can use. A **draw-in** is exactly what it sounds like: it draws your reader into your paper by way of **rhetorical framing**, the manner in which you present and characterize an issue. You may have heard of similar concepts, such as "grabber sentences" or "topic sentences," but draw-ins are strategically used to contextualize an issue while also latching on to your reader's attention. There are numerous ways you might draw a reader in:

- Anecdote
- Shocking statistic to be explained later
- Current event
- Reflection on the topic or circumstance
- A definition of a key term

For your English 1020 research paper, any one of these may help to serve as the first or first few sentences of your submission. This list, however, is non-exhaustive, and you may find other ways to capture the attention of your audience.

There are also not-so-great ways to begin a research paper for an English course. While this may not be the case in other disciplines, a subtle first few sentences are usually more effective than direct statements regarding what your paper will be about. Here are some common lines you might want to avoid when beginning a paper in this genre:

- "My paper will be about…"
- "In the history of the world…"

- Immediate, uncomplicated, and plainly-stated judgments
- "[Insert topic here] is bad," "good," or "easy"

These examples either tell your reader too much about your paper too soon or they simplistically reduce the argument to judgments. If any argument were that simple, then there would be no need to make an argument! Instead, you should realize that your readers may have different opinions than you do, and it is your job to help convince them to, at least, see the issue from your perspective. Most readers will not read a text that insults them or blames them wholly for issues that exist. Likewise, readers will not read a text that immediately denies or rejects their views.

THE IMPORTANCE OF DEFINING KEY TERMS

As mentioned in previous chapters, arguments are simply a stance on something. However, issues are complex, multidimensional, and often have far more than two polar-opposite sides. It is easy to think we all interpret the primary issue of an argument to be the same, but that is not always the case. For instance, think about the national conversations on gun laws that occur during presidential election campaigns and in the tragic wakes of mass shootings. In the past, you may have heard terms and phrases like "gun control," "Second Amendment rights," and "stricter gun laws," but did you ever ask yourself, "What do those terms mean to *me* and what might they mean to *other audiences*?" They may mean very different things to different people:

- To some, these terms are used to describe political actions that, in effect, will only *ban* the purchase of military-grade guns.
- To others, they involve making the requirements of purchasing certain builds of guns *more rigorous*.
- There are also individuals who interpret these terms to mean the gradual and lawful removal of the *entire* Second Amendment.

Imagine three individuals who are attempting to debate with each other on gun laws. Each of them represents one of the three interpretations of what "gun laws" refers to. This conversation would likely not go far because the parties involved do not have the same understanding of the issue at hand. This happens all too often, and it is our duty as rhetors and responsible citizens to take special measures to avoid this type of miscommunication.

HOW TO DEFINE KEY TERMS

One way you may define your term is by stating what it is, what it is not, and an example of how it has been used in the manner you want it to be used. For example, you might write,

> *There are many views on guns in America and the* **Second Amendment**. **The Second Amendment** *of the United States Constitution reads: "A well-regulated Militia, being necessary to the security of a free State, the right of the people to keep and bear Arms, shall not be infringed." However, it does not explicitly state that all citizens have the right to carry all builds of guns in all places and at all times.*

Here, it has been made clear that the Second Amendment is defined as one thing and has been used to argue in conversations regarding who has the right to bear arms, what types of guns can they bear, and where are they allowed to bear such guns.

Make sure to avoid defining common terms and simple words, such as "street," "mailbox," or "mayor." While it may *seem* responsible to cover all of your bases in this way, it can dramatically affect your ethos. To some readers, this type of oversimplification shows that the writer is inexperienced. Even more, it shows that you think very little of your reader's knowledge, and this may insult your reader, which you never want to do! Think of it this way: if you think a 6th grader would know what the word means, it may be too simple to define.

MAKING HISTORICAL ARGUMENTS

While a popular choice among students, contemporary issues don't have to be the focal point of your research paper. Memphis is especially rich with musical, Civil Rights, architectural, commercial, and political histories that lend themselves to research projects like this one. Even more, the University of Memphis has an archive of this history located in the Special Collections of McWherter library on campus. If you are interested in taking a historical approach to this paper, your stance might concern the significance *or lack of significance* of a particular site in Memphis. Or, perhaps, you may argue that more should be done to preserve the history of a site that has fallen to ruin, been replaced, or gone unnoticed.

Concepts at Work: Death of the Shopping Mall

There are certainly ways to make arguments that concern the past and may have effects on the present and future. Here is an example of how you might think about making an argument about the past.

Many people have fond memories of going to local shopping malls. There is always a fun and lively anxiety that characterizes the many sensory experiences you encounter with each visit. The warm aromas of popcorn, coffee, and Auntie Anne's pretzels; the sights of families, first dates, and elderly men and women speed walking down the corridors; and the motley crew of hair salons, skate shops, and department stores are exciting (and odd) to see all in one place! Further, every mall has its own lore, whether it be that the stores in Wolfchase Galleria have better sales at the end of the month or that the horses on the carousel at the Hickory Ridge Mall come to life after midnight. Indeed, for the past several decades, shopping malls across the nation, but especially in Memphis, have embodied the full spectrum of Western consumer culture. However, times have changed, and the reign of the shopping mall is coming to an end. With the rise in popularity of e-commerce and an overall changing market, a growing number of shopping malls are closing their doors each year. In fact, in a 2017 article published by the LA Times, researchers projected that as many as 25% of shopping malls across the nation would close by 2022!

However, this is not simply a national problem with no ties to Memphis. On the contrary, with the closings of businesses, such as Toys R Us in 2018, that help bring shoppers to malls, the decline of malls in Memphis seems to follow in alignment with these trends. For example, the Raleigh Springs mall, once located in Memphis, closed in 2016. And then, of course, there is the late, great Mall of Memphis.

How might this become a research topic?

Unless you lived in the city before 2004, you have probably heard little-to-nothing about the 1.2 million-square-foot attraction to the Hickory Hill area that, in its heyday, featured an ice-skating rink, ribbon-cutting ceremonies, and indoor concerts. Yes, the Mall of Memphis was shut down in 2003 due to a confluence of social and economic reasons as well as having been given the nickname "Mall of Murder" by the local media as crime rose on its property during its last years in operation. It was reduced to a plot of land for many years thereafter, and little was heard about it again.

Here are some potential topics that are rooted in some of the issues presented by the failing state of shopping malls in the Memphis area:

Memorialization: Although native Memphians may have memories of this mall, there are few places around the city that memorialize this site in any way. To take a historical stance on this topic, you could facilitate interviews and conduct research, either by going online or by visiting in-person archives in the city, to argue that there should be a commemoration of this site in a Memphis museum. Of course, this would require you to decide which museum should host the memorial and why that particular Memphis museum should. It would also require you to argue that malls are worth memorializing, and this is where academic research becomes necessary.

Contributions to unemployment rates: Another route you could possibly take in your paper might be to consider how the closing of this mall affected unemployment rates in 2004. You may argue that was an issue that has yet to be resolved and has contributed to Memphis' relatively high unemployment rates since.

Vacant land: With so many shopping malls closing and, in some instances being demolished, what is to be done with the massive plots of land that are left behind? Perhaps, you believe city contractors should use these buildings and plots of land to help serve the local community in some way. Through an **argument for change** or **logistic approach** to your research paper, you may write to convince local leaders that there is potential to revitalize areas of the city by replacing these buildings with services that help the surrounding communities or using the land for urban community gardens.

USING OPPOSITIONAL SOURCES

In your everyday life, having a consensus among you and the people you know is comforting; you like to do the same things, go to the same places, and talk about the same issues in the same ways. In research papers, however, finding sources that present findings and ideas that oppose your stances can actually benefit your argument. When you present your reader with information they may have heard before that conflicts with your views, then you have the rhetorical upper hand; that is, you are able to shape the message your reader is receiving and respond to concerns they may have had about your topic. Once again, this serves as a credit to your ethos and helps to refine your researching skills.

AUDIENCE-DEPENDENT LEXI AND FRAMING

When researching sources that oppose your thesis, you may run into trouble because different sides of similar discourse communities may use different lexi. Sometimes, these different groups use words that implicitly benefit their stances on the issue, framing the issue to be viewed by the public in a particular way. In the chart below, you can see how Democrats and Republicans typically use different words to talk about the same issues to affect the rhetorical effects of the topic (see **FIGURE 7-1**).

Issue	Democratic Terms	Republican Terms
Immigration	Undocumented immigrants	Illegal aliens
Gun Laws	Gun safety	Gun control
Taxes on Homes	Estate tax	Death tax

Figure 7-1. Democrats and Republicans use different terms to discuss the same topics to frame their arguments from Frank Luntz; "The American Lexicon"; 2006

It is easy to see how the differences between using the phrase "undocumented immigrants" and "illegal aliens" may *implicitly* reveal biases about particular issues. In your research papers, it will be important that you recognize these biases and are mindful of the phrases you use to frame your argument and find sources.

YOU SHAPE THE RESEARCH AND THE RESEARCH SHAPES YOU!

In your English 1010 course, you may have learned that writing is a process comprised of pre-writing and planning, drafting, revising, editing, and proofreading. In the case of the research paper, following this process is especially important because the primary objective of the genre is to strategically support a particular stance throughout the entirety of the piece. However, as is the case for many researchers, finding interesting, supportive, and conflicting sources can alter the trajectory of your paper and might even change *your* stance on *your* topic.

Some writers feel that changing their stance after reading more information makes them seem ill-prepared to participate in an argument. As a result, they leave out information that conflicts with their stance or, in light of their change of heart, feel that the work they completed previously is now meaningless. On the contrary, changing how you view your topic is normal and indicative of good researching habits. No one begins a research paper having all of the answers! Researching, like writing, helps you to learn unconsciously while completing tasks for this assignment. This highlights one of the primary purposes for dedicating time to drafting your papers. With proper time management, you can go back to your introduction and other paragraphs to change phrasings and ideas that at one time may have seemed important but now do not serve your stances and goals.

KEEP YOUR PURPOSE IN MIND

Ensuring that your research paper provides the reader with a fair depiction of your topic, effectively communicates the merits of your stance, is well-written, and is well-cited can

7

feel like something of a balancing act. As you write and research, keeping track of your intent for writing the paper becomes more difficult as you place sources that make similar claims **in conversation** with one another while making **nods to the opposition**, recognizing stances and claims that directly oppose your own. In order to write a compelling and sophisticated paper, you should take steps to make certain that your paper is clear, concise, and consistently supports your view on your topic; otherwise, your paper on Memphis's potential to become a thriving economic goldmine for investors may easily devolve into a seven-page description of how the Pyramid downtown became the site for the city's largest Bass Pro Shop. While it is certainly interesting that this decision came down to a bet Bass Pro Shop's owner Johnny Morris made while fishing with a friend, learning the entire context of this story was not your audience's **motive**, or goal, for picking up your research paper.

With this in mind, consider doing the following to help you to avoid losing sight of your purpose as you draft:

- **Maintain an Audience-First Attitude**—Reminding yourself of your and your audiences' purposes can help you to stay on-track as you come across new materials. Remember who your audience is. Think about what knowledge, opinions, and **misconceptions** your audience may have about your topic. Write to clue them into your worldview. You may consider briefly jotting down what you believe the traits, beliefs, and lifestyles of your intended audience may be. This is what technical writing scholar Ginny Redish refers to as a ***persona***. Personas serve as easy references to remind you of what you should consider as you write for an audience.

- **Revisit Your Proposal**—Go back and read your proposal. Revisiting your thesis, the questions you initially sought to answer, your goals for the paper and your purpose can help you to weed-out unnecessary research that does not support or provide a fuller view of your topic and stance. Of course, if your stance has changed slightly, then your proposal may not provide the answers you need. In this case, you may consider responding to the questions you answered in your proposal once again to help you clearly articulate what you are hoping to communicate to your audience.

- **Organize Your Sources**—Organizing *who* said *what* will help you avoid getting lost in a research wormhole. Some researchers color code their sources to tell the difference between sources that provide context, sources that support their stance, and sources that oppose their stance. Others use online citation managers such as RefWorks, provided by the University of Memphis through your tuition, to help them categorize their ideas and cite their work more easily. Over time, you will learn which methods work best for you. In any case, it is important that you use a strategy; avoid simply throwing your content together.

UNTIL GRADE DO YOU PART: A PRE-MARITAL COUNSELING SESSION ON COMMITTING TO YOUR RESEARCH TOPIC

Choosing an appropriate research topic can be a struggle. It requires you to foresee whether there will be enough published research on your topic to construct an interesting argument.

After hitting a snag in your research or feeling as if there is nothing else to write, like many other students, you may develop a wandering eye, becoming all too eager to choose another topic that you perceive to be easier to complete. More often than not, taking this route would be a mistake! Not only does it waste valuable time you could have dedicated to furthering your initial argument, but, sooner or later, you will face a similar issue with your new topic and will not have acquired the difficult-yet-necessary researching skills required to overcome the inevitable barriers we all face when we experience writer's block.

After choosing and writing a proposal on a topic, you have a semester-long commitment to writing a research paper on the subject you proposed. It is for this reason that the topic proposal provides you the opportunity to plan how you might conduct your research, find sources, and ask questions. Think of your proposal as a contract: in it, you vow to honor your topic by sticking with it through ups and downs, free-flowing thoughts and writer's blocks, final submission and shitty first draft—until grade do you part.

During the moments when you feel confused or lost, consider these tips for overcoming researcher writer's block:

- **Revisit Your Primary Argument**—Have you defined key terms that may confuse or become misinterpreted by an audience? Have you identified your stance and the counter-stances that may exist in opposition to yours?

- **Rethink Search Terms**—Which terms are you using to search the databases for sources on your topic? Are there synonyms for the words you're using? Have you considered antonyms to find counter-stances? Ensure that you are searching more than one search engine. The online library at the University of Memphis allows students resources to various databases that can help you find the information you need to better support your stances.

- **Take a Break**—Sometimes the best way to write is to not write at all. If you have dedicated many hours to your paper and can't seem to think of anything else, then simply close your computer or phone (hit "save" first!) and focus on other tasks. After an hour or so, try again. You may find that taking a break allows you return to your work with a fresh pair of eyes and a mind that is ready to work!

- **Visit the CWC**—When in doubt, the Center for Writing and Communication (CWC) is a great resource for students to use. The CWC consultants are great at helping writers to think through writer's block!

Although staying faithful to your topic for an entire semester can be challenging, the experience of doing so will prepare you with the skills required for college-level academic writing.

As this chapter explains, research papers are multifaceted genres of writing that, if done well, can help to effect change in the minds of individuals, in local communities, and beyond. More specifically, they inform the perspectives of academics and other professionals as they make decisions that affect others in society. This genre, then, helps society to function in a reliable, ethically sound, and consistent manner. Further, research papers provide nuance to issues that can, at times, seem black-and-white. This helps us communicate with one another in a citizenly and sensible manner. Because these papers have such important effects, you should always allow yourself enough time to research your topic, write, and organize your paper in a thoughtful and persuasive way.

Writing Prompts and Activities

1. If you've had to complete a research paper before, you may or may not have had a great experience. In either case, recognizing what helped to shape that experience can guide your plans for this research paper. Consider the following questions in order to write a reflection that considers what went well and what you can do differently to help make the process better for you.

   - Was I allowed to choose my topic?

   - Did I like my topic?

   - How did I plan?

   - Did I have to cite? Did I understand how to cite?

   - Did I allow myself enough time to complete the assignment well?

   - Did I write in one sitting or did I work over the course of several sessions?

2. After deciding on a topic, you will have to identify the intended audience of your research paper. This is not always an easy task because most issues impact various groups of people in different ways. You will have to brainstorm which groups of people are affected by or care about your issue. Further, you will also have to think about what their values and concerns may be. After doing research, you will have sources that will help you to respond to these concerns.

   For example, while you may be passionate about limiting the amount of air pollution in Memphis, the cars many of us use every day emit toxic gases. A Memphian who travels to work by car may not know why this issue matters or how they can help. Further, groups that are committed to the protection of wildlife in the Mid-South might already know that this is an issue and would like to know more about statistics related specifically to the effects of pollution on animals. Lastly, the operation of local factories often results in pollution, too. The corporate owners of such factories will probably be more concerned with the costs of alternatives to their current practices. These are three very different groups with very different values and concerns.

   In this exercise, you will practice thinking about your paper from another point-of-view. First, recreate the chart below. Using your topic and your stance, list three groups of people who might be impacted by your topic and identify what their concerns may be.

Topic	Stance	Potential Audiences	Values	Possible Concerns
Limiting Air Pollution	We should limit the air pollution in Memphis	Memphians who travel by car	Taxes Health	How am I impacted? As one person, what can I do?
		Local organization for wildlife protection	Well being of animals	How is the environment impacted? How can my organization help?
		Local factory owners	Money Efficiency	How much will an alternative cost? Will it slow down my production?

Next, think about the order in which you will address the concerns of *one* of the potential audiences. Using the example presented above, you might choose to write for local organizations that are committed to wildlife preservation efforts. In most cases, you would tell your readers how the environment is impacted by pollution in Memphis. Then, you would guide their next steps.

1. Ways air pollution harms the local environment.

2. Ways local organizations help limit air pollution in Memphis to protect the environment.

In your own list, order your audience's potential concerns. In your paper, which would you address first? Second? Third? Do this for each of the concerns you came up with.

1._____

2._____

3._____

4._____

5._____

WORKS CITED

Easter, Makeda. "Up to 25% of U.S. shopping malls may close in the next five years, report says." *Los Angeles Times*, 1 June 2017, www.latimes.com/business/la-fi-malls-closing-20170531-story.html.

Swales, John. *Genre Analysis: English in Academic and Research Settings*. Cambridge University Press, 1990. Print.

Luntz, F. "The New American Lexicon." Alexandria, VA: The Luntz Research Companies. Retrieved from www.dailykos.com/story/2005/2/23/3244/72156 (2005) Print.

COLLABORATIVE WRITING

Skye Roberson

Skye Roberson is pursuing her PhD in Composition Studies at UofM. She teaches first-year writing and works as the Graduate Assistant Director of the Center for Writing and Communication. She's lived in the South her whole life and has learned to love the summer heat. When she isn't writing, you might find her relaxing in the comfy seats at the Ridgeway, walking with her family to Studio on the Square, or setting up a late-night picnic at Summer Drive-In.

As a teacher, I can visualize how my class will react when I mention a group assignment. A group of friends will immediately make eye contact and scoot their desks closer, hoping they will get to pick their partners. Some students stare at me panicked while recollections of horrific group projects flash before their eyes. Others will cross their arms in anger and stare at the floor defeated or suddenly excuse themselves because "they have a dentist appointment they forgot." When I get negative reactions from the class, I don't it take it to heart because I know most students don't have positive experiences with group work. They see my assignment as just another fiasco waiting to happen. I'm here to tell you that it doesn't have to be this way. In fact, this class is about changing many preconceptions you have about literacy, including collaborative writing. The anxieties you have are valid, but moving forward, we are going to face them head on rather than repeat the same mistakes again.

The negative experiences you might have encountered in the past are not because collaboration is inherently bad. In fact, many people have made great careers by writing together, including the Brothers Grimm, Terry Pratchett and Neil Gaiman, and Stephen King and Peter Straub. Likewise, academic writers collaborate all the time. Books, edited collections, and journal articles are often authored by many people. This very textbook is the result of a collaboration between the Director of First-Year Writing and a number of graduate students and instructors from the Department of English. By working together, we accomplished more than we could have working individually. If collaboration is so great, why do so many students have negative experiences with it?

Part of the problem is the way we think about authorship. When we think about "great authors," we usually imagine an individual who spends all their time writing alone. Our preconceptions about writers then create a bias toward single authorship as being more legitimate than collaboration. As writing scholars and collaborators Lisa Ede and Andrea Lunsford illustrate, the culture of higher education rewards individuality (357). Collaboration is sometimes seen as a form of laziness—a way for students to get out of challenging intellectual work. Therefore, when group work is assigned, it's not always taken seriously by students or teachers. Our hidden biases tell us that what we make as individuals is more important than what a group can do together.

Another issue rests in the distinctions between group work and collaborative writing. Many times, the two terms are used interchangeably when, in fact, they are different. In a typical group assignment, each member of the group carves out a task for themselves based on the requirements for the project. Over a set amount of time, each member of the group works on their section individually, until the due date approaches when everyone compiles their work. In this scenario, group work is actually the same as individual assignments, except the workload is split between multiple people. What the group creates as a whole is a collection of individual efforts, combined into one finished project. This explains why many group projects are unsatisfying, because it's essentially the same as working alone, but with a group of strangers who now affect your overall grade. Collaborative writing is something else entirely.

In a collaborative writing assignment, the group works together on each part of the project. No one is solely responsible for an individual element. As a result, the work you create is a representation of the group itself, not a hodgepodge of individual efforts. In a collaboration, each person can use their strengths to make the group shine. For example, one collaborator, Michele, might be good with film equipment, so she explains how to make a video and provides technical support when other group members struggle. Michele isn't solely responsible for the video. She's merely using her talents to help the group be successful. The beauty of collaboration is that everyone gets to share ideas without a single person being in control of what the group does.

I like to think of group work and collaborative writing like a smoothie. If you add all the ingredients to a mixer, some parts become imbedded, while others retain their form. Putting everything into a blender ensures the ingredients meld together into a cohesive, unified whole. Group projects can become a mix, with each member contributing their ideas while still retaining ownership over "their" work. Mixes don't make good collaborations because it's an amalgamation of ideas, whereas blending brings multiple voices together. In blended collaborations, the initial ideas or writing may have been generated by one person, but they become the property of the group through continuous contributions from other members.

Good collaborations don't bring pieces of a project together, they fuse many people's ideas into something new.

Writing research illustrates the benefits of collaborative writing. For example, in Peter Elbow's *Writing Without Teachers*, he uses the metaphor of cooking to describe the collaborative process (48). Like cooking, writing is an interaction between people and ideas. If you're cooking alone, you can make your food to your taste. Most likely though, you are cooking with other people in mind, which means you have to negotiate your ideas for the meal with their tastes. Similarly, when writing multiple authors (or cooks) have to come together to balance their ideas. What emerges as a result is often better than what could be made alone.

Collaboration is also an example of how writing is a social activity. In *Naming What We Know*, a guide to key concepts in writing studies, Kevin Roozen says "writers are engaged in the work of making meaning for particular audiences and purposes, and writers are always connected to other people" (17). In collaborative writing assignments, students act both as writer and audience in the construction of their work. Rather than simply thinking of writing as social, students are put into a situation where exchange is not only encouraged but required to make their writing cohesive. In short, collaborative writing encourages students to grow as critical thinkers and writers through the benefits of writing in social situations.

In English 1020, you will experience collaborative writing during the new media group presentation. For this assignment, your group might be asked to create a handout that explains how to use a digital composition platform step-by-step. Your group might also provide a demonstration of how the platform works by showcasing a sample project you created. It's a good idea to draft notes or write a script to give the presentation structure. This chapter will help you understand how to achieve these goals through collaborative writing. Since you have been asked to work collaboratively to teach the class about a composing software, understanding the core concepts behind collaboration is essential.

TIPS FOR SUCCESSFUL COLLABORATIONS

Although collaborative writing is beneficial, it comes with the complexity of navigating interpersonal work. Many students struggle to make collaborations productive because, in many ways, working alone is easier than trying to work with others and make compromises. With that in mind, here are some practical suggestions for how to get acquainted with your group, how to manage your work, and how to manage any problems that arise.

CREATE OPEN LINES OF COMMUNICATION

The first thing your group should do is exchange contact information through multiple communication platforms. This establishes accountability because it eliminates the potential for excuses (ex: "Oh, I didn't get that message"). If you don't know the members of your group, then it might be uncomfortable to share personal information like phone numbers and social media accounts. The safest form of contact is university email, but if this is the way your group chooses to communicate, then you all need to agree on how often you should check your email. Productivity apps like Slack are good alternatives that allow you to directly communicate while also preserving your privacy. When your group gets together for the first time, give everyone the opportunity to share their communication preferences and then vote on what works for everyone. Likewise, it's appropriate to establish boundaries for out-of-class communication. Conflicts can arise when group members violate each other's comfort zones. Such boundaries might include hours of availability for messages, conduct, language use, etc. Having this conversation on the first day will help your group avoid conflicts later.

GET TO KNOW YOUR COLLABORATORS

It is important to learn about the people you are working with. To open communication, start with basic information like names and majors. From there, ask about each other's strengths and weaknesses when it comes to writing and public speaking. This will allow you to utilize each member's talents effectively. For example, if a group member is comfortable with public speaking, allow them to take a central position in the oral presentation. You'll become stronger by collaborating with someone with a different skill set who can teach you news ways of approaching tasks and problems. Not to mention, getting to know your peers makes collaborative work fun.

TRUST YOUR COLLABORATORS

A problem that can emerge early in a collaborative project is not trusting your partners. Maybe you don't think they will live up to your standards or you won't live up to theirs. Making a judgement about someone early in a project can hurt the group dynamic. If you think your partners are not as capable as you, then it's likely you will take over the workload, denying them the opportunity to participate. Similarly, if you don't think you'll be able to match the group's efforts, you might try to coast through the project, reaping the effects of someone else's work. Neither of these scenarios foster genuine collaboration. Although you may have preconceived ideas about your peers' work ethics, you must dismiss those judgements. Collaborations can bring out the best of a group and its individual members if it's built on mutual trust and respect.

MEET IN DIGITAL PLACES

Everyone in your group is busy trying to balance school work with their private lives. Sometimes, it might not be feasible to meet in person. If necessary, you can take advantage of free services that allow your group to work digitally. Google Docs is a platform that enables sharing documents and collaborating on writing in real-time, which can be helpful when writing a script. If you need to talk, then Skype and Google Hangouts give you the opportunity to discuss ideas with your group wherever you are. The drawback of using these services is that people can become distracted and forget to check-in. Therefore, just like when meeting in physical spaces, set a date and time to get work done. Giving digital meetings guidelines further establishes accountability within the group.

USE CLASS TIME EFFECTIVELY

Many instructors who teach 1020 have built-in workshop days for your group to get things done. Take advantage of these opportunities. Those with laptops or tablets should bring them to class. When the workshop starts, set an agenda (or make a list of tasks) and work through each component of the project. If your group works efficiently, then there shouldn't be much necessity to meet outside of class. At the end of each meeting, make a list of tasks that need to be completed before your next meeting and assign those tasks to individuals so everyone's responsibilities are clear.

TALK TO YOUR INSTRUCTOR

Workshop days are opportunities for the group to get work done, but they also give you time to solicit feedback from your instructor. Your instructor can help your group be successful. Ask them to read drafts, review your project, or listen as you prepare to present. Their feedback can help your group make important edits before the final presentation.

SUGGEST, DON'T DICTATE

Being critical of the group's ideas is part of the collaborative process. However, no one likes to see their ideas changed without their permission. Before the group edits something, make sure each person is involved in the process. If someone has a problem with the changes, then listen to them before making a final decision. Taking this step ensures each person feels involved in the collaborative process. When someone doesn't feel included, they are likely to shut down or become disassociated with the development of the work. Be mindful of this when it comes to decision-making.

REVISE

Revision is a key stage in the collaborative process. As a single author, your perspective of the text is limited. Sharing your work with others helps you consider perspectives other than your own. By editing a project together, collaboration happens through the careful decision-making of the group. Questions like, "Did you intend to use that word?" and "Can you explain this idea further?" push everyone in the group to think deeper about their rhetorical choices.

WHAT TO DO IF THINGS GO SOUTH

Unfortunately, not all collaborations have positive outcomes. Knowing your options will help you make smart decisions if self-preservation becomes a necessity. First, you may wonder when a collaboration has turned sour. If you are doing the bulk of the work, completing milestones of the project by yourself, or communicating without response, then it might be time to ask for help. First, reach out to the problematic group member and let them know how you feel. Yes, this can be awkward, but the problem might be a matter of miscommunication. Try to work things out with the group if possible. On the slim chance the problem persists, contact your instructor, and let them know about the problem. Your instructor might be able to act as a mediator, or they can help your group work through the problem. In some cases, issues with a group member might extend beyond the scope of the course, which is something the instructor is equipped to handle. Collaborations are meant to be beneficial experiences. If you think the collaboration is doing more harm than good, then you owe it to yourself to speak out.

BENEFITING FROM COLLABORATION

When it comes to collaboration, my final piece of advice is to keep an open mind. No matter what this chapter says, the advice won't be meaningful if you've already decided that the new media group presentation is doomed to fail. It's unfair to the members of your group to check-out of the process before it begins. Before you jump to negativity, think about the possibilities of what could happen. Your group could make something awesome together, and you might even make friends along the way. It's good to reflect on the past and understand why things went wrong, but moving forward, focus on how you're going to bring your best self to this presentation.

When I think about the power of collaboration, I'm reminded of one of my favorite writing duos, Amy Poehler and Tina Fey, who have collaborated on many projects throughout their careers. They started acting and writing together at Chicago's ImprovOlympic in 1993. After Tina Fey was hired on *Saturday Night Live*, she spent years trying to get Amy Poehler to join her. When Amy finally decided to join the cast, the sketches they worked on together became iconic (such as their impersonations of Hillary Clinton and Sarah Palin). Separate, they are each comedy powerhouses, but together they bring magic to the screen. Poehler alludes to the benefits of collaboration in her autobiography *Yes Please*, saying "it's easier to be brave when you're not alone" (94). If you're in a group, you're more likely to challenge yourself. Go ahead, take risks together. Through the efforts of your collaboration, what you'll end up with is more interesting than what you might have done alone.

Collaborative writing partnerships can be immensely beneficial. Working in a partnership gives you the opportunity to advance your skills as critical thinkers, audiences, editors, researchers, and writers. These partnerships can continue beyond the scope of one project, transcending into a working relationship and friendship that can enhance your development as a writer and person. For this to happen, you need to start the collaboration with a willingness to listen, learn, work, and share. Following the advice of this chapter will give you the tools to make effective collaboration possible.

8

Writing Prompts and Activities

1. Think about a previous experience you had with a group project. Were you happy working with your group or was it a disaster? Write about the experience and explain why that project was or was not successful. Based on your experiences and the chapter you just read, how can you change your own collaborative practices to ensure success?

2. Each member of your group brings something unique to the table. Before you start planning your project, read the following questions aloud and discuss your answers. Then, use what you know about each other to assign responsibilities.

   - What skills do you have that might help the group? (Are you a natural leader? Do you love speaking in front of people? Are you good with digital design? Are you good at editing? Are you organized or creative?)

   - What are your weaknesses when it comes to group work, writing, or public speaking? (Do you forget deadlines? Are you nervous in front of a crowd? Do you have limited access to a computer?)

   - How can the group put each person in a position where they can use their skills and minimize their weaknesses? (For example, if Rita is charismatic and loves talking in front of people, but she freezes when reading a script, then the group might decide that Rita should practice her speech before presentation day while the rest of the group watches. This will give her a chance to practice and may mean she won't need the script.)

WORKS CITED

Ede, Lisa and Andrea Lunsford. "Collaboration and Concepts of Authorship." *PMLA*, vol. 116, no. 2, 2001, pp. 354–369.

Elbow, Peter. *Writing Without Teachers*. Oxford University Press, 1973.

Poehler, Amy. *Yes Please*. Harper Collins, 2013.

Roozen, Kevin. "Writing Is a Social and Rhetorical Activity." *Naming What We Know*, edited by Linda Adler-Kassner and Elizabeth Wardle, University Press of Colorado, 2015.

CRITIQUING YOUR OWN WRITING

Vincent Kenny-Cincotta

Vincent Kenny-Cincotta is pursuing his PhD in Literary and Cultural Studies at the University of Memphis, focusing primarily on postmodernism and contemporary American literature. A native New Yorker and current proud Memphian, he has experience teaching both first-year writing courses here at the UofM and has also worked at several writing centers (in fact, he is currently a consultant at our very own CWC, which he strongly suggests all students check out, regardless of field). While there are countless aspects of Memphis that he loves, he particularly enjoys the DIY music scene, some of Midtown's more illustrious dives, and savoring delectable local fare with a nice Wiseacre brew.

LET'S STOP AND THINK FOR A MOMENT

Think about the last time you posted something on social media. After drafting your tweet or captioning your Instagram post, did you post it immediately? Did you take a look at what you wrote beforehand to check for any spelling errors? Did you switch up the filter? Did you change which emoji(s) you decided to include? If you answered yes to any of those last three questions, then you are already familiar with the process of critiquing your own writing.

Critiquing your own informal writing is something that comes natural to most. We pretty much do it on a daily basis. Critiquing your own *academic* writing, on the other hand, can be stressful and weird (at least at first). Unfortunately, it is also extremely important. A mastery of critiquing your own writing will help you succeed in not only this class but also in the various other courses you will be taking throughout the rest of your collegiate career—and beyond. Pretty much every career path (everything ranging from the humanities to hard sciences and even to the arts) involves some aspect of writing , especially in this tech-heavy world we live in. This generation of college students is already the most textually focused and adept generation **of all time**. Now you just have to transfer some of the knowledge you've gained on social media to the classroom.

Critiquing your own writing can actually be pretty fun—once you get the hang of it. Learning to critique your own writing is not only important to your success in English 1020 but will also help you conquer fears and anxieties you may have surrounding this admittedly uncomfortable task. This chapter provides you with a handful of techniques and strategies for critiquing your writing and also warns of some pitfalls to avoid.

LET'S TALK PROCESS

By now, you've probably already been told dozens of times that writing is a process. You have also probably been made aware of the fact that the primary difference between a novice writer and an expert writer is revision: the good writers do it; the not-so-good writers don't. If you were not aware of this tidbit, then have no fear: you will be privy to it after reading the chapter on revision towards the end of this book. Generally speaking, critiquing your own writing is a **massive** part of that revision process.

Time for a quick refresher: the four basic steps of writing are pre-writing (invention), drafting (putting your thoughts on paper), revising (moving those words around and adding/deleting in a thoughtful and articulate manner), and editing (tidying it all up). It is important to recognize that this is not a linear process. Some writers draft to invent; others revise while they draft. Don't get bogged down by focusing on what aspect of the process you are in. Focus instead on learning how you write—learning your own process and then improving. Now, the process of critiquing your own writing lies primarily in that "revising" category but also a bit in the "editing" phase as well. We tend to think of "revising" as mostly concerned with peer review, an extremely useful tool in the composition classroom. However, revision really begins (and ends) with the writer.

Although we like to avoid the idea of writing as a solitary activity, writers do not always have access to peer review workshops or even just colleagues with spare time on their hands. We all have deadlines and we all have our own scholarship and social lives. Therefore, the ability to revise and critique your own work is a critical trait for any writer ranging from a high school English student to a bestselling author. Even if a peer reviews your work, you need to have the ability to know when you should take that advice and when you should ignore it. At the end of the day, it is *your* work that will be submitted with *your* name attached to it. Shouldn't you be the one with the final say on how it turns out?

Frankly, the idea of approaching your own work with a critical lens can be kind of scary. As a PhD student in Literary and Cultural Studies, I understand this quite well. My opinion about a paper can vacillate between "this is brilliant" and "this is trash" all in the same day. This is not only normal but, believe it or not, healthy. There are a variety of benefits to being critical of your own writing. Not only are you strengthening your work, improving

9

your writing, and sharpening your critical eye, but you're essentially eradicating the fear of failure. If you can boldly look yourself in the mirror and genuinely say, "this needs work," then you are taking a giant step toward writing success! As writers, we are often our own harshest critics. If we can placate our shrewdest analyst, then we should have no fear of the dreaded peer review (or worse, instructor comments).

It is important to remember that the purpose of critique (especially self-critique) is not only to point out what the writer did *wrong* but also what the writer did *right*. Critiquing is not criticism, and critiquing is also not inherently negative (despite the connotation). Critiquing your own work is all about honesty. What worked? What didn't? This is a golden opportunity to be constructive and improve as a writer—seize it!

That said, it is important to remember that self-critique goes beyond simply editing or proofreading your work; you are taking a comprehensive look at your writing and briefly stepping into the role of "audience." You should be removing yourself from your writer persona and trying your best to view your work objectively.

THE IMPORTANCE OF SELF-CRITIQUE

Self-critique can both instill confidence and correct bad habits. Personally, I find critiquing my own writing to be just as important (if not more important) than peer review. So why, exactly, is critiquing your own writing such a good idea?

Critiquing your own writing can better correct common errors (redundancy, spelling or grammatical errors, etc.) than peer review. Writers often make the same mistakes over and over again. Once you learn what your common mistakes are, then you will know to look for them and address them when you revise and edit. By personally correcting your recurring issues, you will be less likely to make those same mistakes in the future. In this way, self-critique essentially tricks your brain into becoming a better writer.

Critique allows you to take a step back and admire your work. As I mentioned before, typically, writers are their own worst critics. It is natural to feel self-conscious about your work or even paranoid about the idea of someone else reading and critiquing it. Through self-critique, you are able to take a step back and take pride in your work. In this regard, self-critique can be a valuable confidence-building tool. A good chunk of the curriculum in English 1010 was geared towards building confidence in burgeoning writers. Think of critiquing your own writing as a continuation of that: pat yourself on the back when you see something working and take some time to recognize what you have done well.

Critique gives you perspective. By turning a critical eye towards your own work, you can briefly abandon the role of "writer" and step into the audience role. By doing so, you can take an unfettered look at your writing and be able to discern problems in everything from structure and flow to formatting and grammar.

Unfortunately, achieving this perspective is often where writers begin to feel self-conscious about their work. It is important to remember, however, that just because you don't like your work at the moment does not mean that it is beyond repair, and just because you aren't currently in love with your writing doesn't mean that it's objectively awful. Ian Fleming (author of the *James Bond* series of novels) used to destroy novels after completing them if he wasn't completely satisfied with how they turned out. Moreover, in the winter of 1952–1953, renowned playwright Eugene O'Neill burnt the series of plays that he believed to be his *magnum opus* after working on them for nearly **fifteen years**. Clearly, feelings of inferiority affect everyone, even literary visionaries. Obviously, I'm not suggesting that you destroy your work merely because you are dissatisfied, but these examples are simply meant to show you that feelings of inadequacy are normal and can even be constructive. Use this perspective to your advantage and make changes as you see fit. (If you feel like deleting your work, then try opening a new Word document and starting over. Save that old work in case it becomes useful later in your writing process.)

Critique can reveal how you are growing as a writer. Writers often feel the need to churn out their work, hand it in, receive a grade, and move on. By taking a more contemplative and reflective approach to your writing process, you will begin to notice the details of your maturation as a writer. At first, you will notice little things like an expanding vocabulary, a greater command of your authorial voice, and maybe even a stronger sense of grammar and punctuation. Over time, however, you will notice loftier developments: maybe your papers are starting to look more adept format-wise; perhaps you will notice that your sense of content, logic, and structure is gradually improving. By taking time to smell the roses, you will not only feel better about yourself as a writer and more confident in your abilities, but you will actually improve at a faster rate than you would otherwise. This is where metacognition comes in: this thinking about thinking is crucial because reflecting upon your thinking and writing process is key to learning and growing as a writer. When your teachers write comments on your papers, they focus on what is working, what is not working, and how your writing can improve. If you can begin to do this for yourself (before your instructor even has a chance to look at it), then imagine how your writing (and those subsequent comments) will evolve over time.

I'm sure that all of you shudder to think about the papers you wrote in high school (I know I certainly do). This is not just commonplace—it's *good*. Your writing *should* be improving over time. By taking a moment to go over your writing and see what areas you are improving in and which areas you are stagnating in, you can actually speed up your own maturation as a writer. Writing may be an imperfectible craft, but in a sense, that's the beauty of it: you can't top out and you can always improve.

Critique shows you the importance of drafting and emphasizes writing as a process. I'm sure you're getting sick of hearing this by now, but I'll shout it from the mountain tops if I have to: writing is a *process* and it should be treated as such. By critiquing your own writing, you are not only respecting this aspect of composition but engaging with it.

HOW TO CRITIQUE YOUR WRITING

First things first, read everything thoroughly. Every. Single. Word. Read your paper two times, three times, four times, five. The more you review your writing, the greater chance you have in noticing errors in everything from grammar to organization.

Ask yourself questions. And hard ones too. Does this paragraph belong here? What am I trying to say with this sentence? Does this piece fit the genre of the assignment? Is this piece intended to address a distinct discourse community—and if so, is it addressing it properly? Is this a strong enough thesis statement? Does my conclusion really drive my point home or is it just fluff nonchalantly thrown in there to meet a page requirement? These may sound a bit brusque, but I assure you, if you don't ask these questions, then your audience will. Get these preliminary questions out of the way so that by the time your paper reaches the peer review stage (or the grading stage) your audience can focus on the higher-level aspects of your writing. This is how the process of improvement begins.

Reread. This might sound redundant, but it's important. As you read, make necessary changes, answer the questions you asked yourself in the previous step, and wait to edit/ proofread. If you are revising, which means making large-scale changes, then don't waste your time on sentence-level errors that may be deleted in the final draft. As you reread, you may even want to make a list of the more substantive changes you need to make. Then you can return to that list after you are done reading and make the changes you identified. After you make those changes, step away from your paper before reading the paper again. Often, we aren't very self-critical after we just wrote or revised. Time away from a draft can give you a more objective eye and help you see the ways your paper has improved and the places where it still needs work. Repeat this step as necessary. This is the heart of critique and revision. It may feel tedious, but it is absolutely vital.

Summarize and assess. Try to encapsulate what you have read and see if it would make sense to your audience. This can involve outlining, free-writing, or simply taking mental notes. You should compare your writing to the prompt for the assignment and make sure your writing is doing what the assignment asks. Did you answer the prompt? Does your paper meet the requirements? Are you fulfilling the guidelines of the assignment? Most importantly, are you proud of your work?

Ask yourself the "so what?" question. If you took English 1010, then this should be drilled into your head by now. Any time an instructor (or general member of your audience) is reading your paper, they are going to ask themselves, either consciously or subconsciously, something along the lines of "why should I *care*?" Your paper should not really just conclude with a summation of your argument; it should take your argument one step further. What does this analysis and conclusion mean to us? What can we do with the successes or failures of this argument? So *what*?

Follow what you've learned from Peer Review. Naturally, critiquing your own writing is a profoundly different process from simply reviewing a peer's work...or is it? Sure, at first it will be difficult to separate yourself from your own work, to take on the role of audience, and to turn in your writer's card in exchange for one of a critic. However, once you are able to shed the authorial title, critiquing your own work can prove to be a refreshing, even cathartic experience. Just like in peer review, you should think about content, style, organization, and correctness as you critique your writing.

- **Content**. Is this paper actually saying what you want it to? Is your thesis clear? Does the body and conclusion provide enough evidence to support your thesis?

What additional sources do you need to support your claims? Do you need to further develop the connections between your claims and the sources you include?

- **Style**. Is this paper meeting the style and format guidelines of the course and of the discourse community you are writing for? Does your tone align with your audience's expectations?

- **Organization**. Are your paragraphs arranged cohesively? Why have you organized them in this order? Should you move paragraphs around to improve your argument? Are your individual paragraphs organized? Do they focus on a single idea? Do you lead in and out of your quotations, explaining content and connecting them to your argument?

- **Correctness**. Are all your facts in order and supported with citations? Do you notice any glaring errors, inconsistencies, or fallacies? Have you followed the required citation and format guidelines?

STRATEGIES FOR CRITIQUING YOUR OWN WRITING

Read out loud. Surely, you've heard this before—but that's only because it works. Reading your paper out loud is the first line of defense against crappy composition. The main benefit of reading out loud is that it helps you catch editing and proofreading errors. In the hustle and bustle of typing up a paper, our brains are typically light-years ahead of our feverish typing, our weary fingers struggling to keep up with our rapid, off the cuff inventions. In this undeniably hectic process, we make mistakes. We forget words, we make typos, subject-verb agreements can get fuzzy, etc. By reading out loud at a methodical and relaxed pace, we force our brains to slow down and consciously catch the errors we made in our creative haste. That said, we would be remiss not to mention some of the higher order advantages to reading out loud as well. For instance, by reading out loud, you can catch problems with transitions (such as jumping from topic to topic too abruptly) or organization (maybe you'll notice that the first point you make in support of your thesis would pack more of a punch if presented later). You can also catch "awkwardness." Sometimes, a sentence can make perfect sense both grammatically and semantically (meaning, it "makes sense"), but may end up stylistically lacking. Reading out loud can help you pick out instances in which your sentences are redundant, convoluted, long-winded, or just plain strange.

That said, when reading your paper out loud, remember to read at a slow, relaxed pace. This will ensure that you don't miss any words and will also allow you to hear every word in relation to its neighbors. Reading too quickly can prove to be disastrous; you'll end up speeding through sections and missing mistakes, subconsciously filling in missing words. This is why reading *out loud* is so important: when you *hear* your writing, you won't just zip through without noticing errors. It may feel a little silly at first, but the initial goofiness is worth the productive payoff.

It also helps to read from a printed copy so you can hold your writing in your hands and make small edits as you move along. Obviously, you could do something similar to this on your computer or tablet, but don't underestimate the tangible aspect here. By physically grasping your writing and marking certain areas with a pen (as archaic as that may sound) you can better take the whole paper in and maintain a sense of control over your writing.

Let it marinate. Give your writing some space! As a college student, it is easy to get caught up in the industrial mindset of simply churning a paper out and immediately handing it in. It is important for us to remember, however, that writing is not like a math problem. It is not something to be solved; it is a long and winding process.

Our brains are incredibly complex machines. While we write, we are often unable to differentiate the forest from the trees. We easily get caught up in wording and small picture stuff and can miss out on the glaring (and larger) issues that are staring us right in the face. By stepping away from your writing and letting it "marinate," you can return to it with a fresh new perspective. After your initial draft, go for a walk. Have a snack. Maybe even take the rest of the night off and pick things back up tomorrow. By forgetting about your writing for a small period of time, you can return to it refreshed and reinvigorated—not to mention less frustrated.

Obviously, there is a time constraint element to this. If you are writing a five-page paper the night before it is due (which, I might add, is not recommended), you aren't able to let your writing sit. If anything, letting your writing marinate should provide even further encouragement to treat writing like the process it is. The earlier you start this process, the more time you have to let it marinate and the easier it is to catch problems and address them.

Reverse outline. We've all heard of outlining, but *reverse* outlining can be just as useful. Whereas outlining is typically employed before you begin drafting (a tidy organization of loose or concrete thoughts arranged in order to aid in pacing and structuring), reverse outlining is helpful for when you have already written a paper and you could use a little help organizing it. By outlining the content of the paper after it is written (i.e., reverse outlining), you can (re)discover the focus of your paper, see how ideas may work better in a different order, and reorganize your paper.

To reverse outline, follow these steps:

1.   Identify your thesis. Write this at the top of a blank sheet of paper or use the review function in Microsoft Word.

2.   Number each following body paragraph and identify its topic. What is each paragraph's main idea? Write a one to two sentence summary of each paragraph.

3.   Identify how these topics relate to your thesis. Basically, what does each paragraph do? How does the paragraph back up your thesis? Write this down below the main idea of each paragraph. This list of what each paragraph says and does serves as your "reverse outline."

4.   Read through your outline and see if the structure makes sense. Ask if these ideas might better support your thesis if they were presented in a different order. Through a reverse outline, you can determine if your paragraphs all relate to your thesis and are in the most savvy and effective order. As you read through your outline, use the below questions to guide you.

     •   Do all of your paragraphs support your thesis? If not, it's time to think about how they can be restructured or changed (or even removed) to better support the thesis.

- Does the order of the paragraphs make sense? Does your argument flow from one paragraph to the next? Make sure that all your paragraphs relate back to the thesis in a cohesive manner. If there are any paragraphs that talk about your subject but don't support the thesis, then consider removing or revising them. If the flow of the paper feels bumpy or clunky, then consider moving some paragraphs around.

- Is there anything missing? One of the primary benefits of reverse outlining is determining gaps in research/evidence. If you think your paper could benefit from another key point to support your thesis, then consider conducting more research and/or adding another paragraph.

Keep a writing log. The primary difference between skilled and unskilled writers is that skilled writers like to revise whereas unskilled writers resist the urge to remove anything from early drafts. The beauty of keeping a writing log is that it can reveal your own best practices. The writing log is unfixed and nothing in it is set in stone; in it, you can experiment with new forms and styles as well as edits and adjustments. Treat your writing log as a means of reflection, almost like a diary. This will make it much easier to reflect on the ways in which you've grown as a writer as well as a reviser. There is no *right* way to set up your log—do whatever feels most comfortable when tracing your progress. The more familiar you are with writing in a less fixed form, the easier it will be to think of your first drafts as malleable. If you write about what you did each time you write, then this will also allow you to identify the writing practices that work best for you. This will work wonders for your revision process, as you will begin to think of the writing process as just that: a process.

Write a letter to the "author." Now, this can get a little tricky. A common tactic employed by teachers of composition is to have students include a "letter to the reader" as a de facto cover letter for their essay. These letters intend to help the reader (your instructor) understand the writer's aims, thus improving the feedback from your instructor. This version is a bit more abstract; the idea is to read your own writing with a critical lens, intentionally detaching yourself from your writing, and asking the "author" any questions that the piece left you asking. Questions can range from "Does this paragraph belong here?" to "What did you mean by this particular sentence?" to "Do your supporting paragraphs really support this exact thesis statement?" to "Do you think the pacing here works?" You can make critical statements like "This section feels a little long-winded" or "Your conclusion doesn't leave me with a sense of closure." The primary question that you are essentially asking yourself is "Are there any changes I should make?" This is really the essence of stepping into the proverbial shoes of your audience. By writing a letter to yourself from a new perspective, you can begin to address any issues (surface-level or deeper) that you may have missed during the (admittedly frantic) writing process.

COMMON PITFALLS OF SELF-CRITIQUE

The strategies that this chapter has discussed thus far are important to your development as a writer. However, just as significant as these "dos" are the "don'ts." Last but certainly not least, here are some common mistakes or errors in judgment that writers of all experience levels tend to make when critiquing their own work.

Focusing too much on the negative. Don't be too hard on yourself. Your writing will not be perfect (that's impossible, remember?), and you shouldn't harp on the paper's imperfections *too* much. Obviously, a big aspect of self-critique is to notice and correct problems before the person grading your paper can point them out, but this doesn't mean you should attack yourself. Being too hard on yourself is counterproductive and can cause writer's block, so recognize what you did well as well as what can be improved.

Focusing too much on the positive aspects of your writing. This is a slightly less obvious yet equally damaging pitfall. Remember: this is critique. You should not be reading your paper with the intention of stroking your ego; you should be revising, correcting, improving, and growing. Look for places in your paper that can be improved, and remember that at this stage most places can be improved. The negative aspects of your writing are undoubtedly going to need more attention than the positive ones, so don't get too distracted by patting yourself on the back.

Focusing too much on editing and not enough on revision. Just as writing centers and peer review should not be perceived as "grammar garages" or "fix-it shops," critiquing your own writing is not just some glorified version of spell check. Yes, you should take some time to correct the little things like punctuation and spelling, but bear in mind that these aspects of your writing are just that: the little things. Your primary concerns should be content, logic, and structure, not syntax, spelling, and grammar. For more on revision, check out the chapter entitled "Exploring Your Piece's Potential: A Cartographer's Guide to Revision."

Giving in to the urge to be subjective (and not relatively objective) with your critique. You should keep in mind that your work will be perceived by your audience as an entity in and of itself (your name and personality detached). In fact, when academics submit their writing to journals or publishers, the submission process is usually double-blind (meaning that the author does not know who is reviewing his/her work and vice versa). Although many of you may not see yourself submitting work for publication in the near future, when critiquing your own work, it is crucial to keep this in mind. Realize that your intent as a writer might get lost in translation from your mind to the page. When writing, be as clear as possible. When critiquing, be as objective as possible. Be sure to properly take on the role of audience member and resist the urge to brush issues with clarity to the side simply because *you* know what you meant when you were writing; your audience needs you to be as clear as possible.

AN EXAMPLE OF SELF-CRITIQUE

On the pages that follow, you will find a short response paper that I wrote for a Contemporary British Literature course in Fall 2017 with my own critical comments inserted. I employ the reverse outlining technique in this example, but there are other elements of critique as well. When editing and revising, I read aloud. I also didn't go back to this paper for a good five months after my first draft, so bear in mind that it had more time to marinate than your piece might.

Feel free to use this as a launchpad for critiquing your own writing.

Vincent Kenny-Cincotta

Dr. Carey Mickalites

ENGL 8462

16 November 2017

(1) "Think small:" Control as the Rational Retort to Trauma

(2) It is likely no coincidence that Salman Rushdie's *Shalimar the Clown* centers around a character named Maximilian Ophuls, the apparent namesake of Max Ophüls, a Jewish, German-born film director of the 1930s. Ophüls, a gifted and revered filmmaker, spent years in exile evading the rising Nazi regime, bouncing around Europe until eventually resurfacing in Hollywood in the late-1940s. He was known for his captivating and complex camera movements that were before unseen, manipulating the film's action through a combination of subtle yet intricate camera movements and elaborate tracking shots and thus serving as an inspiration for more modern and renowned filmmakers like Stanley Kubrick and Paul Thomas Anderson. It should be noted here that if there is one characteristic that Ophüls, Kubrick, and Anderson have in common, it is the incessant and unapologetic desire for control. This is made abundantly clear in nearly every candid interview regarding these acclaimed directors. Control, it appears, in both Rushdie's opus and Ian McEwan's *Saturday*, is the most rational and understandable response to irrevocable trauma. Reminiscent of Ophüls's own method of conquering his demons following the rise of Nazism in Germany, in the recent subgenre of the "post-9/11 novel," control seems to be the most reasonable and ubiquitous form of therapy in the traumatized, kicked hornet's nest of the early-2000s world.

(3) This idea of control in the wake of anguish is perhaps best epitomized by Theo Perowne's surprisingly profound maxim, "think small:"

> On a recent Sunday evening Theo came up with
> an aphorism: the bigger you think, the crappier it

Margin notes:

(1) Thesis: In the traumatized, post-9/11 world, simply put, people want control; they find it therapeutic and comforting.

(2) Paragraph 1: my introduction. It aims to introduce my thesis. I think I get a little bogged down with the history lesson, but I still like the connection that I found.

(3) Paragraph 2: background information and explanation of "think small."

9

looks. Asked to explain he said, "When we go on about the big things, the political situation, the global warming, world poverty, it all looks really terrible, with nothing getting better, nothing to look forward to. But when I think small, closer in—you know, a girl I've just met, or this song we're going to do with Chas, or snowboarding next month, then it looks great. So this is going to be my motto—think small." (McEwan 35)

Henry Perowne responds to Theo's willfully ignorant mantra with a combination of admonishment and tolerance; a child of the post-9/11 world, all Theo knows is international distress and global catastrophe, desensitized by the sensational and the macabre. Perowne cannot fundamentally blame him for this outlook, yet he cannot bring himself to consciously agree with it, too distracted by the perpetual news programming playing in the corner of his eye to ignore the relentless woes of the world (not to mention the potential disaster he witnessed maybe an hour prior, eerily reminiscent of the World Trade Center attack). He does, however, find Theo's outlook, paired with the lack of "adolescent rage" typical of his contemporaries, to be a bit disconcerting. How is Theo so Zen in such trying times? How does he remain so unabashedly "cool?" Regardless, despite initially looking down his nose at Theo's mantra, Perowne seems to not only accept it but subconsciously live by it. **4**

5 In a world gone mad, Perowne finds solace in his practice. The free indirect discourse of *Saturday* constantly reverts to his neurosurgery firm and his musings on the subject in stream-of-consciousnessesque compulsions. **6** When Perowne is getting his ass handed to him by Baxter and his thugs (a situation in which he has minimal agency, to say the least), his mind retreats to the brain, thoroughly scrutinizing and diagnosing Baxter's neurological ailment as well as determining the savviest manner of defense in order to avoid his own potential brain injury. More notably,

4 I like the transition from the end of this paragraph to the beginning of the next one. It flows nicely. I also like the ordering of the paragraphs. Organization-wise, I think I'm in good shape.

5 Paragraph 3: relates "think small" idea to Saturday by providing textual examples.

6 The language here feels a little too informal given the context.

after he essentially saves Baxter's life towards the end novel and thus towards the end of likely the most absurd and visceral day of his life, Perowne's nerves are calmed and his mind is put at ease simply by knowing that he has performed his duty. After roughly ten consecutive pages of painstaking procedural details, writing that would surely bore a romantic like Perowne's daughter, Daisy, or at least lull the reader into a dull albeit soothed state (clearly a tactical decision on the part of McEwan), Perowne is elated: "For the past two hours he's been in a dream of absorption that has dissolved all sense of time, and all awareness of the other parts of his life. Even his awareness of his own existence has vanished...It's a feeling of clarified emptiness, of deep, muted joy. Back at work and, lovemaking and Theo's song aside, he's happier than at any other point on his day off, his valuable Saturday" (McEwan 266). Here, the reader is given a sense of the sublime, of cathartic and unbridled happiness.

7 This is the crux of the tension that McEwan appears to be negotiating in his book: the macro vs. the micro. All of the universal fears and concerns that plague the world and clearly weigh heavily on Perowne's mind simply disappear when he focuses on the beautifully simplistic task at hand, a tangible problem that he can hold in his palm and personally rectify within a few hours (a far cry from the Hyde Park demonstrations earlier in the day). This is truly the essence of "thinking small," and this is how Perowne, just like his son, finds contentment. Perhaps there is something to Theo's motto after all.

8 9 The comprehensive desire for control following the chaos of September 11, 2001 or a traumatic episode in general may seem understandable and even sensible, but much unlike Perowne's relatively innocuous reversion to his profession in times of strife and confusion, by no means does this inclination always result in a positive and productive outcome. Rushdie's Shalimar is undoubtedly a victim of similar trauma, his life irrevocably altered following his betrayal:

---

7 This, upon further reflection, is inaccurate. The sublime, traditionally speaking, is more so equated with religion. Catharsis is also related to the feelings of emotional purification following the witnessing of the traumatic events of a tragedy. This is the beauty of letting papers marinate!

8 This transition feels a little jagged.

9 Paragraph 4: this relates my thesis to *Shalimar the Clown*. I think one problem I have with this paper is pacing. I seem to methodically take my time when discussing the first novel (*Saturday*) and breeze through the second one (*Shalimar the Clown*).

9

> It comforted him to know that she was there, that
> when he was released from his oath she would be
> right there to kill, defenseless, just as his life had
> been defenseless when she ruined it, defenseless
> and vulnerable just as his heart had once been,
> defenseless and vulnerable and fragile just like his
> shattered capacity for trust. (Rushdie 241)

This passage is oozing with wistfulness and grief and much unlike Perowne's professional/personal inclinations, Shalimar's are rooted in vengeance. The only way for Shalimar to make sense of this trauma and right the wrong that he has been subjected to is through his oath—and his oath is something he can control. Shalimar's alignment with various jihadist organizations throughout his journey seems to directly correlate with the international ramifications of post-9/11 trauma in the United States and, more directly, the rise of Islamic extremism in the Middle East following decades of US intervention. Shalimar's feelings following Boonyi's betrayal mirror those of the American public following that dismal Tuesday morning and, conversely, the dozens of peoples disenfranchised by American international involvement: defenseless, vulnerable, and fragile. [10]

[11] While the desire for control following traumatic events is by no means unhealthy, the pursuit of that control can clearly lead to some disastrous and even immoral consequences. When analyzing the Bush regime through this lens, the War on Terror and subsequent Iraq War, although ostensibly logistical and ethical failures, make sense—a grim yet unsurprising realization. Naturally, however, no party comes out on top: citizens die, terrorists are killed, and countries are invaded. This appears to be part of what Rushdie is attempting to accomplish with *Shalimar the Clown*: in the power struggle following the pandemonium of trauma (whether it be global terrorism or a personal betrayal), there are few winners. If there is one thing that the Bushes, the Cheneys, the Rumsfelds, and

> [10] I would like to hear more about *Shalimar the Clown*. I think there is an opportunity for expansion here.

> [11] Paragraph 5: my conclusion. I think I wrap things up nicely; it's a good combination of closure and a slight branching out to the global/political ramifications of my thesis.

the Shalimars of this world could have stood to learn before they embarked on their primitive quests for authority, they are the wise words of a sheltered, upper-class, eighteen-year-old blues musician from London: think small.

Works Cited

McEwan, Ian. *Saturday*. Anchor Books, 2005.

Rushdie, Salman. *Shalimar the Clown*. Random House, 2005.

FINAL THOUGHTS ON SELF-CRITIQUE

This chapter provided you with the tools and insights necessary to successfully critique your own writing. At the end of the day, your writing is your own. You have ultimate autonomy and the final say. This does not mean to denigrate the importance of peer review in any way, but it is meant to stress the importance of being able to look at your work from outside of your perspective as the writer.

Writing is indubitably weird, and so is critiquing one's own writing. But all weirdness aside, it's a productive activity that can benefit you in innumerable ways. There is a reason why composition courses are basically the only required course throughout colleges and universities in the United States: writing is important and it is hard. Through critiquing your own writing, you can become a better writer; by becoming a better writer, you can more easily succeed in various other courses throughout your college career. Think about it: being a stronger writer will obviously help you out with essays in other humanities courses such as history or philosophy, but I bet you didn't realize that typing up lab reports for Anatomy & Physiology or completing a short answer question on an engineering exam would be less strenuous if you were more adept at critiquing your own writing. Perhaps most importantly, the ability to critique your own writing will aid you beyond the classroom and in your future jobs and careers. After all, you won't have a writing instructor on hand when you're working at a law firm, hospital, or Fortune 500 corporation. By learning to critique your own writing now, you are already setting yourself up for success years (or even decades) down the line.

Remember: be critical with yourself but not hard on yourself. Use the skills and techniques that you learned in this chapter to your advantage, in English 1020 and beyond. Engage with your writing from new perspectives and treat it like the rewarding process it is.

Writing Prompts and Activities

9

1. Break into groups of three. Each student should have a short (1–3 pages), completed paper in hand. Take ten minutes to slowly and deliberately read through your own paper. Then, on a separate piece of paper, write which technique for critiquing your own writing would most benefit this piece in particular and why you think so. Then write one strength of the paper and one weakness. After all parties have completed this, rotate your papers in your group and repeat this process until each paper gets two fresh sets of eyes on it and two new potential techniques and explanations. Once finished, each person in the trio should take a few minutes to discuss their paper with and ask questions to the two other members of the group. Did others agree with your own strengths and weaknesses? If not, then you may have work to do on your ability to self-critique. The idea behind this activity is to get your initial perspective on what your writing needs but also open your eyes to some new possibilities. While rooted in peer review, this activity should also be teaching you some new things about your own revision process that you were hitherto unaware of and helping you learn how to critique your own writing. Take note of what your classmates think and see if you can apply the methods that they suggest you employ to both the original paper and beyond.

2. Think back to the last paper you wrote (for any course). Did you self-critique your writing before you submitted it? If so, then what methods did you use? Were they successful? How could you improve them and thus improve your writing? If you didn't, then pull up your paper and self-critique it now. What are the strengths of the paper? What are the weaknesses? What would you need to do to improve this paper? Did the space from when you submitted it help you see it more critically?

3. Over the course of the semester, continue to reflect on your self-critique and maintain a small, succinct journal that details how you go about critiquing your own writing. For each major assignment, you should not only jot down the self-critique techniques you employ but reflect on how successful those strategies were. As the semester progresses, take note of your tendencies. Do you think you rely too much on reading out loud? Do you tend to avoid letting your writing marinate because of time constraints? Throughout the course, you should make sure that you are using **all** of the techniques and strategies at your disposal. If you notice that you're slacking in some areas, then don't be afraid to branch out and try something new. This activity has a lot to do with metacognition: by being more aware of your own thinking, writing, and critiquing processes, you can more comfortably assess (and thus, revise) your own work.

EXPLORING YOUR PIECE'S POTENTIAL: A CARTOGRAPHER'S GUIDE TO REVISION

Marisa L. Manuel

Marisa L. Manuel is an MFA Fiction candidate at the University of Memphis. She primarily writes horror and magical realism, and she's presented on topics ranging from the relationship of comedy and horror to the origin of zombie and ghost stories. Her classroom often incorporates elements of her creative writing background, and she believes that anyone can be a writer. She loves Memphis for its quirky surprises— from the Mollie Fontaine Lounge to the Peabody Hotel to the Belz Museum of Asian and Judaic Art.

You've found some sources, written your first draft, and shared your essay with a friend or two. You've even submitted it to your instructor and received feedback. What's next? It's a word you probably don't want me to say... a word that fills writers with dread. Yet, here it is, in all of its terror: Revision.

For many writers, revision can conjure painful memories of trying to rephrase a sentence, cutting out chunks of text, or maybe even tossing away hours of work and starting over. It certainly doesn't bring up memories of maps or adventures—though, at its core, revision is a journey as great as any of Indiana Jones's.

Revision is essential to the writing process; it means unearthing the treasure at the end of your journey and finding a text's full potential. It means creating the map to guide your readers and share in this treasure. It means direction, discovery, and purpose. Whether you're revising your Rhetorical Analysis, Researched Argument, or even New Media Project, the revision process is ultimately a matter of making choices. You see where those choices lead and learn from them in order to make new, informed, and better choices.

As we near the end of your textbook, we hit this all-too-important stage of the writing process. So let's take our first steps into revision by exploring exactly what it entails.

REVIEW, REVISE, EDIT, PROOFREAD, REPEAT!

You've likely heard all of these words at some point or another, maybe even interchangeably. Truthfully, they're all connected, and it's difficult to separate one from the other. However, for our purposes, we'll use these terms in the following ways.

Reviewing means looking over what's in your paper, questioning what you're attempting, and deciding how successful your attempt was. This is the *Considering Phase*. Basically, you're considering what you're trying to do with this paper, as well as whether you've succeeded. You can think of this step as viewing your paper through a set of new eyes (hence "re-view," i.e., viewing again).

Revision involves making big changes, the ones that your paper relies on most in order to become what you want it to be. This is the *Big Picture Phase*. These changes will likely deal with main ideas, organization, and arguments. If your argument's not on the page, or if you start with one argument and wind up with another, then the problem could be structural or related to your sources. For instance, you might realize that your sources are outdated and their authors lack *ethos*, or you might have attempted to write a refutation but wound up agreeing with a counterargument. Whatever the problem is, it needs to be fixed. It's also worth noting that while this step is called "revision," the revision process involves this step as well as the others. Thus, sometimes revision refers solely to the big picture changes, while other times it's used as a catch-all for every change involved in this process.

Editing means making the smaller changes, the ones that are important, but not always the most pressing. This is the *Fine Details Phase*. These changes usually involve specific word choices, descriptions, or even grammar. It may be that you have to reword a whole sentence to make it successfully express your content. Editing also considers your tone, which might not match your audience or genre. Additionally, editing could involve removing repetitive sentences that don't add to the paper or rewording parts of sentences to better state your point.

Proofreading is the *Clean Up Phase*, in which we're attempting to spy any last-minute errors in sentence structure, spelling, etc. Proofreading helps shield your essay against distracting mistakes, and it can make all the difference between easily conveying your point and confusing your reader. Proofreading, then, can easily overlap with reviewing; since writing is recursive, an attempt to clean up a piece allows an author to see areas that are less focused or clear. In turn, proofreading can lead to further edits and revisions, along with further proofreading and reviewing, on repeat.

Other Useful Terms

Audience refers to the people who will be reading your piece. Your professor will have different expectations than your friend, and they could also have a different base knowledge of the material. Another way to think of audience is in terms of *discourse communities*—each community has its own *genre*, *lexis*, and insider knowledge. Depending upon which audience you're writing for, the way you write will be different. For instance, if you are writing a book about Memphis for people who have never been here, then you'll want to explain the highlights of the city and explore its background in music and barbecue. If the person you're writing a piece for is a Memphis scholar, then they'll likely already know these basics.

Tone is related to audience because you have to choose how best to convey your material based on who will be reading it. How formal do you want to be? How serious? As writers, we often tone-switch in order to convey our opinions or feelings toward a subject, sometimes employing humor to make a somber topic more approachable, or using a more detached voice in order to adequately present facts. You should also consider the *genre* of the piece you're writing and what that genre usually entails. A professional paper, for instance, requires a different tone than a text.

Grammar is the system or structure of a language and provides rules for writers to follow. For instance, a misspellling can make you look unprofessional (see what I did there?). So too can awkward arrangement of words or misusing a synonym. Worse, these grammar issues can make your sentences difficult to understand. "I'm lost in a dessert" is very different from "I'm lost in a desert." Similarly, consider the following sentence: "Listening to music and barbecue are enjoyed by people in Memphis and also the zoo is great." This sentence is awkward for several reasons. First, the arrangement of words is off—the verb "listen" can easily be applied to both music and barbecue. While someone feasibly could enjoy listening to the simmer of meat on a grill, I'm doubting that's what the author intended. Additionally, the order of words doesn't make sense; why list two things a person in Memphis enjoys at the beginning, only to add a third item at the end? The text is also in passive voice ("enjoyed by people in Memphis"), and generally speaking, a sentence is stronger in active tense. A better version of this sentence would appear as such: "Memphians enjoy music, barbecue, and the zoo." While grammar rules can be hard to learn, knowing them will improve your ability to express meaning.

CREATING MAPS, NOT HOUSES

You may have heard that the writing process is like building a house. First you have the foundation or your main points. Next, you have the walls, which are expert sources and quotes. Finally, you have the windows, doors, and roof—specific details to further your point. But really, writing isn't that straightforward because writing is a constant state of revising: it's messier and more enjoyable, like the map-making I mentioned earlier. In the house example, your house will certainly fall if your sources aren't strong enough, but what if they're entirely the wrong sources? What if you're not sure what sort of house you're making, and instead of building a ranch, you build an igloo?

Thinking of writing as map-making better illustrates the writing process. With map-making, you have a rough idea of where you're going and a rough idea of how to get there, but you have more than one choice, and not every choice will work, so you have to constantly tinker and reassess (there's a lot of re-'s in this process, aren't there?). This reflects the reality that writing is a way to learn. Sometimes, we start a paper with one idea, but we end up making different conclusions than we expected. This happens because writing helps us process our thoughts, and this is another reason why revision is so important. As writers, we need to make sure that what we start off thinking (and writing) matches where we end up.

To simplify, although it might seem useful to think of revising as steps that follow one another, these steps are usually all happening at once. In this way, you're writing the map (your outline) as you're attempting to follow it. You're unearthing the treasure (the piece's main point) as you're trying to find your way toward it (structure). You're adding/deleting and rearranging details and sources as you're learning more about what they're all building up to. Simultaneously, you're creating the map, figuring out where it's leading, and attempting to forge better paths to that destination. Sound confusing? Definitely. No wonder people have problems with revision! But... isn't it also freeing? You're not just following a path—you're discovering your destination, creating the route, and marking the way for others to get there.

After you complete all these steps, take another look at your paper. Then show it to your aforementioned friend or a teacher and see if there's anything else you've missed. Some people consider this a **Repeat** of the stages above, since new eyes might point out new areas that need improvement. In fact, they might suggest the unthinkable: your paper isn't doing what you want, and instead of focusing on editing, you need to do more revision.

ON AVOIDING POTHOLES

Throughout the revision process, you might hit several potholes. These potholes will slow your journey, but don't let them stop your process. Some of these potholes are your own assumptions about what revision entails, or advice given by friends that, though well-intended, might not always be helpful. In fact, advice for one assignment could cause problems with another.

In "Rigid Rules, Inflexible Plans, and the Stifling of Language: A Cognitivist Analysis of Writer's Block," Mike Rose explains how assumptions/advice can lead a writer to enforce strict rules, which are often a disadvantage in the composing process and can even lead to writer's block. Instead, writers should strive for, "open, even adventurous thinking" (543), which involves heuristics, or "guidelines that allow varying degrees of flexibility when approaching problems" (536). For example, you may have been told that you should never use personal pronouns such as "I" when writing. This is a rigid rule, and while it may be true when composing a lab summary or certain kinds of research reports, this rule can make writing a literacy narrative nearly impossible. In the literacy narrative genre using "I" is not only acceptable, it is *necessary*. As a writer, it is up to you to figure out when a rule is helping you and when it is stifling your process.

Furthermore, sometimes a writer might come across a unique problem: too many map-makers. I mentioned earlier that feedback can sometimes be well-intended but not all that helpful. This is especially true when you receive different advice from different readers. Your friends, fellow students, and even teachers are human. They might not always understand where you're going with your essay (which can indicate a problem within the essay itself), but this misunderstanding could also be because they're biased against your point, sleep-deprived, or even struggling with the same question of "how can I strengthen my paper?"

If you ever feel that feedback is not helping your paper, then it's worth asking another person to take a look. If they agree with the previously offered feedback, then it might mean your paper is not clear, and it's worth listening to their advice. However, if they understand where you're going and can help you get there better than your first reader, then it's worth hearing them out and ignoring the other feedback you received. Part of your job as a writer is to know what advice to listen to and to know what advice to ignore. This doesn't mean the first eyes were trying to deceive you; it means they saw a different destination and were trying to navigate there, but since it's not the destination you intended, listening to that advice will make your paper even more confusing than it already is. This confusing feedback is just one of the many potholes you'll likely have to avoid while revising, but that's the good news—these potholes *are* avoidable.

So, now that you have an understanding of what revision is, let's discuss what revision is not. This way, you can focus on where to go instead of where *not* to go.

POTHOLE ONE: REVISION MEANS STARTING FROM SQUARE ONE

Earlier, I mentioned how the entire review-revise-edit-proofread process is interconnected. Another word often used for this process is **Rewrite**, which literally means altering/improving a text by writing it again. That certainly makes it sound like revision means starting from the very beginning, which is a frightening thought! Writing an essay is hard enough to begin with—why would you do it all over again?

If I ask you to revise the ending to your favorite story, however, then I'm implying that there's an original. You're not creating something entirely new; you are making changes to something that already exists. You'll utilize the same (or many of the same) characters and rely on similar plot components, but you'll alter several story elements to get the ending where you want it to go. Essays involve the same process. When your teacher asks you to revise your essay, you'll still be relying on some of the foundational components of your original piece. Only in the most extreme circumstances are you actually starting over completely.

When asked to revise, think about what problems you faced the first time, and avoid making them this second time. Usually, you'll be able to rely on several of the same sources and arguments, but now, you'll have a better idea of what parts are missing or poorly conveyed. Revising research papers almost always means finding additional research.

Unfortunately, these realizations lead us to our second pothole, which is opposite the first but just as problematic.

POTHOLE TWO: REVISION MEANS CHANGING AROUND A FEW WORDS, RESTATING A SENTENCE, ETC.

Ok, so we've reached the other side of our pendulum swing. While revision doesn't mean starting over completely, it also doesn't mean changing a word or two, slamming our laptops shut and shouting "Done!" Certainly, changing words around can help an essay—but if the points we're making don't support our main argument, what good is changing a word?

Oftentimes, early drafts won't yield a discernible argument, summary, etc., because the writer has yet to discover what they want to say. Other times, the author has this part figured out, but not every section of their essay meshes together. As author Anne Lamott says in her phenomenal (and stingingly true) "Shitty First Drafts," "very few writers really know what they are doing until they've done it...we often feel like we are pulling teeth, even those writers whose prose ends up being the most natural and fluid" (528). Thus, even if the words come out easy, they might be the wrong words entirely. A writer may require several drafts before they fully realize what they're writing, so there's no use in attempting to refine what you've written early on in the process, because chances are you're going to change it.

Let's say I'm writing a Researched Argument about the University of Memphis' athletic department. I want to argue that the school should put forth more funding toward the recruitment and retention of student athletes in order to encourage more students to apply to the university. In an attempt to persuade my reader, I write the following (somewhat shitty) first draft:

> The University of Memphis has a great athletic department. My friend Josh is on the football team. Sometimes, he complains about the long hours, but he mostly likes being a student-athlete. I bet other students would want to apply here to be on the football team. There's also the Grizzlies nearby, so that's a plus. I think with more money toward athletics Josh would have more time to study and also be better at football.

In the above example, I've chosen a fairly broad topic, supplied insufficient evidence, and lacked clarity in my argument... But, on the other hand, here's where my ideas are beginning to shape, and once I identify those ideas, I can make them more accessible to a reader.

For instance, I say that the school's athletic department is "great," but I'm not clear what I mean by "great;" in order to be clearer, I could provide statistics/expert opinions on what makes it "great" (especially since the term is subjective). Additionally, I mention that Josh "likes [the team]" and only "sometimes... complains about the hours." By placing this information here, I'm confusing my point. If this paragraph is meant to explore what's great about the team, why am I including a negative aspect?

Also, who's Josh? Why did I mention the Grizzlies? What's the relationship between the University's football team and student applications? I've left the reader confused, and if someone gets confused reading a map, then they won't know where we are heading.

A somewhat clearer version of the above paragraph would be the following:

> In terms of its season wins, the University of Memphis' football team is on the rise and has improved since 2010. During this same period of time, the number of students applying to the UofM has also risen, suggesting there might be a connection between the team's success and the number of prospective students. Thus, the UofM should consider increasing funds to its athletic department, thereby helping the teams win even more games and encouraging even more student applicants.

In this paragraph, I clearly state my argument and provide support. I argue that the athletic department ought to be funded more because of a connection between the strength of the UofM's football team and the number of students applying to the school. However, I'd later have to address the possibility that this relationship is a coincidence, or that other factors might be at play (such as the improvements to the neighborhood surrounding campus). I would also need to insert specific numbers and citations. A better first sentence might explicitly note how many more games the team won in 2016 than 2010. Before I can argue that funding for the athletic department should be increased, I would need to reference sources or ideas that explain why sports teams' success is important to the college experience or retention (for both student-athletes and other students). Right now, I make huge logical jumps without explicitly connecting one idea to the next.

In both of these examples, I could change some words around, say "Josh, my friend of five years" to be more specific, or say "the football team" should be funded more instead of more generally saying "the athletic department." But ultimately, my main argument in the first example is unclear, and in the second, it isn't being supported by any concrete evidence. *Logos* is nonexistent. So even if I use synonyms, they won't help me argue my point. I need to first reevaluate what that point is, then find a stronger way to say it:

> In terms of its season wins, the University of Memphis' football team is on the rise. However, the GPAs of its student athletes continues to drop, and in the case of Dasmine Cathey, a former player, football skills were not enough to get him a degree. If the goal of the University of Memphis is to help its students graduate, then more money should go toward the Center for Writing and Communication (CWC) in order to fund tutors to help its student-athletes graduate. This reallocation would in turn help the athletic department retain its star players, thus increasing the UofM's athletic victories.

Though the above paragraph could still benefit from more information to back my claim, my main argument is clear: student athletes at the University of Memphis need more academic intervention if they are to remain students here, and they can get that help if the school provides more funding to tutors in the CWC.

But wait—originally, didn't I want to argue that we should put more funding into the school's athletic department? Based on the new evidence, it looks like my main argument has changed. Instead, I'm now advocating for more funding to go to the CWC. *That's ok.* Sometimes, your research leads you in directions you didn't expect, and like any good journey, you can follow that new path and see where it leads. In this case, I've discovered that funding could allow the CWC to develop programs specifically dedicated to student-athletes, a service that currently does not exist. I'm now able to argue that point, and through my argument, possibly implement change to help both the CWC and student-athletes.

While the first two examples had the same general purpose, only one of them clearly stated my argument, and neither of them had proper evidence. The third example is more effective because both its claim and its examples are clear. True, it can still be developed more, but that's why we have more than one draft. You can utilize the time between your first and second draft (or even third and fourth) to reflect on any comments you've received, find new evidence, and continue to shape (and improve) your essay.

While writers revise in different ways, revision is almost always an essential part of a writer's process, and this leads to the third and final pothole.

POTHOLE THREE: REVISING IS ONLY FOR "BAD" WRITERS

I like to think of myself as a good writer. I'm sure that Stephen King, Toni Morrison, and JK Rowling also like to think of themselves as good writers. But here's a little secret about all of us good writers: when we start a new piece of writing, we almost never know what we're doing. Whether we are songwriters, poets, essayists, or academics, it's rare that a piece of writing comes out perfectly after just a first draft.

Think back to the reading from English 1010 titled "Revision Strategies of Student Writers and Experienced Adult Writers." In this article, Nancy Sommers examined the revision strategies of student writers and professional, more experienced writers. Both groups attempted to utilize the revision process, but they went about it in different ways. For instance, student writers tended to see revision as a list of rules to follow, and their primary changes focused on finding synonyms, or "stronger" words. Conversely, the more experienced writers sought "to discover (to create) meaning in the engagement with their writing, in revision" (585); furthermore, they adopted heuristics as opposed to set rules, and they viewed revision as a recursive process. Thus, the student writers misunderstood revision as involving only small, uniform changes that were used from essay to essay while the experienced writers understood revision as a holistic process in which they searched for meaning and then tried their best to convey it.

Our writing process is one of constant reevaluation. What am I trying to say? How can I best make my point and be understood? In the previously mentioned "Shitty First Drafts," Lamott views the process as such:

> The first draft is the child's draft, where you let it all pour out and then let it romp all over the place, knowing that no one is going to see it and that you can shape it later. You just let this childlike part of you channel whatever voices and visions come through and onto the page... There may be something in the very last line of the very last paragraph on page six that you just love, that is so beautiful or wild that you now know what you're supposed to be writing about, more or less, or in what direction you might go—but there was no way to get to this without first getting through the first five and a half pages. (528–529)

To rephrase, your first draft is rarely a good draft, and it doesn't have to be! You're given the chance to make changes and improvements—that's exactly the point of revision, and that is why this class has a built-in revision project. Remember, good writing is subjective. Clear writing is less subjective, and that's something we all can work on.

So let's say we write our shitty first draft, then review it, make revisions and edits, and end by proofreading. We've done all the steps, so surely we're finished—we've reached the piece's full potential, right?

X MARKS THE TREASURE

You've finished your review, your revision, your edits. You had a friend offer feedback. And now, you've turned in your paper, but rather than seeing a 100 or a smiley face, you see the

10

dreaded words: *Come talk to me*. Maybe there's an F circled and underlined, or another angry red mark.

How often has a teacher drawn a large X through one of your paragraphs? Don't despair, because the X doesn't mean, "This is terrible." The X means, "There's something here you haven't yet discovered. Keep digging. Keep unearthing. Keep exploring, and you'll find it!"

An X, or a Check Minus, or any variation of these doesn't mean you've failed. It doesn't mean you should give up—that all the time and effort you put into writing was worthless. In fact, it means you've dug some of the treasure out of your first draft, but maybe you haven't found it all. Maybe there's more to unearth in your piece. Maybe it's time to **Repeat**.

It can be discouraging to see notes on your paper that tell you to try something else. But it can also be exciting—you now have permission to experiment, to continue making changes in your paper. Like with literal directions, you sometimes need to choose a different path to get where you want to go. Some paths are more difficult or time-consuming, but in almost all cases, **if one route didn't work, then another one will**.

A Lesson on Drafting: My Original Version of This Piece

While writing this textbook chapter, I had to go through the same revision process I mentioned above. Normally, no one sees your first draft, but for the purposes of showing that, hey, it can start out really badly, here's a look at that initial attempt and how I shaped my draft to where it is now.

My first version of this piece was titled "Re-Envisioning the Re's: How to Get Your Paper to Draft 2 and Beyond. Re-ally!" (...I know, that's a pretty terrible title, and the content within that draft wasn't much better). I began the paper with the following:

> You've researched and written your first draft. Now what? Revision, like anything, is a skill. "All writers are great editors." What, then, is the difference between revising, rewriting, and editing?

> Every sentence can be written a dozen or more ways. Every word has a synonym to consider. Every argument has a counterargument. And, most importantly, I have to remember at all times what I'm attempting with my words; I have to question whether I'm succeeding, and if I'm not, how can I?

> Instead of thinking of rewrites as starting over, think of them as "reconsidering." What parts of your piece work best? What parts work, well, not best?

Ok, so obviously I didn't use all of the content above. In response to that last sentence, a lot of my original text worked "not best." I had reasons for changing the title (it's hard to argue for puns about the prefix "Re"), and I moved around several sentences; rather than front-loading all my questions, I broke them into sections devoted to defining the revision process, identifying common potholes, and showing that all writers can benefit from revision. But most importantly, I realized there was a specific way I could (and should) approach the topic of revision: I could make it into an adventure, not just a process. I could frame revision as a chance to explore rather than a need to confine.

This realization completely changed my approach. I began thinking of revision as a journey involving maps. I realized that, ultimately, I wanted to make the revision process exciting. I could just explain the process and bore both my readers and myself, or I could leap in headfirst, swing from the vines, and invite others to join me.

If I were to continue revising this piece (because let's face it, you can ALWAYS revise more), I'd try to bring this idea of adventure more into the section involving Pothole Two (which I previously called "Rumor Two"), or I might combine the ideas of a journey and a journey in Memphis, specifically. Instead of arguing for university funding, maybe I'd have us explore Beale Street, just to hone in on this idea of "adventure!" Maybe I'd try something else and see how it worked, because it's my writing, so, why not?

There's always more you can play with in a piece, and that's reason enough not to hold back. If you have a million places you can take your piece, don't stop at one; try two, or ten, or three dozen. Just keep trying until it feels complete.

HOW DO I KNOW I'VE ARRIVED?

A common question asked by new and old writers alike is "How can I tell when my piece is finished?" Truthfully, there's no one way to decide. You could always have a goal in mind— get a 100 on my paper, get this piece published, etc.—or you could consider your piece's potential reached when someone else goes, "Oh, I see where you're going with this; I'm with you."

It's another choice, and to help you decide, here are some other questions you can ask yourself. If you answer "no" to any of these, think about why that's the case. Then, question whether that answer should be "yes," and if so, how to make that answer a "yes."

- In a few sentences, can you clearly define what you're arguing? Is that summary on the page? Your reader needs to clearly understand what you're saying in order to continue reading.

- For each paragraph, is the main point clear and helping you build the argument? If there is more than a single point, then you may need more than one paragraph.

- Is every sentence helping develop these paragraphs? Sometimes, less is more, and the points expressed in an especially well-written or fun passage might not fit with what you're trying to say.

- What about individual words? Are they all spelled and arranged correctly? Are they the best words for my purposes? This step falls under *Proofread*, and it can allow a reader to more easily understand what you've written.

- Can your friends or fellow students explain what you're trying to argue? Do they trust your sources? Why? Think of the *rhetorical triangle* and what evidence might be missing.

- Do you include a counterargument? A *refutation*? If you don't, then a reader might come up with a counterargument on their own, and you won't be there to defend your points.

10

- Does this paper fit its intended genre? Is it written toward the proper audience? If not, then you need to rework your tone to better address your audience and discourse community.

- Does your conclusion tie back to your introduction? If it's different, then that means your argument might have changed along the way, and your introduction might need to change, too.

- Have you listened to others' feedback? Why or why not?

OTHER TOOLS TO HELP WITH REVISION

You have several tools at your disposal to help your revision go smoothly. Utilize as many tools as possible to help your paper reach its full potential. For a more in-depth look at some of these strategies (and others!), check out the chapter "Critiquing Your Own Writing."

1. Reverse outline—A reverse outline can help you uncover your point, but backwards. Instead of heading to a destination, start at the end, and make your way back. See if all the steps line up. In other words, write out what you believe to be the topic sentence in each paragraph, and see if those ideas flow, are supported, etc. If not, then move your paragraphs around so your outline (and essay) makes more sense.

2. Robo-reader—It might sound weird to have a robot read to you, but these readers can help you catch snippets that don't sound right, such as misspellings (since you'll hear them pronounced differently than you intended) or missing words. There are multiple tools online that do this, including options on Microsoft Word and Pages. However, if you're scared of robot-takeovers, then you can always read the paper aloud to yourself for a similar result.

3. CWC—If your friends are busy, or you've already asked your classmates for help, then you can always go to the Center for Writing and Communication. Consultants will work with you to understand what you're trying to say, and then they will help decide how to say it as clearly as possible.

4. JSTOR/EBSCO and other databases—Let's say your problem lies not in your writing but in your sources. They aren't trustworthy enough, they're too biased, or you don't know what the heck they're saying. Now that you have a clearer idea of what you want to say and of what you still need to research, you can narrow down on key terms to help you find better sources. Librarians can help you better navigate your search, which will in turn help craft and finish your paper.

5. Spell-check—This one may seem obvious, but it can make all the difference. Before turning in your paper, run it through this system to see what you've missed.

REACHING YOUR DESTINATION

We've been building up to this moment since the start of this chapter. The moment when everything comes together, when you have your map, your treasure, and your piece's full potential all laid out before you. The prize at the end of your journey.

But here's the truth—the real end of the journey is when the audience can get to the treasure without you. You've used specific directions, changed some routes, and added important markers. Your map is done. Now, let them read it.

Writing can always be improved, but at a certain point, it's best to save your doc and move onto the next one. You can't continue writing the same piece forever, and why would you *want* to write it forever? It's only one piece out of dozens that you will write in your college career. But at some point, you have to recognize that you have crafted this one piece of writing as finely as possible, and you should be content and move on. To work on it more would be a disservice to all the other pieces you could work on.

Feel proud of the work you've put into your paper, and reflect on what writing this paper taught you. That way, the next time you write, maybe the revision process will be a bit easier. Share that paper, and take with you all the tricks you've learned on this journey writing it. Writing is a constant process of revision, and you now know what that means, and why it matters.

Thanks for going on this adventure with me. May your writing journey continue in Memphis and beyond. Be fearless, bold, and daring. If your paper loses its way, don't fret—you're the map-maker, and you'll find a way.

Writing Prompts and Activities

1. Think back to a time you were asked to write a paper (preferably, your Rhetorical Analysis) and write about that revision process. If you didn't revise much, then pull up that past essay and think about what you would revise now. Don't forget to review and make edits as well, but most importantly, explore what you were trying to say with this paper—is it clear? Holistically, is every section working toward what you're trying to say? What else can you add or alter, both on a sentence/paragraph level and in terms of meaning?

2. Reflect on what you learned in this chapter. When you began reading, how did you think of revision? Did you, like most student writers, think that revision just meant editing and proofreading? What do you think now? What scares you about the revision aspect of writing? How will you have to change your revision practices to become a better writer? Set three goals for your revision of the researched argument. What revision strategies will you use?

WORKS CITED

Lamott, Anne. "Shitty First Drafts." *Writing About Writing: A College Reader*, edited by Elizabeth A. Wardle and Doug Downs, Bedford/St. Martin's, 2011, 527–531.

Rose, Mike. "Rigid Rules, Inflexible Plans, and the Stifling of Language: A Cognitivist Analysis of Writer's Block." *Writing About Writing: A College Reader*, edited by Elizabeth A. Wardle and Doug Downs, Bedford/St. Martin's, 2011, 532–546.

Sommers, Nancy. "Revision Strategies of Student Writers and Experienced Adult Writers." *Writing About Writing: A College Reader*, edited by Elizabeth A. Wardle and Doug Downs, Bedford/St. Martin's, 2011, 576–589.

ELECTRACY

Scott Sundvall

Scott Sundvall is an Assistant Professor of English and the Director of the Center for Writing and Communication at the University of Memphis. His work has appeared or is forthcoming in *Philosophy and Rhetoric, Composition Forum, Computers and Composition, Enculturation,* and *Media Fields.* He is the editor of *Rhetorical Speculations* published by Utah State University Press. He loves Memphis sports and the unique combination of a "grit and grind" and laissez-faire culture, as well as knowing that Memphis is far superior to Nashville.

You are likely already familiar with the concepts of orality (verbal speech) and literacy (alphabetic reading and writing). Electracy, on the other hand, might be foreign to you, even strange sounding, but it's just another apparatus, similar to orality and literacy. In fact, you'll quickly realize that it's a term for something with which you're actually already familiar, as you live in and with electracy everyday.

We call orality, literacy, and electracy *apparatuses* because they are more than just a method or mode of communication. Gregory Ulmer, who coined the term electracy, notes that "electracy is to digital media what literacy is to alphabetic print," but electracy is *more* than just digital media and literacy is *more* than just alphabetic print. For example, we structure speeches differently than we structure written essays; likewise, we structure digital compositions differently than we structure speeches or written essays. This is because, as apparatuses, orality, literacy, and electracy differ not only in terms of technology, media, and/or medium but also in terms of how they each organize patterns of practice, state of mind, behavior, etc. In this sense, as Ulmer writes, an "apparatus is a social machine, partly technological, partly institutional." While it can be easy to identify the technological differences between the apparatuses of orality, literacy, and electracy, the institutional differences can be more difficult to understand. TABLE 11-1 will help you better understand the institutional dimensions of each apparatus.

Table 11-1. Electracy Chart: An Overview of Gregory Ulmer's Apparatus Theory

Apparatus	Orality	Literacy	Electracy
Practice	Religion	Science	Entertainment
Procedure	Ritual	Method	Style
Institution	Church	School	Internet
State of mind	Faith	Knowledge	Fantasy
Behavior	Worship	Experiment	Play
Philosophy	Mythology	Epistemology	Aesthetics
Ground	God	Reason	Body
Ontology	Totem	Category	Chora
Mode	Narrative	Argument	Figure
Axis	Right/Wrong	True/False	Pleasure/Pain

Source: Ulmer, Gregory. "Introduction: Electracy." The Learning Screen, June 2, 2017, http://ulmer.networked-book.org/the-learning-screen-introduction-electracy/

Each apparatus shift is both rhetorically and historically situated (see **TABLE 11-1**). Prior to the emergence of literacy, when orality figured as the organizing apparatus, the church served as the dominant institution of meaning-making. Accordingly, the primary practice at that time was religion, the behavior was worship, and the mode was narrative. With the advent of literacy, the school functions as the dominant institution of meaning-making. Thus, the primary practice becomes science, the behavior becomes experiment, and the mode is now argument. The theory of electracy contends that we are undergoing yet another apparatus shift, wherein the internet serves as the dominant institution. The dominant practice then becomes entertainment, the dominant behavior becomes play, and the mode becomes figure (literally, we can consider figure as image; abstractly, we can consider figure more broadly as poetics, such as *figurative language*).

Clearly, one apparatus does not negate another: literacy did not get rid of orality (we still give speeches), and electracy did not eliminate literacy (we still write essays and go to church). Nonetheless, each apparatus is entirely different, which is why we do not refer to literacy as "written orality," and such is also why we should not refer to electracy as "digital literacy." But remember: as the chart indicates, an apparatus is more than a mode of technological delivery, media, or medium—an apparatus (and an apparatus shift) changes how we do just about *anything*. As such, electracy means that we must change the way that we consume and produce *rhetoric and composition* because literate methods for consumption and production are not enough once we are engaging with the internet as an institution.

Next, see **TABLE 11-2**, which further contextualizes the differences between literacy and electracy. While **TABLE 11-2** provides just one analogic example of literacy in relation to electracy, an exchange of Plato for Disney may seem intellectually (and even rhetorically) bankrupt. But consider how the institution of the internet structures and conditions our practices, behaviors, modes, etc. The electrate institution of the internet is a fantasy-land of aesthetics, play, pleasure/pain, and as we'll discuss below, it is no accident that the former host of *Celebrity Apprentice* was elected president, regardless of your political opinion of President Trump. The question, then, is not whether or not Donald Duck, for example, should be used rhetorically; rather, it's not a question at all, as contemporary, electrate rhetoric has already been thoroughly Disneyfied. Donald Duck and the logic of celebrity are here to stay.

Table 11-2. Literacy vs. Electracy in Context

Literacy	Electracy
PLATO	DISNEY
Academy School	Disneyland Theme Park
Science Reason Rational	Entertainment Fantasy Visceral
Writing Dialogue	Animation Cartoon
Socrates Dialectic	Mickey Mouse Gag
Idea True/False	Event Attraction/Repulsion
Question	Plasmatic Line

Source: Ulmer, Gregory. "Diagram," Facebook, March 19, 2018.

A BRIEF HISTORY OF ELECTRACY

While Ulmer contends that the initial emergence of electracy started with the Industrial Revolution, the first televised presidential debate between John F. Kennedy v. Richard Nixon (1960) perhaps gives us one of the first culturally and politically significant examples of electrate rhetoric (see FIGURE 11-1). According to the polls, those who heard the debate on the radio (orality) or read the transcript of the debate (literacy) thought Nixon had clearly won. Those who watched the debate on television (electracy), however, thought Kennedy had clearly won. How could this be? While Nixon appeared old and unfriendly, nervous, and sweaty, Kennedy appeared young and charismatic, cool and composed, stylish (see FIGURE 11-1). In other words, the visual rhetoric of Kennedy was a *style that also was the content* (recall TABLE 11-1). The televisual medium did not merely change how the rhetoric was delivered; it changed the rhetoric itself. This is what Marshall McLuhan, a scholar who laid the foundation for the concept of electracy, meant when he said, "the medium is the message" (McLuhan).

Figure 11-1. Kennedy v. Nixon Debate

Source: Wikipedia Commons. "Kennedy v. Nixon Debate." May 28, 2018 https://commons.wikimedia.org/wiki/File:Kennedy_Nixon_debate_first_Chicago_1960.jpg

ELECTRACY TODAY

Flash forward to today, where style still trumps (no pun intended) or otherwise informs content. And with style we include aesthetics, entertainment, fantasy, play, etc., as detailed by TABLE 11-1. It was not an accident that it was after the Kennedy v. Nixon debate that we began to see a stream of celebrities get elected to high office: Ronald Reagan, Al Franken, Jesse Ventura, and Donald Trump, to name just a few. Even Dwayne Johnson ("The Rock") has discussed running with Tom Hanks on a presidential ticket in 2020—that we cannot tell whether or not such is a joke is a clear indication of an apparatus shift to electracy. In fact, celebrities running for office—with increasing success—is now not only common but expected. Moreover, such a rhetorical "logic of celebrity" in the age of electracy is not lost on career politicians, either. Bill Clinton playing the saxophone while wearing sunglasses during primetime television catapulted him in the polls. Barack Obama did something similar: he created a strong social media presence; he participated in conversations about popular culture (e.g., what was currently in his playlist, what his favorite smartphone was, or what teams were selected on his NCAA brackets); and he even won an Emmy for his

comedic routine with Zach Galifianakis on "Between Two Ferns," which he used as a platform to promote the new healthcare plan (see **FIGURE 11-2**).

Figure 11-2. Obama Gets Funny

Source: "Between Two Ferns." "Watch President Obama on 'Between Two Ferns with Zach Galifianakis.'" *The White House Blog*, May 28, 2018, https://obamawhitehouse.archives.gov/blog/2014/03/11/watch-president-obama-between-two-ferns-zach-galifianakis. (Official White House Photo by Pete Souza)

We can understand the rhetorical "logic of celebrity" in the age of electracy more broadly as *persona* or *brand*. Nobody understands the rhetorical efficacy of persona or brand better than our current president, Donald Trump. Trump had been fine-tuning his persona/brand long before his run for president, becoming a central figure in popular culture consciousness, and he then used that refined persona/brand as his central rhetorical strategy during the campaign. For example, many Trump supporters recursively indicate that they are primarily drawn to him because of *how* he says or does something, not necessarily *what* he says or does. For better or worse, Trump is an electrate president *par excellence*.

Electracy has not only changed electoral politics and political discourse; it has also changed fundamental rhetorical values. For example, you are likely familiar with (at least some of) the following terms: post-truth, alternative facts, and fake news. Review the "Axis" column on the chart: it moves from right/wrong in the apparatus of orality, to true/false in the apparatus of literacy, to pleasure/pain in the apparatus of electracy. Of course, this does not mean that the institutions of church or science no longer function as key figures in what we believe or how we behave, but it means that their rhetorical potency is diminishing, giving way to the persuasive power of pleasure/pain (which corresponds with the rest of electracy, such as fantasy, play, aesthetics, etc.).

National news media has also changed in the age of electracy. Consider the layout of a newspaper and the layout of a news website. Whereas the newspaper relies much more heavily on printed words, the news website relies more heavily upon images, videos, and sound bites. For example, consider these newspaper images relative to news websites, taking into account the amount of printed text versus images, videos, sound bites, etc. The use of modes of rhetoric and writing beyond alphabetic print is called multimodality, and as indicated by national news websites, it is central to understanding rhetoric and writing in the age of electracy. Electracy has also changed how national news media can rhetorically approach an audience. For example, consider the image below: the same newspaper edition used two different (even conflicting) headlines so as to rhetorically pander to a certain demographic in a given region (see FIGURE 11-3). The electrate institution of the internet makes selective print dissemination difficult if not impossible, which is likely why many national news media have been forced to adopt an either conservative or liberal position, choosing one market demographic (audience) over another.

Figure 11-3. Different Headlines in the *Wall Street Journal*

Source: Snopes. "Two Editions of 'Wall Street Journal' [sic] Bear Opposite Headlines About Trump," May 28, 2018, https://www.snopes.com/fact-check/wsj-different-trump-headlines/.

This all might sound depressing, namely because we have cherished and embraced the virtues of literacy for centuries. Electracy might seem shallow, tragically lacking in contemplative thought or deliberative action, perhaps even promoting a vapid mind. This is not new, however, as any major apparatus shift entails a certain mourning. Plato feared literacy for the same reasons, thinking that writing would destroy the "metaphysics of presence," obfuscate memory, and damage civil politics and civic engagement. But it is not the apparatus of electracy that should concern us but how we appropriate it. Electrate rhetoric and writing can still be used for the common good and well-being, but a refusal to accept it does little good for the contemporary rhetor. In other words, electracy doesn't make us dumber; we just have to get smarter at using and working with our new electrate apparatus.

YOUR ELECTRATE TASK

Understanding how to appropriate electrate rhetoric into your own compositions requires you to consciously and critically observe your daily life. The institution of the internet is now ubiquitous—what electracy calls "ubiquitous computing" or "ubicomp"—in that you have smart phones, tablets, laptops, desktops, etc. on or around you at all times. You can start by considering the following, unique to electracy:

- Social media—Arguably, you see most political debates on social media, and many people now get their news from links shared on social media platforms (hence the success of fake news during the 2016 presidential campaign).

- Memes—Using what electracy calls "Flash Reason," memes use brevity, humor, and often reference popular culture to make rhetorical points, and social media is inundated with them.

- Viral videos—While some viral videos are merely humorous and have little if any rhetorical import, most viral videos are short and multimodal.

- Commercials/Advertisements—Electracy considers commercials/advertisements to be the pinnacle of electrate rhetoric, and it is likely the rhetoric you consume most frequently on a daily basis.

To add a layer of complexity to this, consider the above in the context of recent rhetoric and writing scholarship. For example, Richard Lanham suggests that what we call electracy is also a shift into an "attention economy." In short, an attention economy means that attention is a scarcity, and as such we have moved from a rhetorical emphasis on *stuff* to a rhetorical emphasis on *fluff* (e.g., the Flash Reason of memes replace long essays). Memes, for example, draw on popular culture, thus serving as an example of why and how popular culture is *not* killing writing (Williams), and why popular culture should not *only* be considered useful as text for criticism (Pepper), especially in the age of electracy. Rather, popular culture now serves as a bountiful and useful index for rhetorical *invention*—even if, as Lanham suggests, such produces more fluff than stuff. Moreover, the digital institution has afforded a multimodality that extends beyond alphabetic text to images, as electrate rhetoric often now uses videos (which includes text, sound, moving images, etc.). As Sarah Arroyo notes, the sharing of (rhetorical) videos within the digital institution also indicates the participatory and circulatory nature of electrate rhetoric as reflected by social media. More recently, we have seen the emergence of augmented reality and mobile rhetorics, as afforded by smartphones, which delivers a new potential dimension to electrate rhetoric and composition.

We can therefore draw from the following threshold concepts to better understand electrate rhetoric and composition: writing is a technology (Brooke and Grabill); writing mediates activity (Russell); all writing is multimodal (Ball and Charlton); and writing is performative (Lunsford). Using these threshold concepts, we can frame electrate rhetoric and writing as: *performative, multimodal rhetoric and writing that, because of the technological conditions of the digital institution in general and ubiquitous computing in particular, is always already mediating our activity*. Yet even this rather specific definition of electracy requires our due attention to the logic, principles, and reasoning of electracy, as given by the above tables.

The goal of your 1020 new media writing assignment is therefore not merely to create a website, video, or multimodal composition. After all, this is not a computer programming, video production, or design course. Rather, the goal of your assignment is to create a digital composition that employs the logic, principles, and reasoning of electracy. Learning how to rhetorically analyze and invent with and within electracy will make you a more critical consumer and civic participant in the free exchange of ideas, especially in our increasingly networked, globalized world. After all, if the historical apparatus shift of electracy has inaugurated a post-truth, alternative facts, fake news *context*, then the *rhetorical text within such* is yours to write and compose.

For better or worse: welcome to electracy.

Writing Prompts and Activities

1. Let's assume that nobody believes in science anymore. How can you use the logic, principles, and reasoning of electrate rhetoric to convince a given audience to protect the environment? Write a series of tweets that uses electrate logic to argue we need to protect the environment.

2. Watch a bunch of random commercials on TV or on YouTube. You'll notice that commercials are rarely selling you the actual product; they're selling you a concept, idea, or ideology. They may never discuss the actual product, but they readily use celebrities, aesthetics, style, popular culture, entertainment, fantasy, play, etc. How would you be able to do the same with an electrate rhetoric that focused on an issue of concern (common good or well-being)? In other words, how can you use fluff to sell the stuff?

3. Identify what makes certain memes and viral videos rhetorically successful or unsuccessful. Make a list. Then use that list to guide your new media writing project.

WORKS CITED

Arroyo, Sarah. *Participatory Composition: Video Culture, Writing, Electracy*. Southern Illinois University Press, 2013.

Ball, Cheryl E. and Colin Charlton. "All Writing is Multimodal." *Naming What We Know: Threshold Concepts of Writing Studies*, edited by Linda Adler-Kassner and Elizabeth Wardle. Utah State University Press, 2016.

Brooke, Collin and Jeffrey T. Grabill. "Writing is a Technology." *Naming What We Know: Threshold Concepts of Writing Studies*, edited by Linda Adler-Kassner and Elizabeth Wardle. Utah State University Press, 2016.

Lanham, Richard A. *The Economics of Attention: Style and Substance in the Age of Information*. University of Chicago Press, 2007.

Lunsford, Andrea A. "Writing is Performative." *Naming What We Know: Threshold Concepts of Writing Studies*, edited by Linda Adler-Kassner and Elizabeth Wardle. Utah State University Press, 2016.

McLuhan, Marshall. *Understanding Media: The Extensions of Man*. The MIT Press, 1994.

Pepper, Mark D. "Popular Culture is Only Useful as a Text for Criticism." *Bad Ideas about Writing*, edited by Cheryl E. Ball and Drew M. Loewe. West Virginia University Libraries, Open Access, 2017.

Russell, David R. "Writing Mediates Activity." *Naming What We Know: Threshold Concepts of Writing Studies*, edited by Linda Adler-Kassner and Elizabeth Wardle. Utah State University Press, 2016.

Ulmer, Gregory. "Introduction: Electracy." *The Learning Screen*, May 28, 2018, http://ulmer.networkedbook.org/the-learning-screen-introduction-electracy/

Williams, Bronwyn T. "Popular Culture is Killing Writing." *Bad Ideas about Writing*, edited by Cheryl E. Ball and Drew M. Loewe. West Virginia University Libraries, Open Access, 2017.

COMPOSING MULTIMODAL TEXTS

Kendra L. Vanderlip

Kendra L. Vanderlip has her MFA in Creative Writing in Nonfiction from the University of Memphis. While definitely a creative writer first, Kendra fell in love with teaching writing and composition while pursuing her MFA and hopes to one day pursue a secondary degree in that field. Her current creative writing projects focus on wrestling and personal relationships. Originally from Michigan, Kendra and her husband moved to Memphis in 2015, and can often be found enjoying the patio life in Cooper Young. She loves many things about Memphis, but two of her absolute favorites include the wrestling community and the brunch culture.

If we think about writing as a skill, and our knowledge as a toolkit, then we learn things in our writing courses that equip us to be more successful writers. As we learn about rhetoric, we can better use rhetoric in our own compositions. The assignments you compose in this course are honing your rhetorical knowledge so that you can later apply that knowledge to new classes and rhetorical situations.

However, there is another genre of writing that you are already knowledgeable about and have been practicing for nearly your entire life: **multimodal texts**. Multimodal texts are everywhere and are composed of just about everything. A basic breakdown of the word shows us that multi means many, and mode means the form that the text takes, but that barely scratches the surface of what multimodal texts are. Multimodal texts are better defined as the "integration of multiple modes of communication and expression [that] can enhance or transform the meaning of the work beyond illustration or decoration" ("Multimodal Literacies"). But what are the modes and how do they transform meaning?

Multimodal texts create layers of meaning in a way that a basic alphabetic text (such as an essay) can't. When the different modes are combined effectively, the meaning and impact of a text is improved. For example, think of your favorite book from childhood. Mine was *The Giving Tree*. For those of you unfamiliar with this book, *The Giving Tree* is about a young boy who grows up in the company of a tree that gives and gives parts of itself to make the boy's life more complete. The tree gives its fruit, branches, and leaves, and finally, even allows the boy to cut the tree's trunk down, leaving only a stump. The significance of the boy cutting down the tree would not have carried the same weight if I couldn't see the tree's progression from a fruit-bearing and healthy tree to the final result: a stump. It is the combination of words and images that makes children's books effective, and that increase in impact is why multimodal texts are so fascinating for readers and useful for rhetors.

You encounter multimodal texts all the time, but you probably don't recognize them as such, so let's look at some examples. Let's start with my favorite: Memes. Memes are a popular example of a multimodal text. Memes, a form of communication on social media, are typically a combination of an image with a few words to make a point, typically with the purpose of sharing a humorous or sarcastic point. In **FIGURE 12-1** below, we see a meme that was popular several years ago.

Figure 12-1. Ain't Nobody Got Time for That Meme

Memes have become such a popular multimodal text, that they have evolved to use gifs and are now available even when we aren't on popular social platforms like Facebook or Twitter via Gif keyboards. They also have become a huge part of fan engagement with popular television shows, with audience members creating meme reactions to poignant moments as the show unfolds. These memes serve as a way to bring layers of meaning to a moment and create a more nuanced form of communication. But multimodal texts aren't just digital. A multimodal text can also be a research paper that uses graphs and figures, or a poster for a geology class with pictures and mathematical equations. Such texts just have to contain more than one mode.

Think About It

1. Can you think of other examples of multimodal texts based off what you learned about them thus far?

2. Are all texts multimodal? Can you think of one that isn't?

3. Why might multimodal texts be more effective than other texts?

THE MODES: GETTING TO KNOW THE SPECIFICS

A wide variety of texts can be described as multimodal, and these texts are everywhere. For example, think of the dreaded SPCA commercial currently on air. You know the one I'm talking about: Sarah McLachlan's "In the Arms of the Angels" plays while the audience is shown video clip after video clip of animals looking sad and desperate and sometimes even injured. Sarah McLachlan herself appears, petting an animal while talking about the atrocities that occur to household pets on a daily basis. She informs the audience how they can help save these animals, to please call the number on the screen (which flashes in bold white lettering as she speaks), and to donate X dollars a month (only pennies a day to save animals!). The combination of music with sad images and a celebrity spokesperson work together and usually cause the viewer to either look away/change the channel or motivates them to donate. The text that flashes across the screen provides useful information for viewers who are persuaded to donate. This commercial uses visual and aural modes to encourage people to donate to their cause and the linguistic mode to share the website and/or phone number the audience needs to help them.

To better understand the texts you see on a daily basis, it helps to understand the modes that are used in multimodal texts. Multimodal texts use at least two of the New London Group's five modes to convey an effective message. Those modes are: **Linguistic**, **Visual**, **Aural**, **Spatial**, and **Gestural**.

Once you understand these modes, you will be better prepared to compose your digital composition for English 1020. Understanding what these modes can do will help you make decisions about which modes will be most persuasive for your audience and choose a genre of digital composition accordingly. According to Digital Rhetoric and Composition scholars Cheryl E. Ball and Colin Charlton, "the definition of mode is complicated to distribute equal emphasis on how the meanings are created, delivered, and circulated through choices in design, material composition, tools, and technologies, delivery systems, and interpretive senses. That is, mode isn't just words, but sound, texture, movement and all the other communicative acts that contribute to the making of meaning" (Ball, Charlton 42). So, if you want to use the aural mode, then you will likely decide to compose an animation, video, or podcast. If you need to use the visual mode to include lots of graphs and figures, then an infographic will probably suit your needs best. Different arguments will rely on the modes differently, so consider your own argument as you read about the modes and ask yourself which modes are most important for your rhetorical purposes.

LINGUISTIC

The linguistic mode refers to language, whether spoken or written. The mode makes its meaning through how it is presented. So, for example, vocabulary, structure, and grammar shape the linguistic mode. Consider the two sentences below:

"I'm finna get to it."

"I've been meaning to get around to that."

Both sentences present a similar message, but the meaning changes slightly because of changes in the vocabulary. We could also argue that one might be more effective than the other, depending on who wrote it and who hears or reads it. We probably wouldn't expect someone who hails from the northern side of the country to use the word "finna" while writing, but it would make perfect sense if the writer was a Southerner writing for other Southerners, both of whom would know that 'finna' is a slang conjugation of "fixing to."

Why does the linguistic mode matter? Consider this for a moment: different regions have different lexis, as we've discussed above. For example, in Michigan (where I'm from), we call carbonated beverages "pop," while the majority of the population here in Memphis calls it "soda." But even that changes as you go explore some of the less populated areas in Tennessee, where locals sometimes refer to all sodas as "coke." In order to cut down on confusion when going out to dinner, I learned to call pop soda. If I hadn't learned, then I would still get blank stares when I asked my waitress for a "pop." Even now, sometimes I forget, and it almost always causes confusion. Being aware of my audience and adapting to their expectations allowed me to communicate more fluently.

In digital spaces, the linguistic mode can be further utilized by playing with things such as academic tone, slang terminology, or abbreviations. For example, if you are writing something intended to be read by a more academic audience, then you would likely not choose to use slang, but if you are trying to engage an audience who relies heavily on texting, then you might use a large amount of text abbreviations such as "lol" or "imho." Using slang or text speak allows the conversation to seem less formal and creates a more casual and relatable tone. For some topics, that informal tone may be just the thing you need to strengthen your pathos for an argument or to change the rhetoric of an argument you may have heard several times over. For example, if a student wanted to write about the implications of deporting immigrants from Memphis, having an informal tone would allow them to seem more relatable to their audience and build personal connections while a formal tone would make it more difficult to establish a connection with their audience.

VISUAL

This mode refers to images (either still or moving) or other elements of a document that might shape how a reader sees the text. For example, the visual mode can refer to color, page layout, style, size, and perspective.

Figure 12-2. Two Perspectives, One Image

For example, see **FIGURE 12-2** for a visual that plays with the idea of perspective. There are two potential viewings of this image: one as a rabbit and one as a duck. Sometimes people only see one of the animals and not the other, and it might be necessary for someone to show them where the other animal is in the picture. This effect is deliberate. The dual potential of the image causes the reader to dwell on the image longer than they would if it could only be viewed in one way. By creating this visual "trick," the artist forces the audience to consider multiple perspectives, and in turn, starts a larger conversation about what the audience might be missing if they accept only what they see at first glance. It's an effective use of the visual mode because we not only appreciate the work itself, but also the work that the artist had to put in to create such an illusion, extending the conversation beyond the image itself.

In digital spaces, you can further utilize the visual mode by incorporating pictures, background colors, or altering page layout. For example, if you were talking about the systematic oppression of people of color in Memphis, you might rely on somber colors since having bright colors might seem insensitive to your audience or inappropriate for the tone of your project. Or, if you were crafting a project on the Memphis aquifer, you might choose to utilize blue colors because it is indicative of water, and therefore, relevant to your material.

AURAL

The aural mode refers to the use of sound. Elements that fall under this mode include music, sound effects, ambient noise, silence, volume of sound, emphasis, and accent. Whether it's sound effects for a Snapchat filter, music in the background of a commercial, or even the deliberate omission of sound, sound has an impact in how we perceive a message. In "The Body" episode of *Buffy the Vampire Slayer*, a show that is usually filled with sound effects and dramatic music, the writers created an episode almost completely devoid of sound, including only extremely muted background noises in order to highlight the absence of a main character that had died in the previous episode. The absence of sound was intended to mimic the absence of the presence on the show and symbolized how the world seems a little different when someone close to us has passed. Because it was such a departure from a normal episode, it resonated as being one of the most powerful episodes with the show's dedicated fanbase.

For another example of how sound is used to present messages, have you ever noticed how much louder commercials seem than the television programs we are watching? This is a deliberate choice on the part of the advertisers, as the increase in sound grabs your attention when you were just getting ready to look at your phone or walk out of the room for a moment. Similarly, consider how a scary movie will put a lull in the soundtrack before a surprising moment, or how when the bad guy jumps out, there is a shrill/loud/freaky noise to pair with what you are seeing. These auditory moments serve as cues and also help to create meaning. There are rules that these genres follow, and those rules create expected behavior. As an audience member, you understand that tense or dramatic music is indicative of something major about to happen on the screen, and because we are familiar with the rules, we understand subconsciously that we are about to be scared. Being aware of the rules allows you to use the aural mode effectively.

In digital spaces, you might decide to utilize a background soundtrack to go with the argument you are presenting. A jaunty tune might be used to draw an audience in and persuade them to be more engaged with the rest of the text. For example, if you are composing an argument on the benefits of converting the Midsouth Coliseum into a wrestling museum, you might use iconic wrestler's entrance music as background or use specific sound effects to highlight the excitement of wrestling. Or, if you were composing an argument on the economic disparities between races in Memphis, then you might go with a more somber soundtrack to mimic the tone of your argument.

SPATIAL

A common misconception is that multimodal texts are always digital or related to technology, but that is not always the case. Sometimes multimodality is part of the structure around you. The spatial mode relies on characteristics such as environment, architecture, proximity, position, and organization. Following this same line of thought, one can argue that anytime an architect designs a new building, he is adding to the larger text of the city. When entering an unfamiliar neighborhood, you may notice a stretch of houses that seem to all be similar builds or utilize the same color scheme. These are deliberate choices intended to reflect a city's culture and aesthetic.

12

Figure 12-3. The Two Towers

Figure 12-4. The Freedom Tower

Let's consider the Two Towers in New York City that were attacked on September 11, 2001. The Two Towers (seen in **FIGURE 12-3**), were highly visible within New York's skyline. As such, they were filmed in many movies while they stood. However, after the Towers fell as a result of the attacks, a single Tower was built in their place. The choice to build one tower instead of two was deliberate, and the tower was renamed The Freedom Tower (seen in **FIGURE 12-4**). Instead of continuing on as only an office building, the Tower was turned into a museum and a memorial pool was placed where the other tower stood. At the museum dedication of The Freedom Tower in 2014, Former President Barack Obama used the architecture and design to introduce the United States to this new symbol.

Here, at this memorial, this museum, we come together. We stand in the footprints of two mighty towers, graced by the rush of eternal waters….Here we tell their story, so that generations yet unborn will never forget. Of coworkers who led others to safety. Passengers who stormed a cockpit. Our men and women in uniform who rushed into an inferno. Our first responders who charged up those stairs. A generation of servicemembers—our 9/11 Generation—who have served with honor in more than a decade of war. A nation that stands tall and united and unafraid—because no act of terror can match the strength or the character of our country. Like the great wall and bedrock that embrace us today, nothing can ever break us; nothing can change who we are as Americans.

The choice to rebuild one tower rather than two was deliberate. Indeed, it was an acknowledgement that the past can't be changed, but as the Former President's speech indicates, the design of the Freedom Tower makes the importance of the spatial choices evident and resonant and illustrates the potential power this spatial structure carries as a text. It is taller than the two previous towers, standing at 1776 meters tall, in observance of America's year of independence (1776). Like the Two Towers, the single building stands out in the New York City skyline, but its missing twin tower reminds us to "Never Forget," acknowledging the many lives lost on that day. While Freedom Tower represents American resilience and perseverance, the missing building reminds New Yorkers and visitors of the traumatic day. This example illustrates how the spatial mode can be used to create meaning that other texts may not be able to completely convey.

In digital spaces, you might utilize the spatial mode by zooming in on something in a photo, or by creating a text box in an unexpected place to garner your audience's attention. Or perhaps, one might choose to organize the space a little bit differently, such as going through facts counting backward so as to build tension while working towards number 1 on a list. If you were constructing an argument about gang violence in Memphis, then you might use this mode to highlight a quote from someone you interviewed or from your research. Or if you were constructing an argument on the geographical values of Memphis as a community, then you might include maps and zoom in on important areas.

GESTURAL

Gestural mode refers to how the body and its movement can convey a message. This category relies on characteristics such as eye movement, hand gestures, facial expressions, body language, and even interaction between people. The classical thinkers that began our study of rhetoric (Aristotle, Cicero, and others) devoted a great deal of time discussing gesture because it is an important part of persuasion. Gesture is a rhetorical device that successful rhetors consciously craft to reflect their speeches. For example, when saying thank you to a cheering crowd at her presidential race announcement in 2016, Hilary Clinton held her hand over her heart. This was likely a calculated movement, made to emphasize and highlight points of the verbal speech. A move as simple as placing a hand over a heart makes the speaker seem more genuine while a speaker that gestures inappropriately (or doesn't gesture or move at all) while they speak may be perceived as incompetent even if their words are logical and persuasive.

Figure 12-5. Former Presidents Barack Obama & Laura Chinchilla have a discussion prior to photo op during their presidencies.

In FIGURE 12-5 (taken during both their presidencies), former President Barack Obama is speaking to Laura Chinchilla, the former President of Costa Rica. By looking at their body language and eye contact, we can see that they are engaged in a serious conversation with one another, and we can also assume that they have a certain amount of respect for one another. Former President Chinchilla is leaning in with her hand raised, which we could read as her being earnest or trying to emphasize a point. Both people have serious facial expressions, and they are looking at each other, not the camera, so we can read this as a candid moment unlike the formal pictures that are often taken during these visits when politicians pose and smile for the camera. The reason we might look at a photo like this, versus the formal photos so often circulated after the visit, is because we can analyze some of the more candid moments between the two officials. When most people are aware of a camera nearby, they physically change their behavior, shift their posture and placement in the seat, and smile. Or they "pretend" to act natural, which rarely passes for an actual candid shot. A candid shot shows the audience a more honest representation of that moment. It allows us to get a real sense of the professional and respectful relationship between these two politicians through unaltered body language.

In digital spaces, you might consider highlighting or focusing on a particular facial expression to effectively create a mood. If you are recording a person speaking, then you will need to make sure their facial expressions and hand and arm movements appropriately reflect the situation. If you are creating an animation and need to emphasize the importance of a moment, then you might make a character do things with their arms or have them jump around in order to get your audience's attention.

12

Think About It

1. Review your list from before, are all your examples multimodal? What modes does each text you listed use?

2. Think about past assignments you've completed in English classrooms. If you could revise them, how might you make them multimodal? For example, would you consider an aural literacy narrative? How about a rhetorical analysis that uses visuals?

3. What modes are you currently using in your Researched Argument?

WHY LEARN ABOUT THIS NOW?

Multimodal texts are effective because of how they can create layers of meaning within a text. Most texts that have resonated with you over the course of your life were very likely multimodal. The idea that a text can exist in just one mode is a fairly romantic and outdated notion. According to Ball and Charlton, "There is no such thing as a monomodal text. An example of a text often referred to as being monomodal is the traditional first-year composition research essay. Yet such a text is recognized from its linguistic mode and its visual and spatial arrangement on the page (title, name block, double spacing, margins, default font size, formulaic structure, etc.)" (Ball, Charlton 43). Put more simply, the choices we make when formatting a paper, such as following MLA or APA format requirements, are not only linguistic. Indeed, first-year composition texts often use the spatial and visual modes to accompany the linguistic mode; this means that even the essays you write for class are multimodal.

Keep in mind that when you revise your argument over for the New Media project, you no longer need to follow the requirements of the academic genre. Changing the genre of your text will, however, impact your rhetorical situation. The reason we might choose a different genre to persuade our audience is that our text now reaches different audiences and follows different rules. Instead of six pages of carefully chosen words, you might have two minutes to persuade an audience. The rules (or genre conventions) change because your audience's expectations have changed. By persuading an audience in a different format, you may think about your argument differently, which will make for a stronger argument overall. Thinking of your digital composition as another draft of your researched argument will not only allow you to create a version of your argument that can reach different audiences but also can help you improve your researched argument when you return to it and revise.

Following the restrictions of a traditional research paper can limit your creativity and hinder your ability to see new avenues into your argument. Alexandria Lockett, an author in the *Writing About Writing* textbook from English 1010, talks about this briefly: "Although traditional research papers undoubtedly address the problem of how to evaluate and integrate sources, a contemporary first-year college writing student will probably be sensitive to [their] limitations as a single writer. What kind of original contribution can teachers reasonably expect the average college student to create that they can't instantly access via the Internet?" (Lockett 237). By composing your argument outside of the academic genre, however, you can not only be creative and make an argument for a new audience, but you can also create something with your own voice, and this may end up shaping both your digital composition and your final revision.

MOVING FORWARD

Now that you know how the modes work, you can start thinking about how to make strong rhetorical moves when composing in different mediums. As you begin to think about how to make your researched argument successful as a digital text, consider the modes your argument needs as you choose the software you will use to create your project. Consider how you might use visuals or sound to shape your argument. If you pair a certain style of music with the new media project, then it can help strengthen the pathos of your argument. If your argument requires a lot of statistics, perhaps relying on an infographic that can incorporate bar graphs would be the best choice. If you are focusing on Memphis's long history with music, then utilizing a medium that can play music would be a smart choice. As you decide on the software you want to use to compose your argument, think thoroughly about your research question and how certain modes can help you persuade your audience.

When considering which genre you want to use for your new media project, consider the strengths of each platform and how they can strengthen your argument in a new genre.

INFOGRAPHIC

This platform's strengths are in the linguistic, visual, and spatial modes. An infographic allows you to emphasize statistics through innovative graphics and visuals, while still incorporating traditional text. The ability to design either using one of their preloaded templates or by creating your own allows some creative flexibility when writing your argument on this platform. You might consider this platform if you think statistics and/or graphs are going to help persuade your audience. For example, one might choose an infographic if they wanted to show the economic impact of the Grizzlies in Memphis, using graphs to show the statistics around income/revenue for the NBA team and designing a cohesive background with the team's colors/logo.

PODCAST

This platform's strengths are in the aural and linguistic modes. A podcast allows you to highlight either yours or others' natural ability as a storyteller or a public speaker. A podcast allows you creative flexibility by splicing in other sounds in addition to your own voice, such as music, sound effects, or interviews. You might consider this platform if you think personal interviews or your own strengths as a public speaker can help make your argument its most effective. For example, you might choose to make a podcast if you want to talk about rape on college campuses in Memphis so that you can include snippets of personal interviews without showing survivors' faces or public statements made by officials.

VIDEO

This platform's strengths are in the visual, aural, spatial, and gestural modes. A video allows you to bring a lot of different elements together in a visual format. It is one of the most popular forms of persuading an audience, especially on social media platforms. A video allows you to incorporate either a visual of you speaking or a voiceover, in addition to music/sound elements, images, and other video clips. You might consider this platform if you hope to persuade your audience through your own talents as a public speaker, or if visual clips would be effective for persuading your audience. For example, you might choose a video if you are writing about the number of traffic accidents that occur in Memphis, and you might choose to include photos of damaged vehicles, clips from news sources about bad accidents in the area, or interviews with people who are affected by accidents in Memphis (ex. police officers, victims, business owners).

ANIMATION

This platform's strengths are in the visual, aural, linguistic, and spatial modes. An animation, like a video, allows you to splice in a lot of different elements in order to persuade your audience. With an animation, you can incorporate a voiceover or music to go with moving animations on the screen or photos/other visuals to persuade your audience. The moving elements of the templates create a textured background, highlighting the design of the animation. You might consider this platform if your argument needs visuals to make it more effective. For example, one might choose an animation if they wanted to talk about the Greensward in Memphis but wanted to incorporate visuals of what the Greensward is and its proximity to the zoo, as well as maps of zoo parking in order to demonstrate why it is such an important issue to Memphians.

GRAPHIC NOVEL/COMIC

This platform's strengths are in the gestural, visual, and linguistic modes. A graphic novel or comic strip allows you to create characters who can show emotion through facial expressions and body language. It also allows you to create different settings for the characters. Genre expectations of the graphic novel/comic also allow for some humor to be incorporated. One might choose the comic as their platform for the New Media writing project if their Researched Argument could benefit from moments of humor or action. For example, one might choose the graphic novel/comic if their Researched Argument is about gentrification in Memphis, moving characters around in different sceneries to talk about the ramifications of gentrification.

It is important to remember that the modes need to be used strategically to strengthen an argument. For example, if talking about gang violence in Memphis, there are several platforms that could work. Video would be an excellent platform, combined with the right elements. However, if I chose the wrong interview clips or incorporated a voiceover recording where I stumbled over my words or played music too loud in the background that distracts from the other modes, I'm not using the modes as effectively as possible. However, when these elements all work together, they can send a powerful message.

As you compose your digital composition, remember to have fun. Sometimes, when composing in new genres, we struggle to create the most effective text, especially as newcomers encountering previously unused technologies. This is a necessary part of learning the software and exploring different options, but once you get used to the software, this should be fun. Play with the different modes—the different colors, different visuals, different sounds, etc.—until you are happy with the result. The most successful projects result from students playing to their strengths: a student with a gift for public speaking using her own voice to tell a narrative; a student with a visceral sense of humor creating a comic that tears apart the rhetoric of popular public figures; a student with strengths in math or design creating an infographic that incorporates and examples graphs and figures. Now that you've been given this new blank slate with new modes to play in, what can you bring to this project to make it stand out?

Writing Prompts and Activities

1. Think about a commercial that's jingle stayed with you or a movie that touched you deeply. How about a dance that took your breath away? Did you get goosebumps? Did you cry? What was it that made it so effective? If you took away one of the modes, then would the text work as well?

2. Refer to FIGURE 12-1 at the start of this reading. Can you identify all the modes used? Is the meme effective? Why or why not?

3. What are your strengths as a writer and with digital technologies? How can you incorporate them into the New Media Writing Project?

4. Who do you want your audience to be for the New Media version of your argument? What modes will best address and persuade the audience?

5. Consider the video at this link: https://www.youtube.com/watch?v=8v5l6j-x9Rl With a partner, identify all the different modes in this video. Be specific and be prepared to share your answers with the group. What mode is missing? What does that take away/add to the video? Defend your answer.

6. Using the technology available to you, search for another image/video that contains at least 4/5 modes. Applying your knowledge from the chapter, talk about the choices made in the video. Were all the modes used effectively? Why or why not?

WORKS CITED

12

Ball, Cheryl E. and Colin Charlton. "All Writing is Multimodal." *Naming What We Know: Threshold Concepts of Writing Studies*, edited by Linda Adler-Kassner and Elizabeth Wardle, Utah State UP, 2015, pp. 35–47.

Mann, Austin. "Optical Illusion Rabbit and Duck." *Wikimedia*, Creative Commons, 1 Mar. 2018, upload.wikimedia.org/wikipedia/commons/thumb/1/13/PSM_V54_D328_Optical_illusion_of_a_duck_or_a_rabbit_head.png/1024px-.

"Multimodal Literacies." *National Council of Teachers of English*, 25 Oct. 2017, www.ncte.org/positions/statements/multimodalliteracies.

Souza, Peter J. "United States President Barack Obama Participates in a Restricted Bilateral Meeting with President Laura Chinchilla of Costa Rica at the Ministry of Foreign Affairs in Casa Amarilla, San José, Costa Rica on 3 May 2013." *White House*, Wikimedia/Creative Commons, 5 May 2013, en.m.wikipedia.org/wiki/File:Barack_Obama_meets_Laura_Chinchilla.jpg.

Unknown. "Ain't Nobody Got Time Fo That." *Create a Meme Image | Meme Generator*, 31 Mar. 2013, memegenerator.net/AinT-Nobody-Got-Time-Fo-That.

STUDENT EXAMPLE 1

Amoriana Davis

Reflecting on English 1020

When we began the semester, each student was aware of the 4 major assignments that we would have to complete: a rhetorical analysis, a research paper rough draft, a new media project, and a final research paper revision. We had the option of choosing any topic related to Memphis for the rhetorical analysis. When I began my research for the paper, I was looking for something fashion related, but when I typed "fashion in Memphis," the first site that popped up was, "Blacks in Memphis Lose Decades of Economic Gains." It was a stroke of luck, but it led me from my rhetorical analysis to the revision of the researched argument.

After the rhetorical analysis, I thought that I would be able to simply research the income gap in Memphis and have the perfect paper. However, once I turned in my rough draft for the researched argument, I realized that I had found good statistics from the U.S. Census Bureau, but that's about all I had. I didn't have enough academic sources, and I couldn't even reach the 5–6-page minimum for the research argument rough draft because I was simply repeating everything that I read from online articles. After our rough draft, we had to do a new media project assignment based on the information we'd gathered for our research paper. I chose to do an infographic and it completely changed my views on PowerPoint or presentations in general.

Even though my new media project turned out well, it was obvious that I would need more credible academic sources. I also needed to narrow my topic so it wasn't as broad. When I met with Dr. Fredlund, she helped me use JSTOR in order to find some of the academic sources that became crucial to my revision. As we reread my paper, we realized I could turn my paper into a proposal, using the research I did for the draft as my introduction and my new research to frame my argument. In my final paper, I included more academic sources and my writing wasn't simply scattered statistics because I had a sense of direction and a path to follow. So while my topic remained related to the income gap, my argument changed from simply claiming it existed to presenting a proposal for how to fix the problem of the income gap in Memphis.

RHETORICAL ANALYSIS

Amoriana Davis
Dr. Fredlund
English 1020
13 February 2017

An Analysis of "Blacks in Memphis Lose Decades of Economic Gains"

The article, "Blacks in Memphis Lose Decades of Economic Gains", written for *The New York Times* in 2010 by Michael Powell explores the links between a failing black middle class and Wells Fargo Banking. Powell interviews homeowners with foreclosures like Tyrone Banks, public officials like mayor A.C. Wharton, and Wells Fargo officials in order to expose the root of the financial plight for African Americans in Memphis. He unearths the startling truth that Wells Fargo targeted black homeowners by marketing the most expensive loans to black applicants, even when they qualified for cheaper loans (Powell 1). When the recession hit, it put all the pressure on black homeowners in Memphis causing foreclosures and plummeting black credit into the abyss. He concludes that even though Wells Fargo refuses to accept accountability, the statistics show that they unfairly charged black homeowners and their greed helped to create an economic gap between blacks and whites in Memphis that hadn't been seen since 1990. Michael Powell proficiently wields digestible organization, expressive description and imagery, and logos in order to further his claim that Wells Fargo's high interest loans were a factor that led to a financial decline for blacks in Memphis, TN.

Michael Powell organizes his article effectively by moving seamlessly through dialogue and description. His organization allows for a purposeful shaping of necessary context around core content, making the information more digestible in order to proficiently reveal his findings about Wells Fargo's part in the downfall of black economy in Memphis, TN to the public. Powell explains the context of financial situations throughout America, "Federal and state officials say that high-cost mortgages leave hard-pressed homeowners especially vulnerable and that statistical patterns are inescapable" (Powell 3). He then allows Thomas E. Perez, the assistant attorney general for the Justice Department's civil rights division, to provide core content that lead to Powell's findings in Memphis: "the more segregated a community of color is, the more likely it is that homeowners will face foreclosure because the lenders who peddled the most toxic loans targeted those communities" (Powell 3). By shaping his information in

13

an easily comprehensive context/content format, his readers are allowed to easily navigate through his findings. In a similar fashion, Powell explains Howard Smith's financial decline, "he was laid off. He sent out 60 applications, obtained a dozen interviews and no call backs. A bank foreclosed on his biggest house" (Powell 4). He uses Howard's dialogue, "it all disappeared overnight" in order to give content to the context (Powell 4). He could have easily used Howard's dialogue to explain his financial situation, but he instead contextualizes the information in order to make it more coherent for the audience. His organization then lends a purposeful tool in ensuring that the information reaches the audience.

Powell's use of description in and around his interviews helps to further his findings by creating a story that people can connect to. He describes settings and personal situations in an expressive manner that allows people to create a picture or person that the readers can easily connect with. As he describes Tyrone Banks financial plight, "He worked for FedEx and also as a custodian, built a handsome brick home, had a retirement account and put his eldest daughter through college... Then the great recession hit...Mr. Banks now faces bankruptcy" (Powell 1) He gives Tyrone Banks more dimension by giving his audience a full and rounded perspective of Mr. Banks as a human being. Powell reveals that Tyrone Banks is a person and had a full life before he was faced with his financial troubles. Presenting a rounded individual allows for the audience to receive the information from a 3-dimensional source in order to introduce Powell's findings and its effects on the financial plight of black people in Memphis, TN. Powell proceeds to describe the setting of the financial plight in Memphis, and it gives the audience a vivid picture of what companies like Wells Fargo leave behind when they unfairly target black communities with high interest loans. Powell describes Soulsville as, " a neighborhood south of downtown Memphis, is to find a place where bungalows and brick homes stand vacant amid azaleas and dogwoods, where roofs are swaybacked and thieves punch holes through walls to strip the copper piping. The weekly newspaper is swollen with foreclosure notices"(Powell 3). Powell presents the solemn picture of a number of black neighborhoods that happened to be targeted by Wells Fargo in Memphis, TN. These neighborhoods were once a thriving part of a bustling city and have now plummeted into deserted wastelands. As the recession hit and homeowners were unable to afford predatory loans that should never have been promoted to them by Wells Fargo. Powell uses the description of Soulsville and Tyrone banks to express the damages that occurred to black homeowners when Wells Fargo knowingly targeted their neighborhood for high-interest loans.

Powell utilizes logos, primarily though his presentation of statistics and a range of credible sources, in order to strengthen his relationship to the audience. This use of logos further his argument that Wells Fargo targeted black communities with high interests loans that aided in the financial decline of black economic growth in Memphis, TN. Powell explains that, "As of December 2009, median white wealth dipped 34%, to $94,600; median black wealth dropped 77%, to 2,100" (Powell 2). He notes that this information was from the Economic Policy Institute, supplementing logos in two ways; it uses a factual and numeric source that the audience can reference in order to more aptly understand the impact of the recession and provides a credible source that the audience can rely on. He could have gotten this statistic from a number of sources, but Powell chose a source that has developed a certain level of credibility. Powell's use of credible sources aids in insuring that his audience will receive the information while trusting that his article is a trustworthy source of information as well. He also uses a range of information from Wells Fargo employee, Camille Thomas, who explains, "Your manager would say 'let me see your cold call list. I want you to concentrate on these zip codes... African American Neighborhoods'... We were told, 'oh they aren't too savvy'" (Powell 5). He also quotes Wells Fargo's law representative, Andrew L. Buckler, who states, "people who have less tend to be more vulnerable during downturns" (Powell 6). By gaining information from a broad range of sources and people, Powell developed a well-rounded perspective, creating a stronger foundation to in order to further his claim that Wells Fargo was a factor that led to a financial decline for blacks in Memphis, TN.

Powell presents a well-organized, descriptive and reliable expose that reveals how Wells Fargo targeted black communities with high interest loans, when they qualified for better loans. They did this because they felt that majority black communities in Memphis, TN would more likely accept said loans. He continues to explain that because Wells Fargo targeted these communities, when the recession hit, these black communities were dragged down into economic plight by the weight of high interest loans promoted by Wells Fargo. Ultimately, his combination of statistics and interviews presents a compelling argument.

WORKS CITED

Powell, Michael. "Blacks in Memphis Lose Decades of Economic Gains. *The New York Times*, http://www.nytimes.com/2010/05/31/business/economy/31memphis.html. Accessed 19 February 2017.

RESEARCH PAPER DRAFT

Amoriana Davis
Dr. Fredlund
English 1020
20 March 2017

Income Gap in Memphis, TN

Income inequality or the extent to which income is distributed in an uneven manner among a population, has been a raving topic for decades, even centuries throughout the United States of America and many other countries. The discussion about the distribution of wealth has been a recurring topic for the past decade but it seems that the numbers become more dismal each time the income gap is mentioned. As we progress with technology, medicine, and public policy, it seems that most cities in America leave the income gap to simply fester within itself, Memphis is no different. In recent years, each edition of Memphis's Commercial Appeal that discusses income inequality, reveals another unimpressive statistic about the widening income chasm in Memphis, TN. Memphis unlike the other top 50 metropolitan cities, with the exception of ATL, GA, has a vastly uncommon population distribution with 63.3% of its population being African American as of 2010's census. The uncommon population distribution adds another layer to the complexities of income inequality in Memphis and seem to aid in the manifestation of income inequality in Memphis, Tn. Income inequality in Memphis, TN is not only race related but it is also aided by the marginalization of the odd majority, minority complex that lives within Memphis, TN.

The Income Gap in America is one symptom of Memphis, TN's vast income gap. The fact that "various studies show the income gap is wider than any time since 1928… months before the stock market crash in October that started the Great Depression" (Appeal 2011) is indicative of large national patterns. Because we live in an economy where what affects the whole will inevitably affect the parts, it would be unlikely that Memphis would not have an income gap. However, the degree to which Memphis has been affected is both uncommon and the lack of promise to close the gap in Memphis is unsavory.

According to the Federal Census Bureau's 2010 census, Memphis has a population of 646,889 residents (this does not include the surrounding areas of Memphis: Cordova, Germantown, etc.). 408,675 (63.1%), of the residents are African American, while 177,735 (27.7%) of the residents are white, 41,994(6.5%) of the residents are Hispanic or Latino, 10,146 (1.6%) of the residents are Asian with the remaining 1.1% as native American or Pacific Islander. These numbers become much more purposeful when compared to the median income of the residents. City Data states that the median income for African Americans in Memphis is $30,464. The median income for Whites is $56,264 while Hispanic residents have a median income of $34,100, and Asian residents have a median income of $75,774. Altogether, the median income for Memphis is $36,908 and the aggregate income is $14,070,784,800. These statistics by City Data in 2015 follow the trend of the Federal Census in 2010: "In metro Memphis… The most recent Census…top 5% of wage earners…making at least $165,411 a year, take home 22% of all the income in the area. The richest 20% get a total of 50.5% of all the income…bottom 20%, earning less than $18,725 3.2% of the pay" (Charlier 2011).

The data presented can seem daunting but at the base of the matter there are stark parallels between race and income in Memphis. For example, black Memphians make 63.3% of the residential population yet they have the lowest median income of the residential population. On the other hand, white Memphians (27.7% of the population) and Asian Memphians (1.6 of the population) have the highest median income with $56,264 and $75,774. There are 35.6% more black residents than white residents yet the median household income is 25,800 more than the black median household. Even if the number would be lower based on statistical probability, the gap is uncanny. Even more shocking is the gap between Asian Memphian Income and black Memphian income, $45,310.

Looking at the aggregate income of $14,070,784,800, the top 5% of Memphians get 22% or 3,095,572,656 of the income, the richest 20% obtain $7,105,746,324 of the wealth, and the middle 40% acquiring $3,419,200,706.4 while the bottom 20% only earn $450,265,113.6 of the wealth. The income gap between the richest 20% and the middle 40% of 3,686,545,617.6 is startling but even more saddening is the remainder of the income that is allocated to the bottom 20% of income earners. Couple these startling statistics with the fact that in Memphis, "one of three families are poor or impoverished" (Evanoff), the effects of the income gap are a sign of the burden on the modern Memphian family.

The income gap in Memphis is generally viewed as more vast than most: "in many other Metro areas, the middle-income groups receive a greater share of the total pay" (Charlier). The income inequality in Memphis is quite drastic, even in the sense that there are such deeply divided income sects in such short distances from one another. In 2011, the Commercial Appeal reported that Tract 231.10 in East Memphis is among the most unequal, income-wise, in the city: "1,100 of the tracts 3,705 households have incomes of at least $150,000 Census figures show, nearly 1,000 others make less than 30,000" (Charlier). The income gap of $120,000 within the same tract is indicative of the vast depth of the income inequality in Memphis. The income inequality in tract 231.10 also reveals that, "the richest 5 percent of households—those earning more than $443,000—take in more than one-third of all income in the tract." (Charlier). Not only is the income gap between the richer and poorer vast but it also consumes any fair distribution of wealth to the less wealthy.

The more aware statisticians and think tanks become of the widening income gap in America, "a report by the Congressional Budget Office...found that between 1979 and 2007, the richest 1 percent of Americans enjoyed an average income increase of 275 percent, while middle-income wage-earners, on average, saw less than 40% rise in the pay", the more questions begin to spring from said think tanks. (Charlier) These think tanks now begin to question the differing effects of the wage gap on minority/majority populations in America: "census data... the median wealth of Hispanic households fell 66 percent from 2005-2009. African Americans' wealth dropped 53 percent... it dropped 16 percent for white households" (Commercial Appeal). These patterns of median wealth throughout America are indicative of majority/minority race related statistics in Memphis as well.

In Memphis, specifically, "The wealth disparity that separates white Americans from African-Americans and Hispanics is so wide that even an improving economy will have little impact on closing the chasm" (Commercial Appeal). Most statisticians are aware of the link between the wage gap and minority/majority wealth but in the case of Memphis, TN, blindly connecting the two can become problematic. As of the 2010 census, the American population of 308,745,530 million people, 196,817,552 or 63.3% of the population are white, 37,685,848 or 12.2% of the population is black, 50,477,594 or 16.3% is Hispanic, and 14,465,124 or 4.7% if the population is Asian. In Memphis those statistics are drastically different 408,675 (63.1%) of the residents are African American, while 177,735 (27.7%) of the residents are white, 41,994 (6.5%) of the residents are Hispanic or Latino, 10,146 (1.6%) of the residents are Asian with the remaining 1.1% as native American or Pacific Islander. From the statistics presented, it is obvious that Memphis has a different majority/minority population dynamic than the majority of America. Memphis is majority Black in a country that is majority white. The issues that are typically presented as a result of the income gap have different implications when attached to Memphis's population dynamic.

WORKS CITED

www.city-data.com. (n.d.). Retrieved 2 27, 2017, from City-Data.

Charlier, T. (2011, November 20). Area Income chasm vast—Only N.Y. Miami, L.A. have a greater income gap. *Commercial Appeal* .

Evanoff, T. (2012, September 12). Gap Keeps Growing—Joblessness, Income loss keep eonomy weak . *Commercial Appeal.*

factfinder.census.gov. (2015). Retrieved 2 27, 2017, from American Fact Finder.

Income Gap hits Minorities hard. (2011, July 29). *Commercial Appeal.*

http://statisticalatlas.com/place/Tennessee/Memphis/Race-and-Ethnicity. (2015, April 8). Retrieved 4 10, 2017, from Statistical Atlas.

Powell, M. (2010, May 30). *Blacks in Memphis Lose Decades of Economic Gains.* Retrieved from The New York Times.

sosmemphis. (2000). Retrieved April 4, 2017, from http://sosmemphis.org/uploads/ Orange%20Mound%20Demographic%20data.pdf.

RESEARCH PAPER REVISION

13

Amoriana Davis
Dr. Fredlund
English 1020
20 March 2017

The Income Gap in Memphis: Higher Education and Closing the Gap

Income inequality, or the extent to which income is distributed in an uneven manner among a population, has consistently been a topic for decades throughout the United States of America and many other countries. Even with the popularity of said discourse, it seems that the numbers become more dismal each time the income gap is mentioned. As we progress with technology, medicine, and public policy, it seems that most cities in America leave the income gap to simply fix itself, and Memphis is no different. In recent years, each edition of Memphis's *Commercial Appeal* that discusses income inequality reveals another unimpressive statistic about the widening income chasm in Memphis, TN. Memphis, unlike the other top 50 metropolitan cities, with the exception of Atlanta, GA, has a vastly uncommon population distribution with 63.3% of its population being African American as of 2010's census. The uncommon population distribution adds another layer to the complexities of income inequality in Memphis and seem to aid in the manifestation of income inequality in Memphis, TN. Income inequality in Memphis, TN is not only race related but it is also aided by the marginalization of the odd majority, minority that lives within Memphis, TN. However, though most statisticians are aware of the effects of the race-related income gap in Memphis, few have pushed the rhetoric necessary to lessen the income gap in Memphis, TN. Higher education is the key to lessening the income gap between races in Memphis, TN.

In order to better understand the effects of higher education on the income gap in Memphis, TN, it's important to understand the context within which the income gap has manifested. According to the Federal Census Bureau's 2010 census, Memphis has a population of 646,889 residents (this does not include the surrounding areas of Memphis: Cordova, Germantown, etc.). 408,675 (63.1%), of the residents are African American, while 177,735 (27.7%) of the residents are white, 41,994(6.5%) of the residents are Hispanic or Latino, 10,146 (1.6%) of the residents are Asian with the remaining 1.1% as native American or Pacific Islander (see fig. 1).

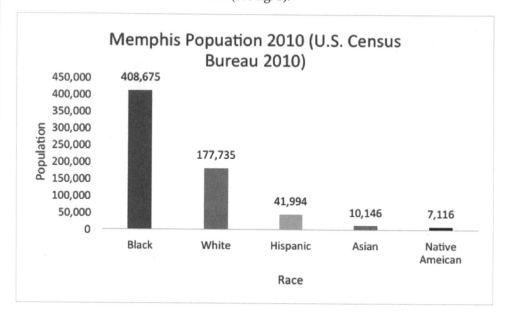

Fig. 1. Memphis population distribution by race.

These numbers become much more meaningful when compared to the median income of the residents. City Data states that the median income for African Americans in Memphis is $30,464. The median income for Whites is $56,264 while Hispanic residents have a median income of $34,100, and Asian residents have a median income of $75,774. Altogether, the median income for Memphis is $36,908 and the aggregate income is $14,070,784,800. These statistics, prepared by City Data in 2015, follow the trend of the Federal Census in 2010: "In metro Memphis...the top 5% of wage earners...making at least $165,411 a year, take home 22% of all the income in the area. Richest 20% get a total of 50.5% of all the income...bottom 20%, earning less than $18,725 3.2% of the pay" (Charlier 2011). The data presented can seem daunting but it's necessary to comprehend that at the base of the matter there are stark parallels between race and income in Memphis. For example, as seen in fig. 2, black Memphians make 63.3% of the residential population yet they have the lowest median income of the residential population.

13

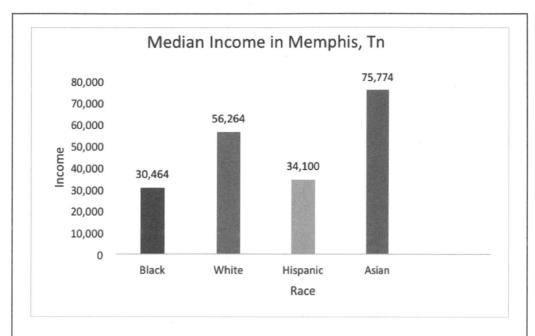

Fig. 2. Median income in Memphis by race.

On the other hand, white Memphians (27.7% of the population) and Asian Memphians (1.6 of the population) have the highest median income with $56,264 and $75,774. There are 35.6% more black residents than white residents yet the median household income is $25,800 more than the black median household. Even if the number would be lower based on statistical probability, the gap is uncanny. Even more shocking is the gap between Asian Memphian income and black Memphian income: $45,310. Looking at the aggregate income of $14,070,784,800, the top 5% of Memphians get 22% or $3,095,572,656 of the income, the richest 20% obtain $7,105,746,324 of the wealth, and the middle 40% acquiring $3,419,200,706.4 while the bottom 20% only earn $450,265,113.6 of the wealth. The income gap between the richest 20% and the middle 40% ($3,686,545,617.6) is startling but even more saddening is the remainder of the income that is allocated to the bottom 20% of income earners. Couple these startling statistics with the fact that in Memphis, "one of three families are poor or impoverished" (Evanoff), and the effects of the income gap are a sign of the financial burden on the modern Memphian family. This information about the wide race-related income gap is vital to changing the course of the income gap through education.

The income gap in Memphis is generally viewed as more vast than most: "in many other Metro areas, the middle-income groups receive a greater share of the total pay" (Charlier). The income inequality in Memphis is quite drastic, even in the sense that there are such deeply divided income sects in such short distances from one another. In 2011, the Commercial Appeal reported that Tract 231.10 in East Memphis is among the most unequal, income-wise, in the city: "1,100 of the tracts 3,705 households have incomes of at least $150,000 Census figures show, nearly 1,000 others make less than 30,000" (Charlier). The income gap of $120,000 within the same tract is indicative of the vast depth of the income inequality in Memphis. The income inequality in tract 231.10, illustrated in fig. 3, also reveals that, "the richest 5 percent of households—those earning more than $443,000—take in more than one-third of all income in the tract" (Charlier). Not only is the income gap between the rich and poor vast but this also reveals that the income gap is present both throughout and within the greater Memphis area. The income gap is not simply two separate parts of a city; it persists within small communities and among neighbors.

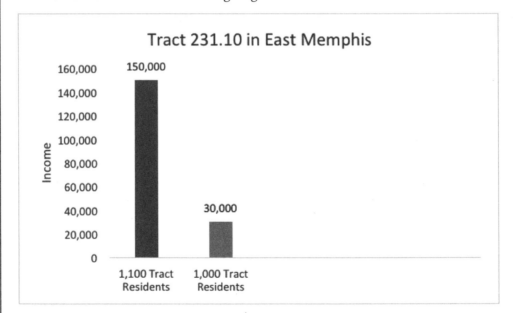

Fig. 3. Tract 231.10 income.

The more aware statisticians and think tanks become of the widening income gap in America, the more questions begin to spring from said think tanks: "a report by the Congressional Budget Office...found that between 1979 and 2007, the richest 1 percent of Americans enjoyed an average income increase of 275 percent, while middle-income wage-earners, on average, saw less than 40% rise in the pay" (Charlier). These

13

think tanks now question the differing effects of the wage gap on minority/majority populations in America: "census data...the median wealth of Hispanic households fell 66 percent from 2005–2009. African Americans' wealth dropped 53 percent...it dropped 16 percent for white households" (2011). These patterns of median wealth throughout America are indicative of race related statistics in Memphis as well. However, these statisticians are not necessarily as invested in a solution to the income gap as they are to the reasons for, the effects of, or the ramifications surrounding the income gap. If Memphians are concerned with lessening the income gap, then knowing the statistics isn't enough. Memphians need to consider ways to close this gap.

Sadly, in Memphis, "The wealth disparity that separates white Americans from African-Americans and Hispanics is so wide that even an improving economy will have little impact on closing the chasm" ("Worrisome"). Most statisticians are aware of the link between the wage gap and majority/minority wealth, but in the case of Memphis, TN, blindly connecting the two can become problematic: "inequalities in the distribution of income and wealth have grown steadily over the last 30 years, creating greater differences in opportunity and challenging the longstanding American belief in equality of opportunity" (Hoschild 1995). From the statistics presented earlier, it is obvious that Memphis has a different majority/ minority population dynamic than most of America. Memphis is a majority black city in a country that is a majority white city; the issues that are typically presented as a result of the income gap have different implications when attached to Memphis's population dynamic. With this knowledge in mind, a solution to the income gap in Memphis, TN is more important than ever. Part of the solution lies within higher education.

Higher education is at the core of the initiative to lessen the income gap. In a section entitled "News and Views," *The Journal of Blacks in Higher Education* reported, "blacks with a four-year college degree now earn on average more than twice the income of blacks with only a high school diploma" ("The Power" 34). The same source also stated, "African Americans with a two-year associates degree improve their income by only 20% over blacks with only a high school diploma" (34). Blacks with a four-year degree not only outperform blacks with a high school diploma by 98.3%, but they also have incomes that, on average, are more than double the incomes of blacks with only a high school diploma (Higher 6). Unfortunately, as of 2004, only 11% of all black adults in the United States hold a 4-year college degree (Higher 7).

Not only do blacks who complete a four-year education achieve a far greater median income than blacks with a high school diploma, but statistics from 1998 show that African Americans with a four-year degree also lessen the income gap between themselves and whites with a four year degree by 89% (Power 34). Although black men only made a median income of $36,433 (or 79% of white male's median income of $45,825), black women with a 4-year degree made 117% of white women's income in 1998 (mostly because black women have a higher retention rate, of 64% rather than 49.2% of white women, for full time jobs). It would seem, the higher the level of degree, the more we lessen the income gap: "In 1998 blacks with a master degree had an income of $39,788...88.7% of the median income of whites" (Power 35). However, this trend does not always continue, because in 1998 blacks that have obtained professional degrees have a much lower median income than whites with professional degrees, "blacks with professional degree had a median income of $51,196...only 78.5% of the median income of whites with a professional degree" (Power 36). As of 2004, blacks with a four-year degree have lessened the income gap between themselves and whites with a four-year degree by 90%. Blacks with master's degrees earned 98% of whites with master degrees income. These trends for 2004 also positively affected the income gap for professional degrees, Blacks with professional degrees were able to lessen the income gap by 94% with whites with professional degrees. (Higher 7) Thus, encouraging Black enrollment and retention in higher education is the key to closing the race-related income gap.

Even with the positive trends that have been presented from 1998 to 2004, many still believe that higher education is not the solution to the income gap because these encouraging statistics apply to only one in nine blacks. The problem is the median income gap is 61% between blacks and whites normally, and the gains through higher education only marginally effect the income gap: "It turns out that the much greater earnings produced by more blacks who have completed college make little difference to the median income figure because only 18% of all black adults over the age of 25 have completed a four-year education" ("Higher" 7). However, that type of logical reasoning can be problematic. If it's proven that higher education is a guarantee to lessen the income gap between black and whites, and the rebuttal is that not enough African Americans have pursued and completed a higher education, the problem is not the solution of obtaining higher education. The problem is the road to which blacks reach the solution of obtaining higher education. In other words, black enrollment and retention levels in colleges must consistently increase in order to lessen the income gap.

The solution of higher education is especially important to the black population of Memphis. Memphis is a city where the pressures of a minority-majority dynamic may seem to be null and void in the income gap. However, the problems linked to a lack of higher education within the black population in Memphis has yet to discussed. The statistics of higher education within the black community for ages 25 and up provide context for the problems with which black Memphians are faced. As of 2015, the Census Bureau report states that out of 108,883 black men over the age of 25 in Memphis, TN, only 12,779 or 12% achieved a 4-year bachelor's degree or higher. Furthermore, only18% of black Memphian women over 25 have achieved a 4-year bachelor's degree or higher. Altogether, that means that less than 15% of African Americans over the age of 25 in Memphis have obtained a four-year college degree. However, a lot of black Memphians have obtained at least a high school diploma (37%) and others have some college or associates degree education (31%). If the 31% of blacks that had some college education or an associate's degree education had continued to obtain a bachelor's degree, it could have vastly lessened the income gap between blacks and whites in Memphis. If the 37% of black Memphians who only obtained a high school diploma had continued to an associate's degree, then that would help lessen the gap as well. These numbers reveal an issue of college retention for black Memphians, as well as, an issue with continuance of education past high school.

The University of Memphis is a prime example of how the necessity for higher education is oftentimes overlooked or may seem unattainable in the black community in Memphis. In a city where 63.3% of the population is black, The University of Memphis has an almost flipped population distribution with 50% of the population being white and 30% of the population being black (University of Memphis). In 2007, out of 735 African American first time, full time students, 51.40% of students completed 4 years of college education and 43.70% completed 8 years of college education. For white first time, full time students in 2007, 55% of 1148 students completed 4-year college educations and 55.10% also completed 8-year college educations. The numbers of retention for white first time, full time students in 2007 at the University of Memphis was 4% higher for a four year education but more than 11% higher for completion of an eight year education (University of Memphis). These numbers are important because statistics collected from 1998–2004 have shown that blacks who receive master's degrees are able to close the income gap by 98%. Blacks with professional degrees (education beyond a Masters degree) are able to lessen the income gap by 95%, and blacks with doctorates are able to surpass the median income of whites with doctorates by making 100.3 % whites median income ("Higher").

Every week or two, there seems to be another conversation about the widening chasm of the income gap in America. Rarely, do Americans hear about a solution. The focus of the income gap needs to shift. Most Americans are aware that there is an income gap, and they simply need the resources and tools to fix it. The statistics about education continuance, college retention and their effects on the wage gap serve as the resources necessary to understand the effects of higher education on the race-related income gap. The tools, however, will be finding methods to explain to the youth the necessity of higher education or programs that ensure college readiness in 9th–12th grade in lower-income communities. Fixing the race-related income gap is not as simple as going to college; there are too many factors related to race in this country for only one solution to erase the race-related income gap. However, higher education has proven to be a means by which many African Americans in Memphis may be able to succeed in lessening the income gap.

WORKS CITED

___. "Higher Education is the Major Force in Closing the Black-White Income Gap." *Journal of Blacks in Higher Education*, 2007, pp. 6–8.

"Memphis, TN Income Map, Earnings Map, and Wages Data." *City-Data*, 12 April 2017, http://www.city-data.com/income/income-Memphis-Tennessee.html.

Charlier, Tom. "Area Income Chasm Vast: Only N.Y., Miami, L.A. Have Greater Gap between rich, poor, Census finds." *Commercial Appeal*, 2011.

Evanoff, Ted. "Gap Keeps Growing—Joblessness, Income Loss Keep Economy Weak. *Commercial Appeal*, 2012.

"Worrisome Trend: A Widening Wealth Gap Between White Americans and Minorities Portends Trouble for the Economic Recovery." *Commercial Appeal*. 29 July 2011.

"Memphis city, Tennessee." *United States Census Bureau.* 8 March 2017. https://fact-finder.census.gov/faces/nav/jsf/pages/community_facts.xhtml?src=bkmk.

"Race and Ethnicity in the Memphis Area." *Statistical Atlas.* http://statisticalatlas.com/metro-area/Tennessee/Memphis/Race-and-Ethnicity. Accessed 9 March 2017.

Powell, Michael. "Blacks in Memphis Lose Decades of Economic Gains. *The New York Times,* http://www.nytimes.com/2010/05/31/business/economy/31memphis.html. Accessed 19 February 2017.

SOS Memphis. "Orange Mound Demographic Information from 2010 US Census." *SOS Memphis.* http://sosmemphis.org/uploads/Orange%20Mound%20Demographic%20data.pdf. Accessed 18 March 2017.

Stonecash, J.M. "The Income Gap." *Political Science and Politics*, vol. 39, no. 3, pp. 461–465.

___. "The Power of Higher Education to close the Black-White Income Gap." *Journal of Blacks in Higher Education*, 2000–2001, 34–36.

University of Memphis. "Retention Consolidation 2007–2015." *University of Memphis* http://oir.memphis.edu/WebReports/Retention/RetentionConsolidated.pdf. Accessed 15 April 2017.

13

STUDENT EXAMPLE 2

Joshua L. Maddock

English 1020 Reflection

When I began my freshman year at Memphis, I was having a tough time transitioning to college. My plan was never to go to the University of Memphis, but circumstances sent me here for my first year of prerequisites. When I came to English 1020, I was somewhat hesitant about participating in the work for a class that focused on a city I was not particularly happy to be in at the time. We were told early on that we would be working on a large research and writing project that encompassed one aspect of Memphis, and I spent a good amount of time trying to figure out what I found interesting about Memphis and, to be honest, at the time there wasn't much. As a film major, I eventually decided to tackle the filmmaking scene in Memphis, or lack thereof. My original plan was to inspect tax incentive programs offered by the city and state, using *Bluff City Law* as an example. However, as I was working on my rough draft I ran into a somewhat sizable barrier: there simply aren't many academic sources revolving around the filmmaking scene of Memphis. I was quick to think that it was an impossible essay to write, but then Dr. Fredlund suggested that I approach a librarian about the topic. I made a research appointment online, and I was met with terrific advice: instead of searching for articles about my exact topic, find articles about a similar topic and use them for comparison. For example, Memphis does not have a sizable film market, but another similar city in Louisiana did. This led me to many sources on the subject of tax incentive programs for filmmaking in other states.

After this, I decided to change my approach to my paper: instead of focusing on only the filmmaking scene in Memphis, I found a more argumentative approach in what the filmmaking scene *should be*. Having come from a high school where writing and rhetoric was stressed above all else, the format and pace of the paper came very naturally to me, but the biggest takeaway from class was to not stress over the first draft. As someone who normally treats their first draft as their last, I decided to take this more calm approach. I started by writing a two page outline of how I would structure my argument, and I filled in the details, stretching it to six pages. By not stressing over what I was writing down, I had written a first draft that I was actually happy with (which I purposely titled *A Bad First Draft* to remind myself not to worry). Another aspect was that I was writing about something I loved, and so I ended up going above and beyond in terms of detail. By the time I finished my rough draft, I had restructured my entire paper, using *Bluff City Law* as an example, rather than my initial idea to use it for the whole structure of my argument. It was hard at first to change the structure as I originally believed I knew what I wanted, but I ended up using my original idea in a much better capacity later on.

Though I was happy with my draft, it was far from done. There were sections that lacked support and overall message, acting as filler. I knew I needed to change something. The second time around the research was purely my own, and I ended up finding even more academic sources revolving around the subject which gave me the extra information I needed to make a clear and concise argument. I filled in details and added more support to my argument, ultimately creating a much more comprehensible message. I took most of Dr. Fredlund's comments into account when revising my essay, but for certain parts that she thought were not connected, I saw as examples that I needed to better flesh out and connect to my central argument. Ultimately it was up to me what to keep and what to eliminate, and I decided to pick and choose what details I left in. My revision was similar to my first draft, however, it was much more streamlined and precise.

For the New Media Project, I decided to use my skills as a film editor to turn the paper into an argumentative video essay, presenting a mix of film footage, interviews, narration, and music to create a clear and concise point. I used multiple examples to discuss the film scene in Memphis and included elements from my paper, but I decided to spend a majority of the video on my original idea (the positive effect of *Bluff City Law*) because of the availability of footage and because I didn't have to focus on the same academic audience. This was easily my favorite part of the entire process because I was able to take the thing that I love to do most and use it for educational purposes.

English 1020 was incredibly fulfilling for a multitude of reasons. The entire process allowed me to come closer to the city that I lived in my whole life, with a new appreciation and love for where I was at a time when I frankly didn't want to be there. Another reason is because I was studying filmmaking, which is what I want to pursue as a career. Despite not taking any film-centered courses that first semester, I was able to do my own research into the craft and gain a greater understanding of the business side of filmmaking because of the course. My two biggest pieces of advice would be to look for a subject that you find interesting, because if you enjoy what you're writing about it isn't as challenging, and to not stress over your first draft. Doing this will help you in the long run.

Because I did those two things, my semester in English 1020 was extremely satisfying for me, and I found that out of all the classes I took my first semester, I was happiest with my work in this class.

RHETORICAL ANALYSIS

Joshua Maddock
Katherine Fredlund
ENGL 1020
9/24/19

Analyzing "Memphis Burning": Exploring Racism through Housing in Memphis

If you want to discover the racism that's overthrown our country for the past hundred years, look no further than the housing crisis in Memphis during the mid twentieth century. At least, this is how Preston Lauterbach explores this issue in his article titled "Memphis Burning." Published in 2016, over six decades after the event it specifically centers around, the article tells a cautionary tale about two men, using this tale as a means to explore racial inequality within America and more specifically housing segregation. Preston uses three linearly connected ways of preaching these tales. He starts with carefully picked expository details that fill in the backdrop of a notorious house burning in Memphis. These details pull the reader out of the real world and set him or her in the past. He then relates the event to the modern day political scene, and through doing this ultimately appeals to our emotions regarding the current political climate.

This recounting of history basically revolves around Robert Church Jr, an African-American businessman who was the president of the first black-owned bank in Memphis, and Boss Crump, a white Democrat who dominated the political scene in Memphis throughout the 20s, 30s, and 40s. At first, it would appear the two men were meant to be mortal enemies, representing different communities and being polar opposite types of individuals: Crump a white Democrat and Church a black Republican. However, their relationship started out in a positive light. They seemed to be working together, and then the Great Depression hit. It was during this time that Boss Crump betrayed Church; it seemed that because Roosevelt was now in office, Crump no longer needed Church as a political ally. And then, his success was spotlighted by fumes and burning ash. The city administration took Church's real-estate holdings and began harassing businesses allied with Church. Crump decided how the city would use the house that used to belong to Church and represented Black success. And with a single spark for a demonstration of new equipment to fight fires, on February 26, 1953, he burned it to the ground. Preston uses such vivid detail in recounting the story, that it's hard to not feel like you're witnessing the crumbling infrastructure of Church's mansion. He uses details to paint a picture and induce empathy. For example, he writes, "Firemen in black helmets and black slickers fought flames" (Lauterbach 183) and "a low-rise, 900-unit public housing complex" (Lauterbach 188). These phrases aren't just for show, they are used to grab the audience. Preston weaves details throughout his article in order to illustrate how housing problems of today are defined by racial tensions of the past, and he associates the overall issue of inequality within America's real estate ventures to the tale of Crump and Church. By giving all these details, the reader can understand every point, hopefully.

There's a real life issue that this recounting has to offer, and it's the harsh living conditions beset upon certain individuals. In the era of the 30s and 40s, owners of land were openly opposed to letting African Americans move on to their land. Lauterbach explains that this led to redlining properties, forcing many to live in harsher conditions than what they deserved. For years on end, African Americans had to face inflation and poor housing conditions in order to live where they wanted to. This is the story of a political organizer whose entire foundation crumbled, leading to the deterioration of once great neighborhoods. The once grand house was sold off at an auction after the low-income housing Crump helped plan around a neighborhood resided in by the wealthy regardless of their race. Preston describes the decay stating, "Surrounded by dense, low-income housing, the fine Victorian homes were subdivided and turned into cheap rooming houses" (188). It's easy to see how this relates to the real world, which is ultimately Lauterbach's main goal here. To understand where we came from, and where we're going. And it's through this that Preston tries his greatest tactic: an appeal to our emotions.

The history Lauterbach presents details how a powerful white politician turned on a fellow politician and business leader, one who had given chances to many who didn't have a voice, ran him out of town, and burned down everything he had built, both metaphorically and literally. It's hard for an audience to not sympathize with this story. And Preston slowly tells this history, and then helps the audience see connections to a much bigger picture. He appeals to the emotions of people who have seen, first hand, restrictions set on individuals in our society who simply live through hardship because of their different skin color. Due to the way Lauterbach structures

14

his argument, it's hard not to sympathize with this even if you haven't seen it up close. It's hard to avoid it; Preston makes us examine this by seeking out sources within the centuries of hardship that have been endured by so many people. Tiny incidents that may not seem big out of context, but which fit within the greater realm of understanding. Crump's reign was for his own greed, and it came at the expense of Church. By tying what appear to be unrelated and small instances together, Lauterbach tells an untold history of Memphis housing that helps the reader understand the problematic contemporary conditions of race and Memphis housing. Church was a man who gave a voice to people, and though the voice was left even after he was gone, Crump made it very hard to hear the words by burning down what should be a museum today. Preston details how Crump single-handedly "converted one of the black community's greatest strengths into a monument to inequality" (188). And now we see this life for how it is. One of unfair chances and a disintegration of trust for one another because of how people view the colors of people's skin.

Ultimately, Preston's main goal is to is persuade the audience with details and facts, and then side sweeping them with a brutal but realistic tale of what African Americans go through on a daily basis. It's not fair, and it certainly isn't moral, but it's been set in stone by generations of people. Crump and Church are ultimately just pieces of the puzzle. Preston realizes this, and he wants you to analyze it for yourself. Is this really where we are now? If it is, then how did we get here? Take a moment out of the history books and you'll likely find your answer. This small meeting between two men in a city of blues and BBQ has a much bigger meaning when you realize how everything is a domino. By using detail to create empathy, Lauterbach shows us that we have to look no further than a once wealthy and great black neighborhood in Memphis that now is occupied by cheap public housing and proverty for proof of the racial disparities in both housing and economics in Memphis.

WORKS CITED

Lauterbach, Preston. "Memphis Burning: Housing and Inequality." *Writing Memphis*, 2nd ed, edited by Katherine Fredlund, Macmillan Learning, 2018, pp. 183–201.

FIRST DRAFT REFLECTION LETTER

Dear Dr. Fredlund,

My essay is about tax incentives for filmmaking in Memphis. There really is only one group that this would fall into in terms of an audience: the filmmaking community and the tax faculties of Memphis, though this is not as direct. I appeal to this audience by trying to show the possibility of what Memphis is capable of through comparisons with Louisiana's tax program.

I really chose this topic because I've always found the filmmaking scene of Memphis interesting. However, the first roadblock came through research. It was hard finding good research related to Memphis and filmmaking but after talking with a librarian it was easy to find sources to compare it to. It's very easy to write about filmmaking for me and I actually enjoyed doing research on tax incentives (which sounds as boring as ever when I say it out loud). I'm not really satisfied with the first and last paragraph, I think both sound a little forced. These are the big weaknesses in my essay. I think the actual research portions were easier to write because it was all fact based and not just coming out of my mouth. I just couldn't crack the opening and conclusion. I was able to back pretty much everything with facts except the part where I propose a tax incentive plan, however I was able to back this section with actual companies in Memphis.

My plan is to first go at the inside research, maybe dusting off the rather unnecessary details and adding a bit more into the strengths of Louisiana's program and how it could be compared to Memphis. Then I need to combat the opening and closing, making it a bit more professional and readable. My main question for you is how to do this.

Thanks,

Joshua

RESEARCH PAPER DRAFT

Joshua L. Maddock
Dr. Fredlund
English 1020
1 November 2019

A Bad First Draft

If you're out late one night in Memphis, enjoying dinner at one of Overton Square's ever growing center of spots for food and drinks, you may look across the street and find a crowded movie theater. This is even more likely if it's the first weekend of November; this is because what you're likely witnessing is a screening during the near week-long run of Memphis yearly film festival: Indie Memphis. This is merely a snippet of the kind of underground lair that the city built on blues and BBQ has been building for the past two decades. But when you look on a website or a piece of paper that are telling you where to shoot your next film, you will never see a picture of BB Kings lit up, rather the Hollywood Hills of California or the French Quarter of Louisiana. Despite this, The Bluff City has its fair share of films and has been the setting for many famed films. Whether it be the courtrooms of *The Firm*, the famous Sun Studio in *Walk the Line*, or just Memphis in general in *Mystery Train*, this city is alive and breathing with filmography. But why is it, that a city with a rich and vibrant film scene has yet to get the proper close up it deserves? Well, we have to first look at what Memphis has to offer and why people, at this time, would rather shoot in another state.

For decades, the mid-south went rather unheard of when it came to filming. Films such as *A Face in the Crowd* or *The Reivers* showcased a bit of the southern charm Memphis had to offer, but outside of location scouting not much made it to the screen. Then, in 1989, the Memphis Film Commission (MFC) was created as well as the job of the Film Commissioner. The MFC work "hands-on" recruiting and assisting productions all throughout the county. After this creation, film shoots in Memphis began to pop up, though not frequently but more regularly. But more often than not, the films will probably be lying to you. Often, Memphis will double for a rural area unrelated to Shelby County. For example, in the film *A Family Thing*, the main character lives in Arkansas, however it was filmed just outside of Memphis. Though this is a common occurrence, Memphis does have its prominent features as well as local film legends.

14

Critically acclaimed filmmaker Craig Brewer has shot over half of his filmography in the city (prominently showcased in *Hustle & Flow* and *Black Snake Moan*) and gave Memphis the opportunity to see his latest work, *Dolemite Is My Name*, three weeks before the Netflix, Tom Shadyac, director of *Ace Ventura: Pet Detective* and now currently a teacher at the University of Memphis, shot his latest work, *Brian Banks*, in Memphis, director of the Academy-Award winning film *Moonlight*, Barry Jenkins, recently headlined Indie Memphis. But big names aren't the only thing that showcase the possibilities of filmmaking here. Festivals run by locals are what sometimes bring the crowds in. Indie Memphis has flourished from its original roots, now the spotlight of politics, art, music, and the weird surreal that could only exist in a town as weird and surreal as Memphis. This festival's main goal is a showcase of what one close but diverse community can offer. Another similar attraction is the year round Time Warp Drive In. Now in its sixth year, the series is a year long celebration of film and music. Each month on a Saturday night, a collection of throwback movies are shown at the only remaining drive-in in Memphis from dusk till dawn, usually accompanied by a band pre-show. The event is put on by the local video store Black Lodge Video, a store which has just recently reopened its doors to a much bigger venue than previously, now renting out movies, hosting concerts, and other events in the realm of film cult lore. These are just a few examples as to how Memphis is proving itself to be a small but effective force in this collective nationwide goal of moviemaking. And it is clear that Memphis has the framework of city that should be known for its moviemaking, with local famed directors, a lauded festival, and an underground scene that takes the spotlight more often than not. But why are so few big movies made in this city? It starts with something called tax incentives.

Tax incentives on film productions are tax benefits offered throughout the United States, determined by individual states, to encourage film-production. Beginning in the 90s, these benefits were introduced when a wave of productions began outsourcing to countries such as Canada, and thus states began to give out incentives (the word literally meaning a thing that motivates or encourages one to do something) in order to bring business to their states. States will offer productions a percentage on their budget through rebates on their tax bills. The films involved in these programs are known as flight productions, better known as "runaway productions." This is where a film is developed in Hollywood and then outsourced to a state that offers the cheapest incentives and is tonally in the realm of what kind of film they are dealing with. Nowadays its become a competition of which state has the best offer in terms of rebates. A case study written by Stephanie Leiser was quick to point out how "In 2000, only six states had programs to provide financial incentives for the television and movie industry to shoot and produce films in their states" (1) and that "By the end of 2010, all but six states had enacted film incentive legislation." (1) States usually open up to these programs to offer numerous job programs (however it is not the creation of jobs, rather in influx of jobs from another state) and bring in new blood to the cities in the form of tourism. An article in the *Virginia Sports and Entertainment Law Journal* states how if "state incentive programs are successful in attracting films and creating an industry infrastructure within the states, then states may also have the opportunity to offer film productions a variety of attractive in-state resources such as local crew members, costume and design services, lighting and sound equipment, and even legal services." (213) In the past, Memphis has lacked a program that offers incentives on the scale of other states. To show this, let's look at a state that is excelling to top ranks in its tax incentive program: Louisiana.

Ever since establishing a tax incentive program in 1992, Louisiana has recently been at the forefront of filming for mainstream American entertainment. This decade showed a number of big-budgets Hollywood films come out of Louisiana, including *Looper*, *Killing Them Softly*, and *Oblivion*. An academic journal by Jade Miller under the title "Louisiana Disguised: Film Tax Incentives and Location Representation in Contemporary Hollywood Films" was quick to point out how Louisiana would offer "more than a third of a film's budget in an uncapped tax credit program," as well as "their own buyback program at eighty-five cents to the dollar, guaranteeing productions a buyer for their unused incentives: the state of Louisiana." (469) Through this program, Louisiana is able to benefit in the easiest way: owning what comes through their state. If Memphis wants to become the filmmaking hub it is trying to be, then it has to integrate a similar program. And it seems very close to doing so.

This year saw the premiere of *Bluff City Law*, a primetime network television show following the lives of a family of lawyers fighting for justice in Memphis, Tennessee. When this was announced, many were skeptical as to whether or not Memphis would be the main shooting location for the show. A similar Memphis-based show, the short-lived *Memphis Beat*, failed to receive tax incentives from Memphis and was hauled off to cities in Louisiana such as Laplace, and New Orleans. It seemed *Bluff City Law* was on track for a similar situation, until news came that the Economic Development Growth Engine (EDGE) for Memphis and Shelby County was to fund a $1.4 million tax break in order to save the show from not being able to afford the costs of filming in Memphis. This added on to an already large incentives package of $4.25 million, of which the state of Tennessee gave $2.5 million to and Memphis Tourism contributed $350,000. This is equally as shocking when you realize that this is the first time they have done so for a television show. This information was revealed in an article published in *The Commercial Appeal*, noting that, "While taxes on "personal property"—manufacturing machinery, furniture, phones—are often reduced as part of a PILOT, the bulk of the savings for the company is usually in reduced property taxes on "real property"—buildings and land." This is a landmark moment for Memphis filmmaking, and it seems ever so clear that the city is building towards better chances for these filmmakers. This begins with the recently created Memphis Production Incentive Program and the Shelby County Production Crew Workforce Development Program in 2018, however that's not enough. *Bluff City Law* has possibly opened up both the state and city's eyes on the possibilities of tax incentives on a show by show or film by film basis. This will give Memphis the control it needs over these productions to ease their mind. Just like the journal article by Miller says, "Tax credit funding is normally channeled through economic development agencies or is incurred as tax expenditures, giving the state more or less control over spending, respectively. In exchange, states typically require that production activity occur in designated jurisdictions, that a percentage of wages be paid to local employees, or that spending meet or exceed a specified threshold." Memphis is at the precipice of something great; it's ready to jump off and explore new territory.

Bluff City Law just finished filming. Even though NBC ordered the cancellation of the additional six episodes they previously added for the first season, this doesn't change the massive case that EDGE has created for other potential shows and movies to be funded through the city and state. And despite overwhelming fears that taxpayers will be wasting money with a show that faces the possibility of cancellation, Linn Sitler of the Memphis Film Commission put people's fears to rest. In an article published by LocalMemphis.com, Sitler was stated as saying, "In the case of the incentives used to attract 'Bluff City Law,' there has been no 'waste of taxpayer dollars.' This is because the

City, County, and EDGE incentive was designed to kick in per episode. So the annual potential incentive of $1.4 million will be pro-rated as a payment per episode aired." Now it's just a question as to where we are going. Memphis is breathing film. It is alive, and no one is saying anything. The city has slowly hidden itself away from the world, building on its own influence and creating a rich and vibrant setting. People here have curated a culture built on artistic expression and a love for creating and it shows in what we have to offer. We lack a completely fleshed out incentive program, but with a little support Memphis could be at the top of these "top filmmaking cities" lists in no time. So the next time you pass by one of these festivals, go in. Show your support. Enjoy a night of movies, music, and fun. Even if Memphis doesn't venture into the realm of big budget Hollywood films, it will still have this culture of love and respect for each other. And that's what moviemaking is all about.

WORKS CITED

Leiser, Stephanie. "The Diffusion of State Film Incentives: A Mixed-Methods Case Study." *Economic Development Quarterly*, vol. 31, no. 3, 2017, pp. 255–267., doi:10.1177/0891242417710715.

Miller, Jade L. "Louisiana Disguised: Film Tax Incentives and Location Representation in Contemporary Hollywood Films." *The Journal of Popular Culture*, vol. 50, no. 3, 2017, pp. 466–489., doi:10.1111/jpcu.12551.

Mathis, Tim. *Louisiana Film Tax Credits: Costly Giveaways to Hollywood*. Louisiana Budget Project, 7 Aug. 2012, https://www.labudget.org/wp-content/uploads/2012/08/LBP-Report.Louisiana-Film-Tax-Credits.pdf.

Joseph, Robert Gordon. *Playing the Big Easy: A History of New Orleans in Film and Television*. Graduate College of Bowling Green State University, May 2018, https://etd.ohiolink.edu/!etd.send_file?accession=bgsu1522601211962016&disposition=inline.

McIntire, Amy. "Louisiana's 'Motion Picture Investor Tax Credit': A Uniquely Effective Economic Policy." *Virginia Sports and Entertainment Law Journal*, vol. 13.2, 2014, pp. 211–240.

Stennett, Desiree. "'Bluff City Law': EDGE Leaders Approve $1.4 Million Tax Break to Film Show in Memphis." The Commercial Appeal, 21 Aug. 2019, https://www.commercialappeal.com/story/money/business/development/2019/08/21/bluff-city-law-nbc-legal-drama-tax-breaks-memphis-tv-shows/2060481001/.

Thom, Michael. "Lights, Camera, but No Action? Tax and Economic Development Lessons From State Motion Picture Incentive Programs." The American Review of Public Administration, vol. 48, no. 1, May 2016, pp. 33–51., doi:10.1177/0275074016651958.

McCarthy, Caitlin. "'Bluff City Law' to Stop Filming after First Season, so What Does That Mean for Memphis?" WATN - Local 24, 20 Oct. 2019, https://www.localmemphis.com/news/local-news/bluff-city-law-to-stop-filming-after-first-season-so-what-does-that-mean-for-memphis/.

REVISION REFLECTION LETTER

Dear Dr. Fredlund,

I've always been very passionate about filmmaking in Memphis, especially when it comes to our representation. I can name over a dozen films set in Detroit, New Orleans, and New York. But it's rare to see a film in Memphis, and when there is one set in Memphis it's outsourced to another city. I believe Memphis has a rich and flourished film community that has the possibility to be something greater. My audience is mainly EDGE or the Shelby County Commerce, but it's really for anyone who believes the same. I'm hoping I can appeal to the artist in people when they read this, to show what Memphis is doing right in terms of moviemaking. You could argue it's not as important as other issues, but it's something I really believe in.

This is why the process came naturally to me. When I began writing, I didn't stop. I enjoyed doing research, I enjoyed finding out more about the filmmaking community in the city. Research was difficult because of how little there was, but this roadblock was overcome quickly when I realized it didn't have to specifically focus on Memphis.

I think the strengths are my knowledge on filmmaking, and the evidence I presented for Louisiana's tax incentive program in reference to Memphis's lack of one. I think I make a strong argument as to why Memphis should have a film incentive program.

I think my first draft had weak arguments and unstructured support of a tax incentive program, especially for Louisiana. Hopefully, I've rectified that in my revision.

This is something that I believe in, deep down in my heart. It's something I'm passionate about and want to pursue. I'm hoping that by the end of this, if I showed this to someone, I persuaded them as to why Memphis is so important when it comes to filmmaking. If someone took the time out of their day to think about this, to go see a movie, to advocate for one of these programs, then that's what I want out of this.

I've enjoyed this semester, this project and the new media assignment. I've learned a lot about writing and I'm hoping it shows in my revision.

Thanks,

Josh

RESEARCH PAPER REVISION

Joshua Maddock
Dr. Fredlund
English 1020
6 December 2019

The Hidden Filmmaking Giant of Memphis

When you think of movie-making cities, there are a few that come to mind: the bustling and tourist ridden city of Los Angeles or the muggy and evergrowing hub of Atlanta. The South in general is beginning to be noticed for its emerging growth of filmmaking, but one city is still stuck in the weeds: Memphis. The city built on blues and BBQ has been building a steady collection of evidence to support its showcase of filmmaking for the past two decades, and has been a spot for filming movies ever since the fifties. The Bluff City has been the setting for many famed films, whether it be the courtrooms of *The Firm*, the famous Sun Studio in *Walk the Line*, or the classic Arcade Diner in *Mystery Train*. This city is alive and breathing with filmography. However, when filmmakers look for a location to shoot their next film, they will never see a picture of BB Kings lit up. Instead, they'll be encouraged to film near the Hollywood Hills of California or the French Quarter of Louisiana. But while Memphis is certainly capable of becoming a center for filmmaking, the city lacks a government funded tax incentive program. Other cities have used such incentive programs to effectively employ filmmaking as a viable and economically friendly medium. If Memphis wants to build their filmmaking community, the next step is to employ one of these programs.

For decades, the mid-south went rather unheard of when it came to filming. Films such as *A Face in the Crowd* or *The Reivers* showcased a bit of the southern charm Memphis had to offer, but outside of location scouting not much made it to the screen. Then, in 1989, the Memphis Film Commission (MFC) was created along with a job for a Film Commissioner. The MFC's work includes "hands-on" recruiting and assisting productions all throughout the county. After the creation of the MFC, film shoots in Memphis began to pop up, though still not frequently just more regularly. But more often than not, the films will probably not be shot in the location of their setting. Often, Memphis will double for a rural area unrelated to Shelby County. For example, in the film *A Family Thing*, the main character lives in Arkansas, however it was filmed just outside of Memphis.

Memphis does have its prominent features in films as well as local film legends. Critically acclaimed Memphis native filmmaker Craig Brewer has shot over half of his filmography in the city, and he prominently showcased Memphis in *Hustle & Flow* and *Black Snake Moan*. He also gave Memphis the opportunity to see his latest work, *Dolemite Is My Name*, three weeks before its release on Netflix. Tom Shadyac, director of *Ace Ventura: Pet Detective* teaches at the University of Memphis when he isn't working on a new film, and he also shot his latest work, *Brian Banks*, in Memphis. Director of the Academy-Award winning film *Moonlight*, Barry Jenkins, also recently headlined Indie Memphis.

Big names aren't the only thing that showcase the possibilities of filmmaking in Memphis. Festivals run by locals are what sometimes bring the crowds in. An underground world of filmmakers brings together a year-round drive in movie festival as well as other events throughout the city. These are just a few examples as to how Memphis is proving itself to be a small but effective force in this nationwide passion for moviemaking. It's important to take this into consideration because this is how all good filmmaking cities begin. They start out small, building upon their legacy and sourcing locally in terms of stardom and talent. But why have we stayed local and not started creating big blockbuster films? Well, once you have built this legacy and foundation of local trust, then you need to add in help from the government. This is what is called a tax incentive program.

Tax incentives for film productions are tax benefits offered throughout the United States, determined by individual states, in order to encourage film-production. Beginning in the 90s, these benefits were introduced when a wave of productions began outsourcing to countries such as Canada, and thus, individual states began to give out incentives in order to bring business back to their states. States will offer a film production a percentage on their budget through rebates on their tax bills. The films involved in these programs are known as flight productions, better known as "runaway productions." This is where the film is developed in Hollywood and then filming is outsourced to a state that a) offers the best incentives and b) can match the type of city they are setting the film in, such as when a film set in New York can be filmed in a similar city like Toronto. Nowadays it has become a competition of which state has the best offer in terms of rebates. A case study written by Stephanie Leiser was quick to point out that "In 2000, only six states had programs to provide financial incentives for the television and movie industry to shoot and produce films in their states" and that "By the end of 2010, all but six states had enacted film incentive legislation" (255). States usually open up to these programs to produce jobs, however not all positions are filled locally and often there is an influx of jobs from another state and this can bring in money as those people need places to live and spend money in the city supporting the economy. An article in the *Virginia Sports and Entertainment Law Journal* states how if "state incentive programs are successful in attracting films and creating an industry infrastructure within the states, then states may also have the opportunity to offer film productions a variety of attractive in-state resources such as local crew members, costume and design services, lighting and sound equipment, and even legal services" (McIntire 213). Memphis has lacked a program that offers incentives on the same scale of other states.

In order to see how other states have implemented such programs, let's look at a state that is excelling with its tax incentive program: Louisiana. Ever since establishing a tax incentive program in 1992, Louisiana has been at the forefront of filming for mainstream American entertainment. The nineties showed a number of big-budgets Hollywood films come out of Louisiana, including *Looper*, *Killing Them Softly*, and *Oblivion*. In "Louisiana Disguised: Film Tax Incentives and Location Representation in Contemporary Hollywood Films," Jade Miller is quick to address how Louisiana would offer "more than a third of a film's budget in an uncapped tax credit program," as well as "their own buyback program at eighty-five cents to the dollar, guaranteeing productions a buyer for their unused incentives: the state of Louisiana" (469). Louisiana is one of fifteen states that has this program. Basically tax credits become refundable, which allows buyers to sell their credits back to the state, which the state will buy back (in Louisiana's case, 85 cents on the dollar). According to the *Louisiana Budget Project*, "the amount directly paid to film productions rose from zero in 2008-09 to $110 million in 2011-12. The buy-back program now constitutes 48 percent of the film subsidy program." (4) See fig. 1 for more information on Louisiana's tax incentives.

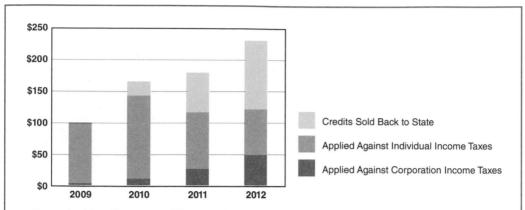

Source: Louisiana Department of Revenue *Investment, Employment and Infrastructure

Fig. 1. Louisiana Tax Incentive Revenue

Louisiana is effectively owning the films produced there by providing tax credits on film production and then taking a percentage of profits when they are sold. Louisiana, and New Orleans in particular, are now structuring part of their economy around filmmaking. Joseph notes that "Particular attention is given to developments in the twenty-first century, especially how the devastation of Hurricane Katrina and the recent tax credit laws affected popular understandings of the city. Hollywood's representations have largely reinforced New Orleans' exceptional, "Big Easy" identity by presenting the city's unique cultural practices as every occurrences and realities for New Orleanians" (3). This state now uses its otherworldly qualities to create films, and with a flourished tax credit program it has been at the forefront of moviemaking since the early 2000's. If there is one way to portray Memphis, it's as otherworldy. It's strange odyssey of music and food on the outskirts of the South makes it an obvious center of culture for movies. But historically, Memphis has not provided an incentive program similar to Louisiana's, or any other state for that matter. This changed in 2019.

In 2019, *Bluff City Law*, a primetime network television show following the lives of a family of lawyers fighting for justice in Memphis, TN, premiered. When this was announced, many were skeptical as to whether or not Memphis would be the main shooting location for the show. A similar Memphis-based show, the short-lived *Memphis Beat*, failed to receive tax incentives from Memphis and was hauled off to cities in Louisiana such as Laplace and New Orleans. It seemed *Bluff City Law* was on track for a similar situation until news came that the Economic Development Growth Engine (EDGE) for Memphis and Shelby County was to fund a $1.4 million tax break in order

14

to save the show from not being able to afford the costs of filming in Memphis. This money contributed to an already large incentives package of $4.25 million, of which the state of Tennessee gave $2.5 million to and Memphis Tourism contributed $350,000. This is equally as shocking when you realize that this is the first time they have done so for a television show. Stennett, writing for *The Commercial Appeal,* notes that, "While taxes on "personal property"—manufacturing machinery, furniture, phones—are often reduced as part of a PILOT, the bulk of the savings for the company is usually in reduced property taxes on "real property"—buildings and land." By providing such reductions on property taxes, the city of Memphis and state of Tennessee were able to keep *Bluff City Law* in our city.

With *Bluff City* Law Memphis invested in a TV show, something it hasn't done before. Despite the critical reception and viewership, this is a landmark moment for Memphis filmmaking. Now, it seems ever so clear that the city is building towards better chances for these filmmakers. This begins with the recently created Memphis Production Incentive Program and the Shelby County Production Crew Workforce Development Program created in 2018, however, that's not enough. *Bluff City Law* has possibly opened up both the state and city's eyes on the possibilities of tax incentives on a show by show or film by film basis. This will give Memphis the control it needs over these productions to ease their mind. Miller explains,

> Tax credit funding is normally channeled through economic development agencies or is incurred as tax expenditures, giving the state more or less control over spending, respectively. In exchange, states typically require that production activity occur in designated jurisdictions, that a percentage of wages be paid to local employees, or that spending meet or exceed a specified threshold. (470)

Louisiana did not officially begin their tax incentive program until 2002, when the Louisiana Legislature enacted the Louisiana Motion Picture Tax Incentive Act. No legislative move has been made for Memphis yet, but EDGE started this process early by offering a tax credit program on a TV show, and the city should build on this one-time tax reduction by creating a formal program for the city.

Bluff City Law just finished filming. Even though NBC ordered the cancellation of the additional six episodes they previously added for the first season, this doesn't change the massive case that EDGE has created for other potential shows and movies to be funded through the city and state. And despite overwhelming fears that taxpayers will be wasting money with a show that faces the possibility of cancellation, Linn Sitler of the Memphis Film Commission put people's fears to rest. In an article published by Local Memphis, Sitler explained, "In the case of the incentives used to attract 'Bluff City Law,' there has been no 'waste of taxpayer dollars.' This is because the City, County, and EDGE incentive was designed to kick in per episode. So the annual potential incentive of $1.4 million will be pro-rated as a payment per episode aired" (McCarthy). By tying the incentives to the number of epiodes, Memphis protected itself from losing money due to a series cancellation. Because *Bluff City Law* was cancelled, the remaining money can now be used to provide funds to future filmmaking opportunities.

Now it's just a question as to where we are going. Memphis is breathing film. While the city is known for The Blues and the king of rock and roll, it can continue to build its cultural influence by showcasing itself as a rich and vibrant setting for films. People here have curated a culture built on artistic expression and a love for creating and it shows in what we have to offer from the banks of the Mississippi to bright lights on Beale to the Buffalo in Shelby Farms. Currently, we can't showcase all we have to offer because we lack a completely fleshed out incentive program, but with a little support, Memphis could be at the top of these "top filmmaking cities" lists in no time. So the next time you pass by a film festival in Memphis, go in. Enjoy a night of movies, music, and fun. Show your support. Even if Memphis doesn't venture into the realm of big budget Hollywood films, the more Memphian's support local film, the more our city leaders will understand the potential economic boom a tax incentive program could provide. In Memphis, we still have this culture of love and respect for each other and for the arts. And that's what moviemaking is all about.

WORKS CITED

14

Joseph, Robert Gordon. *Playing the Big Easy: A History of New Orleans in Film and Television.* 2018. Bowling Green State U, PhD Dissertation.

Leiser, Stephanie. "The Diffusion of State Film Incentives: A Mixed-Methods Case Study." *Economic Development Quarterly*, vol. 31, no. 3, 2017, pp. 255–267.

Mathis, Tim. Louisiana Budget Project. *Louisiana Film Tax Credits: Costly Giveaways to Hollywood.* Baton Rouge: Louisiana Budget Project, 2012, https://www.labudget. org/wp-content/uploads/2012/08/LBP-Report.Louisiana-Film-Tax-Credits.pdf. Accessed 2 Nov. 2019.

McCarthy, Caitlin. "'Bluff City Law' to Stop Filming after First Season, so What Does That Mean for Memphis?" *WATN - Local 24*, 20 Oct. 2019, https://www.localmemphis. com/news/local-news/bluff-city-law-to-stop-filming-after-first-season-so-what-does-that-mean-for-memphis/. Accessed 1 Nov. 2019.

McIntire, Amy. "Louisiana's 'Motion Picture Investor Tax Credit': A Uniquely Effective Economic Policy." *Virginia Sports and Entertainment Law Journal*, vol. 13.2, 2014, pp. 211–240.

Miller, Jade L. "Louisiana Disguised: Film Tax Incentives and Location Representation in Contemporary Hollywood Films." *The Journal of Popular Culture*, vol. 50, no. 3, 2017, pp. 466-489.

Stennett, Desiree. "'Bluff City Law': EDGE Leaders Approve $1.4 Million Tax Break to Film Show in Memphis." *The Commercial Appeal*, 21 Aug. 2019, https://www. commercialappeal.com/story/money/business/development/2019/08/21/bluff-city-law-nbc-legal-drama-tax-breaks-memphis-tv-shows/2060481001/. Accessed 11 Oct. 2019.

Thom, Michael. "Lights, Camera, but No Action? Tax and Economic Development Lessons From State Motion Picture Incentive Programs." *The American Review of Public Administration*, vol. 48, no. 1, May 2016, pp. 33–51.

NARRATIVES
AND TESTIMONIES

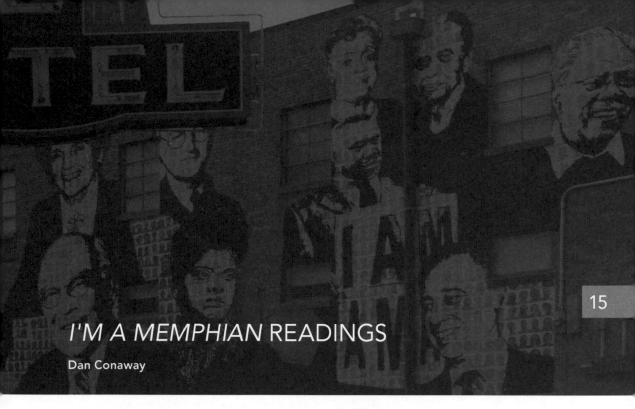

I'M A MEMPHIAN READINGS

Dan Conaway

I'm a Memphian is a 2013 collection of expository and analytical short essays by freelance writer/columnist and lifelong Memphian Dan Conaway. Simply put, Conaway is a Memphian through and through: he has worked for advertising agencies promoting everything from the Peabody Hotel to the Memphis Grizzlies and has a weekly column called "Memphasis." Originally published as a newspaper column, the short vignettes within *I'm a Memphian* are concerned with the uniqueness of the city of Memphis and the characters that inhabit it. His column eloquently illustrates the balance between fascination and frustration for his beloved hometown, all the while expressing this in his unique yet distinctly Memphian voice. Included in this anthology are selections regarding everything from race and community to civic duty and local politics. For example, in "Howard and Bill," Conaway tells the story of the unlikely friendship between Howard Robertson, a black postal carrier and waiter, and Bill Loeb, a wealthy white businessman, in 1960s Memphis. Here, Conaway outlines the importance of respecting each other's differences while advocating for inclusion and cooperation above all else. He appeals to both the reader's pathos and logos. In "Building Models," he details the favorable results of after school programs in Memphis and the ignorance of the white, over-50 aristocracy. By providing a variety of statistics that speak to the positive impact that Memphis City Schools and various after school programs have on the youth of the city, Conaway implores his audience to think critically and logically before becoming a part of the loud yet uninformed majority. By appealing to the reader's emotions, ethics, and logic, Conaway captures the good, the bad, the ugly, and the beautiful of Memphis, often arguing and advocating for societal change.

Look Who's Here

As published June 25, 2010

If you let it, the passing parade that is this city will pass you by. If you pause to take it in, a chimp might sell you a suit.

"38 regular," I told the chimp.

Take a minute and look around. You may see a story. And it may last a lifetime.

Before he was Prince Mongo, he was Robert Hodges. Oh, he was clearly from a place far, far away, but he had not yet assumed the title. When I first became aware of him, the heir apparent to the house of hinky used to ride around town on a motorcycle in a leather jacket and goggles. Sitting behind him was a chimp... in matching leather jacket and goggles. It was the late 60s, and sightings of the weird and wonderful, both natural and chemically-induced, were commonplace, but this caught your attention.

Hodges owned a men's store in those days...no, really...called Dalian et Rae. I went in there one day to look around and saw no one, no one human at least. The chimp appeared from behind a clothes rack, in a nice little jacket and pants, and held up his hand. At this point, you have to make a decision—either go for the whole experience or turn around and walk out. Either way, you've got a story, but what makes Memphis Memphis is that the stories can always get better.

I took his hand.

He walked me to the men's suits, and stepped back as if to say, "You look like a 38 regular." That's where he stopped, and that...a couple thousand super-sized fries ago...was my size. He smiled, and, buddy, chimps can smile. I was about to ask him, I swear, what he had in a double-breasted blazer, when I heard a voice. No, not the chimp, but a guy who worked there who had been in the storeroom. I never saw the chimp again but his bananas owner went on to cosmic infamy.

The truth of what you can see every day in Memphis is better than the fiction other cities have to come up with to make them interesting.

Like that day in 1965 when a 16-year-old in his mamma's convertible pulled up to the light at Union and Cooper. A Harley pulled up next to him, and, with a big smile, Elvis said to the kid, "Nice car." I might still be sitting at that light if the guy behind me hadn't laid on the horn.

Or the time I ran into Isaac Hayes in a break room and we spent an hour talking about bathroom renovation and fireplaces.

Or when I was screwing around with a wedge in my parents' front yard when Cary Middlecoff walked by, and spent 30 minutes showing me how to hit down on the ball.

I have hundreds more, and whether you realize it or not, so do you. Start looking around for your stories. They're everywhere in this town because giants...giant heroes, giant goats, giant characters...have walked and continue to walk among us.

I'm a Memphian, and I have a story.

────────

All Funked Up

As published April 9, 2010

Memphasis, my new weekly column in *The Daily News*, begins Friday, April 9, and will appear every Friday and over the weekend in *The Memphis News*, the paper's weekly. It's all about what I think Memphis is all about. Let me know what you think. But think first. There's far too little of that going around.

Face it. You're funky. *funky 1 \f ng k \ adjective (funkier, funkiest) informal 1 (of music) having or using a strong dance rhythm, in particular that of funk: some excellent funky beats. • modern and stylish in an unconventional or striking way : she likes wearing funky clothes. 2 strongly musty: cooked greens make the kitchen smell really funky.*

Rufus Thomas understood. If a chicken could get funky, it would be in Memphis. Just look at the definition. It includes quintessential Memphis words. Rhythm. Beats. Unconventional. Striking. And, yes, greens and kitchen are in there, too.

This part of the world, and Memphis as its capital, gave the rest of the world rhythm and blues, the beat of rock and roll, the king and court of unconventional and striking. And, yes, we gave them greens and cornbread, too, and grits and chitterlings and fried green tomatoes and fried chicken.

We gave them the stuff that sustains life in hard-to-live lives. Soul-stirring music born of abject poverty. Mouthwatering flavor from food easy to come by out in the yard, over in the field. A sense of, "I can make it," "I can change it," "I can create it," because the most ordinary of origins have sent such extra extraordinary gifts to the world from here.

Elvis and Holiday Inns. Self-service groceries and Federal Express. Three 6 Mafia and modern orthopedics. Stax and St. Jude. Isaac, Al and B.B. Clarence, Fred and Kemmons. Billy Dunavant and Billy Kyle. Pit barbecue and Pitt Hyde.

We have over the years in no particular order and without argument been known as the world's foremost city for cotton, hardwood, juke joints, mules, blues, rock 'n roll, yellow fever, soul, keelboater fights, air freight, trauma nails, and barbecue.

And the assassination of Martin Luther King, Jr.

All of that, mixed in our rich and dangerously spicy diversity, baked in our sweat-through-everything summers, and left to stand on the kitchen, restaurant and church tables where we all gather, has made us one of the funkiest dishes this country serves. And people from everywhere can't wait for a taste.

We're known the world over for the beat of our mojo, for the depth and breadth of our creativity, the warmth of our hospitality, and as the most giving city of our size anywhere. Yet, if you listen to us, you'd never know it.

We think it's all about crime—or who the mayor is, was, or isn't—or consolidation—or taxes—or what we'll do about my street/neighborhood/school/Bible/gun. Those are real concerns needing real solutions, but people from everywhere have them, and when we bitch mightily as if they were ours uniquely, we can lose sight of what others see in us.

Look at it this way, if everybody sees that funky person you're with as attractive, fun, imaginative, intelligent, capable, different, open and loaded with potential and you don't...you're the one who's wrong. As John Cleese purportedly said, "If you walk into a room dressed in a suit and everyone else is dressed as a chicken, you're the one who's out of place." Rufus would have understood.

Work on our faults, but build on our strengths.

I'm a Memphian, and I'm funky.

————

Worldview
As published April 23, 2010

We seem to worry a lot about who we aren't, what we aren't and where we aren't. Memphians are always asking, "What in the world will they make of that?" Well, in my experience, we seem to make the world happy. Not a bad thing.

This week begins in Paris.

You may not know them, but they know you.

Paris.

Cabs in Paris are about the size of clown cars, and putting more than three passengers in one has the same effect. So, when the five of us arrived—us, our kids and my mother-in-law—we split up in two cabs. Gaines, five at the time, and I had the all-guy cab. The front seat passenger was a dog, part poodle and part Charles De Gaulle, complete with his water bowl in the passenger well. The driver introduced him as, "le navigateur." The driver spoke no English. I spoke even less French. Somehow, with Gaines and the dog laughing at both of us, I realized he was asking me where we were from—a place, not a country. He knew we were Americans. Americans stand out in Europe like Hawaiian shirts at a funeral. "Memphis," I said. What happened next was a six-ticket ride. He took a hard right, and a death-defying run around the Arc de Triomphe on the Champs-Elysées. A couple hundred

15

lanes of traffic anarchy. Like NASCAR, except no caution flags and less courtesy. Sweeping into a side street and braking hard enough to turn over Charles De Gaulle's water bowl and my stomach, he stopped in front of a nightclub. Sticking out of the wall was the rear end of a 1959 pink Caddy. "Elvis!" the driver exclaimed.

Amsterdam.

So we're in line with another Memphis couple at the Anne Frank House. It's going to be a while, so the guys go to get everybody a snack. French fries. Stands sell them everywhere in Amsterdam. With mayonnaise. No, really. But I digress. One particular stand gets our business because the entire thing was painted with the scene from the Sistine Chapel where Michelangelo depicts God giving life to Adam...except, in this case, God is giving Adam an order of French fries. "French fries," I said. "What part of the southern United States are you from?" the vendor asked in perfect English. "Memphis," I drawled. "Friendliest city I know," he said. Seems he takes his family to the United States for two weeks every year, picking a different state for the whole two weeks. Been to Memphis twice. "We had the children with us one night, having a wonderful time walking around when we got a little lost," he related. "We walked several dark blocks when we saw spinning bright lights. Black people, white people dancing and laughing," he said, laughing himself. "They adopted us, gave us huge beers, taught the kids new dances...and called us a cab. Best time we had on that whole trip. Can't remember the name...it's, uh...," he struggled. "Raiford's Hollywood?" I guessed. "Yes, yes," he said, clapping his hands together, "that's it!"

You can't make this stuff up.

I have three packages of Memphis cigarettes from Germany, and a Memphis ashtray I talked a bar owner out of in Munich. I walked by a Volkswagen Memphis model in Salzburg, and I've been to a show in Rome featuring work from a whole design school called Memphis.

In Galatoire's in New Orleans...yes, that's an international city...the waiter engages us in conversation with a heavier European accent than the French fry guy in Holland. "Where are you from?" We tell him. He doesn't tell us about the signature trout or crab dishes, or the wine list, or anything about one of the country's great menus. He simply asks, "So where do you go for your barbecue?"

I'm a Memphian, and I'm world famous.

———

One of a Kind

As published June 11, 2010

A number of places have a certain thing about them that is aptly described as unique, but just one or two things in most cases. Duck Hill, Mississippi, for instance, has trees that grow damn near sideways out of that namesake hill. It takes a bunch of things like that before the whole place can be thought of as unique.

Folks, this place is unique.

Really unique is really not. Memphis is.

Nothing is really unique. Unique is unique. If there is more than one of it, it isn't.

Memphis is et up with unique.

The Peabody is unique. Two hammered duck hunters dump their live decoys in the lobby fountain. One is actually the hotel manager, and instead of getting him fired, that drunken prank makes the place world-famous. Almost 80 years later, ducks are still in that fountain by day, live in an air-conditioned penthouse by night, march back and forth twice a day to a packed crowd, and are on TV as much as Daffy and Donald.

Unique.

Graceland is unique. Depending on who you talk to, Elvis has been dead since 1977. Visit Graceland today and tell me you don't think he's still in there somewhere. Somebody has just been napping on that ginormous couch. Those dark TVs are still warm, and somebody's screwing around with a guitar in the jungle room. Walk by the kitchen and you can smell peanut butter and banana sandwiches. There's a reason they won't let us go upstairs.

Unique.

Memphis in May is unique. "I've got an idea," someone certifiable said at the first meeting, "Let's have a barbecue cooking contest. Contestants will come from all over the world, bring smokers that look like locomotives, set up booths 30 feet tall, and 100,000-plus will come down to the river to watch them cook food they can't eat."

Unique.

The National Civil Rights Museum is unique. There is one Lorraine Motel, one balcony, one bathroom window through which a modern-day prophet was killed but his dream refused to die. What fed that dream and what feeds it still is on display in one place.

Unique.

St. Jude Children's Research Hospital is unique. What all those unbelievably dedicated people drink over there isn't Kool-Aid, it's great big gulps of hope. What they do every day to give children a chance at life shines a bright light from Memphis the whole world can see.

Unique.

The Rendezvous is unique. It's in a basement. You walk by a dumpster and step over a couple of puddles of God-knows-what to get in. Not only do they charbroil their ribs down there, the restaurant itself has burned twice. The beams are still charred. Everything in this city's collective attic is hanging on the walls or from the ceiling. Their ribs started and continue to fuel a worldwide debate. Wet or dry.

Unique.

Cozy Corner is unique, a barbecue joint famous for...Cornish hens? The National Ornamental Metal Museum is unique, both for what it is and the river view from where it is. Dyer's is unique, deep frying hamburgers in a vat of grease I think Andy Jackson brought with him when he founded the city.

The list goes on and on, and that's the point. Beyond and because of music, and barbecue, and cotton, and race, and hospitality, and river, and creativity, it goes all the way to soul. Uniquely.

I'm a Memphian, and I'm unique.

————

Howard and Bill

As published April 30, 2010

Just as this city is different from any other, each of us is different. If we were all the same, what a great large snore life would be. However, if we fail to respect our differences, or fail to treat each other with simple dignity and common courtesy, what a nightmare awaits us all.

This week you'll meet Howard and Bill.

Two halves make a whole.

In the 60s, Howard Robertson was a black postal carrier moonlighting as a waiter at the capital of white money dining in Memphis, Justine's, housed in an antebellum mansion. Bill Loeb was a successful white businessman, owner of ubiquitous laundry branches about town, and the brother of Henry Loeb, mayor during the 1968 sanitation strike. Loeb lived in a home literally bordering the Memphis Country Club. Robertson lived in the other Memphis those of us who grew up white then never really acknowledged.

They would meet amid crisp white tablecloths set with crystal and crabmeat, one hosting, the other serving.

One evening at Justine's, Robertson did something that displeased Loeb. In front of his guests and the entire restaurant, Loeb wore him out. Loud and personal. Putting someone "in his place." But that wasn't Robertson's place. He returned the verbal fire, shot for shot, then returned to the kitchen and quit. That took the kind of dignity and courage that comes from deep inside. The kind that says even though this will cause sacrifice for my family, even though that kind of behavior was the norm, I will not take it. Loeb's brother, Henry, would later see that sentiment expressed on posters, "I am a man."

This is when this becomes a different story. This is when Loeb would show his own dignity and courage. As he talked with his guests, he realized he had been in the wrong. He invited all of them back the following evening, and asked for Robertson. When told he had quit, Loeb asked Justine if she could please try and get him there. It took some doing, but she did, and for the second night in a row, Loeb and Robertson became the center of attention for the restaurant. Except, this night, Loeb apologized. Man to man. They talked. They decided to meet again.

And they kept meeting for the rest of Loeb's life. They watched games together. They talked life. They talked business. When Loeb converted his laundries to very popular barbecue shops, he brought Robertson on as a partner in two of them.

That was then, and that is now. The sense of two cities in one, a tale like Dickens' "It was the best of times, it was the worst of times," is not only still with us, it divides and defeats us. What Robertson and Loeb did, when it was much more difficult to do, is the common ground we must all find.

Bill Loeb's children have continued to show leadership in the business, arts and causes of our city. Howard Robertson's son—Howard, Jr.—is an involved citizen and business owner, and married to the executive director of the National Civil Rights Museum. Howard, Jr. once told me, "A father is how a son learns to be a man."

Good job, guys, you taught them well, and there's a lesson in it for us.

I'm a Memphian, hopefully, like Howard and Bill.

———

Two Ways to Look at It

As published April 8, 2011

Most cities are looking for something to hang a civic hat on—a single thing that can define and attract and separate.

Might be they're the birthplace of something or someone significant enough to brand a whole city. Or perhaps they're known as the center or capital of some enterprise, the place where something is made or from or named after.

If they're really lucky, really rare as cities go, they'll have more than one such thing and a few, incredibly few, might have such things from both the right and left brain, both cool and profitable.

Of course, they'd have to realize it.

It all depends on your point of view.

Coming from Arkansas, it looks like Oz.

It appears suddenly, just past that truck in front of you, between that truck and the one next to you, glimpsed between rearview mirror checks of that truck behind you. You've somehow survived the concrete gauntlet of West Memphis and the semi cowboys whipping their rigs into a frenzy, driving them to market across the modern day trails of I-40 and I-55.

There in front of you is a city on a hill. It's an urban island; surrounded by the agrarian sea of cotton, soybeans and rice you've just navigated. You'll reach it by crossing a bridge of lights and a river so great that a great nation uses it to define its east and west. You see the city spread out across the horizon, and to my taste, a feast for both eyes and spirit.

Okay, that's a truckload of metaphors, but I think the view is pretty trucking impressive.

You're looking at a place where new ideas come out of nowhere and go everywhere, where cultures, races, circumstances and history all come together and give rise to new ways to see, hear and heal. From here—from a brand-new waterfront town and a 30-story stainless steel pyramid on one side to an old city makeover and fledgling arts district on the other— you can't see the problems, but you can still see the possibilities.

Coming from Mississippi, it looks like a Star Wars set. It appears to the right, just past that truck in front of you, between that truck and the one next to you, glimpsed between rear-view mirror checks of that truck behind you. You've somehow survived the challenge of the Lamar corridor where Mississippi turns into Tennessee and farm turns into industry as suddenly and chaotically as a five-truck pileup.

There beside you at Shelby Drive is the old Tennessee Yard, the new Memphis Intermodal Facility. BNSF dropped a $200 million upgrade here and rolled in those ginormous cranes that look like Empire war engines and can lift the national debt. The wheels are bigger than my house. They pick up 40-foot containers from railcars and put them on trucks and vice versa, and they do that 600,000 times a year with capacity to do it a million times a year.

You're looking at a place where things come from everywhere and go everywhere else, where river, rail, air, road and geography all come together. From here—from the permanent ruts in the road made by the world's heavy loads—you can see what made Memphis storage closet and delivery service to the known universe.

Two views, one of a city of imagination, an incubator where new things are born and grow strong in the Delta heat, and another of a city of purpose, a critical transfer point where whatever's wanted comes to be sorted and sent.

One city.

I'm a Memphian, and our original music includes the sounds of boats, trains, trucks and planes.

———

Building Models

As published May 27, 2011

Most of the solutions we're being offered for our various and sundry urban problems seem to have several things in common:

The loudest come from white people over 50 and usually start with, "And I'll tell you another damn thing..."

They are simplistic so as not to strain simple minds.

They are not merely dogmatic, but red-in-the-face, a-little-spit-at-the corner-of-your-mouth dogmatic.

They are based on some time in the past, generally a hybrid of King Arthur's Camelot, Robert Young's "Father Knows Best," and your choice of John Wayne movies.

They are most often voiced with the greatest volume by those with the least knowledge of the subject at hand and the least experience in dealing with or managing it.

So let's get started with this week's column, and I'll tell you another damn thing...

A 99.6 percent success rate.

We've seen the letters to the editor, heard the guy two stools down, the geniuses spitting into talk show microphones, "It's not the teachers, it's the parents."

If I'm 17 in south Memphis right now, we don't have time to teach or reach my parents to teach or reach me. I have little brothers and sisters I'm responsible for, they're hungry, I'm mad. And I just put a gun in my pocket and walked out the door.

When there's one exhausted parent or no parent at home, where would you have me go? When home is no place I can safely come home to, when the corner is my mentor, the street my support, what would you do with me? When there are thousands of me one meltdown away from you, can you actually pretend that we have nothing to do with each other?

I'm next door. What happens to me tonight when I walk out that door happens to you as a city tomorrow.

The flat earth Tennessee legislature—declaring war on teachers and marching education backwards in lockstep—doesn't get it. People who talk just in terms of what used to be or in terms of 20 years from now—or just talk—don't get it either. We need to stop *these* teen pregnancies, graduate *these* kids, save *this* generation so it can save the next.

We need to stop that kid at that door and open another one right now.

There are people who get it. Alisha Kiner, principal at Booker T. Washington High School, gets it, and the tough love she gives out keeps kids from giving in. Digger Phelps, legendary coach and motivator, gets it, recently telling an audience of prominent Memphis business people to get off their assets and get into a mentoring program. President Obama gets it, coming here for the BTW commencement in recognition of what that amazing inner city class did, raising their grades, raising their graduation rate more than 20 percent, raising the hope of a city, and symbolically through his appearance, the hope of a nation for inner city schools.

There are programs that get it. The Boys & Girls Club, building model citizens from the very raw product of urban reality, gets it.

15

Half of BTW's graduating class went to the Porter Boys & Girls Club across the street instead of staying on the street. For mentoring and guidance. For role models, reinforcement, and a sense of self-worth. For what can happen when parents can't be there but others are willing and able to step in and stand up.

The graduation rate for Memphis City Schools is in the low sixties. Last year, the Boys & Girls Clubs had a graduation rate of 97.6 percent among the seniors in their six clubs. This year, with three times as many seniors, the graduation rate was 99.6 percent.

Our kids can do anything, but not if we do nothing.

I'm a Memphian, and our kids can inspire Presidents.

Questions for Discussion and Journaling

1. Conaway uses repetition, beginning each article's conclusion with a resounding "I'm a Memphian," an expression of pride. What effect does this technique have on the audience? Why would an author choose to use repetition in this way?

2. With "I'm a Memphian," Conaway invented his own genre that simultaneously challenges and celebrates Memphis. Mimic his style and genre to write your own "I'm a Memphian" essay. If you aren't a Memphian, then write an "I'm not a Memphian" essay or write about the city or place you call home.

3. Which of Conaway's articles speaks to you or interests you the most? Reflect on what it is that pulls you to that article. It is his tone? The content? His argument?

4. While Conaway's arguments are often implicit, choose one of his articles and analyze his argument using the "Analyzing Arguments" chapter. What rhetorical moves make you agree with his argument? Where does he lose your attention?

SPUN CITY

Paula Hayes

Paula Hayes wrote "Spun City," published in the *Memphis Flyer* on February 8, 2018, as part of her exploration of what it means to be an authentic Memphian. She initially wrote the article for her composition classroom to show her students how to write a short work concerning the selection of a Memphis landmark or popular venue. Inspired by Dan Conaway's "I'm a Memphian" series, she wrote this while teaching English 1020. Her narrative on the closing of the iconic Spin Street Music store intends to stir memories of nostalgia. The piece explores how everyday places in Memphis hold meaning for Memphians. Spin Street Music store was Memphis' last major record store, though smaller music stores Goner Records and Shangri-La Records remain open. She argues that the closing of the last major record store in Memphis is significant in a city where local history is steeped in memories of Southern style sounds such as rhythm and blues.

Elvis, the Patron Saint of pop culture and Poplar Avenue, has left the building.

It is with melancholy that I find myself saying goodbye to Spin Street. Walking through the big record store at Poplar and Highland felt like walking through a time capsule, but with a slightly B-grade movie atmosphere. The store's odd array of eclectic items carried a silent scream against pragmatism and reinforced the efficacy of pop culture: An authentic *Star Trek* lamp in the shape of the Starship Enterprise, a red-hot lava lamp, slightly frightening-looking bobbleheads, giant house slippers in the shape of a Marvel comic book hero, a retro record player, or the old, crumbling tattered record covers of Isaac Hayes.

"Spun City" by Paula Hayes. From *The Memphis Flyer*, February 8, 2018. Reprinted by permission of the author.

These weren't items I needed in a society that plays music on its phones. Just items I wanted. In our quick evolution into a digitalized society, CD and record stores are going the way of chain bookstores, assigned to be relics of history and, sadly, to a soon-to-be-forgotten part of the city's past.

What I will miss most about Spin Street is the larger-than-life Elvis that hung over the store's entrance. He was hard to miss. Two stories high, hovering inside a glass encasement, this Elvis was an ubermensch. This Elvis could represent anything to the imagination; Elvis preserved for posterity as a specimen in a high school biology vial; Elvis the extraterrestrial alien sandwiched between flying-saucer-shaped disks on both sides of the glass; Elvis flying off in a space capsule with the glow of blue neon lighting the way. It was Saint Elvis, the resurrected one, in his shining glory, with a halo of light circling his head, as he ascended into the heavens. It was Elvis, the forerunner of Justin Timberlake, the on-call performer, standing ready, in suit and tie, for the next big show. It was the uniquely Memphis Elvis, not the Las Vegas Elvis.

When I first moved to Memphis, one of the first "Elvis spottings" I had was of the Spin Street Elvis. It always felt a bit like this Elvis offered his watchful gaze over the traffic, hovering 10 feet off the ground of Highland and Poplar (not 10 feet off of Beale; sorry, Marc Cohn), a protector of the crossroads. It seemed a bit as though this Elvis was looking out for me, the new girl in town.

16

Many a summer day, in the suffocating, mosquito-charged, thick-as-a-slice-of-bread heat, I would make my way into Spin Street, arms chock full of my used CDs. In shorts, a T-shirt, and flip flops, I would wait in a 30-minute line, until a friendly, slightly grungy dude, who looked like he had smoked a little too much of the herb the night before, held each of my individual CDs up to the light with his shaky hands. I would watch the sunlight bounce off each CD rim, finally to be given an offer: "Cash or credit in the store?" I was always broke, and I always responded with "Cash, please."

As a young woman, that extra $10, $20, or, on a good day, $30, could buy a pack of Diet Cokes and enough survival food to make it a few more days in the city.

Now, I am just another aging Generation X-er but, in my youth, CDs meant more than just entertainment. Sometimes, they meant fast cash and food. CD stores like Spin Street meant a place where one could get lost, nights of getting absorbed by the racks of music, where the tension of the outside world gave way to aisles marked "Rap" or "Rock."

Some people believe in the patron saints of the Holy Apostolic Catholic Church or in the Virgin Mary of Guadalupe, and that is all well and good and fine. I just happen to have believed in the Spin Street Elvis, the patron saint of pop culture and Poplar Avenue.

Once a part of the unique Memphis Kitsch, that Elvis has now left the building.

Questions for Discussion and Journaling

1. What methods of voice does Hayes use to mimic Conaway? How does her voice differ from Conaway's? For help, see the section on "How to Construct *Your Voice*" in Chapter 6 for detailed explanations about how voice is created by diction, details, imagery, syntax, and tone.

2. Choose an iconic Memphis landmark. Write a reflection on what makes this landmark important to you and to Memphis. Try to weave the personal together with the Memphian like Hayes did.

3. Often writers learn to write or begin to write something new by mimicking the writing of another author like Hayes did here. Have you ever tried to mimic another writer? Why might this be a useful tool for a new writer?

17

LETTER TO MY CITY

Troy L. Wiggins

While not born in Memphis, Troy Wiggins and his family moved here when he was 5. A product of Legacy Memphis City Schools, he grew up in an unnamed neighborhood in North Memphis where he experienced both extreme poverty and loving community. As his two articles included in this textbook illustrate, his experiences navigating Memphis as a Black man inform his writing. In "Letter to My City," (originally published in the Opinion section of the *Memphis Flyer*), Wiggins reflects on his life as a millennial in Memphis, reminding us that discussion pieces about millennials aren't really talking about him while making connections to the national conversation about police violence. He uses the landmarks he encounters and experiences he has on his drives through midtown Memphis to expose the hypocrisy of the "Memphis Loves Everybody" claim seen on one midtown wall.

All millennials do not share the same Memphis experiences.

There are dead and dying black people everywhere.

I haven't logged on to Facebook in two weeks, partly because people talk too damn much, partly because I don't want to watch endlessly looped videos of black and brown people's slaughter and share sadface emojis because I don't have any more meaningful words about their deaths.

Words are data-mined and used in targeted ads: Quality proofreading services, Marvel's *Defenders* series, black and brown people vomiting blood from gunshot wounds in 4k resolution on your screen—aren't these new phones amazing? Look at that quality; you can see each individual shudder in that death rattle. Check out these suggested videos. Repeat, repeat, repeat. Cry.

I love Memphis, but does Memphis love me? Photo: Author.

Last night, I was driving home from dinner in my mom's car. My neighborhood is belted by extreme affluence on one end and extreme poverty on the other. I live squarely in the middle, in the liminal space, which is lowkey my existence because I'm the kind of millennial that people aren't talking about when they talk about millennials. Charleena Lyles was a millennial, too. I wonder if her love of avocado toast is to blame for our failing economy. I wonder how many degrees of separation there are between avocado toast and her murder. There are dead and dying black people everywhere.

I was driving my mom's car last night to get dinner for my family. My route is always the same when I'm heading west toward home: turn on the rich people's street to get to the street designated for the not-rich black people, most of whom are dying from incarceration, from poverty, from generations of advancing bare centimeters and you all should be grateful, we could just wall off your part of the neighborhood and leave you in Memphadishu, dude, but I'm cool, bro, so here, have a swig of my 201 Hoplar what do you mean you don't like IPAs? I don't even know who Duanna Johnson is, dude. Forget it, we're building the wall, don't say we never tried to give you anything.

The rich people's street on my side of the 'hood has 24-hour security patrols. The rich people's street on the other side of the 'hood has 24-hour security patrols and those police blue eyes in the sky that are possibly the blue eyes of the precogs rifling through our black minds for prethoughtcrimes against the white supremacist order, the better to justify our murders. Data-driven probable cause, but all the artificial intelligence is racist.

My route is always the same. I turn on the rich people's street to get to my street. As I am sitting in the lane to turn on the rich people's street, a blue eye—a blue life?—pulls up short, creeps behind me as I am sitting in my mom's car, a bag of food in my wife's lap. The other blue eye winks from across the street, as if to say to the blue life behind me, "Do what you gotta do. Fear for your life if you need to."

Thankfully, my child hasn't been born, so they won't have to see my black life taken by this blue life. All I've done is buy dinner. I have guacamole in the bag. How many avocadoes is my black life worth? I contemplate having my wife turn on Facebook Live—if I go, I'm going out in 4k. But we're working-class blacks and we can't afford 4k tech on a writer's salary, so I don't bother. I haven't committed a crime, but neither did Philando or Sandra or Tamir or Darrius or eight-year-old Aiyana or Laquan or anyone else on this charnel house list that started, really, in 1619. There are dead and dying black people everywhere. Listen to the high definition sound quality of those rattling chains.

That winking blue eye followed me through my dreams. On my way to work, I pass two signs: "I <3 Memphis" and "Memphis Loves Everybody." Let's do the math: One of those is true; the other is bullshit. Memphis don't love me. Memphis loves those other millennials, the ones who think quality avocado toast goes well with craft IPAs. Memphis don't love me. Memphis glares at me suspiciously in its tourist sandals while I'm going to pick up my slices from Memphis Pizza Cafe, even though I've been going there since I was 16 and the millennials Memphis loves just got here last year. Memphis loves grit and grind. Memphis loves urban displacement, platitudes, preserving historic standards, saving the Greensward. Memphis loves being number 3 on the Best New Mid-Sized Cities for Millennial Homebuyers list. Memphis loves progress as long as it comes with a shaggy surfer haircut, a pantsuit, a start-up with a Grizzlies blue-and-gold material UI logo, a digital rendering of a pistol, and an insensitive ironic slogan because that's the new Memphis, man. Memphis loves not loving me and people like me.

I finally log on to Facebook. People are still talking. Dana Loesch is in an NRA ad calling for people to take up arms and defend America in its noble struggle against its oppressed. City, county, and state politicians are still debating whether it's more economically viable to smother us slowly or to bleed us out with a single bullet. The *Commercial Appeal* is "exploring" Memphis' problem with gun violence. A blue life creeps by, armed and armored in the same kind of van that Freddie Gray was killed in. Memphis loves Everybody. There are dead and dying black people all over this city. I love Memphis.

Questions for Discussion and Journaling

1. Throughout this piece, Wiggins uses what writing scholar Vershawn Ashanti Young calls code-meshing ("blending minoritized dialects and world Englishes with Standard English"). Identify two examples of code-meshing in this piece, and consider how this code-meshing works for rhetorical effect. Why would an author code-mesh? How does doing so further support the argument presented in this article?

2. Vershawn Ashanti Young argues that code-meshing is a more appropriate and ethical form of writing to encourage in college writing classrooms. That said, most writing teachers encourage code-switching which asks students to learn how to switch from their own dialects of English to the academic (and traditionally white) dialect of Standard English. Have you been asked to code-switch by English teachers? How did this impact you? If not, then why haven't you been asked to code-switch?

3. Wiggins uses repetition for rhetorical effect throughout his piece. What phrases does he repeat? How does this repetition support his argument? Why do you think he made the rhetorical choice to repeat these phrases?

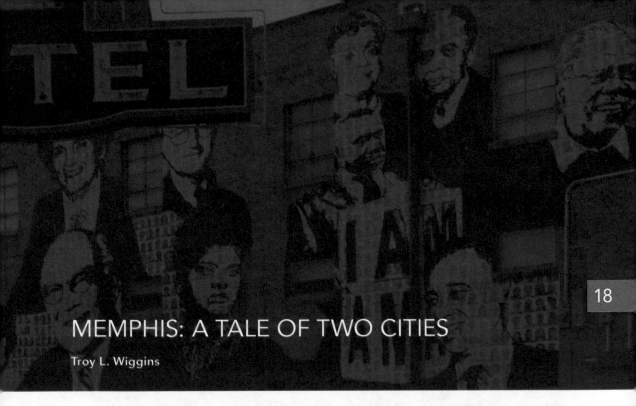

MEMPHIS: A TALE OF TWO CITIES

Troy L. Wiggins

While not born in Memphis, Troy Wiggins and his family moved here when he was 5. A product of Legacy Memphis City Schools, he grew up in an unnamed neighborhood in North Memphis where he experienced both extreme poverty and loving community. As his two articles included in this textbook illustrate, his experiences navigating Memphis as a black man inform his writing. In "Memphis: A Tale of Two Cities," published in the *Memphis Flyer*, Wiggins remembers driving by the Sears Crosstown Tower with his grandmother and discusses the opening of Crosstown Concourse. He presents his memories alongside a number of depressing realities for non-white Memphians in order to illustrate how the development happening around Memphis seems to forget (or worse ignore) Memphis's largest constituency, time and time again.

My paternal great-grandmother abandoned rural Mississippi in the 1960s in order to escape her husband, an abusive man who decided early in their marriage that he wanted a farmhand instead of a wife. My great-grandmother—affectionately called "Granny" by her great-grandchildren—survived assaults from men who wanted to claim her body, a wage-slavery system that wanted to claim her soul, and a concentrated dose of white supremacy that had no qualms about making a feast out of her bones as well.

In her old age, my Granny's favorite pastime was riding around the city to visit shopping malls and department stores, but she couldn't drive, so when one of her children or grandchildren was too busy to serve as chauffeur, we rode the bus. During the face-meltingly hot Memphis summers of the early 1990s, I was frequently her co-pilot and traveling companion. One of my fondest memories of her was a summertime bus ride where we rumbled past the Sears Crosstown tower on Cleveland, which by then had been long abandoned. As we passed the building, Granny looked up at it, cursed (she only cursed when she was mad), and sighed.

"Memphis: A Tale of Two Cities" by Troy L. Wiggins. From *The Memphis Flyer*, August 31, 2017. Reprinted by permission of the author.

My Granny had given most of her life to affluent white Memphians who visited our house whenever they wished to slip silver dollars from behind our ears like stale magic, praising my Granny for her hardworking nature and her homespun wisdom even as they worked her to her grave. Her sigh that day as we passed Sears Crosstown wasn't wistful. She did not long for bygone days, and she was not lamenting lost fondness; my Granny had lived through so much pain at the hands of men, white-folks, and crushing poverty that she rarely ever seemed fond of anything other than her grandchildren and great-grandchildren.

Crosstown. Justin Fox Burks

I carried her memory and her history with me more than 10 years after that bus ride when I crossed Cleveland and stepped into the brand new Crosstown Concourse. I was there to witness firsthand the realization of a project purported to bring new life into central Memphis. New life, of course, because the old ones are less meaningful in the face of developments like this one.

I can't lie, the Crosstown Concourse is a nice building. The idea of a "vertical urban village" is a concept out of my futurist fantasies, and the Crosstown Concourse looks the part. The updated construction has managed to retain the massive look and feel of the building from my childhood while also making the new space feel fresh and modern. The public servant in me is impressed by the convergence of commercial and civic interests into a single public-use space.

But Memphis is full of disrespected dead, and their spirits still cry out for justice. On the afternoon of Saturday, August 12th, our city was at the crux of an interesting convergence: Less than three miles from the celebration of Crosstown's shining beacon, hundreds of protesters (many of whom are descendants of the slaves that kept Memphis living in high cotton) decided to use their bodies and lives to demand that our elected representatives stand on the correct side of history and remove hateful edifices from our taxpayer-funded parks. While the people who Memphis prioritizes bobbed their heads to performances from some of our most brilliant black artists, immigrant Memphians marched to defend themselves and their families from forces that threaten to rupture their families and destroy their livelihoods.

We are living in a literal tale of two cities.

I want to know: How can I be excited about the Crosstown Concourse when the grocery store inside of it is explicitly not marketed to the disenfranchised residents of Klondike and Smokey City? How can I be excited about the Crosstown Concourse when there are thousands of unemployed and underemployed Memphians in a two-mile radius of its doors? How can I be excited about the Crosstown Concourse when entire swaths of the city remain blighted and infested with vermin and waste? How can I be excited about the Crosstown Concourse when white supremacy, the system that makes Memphis great (for white residents) is still deeply ingrained in every facet of our city's operation, from the police to the politics to the food and employment deserts, and is still killing people in whatever way it deems best—just like it killed my Granny?

Just last week, I was visiting South Memphis, talking to residents in an area infamous for having lead soil contamination readings higher than 1,700 parts per million (the federal standard for lead soil contamination is 400 parts per million). One woman caught my eye—her resemblance to my Granny struck me so deeply that it nearly brought tears to my eyes.

She was hurt and disgusted. Everyone in Memphis seemed to be on the receiving end of such great developments. Her neighborhood had changed too, with new housing and freshly constructed green space, but she was still not impressed. Where were the opportunities for her children and grandchildren to escape the chains of poverty that had held her in place for generations? Where were the nearby jobs? The adequately funded schools? There isn't a full-service grocery store within three miles of her house. Those seem to be very basic requests, and I thought that Memphis was in the business of being brilliant at those. At one point during our conversation, she sighed and shook her head. For a moment, I was back on that bus with my Granny, my 10-year-old self finally understanding the weight of her sigh.

18

Time and again, our city's leadership proves to folks like me that it does not care about our poor black grannies, our immigrant friends and family, or anyone else who dares to speak up and demand that all of the edifices to hate and white supremacy—mounted or not—be removed from this place where we've planted our roots. In the face of all these past memories and current pain, tell me: Why should I, or any Memphians like me, be excited about these future developments?

Questions for Discussion and Journaling

1. Wiggins juxtaposes the 2017 opening celebration of Crosstown Concourse with protests happening around the city. How does this juxtaposition support his argument? Why do you think he made this rhetorical decision? What kind of rhetorical appeal is such a juxtaposition?

2. Wiggins blends personal narrative (pathetic appeals) with facts (logical appeals). His combination of personal and informational writing is quite persuasive. Why do you think this blend works? How do these two appeals work together to develop his ethos? How else do you see him developing his ethos?

3. Wiggins notes a number of different things happening around Memphis. Briefly reread the article in order to generate a list of 5 potential topics for a research paper. Then choose the two that you are most interested in. Turn to the "Choosing a Topic" chapter in your textbook and ask yourself the three questions intended to help you choose a topic successfully.

REAL MUSEUMS OF MEMPHIS

Zandria F. Robinson

19

"Real Museums of Memphis" is a reflection on the conflicting realities of the MLK 50 celebration, the Civil Rights Museum, and gentrification, poverty, and continued racial segregation in Memphis. Written by Zandria F. Robinson—a Memphis native, renowned sociologist, author of 3 books and many more articles, and professor at Georgetown University—the article was originally posted to her blog and was later published in *Scalawag*, "a journalism and storytelling organization that illuminates dissent, unsettles dominant narratives, pursues justice and liberation, and stands in solidarity with marginalized people and communities in the South." She testifies with memories of her experiences going to The Civil Rights Museum on school trips and reflects on the events surrounding the 2018 MLK 50 Celebration, happening when she wrote this blog. She also presents other stories about Memphis, and particularly about downtown, that may make you uncomfortable by criticizing Memphis institutions that you are used to being celebrated, or her testimonies and critiques may make you nod your head in agreement and excitement. No matter your reaction, her words are likely to generate an emotional reaction, and as you read, you should keep in mind that if and when you have an emotional reaction to something, you should question that reaction and how it is making you respond to the author's argument.

I wasn't well able enough to be a live and in-person witness to the April 4th celebration/ commemoration/reflection of/upon the life, lynching, and legacy of Dr. Martin Luther King, Jr. in Memphis. I don't know how long my sickness had been creeping, but I took note of it several Fridays ago, when I stood on my porch and watched the red-lettered "I AM MEMPHIS" slogan float onto my street all tall and blaring on the side of a sanitation truck on pickup day. "*Who* is Memphis?" I snapped at no one in particular, adjusting my raggedy pink flannel robe and my bonnet because I had been so assaulted by the declaration. The sound of my voice hit the street and a "Shiiiid, sista, Ion'teeno" bounced back from a sanitation worker grabbing up and dumping the contents of green cans. I waved weakly in the direction of the voice, and whispered a "mane" in response, and then, more definitively, a "THANK, Y'ALL!" as the truck and its logo made its way on down the street.

Lately Memphis been engaged in a kind of gross boosterism that prefigures the spectacular simulacra that is MLK50. There is a new Memphis afoot, built on the post-racial capitalist fantasy of "grit and grind," that aims to attract new Memphians to teach in the rapidly expanding charter school sector, to endow our country town with the sophisticated art cultures they bring as they flee the rising rents in their better cities, and to innovate new ways for more new Memphians to live off poverty via the city's expansive foundation and non-profit landscape. In exchange, the city rewards these new Memphians for their sacrifices, for living in such a poor Black town, with no sufficient public transportation to reduce their carbon footprints, where good coffee and cocktails and neighborhood bars are only just coming into reach, by highlighting their valiant choice of Memphis as their new home. There are institutes and trainings and leadership seminars for these new Memphians, where they learn their role in and worth to the city, as well as all of the requisite statistics about infant mortality rates (answer: get well-meaning white women to help Black pregnant people love themselves!), food deserts (answer: grow your own food, Blacks!), and health disparities (answer: bike lanes!). Beyond the usual tensions between the tourist version of a city and the "real" city, this new Memphis, which perhaps is the real cause of all our sickness, obliterates *now* Memphis and buries *then* Memphis, in all of its complexity and depth, at the Lorraine Motel.

The fiftieth anniversary of the assassination of Martin Luther King, Jr., is to Memphis what the Olympics was to Atlanta over 20 years ago, which is about right for how many years we are behind Atlanta in other things. As communities have been reshaped, neglected, obscured, and obliterated in the lead-up to this moment, and as they will continue to be from here on out, we have to assess that *then* Memphis. We also have to tell the world loudly about the *now* Memphis, tell it straight from the mouths of the people whose necks the now Memphis, like the then Memphis, keeps its foot on. And we have to keep track of how our memories and experiences are being gentrified in a notion of progress that has no meaningful proof or original referent.

The discursive destruction of then Memphis and now Memphis ain't start when I saw that sanitation truck, of course. It started 27 years previous, when the National Civil Rights Museum opened that July and the city of Memphis finally elected its first Black mayor (right on time, almost 20 years after Atlanta) that October. There was a museum about our history, about American history, and a Black mayor. It was Obama and the Blacksonian before Obama and the Blacksonian were a twinkle in the chocolate city's eye.

I was nine when the Museum opened, which meant I was already 23 years into the mourning that got in everybody's blood within a 25-mile radius that Thursday evening, April 4, 1968. That mourning had gotten in our blood so much so that the next generation of folks who bore babies here were more likely to lose they babies than anyone else in any other city in this country. Being born with an extra 14 years of mourning, plus learning in your own nine years just as soon as you could comprehend your own name what you should know about that mourning, and why you had to carry it just as you carried yourself—so tall and proud and better than the worst of you and the worst of white folks, too—made me tired before I ever even could really know tiredness. Like Fannie Lou Hamer sick-and-tired-of-being-sick-and-tired kind of tired. The kind of tired that made me extra musty as a little girl for no apparent reason.

The Museum was added to our annual school field trip rotation alongside trips to the zoo, which, thanks to the miracle of desegregation, we could now go to any day we pleased. We went on His birthday, on free Tuesdays, during Black History Month, and sometimes for the anniversary, and sometimes because we were on the civil rights unit in social studies. I came to expect the funkiest feeling in my heart and stomach when we got to the bus and Rosa Parks and the bus driver and the other sculptural figures were still sitting there in silent history. I hoped Ms. Parks got up in the night after the museum was closed, put her makeup on to bring her color in good, got up from her seat, and marched up the aisle and slapped the dog shit out that bus driver. Every time I returned to the Museum, to that bus, there was no evidence that she had done any such thing. I jumped at the bus driver in the way we thrust our shoulders forward and furrowed our brows to threaten a fight on the blacktop.

"My Mama was alive during them times," I whispered not quietly to classmates on those trips, nodding with a practiced gravity. That museum told me them times was over. I wish that museum had told me that these was them times. My Mama Museum told me that these was still them times, and that them times would always be these times as long as we were Black and alive, and probably even after we were Black and dead. I hadn't yet registered that I arrived in this life with 14 years of mourning that, like the stank of my right underarm, told me that these was them times. Sometimes I felt silly for thinking that these times was them times, because there weren't dogs and hoses and nooses and crosses burning and white women's teeth. Then I felt silly for ignoring all the evidence that told me these was them times and had always been them times.

Mama had shown us so many of her artifacts, in fact, that by the time people were talking about how hard Black folks (and don't forget the good white folks) fought to open this museum, and how we all needed to go to better ourselves and know our histories, I felt I had seen and heard and inherited enough. In summer 1991 when the Museum opened, I sure smelled like it. I wondered why there had to be a fight to get a museum. I wondered if white folks didn't want there to be a museum because they didn't want us to find out that somebody from right in our town, and not the lone wolf outside agitator James Earl Ray, killed King. That maybe they had done it.

Being 16 when King was killed, Mama spent her whole life knowing. I don't know how many years of extra mourning she was born with. Nor do I know which cataclysmic rupture in the Memphis history that happened to her before she was born—the lynchings of Calvin McDowell, Thomas Moss, and William Stewart? The burning of Ida B. Wells's newspaper offices?—was the source of that extra mourning. Growing up, Mama's stories of her every day and emotional life after that Thursday, April 4, 1968, made me know that she was herself a museum, archiving all the things of her life and rotating what was on view. She was the docent of her life and of Black southern women's lives and Black Memphis life, guiding us through her exhibits. Mama was an activist for being a museum and for just thinking she deserved freedom. She taught us the Black folk cogito: I think therefore I am free.

Every time we came out of that place, musty and ashy with grief from what the museum said the white folks did to our mamas and grandmas and other folks who looked like us, we were sad and heavy as a patch of winter interrupting a good spring. Even though we had learned that we were a people of hope and resilience and we kept on fighting and pushing and moving and singing spirituals, precious Lord, we still had little explanation as to why white folks acted like that towards us for so long, so we tended to think one of us or some of us had done something wrong to earn that treatment. Like when the teacher punish the whole class for talking and say we can't go outside when it was really only Marcellus and Keon talking but won't nobody tell because we'd rather miss recess once than be a snitch forever.

When we got back into the light, we were right back at the scene of the crime, the centerpiece out of which the museum grew northward and westward, an extra arm and an extra leg. We came fresh out into the air funky not with the stank of what happened before to people who looked like us, but rather with the feeling that it was happening to us, too, seeing as we had fewer and fewer white kids in our classes, and some of the remaining ones usually got sick on museum day.

What really did us in afterward was seeing that balcony and getting close enough to it so it could talk shit to us. People used to say the stain of King's blood was still there from 1968 and that you could see it and the spatter in the concrete outside of the room if you squinted and stretched your neck. That balcony said, you don't know nobody being murdered by white folks like this now, knocked clean up out they shoes. Nobody blood on the concrete now. Act right and read *To Kill a Mockingbird*. Except you, skinny little you, want to tell that balcony about your cousin who got shot because the police say he pulled a gun on them, but the autopsy say the bullets entered his back. That balcony said to us, this is what will happen to y'all ashy ass if you speak out, too. And also, you free now, so be grateful and take your math test seriously and register to vote. It also said, by this blood, white people have been made maybe a little bit less likely to explicitly infringe on your First Amendment rights. James Earl Ray was just one sick white man, not at all representative of all white folks. Your cousin was a bad Black boy called Boo who thought he was free. James Earl Ray and those cops that pull us over and threaten us and the cops that beat Rodney King (maybe folks are just really mad at people whose last names are King?) are anomalies, bad apples, who just haven't yet been to the museum. Even though they were living in houses and spending money that was the rotten spoil of what they had done to Black people, most white folks just didn't know what some of them had done to us. The textbooks kept them ignorant of the role they had played and how they benefited, so it really wasn't their fault that they didn't know. But now they know so everything is repaired now. White people are better now because of this museum. By His blood on the balcony—can you see it there? Look harder—all lives are saved.

We wasn't actually allowed to tell nobody we was tired afterwards, in our bones and blood, so we kept our weariness deep inside us, simmering on low with a little salt. We were the young, strong inheritors of King's dream, made flesh through our grit and grind and good grades. We had a lot of opportunities our daddies and grandmama 'nem didn't have. Like the opportunity to not be terrorized with dogs or hoses or white ladies with their mouths pulled wide open with wishes for our deaths, only with bullying and displacement and resentment, when we try to go to school with them. Or the opportunity to live in neighborhoods the white folks left in good condition for us, even though they might have been adjacent to chemical plants. And, of course, and perhaps most important, we now have the opportunity to wonder, wander, wonder, through the simulacra of post-racial America, whether that unjust thing that happened to us (when white folks were coincidentally involved) had to do with our race or our individual karma.

We also wasn't really allowed to be mad about the death of King or what we had seen in that museum, just like we wasn't allowed to say we was tired. It was time for our sack lunch on the sidewalk under that wreath, under that balcony. You have more opportunities now. Wasn't no museums like this when we were growing up. (But my Mama is a museum, and I know my grandmama was a museum when she was only a mama.) You better stop mumbling under your breath. Anyway, like Jesus you know from Sunday School and from listening outside your auntie door at night when her friend is over, Martin Luther King, Jr., was a King who did miracles. And like Jesus, he was destined to die. That was just that. He died for our sins of protesting and rioting that brought him here and embarrassed him when he was here. His prophecy came in dreams. He went to the mountaintop in them. And he died so we could be free. Say your grace over your sack lunch. Be glad you got a sack lunch.

Ms. Jacqueline Smith was down there across from the Museum talking about gentrification before white folks even came up with terms like "preservation" and "revitalization" to describe the foolproof Negro removal in which they had been engaged since the 1950s in downtown Memphis. We didn't know what gentrification was because we lived in neighborhoods white folks would never be interested in, in the neighborhoods they had fled on their ever-extending trek to the east of the city. But Ms. Jackie did, and she knew the Museum was part of it way before the first brewery popped up. She knew the end of the Lorraine meant the inevitable end of all kinds of low-income housing, and therefore Black housing, around downtown. Atlanta had begun the demolition of housing projects to make room for Olympic possibilities. Memphis would be next, and there would be no affordable housing for us. King would have wanted affordable housing instead of a Museum, she would say.

They never let us get close to Ms. Jackie on the school fieldtrips, but we might sneak as close as we dared if we finished our sack lunches early and the teachers were still huddled talking while we waited for the yellow buses to come and take us back to our segregated schools. She had worked as a clerk at the Lorraine Motel and also lived there for a time, we learned in our brief conversations with her, always looking over the shoulder to see if the teachers were looking. When the Lorraine closed in the 1970s, she did not imagine it would return as what she might call a worship site for King's death. The Museum was like a long Groundhog Day funeral, King living and then dying and then being resurrected by each visitor to die again on the balcony. Ms. Jackie, her signs, her table, her literature, her seats, her sofa—they were all artifacts of a protest present and future. Her signs told us this museum was wrong and we were wrong for looking for King's bloodstains. We needed more than our Mama Museums, who would get fragile. But we needed places to live, too. I didn't know then that Jackie was the real museum to visit.

By 18, we had stopped going to the museum like we stopped going to church (or at least our Mama or grandma 'nem church) after we moved out from under grown folks' roof. The museum hadn't changed much, but we had in the nine years since it had opened, over those nine years of semi-annual trips: inside to learn about a lot of white bad apples and the resilience and hope of our heroes and leaders, outside ashy to squint at bloodstains, down to pray over our sack lunches under the balcony, and over to ease our musty selves close to Jackie, curious to learn something we hadn't in the museum. The clash of its sameness and our difference made us impatient with its fixity. In particular, I had learned how truly gangsta Rosa Parks was, and I was fire hot with how they had her stone figure sitting there. I knew damn well she ain't want to be no stone figure, and I knew damn well how much restraint it took for her not to beat that bus driver every night.

When the Museum opened the conspiracy appendage of itself across the street in the building where James Earl Ray allegedly took that shot, or where he said he took it and then later said he didn't, it was clear the Museum had doubled down on the themed experience of this One Spectacular Black Death. From that building, you could look out onto the balcony just like James Earl Ray said he did then didn't, aim your eyes at the wreath outside Room 306 like a posthumous target, and imagine what Ray, a bad apple, was thinking before he might have done it.

Then when the Museum redesigned itself in the Obama era, bringing in the best Negro historians from all over the country to gentrify the story of civil rights, it was clear it had doubled down on the interests of its white funders and the containment of history in a dark building, rather than pivoting towards the diverse Black history happening right then, bright and messy in the now Memphis streets. Stationed in the "Black Power" section of the Museum last fall to provide some additional context for students matriculating the liberal arts college that semester, I watched on loop a video that subsumed the Black Lives Matter movement, perhaps the clearest contemporary tie to the Museum's narrative, under an umbrella of "global protest" that included all kinds of uprisings of the decade. There is only one movement, however diversely populated, concerned explicitly with eradicating anti-Blackness from the core of our nation's social institutions, I told the freshmen, these new Memphians I had influence over and desperately needed to be on the side of now Memphis.

When those good Negro historians came, unaware of the now Memphis, the Museum underwent its own kind of internal gentrification, or revitalization, in tandem with the changes around it. Long a bastion of the respectable history of the civil rights movement, and in particular a proponent of respectable, non-violent forms of protest, it increasingly applied these logics to its interpretation of Black Memphians and its interpretation of itself as a social justice brand. It brought James Pate's charcoal series "Kin Killing Kin," which depicts young Black men in Ku Klux Klan hats in the act of shooting each other, to provoke a conversation about youth violence, or, to divert attention from its complicity in conditions that destabilize Black communities. Most recently, at the behest of funders, it attempted to silence a journalist's structural critiques of ongoing racial disparities in Memphis. We belong in the Museum less now than we did on our school fieldtrips.

Maybe that's what Ms. Jackie was trying to tell us about gentrification. I would call the condos that have gone up around the Museum, around the site of King's last breath, "luxury" because that is the parlance today that lets everyone know that we are now talking gentrification, displacement, and inequality. But there's nothing luxury about the trite, overpriced white boxes with their kitschly refurbished historic exteriors that people are willing to live in to avoid poor people and Black people and especially poor Black people.

Jackie had called the Museum a tourist trap, but they called it an anchor institution, a community good, a force for change, a site of social justice. They talked about it in terms of tourist dollars and economic impact. An arts district grew up around it, complete with warehouses-turned-artist-housing, galleries, microbreweries, fine dining, yoga studios, and distilleries. The Museum is the Black hole around which this constellation of white economies, the ones of new Memphis, thrives.

Memphis might be the only chocolate city in which the quintessential Martin Luther King, Jr. Boulevard is not in a Black neighborhood. That's because its new name came after Black folks had mostly been moved away already, after Obama was president. Its renaming encourages and emboldens the gentrification along its two miles, which begins in the east near the medical district, passes the FedEx Forum basketball arena, and ends at the river. I be sitting at the bar at the southeast intersection of Main and Martin Luther King, Jr. Avenue and having a $12 cocktail with my last cash and looking out the window and seeing that sign and thinking, "Thank you, Dr. Martin Luther King," for the money to enjoy this rosemary garnish in this bar with mostly white patrons and white owners and white staff. If I am lucky, I'll get a new Memphis job at a company that will rent out the Museum for a fun end-of-the-year event so we can have an opportunity to go there without an ancestral or curricular imperative. Though one of my white co-workers might regale me with their love and knowledge of civil rights history and how their "kinda conservative" parents were brought to tears when they brought them to the Museum and so forth, those microaggressions will be a small price to pay for a less dutiful sort of trip to the Museum. Or maybe I won't never have one of those new Memphis jobs. Syke. New Memphians don't have cousins who been shot by the police or daddies whose noses were broken by the county cops. Maybe new Memphians don't have cousins at all.

What is the mood like in Memphis 50 years after the assassination of King? What's it like to be the poorest large Black city in the country and the city that killed a man leading a campaign advocating for poor people at the same time? What about that bankruptcy and environmental racism and foreclosure and infant mortality? How you—is it "y'all"?—feel about all of this police surveillance? Where is the best barbecue/soul food? You say your little cousin was shot in the back by police before social media? Is the dream continuing here, where his blood was spilled? Is this ground zero for the civil rights movement? Is the dream now a nightmare? How can we keep King's dreams alive? Do you know a sanitation worker? About this mountaintop: Are we there yet? Will we ever get there? Was his blood the magic?

Our mood is that low, salty, stank ass simmer of weariness of the same, that stale midsummer mustiness, that heaviness of a viscous mourning we haven't been able to put down because King and our cousins and friends are murdered and resurrected to be murdered again. We are tired of unfulfilled dreams, dreams deferred, cranes in the sky, and raisins in the sun. If we must be committed to the grotesque—the spectacle of our deaths as well as of the impunity with which our murderers smile and strut about like roosters—then we want some different kinds of museums. A museum for Duanna Johnson in North Memphis that houses Black trans folks. Ones for Steven Askew in that apartment parking lot not too far for my old high school, for Darrius Stewart on Winchester, for the baby Dorian Harris in that North Memphis yard, and for my cousin Boo in South Memphis, that house young Black folks. Some Mama museums.

We been trying to adjudicate the meaning of the civil rights movement since before we were born, since people died for us to vote, and to sit with white folks, to live with white folks, to have our silver rights, our equal opportunity, our integrated schools, our affirmative action. Or, we have been doing it since the state and its extrajudicial arms, radicalized by the Constitution, have been murdering Black people. We been doing it since 1968. We been wanting to know who really did what and thought what, and to what end, because we are trying to figure out why it didn't take. In Memphis in particular, because we been taught that King's death made us free, we especially have been trying to understand by so many means what exactly went wrong. Moreover, we want to know, what kind of freedom is this? As we lay dying, we here have been unlearning that lie.

Questions for Discussion and Journaling

1. As you read, take out a piece of paper or open a blank document on your computer and write down any word, phrase, or name you don't know or understand. Each time you write something down, pause and do some research online in order to define that word or learn about the phrase or person. As you do your research, write what you learn down. Bring this list of words, phrases, names, and definitions to class (note: write down both words that you don't know because they are slang and words you don't know because they are academic). When you come to class, you and your classmates will discuss the words you all didn't know, the words only some of you didn't know, and the reasons for the similarities and differences in your lists. As you create your list, remember that there is no shame in not knowing a word. Not understanding something is simply an opportunity to learn something new.

2. Robinson writes, "But my Mama is a museum, and I know my grandmama was a museum when she was only a mama." What do you think she means by this statement? How is this statement important to the article and to the author's argument? Keeping this in mind, what is the thesis of "Real Museums of Memphis"?

3. Write a 2-page reflection on your emotional reaction to Robinson's words. What emotions did you experience as you read? Sadness? Anger? Guilt? Nostalgia? Grief? Something else? What lines or memories conjured these emotions? Did Robinson's words challenge or support beliefs about the U.S., Memphis, or life more generally that are important to you? If so, which beliefs did she challenge or confirm?

    To help you understand your emotional reaction to the piece, try using self-distanced language as you think and write. Self-distancing is a technique discovered by psychologists that helps with emotional self-regulation. To do this, don't ask yourself "why do I feel this way"? Instead, replace "I" with your name (i.e., Why did Katie feel/react in this way?); by changing the language you are using to think and write, you can distance yourself from your emotions and better evaluate them. Doing this is especially important when reading about a topic you feel strongly about (whether those strong feelings are in agreement or disagreement with the author's claims) because we are less likely to critically examine an argument if we agree with the argument's conclusions, and we are more likely to dismiss an argument without critical examination if we disagree with the conclusions or if they challenge our beliefs. Thus, as you continue to hone your critical reading and thinking skills, learning to pause and reflect on your emotional response is an important skill that allows you to be more open-minded and empathetic, and both of these qualities will improve the rhetorical skills that you use when reading and creating your own arguments.

THE SOUL OF MEMPHIS

Jamie Katz

In Jamie Katz's "The Soul of Memphis," we are given a succinct yet intimate review/travel story of the writer's trip to the birthplace of rock 'n' roll and home of the blues. Written for the *Smithsonian* magazine website in April 2010, Katz effortlessly captures the flavor of Mid-South and Mississippi River Delta culture, praising Memphis for its "realness" and the inspiration that seemingly flows through the city's veins. His tone is undoubtedly romantic and tinged with local color, despite this being his first visit. Note how he appeals to the reader's sense of adventure (a pathetic appeal), arguing that despite the often negative portrayal of the city at the national level, Memphis matters. In his conclusion, Katz proudly argues that Memphis is a metropolis worth cherishing—a town that can at once be revered for its significant cultural contributions and wear its scars for all to see.

Forty years after Martin Luther King's assassination, a feisty city fights to get its groove back.

IF YOU LOOK CAREFULLY, you can find dozens of white birdhouses perched atop tall metal poles all over downtown Memphis—a chalet here, a pagoda there—each one carefully fashioned. They add a touch of whimsy to a town that has known its share of trouble. "People like them," says Henry Turley, the philanthropic-minded real-estate developer who erected them. "I'm proud of those birdhouses."

There's more to those little birdhouses, though, than you might suppose. They sprung up because Turley has concentrated his business efforts in and around the older, westernmost part of his hometown—territories that are all within attack range of the Mississippi River, if you happen to be a mosquito. That's no small matter in a city whose population was decimated by yellow fever epidemics in the 1870s.

"People complained that it's impossible to live near the river because it breeds mosquitoes," Turley says in an elegant drawl. "So I put up the birdhouses to attract purple martins, which are supposed to eat thousands of mosquitoes on the wing. But mosquitoes don't like flowing water. So it's bullshit." He savors this last word, breaking it in two, even singing it slightly. "And it's bullshit about the purple martins killing them," he adds. "I'm fighting a myth with a myth."

A man of sly humor and earthy charm, the silvery-haired Turley, 66, fits in with a long line of original characters in local lore—from Gen. Andrew Jackson, who co-founded Memphis in 1819 on what was then known as the fourth Chickasaw bluff, to E.H. "Boss" Crump, the machine politician who ran the city for the first half of the 20th century, to W.C. Handy, B.B. King, Elvis Presley and a disproportionate number of other musicians who've inspired and delighted people across the globe.

In fact, you can't get much more Memphian than Turley. His great-grandfather, Thomas Battle Turley, was the grandson of one of the Bluff City's earliest white settlers; he served as a Confederate rifleman, was wounded at Shiloh and Peachtree Creek, and later became a prominent lawyer and populist U.S. Senator (D.–Tenn.) at the turn of the 20th century. But Henry Turley's stellar reputation has nothing to do with rebellion—or birdhouses—and everything to do with what happened in Memphis after the Rev. Martin Luther King Jr. was assassinated on the balcony of the Lorraine Motel on April 4, 1968.

Forty years have passed since that traumatic event and the riots that followed. The more immediate consequence, however, was an acceleration of inner-city decay that was already well underway, thanks to continuing racial disharmony, white flight, tax-advantaged suburban development, the rise of automobile culture and the decline of Memphis's economic mainstays—especially King Cotton. Many businesses and homeowners gravitated toward paler suburban havens east of Memphis, such as Germantown and Collierville. But a hardy few, notably Turley and his oft-times partner Jack Belz—who reopened downtown's historic Peabody Hotel in 1981—stood firm. And the heart of old Memphis has steadily regained its rhythm ever since. Several Turley-Belz developments have earned widespread acclaim, such as Harbor Town, the New Urbanist community on Mud Island, or South Bluffs, a cobble-stoned enclave overlooking the Mississippi not far from the old Lorraine Motel, a slice of which survives as a wing of the National Civil Rights Museum.

Especially close to Turley's heart these days is an ambitious, racially integrated, mixed-income project called Uptown that he has undertaken with Belz and the city government. They're creating some 1,000 attractive single-family homes, fostering small businesses and carving out green spaces throughout a residential area just north of the renowned St. Jude's Children's Research Center—a 100-block section Turley says was probably the most degraded part of the city. And the new houses don't all look alike. "We're trying to make a nice neighborhood to live in, even if you happen to be poor," he says.

Though he helped turn the tide downtown and transform whole neighborhoods, Turley denies having grand visions. He's more like a blues guitarist who builds a solo gradually, from one chorus to the next. "We set out in a sort of dreamy Memphis way," he says. "And remember, Memphis has a lot of freedom, Memphis is a place of creativity. I mean a pretty profound freedom, where there aren't so many social pressures to behave a certain way. In Memphis you can do any goddamned crazy thing you want to do."

On a broiling afternoon last July, Turley took me around to see a few of the crazy things he has done and tell me about some of the other Memphis mavericks he has known, such as his late buddy Sam Phillips. A white man from Florence, Alabama, Phillips broke the rules by embracing both country music and rhythm & blues; as a young DJ and sound engineer in Memphis, he recorded black bluesmen like B.B. King and Howlin' Wolf, and, in 1952, founded Sun Records, whose roster would eventually include not only Elvis, but Johnny Cash, Jerry Lee Lewis, Carl Perkins and Roy Orbison. Then there was Fred W. Smith, the ex-Marine fighter pilot who created overnight package delivery (Federal Express, in 1971), and Kemmons Wilson, who spotted opportunity in America's burgeoning highway culture and founded the first modern motel chain (Holiday Inn, in 1952). Another local visionary of commerce, Clarence Saunders, opened the nation's first self-service grocery store in Memphis in 1916, featuring such novelties as shopping baskets, aisle displays and checkout lines. He named it Piggly Wiggly. Within six years, there were 1200 of them spread across 29 states.

We ended the day at Turley's South Bluffs home, tearing into some carry-out from Gus's Fried Chicken along with Henry's wife, Lynne, who's a musician and teacher, and their guest Ann Coulter (no, not that one), who'd been named the first Turley Fellow in urban planning at the University of Memphis. As the sun finally melted into the pristine Arkansas woodland across the river, we sank into some sofas to enjoy a two-hour PBS documentary co-directed by Memphis author and filmmaker Robert Gordon called *Respect Yourself: The Story of Stax Records*, the Memphis label that rivaled Detroit's Motown Records in the 1960s as a purveyor of first-class soul music—think Otis Redding, Carla Thomas, Sam & Dave, Isaac Hayes, the Staple Singers, Booker T. and the MG's. Stax' raw, high-spirited music is a perfect emblem for Memphis. And Gordon's film is a powerful reminder of the racial currents and collisions—some of them positive—that have long given this city its distinctive cultural imprint.

THE TOURIST BROCHURES tout Memphis as the home of the blues and the birthplace of rock 'n' roll. Without a doubt, there are musical shrines and experiences few visitors would want to miss: the rollicking blues bars up and down historic Beale Street; the original Sun Studios on Union Avenue where that hopeful 18-year-old named Elvis wandered in one day from the nearby Lauderdale Courts public housing project; and, of course, the slightly eerie theme park that is Graceland. On top of that, Memphis has two remarkably lively museums devoted to its musical heritage—the Rock 'n' Soul Museum (a Smithsonian affiliate) and the Stax Museum of American Soul. Between them, they pay proper homage to the broad streams of influence—Delta blues, spirituals, bluegrass, gospel, hillbilly, Tin Pan Alley, Grand Ole Opry, rhythm & blues, jazz and pop—that converged in Memphis.

That rich culture is by no means moribund. As in New Orleans, especially before Katrina, music still thrives in Memphis in many of the traditional forms, but also in contemporary ones—a feisty alternative rock scene and a bouncy, bass-driven urban sound that influenced much of Southern hip-hop. There are great juke joints and blues bars nowhere near Beale

Street, and independent record stores, such as Midtown's Shangri-La and Goner Records, that strongly support Memphis artists. Local boy Justin Timberlake has conquered the international pop charts in recent years, and the Memphis rap group Three 6 Mafia won an Academy Award in 2006 for their song, "It's Hard Out Here for a Pimp" from the excellent film *Hustle & Flow*, directed by another Memphian, Craig Brewer. That side of Memphis life is omitted from the visitors' guides; the gritty Storyville district of Louis Armstrong's youth was no kiddie ride, either.

The assumption that Memphis's glory lies entirely in the past doesn't sit well with some of the younger musicians. "There's a little bit of resentment that when people talk about Memphis, they only talk about the blues and Elvis, limiting the possibility of Memphis as a cultural or progressive place," says Benjamin Meadows-Ingram, 29, a native Memphian and senior editor at *Vibe* magazine. But they agree that something about the city fosters their creativity. "Everyone is proud of Memphis, to a degree, even the people who hate it," Meadows-Ingram says. "Everyone feels they're from a place that *is* a place."

BEFORE I ARRIVED IN MEMPHIS, I hoped to get a better sense of just what makes it such a singular American place, to at least begin tapping into what Robert Gordon calls the "invisible bayou" that runs through the city's essence. As a first-timer, I also knew I'd have to bone up some, in advance.

The syllabus included movies set in Memphis, such as Jim Jarmusch's *Mystery Train*, and must-reads like Peter Guralnick's two-part Elvis biography and Taylor Branch's *At Canaan's Edge*, about America in the King years. The city crops up regularly in fiction, too. "Memphis aint a bad town, for them that like city life," writes William Faulkner, in *Light in August*. "It is a beautiful city, nobly situated on a commanding bluff overlooking the river," Mark Twain says in *Life On The Mississippi*, adding, "The streets are straight and spacious, though not paved in a way to incite distempered admiration." That's a polite way of saying he got some mud on his boots.

I also paid a call on Kenneth T. Jackson, 68, the well-known urban historian who holds the Jacques Barzun chair in history and social sciences at Columbia University and is a proud son of Memphis to boot: Four decades on New York's Morningside Heights haven't put a dent in his mid-South cadence. We were joined by his wife of 45 years, Barbara, a former high school English department chairman. They were college sweethearts at Memphis State (now the University of Memphis), and she keeps a Southern magnolia in their Mt. Kisco, N.Y., front yard as a reminder of home.

The couple has many fond memories of the Memphis they knew in the 1950s, when Boss Crump himself might appear with his entourage at a Friday night football game, passing out candy bars to the cheerleaders. "He had this long white hair, and he'd wear a white hat and a white suit—he was so dapper," Barbara said. "It was as if the guardian angel of Memphis had come down to mix among the people."

The Jacksons also remember tuning in to a wild man of a disk jockey named Dewey Phillips (no relation to Sam), who flagrantly disregarded the usual radio formats and conventions on his nightly WHBQ broadcast, *Red Hot & Blue*. His was possibly the first program of its kind in the U.S. with a devoted following in both the white and African-American communities, not only because of his zany, trash-talking style, but because he was spinning rhythm & blues records with an irresistible beat, regardless of whose feathers might be ruffled. (Rufus Thomas, the popular black Memphis DJ and R&B singer who recorded for Sun and eventually Stax, paid Phillips the wry compliment of calling him "a man who just happened to be white.") Dewey also had what Sam Phillips called "a platinum ear"—an unerring instinct for what would catch on, especially with a little push. It was Dewey Phillips who catapulted Elvis's career on the night of July 8, 1954, when he previewed Presley's spirited debut single, "That's All Right, Mama," playing it and praising it over and over into the evening until teenagers all around town were in a fever, then hauling the astonished young crooner out of a neighborhood movie theater to submit to his first interview ever. "Just don't say nothin' dirty," Phillips instructed him.

Though forward-looking music people like Dewey and Sam Phillips were playing havoc with the color line, segregation was still the law of the land throughout Dixie, and Ken Jackson tells of a systematic wrong that, needless to say, went considerably deeper than the oft-cited indignity of drinking fountains marked WHITE or COLORED.

Late one night in 1960 or '61, Jackson recalls, he was heading home from a date with Barbara when he came upon a horrific traffic accident. A bloody-faced man lay motionless in the street, and Jackson heard people moaning inside a flipped-over Oldsmobile. "I ran to a telephone to call for help, and the first question they asked me was, 'Are they colored or white?'" Jackson says. "I was totally unprepared for the question, because I hadn't really looked. But that's what they wanted to know, what kind of ambulance do you want us to send?" Even with lives on the line—and two people were killed—the dispatcher's priorities were skewed by color.

Race is the inescapable starting point for understanding Memphis, Jackson maintains. "There's a famous saying that the Mississippi Delta begins in the lobby of the Peabody Hotel and ends on Catfish Row in Vicksburg. It's a rich agricultural area, drained by the river, that is part of what's known as the Black Belt—that's where the highest percentage of the African-American population lives in the state of Mississippi. And Memphis is the only large city between St. Louis and New Orleans, a good 700-mile stretch of river," he said.

"Memphis grew up as a commercial *entrepôt*, a trading center for cotton, slaves, hardwood lumber and livestock—it was even the world's largest mule market, right into the 1950s," Jackson said. "By the turn of the last century, Memphis had become the unofficial capital of both cotton culture and the Black Belt. Beale Street was the cultural heart of the African-American world and arguably the most famous black street in the United States."

Today, Memphis's population of over 670,000 is 64 percent black. Not coincidentally, the nation's 17th largest city is also the eighth poorest (trailing Cleveland, Miami, St. Louis, Cincinnati and a just a few others), and it has the sad distinction of owning the highest infant mortality rate in the U.S., with twice the national average.

In October 2006, Jackson challenged an audience of local notables at Memphis's Rhodes College to recognize that the city had partly itself to blame for losing ground over the past half-century to Atlanta, Dallas and other Southern cities. High crime, political corruption, a failure to address race relations constructively, the abandonment of downtown—all played a part, he said. Yet Jackson hasn't given up, either. "I think cities can change," he said. "If New York can do it, why the hell can't Memphis do it?" At a time when many cities have lost their distinctive character, Jackson thinks it's worth it. "Memphis still has soul," he said simply.

I CLOSED MY EYES on the flight from New York, lulled by an all-Memphis iPod playlist heavy on soul legend Al Green and underappreciated jazzmen such as Phineas Newborn Jr., George Coleman, Charles Lloyd and Jimmie Lunceford (who recruited the nucleus of his famed Swing Era band from his music students at Memphis's Manassas High School). When the pilot announced our descent to Memphis International Airport, I flipped up the window shade to find column after column of fiercely billowing thunderheads, awesomely charged by the energy and heat below. We shuddered through the clouds into a vista of flat, lush farmland edging into suburban developments with curlicued street plans, then, near the airport, a series of immense truck terminals and warehouses. On the runway, I glimpsed the vast fleet of purple-tailed FedEx jets that largely account for Memphis International's ranking as the world's busiest cargo airport—beating Hong Kong by a neck. LAX handles about half the tonnage, by way of comparison.

All this impersonal hugeness teed me up for the genuinely warm greeting I received at the Talbot Heirs Guesthouse, within a few blocks of Beale Street and the major downtown enticements. Tom and Sandy Franck have run Talbot Heirs since 2005, when their middle daughter Dana, a Hollywood film and TV producer and University of Memphis alumna, made an offer to buy the place if her parents would consent to operate it. "I never thought she could swing the deal, so I agreed," Tom said. "And here we are."

They run it as if guests were family. It's a tiny boutique hotel across South 2nd Street from the much grander Peabody, and it's easy to miss. As I pulled up the block, there was Sandy, looking like a coffeehouse singer in her blue jeans and straight blonde hair, waiting to flag me down. We were fast friends by the time she showed me up to my room, one of only eight in the hotel, each with its own personality and witty touches. On one wall, there was a colorful hand-painted sign reading BE NICE OR LEAVE, in a wooden frame fringed by beer bottle caps, by New Orleans folk artist Dr. Bob. (Another version of it hangs in the nearby Center For Southern Folklore.) And on the bathroom wall, they'd hung a small portrait of Sigmund Freud, looking awfully stern. "Some of our guests are amused by that photo," Sandy said. "But one lady wasn't. After she checked out I found the picture hidden in the vanity under the sink."

Best of all, my digs came equipped with a stereo system and a baby grand piano that once belonged to Bobby Whitlock, of Derek and the Dominoes (who recorded "Layla" with Eric Clapton). And the walls were thick enough that you could make a joyful noise without disturbing hotel guests.

It was time to hit the streets. To get the lay of the land, I jumped aboard the Main Street trolley at the Union Avenue stop around the corner. It was a pleasant initiation: The trolley lines loop through downtown and along the river, passing a number of local landmarks, and the trolleys themselves are beautifully restored trams from cities as far-flung as Oporto, Portugal, and Melbourne, Australia, with brass fittings, hand-carved mahogany corbels and antique lighting fixtures. At every turn, the conductor pointed out highlights and curiosities in a melodious accent that was hard to pin down. Louisiana Cajun, maybe?

"No, sir, I'm from Kurdistan, in Iran," allowed the conductor, Jafar Banion. "I've been in and out of Memphis since '85. I trained to be an aviation mechanic, but now I'm doing this. I enjoy showing people what's what. There's plenty to talk about."

One of those things, nestled in the heart of downtown, is AutoZone Park, home of baseball's Triple-A Memphis Redbirds; Banion informed us that the new ballpark—the minor leagues' answer to Baltimore's delightful Camden Yards—is also earthquake-proof. It's a good thing, too, since Memphis lies at the southern end of the New Madrid seismic fault system; in 1812, a titanic quake temporarily caused a portion of the Mississippi to run backwards. Banion also pointed out the 29-story Sterick Building, which was the tallest building in the South when it was built in 1930, but now stands empty. Soon we caught sight of the Pyramid—the 32-story stainless steel-clad arena on the banks of the Mississippi—a nod to Memphis's Egyptian namesake (and sister city) on the Nile. Though the Pyramid has been eclipsed as a sports and convention center by the newer FedEx Center, it remains the most striking feature of the Memphis skyline. "Every time I see it, it reminds me of my uncle and his camels," Banion said, laughing.

The lower end of the trolley route swings through the South Main Arts District, which is dotted with lofts, galleries and eateries, among them the Arcade Restaurant, Memphis's oldest, where you can sip a malted in Elvis's favorite booth or imagine GI's drifting in from the train station down the block for a home-style Southern breakfast, with country ham & eggs & grits & biscuits & gravy, and a bottomless cup o' joe...

THE LORRAINE MOTEL is just a short walk from the Arcade and a half-mile south of Beale Street. In its day, it beckoned as a clean, full-service establishment with decent food—one of the only lodgings in Memphis that welcomed African-Americans, among them visiting celebrities such as Count Basie, Sarah Vaughan and Nat King Cole. Even after the Civil Rights Act of 1964 dismantled legal barriers, the Lorraine was that rare place where blacks and whites could mingle comfortably. In hot weather, a mixed group of musicians might drop in from recording sessions at Stax, which had no air conditioning, to cool off in the Lorraine swimming pool. They also got some work done. Guitarist Steve Cropper—one of several white artists who were integral to the Stax sound—co-wrote "In the Midnight Hour" with Wilson Pickett just a few doors down from No. 306, the $13-a-night room where Dr. King customarily stayed.

Shortly after 6 p.m. on the evening of April 4, 1968, the civil rights leader stood outside that room, bantering with friends down in the parking lot. One of them was a respected Memphis saxophone player named Ben Branch, who was scheduled to perform at a mass rally later on. "Ben, make sure you play 'Precious Lord, Take My Hand' in the meeting tonight," Dr. King called out. "Play it real pretty." Those were his last words. There is no sight in Memphis more heart-stopping today than the Lorraine Motel.

Barbara Andrews, 54, has been curator of the adjoining National Civil Rights Museum since 1992, but she is still moved by the reaction of people who make the pilgrimage. "It is a very emotional place," she said. "You see people crying, you see people sitting in silence, thinking about what they're seeing."

The exhibits wind through a series of rooms that march forward in time, recapitulating the movement's painful yet determined journey from abolitionism and the Underground Railroad to the breakthroughs of the 1950s and '60s. You can board a early '50s–vintage city bus from Montgomery, Alabama, and sit up front near a life-sized plaster statue of Rosa Parks; every minute or so, a looped recording of the driver commands her to get back. ("No!" snapped 16-year-old Durand Hines of St. Louis, in town for a family reunion.) The narrative moves on to Birmingham and Selma and Dr. King's work in Chicago and the Memphis sanitation workers' strike of 1968. And then, as you approach his carefully preserved motel rooms and the balcony door, you hear a recording of Mahalia Jackson singing "Precious Lord" with a calm, irresistible power, as she did at Dr. King's funeral:

Precious Lord, take my hand,

Lead me on, let me stand,

I am tired, I am weak, I am worn.

Through the storm, through the night,

Lead me on to the light.

Take my hand, precious Lord,

Lead me home.

Not everyone makes it all the way to the balcony. "I remember walking the late Barbara Jordan through the museum—actually I was pushing her wheelchair—and she did pretty well through most of the exhibits," Andrews said. "But by the time we had come around by Chicago—you could hear Mahalia singing—she asked that I turn back. She said she knew how this ends. It was just too much for her to bear."

I asked Andrews about the lingering effects of the assassination on Memphis, and about race relations generally.

"This is still a very race-driven city, it's always about black and white, and I think a lot of that has to do with the fact that Dr. King was killed here," she said. "But Memphis has opened up and changed quite a bit. When I first came here I felt like there was a cloud, a very low ceiling over the city. Somehow it hadn't made the leap to the 20th century. Now there's an overwhelming number of organizations that are attempting to build bridges, to address the issues of race, the separateness. But I'm not sure it's really getting at the heart of the matter, which has to do with economics as much as race."

Andrews says she is taken, though, with the change she sees in the generation coming up now. "They're not interested in anything that separates people, whether it's the music, the food, whatever—it's all Southern. People are really rooted here, especially in the music. You can find white folks in their 30s and 40s who know every word to a Rufus Thomas song, and I know that in Dayton, Ohio, where I grew up, I'd have to look long and hard to find somebody who knew all the words to a Rufus Thomas song. So even though people were separated, in many ways they share the same kinds of affinities and affection for the things that make Memphis Memphis," she said.

EXACTLY FIVE YEARS AND 13 DAYS after the King assassination, on April 17, 1973, a single Dassault Falcon 20C—a small, French-built aircraft modeled on the Mystère fighter—took off from Memphis bearing the first Federal Express overnight package. That night, 14 Falcons carried 186 packages to 25 cities. The original jet is now on display at the Smithsonian National Air and Space Museum.

Fred W. Smith had dreamed of creating such a service as an undergrad at Yale, where he was a flying buddy of John Kerry and a frat brother of George W. Bush. During two tours of duty in Vietnam, where Smith flew more than 200 combat missions, he gained valuable exposure to complex logistical operations. It paid off. Today FedEx is a $35 billion company serving 220 countries and handling more than 7.5 million shipments daily. Its 672 airplanes constitute the largest civilian fleet in the world. Needless to say, its impact on Memphis, where FedEx has its world headquarters, is enormous. "Memphis without Fred Smith and FedEx is hard to conceive," says Henry Turley. "I mean, when they talk about the Second Coming, I always think, which one? FedEx is the economic engine. Everything else is drawn by FedEx."

A sizable percentage of the stuff America buys, sells and transports passes through Memphis: Even apart from its air cargo supremacy, it is the fourth largest inland port in the U.S., it ranks third in Class I rail freight service, and, with seven intersecting Federal and Interstate highways, it is the third-leading trucking corridor in America, within an overnight haul of 75 percent of the nation's population. A long list of companies, such as Williams-Sonoma, Nike, Pfizer and Ford Motor, have set up major distribution operations in and around the city, as have time-critical enterprises from law firms to medical device manufacturers, who benefit from the later drop-off deadlines. Memphis also has a significant concentration of expertise in supply-chain management and logistics.

With all that in mind, I felt that one of the quintessential Bluff City experiences had to be a visit to the FedEx SuperHub, where an average of 3.3 million packages are sorted and loaded onto planes and trucks every day. Unfortunately, the facility is generally off-limits to visitors, for security reasons. Luckily, their PR folks are sympathetic to an itinerant scribbler, though not before you pass a background check.

I was shepherded around by Steve Taylor, 43, who began here as a package handler in 1984 and is now a manager in the SuperHub control room. He took me into the cavernous West Matrix (there's also an East Matrix)—where 42 automated sorting lines distribute a rapid flow of packages. The noise level is deafening. Handlers must wear ear plugs, back belts and steel-toed shoes. Some 300 miles of conveyor belt criss-cross the sprawling facility, whose pace intensifies after 11 p.m. to honor the company's on-time delivery promises. "At night, we gang-tackle everything, we double-team everything," Taylor said. "We're sorting 160,000 packages an hour."

The cargo isn't always inanimate: Tian Tian and Mei Xiang, a pair of giant pandas from Chengdu, China, were FedExed to the National Zoo in Washington, D.C., in 2000. Rumor has it they were upgraded to business class for better paw-room and tossed fresh bamboo shoots instead of the usual bag of peanuts. Taylor took me aboard a DC-10 to see the bare metal interior of the fuselage, which included a handful of jump seats that once allowed FedEx people to hitch rides all over. "That ended on 9/11," he said.

FedEx employs 280,000 people, 30,000 in Memphis, where they are by far the city's largest employer. Glenn D. Sessoms, 53, an executive vice president who has been with FedEx since 1982, sees those jobs as a key to undoing the legacies of poverty and racial inequality. "Think about it—there's probably about 2,000 or more African-Americans on my 3500-person shift here," he said. "Well, a lot of them are managers, team leaders and ramp agents. A lot of them make a lot of money because of FedEx. If they weren't here, what would they be doing? A lot less, maybe."

Sessoms, who is himself African-American, came to Memphis in 1994 and never looked back. "I jumped into the city," he said. "I got very involved with the Civil Rights Museum. It is a springboard for telling people how you can transform a place—it's not just what an individual can accomplish, but a group of people. I feel good about the sports here, the energy around the University of Memphis Tigers, about the new NBA team, about my golf game. I can play golf where I want to."

Not infrequently, Sessoms said, he finds himself in settings where the clientele is all affluent whites, the help all black.

"This is still fundamentally a racially divided city," he said. "But I think people are starting to figure out how can we live better together, support one another's agendas." He serves on several charitable boards and has chaired Memphis's United Way drive. "You've got kids, right? Your kids are crazy, right?" I took the Fifth. "My kids are crazy, too!" he continued, undeterred. "We've got the same issues goin' on, whether we're black, white, male, female, Jewish, Hispanic, Asian, whatever. We're trying to raise a family, take care of business, enjoy life, take a vacation every once in a while. And hopefully, people will remember us when we die. The goal is, how do we get along better, and how do we make it so everyone can achieve what they want to achieve?"

Sessoms pointed out his office window to the airport tarmac, where FedEx handlers were toiling on one of the hottest days of the year. "It's hard work out here," he said. "Especially when it's 98 degrees out, which means it's 110 down there. But people who work here have pride. They can say, 'I'm throwing packages out here in the heat, but I've got a good job with good benefits. I'm wearing a uniform.'" And they're the backbone of FedEx, Sessoms said. "I'm an executive vice president. If I don't come to work, we're okay. If *they* don't come to work, we're S.O.L."

"What's that?" I asked.

"Shit outta luck."

ONE OF MEMPHIS'S MOST CHERISHED rituals has been around twice as long as FedEx, with a similar record of punctuality: the daily procession of the Peabody Ducks. At precisely 11 a.m. and 5 p.m., as hundreds of delighted spectators look on, the famed mallards waddle through the hotel lobby to the strains of John Philip Sousa's "King Cotton March," commuting to and from their day job, which consists of splashing around an ornate travertine fountain and nibbling on cornmeal treats. For half a century, the ducks were marshaled through this ceremony by the late Peabody bellman Edward Pembroke, whose portrait now hangs in the hotel entrance. Today the responsibility rests with 34-year-old Jason Sensat, who acquired one of the world's great job titles—Peabody Duckmaster—in 2007. "They asked me in the interview if I could handle five ducks," he said. "I told them, I've got a 5-year-old daughter and 2-year-old son. Five ducks are gonna be no problem."

The hotel was kind enough to offer me an honorary duckmastership for a day, which would have put me in the rarefied company of such past transients as Emeril Lagasse and Queen Noor of Jordan. On the day I came, however, that role was already being filled by 11-year-old Ian Murtha, of Harrisburg, Pa., whose parents had evidently sprung for the hotel's $290 Ducky Day family package. I tagged along as the ducks marched from their rooftop cage into a wood-paneled elevator, where they patiently mingled with the Murthas and the crimson-jacketed duckmaster. As we descended, Sensat was alerted via intercom that the music was cueing up. "Now, the hardest part of my job," he said, counting....*one, two*... "It's all a timing thing. Downstairs they're playing a little narration, and it should be timed perfectly so that by the time we get down there, there's a little drum roll, then Sousa's march will start playing, the doors will open, and we'll head right out on the red carpet." It all went according to plan.

Since there are several restaurants on the premises, I asked Kelly Earnest, the hotel's PR director, the obvious question.

"No, we don't serve duck *à l'orange* anywhere in the Peabody," she reassured me. "We have probably the only French restaurant in the world that doesn't serve duck."

ACTUALLY, THERE ARE SAID TO BE some excellent high-end restaurants in Memphis. I never found out. I came for the fine swine: barbecue. The Memphis variety is all about pork—ribs or shoulder meat, prepared "dry" (with a spicy rub) or "wet" (with a basted-on sauce). Is Memphis the barbecue capital of America? Damned if I know. But I can report that local standards are mighty high, and Memphians do swap mouth-watering tales about obscure neighborhood rib joints: Fantasizing about barbecue may be the next best thing to pigging out. If you feel the urge, you can join the 90,000 hog-heaven seekers who gather down by the river each May for Memphis's World Championship Barbecue Cooking Contest. I can think of worse ways to achieve heartburn.

I tried hard, popping Tums all the way. The best of the best? I'm tempted to nominate the much-celebrated Rendezvous, tucked away in a downtown passageway called General Washburn's Alley (after a Union general who fled in his nightclothes during the famous cavalry raid led by the rebel Gen. Nathan Bedford Forrest in 1864). But then there's this converted Exxon service station out on Lamar Avenue. That would be Payne's Bar-B-Q. Walk past the gumball machine into a large room with a salmon-colored cinderblock wall. Belly up to the counter and order one "chopped hot"—a pork shoulder sandwich on a soft bun with hot sauce and some mustardy slaw. Crunchy on the outside, smoky tender inside. With a can of Diet Coke, it comes to $4.10—possibly the greatest culinary bargain in America.

Payne's was opened in 1972 by the late Horton Payne, whose widow, Flora Payne, 59, carries on the tradition. I asked her how business was going. "It's holding its own," she said. "Damn right!" thundered a customer nearing the counter. "Give me two just like his, all right, baby?" She flashed a tiny smile and turned toward the kitchen.

But the heavyweight champ has to be Cozy Corner, at the intersection of North Avenue and Manassas. The sign over the front door is hand-lettered. The charcoal cooker is just inside. The founder and original pitmaster, the late Ray Robinson, was Memphis barbecue royalty. I ordered the ribs. White bread makes a good napkin to sop up what happens next. My sauce-splattered notes from that foray consist of two words: the first is "Holy"; the second is unreadable. Smokes, maybe.

SORRY, MR. STEINBRENNER, but the eats at a Memphis Redbirds game are *way* better than anything at Yankee Stadium. You can even get some of the same Rendezvous grub they serve at the restaurant, just a block away. Not only that, but the tickets are cheap, the people are friendly, the sightlines are all good, and the ballpark is just around the corner from most of the downtown hotels. But even in commodious, family-friendly AutoZone Park, it's baseball, not food, that's the attraction.

I ambled over one night to see Memphis take on the Sacramento River Cats, and especially to watch the Redbirds' Rick Ankiel—whose improbable tale will be familiar to most baseball fans.

Ankiel shined as a flame-throwing 20-year-old rookie in 2000, pitching for the parent club, the St. Louis Cardinals. But then he suffered a spectacular meltdown in the playoffs, throwing five wild pitches in a single inning—after which he was never quite the same. Now, having reinvented himself as a slugging center fielder, he was leading the International League in home runs and was clearly on the verge of a dramatic return to the majors.

Ankiel didn't hit one out that night against the River Cats, but he did make a defensive play I won't soon forget. With a runner on third and one out, a batter hit a high fly to center. As Ankiel parked under it, the runner tagged, challenging the ex-pitcher's famed arm. He uncorked a cannon shot straight to home plate without a bounce, freezing the runner at third. The guy who had lost the ability to throw strikes from the pitcher's mound had just thrown one from dead center.

A week later, Ankiel was shipped upriver to St. Louis, where he made a theatrical re-entrance, lofting a three-run homer on his comeback night and continuing his torrid hitting for weeks. Invigorated by Ankiel's storybook return, the Cardinals made a serious charge for the pennant—until he confirmed a published report that he had taken human growth hormone three years earlier—and the drive to the top stalled.

Oops, wrong storybook.

THE MIGHTY MISSISSIPPI has spawned triumph and tragedy, song and legend—and, as I learned one sultry afternoon, a great number of scary-looking catfish. The kind with faces as big as a baby's and bodies that weigh more than your mama. In *Life on the Mississippi*, Twain tells of a catfish more than 6 feet long, weighing 250 pounds. It's all so unbelievable that some catfish competitions require anglers to strap on lie detectors to verify they didn't cheat, say, by submitting the same fish that won last time.

20

At the Bass Pro Shops Big Cat Quest Tournament, which I attended on Mud Island, the catch must be brought in live ("No catfish on ice," the rules state.) They are eventually released. This was all patiently explained to me by one of the judges, Wesley Robertson, 78, in for the day from Jackson, Tennessee. "I'm a little-town guy," he said, glancing none-too-warmly toward the Memphis skyline a short monorail ride away.

The event was part of a 12-tournament series offering $75,000 in cash prizes. As a long line of trailer-towed river craft inched toward the official weigh-in, bristling with rods and nets, Robertson told me the world record catfish was actually about 124 lbs. (Researchers once landed a freakish 646-lb. catfish in Thailand's Mekong River—but it wasn't in a sanctioned tournament.) The best bait? "Drift fish or anchor fish. Shad and skipjack," he said. The nation's best catfishing spot? "James River, Virginia." The one he dreams about? "I'll take three dams on the Tennessee River. There's a world record in there." I observed that he wasn't being very specific about just where he meant. He shot me a sidelong grin that made me feel I just might be starting to understand things.

Mud Island is also home to the very pleasing Mississippi River Museum, with its Indian artifacts, boat models and stories about mythic characters like keel-boatman Mike Fink, who boasted he was half-horse, half alligator. You can climb aboard a full-sized riverboat replica laden with bales of cotton, or relive the 1862 Battle of Memphis—artillery sounds included—from the vantage point of a Union ironclad gunboat.

The best part lies outside, however: a five-block-long scale model of the Mississippi, with every bend of the river, its terraced banks, major towns, flood plains and levee systems all faithfully rendered in concrete. A cool stream of water flows through the miniature river—perfect for kicking off your shoes and wading the whole way. And when you arrive at the "Gulf of Mexico," an expansive pool where you can rent a paddleboat, why not just jump in and cool off? On a grassy slope facing west, away from the city, you can dry off, lie under a shade tree and let your spirit roam free like Huckleberry Finn, while Ol' Man River—the real one—rushes by on its inexorable, muddy course.

IF I HAD ONLY A DAY OR TWO to plunge into Memphis, I'd call Tad Pierson at American Dream Safari tours and hitch a ride in his creamy pink 1955 Cadillac. Pierson, 56, a straw-hatted blues aficionado originally from Kansas, is the Zen master of tour operators, a one-man google of local knowledge who can guide you through every corner of Memphis and the Delta blues Holy Land to the south. "I do anthro-tourism," he told me.

I rode shotgun in the Caddy for a deliberately random, free-associative couple of hours, during which we took in a few of the lesser-known Elvis sites, such as McKellar Lake, where the King used to water-ski, and his alma mater, Humes High School, which is now a middle school. "It was all-white back then," Pierson noted. "Now it's 99 percent black." We nudged by the National Ornamental Metal Museum, where they hold the summertime Blues on the Bluff concerts sponsored by WEVL radio—one of the nation's great homegrown stations—showcasing contemporary Memphis artists like Sid Selvidge and Daddy Mack. Then

Pierson steered us up to Daddy Mack's garage on Jackson Ave., where the bluesman spends his days repairing cars and regaling visitors. He was out, so we looped around to see the juke joints on Thomas Street, which some people call "the real Beale Street." The more interest you show, the more Pierson lights up. "I get a sense that people are *called* to Memphis, in a Joseph Campbell sense," he said. "They have to fulfill their mission. It's cool being with people like that and bringing them to the altar of experience."

THE ALTAR THAT ATTRACTS the largest number of Memphis bliss-followers is, of course, Graceland, which is in fact a cluster of attractions—including the Heartbreak Hotel & RV Park, the Elvis After Dark exhibit, Elvis's private jet, and so on—all approached from the dreary, strip-mall-lined Elvis Presley Boulevard. Maybe I was just in a bad mood, but the whole trumped-up Elvis-land experience seemed to me a betrayal of what was most appealing about the King himself—the early Elvis, at any rate—namely his fresh, even innocent goodness and musical sincerity. There's also an undercurrent of cultural tension there, with some visitors reverentially fawning over every scrap of Presleyana, while others snicker, secure in the knowledge that their taste is greatly more refined than a slick-coiffed rocker born in a two-room shotgun shack in Mississippi at the height of the Depression—who, even posthumously, earns $49 million a year. Actually, the white-columned house and grounds he bought for his family are quite pretty. And it was a pleasure walking through them with the four good-natured Paul sisters from Rural Shade, Texas, aged 59 to 75, outfitted in matching magenta T-shirts with the slogan, "What Happens With the Sisters Stays With the Sisters." The youngest of them, Mary, told me they had two more sisters (one living, one deceased) and seven brothers. "We have a family reunion in Corsicana every year with over a hundred people," she said.

I WAS PARTICULARLY STRUCK by the fact that Elvis's humble white-clapboard birthplace—there's a scale model of it at Graceland—was almost identical to W.C. Handy's Memphis home, which now houses the W.C. Handy Museum on Beale Street. Handy was the godfather of Memphis blues composers; the first of his published works, 1912's "Memphis Blues," began as a jaunty campaign song for Boss Crump, and Handy eventually wrote many popular songs, including "St. Louis Blues" and of course, "Beale Street Blues":

> *If Beale Street could talk, if Beale Street could talk,*

> *Married men would have to take their beds and walk.*

Late one afternoon, hours before the street ginned up for real, I was leaning into the open-air bar window of B.B. King's Blues Club at Beale and South 2nd, checking out a singer named Z'Da, who's been called the Princess of Beale Street. Across the street is the Blues City Café, an eatery whose motto is "Put Some South in Your Mouth." A tall black man with a white T-shirt and salt-and-pepper hair approached me, pulling on a cigarette.

"I saw you taking pictures of W.C. Handy's house a little while ago," he said, in a friendly tone. "Did you know they picked up that whole house from Florence, Alabama, where he came from, and they moved it here to Beale Street?" No, I didn't. (And when I later checked, it wasn't even true—the house had been moved from its original spot elsewhere on the south side.)

But we got to talking. He told me his name was Geno Richardson, he was 54, born and raised in Memphis, did odd jobs for a living. "I bring water for the horses," he said, pointing over to one of the carriages that take tourists around the area; its driver was a young woman with Paul-sisters magenta hair.

He had heard stories about Beale Street in its 1920s heyday, when prostitution and gambling flourished and Machine Gun Kelly was a small-time bootlegger here. Talented bluesmen could always find work, but it wasn't a place for the faint-of-heart. Even years later, the air of menace remained. "Elvis was about the only white guy who could come here after dark," Richardson said. "And that was because B.B. King, Howlin' Wolf and those guys sort of took him under their wing."

Today's throbbing two-block entertainment district is well-patrolled by Memphis police, but it's just a piece of the old Beale Street, which stretched eastward with respectable shops, churches and professional offices that were the heart of black Memphis and a nexus of American history. Across the intersection from the Handy museum, in the basement of the First Baptist Beale Street Church, the famed civil rights advocate and feminist Ida B. Wells founded her newspaper, *Free Speech*, in 1889. After the lynching of three black grocery store owners—friends of hers—who were targeted because they might be taking business away from whites, Wells urged blacks to pack up and leave Memphis; in 1892, her office was ransacked and she fled the city herself. Seven years later, on an expanse of land adjoining the same house of worship, Robert R. Church Sr., a former slave who became the South's first black millionaire, created Church Park and Auditorium—the city's first such amenities for African-Americans—and later hired W.C. Handy as the park's orchestra leader. Booker T. Washington spoke there, and President Theodore Roosevelt once addressed a throng of 10,000 on this patch of downtown turf that now looks empty and forgotten, except for an historical marker. Few tourists venture here.

Much of historic Beale Street was razed in misbegotten urban renewal schemes during the years that followed the King assassination, which I asked Richardson about. "I remember that day very well," he said. "I was at Carver High when the news came over, and we all wanted to take off from school. But they tried to make us go back. The police were chasing us with sticks, but we took off. That was a bad day for Memphis."

He asked where I was from, and when I told him, Richardson touched the Yankees logo on his baseball cap and smiled. Then he handed me a copy of the weekly *Memphis Flyer*, folded open to the music listings. "This has everything you need," he said. I gave him $5 and we wished each other well.

THROUGH HIS FILMS AND WRITINGS—which include a biography of Muddy Waters and *It Came From Memphis*, a captivating study of the Bluff City's racial and musical gestalt during the pivotal Sun-to-Stax era—Robert Gordon, 47, has become a beacon of Memphis culture.

I had the pleasure of meeting Gordon for lunch one day at Willie Moore's soul food place on S. 3rd Street, which, he pointed out, is the continuation of Highway 61, the fabled blues road that slices through the Mississippi Delta on its journey from New Orleans to Memphis and points north. "Memphis is the capital of the Delta, and we're on the spine—Highway 61," Gordon said. "All roads in the Delta lead to 61, and 61 leads to Memphis. This is the south side of town—the Delta side. The way the moon creates tidal flows, the Delta creates social patterns in Memphis."

We drove around Soulsville, USA, the predominantly black section where Aretha Franklin and several other important music figures came from, including Memphis Minnie and Maurice White of Earth, Wind & Fire. I was especially glad when Gordon turned down S. Lauderdale to show me the studios of Hi Records, the label best known for recording the charismatic Al Green—now known as the Rev. Al Green—who is still actively performing. The street has been renamed Willie Mitchell Boulevard, after the musician and producer who is to Hi Records what Sam Phillips was to Sun. There's common ground there, Gordon suggested.

"I think that what runs through much of the stuff in Memphis that has become famed elsewhere is a sense of individuality and of independence, establishing an aesthetic without being concerned about what national or popular trends are," Gordon said. It's not a quality that's restricted to musicians, he added. "I think the best example may be William Eggleston's photographs. His photographs are my favorite rock song."

Just a few blocks farther along we approached the Stax Museum and the adjoining Stax Music Academy, where neighborhood teenagers enjoy first-class facilities and instruction from a dedicated staff. I had a chance to meet some of the students and teachers at a Stax event the next evening; you can't help but be moved by the spirit of regeneration they embody and their proud (but also fun-loving) manner. The hope is that the new Stax complex, which opened in 2003, will anchor a turnaround in this historically impoverished community, the one Gordon said had essentially pushed up Highway 61 into south Memphis.

"I like the whole *message* of what's happened to Delta culture, that it's gained respect," Gordon said. "It didn't yield to pressures, it maintained its own identity, and ultimately, the world came to it, instead of it going to the world. And I feel like you can read that in the buildings and streets and history and people and happenstance exchanges—all of that."

"PUT YOUR HANDS TOGETHER for Miss Nikki, all the way from Holly Springs, Mississippi!" the emcee yelled to a packed house.

It was Saturday night at Wild Bill's, a juke joint wedged into a little strip mall on Vollentine Avenue. The drummer was laying down a *heavy* backbeat, accompanied by a big fat bass line. Wild Bill's house band, the Memphis Soul Survivors, includes veteran sidemen who have backed just about all of the great Memphis blues, R&B and soul musicians—B.B. King, Al Green, everybody—and the groove they establish is irresistible. Then Miss Nikki herself, a full-figured, big-voiced singer with charm to spare, stepped to the mike.

By sad coincidence, the club's owner, "Wild Bill" Storey, 88, had died earlier that week and been laid to rest at the veterans' cemetery in Germantown just the day before. Miss Nikki was still feeling tender. "I almost didn't come. I cried my eyes out," she said.

Well, they say there are two very good times to sing the blues—when you're feeling bad, and when you're feeling good. And sometimes they overlap, like good and evil, the sacred and the profane. So Miss Nikki decided to show up. "Y'all came to the best doggone blues joint this side of the moon!" she declared, reaching deep and belting out one impassioned verse after another in Wild Bill's honor. Records may be great, but the real thing makes your body move and your skin tingle. And Miss Nikki's a throwback, the kind of singer who doesn't need a mike. She turned up the heat with a B.B. King blues:

Rock me baby, rock me all night long.

I want you to rock me—like my back ain't got no bone.

Wild Bill's is a long, narrow space—a shotgun room—with red walls and ceiling fans and a tiny bar and kitchen in the back. People were drinking 40-ounce beers in plastic cups at communal tables, laughing and carrying on, black and white, all ages. Fourteen dancers crammed into a space big enough for eight, right up where the band was playing. An elegantly turned-out 70-something black gentleman sporting a leather cowboy hat and a large diamond pinky ring invited a young white lady with a red flower tucked behind her ear— maybe a student from nearby Rhodes College—for a dance. She complied happily, since her boyfriend didn't seem too interested in standing up. From a corner table in the back, under a bulletin board festooned with hundreds of snapshots, three smartly-dressed young women spontaneously launched into a backup vocal riff borrowed from an old Ray Charles hit—*night n'day*…[two beats]… *night n'day*—spurring on both the band and the dancers. The Raelets would have been proud.

"Anyone here from the Show-Me State?" Miss Nikki asked the crowd between songs. A 40-ish woman in a low-cut dress raised her hand.

"You look like a *show-me* girl!" Miss Nikki said, to raucous laughter. Then she piped up:

I was born in Missouri, 'cross the line from Arkansas.

Didn't have no money, so I got in trouble with the law.

Actually, Miss Nikki was born in 1972 in Holly Springs, Mississippi, just like the man said, and she's about the sweetest person you'd ever want to meet. Nicole Whitlock is her real name, and she didn't even *like* the blues when she was growing up. "My real taste of the blues came after I got to Memphis," she told me. "Back home, we were *church* folks—gospel, gospel, gospel."

ON SUNDAY MORNING, I headed over to the First Baptist Beale Street to attend services and hear the choir. I'd been planning to visit the Rev. Al Green's Full Gospel Tabernacle Church—sometimes he leads the music himself. Or I thought I might even drive out 20 miles into the eastern suburbs to the Bellevue Baptist megachurch, whose Web site portrays something more like a campus or a God-themed suburban mall than anything I'd ever seen. But then my hosts Tom and Sandy Franck recommended the gospel service at First Baptist Beale right nearby, and by now, I completely trusted their advice.

When I arrived at the historic church, though, I discovered that once every five weeks they switched the Sunday school session with the main service, and this was that week—so I had just missed the service. It was a major disappointment, but what could I do? Move on to the day's primary mission, that's what: a day trip through the Delta.

I jumped in the car, tuned in to a gospel station at the upper end of the AM dial, picked up S. 3rd St. and pointed southward toward Highway 61. Destination: Clarksdale, Mississippi, the very cradle of the blues. It's where—at the crossroads of Highways 61 and 49—the legend says bluesman Robert Johnson sold his soul to the devil to gain his talent. It's where Bessie Smith died (not in Memphis, as Edward Albee seems to have believed). It's where the Delta Blues Museum lives. And it's only 80 miles down the road.

The transition from urb to herb didn't take long. Within 15 minutes, I was passing men in overalls selling humongous watermelons off an old flatbed truck. You see billboards luring Memphians down to the Tunica, Mississippi, casinos for the slots and craps action. A restaurant ad promised 48-oz. steaks—the term doggie bag seemed suddenly inadequate. Pretty soon, I was in the Magnolia State, easing by rice and cotton fields that stretched off to the horizon. The soil looked awfully rich to my non-expert eyes.

En route, I couldn't resist a quick detour into Tunica's gambling emporia, choosing the Horseshoe Casino because it looked less generic and because it sits next to the Bluesville Club, whose marquee advertised upcoming visits from Booker T. & the MGs and B.B. King himself. Hey, I was feeling lucky, and no sooner had I shaken hands with the one-armed bandit than I won a $35 jackpot. Good time to scoot. (Ethical dilemma: Should my expense report reflect dollar inflows as well as outflows? I ruled in my own favor—surprise!—reasoning that since I wouldn't have dared to expense any losings, I was entitled to keep my winnings. Mark Twain might have appreciated this self-serving logic.)

I soon veered off onto Old Highway 61, a back road dotted with shacks—a corrugated community, you might say—leading after a while into the sun-drenched main square of old Tunica. I wondered about this musical place name, which sounds like it could be a tuneful cousin of the harmonica. In fact, I learned later, Tunica is named for the Indian tribe once that lived in the area and now shares a reservation with the Biloxi tribe in Marksville, Louisiana. The Tunica were much put upon by the more aggressive Chickasaw, who even sold a number of them into slavery in South Carolina about 300 years ago. Interestingly, the Tunica language, now extinct, is said to have no connection with any other family of languages—a kind of North American Basque. Since the Tunica and the Biloxi couldn't understand each other, they both resorted to French.

I stopped for lunch at the delightful-looking Blue & White Restaurant back on 61. It's been there since 1937, and from all appearances, hasn't changed much. (Hollywood location scouts, take note.) My genial waitress, Dottie Carlisle, recommended the $9 all-you-can-eat Sunday buffet special. I heaped on some fried chicken, mac 'n' cheese, Brussels sprouts, yams, turnip greens and black-eyed peas, created a little puddle of gravy, and got down to work. Afterward, Dottie insisted I sample the peach cobbler, which later caused me to slide the driver's seat back an inch or two. Before Dottie would let me go, though, she led me into the kitchen to meet Dorothy Irons, who had cooked up this feast. She said she'd worked at the Blue & White for 43 years. I quickly did the math and realized this meant Irons had begun there in 1964, an especially tense time in Mississippi. But as I looked around the restaurant—where white and black employees acted like sisters, where an elderly black woman in her Sunday finery took her place right next to a table of plaid-shirted good ole boys without anyone seeming to take notice—I had to conclude that while the legacy of that past persists, there was no question a whole lot had changed, too.

FINALLY, I APPROACHED CLARKSDALE. Looking across the flat terrain, there were major storm clouds ahead and as I entered town, it was kicking up pretty good. I got lost trying to find the Delta Blues Museum, and there seemed to be no one around who could even give me directions. At last I stumbled upon the museum, which sat across an empty lot—not a good omen.

As I walked across the deserted space, I caught sight of the only other human who had ventured out in Clarksdale on this steamy Sunday afternoon—a barefoot, freckle-faced white boy splashing through the puddles like Gene Kelly. The kid eyed me from a safe distance.

"It's closed," he yelled.

"Looks like it," I conceded, wondering about this little guy playing freely all by himself. He was small, but had the toughened air of a much older boy. "How old are you?" I asked.

"Nine."

"Are you with your parents or somebody?"

At that, his eyes widened and he tore off across the lot, looking back warily every ten yards or so.

I think I just met Huckleberry Finn.

SO NOW I'D MISSED BOTH the gospel service in Memphis and the Delta Blues Museum, but I still had this growing feeling that there's something powerfully different about this corner of the world. I just couldn't quite put my finger on it, and realized it might be a long time before it really sunk in. I decided to head east toward Oxford, carrying thoughts of Faulkner, the University of Mississippi, John Grisham and the *Oxford American*. Sounded like a civilized place, on the whole—with more than a whiff of the dark side of American history, as well. In 1962, when U.S. Air Force veteran James Meredith attempted to enroll at Ole Miss as the university's first black student, it sparked riots that required a show of force from President Kennedy to tamp down: A century after the Civil War, 28 federal marshals were shot during the fray, and two people were killed. Today, some fans still wave the Stars-and-Bars and sing "Dixie" at football games—but there is also a statue of James Meredith on campus. His late son Joseph earned a doctorate at the university's business school in 2002, and black students represent more than 10 percent of the school's enrollment—far lower than one might hope for in a state that is 40 percent black, but certainly an advance in the decades since Meredith bravely crossed the school's threshold.

NOT FIVE MINUTES OUT OF CLARKSDALE, the torrential rains caught up with me again. Radio reception cut out, the road disappeared under water, and an 18-wheeler rumbled by at about 75 in the opposite lane, sending a small tsunami my way. I barely saw it coming. I decided to play a stupid game: I'd count to 30, and if the visibility didn't improve, I'd pull over and wait it out. At 23 or 24, it started to relent. I kept going.

Halfway to Oxford, you pass though the town of Marks, Mississippi, which happens to be the birthplace of FedEx's Fred W. Smith. But its claim on history comes mostly from Dr. King, who was stirred to tears by the conditions he found there in 1968—poverty so entrenched that hundreds of children went without shoes or regular nutrition. He decided to begin his Poor People's March to Washington, D.C.—an epic campaign he didn't live to see concluded—from Marks. Bobby Kennedy also visited the town that year in solidarity with Dr. King's cause, and in 2007, Sen. John Edwards made a point of coming to Marks as part of his presidential campaign. One-third of Marks's residents still live in poverty.

Oxford, Mississippi, deserves a journey of its own—I'm afraid my drive-by shooting (by camera) through the Ole Miss campus and some charming downtown streets only whetted my appetite. Having just fallen under Miss Nikki's spell, though, I was more curious to continue on to her native Holly Springs, to complete the circle.

There are other important Memphis connections in Holly Springs. It was the birthplace of both Boss Crump and Ida B. Wells, and one of the hometowns of Gen. Nathan Bedford Forrest, who was so lionized in Memphis that the city erected an impressive equestrian statue of him in the Union Avenue park named for him. Considered a brilliant military tactician, Forrest has also been held responsible for war crimes that included the 1864 massacre of black Union prisoners under his command at Fort Donelson, and he was the first Grand Wizard of the Ku Klux Klan. For his Confederate zeal, he is still revered by white supremacists, more so than the kinder, gentler Robert E. Lee, for example. Needless to say, Forrest's continuing place of honor in a majority African-American city sparks some controversy.

Holly Springs itself looked lovely, with a satisfying old main square that made Oxford's even look a little fussy. There were notable sights I'd probably never get to see, such as the juke joint Robert Gordon described as his all-time favorite, which he was once led to by Junior Kimbrough, a local bluesman. "It was in a house in the middle of a cotton field," Gordon recalled. "The party was roaring. They were selling fruit beer in the kitchen, and Junior was *throwing down* in the living room." In case you're unfamiliar with that expression, it's a high compliment.

IT WAS ONLY AFTER I RETURNED to Memphis that I got to meet Henry Turley. He invited me up to his office in the historic Cotton Exchange Building—the Grisham best-seller and movie *The Firm* was partly set there. The landmark building stands at the corner of Union Avenue and Front Street, once known as Cotton Row, and the ground floor houses the Cotton Museum, an excellent exhibit devoted to the cash crop that largely gave Memphis its place in the world. In fact, Turley told me, a high percentage of the nation's cotton trading still takes place in Memphis. And the traders have the same damn-the-torpedoes attitude that gave Memphis so much of its character through the years.

"They're wild and free, and they do what the hell they want to do," Turley said. "A lot of these cotton guys, they're mad gamblers, you know, betting on cotton futures with money they never dreamed they had, leveraging things at a huge multiple. A lot of 'em are quite mad."

Turley describes himself and his approach to real-estate development in more modest terms. "I have small ideas," he said. "I tend to think those are better ideas, and I tend to think that they become large ideas if they're replicated in discrete and different ways, sufficiently. My small idea is to create neighborhoods where life is better, and richer, and more interesting and just more fulfilling for the people who choose to live there. That's a small idea."

One more thing about Henry Turley: he seems to know everybody in Memphis—from the mayor to the local newspaper reporters to the musicians and the street people. He doesn't make a big deal about this, but it's impossible to drive around with him without stopping every block or so for another friendly exchange.

"Hey, you're lookin' good, man," he called out to a young black homeowner in Uptown who'd been ailing the last time they spoke. Within the next five minutes, they swapped spider-bite remedies, Turley dispensed some legal advice, and the man passed on a suggestion about putting more trash cans in the neighborhood—with the slogan "Two Points" on each one to encourage the basketball-minded. Even as he said this, Turley punched up a number on his cell to tell someone in his office about the idea, which he liked. "Let's get somebody to put a few out," he said cheerfully.

"I knew a guy who once said to me, 'You know, Memphis is one of the few real places in America,'" Turley said. "Everything else is just a shopping center.' He's right. Memphis is a *real* place."

He pulled up in a pleasant new square hacked out of an abandoned lot and pointed out the window. "Look at that!"

I poked my head out and peered up to see a miniature, octagon-shaped white house perched on a tall metal pole.

"Looks like a *birdhouse* to me," Turley said, savoring the word, even singing it slightly.

Questions for Discussion and Journaling

1. Katz uses description and imagery throughout the article. One example of this is his discussion of white birdhouses in the introduction. Why does he choose to describe these in great detail? What words does he use? What effect do those words have? Why does he return to the birdhouses as he concludes the article?

2. While Katz's piece jumps around Memphis, noting bits of history before turning to a discussion of BBQ and then moving to discuss race relations and more, his conclusion notes "Memphis is a *real* place." This seems to be his implicit argument, but what does that mean? Using quotations from the article as evidence write a 10–12 sentence paragraph that explains what he means by "Memphis is a *real* place."

3. Katz's travel narrative touches on tons of potential research topics. Briefly reread the article in order to generate a list of 5 potential topics for a research paper. Then choose the two that you are most interested in. Turn to the "Choosing a Topic" chapter in this textbook and ask yourself the three questions intended to help you choose a topic successfully.

THE ALIEN HAS LANDED

Bob Norman

Bob Norman's "The Alien Has Landed" is a bizarre yet undoubtedly enthralling narrative of the life of Prince Mongo, the allegedly 333-year-old local celebrity/extraterrestrial that hails from the planet Zambodia and is hell-bent on saving humanity. In this biographical piece written for the *Miami New Times* in 2006 (a free weekly tabloid-style newspaper serving the Miami Metro area since 1987), Norman examines the zany day-to-day life of Mongo and his relations with the rest of Memphis, chronicling everything from his various mayoral campaigns to his one-of-a-kind style. Whether he is a shoeless alien from a planet nine light years away or simply a peculiar fellow proudly living on his own terms, Mongo is indubitably a man (or Zambodian) worthy of examination. Norman uses Mongo's exploits to implicitly argue that no one is more comfortable than one who lives comfortably in one's own skin.

The extraterrestrial sits on a couch and looks up at a blank artist's canvas hanging crookedly on the wall. Only it's not blank. There are vague grayish shapes and blotches in the white background.

"That picture is transforming right now," Prince Mongo proclaims. "It's the resurrection of the world. The Earth doesn't have much time left. We're on the second run right now. That painting is the tunnel to life."

When will it be finished?

"It won't end until the world ends. Then I will take the people I'm going to save back to Zambodia."

It may sound like the ravings of a demented street person, but Prince Mongo isn't homeless. He's sitting in his two-million-dollar Fort Lauderdale home with a pool and an elevated wooden deck on a canal. He also owns homes in Virginia Beach and Memphis, and he skis in Vail.

But when Mongo sleeps, he does it on a little mat in the family room, like a poverty-stricken college student. He wears old T-shirts and never wears shoes, even when walking in the snow in Vail.

Prince Mongo is maybe five feet seven inches tall, and he's got a good-size belly. When I paid him a surprise visit last week, he offered me radishes, sushi, goat's milk, vegetable soup, and a ham sandwich.

His property suffered no damage during Hurricane Wilma, while almost all of his neighbors' homes did. "My aura protected it," he says.

Mongo looks to be in his fifties, but he says he's 333 years old. Three is his favorite number —it has some special significance in Zambodia, his original home nine light years away. "When I hit Earth, I fragmentized and went all over the world," he explains. "I then began assembling myself and still am."

His first identity on Earth was that of a Blackfoot Indian chief in the Dakotas. Since then, he's had 33 wives, all of whom have died. "They can't last like I can," he explains.

He says he's gone to several universities—including the University of Virginia, Tulane, Columbia, and William and Mary—and has a doctorate, though he won't divulge in what. He says he's been living winters in Fort Lauderdale for 33 years, but property appraiser records indicate he's owned the home since 1985. When he leaves for parts north, he doesn't lock the doors. "Anybody can come in here anytime and take what they please," he states.

Only those with eclectic tastes could appreciate Mongo's household goods. The walls are filled with paintings, as well as kites, model planes, fossils, and a few things that can be described only as dried-up sea creatures. Everything is crooked or upside down.

In the living room is a poster of him wearing mirrored welding goggles, a long gray wig, and a rubber chicken around his neck as he walks across a road, triumphantly holding a large bone in his hand.

On his front porch six Christmas trees surround the door. "My Christmas doesn't begin like y'alls'," Mongo says.

In the back yard, near the water, an upside-down toilet sits by itself. His neighbor Concha says there used to be 50 toilets on his property, but he's cleaned it up a bit. Mongo has been hit with a few code violations for the "artwork" he's kept outside his home in years past. "We had a war once," he says. "I won. They moved away. I'm still here."

On the water is a yacht he takes out regularly. He fishes but doesn't golf. ("I once hit a golf ball so hard it caught on fire, so I quit that game.")

When I first asked Mongo for his given Earth name, he skirted the question. But he did tell me he had run for every political office there was in Memphis. And he said he'd grown up in Virginia and that his "Earth parents" were named Roebuck and Minnie and had already returned to his home planet.

It was Concha who gave me Mongo's given name: Robert Hodges. With a quick Internet search, I learned Hodges is famous in Memphis, where he has owned several large nightclubs, including the giant Prince Mongo's Planet—three stories and 30,000 square feet of partying—and another called The Castle, which was housed in a century-old stone mansion.

If previous published reports in Memphis newspapers are correct, he's now 58 years old. The first reference I found to the fact that he never wears shoes dated back to a mayor's campaign in 1978, when he was just 30. He has run for office countless times, always losing. His favorite epithet for politicians seems to be "skunk bat."

Hodges has been jailed a handful of times, mostly for contempt of court. He made national news when he appeared before a judge in 1983, covered in green body paint and wearing a fur loincloth. The Tennessee Supreme Court overruled the conviction on the grounds that Hodges was practicing his religion.

"On the Mongo question, Memphis is generally divided," wrote nationally syndicated columnist Bob Garfield in 1987. "Some regard him as a crackpot, others as a shrewd businessman assiduously cultivating a weird persona for the purpose of selling more pizza and beer."

In 2002, *Commercial Appeal* columnist Michael Kelley bludgeoned Prince Mongo in print. "I've watched as you annoyed one neighbor after another with yard displays and antics that lack creativity and fail to make a statement about politics or culture or anything else," he wrote. "It has become apparent that you're just a provocateur."

When I mentioned his life in Memphis, Mongo said he's been the victim of harassment for decades there. "When I ran for office and gave speeches, I'd always express myself in a fanatical way," he says. "I'd call the other guy a fabulous thief, and every time he'd prove me right."

Okay, Mongo is definitely not crazy. And he's also not perfect. But he most definitely is one of those rare things on this planet—a man who lives life on his own terms. After I spent a couple hours with Mongo, he showed me the cooler in the back of his truck, full of ice and leftover food from a morning delivery. "I try to help unfortunate families who can't pay their bills," he says. "There is no mercy on Earth to help those people."

Good thing there's mercy on Zambodia. Long live Prince Mongo.

Questions for Discussion and Journaling

1. Norman uses vivid description to describe Mongo's home. Why was this description necessary for his purposes? How does this description add to the portrait of Prince Mongo?

2. Throughout the article Norman provides quotes from Prince Mongo. What effect do these quotes have? Consider how he introduces (or doesn't introduce) each quote. How does their placement impact the audience's reading of the article? Why does he place the quotes where he does?

3. Norman ends his portrait of Mongo with a reference to Mongo feeding the poor. How does ending with this tidbit rather than Mongo's court exploits in green body paint and a loincloth impact your conclusions about Mongo? What does this conclusion tell you about how Norman feels about Mongo?

WRITING ABOUT CULTURE

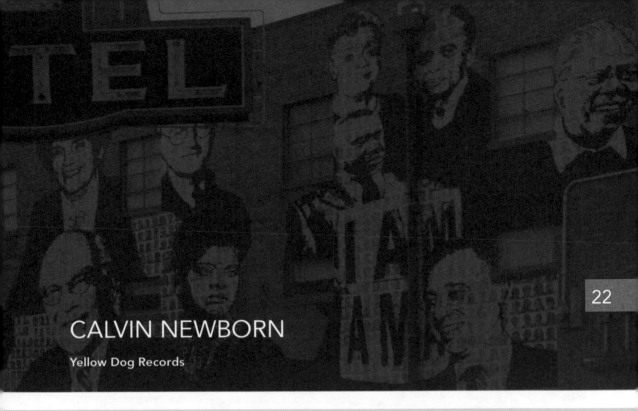

CALVIN NEWBORN

Yellow Dog Records

"Calvin Newborn" provides a short but sweet argument for considering Memphis the "Home of the Blues." This vignette also delivers a vivid description of Newborn's musical journey from a child with a guitar in his hand to a legendary Memphis musician and "one of the great unsung heroes of blues and jazz." Initially written as a brief biography of the prolific jazz guitarist for the Yellow Dog Records website, this article seeks to enlighten readers to the musical magic of Memphis and the undeniable talent that it is able to foster. Note how the thesis of this article (that Calvin Newborn is essential to blues and jazz history) does not appear until the last paragraph, a rather unorthodox approach. What effect might this have on swaying the audience's opinion?

Memphis, Tennessee, is known as the Home of the Blues for a reason: Hundreds of bluesmen honed their craft in the city, playing music in Handy Park and in the alleyways that branch off Beale Street, plying their trade in that street's raucous nightclubs and in juke joints across the Mississippi River. Mississippians like Ike Turner, B.B. King, and Howlin' Wolf all passed through the Bluff City, often pausing to cut a record before migrating northward to a better life. Other musicians stayed in Memphis, bristling at the idea of starting over in unfamiliar cities like Chicago, St. Louis, and Los Angeles.

Drummer Finas Newborn was one of the latter—as a bandleader and the father of pianist Phineas and guitarist Calvin Newborn, and as the proprietor of his own musical instrument store on Beale Street, he preferred the familiar environs of Memphis. Finas' sons literally grew up with musical instruments in their hands. While they were still attending elementary school, the two took first prize at the Palace Theater's "Amateur Night" show, where Calvin brought down the house singing "Your Mama's On the Bottom, Papa's On Top, Sister's In the Kitchen Hollerin' 'When They Gon' Stop.'"

Before Calvin followed his brother Phineas to New York to pursue a jazz career, he interacted with all the major players on Memphis' blues scene. In fact, B.B. King helped Calvin pick out his first guitar. The favor was repaid when the entire Newborn family backed King on his first recording, "Three O' Clock Blues," recorded for the Bullet label at Sam Phillips' Recording Service in downtown Memphis. Hanging out in his father's music store, Calvin even taught the great Howlin' Wolf how to read sheet music.

Then the Newborns were tapped for another big project: accompanying Ike Turner on a tour promoting his '51 smash "Rocket 88" (allegedly the world's first rock'n'roll single), also cut at Phillips' studio. As Calvin recalls, he taught Turner—then a boogie-woogie pianist—how to play guitar; in return, Turner taught him how to drive. "We made a deal," Calvin says. "He just slid out from under the wheel—and that's how I learned how, on the way back from Clarksdale, Mississippi. As far as his guitar lessons went, I didn't really get a chance to teach him more than a few chords—I just got him started."

For four years, the Newborn Orchestra performed at the Plantation Inn in West Memphis, Arkansas, before moving back across the river to Clifford Miller's Flamingo Room in downtown Memphis. Incendiary photographs by Ernest Withers and George Hardin capture Calvin's onstage energy: He danced, leapt, and slid across the floor with his guitar in his hands, never missing a note. "My hang time was like Michael Jordan's, but I was dunkin' the guitar!" Calvin boasts today. "I was known as Flying Calvin, the king of after-hours blues on Beale Street."

In 1955, however, Calvin moved to New York, where his brother had already established a regular gig opening for Count Basie. Calvin accompanied Phineas on his first solo recordings for Atlantic and RCA Victor, then joined groups led by Wild Bill Davis, Jimmy Forrest, and Earl Hines. He also played on dozens of sessions led by such greats as Charles Mingus, Roy Milton, Ray Charles, Sun Ra, and Hank Crawford, gigging on the east and west coasts. Phineas, meanwhile, became known as one of the greatest piano virtuosos to ever enter the jazz world, dazzling audiences with his prowess and brilliancy at the keys. Unfortunately, by the late '60s, his physical and mental problems had forced him from the New York scene.

When Calvin returned to Memphis to take care of an ailing Phineas in the early '80s, he discovered an entirely different Beale Street. He saw "tourists gazing at a map and looking puzzled outside the Visitor's Information Center," and "a station wagon stopping at W.C. Handy's house," where its driver took a snapshot then sped off. Musicians like Calvin Newborn were no longer so welcome in the rebuilt entertainment district. Nevertheless, he never forgot his blues roots. Calvin picked up gigs wherever he could, and began to focus on other outlets. He wrote *As Quiet As It's Kept*, an autobiography of his brother, who died of cancer in '89.

Calvin worked as assistant director of Jazz Studies at LeMoyne-Owen College, where he earned a B.A. in Humanities. He taught underprivileged children at the Stax Music Academy, and he wrote a handful of stage plays and operettas. Calvin also recorded two solo albums: 1983's *From The Hip*, released on Rooster Blues Records, and *Flying Calvin/UpCity*, originally released on his own Omnifarious label. Although he performed regularly in Memphis, he largely slipped under the radar.

22

Today, the 70-something year old Calvin Newborn is ripe for a comeback. He still steps lively, while his entire body glows with a mixture of divine intelligence and unbridled energy. He's writing another book, *Rock 'N Roll versus Rock 'N Soul: How the King Won*, an account of his friendship with Elvis Presley. He's working on a documentary film called *Triumph Over Chaos!* which details the Newborn family's musical legacy.

Calvin just recorded a brand new album, *New Born*, for Yellow Dog Records, which is also reissuing *UpCity*. The compositions on *New Born* reflect Calvin's determination to persevere. "When Kingdom Comes/Sho' Nuff" and "Restorations," point toward a new beginning, while "The Streetwalker's Stroll" and his interpretation of the standard "Lush Life" take inventory of the life he's left behind.

Listen to "Newborn Blues," or "After Hours Blues," and you'll hear the lineage that began with sessions for B.B. King's first record, recorded by Sam Phillips at his Sun Records studio in 1950, and ends with *New Born*, recorded, appropriately enough, by Roland Janes at Sam Phillips' Recording Studio (located right around the corner from Sun) more than half a century later. Meanwhile, tracks like "Blues & Beyond" and "Spirit Trane/Omnifarious" outline Calvin's impeccable jazz pedigree, honed at New York City recording sessions and in the many smoky after-hours joints.

Musician, playwright, author: Calvin is a piece of living history. With astonishing clarity, he can recall hundreds of stories about "the old days"—magazines like *Living Blues*, *Mojo*, *G.Q.*, and *Cadence* have mined dozens of tales about his work with Howlin' Wolf, Ike Turner, Count Basie, and others—and his image (George Hardin's "Flying Calvin" photo) was even co-opted by the Smithsonian Institution as the logo for their Rock'N'Soul exhibit. One of the great unsung heroes of blues and jazz, it is high time that the world found out more about Calvin Newborn.

> "I always did like the blues because I could get attention playing the blues. I could do something with the guitar that a lot of guys couldn't do. I had expression, and I moved with the guitar. I got that from my granddaddy—he used to play his guitar in his church, and walk all over the church playin'. I guess I inherited that."
>
> **–Calvin Newborn in *Living Blues***

> "Calvin's playing is infinitely expressive. He has that same gift that Charlie Parker had to play a note a million different ways with a million different tonalities: gentle, soft, rough, smooth. He's just a total master of tone."
>
> **–Stanley Booth, *Rythm Oil***

> "Calvin Newborn—man, do I love that fella! He came to New York and sat in with us at a gig at Minton's Playhouse, way back in the day. He tore the place up! When I found out who his brother was, I said no wonder! There's no slack in that family name!"
>
> **–George Benson**

> "Newborn's guitar phrasing, equally tough and tender, is supreme. He can coax satiny Wes Montgomery licks out of a ballad, swing a blues or relish an R&B groove all in his edgy style. This [music] wasn't learned, it was lived in."
>
> **–*The Commercial Appeal***

"Despite his imaginative approach to his instrument, Calvin Newborn has never fully received the attention he's due, and has spent a lifetime in the shadow of his brother's legacy. Rest assured, this has little to do with Newborn's musicality, but instead can be linked to the lack of availability of his recordings and the lack of recording situations themselves."

–**Jon Morgan,** *Cadence*

Questions for Discussion and Journaling

1. This article mentions a variety of musicians, including greats like B.B. King, Count Basie, and Elvis Presley, along with several specific songs. At one point, the author tells the reader to listen to Calvin Newborn's music in order to hear Newborn's impact on the blues genre. Newborn's song "When Kingdom Comes/Sho'Nuff" is easy to find online by simply searching for the song title or for the title of the record, *New Born*. Find and then listen to at least one song by Newborn and consider how his music has or has not affected the music you prefer. Identify two or three similarities and/or differences between Newborn's music and your own favorite artist(s).

2. For which specific audience was this article written? Who would be most likely to read this article for both enjoyment and edification? Why do you think so? Write a paragraph in which you name the audience and determine if that audience is a discourse community. Share your analysis with your small group; if classmates do not agree with your analysis, then attempt to persuade them to see your reasoning.

3. Look at the end of the article and read the various quotes provided about Newborn. Consider why the author chose to include these quotes, and determine the purpose of the author providing such quotes about Newborn at the end of the article (rather than at the beginning or in the middle).

23

MEMPHIS ACTIVISTS TELL THE TALE OF FIZDALE OFF THE COURT

Tonyaa Weathersbee

"Memphis Activists Tell the Tale of Fizdale off the Court" by Tonyaa Weathersbee was published in the *Commercial Appeal* on November 29, 2017. In this article, Weathersbee details the influence and activism of David Fizdale, former Memphis Grizzlies head coach. Using the testimonies of two specific activists in Memphis, Tami Sawyer (a leader of the Take 'Em Down 901 group which pushed for the removal of Confederate monuments) and Terri Freeman (the president of the National Civil Rights Museum), Weathersbee shows how Fizdale's tenure in Memphis had a positive impact on the city. Weathersbee paints a picture of Fizdale that forces readers to consider him as more than just a basketball coach, ultimately persuading readers to agree that Memphis needs more men like Fizdale—men who fight to empower those in the minority. As you read, consider how and why the author interweaves other narratives, such as those of NFL football player Colin Kaepernick, into her argument.

Tami Sawyer said she believes that when she and other activists laid in front of the FedEx Forum in October to demand that Memphis purge its parks of the blemishes that are Confederate monuments, a certain person had a hand in them not being hauled off by the police.

That person, she believes, was Grizzlies coach David Fizdale.

"I feel like, were it not for our coach, we would have been removed," said Sawyer, one of the leaders of Take 'Em Down 901—a group that has been pushing to remove the monuments. "Then, the last thing he said in his press conference that night was, 'Take 'em down now.'

"That was empowering...at a time when we have to push coaches across the nation to even admit racism, that, that, for me, was very empowering."

Which is why many people who are fighting for social justice here, as well as for ways to empower African-American men, say they will miss Fizdale—who was recently fired by the Grizzlies' organization.

And while the reasons for his firing are being debated on social media, what's not debatable is that, as an African-American man and a professional sports coach, Fizdale paid extraordinary attention to the mark he was leaving on Memphis, and not just on the basketball court.

Terri Freeman saw it firsthand.

Freeman, president of the National Civil Rights Museum, recalled how, in the spring of 2016, during a time when then-presidential candidate Donald Trump was whipping up fears about Mexicans and Muslims, Fizdale gave her a call.

"He invited me to come over and talk [to the Grizzlies players] about why voting was so important," Freeman said. "It [her talk] was posted on the NBA channel...

"What we found was that a good number of the players were not registered, and we got them registered out of the state."

That wasn't Fizdale's only collaboration with Freeman.

In September of 2016, he was part of a conversation titled, "A Bridge of Opportunity," in which he and others discussed the parallels between sports and social justice.

It was a conversation that was necessary and, to a point, overdue during a season in which NFL quarterback Colin Kaepernick was vilified for taking a knee to protest police brutality and injustice.

But Fizdale could relate.

For one thing, he was reared in South Central Los Angeles, where friends and relatives were snuffed out by the sort of gun violence that Memphis is experiencing. He also knew that joblessness and aimlessness is what leads many young people, especially young African-American men, to succumb to the streets. Fizdale also experienced police brutality and police profiling.

That's why he used his platform to encourage others to empathize with young black men and their predicament.

"I'm very concerned about our young black men in Memphis," Fizdale told The Undefeated, an ESPN news site which examines the intersection of sports and race, in 2016. "Not only them killing each other, but them having to deal with anything with the police...

"...I always said that when I became a head coach, my passion is going to be, outside of basketball—it's going to be, how do I help young African-American males, young minority males...

"And that's my passion. How do I help these guys stay in school, stop killing each other, get a job?"

At a time when many sports figures use their celebrity as a reason to isolate themselves from real world problems, or to put a wall up between themselves and the environments in which they were reared, Fizdale stood out.

He stood out when he stood for removing Memphis' Confederate monuments, abominations that are poised to dampen the 50th anniversary of Martin Luther King Jr.'s assassination here, and for the rights of athletes to take a knee to protest injustice.

In doing so, Fizdale gave further lie to the notion that success means black athletes and sports celebrities should be aloof to injustices that could ensnare them; that wealth and fame insulates them from unfairness, and that they should be grateful and, most of all, silent.

"From the perspective of someone who had local celebrity, he was very engaged," Freeman said. "I do think it [Fizdale's firing] is a huge loss, because he didn't just care about himself. He cared about Memphis. He also is a real good guy."

"It meant a lot to have a coach to speak out like that," Sawyer said. "I think it's a huge loss, and I'm devastated."

Certainly, she's not the only one.

Questions for Discussion and Journaling

1. Consider these lines from the article: "In doing so, Fizdale gave further lie to the notion that success means black athletes and sports celebrities should be aloof to injustices that could ensnare them; that wealth and fame insulates them from unfairness, and that they should be grateful and, most of all, silent." Do you agree with the author that African-American celebrities and athletes should resist becoming insulated from and unaffected by the injustices so often found in America? Can you think of a particular celebrity who uses his or her fame for social justice? What are the pros and cons of celebrities using their fame in such a way?

2. This article argues that losing David Fizdale is bad for the city of Memphis. However, there are several other arguments within this primary argument. Identify one or two of the mini-arguments within the article. Explain why the author chose to include them within the broader argument about Fizdale.

3. Take 'Em Down 901 is a discourse community featured in this article, but there are at least three others. How many discourse communities can you identify? How can you be certain these communities qualify as discourse communities?

THE RESISTANCE: MEMPHIS ACTIVISM SPROUTS EVERYWHERE

Flyer Staff

"The Resistance: Memphis Activism Sprouts Everywhere" first appeared in the *Memphis Flyer* in February 2017. The article is a clear-cut proposal to its audience, attempting to persuade the reader to get involved at the local level in order to implement change at the national level. The article is teeming with instances of racial injustice, economic disparity, and hegemonic oppression. The *Flyer* Staff use a combination of imagery and first-person accounts of activism in the local area, and the article concludes with a partial list of grassroots organizations in the greater Memphis area. The goal of the article is simple (show readers the many ways to become active in the community), and the argument is even more straightforward: it's never too late to get involved.

The Black Lives Matter photo was from a Darrius Stewart rally outside of 201 Poplar. Micaela Watts/*Memphis Flyer*

We've planned this cover [story] for a couple of weeks, calling on sources, digging through social media, and going to rallies and marches to find the faces of Memphis resistance. Turns out, all we really had to do was check with City Hall. The city of Memphis has a list.

The Commercial Appeal's Ryan Poe uncovered the Memphis Police Department's "escort list" through an open records request and revealed it in a story Friday. The list features the names of dozens of Memphis activists, organizers, disgruntled former employees, and others. Those on the list "have to be escorted inside City Hall at all times," according to a note on the list signed by MPD Lieutenant Albert Bonner.

Mayor Jim Strickland said he hadn't seen the list before Poe's story surfaced and said he will review it with MPD director Michael Rallings to discuss its future.

"It is the professional assessment of the Memphis Police Department's Homeland Security Bureau that individuals on the list pose a potential security risk," Strickland said in a statement, Saturday. "It's important to note that these individuals have not been banned from City Hall. They simply require an escort."

Citing ignorance of the City Hall security list is one thing, but we do have insight into how Strickland handles protests. When Greensward supporters took to the grassy field in Overton Park last April (armed with protest signs, streamers, guitars, and kids in costumes), Strickland ordered 88 security staffers (including MPD, Memphis Fire Services, Memphis Animal Services, and more) to the site. The show of force included clandestine surveillance units, mounted police, a fleet of police cruisers, and a cop chopper circling overhead. All of this cost taxpayers around $37,000.

A few months later, about 1,000 protestors shut down the Hernando de Soto Bridge in an action aimed at drawing attention to the deaths of several black men at the hands of police across the country. MPD officers, and Rallings, himself, ensured that protestors marched peacefully and safely through downtown streets and onto the bridge. Once there, they were met with a sea of blue lights, a squad of cops clad in black riot gear, and a police helicopter.

Both protests ended peacefully, and the overwhelming police presence may have had some thing to do with it. The City Hall list, though, feels like overreach—targeted and possibly aimed at intimidation.

The original introduction to this piece described a city that lauds the efforts of its resistors. We paint their faces 15 feet high on the sides of buildings and call them "Upstanders." We turned the site of Dr. Martin Luther King Jr.'s final moments into the iconic National Civil Rights Museum, which helps visitors and locals alike learn about what King and other civil rights leaders fought and died for. Through that lens, we've watched with some pride as grassroots efforts in Memphis have sprouted and grown since the inauguration of President Donald Trump. If any city is going to respect those who rise up and resist, it should be Memphis.

Maybe future generations will paint visages of the new resistance on another Upstanders Mural, like the one in South Main. Though the spectrum of resistance and activist groups in Memphis is wide and diverse, we've selected a few to highlight. Memphis, meet (some of) the resistance. —*Toby Sells*

BLACK LIVES MATTER, MEMPHIS CHAPTER

24

Perhaps the most recognizable of the social justice-oriented groups, Black Lives Matter faces ample scrutiny from law-enforcement supporters and, well, white people, though there has never been an "Only" in front of the group's name.

BLM as a national organization formed after the death of Trayvon Martin, the unarmed Florida teenager stalked and killed by George Zimmerman, a self-proclaimed neighborhood watch vigilante. BLM has grown in size and reach, often in conjunction with protests against police killings of unarmed African Americans.

Shahidah Jones, a Memphis chapter representative, says that people's involvement in the Memphis chapter tends to rise and recede. "It's not a growing trend, necessarily, but people will be motivated by a particular incident and come out," Jones says, adding that "it really depends on public traction, but also accessibility."

Shahidah Jones, an organizer with Black Lives Matter. Joey Miller/*Memphis Flyer*

In this case, accessibility refers to how much time someone is able to commit to BLM, which is why the chapter is comprised of regular members who stay steadily involved, like Jones, and volunteers who can help organize around a specific event.

"The basic core of what we're doing is we are fighting for the liberation and equality of all black people," said Jones.

Like most social justice groups organizing under a national presence, the local group adheres to national guiding principles. For BLM locally, the economic equality they are pursuing has many components. This year, the chapter decided that pursuing transformative justice in Memphis means working on bail reform and decriminalizing marijuana—two components of the criminal justice system that disproportionately work against people of color.

Jones advises anyone wanting to get involved with BLM Memphis to send an email and let organizers know how they would be able to contribute in terms of time and skill set. —*Micaela Watts*

SHOWING UP FOR RACIAL JUSTICE (SURJ)

As more and more community activism takes aim at dismantling long-standing institutional structures—and centuries-old repercussions—on people of color, there's a call for white individuals to join in efforts to fight racism.

For many whites, answering that call is not always a clear-cut process, particularly when it comes to grassroots movements. How to combat racism without being, well, kinda racist isn't always clear to the race that has been at the top in this country since its founding.

SURJ exists to engage white people who want to dismantle racism. Like Black Lives Matter, SURJ is a national organization, and the Memphis chapter formed in the latter half of 2016.

Allison Glass, a representative of SURJ. Micaela Watts/*Memphis Flyer*

Allison Glass, one of the representatives of the group, said the catalyst to the Memphis chapter's formation came in July, shortly after more than 1,000 people shut down traffic on the I-40 bridge.

"It was such a powerful moment in Memphis that I think people felt really inspired," says Glass. "If these folks are going to commit such a courageous act, then we as white people need to organize other white people to join this effort."

In September, SURJ members dispersed through the crowds of the Cooper-Young Festival in their first action and signed up people interested in learning how to combat racism.

They also sold Black Lives Matter yard signs, with the proceeds going to the national BLM organization.

"One of the core principles of SURJ is about accountability, specifically to people-of-color-led organizations. So, SURJ signed on as an organizational partner to BLM," says Glass.

Like many community organizing groups, the interest in SURJ has risen following the election of President Trump. The organization will host its next direct training action on March 4th at Evergreen Presbyterian Church in Midtown. —*MW*

COMUNIDADES UNIDAS EN UNA VOZ

Though the Memphis chapter of Comunidades Unidas en Una Voz (United Communities in One Voice) formed in 2010, it made local headlines after organizing the 3,000 strong Memphis We Belong Here march on February 1st, in downtown Memphis.

"We never imagined the magnitude that this march would have and all the support we have received from people," says CUUV organizer, Christina Condori. "The actions are a response to the erroneous measures being implemented that hurt our families," she adds.

The erroneous measures Condori refers to may have come into the spotlight after President Trump's travel ban, but CUUV has been rallying against the lesser-known immigration practices that have been dividing families in the Mid-South for years.

Christina Condori, an organizer with CUUV. *Memphis Flyer*

They've called upon Shelby County officials to not work with ICE (U.S. Immigration and Customs Enforcement) in executing raids in Spanish-speaking communities, where individuals often do not know their rights as undocumented residents in Memphis.

"When there was a raid and people did not know their rights, we started attending TIRRC (Tennessee Immigrant and Refugee Rights Coalition) workshops and would then transfer the learned information regarding our rights," Condori says. CUUV has started hosting "Know Your Rights" workshops in churches, schools, and businesses within vulnerable communities.

CUUV has aligned with multiple organizations on the local and national level, including Black Lives Matter, LGBTQ-focused groups, and Fight for $15, the national living wage reform group. The diversity among their affiliated causes is linked to a core tenet, "No to xenophobia."

CUUV plans to continue organizing against policies that harm minority communities and will strive to make Memphis a place that welcomes immigrants and refugees. "We know we are not alone," says Condori. "We have many allies who are willing to support us." —*MW*

PROTECT OUR AQUIFER

Ward Archer is no stranger to matters of the environment and public interest. Several years back, he helped raise $4 million to buy endangered property along the Wolf River from would-be loggers on behalf of the Wolf River Conservancy.

In the process, Archer ended up well grounded (in every sense of that term) with the fact that the headwaters of the Wolf—the Baker's Pond area in northern Mississippi—served as a recharge area for the Memphis Sand aquifer, the source of Memphis' unusually pristine drinking water. Fascinated, Archer learned everything he could about the subject of ground water in general and the Sand aquifer in particular.

Archer, who is also a board member of Contemporary Media, Inc., the *Flyer*'s parent company, remains sensitive to any news regarding the aquifer and responded to the alarm raised last year by Scott Banbury of the Sierra Club about what had been a virtually unpublicized plan by the Tennessee Valley Authority to do some massive drilling into the aquifer to acquire coolant water for TVA's forthcoming natural-gas power plant.

Banbury and experts like Brian Waldron, of the University of Memphis, made a compelling case that the drilling—five wells, three of them already approved and some of them arguably ill-placed—could result in possible contamination of the aquifer's water supply.

Archer formed an ad hoc non-profit citizen's group, Protect Our Aquifer, which has held numerous public meetings to raise awareness of the issue and has participated in various actions to halt the TVA drilling. The group has joined the Sierra Club in an ongoing legal appeal, now in Chancery Court, to reverse the preliminary approval of the TVA drilling by the Shelby County Groundwater Control Board.

Protect Our Aquifer has a governing board of 10 and, perhaps more important, has an informal membership core of 1,800, communicating full-time via Facebook and fully able, as circumstances have demonstrated more than once, to mount an organized public presence. —*Jackson Baker*

24

THE LEFTIST COMEDY SHOW

It was the one-year anniversary of the Leftist Comedy Show, and show host Stan Polson thought he had one more joke—but, just to be sure, he checked an index card tucked in his breast pocket. "I'm really good at this," he mumbled. "Oh yeah, yeah," he said, reading deadpan from the card: "Men and women are really different. [laughter] Like, if you look on the internet, you can really see a lot of that. [laughter] Women are like, 'Quit harassing me!' And men are like, 'Nobody's harassing you, whore! Shut up! Kill yourself!' [pause] That seems different."

Resistance can be funny. At least, that's the take of those involved with the Leftist Comedy Show. It was born in the backyard of the Lamplighter Lounge and was supposed to be a one-off event, created by a group of friends with similar political interests. Turned out, the idea had legs, and the crowds are getting bigger.

The first events were planned with the goal of creating "safe space" comedy for audiences who might not feel comfortable at regular shows and open mics.

"A lot of people think we get offended by offensive material," he says. "But that's not really the case so much as we believe people when they tell us why they don't come to comedy shows. At a leftist show, you're not going to hear any rape jokes. You're not going to hear any racial slurs. We heard women didn't feel safe at open mics, comedy in Memphis was too segregated, and a lot of our transgender friends wouldn't go because they'd hear jokes that made them uncomfortable." The result is a comedy showcase with a lot of familiar faces on stage, but a unique audience.

The next Leftist Show is slated for April 15th at Midtown Crossing. It will be hosted by the Living Room Leftists, a local pro-union folk band. —*Chris Davis*

MID-SOUTH PEACE AND JUSTICE CENTER

"It's all about poverty at the end of the day," says Brad Watkins, executive director of the Mid-South Peace & Justice Center (MPJC). "Our organization was founded on the birthday of Dr. Martin Luther King Jr. because our founders believed, as Memphians, we have a special responsibility, as this was the city in which King was murdered. [They wanted to build] on the work of Dorothy Day, of Chavez, of King. This organization stands to push that vision forward."

MPJC launched in 1982 and originally had a wide-ranging, four-pronged mission: opposing apartheid; targeting industrial polluters; calling for nuclear disarmament; and opposing U.S. military involvement in Central America. Some 20 years later, the focus was narrowed to local issues when Jacob Flowers, whose parents were active at the center in the 1980s, became executive director. The center has now become a mother ship, of sorts, for other fledgling organizations, including the Memphis Bus Riders Union, Memphis United, and H.O.P.E. (Homeless Organizing for Power & Equality).

Watkins became executive director in 2014. "If you look at homelessness," he says, "if you look at public transit, if you look at our work with low-income tenants or immigrants or criminal-justice reform—all of that has its roots in poverty. And not just poverty like it's just something that happens, like the weather.

"Low income people pay all the late fees; they pay all the reactivation fees," Watkins continues. "The system bleeds people dry and keeps them trapped in poverty. If you wanted to sum up all of the issues we work on, it comes from a place of liberation from oppression, and poverty is the means to oppression."

Watkins says the center's role in the current spate of activism is a supportive one. He says activism works best when a movement is led by the people most affected by an issue.

"Here's what I want to say," says Watkins. "It's never too late for someone to get involved. None of us were here at the beginning of the movement, and none of us are too late to be a part of it." —*Susan Ellis*

ACTIVIST GRASSROOTS GROUPS IN MEMPHIS (PARTIAL LIST):

M.A.R.C.H. (Memphis Advocates for Radical Childcare)
Fight for $15
Healthy and Free Tennessee
Memphis Bus Riders Union
Memphis Feminist Collective
Comunidades Unidas en Una Voz
Home Health Care Workers
Memphis Voices for Palestine
Showing Up for Racial Justice (SURJ)
Official Memphis Chapter of Black Lives Matter
Sister Reach
Save the Greensward
OurRevolution 901
Preserve Our Aquifer
Mid-South Peace & Justice Center

Questions for Discussion and Journaling

1. The best research projects often begin when a person learns some tidbit of information that she finds intriguing, and so she attempts to learn more. You probably do this when you hear something scandalous about a favorite musician, actor, or athlete. Maybe you check Twitter, YouTube, or ESPN until you find more information. Because the initial information catches your attention, you intentionally go find more details. The same principle should apply to academic research. The best projects often emerge from some small idea that caught the researcher's attention. Keep this in mind as you seek out projects to research. In this article, the authors mention a piece of Memphis art called the "Upstanders Mural," located on South Main. The mural is a fascinating piece of Memphis history that all residents should know. You can find information about it at https://engage.facinghistory. org/mural/. Go to the website and choose one of the activists on the mural you'd like to read more about. Provide a summary of one of those activists along with why he or she is important to Memphis.

2. This article mentions many of the resistance efforts at work in Memphis. How many of these organizations were you familiar with before reading this article? Choose one of the organizations that is "new to you" and write a reflection in which you consider the pros and cons of that group. If you were to write a persuasive paper about that particular organization, what information might you need to help you and your readers decide whether the organization is worthwhile?

WEED!

Toby Sells and Micaela Watts

The aptly-named "Weed!" was a cover story from an October 2016 edition of *The Memphis Flyer* addressing recent changes to Memphis's marijuana ordinance and the impact it might have on the rest of the Mid-South region. Authors Toby Sells and Micaela Watts analyze the traditional strictness of marijuana laws in the South and discuss how laws have evolved over the years. They use emotional appeals to explain how the recent city ordinance relates to the regulations of neighboring states Arkansas and Mississippi and detail how stricter marijuana laws traditionally affect black citizens at a disproportionately high rate compared to their white counterparts. They appeal to the reader's sense of logos using statistics, charts, and data to argue that marijuana law reform is not just reasonable; it's inevitable.

What Memphis' new marijuana ordinance means—and what future changes may be in store (think Arkansas) for marijuana in the Mid-South.

Marijuana had smoldered in the minds of Memphis City Council members for six weeks, and, with the dramatic final vote only minutes away, Berlin Boyd had one last push to make his case.

Boyd wanted to soften city penalties for the simple possession of marijuana. It was the highest-profile piece of legislation he'd ever brought to City Hall. It had gained the attention of lawmakers, law enforcement officials, and marijuana advocates from across the state and beyond. And, without a doubt, they were all watching the council meeting, and especially watching Boyd that Tuesday night.

Boyd's mic went hot, and he began to speak. It was his last shot. If he was going to change some minds, he needed some magic, some blow-your-mind evidence, and some shut-you-down logic

"A person high on marijuana is in a chill mode," Boyd said. "But a person that's drunk with alcohol, they're very belligerent and want to talk all over you and slob everywhere over you, and that's not cool."

No, it didn't remind anyone of Ronald Reagan's "shining city on the hill" rhetorical moment. And, to be fair, it was only a part of the argument Boyd delivered that night. But it's what he said in the final moments before the vote.

And it worked. In true Memphis style, it worked. In truth, though, Boyd did not need to win hearts and minds on weed that afternoon. The votes, it seemed, were in.

Boyd's "chill mode" moment capped six weeks of what was at times a funny (sometimes odd) marijuana debate, rife with jokes about the munchies and not inhaling (à la Bill Clinton). But the debate was also sober, even somber at times.

Council members would sit silently with their eyes cast downward, acknowledging the massive disparity between African Americans and whites arrested for marijuana in Memphis. These facts are undisputed, the silence said, and this is a system we've allowed—and need to change.

Changing that system was at the heart of Boyd's motives. He'd repeatedly stated (as he did before the final vote) that lowering marijuana charges wasn't about marijuana at all, but about helping to break the chain of poverty for African Americans in a city that is predominately African-American.

NEW LAW IN TOWN

The council passed Boyd's ordinance—which was later co-sponsored by council member Martavius Jones—by the slimmest of margins: seven for; six against. The vote breakdown was not along the traditional racial or district lines often seen in council votes.

Those voting for the ordinance pushed the need to do something different to aid African Americans in Memphis, to level economic disparities, and help keep them out of the criminal-justice-system quagmire.

Those opposed questioned the details of the rule's implementation, questioned if the city had a right to set such a law, and seemed influenced by local law enforcement officials, who were wary of the rule's effects on the streets of Memphis.

Here's what the new law does and doesn't do (h/t to council Chairman Kemp Conrad):

- It gives Memphis Police Department (MPD) officers two choices when they catch someone in possession of a half ounce or less of marijuana or paraphernalia.
- They can issue a $50 city fine, which is like a traffic ticket and comes with no criminal record.
- Or they can go with the current state charge, which is a Class A misdemeanor that comes with a maximum $2,500 fine, up to a year in prison, and a mark on your criminal record.

- City Court judges can waive the $50 fine and instead require community service.

- The law does not impact minors.

- The law does not change D.U.I. laws.

- It does not prevent employers or landlords from drug testing and/or prohibiting drug use on their properties.

- MPD will report annually the number of $50 fines issued for pot possession versus the state's misdemeanor charge. That report will break down those charges by race and gender.

DON'T BE 'IGNORANT'

The big question now is: Can you smoke dope openly in front of Memphis police? Thankfully, council member Janis Fullilove gave us a totally nuanced breakdown of the question before the vote last week. "We're talking about an ordinance that some people in this city believe they will have free rein to walk up in front of a police officer, take a hit off a joint, and say, 'now you can't do a doggone thing to me'," Fullilove said to a smattering of laughter. "You are laughing but... we have some ignorant people in our city. When I say 'ignorant', I don't mean it degradingly. That they just don't know. Because they have not listened long enough or been instructed long enough that this is not what this ordinance is about."

Here is the straight dope (heh) from MPD director Michael Rallings: "Marijuana is not legal in the state of Tennessee; it is not legal in the city of Memphis," Rallings said in a MPD Facebook video released after Tuesday's vote. "If you are found in possession of less than a half ounce [of marijuana], it is still a violation of the law."

Last year, 655 adults were arrested by the MPD on misdemeanor marijuana charges. From January 1st to September 4th this year, 521 adults were arrested on the same charges. In Shelby County last year, about 3,800 people were arrested for possessing less than a half ounce of marijuana, according to numbers from Conrad.

Those same numbers revealed that nearly 90 percent of those arrested for misdemeanor weed in Shelby County were black. The American Civil Liberties Union (ACLU) says blacks in the Memphis area are 4.2 times as likely to be arrested for marijuana possession as a white person, though the two groups use marijuana at comparable rates.

"For too long, thousands of Memphians have been arrested for possession of tiny amounts of marijuana—leading to disastrous consequences for their lives, including the loss of jobs, education, and housing opportunities," Hedy Weinberg, executive director of the ACLU of Tennessee, said in a letter before the final marijuana vote here. "Make no mistake—this is an issue of racial justice."

Council member Patrice Robinson said she did not support drug use, but she supported "doing the right thing." In her case, that meant voting for the weed ordinance. "We know that there is a disparity between African-American and white males, especially with this issue," she said. "We no longer can continue doing the exact same thing that we've been doing in the past to create a new reality. That does not work."

DECRIMINALIZATION?

Proponents of the ordinance argued the new rule was not as much about marijuana legalization, as it was about criminal justice. Council member Worth Morgan said it wasn't about decriminalization. But most news headlines that were posted after the vote included that word.

However the definition of "decriminalization" from the Marijuana Policy Project (MPP) and the National Organization for the Reform of Marijuana Laws (NORML) goes beyond the Memphis ordinance to mean, basically, no penalty for possession of marijuana.

No matter what you label it, the new ordinance is a type of criminal justice reform. Josh Spickler, executive director of Just City, said the new rule is a very small reform, one that likely won't give rise to the sweeping changes his nonprofit, criminal reform advocacy group would like to see. But it's at least a recognition, said Spickler, that there is "disproportionate policing" in Memphis for marijuana possession.

"So, in a time when we've had a Black Lives Matter protest shut down the (Hernando-DeSoto Bridge) in Memphis, this is a recognition of one of the reasons why that segment of the population is so frustrated," Spickler said. "Young men of color are targeted and are vastly over-represented in our courts."

While Spickler was hesitant to say the move will make a large difference, he did call it, "a step in the right direction."

But will it really help?

Not much, according to Shelby County District Attorney General Amy Weirich.

Reform proponents said lowering charges would also help clean up court dockets and, perhaps, lower jail populations. But Weirich said of the 3,800 arrested in the county on pot charges last year, only about 300 faced prosecution by her office.

"So, the notion that there are thousands and thousands of people in custody on misdemeanor marijuana charges is false," she said.

Spickler agreed. Though, he pointed out, marijuana charges are often piled on top of a litany of other charges, such as a broken taillight, too-dark window tint, or other offenses. MPD officials said other offenses often include handgun possession. The marijuana charges help send people to 201 Poplar or pile up their charges.

NEXT STEPS

Director Rallings said he would not allow his officers to issue city citations on simple possession until he has cleared an implementation strategy with the Memphis City Court Clerk and city prosecutors. He did not offer a timeline for the process. But he noted in a Facebook video that no city citations will be issued until after the minutes of last week's meeting are approved by council next week. Then, he said, Memphis Mayor Jim Strickland has 10 days to sign those minutes.

So, it would be wise to wait for the final word before you go out ridin' dirty. However, when those citations are ready to go, MPD officers will have a choice: the arrest on state charges or issue a city ticket. So, who gets what, and might that not lead to a different of type disparity?

MPD spokesman Louis Brownlee refused to offer any details on what factors will inform an officer's decision to charge individual violators. When asked how they will decide, Brownlee only wrote, "It's the officer's discretion."

This is one of the problems with the new rule, said Bill Gibbons, the former Shelby County district attorney general and former head of the Tennessee Department of Safety and Homeland Security who is now president of the Shelby County Crime Commission.

"If it's left up to the individual officer to make that decision, arguably, you can see a serious disparity in terms of how individuals are treated, based on who the officer is and what part of town it's in. And that can create a whole new set of problems," Gibbons said. "Is that officer going to cite someone under state law, which means it's a misdemeanor? Or, is he going to cite someone under the ordinance, which means it's not. That could create some serious disparities."

This is why Boyd tweaked his original ordinance to include that an annual report be delivered to the council. It will show if MPD officers gave more state charges to African Americans, and/or whether they were more lenient when dealing with whites and other ethnicities. Nashville Metro Council members, who passed a similar weed ordinance two weeks before Memphis did, are now attempting to include a similar report to go with their legislation.

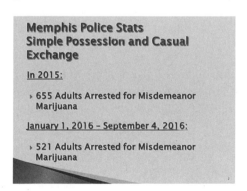

Memphis Police Stats Simple Possession and Casual Exchange

In 2015:

▸ 655 Adults Arrested for Misdemeanor Marijuana

January 1, 2016 – September 4, 2016:

▸ 521 Adults Arrested for Misdemeanor Marijuana

Marijuana and Handgun STATS

January 1, 2016 thru September 4, 2016

Since January 1, 2016, the Memphis Police Department has made 132 Arrest involving individuals in Possession of Misdemeanor Amounts of Marijuana with a Handgun

January	February	March	April	May	June	July	August	September	TOTAL
20	16	16	28	18	19	7	12	2	132

MEANWHILE, IN NEIGHBORING STATES...

Memphis borders Mississippi and Arkansas. That means that those living here are dealing with three states—and three different sets of marijuana laws.

In Mississippi, possessing 30 grams or less carries no charge or jail time, with a maximum fine of $250 for a first offense. The punishment gets a little steeper for the second and third offenses, with fines capping at $500, and the possibility of serving from five days to six months in prison.

Though possession of a small amount of marijuana is basically decriminalized, the distribution of marijuana is still illegal and categorized as a felony. Being caught with the smallest amount deemed to have been packaged for sale will earn you three years in jail at a minimum, as well as $3,000 in fines.

In Mississippi's 2016 legislative season, state Representative Joel Bomgar filed a bill that would have allowed seriously or terminally ill patients access to medical marijuana. Despite being filed by a Republican in a red state, the bill didn't make it out of the committee. However, it's not unusual for medical marijuana efforts to take years to pass at the state level.

Things appear to be moving considerably faster in Arkansas. The Natural State will have two medical marijuana measures on the November 8th ballot. If both measures pass, the measure receiving the most "yes" votes will become law.

Though similar in that both measures will mean some form of marijuana legalization, the two initiatives differ when it comes to whom they impact, said Melissa Fults, an organizer with Arkansans for Compassionate Care, the organization that's pushing for the Arkansas Medical Cannabis Act (AMCA). "Our [measure] is designed to protect patients, and not use patients to get rich," Fults said. AMCA will allow some patients to grow up to six plants for personal use. Fults claimed that the competing measure, the Arkansas Medical Marijuana Amendment (AMMA), has language designed to protect would-be profiteers, who could begin selling medical marijuana.

The key difference between the two measures lies in who can grow and sell pot. Under AMMA, personal cultivation would not be allowed, and there would be no cap on patient fees. So access to needed medical marijuana would be limited to dispensaries that, like any business, could charge whatever amount they wanted.

"I would never tell anybody not to vote for anything, but we do want folks to read up on the language of Issue 6 (AMMA)," explained Fults. "Theirs is designed for people to make money, ours is designed to protect patients and their families who need this medicine," Fults said.

The AMMA measure will put Arkansas more in line with states that have legalized medical marijuana via dispensaries, such California.

It's possible that neither measure will pass come November 8th, but Fults—as do many others in Arkansas—believes one of the two measures will become law. Should that happen, legal marijuana will be available for sale just across the Mississippi from Memphis. Kind of like fireworks.

"If Arkansas were to legalize medical marijuana before Tennessee, I think you'd see something like what happened in the 1990s before Tennessee liberalized its beer laws," Scott Banbury, a local environmental activist, said.

"You couldn't buy most craft beers in Tennessee. Due to restrictions on alcohol content, you could only buy weak domestic beer in convenience stores and high-gravity beers in liquor stores."

It was not uncommon 20 years ago for Memphians to drive to West Memphis for beer because of the variety of brews that were available. Tennessee's strict beer laws and keg-size limits prevented state residents from buying beer that wasn't produced by large, corporate-owned breweries such as Anheuser-Busch and Miller.

Will the same dynamic happen with marijuana? There's little doubt that it will. Memphis would be by far the largest potential market for legal pot in the Mid-South.

Arkansas residency would be required to access medical marijuana regardless of which measure, if either, is passed. Potentially, residents of the surrounding states could relocate to Arkansas to gain access, or create other end-around moves, such as fake IDs, to "prove" Arkansas residency. According to Banbury, that creates "a serious social and economic injustice."

"Folks that can afford to go to Arkansas, visit a doctor, and get a prescription, will, and they'll leave their tax money in Arkansas," Banbury said. "Other people, with no transportation, or unable to afford the costs of getting a prescription, will be left to the black market in Memphis."

Needless to say, a lot of people will be watching and waiting to see what happens when the smoke clears on November 8th.

Questions for Discussion and Journaling

1. The article explains that City Councilman Berlin Boyd argued that "lowering marijuana charges wasn't about marijuana at all, but about helping to break the chain of poverty for African Americans in a city that is predominately African American." Using statistics and testimony from the text, provide 2–3 examples that support Boyd's claim.

2. The authors reference a debate concerning whether the new legislation is concerned with decriminalization or criminal justice reform. How do these words differ? Why is the difference important to the authors' argument? What other terminology is important to the authors' argument? How do they (or don't they) define these terms?

3. Sells mentions that ordinances in the bordering states of Mississippi and Arkansas differ from Memphis ordinances. What are some ways in which they differ, and what is Sells and Watts' purpose in mentioning these differences? How does drawing attention to these differences support their argument?

WELCOME TO MEMPHIS!

Toby Sells

"Welcome to Memphis!" by Toby Sells provides an entertaining look into the tourism business in Memphis. The article, originally published in *The Memphis Flyer* on May 11, 2017, describes several specific events and locations that attract the city's tourists, including Memphis in May, Bass Pro Shops, and Graceland. Not only does Sells provide specific numbers to show the effect of tourism on Memphis' economy, but he also relays his own experiences visiting several popular destinations, thus imbuing the article with both factual data (logos) and personal anecdote (pathos). He also interviews several prominent figures in the tourism industry, using primary research to explain what Memphis has to offer, not just to tourists, but to native Memphians as well.

Tourism is paying big ($3.2 billion a year) dividends for the Bluff City.

Last year, about 11 million people visited the city of Memphis. That's roughly the population of Cuba or the American state of Georgia. There's no official tourist season in Memphis, really, like spring break or summertime at beaches. But there are some high tides—Elvis Week and Memphis in May (MIM), for example.

Some 265,000 people came to the east bank of the Mississippi River in May last year for the Beale Street Music Festival, World Championship Barbecue Cooking Contest, 901 Fest, and the Great American River Run. About 60 percent of those visitors came from outside of Shelby County—from all 50 states and from all over the world.

May is easily the biggest blip on the Memphis tourism radar. But Robert Griffin, marketing director for MIM, said that's largely because the festival is a month long with many diverse events, adding that, "Elvis Week is huge, but it's only a week."

"Welcome to Memphis!" by Toby Sells. From *The Memphis Flyer*, May 11, 2017. Reprinted by permission of the publisher.

Hospitality is the bedrock of the tourism industry. And as I found out in reporting this story, those in the Memphis tourism industry are also hospitable to each other. The competition is healthy, but the players are cooperative, not cutthroat. That's largely due to the many different types of tourists who come here and the many different experiences Memphis can offer them. There's plenty for everyone, it seems.

Memphis tourism was a $3.2 billion industry in 2015, according to the latest numbers from the U.S. Travel Association.

About 67,800 people are employed in the "leisure and hospitality" business in Shelby County, according to the freshest figures (April 2017) from the United States Bureau of Labor Statistics. Tourism is the fifth-largest employer in Shelby County, only behind industries transportation (read: FedEx Corp.), education, health care, government, the very-broad "business services" category.

WHERE ARE THE TOURISTS?

As a Memphian, you probably think about Beale Street, Graceland, Bass Pro Shops at the Pyramid, and those riverboats—places you may not go to regularly. Intellectually, you know those places are filled with tourists, but as we go about our workaday world, most of us rarely see those folks. When my folks came in town for a visit last year, my stepfather wanted to see Bass Pro, so off we went.

We stood by the gleaming glass fish tank by the kids' section, along with 40 or so other visitors, watching as catfish, bass, and crappie swim around. Then a voice broke from the ether.

"Hello, how are you today?"

A man in a black dive suit had climbed into the tank and was waving and talking to us from behind his swim mask. We went from amused to entranced. The man fed the fish from a plastic bag, describing the different species that were swimming around him and nipping at his fingers.

"Thanks for joining me today," the man said, wrapping up his show. "Let me ask, how many of you are from out of town?"

Every hand but mine went into the air. It was 10:30 a.m. on a Wednesday. Ordinarily, I'd be at *The Memphis Flyer* office, but on this day I had found the tourists—and I was one, myself.

"When you got a glimpse of the visitor economy that day at Bass Pro, I'm sure you went 'Wow!,'" said Kevin Kane, president of the Memphis Convention and Visitors Bureau. "That's when it hits home: There's a lot of power in [tourism]. It's a $3.2 billion industry in Memphis. It's a big deal. It's important."

That's why we're taking a closer look at the fun-having industry here. (And, look, y'all, I promise I had no idea that this week is National Travel and Tourism Week. Seriously.)

THE AMERICAN DREAM SAFARI

26

Tad Pierson drives a time machine, a 1955 Cadillac, and he'll pick you up from your hotel.

That's how it works with his American Dream Safari tour company. Since 1996, Belgians, Brazilians, Taiwanese, Texans, and a whole bunch of Brits, and hundreds of others from around the U.S. and the world have piled into Pierson's Caddy to see history through its windows and, perhaps, get a few "psychic souvenirs" (more on that later).

"It's a beautiful town to cruise around in," Pierson said, "Because a lot of subjects come up."

Pierson's clients know they're getting a general tour of Memphis, but those conversations easily swing to the city's music, its place in the civil rights movement, the Civil War, and, of course, Elvis.

Pierson hones in on their interests and tailors the tours to his customers. While he hits the typical "must-sees," he also takes visitors to some out-of-way spots—like the place where Johnny Cash met the Tennessee Two, or to B.B. King's first house in Memphis.

Pierson calls what he does "anthro-tourism." It's the same idea as eco-tourism, he said, but with history as the focus. He hopes that the upsurge of new development here won't spoil the city's most essential asset: "Memphis is real," Pierson said. "People come here for that reason. They don't come here because it's, say, an artificially rebuilt waterfront that rips them off. It's an authentic scene here, and we have to protect that."

Pierson will also send you home with a bit of that Memphis realness. Instead of tchotchkes or a T-shirt, Pierson hopes his clients go home with a powerful Memphis memory, like, say, the aroma of barbecue wafting over the parking lot at Cozy Corner.

"These psychic souvenirs are just moments that go by the window of the car and you're like—ah!—I gotta remember that one forever," Pierson said.

OUR "BIG HOOKS"

Kane, who is basically the mayor of Memphis tourism, would rather talk about our city's "big hooks" rather than give some clinical listing of our top, most-visited attractions.

Music, he said, is without a doubt our "biggest hook" here, whether it's Graceland or Sun Studios or the Stax Museum or Beale Street, or the Center for Southern Folklore or the Rock 'n' Soul Museum or the Blues Hall of Fame—all places Kane cited off the top his head.

"I think our music heritage gives us a cool factor that only a few cities can boast about," Kane said. "Memphis, Nashville, Chicago, Kansas City, and Austin—only a handful of cities can lay claim to music and do it legitimately."

Kane thinks another big hook for Memphis is its Southern culture and, largely, that means food. Barbecue is likely the city's second-largest cultural export, after music. That's evidenced by lines that stretch out the door at Central BBQ's downtown location or the fact that the Rendezvous' waiting area is big enough to house a bar. But, also, consider that the

MIM barbecue contest drew 37,146 tourists last year, who spent about $17 million while they were here.

But Kane notes that Memphis' culinary scene is growing beyond barbecue. Chefs here are regularly opening diverse new spots and further defining the Memphis dining landscape.

"The Southern product we're able to roll out—with Southern art and food and friendliness—is huge for us," Kane said.

The big hooks for Memphis tourism also include "family fun stuff" like the Children's Museum or the Memphis Zoo. It's also important historical attractions such as the National Civil Rights Museum, and outdoor attractions like Shelby Farms Park and Big River Crossing, Kane said.

For the record, Memphis' top 10 tourist attractions in 2015 were, in order, by attendance: Beale Street (5 million visitors), Bass Pro (2 million), Agricenter International (1.3 million), Memphis Zoo (1.1 million), Overton Square (1 million), Memphis Grizzlies (820,000), The Peabody Grand Lobby (750,000), Golf & Games Family Park (634,000), Mike Rose Soccer Complex (620,000), and Graceland (600,000). These figures are according to the *Memphis Business Journal*'s 2016–2017 Book of Lists.

A TOUR OF POSSIBILITIES

Carolyn Michael-Banks knows her tour is nontraditional—and it may even make some people uncomfortable. But her goal in founding A Tour of Possibilities was to "share the historical and cultural gems that African Americans have contributed to Memphis." It does so with stops at Beale Street, Robert Church Park, Slave Haven Underground Railroad Museum, Soulsville, Stax, and more.

Michael-Banks spent years doing tours for other companies in Philadelphia and Washington, D.C. She included African-American history in those tours, as well, but her bosses felt it made some uncomfortable.

"The thing about history is that there are parts of it that are definitely uncomfortable," she said. "But just because they are uncomfortable doesn't make them not exist. Our tag line [at her former company] was 'reliving history.' I felt compelled to relive it completely and [my company] is doing that now."

Hop on Michael-Banks' van (which she calls the Van of Possibilities) and you may find Brits, other Europeans, Australians, and Americans, many from Chicago, Texas, and California, she said. People from all over, except Memphis (more on that later).

Her tour is designed to stop at a place "that will probably make you feel uncomfortable" but leave within 10 minutes and head off to something else. She's not doing a documentary, she said, and she's not a professor giving a lecture. "So, I believe there's a way to blend history without sugarcoating what is difficult," said Michael-Banks. "You go through a rollercoaster of emotions, and that is intentional."

Having a small van (10 passengers) allows her clients to feel comfortable enough to express themselves. Most respond positively to the tour, she said. And Memphians might change their minds about their own town if they'd come along.

"If Memphians actually got why 11 million come here every year, they would feel a little different about themselves," she said. "They wouldn't be saying, 'Oh, no, you don't want to come here.' I'm working on trying to get to them to say, 'Oh, you have to come here.'"

HOW'RE WE DOING?

Memphis has held steady at number two in Tennessee tourism for many years. Nashville is a regional tourism powerhouse, pushed farther and faster now by the newly built, $623-million Music City Center convention center.

Kane said he uses two barometers to gauge the health of Memphis' tourism industry: attraction attendance and occupancy room rates at area hotels and motels. The city is healthy, he said, and its future is "very, very bright."

Last year, about five million tickets were sold for paid attractions here like the zoo, museums, and other attractions. Hotel occupancy spiked 10 percent three years ago, Kane said, and the figure has been slightly up or flat ever since (but it hasn't receded) from about 5.4 million paid room nights per year.

Kane bemoaned some near-misses that could've boosted tourism, such as not attracting the Tanger Outlets to the Pinch District near the Cook Convention Center. But an update to the Convention Center is in the works. Renovation construction will begin there as soon as September, Kane said. It's a $60-million facelift project aimed at modernizing the space with a "total interior and exterior renovation."

The project will bring functionality to the building, including more loading docks with easier access. It'll also bring aesthetic upgrades, such as views of the Mississippi River and what Kane calls a "21st-century feel" to the inside of the building.

"We're not going to build the Music City Center; we don't have the money for that," Kane said. "We are going to make a substantial investment in our convention center, and I think it'll pay huge dividends for us."

SPROCK N' ROLL

Call it a pedal bar, a party bike, a rolling tavern, a bar bike, or something else, but Ashley Coleman wants you and your friends to come try it.

Sprock N' Roll brought their party bike (let's just call them party bikes, okay?) to Memphis two years ago. Since then, hundreds have mounted the oversized bike seats and pumped the mobile bars around downtown or Midtown.

Not clear on the concept? Imagine a small bar with five bar stools on each side, a bench in the back—under a tin roof and on four wheels. A bartender hangs out in the middle, and a driver mans the steering wheel and brakes at the front. You and your friends provide the power by pedaling. The more people, the easier the pedaling.

Coleman said the company's most popular tours are two-hour pub crawls. But the company also offers an "Artsy Fartsy Tour" (which begins at the Art Project), progressive dinner tours, and brunch tours.

While most of Memphis' tourists stay downtown, Coleman said she tries to lure them to Midtown with a tour that rolls between Overton Square and Cooper-Young (and several bars en route). Coleman bills the tour as "where the locals like to go."

"Some aren't coming for the Beale Street party," Coleman said. "They want to see other cool parts of town. Many [tourists] aren't familiar with Midtown. We take them off Cooper down Rembert, and everyone enjoys seeing the houses. They'll say, 'We love this part of town!'"

Coleman said it's likely that more locals ride her party bikes than tourists, but plenty of tourists still ride through Midtown, she said, remembering a time a group of Australians rode down Cooper with a group of Iowans.

"They end up staying in that part of town," Coleman said. "They'll get off the bike and explore some more. It's a great way for us to get the tourists to Midtown and get them spending some money there."

May is a big season for Sprock N' Roll, Coleman said, noting that they have to work to make sure there's enough availability to meet the demand.

"It's just a fun way to see the city."

THE REAL DEAL

Attracting more conventions and conferences has long been a goal of the CVB, and a theme of many of the group's annual meetings. The renovated convention center is supposed to help with that, but Kane said the convention center still needs a large, nearby, full-service hotel. "We've got the Sheraton, the Peabody, the Hilton out East and, now, the Guest House at Graceland, but none of them are within walking distance of the convention center," Kane said.

Kane added that another missing piece of the tourism puzzle is an indoor sports complex. Kane and the CVB were major supporters of a plan formulated a few years ago that would transform the Mid-South Fairgrounds into a mammoth youth sports complex, with sports fields, indoor arenas, a hotel, and big-box retailers.

"We're ready for that type of a complex somewhere in Memphis," Kane said. "I don't know if it'll be at the Fairgrounds or if it'll be out in Cordova or downtown. I don't know where the darned thing will be located. But we're really aggressively working on that now."

Kane, who has spent more than 25 years selling the Memphis experience to potential visitors around the globe is, indeed, bullish on Memphis tourism. For him, there is a "cool factor and an intrigue and mystique about Memphis." It's also authentic, he said.

"I don't know if you saw it that day you were in Bass Pro, but overwhelmingly most of the visitors who come here are impressed by the friendliness of our people," Kane said. "They genuinely find that Memphis is real and it's not manufactured, not some made-up experience. It's a real, natural, real-deal type of experience. So, we've kept it real, and people appreciate that."

Questions for Discussion and Journaling

1. Although Sells mentions specific events and places that attract tourists, his emphasis seems to be on the latter. What effect might it have had if Sells had detailed his experiences at the aforementioned events as well? Why do you think he focused primarily on the locations instead?

2. Use this article to generate three topics for a potential research project. What are some of the "hooks" mentioned in this article? What could you research about them?

3. Who is the primary audience of this article? What helped you determine this audience? Was it the tone, the publication venue, or other information found within the text? If you wanted to write on this topic for an academic audience, what would you need to do differently?

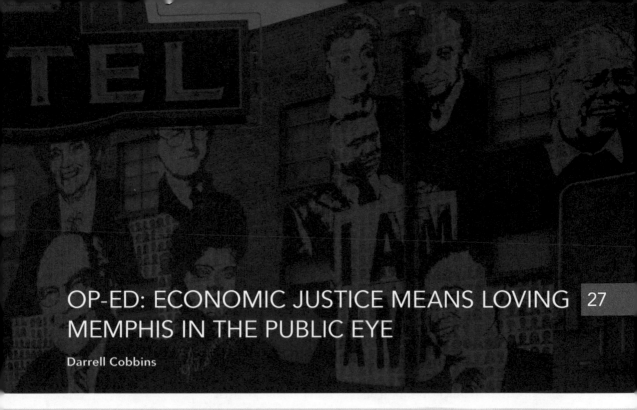

OP-ED: ECONOMIC JUSTICE MEANS LOVING MEMPHIS IN THE PUBLIC EYE

Darrell Cobbins

"Op-Ed: Economic Justice Means Loving Memphis in the Public Eye" is an opinion editorial by Darrell Cobbins (president and CEO of Universal Commercial) which appeared in *High Ground News* in February 2017. Cobbins makes an empathetic plea to his audience by describing the economic injustice that has afflicted the city of Memphis for years. What Cobbins wants regarding economic justice is as idealistic as it is simple: a "unified collective response with responsibility, accountability, and periodic reporting to the broader community on moving the needle in the opposite direction of where it is pointing today." In this sense, Cobbins's editorial can be viewed as a proposal, and his argument intends to move his audience to action. Through this potent combination of rhetoric paired with first-person perspective, Cobbins makes a successful and engaging appeal to his audience, arguing for some much needed harmony in the community and, perhaps most importantly, for love.

The respected theologian and professor Dr. Cornel West says that "Never forget that justice is what love looks like in public."

In the context of economic justice, in Memphis and beyond, we must ask ourselves continually "where is the love?" How have we manifested our love for Memphis, and more importantly our fellow Memphians, through the prism of economics?

There is no doubt that to examine our economics and history, we must not be apprehensive to examine race as a component if we are to be authentic and honest in our pursuit of real solutions.

Memphis' history as a cotton metropolis for centuries created generational wealth that still benefits Memphis' economic and philanthropic initiatives to this very day.

Conversely, that same history has also contributed to generations of Memphians on the outside looking into the window of prosperity. We cannot shy away from acknowledging this reality of historical economic imbalance if our goal is to create a better Memphis for future generations.

In late 2012, the Commercial Appeal published several installments of "POVERTY, Inc." where reporters delved deeply into local poverty as an engine within the Memphis economy estimated at $200M+ annually. It highlighted personal stories of the daily struggles of many individual Memphians as well as the public policy that funds and subsidizes initiatives and families in Memphis.

After reading this important piece of work, I have long awaited the follow-up piece that should be entitled WEALTH, Inc., to illuminate the wealth and prosperity that exists in Memphis in spite of the high poverty rate that has persisted for so long. Maybe this could better assist us in understanding this "Tale of Two Memphises" that exists since we have for decades focused so much attention on how much poverty exists.

In 2015, a study performed by New York-based financial technology firm Smart Asset had Shelby County was ranked the No. 1 county in Tennessee for inherited wealth and No. 78 in the nation, which is ahead of Nashville/Davidson County by a wide margin. No county in Georgia, Alabama, Louisiana, Mississippi, Arkansas, Missouri or Kentucky ranked higher.

In mid 2015, the bipartisan economic think tank Economic Innovation Group, in a report published in the Washington Post, ranked Memphis as the city in the nation with the highest economic disparity citing that 68 percent of its population lives in distressed areas. Coming in a distant second was Fresno, California with 48 percent.

A thorough examination at both ends of this spectrum would be beneficial to Memphis in fostering a deeper understanding how we arrived where we are today, in an economic context, and help us chart a path forward that can effectively help grow prosperity in more corners of Memphis.

The esteemed author and social critic James Baldwin wrote, "Not everything that is faced can changed, but nothing can be changed until it is faced."

We can all agree that there have been significant strides socially in our community over time. We eat together, socialize, attend sporting events, concerts, serve on our boards and work hand in hand together all in the "grit-n-grind" spirit that has come to define Memphis and being a Memphian.

The one area that plagues and impedes our progress is that of the economic imbalance that has persisted for generations and the opportunity cost for our city that accompanies this imbalance. The business term "opportunity cost" is defined as "the loss of potential gain from other alternatives when one alternative is chosen."

Crime, fatherless households, inadequate educational attainment, workforce readiness, blighted neighborhoods all have a root that connects back to the symbolic albatross of too many Memphians not fully participating and contributing to the local economy.

This is why privately I have urged specific local philanthropic and civic institutions to invest in the creation of a comprehensive plan to address the entrenched systemic poverty in Memphis.

We have many social service organizations working tirelessly to address issues that derive from our severe economic imbalance. They should be lauded for their commendable love and dedication to deal with what most consider an intractable issue.

My desire, however, is to see a knitting together of the work of these organizations into a unified collective response with responsibility, accountability, and periodic reporting to the broader community on moving the needle in the opposite direction of where it is pointing today.

We have a plan for our parks and greenways, our Downtown, our workforce development, then why not a plan to address the biggest obstacle staring us in the face? A locking of arms that says we will not be a community where this economic imbalance exists for future generations to toil over.

It ends on our watch. Then, and only then, will we be able to demonstrate to the nation what loving Memphis looks like in public.

Questions for Discussion and Journaling

1. Cobbins opens his article with a quote from respected professor/theologian Dr. Cornel West, a strong and immediate appeal to the reader's sense of authority (ethos). As a reader, how did this ethical appeal introduce you to both the author and their argument? How else does Cobbins build his credibility throughout the article?

2. Cobbins presents data on economic disparity in Memphis, comparing and contrasting this data to data from other major cities. What kind of rhetorical appeal is this? Did you find the rhetorical comparison compelling? Why or why not? Were the facts he presented surprising? How so?

3. Cobbins argues that Memphis needs to address the economic disparity of wealth distribution. He invites readers to think of solutions to this problem and also proposes some of his own. If you were to develop a 'proposing a solution' argument about decreasing poverty in Memphis for your research paper, what other kind of data would you want to look for? What kind of sources would you need?

INVESTIGATIVE JOURNALISM

SELECTIONS FROM

SOUTHERN HORRORS:
LYNCH LAW IN ALL ITS PHASES

Ida B. Wells-Barnett

These selections by journalist Ida B. Wells-Barnett first appeared in *The New York Age* and then in a pamphlet entitled *Southern Horrors: Lynch Law in All Its Phases* in 1892. The name of the pamphlet is as powerful as it is evocative, simultaneously tugging at the reader's heartstrings and intentionally making them more than a bit uncomfortable. Wells-Barnett's essays detail the nineteenth-century South's justification of lynch mobs, uncovering the excuses and fabrications made by the White Press. Wells-Barnett specifically examines the role of the press, explaining that, "Not content with misrepresenting the race, the mob-spirit was not to be satisfied until the paper which was doing all it could to counteract this impression was silenced." She argues that the white press was not merely condoning lynch mobs but encouraging them by deliberately producing misinformation while simultaneously repressing free speech. This combination seems to invoke within the reader both a sense of empathy as well as an almost overwhelming feeling of dread. As you read, ask yourself how Wells-Barnett managed to appeal to resistant white audiences with this disturbing yet poignant report on the horrors of lynch law in the South.

[Transcriber's Note: This pamphlet was first published in 1892 but was subsequently reprinted. It's not apparent if the curiosities in spelling date back to the original or were introduced later; they have been retained as found, and the reader is left to decide. Please verify with another source before quoting this material.]

Selections from *Southern Horrors: Lynch Law in All Its Phases* by Ida B. Wells-Barnett. 1892.

PREFACE

The greater part of what is contained in these pages was published in the *New York Age* June 25, 1892, in explanation of the editorial which the Memphis whites considered sufficiently infamous to justify the destruction of my paper, the *Free Speech*.

Since the appearance of that statement, requests have come from all parts of the country that "Exiled" (the name under which it then appeared) be issued in pamphlet form. Some donations were made, but not enough for that purpose. The noble effort of the ladies of New York and Brooklyn Oct. 5 have enabled me to comply with this request and give the world a true, unvarnished account of the causes of lynch law in the South.

This statement is not a shield for the despoiler of virtue, nor altogether a defense for the poor blind Afro-American Sampsons who suffer themselves to be betrayed by white Delilahs. It is a contribution to truth, an array of facts, the perusal of which it is hoped will stimulate this great American Republic to demand that justice be done though the heavens fall.

It is with no pleasure I have dipped my hands in the corruption here exposed. Somebody must show that the Afro-American race is more sinned against than sinning, and it seems to have fallen upon me to do so. The awful death-roll that Judge Lynch is calling every week is appalling, not only because of the lives it takes, the rank cruelty and outrage to the victims, but because of the prejudice it fosters and the stain it places against the good name of a weak race.

The Afro-American is not a bestial race. If this work can contribute in any way toward proving this, and at the same time arouse the conscience of the American people to a demand for justice to every citizen, and punishment by law for the lawless, I shall feel I have done my race a service. Other considerations are of minor importance.

IDA B. WELLS

New York City, Oct. 26, 1892

To the Afro-American women of New York and Brooklyn, whose race love, earnest zeal and unselfish effort at Lyric Hall, in the City of New York, on the night of October 5, 1892—made possible its publication, this pamphlet is gratefully dedicated by the author.

THE OFFENSE

Wednesday evening May 24, 1892, the city of Memphis was filled with excitement. Editorials in the daily papers of that date caused a meeting to be held in the Cotton Exchange Building; a committee was sent for the editors of the *Free Speech* an Afro- American journal published in that city, and the only reason the open threats of lynching that were made were not carried out was because they could not be found. The cause of all this commotion was the following editorial published in the *Free Speech* May 21, 1892, the Saturday previous.

Eight negroes lynched since last issue of the *Free Speech* one at Little Rock, Ark., last Saturday morning where the citizens broke(?) into the penitentiary and got their man; three near Anniston, Ala., one near New Orleans; and three at Clarksville, Ga., the last three for killing a white man, and five on the same old racket—the new alarm about raping white women. The same programme of hanging, then shooting bullets into the lifeless bodies was carried out to the letter.

Nobody in this section of the country believes the old thread-bare lie that Negro men rape white women. If Southern white men are not careful, they will overreach themselves and public sentiment will have a reaction; a conclusion will then be reached which will be very damaging to the moral reputation of their women.

The *Daily Commercial* of Wednesday following, May 25, contained the following leader:

Those negroes who are attempting to make the lynching of individuals of their race a means for arousing the worst passions of their kind are playing with a dangerous sentiment. The negroes may as well understand that there is no mercy for the negro rapist and little patience with his defenders. A negro organ printed in this city, in a recent issue publishes the following atrocious paragraph: "Nobody in this section of the country believes the old threadbare lie that negro men rape white women. If Southern white men are not careful they will overreach themselves, and public sentiment will have a reaction; and a conclusion will be reached which will be very damaging to the moral reputation of their women."

The fact that a black scoundrel is allowed to live and utter such loathsome and repulsive calumnies is a volume of evidence as to the wonderful patience of Southern whites. But we have had enough of it.

There are some things that the Southern white man will not tolerate, and the obscene intimations of the foregoing have brought the writer to the very outermost limit of public patience. We hope we have said enough.

The *Evening Scimitar* of same date, copied the *Commercial*'s editorial with these words of comment:

Patience under such circumstances is not a virtue. If the negroes themselves do not apply the remedy without delay it will be the duty of those whom he has attacked to tie the wretch who utters these calumnies to a stake at the intersection of Main and Madison Sts., brand him in the forehead with a hot iron and perform upon him a surgical operation with a pair of tailor's shears.

Acting upon this advice, the leading citizens met in the Cotton Exchange Building the same evening, and threats of lynching were freely indulged, not by the lawless element upon which the deviltry of the South is usually saddled—but by the leading business men, in their leading business centre. Mr. Fleming, the business manager and owning a half interest the *Free Speech*, had to leave town to escape the mob, and was afterwards ordered not to return; letters and telegrams sent me in New York where I was spending my vacation advised me that bodily harm awaited my return. Creditors took possession of the office and sold the outfit, and the *Free Speech* was as if it had never been.

The editorial in question was prompted by the many inhuman and fiendish lynchings of Afro-Americans which have recently taken place and was meant as a warning. Eight lynched in one week and five of them charged with rape! The thinking public will not easily believe freedom and education more brutalizing than slavery, and the world knows that the crime of rape was unknown during four years of civil war, when the white women of the South were at the mercy of the race which is all at once charged with being a bestial one.

Since my business has been destroyed and I am an exile from home because of that editorial, the issue has been forced, and as the writer of it I feel that the race and the public generally should have a statement of the facts as they exist. They will serve at the same time as a defense for the Afro-Americans Sampsons who suffer themselves to be betrayed by white Delilahs.

The whites of Montgomery, Ala., knew J.C. Duke sounded the keynote of the situation— which they would gladly hide from the world, when he said in his paper, the *Herald*, five years ago: "Why is it that white women attract negro men now more than in former days? There was a time when such a thing was unheard of. There is a secret to this thing, and we greatly suspect it is the growing appreciation of white Juliets for colored Romeos." Mr. Duke, like the *Free Speech* proprietors, was forced to leave the city for reflecting on the "honah" of white women and his paper suppressed; but the truth remains that Afro-American men do not always rape(?) white women without their consent.

Mr. Duke, before leaving Montgomery, signed a card disclaiming any intention of slandering Southern white women. The editor of the *Free Speech* has no disclaimer to enter, but asserts instead that there are many white women in the South who would marry colored men if such an act would not place them at once beyond the pale of society and within the clutches of the law. The miscegnation laws of the South only operate against the legitimate union of the races; they leave the white man free to seduce all the colored girls he can, but it is death to the colored man who yields to the force and advances of a similar attraction in white women. White men lynch the offending Afro-American, not because he is a despoiler of virtue, but because he succumbs to the smiles of white women.

THE MALICIOUS AND UNTRUTHFUL WHITE PRESS

The *Daily Commercial* and *Evening Scimitar* of Memphis, Tenn., are owned by leading business men of that city, and yet, in spite of the fact that there had been no white woman in Memphis outraged by an Afro-American, and that Memphis possessed a thrifty law-abiding, property-owning class of Afro-Americans the *Commercial* of May 17, under the head of "More Rapes, More Lynchings" gave utterance to the following:

> The lynching of three Negro scoundrels reported in our dispatches from Anniston, Ala., for a brutal outrage committed upon a white woman will be a text for much comment on "Southern barbarism" by Northern newspapers; but we fancy it will hardly prove effective for campaign purposes among intelligent people. The frequency of these lynchings calls attention to the frequency of the crimes which causes lynching. The "Southern barbarism" which deserves the serious attention of all people North and

South, is the barbarism which preys upon weak and defenseless women. Nothing but the most prompt, speedy and extreme punishment can hold in check the horrible and beastial propensities of the Negro race. There is a strange similarity about a number of cases of this character which have lately occurred.

In each case the crime was deliberately planned and perpetrated by several Negroes. They watched for an opportunity when the women were left without a protector. It was not a sudden yielding to a fit of passion, but the consummation of a devilish purpose which has been seeking and waiting for the opportunity. This feature of the crime not only makes it the most fiendishly brutal, but it adds to the terror of the situation in the thinly settled country communities. No man can leave his family at night without the dread that some roving Negro ruffian is watching and waiting for this opportunity. The swift punishment which invariably follows these horrible crimes doubtless acts as a deterring effect upon the Negroes in that immediate neighborhood for a short time. But the lesson is not widely learned nor long remembered. Then such crimes, equally atrocious, have happened in quick succession, one in Tennessee, one in Arkansas, and one in Alabama. The facts of the crime appear to appeal more to the Negro's lustful imagination than the facts of the punishment do to his fears. He sets aside all fear of death in any form when opportunity is found for the gratification of his bestial desires.

There is small reason to hope for any change for the better. The commission of this crime grows more frequent every year. The generation of Negroes which have grown up since the war have lost in large measure the traditional and wholesome awe of the white race which kept the Negroes in subjection, even when their masters were in the army, and their families left unprotected except by the slaves themselves. There is no longer a restraint upon the brute passion of the Negro.

What is to be done? The crime of rape is always horrible, but the Southern man there is nothing which so fills the soul with horror, loathing and fury as the outraging of a white woman by a Negro. It is the race question in the ugliest, vilest, most dangerous aspect. The Negro as a political factor can be controlled. But neither laws nor lynchings can subdue his lusts. Sooner or later it will force a crisis. We do not know in what form it will come.

In its issue of June 4, the *Memphis Evening Scimitar* gives the following excuse for lynch law:

Aside from the violation of white women by Negroes, which is the outcropping of a bestial perversion of instinct, the chief cause of trouble between the races in the South is the Negro's lack of manners. In the state of slavery he learned politeness from association with white people, who took pains to teach him. Since the emancipation came and the tie of mutual interest and regard between master and servant was broken, the Negro has drifted away into a state which is neither freedom nor bondage. Lacking the proper inspiration of the one and the restraining force of the other he has taken up the idea that boorish insolence is independence, and the exercise of a decent degree of breeding toward white people is identical with servile submission. In consequence of the prevalence of this notion there are many Negroes who use every opportunity to make themselves offensive, particularly when they think it can be done with impunity.

We have had too many instances right here in Memphis to doubt this, and our experience is not exceptional. *The white people won't stand this sort of thing, and whether they be insulted as individuals are as a race, the response will be prompt and effectual.* The bloody riot of 1866, in which so many Negroes perished, was brought on principally by the outrageous conduct of the blacks toward the whites on the streets. It is also a remarkable and discouraging fact that the majority of such scoundrels are Negroes who have received educational advantages at the hands of the white taxpayers. They have got just enough of learning to make them realize how hopelessly their race is behind the other in everything that makes a great people, and they attempt to "get even" by insolence, which is ever the resentment of inferiors. There are well-bred Negroes among us, and it is truly unfortunate that they should have to pay, even in part, the penalty of the offenses committed by the baser sort, but this is the way of the world. The innocent must suffer for the guilty. If the Negroes as a people possessed a hundredth part of the self-respect which is evidenced by the courteous bearing of some that the *Scimitar* could name, the friction between the races would be reduced to a minimum. It will not do to beg the question by pleading that many white men are also stirring up strife. The Caucasian blackguard simply obeys the promptings of a depraved disposition, and he is seldom deliberately rough or offensive toward strangers or unprotected women.

The Negro tough, on the contrary, is given to just that kind of offending, and he almost invariably singles out white people as his victims.

On March 9, 1892, there were lynched in this same city three of the best specimens of young since-the-war Afro-American manhood. They were peaceful, law-abiding citizens and energetic business men.

They believed the problem was to be solved by eschewing politics and putting money in the purse. They owned a flourishing grocery business in a thickly populated suburb of Memphis, and a white man named Barrett had one on the opposite corner. After a personal difficulty which Barrett sought by going into the "People's Grocery" drawing a pistol and was thrashed by Calvin McDowell, he (Barrett) threatened to "clean them out." These men were a mile beyond the city limits and police protection; hearing that Barrett's crowd was coming to attack them Saturday night, they mustered forces, and prepared to defend themselves against the attack.

When Barrett came he led a *posse* of officers, twelve in number, who afterward claimed to be hunting a man for whom they had a warrant. That twelve men in citizen's clothes should think it necessary to go in the night to hunt one man who had never before been arrested, or made any record as a criminal has never been explained. When they entered the back door the young men thought the threatened attack was on, and fired into them. Three of the officers were wounded, and when the *defending* party found it was officers of the law upon whom they had fired, they ceased and got away.

Thirty-one men were arrested and thrown in jail as "conspirators," although they all declared more than once they did not know they were firing on officers. Excitement was at fever beat until the morning papers, two days after, announced that the wounded deputy sheriffs were out of danger. This hindered rather than helped the plans of the whites. There was no law on the statute books which would execute an Afro-American for wounding a white man, but the "unwritten law" did. Three of these men, the president, the manager and clerk of the grocery—"the leaders of the conspiracy"—were secretly taken from jail and lynched in a shockingly brutal manner. "The Negroes are getting too independent," they say, "we must teach them a lesson."

What lesson? The lesson of subordination. "Kill the leaders and it will cow the Negro who dares to shoot a white man, even in self-defense."

Although the race was wild over the outrage, the mockery of law and justice which disarmed men and locked them up in jails where they could be easily and safely reached by the mob—the Afro-American ministers, newspapers and leaders counselled obedience to the law which did not protect them.

Their counsel was heeded and not a hand was uplifted to resent the outrage; following the advice of the *Free Speech*, people left the city in great numbers.

The dailies and associated press reports heralded these men to the country as "toughs," and "Negro desperadoes who kept a low dive." This same press service printed that the Negro who was lynched at Indianola, Miss., in May, had outraged the sheriff's eight-year-old daughter. The girl was more than eighteen years old, and was found by her father in this man's room, who was a servant on the place.

Not content with misrepresenting the race, the mob-spirit was not to be satisfied until the paper which was doing all it could to counteract this impression was silenced. The colored people were resenting their bad treatment in a way to make itself felt, yet gave the mob no excuse for further murder, until the appearance of the editorial which is construed as a reflection on the "honor" of the Southern white women. It is not half so libelous as that of the *Commercial* which appeared four days before, and which has been given in these pages. They would have lynched the manager of the *Free Speech* for exercising the right of free speech if they had found him as quickly as they would have hung a rapist, and glad of the excuse to do so. The owners were ordered not to return, the *Free Speech* was suspended with as little compunction as the business of the "People's Grocery" broken up and the proprietors murdered.

SELF-HELP

In the creation of this healthier public sentiment, the Afro-American can do for himself what no one else can do for him. The world looks on with wonder that we have conceded so much and remain law-abiding under such great outrage and provocation.

To Northern capital and Afro-American labor the South owes its rehabilitation. If labor is withdrawn capital will not remain. The Afro-American is thus the backbone of the South. A thorough knowledge and judicious exercise of this power in lynching localities could many times effect a bloodless revolution. The white man's dollar is his god, and to stop this will be to stop outrages in many localities.

The Afro-Americans of Memphis denounced the lynching of three of their best citizens, and urged and waited for the authorities to act in the matter and bring the lynchers to justice.

No attempt was made to do so, and the black men left the city by thousands, bringing about great stagnation in every branch of business. Those who remained so injured the business of the street car company by staying off the cars, that the superintendent, manager and treasurer called personally on the editor of the *Free Speech*, asked them to urge our people to give them their patronage again. Other business men became alarmed over the situation and the *Free Speech* was run away that the colored people might be more easily controlled. A meeting of white citizens in June, three months after the lynching, passed resolutions for the first time, condemning it. *But they did not punish the lynchers.* Every one of them was known by name, because they had been selected to do the dirty work, by some of the very citizens who passed these resolutions. Memphis is fast losing her black population, who proclaim as they go that there is no protection for the life and property of any Afro-American citizen in Memphis who is not a slave.

The Afro-American citizens of Kentucky, whose intellectual and financial improvement has been phenomenal, have never had a separate car law until now. Delegations and petitions poured into the Legislature against it, yet the bill passed and the Jim Crow Car of Kentucky is a legalized institution. Will the great mass of Negroes continue to patronize the railroad? A special from Covington, Ky., says:

Covington, June 13.—The railroads of the State are beginning to feel very markedly, the effects of the separate coach bill recently passed by the Legislature. No class of people in the State have so many and so largely attended excursions as the blacks. All these have been abandoned, and regular travel is reduced to a minimum. A competent authority says the loss to the various roads will reach $1,000,000 this year.

A call to a State Conference in Lexington, Ky., last June had delegates from every county in the State. Those delegates, the ministers, teachers, heads of secret and others orders, and the head of every family should pass the word around for every member of the race in Kentucky to stay oil railroads unless obliged to ride. If they did so, and their advice was followed persistently the convention would not need to petition the Legislature to repeal the law or raise money to file a suit. The railroad corporations would be so effected they would in self-defense lobby to have the separate car law repealed. On the other hand, as long as the railroads can get Afro-American excursions they will always have plenty of money to fight all the suits brought against them. They will be aided in so doing by the same partisan public sentiment which passed the law. White men passed the law, and white judges and juries would pass upon the suits against the law, and render judgment in line with their prejudices and in deference to the greater financial power.

The appeal to the white man's pocket has ever been more effectual than all the appeals ever made to his conscience. Nothing, absolutely nothing, is to be gained by a further sacrifice of manhood and self-respect. By the right exercise of his power as the industrial factor of the South, the Afro-American can demand and secure his rights, the punishment of lynchers, and a fair trial for accused rapists.

Of the many inhuman outrages of this present year, the only case where the proposed lynching did *not* occur, was where the men armed themselves in Jacksonville, Fla., and Paducah, Ky., and prevented it. The only times an Afro-American who was assaulted got away has been when he had a gun and used it in self-defense.

28

The lesson this teaches and which every Afro-American should ponder well, is that a Winchester rifle should have a place of honor in every black home, and it should be used for that protection which the law refuses to give. When the white man who is always the aggressor knows he runs as great risk of biting the dust every time his Afro-American victim does, he will have greater respect for Afro-American life. The more the Afro-American yields and cringes and begs, the more he has to do so, the more he is insulted, outraged and lynched.

The assertion has been substantiated throughout these pages that the press contains unreliable and doctored reports of lynchings, and one of the most necessary things for the race to do is to get these facts before the public. The people must know before they can act, and there is no educator to compare with the press.

The Afro-American papers are the only ones which will print the truth, and they lack means to employ agents and detectives to get at the facts. The race must rally a mighty host to the support of their journals, and thus enable them to do much in the way of investigation.

A lynching occurred at Port Jarvis, N.Y., the first week in June. A white and colored man were implicated in the assault upon a white girl. It was charged that the white man paid the colored boy to make the assault, which he did on the public highway in broad day time, and was lynched. This, too was done by "parties unknown." The white man in the case still lives. He was imprisoned and promises to fight the case on trial. At the preliminary examination, it developed that he had been a suitor of the girl's. She had repulsed and refused him, yet had given him money, and he had sent threatening letters demanding more.

The day before this examination she was so wrought up, she left home and wandered miles away. When found she said she did so because she was afraid of the man's testimony. Why should she be afraid of the prisoner! Why should she yield to his demands for money if not to prevent him exposing something he knew! It seems explainable only on the hypothesis that a *liaison* existed between the colored boy and the girl, and the white man knew of it. The press is singularly silent. Has it a motive? We owe it to ourselves to find out.

The story comes from Larned, Kansas, Oct. 1, that a young white lady held at bay until daylight, without alarming any one in the house, "a burly Negro" who entered her room and bed. The "burly Negro" was promptly lynched without investigation or examination of inconsistant stories.

A house was found burned down near Montgomery, Ala., in Monroe County, Oct. 13, a few weeks ago; also the burned bodies of the owners and melted piles of gold and silver.

These discoveries led to the conclusion that the awful crime was not prompted by motives of robbery. The suggestion of the whites was that "brutal lust was the incentive, and as there are nearly 200 Negroes living within a radius of five miles of the place the conclusion was inevitable that some of them were the perpetrators."

Upon this "suggestion" probably made by the real criminal, the mob acted upon the "conclusion" and arrested ten Afro-Americans, four of whom, they tell the world, confessed to the deed of murdering Richard L. Johnson and outraging his daughter, Jeanette. These four men, Berrell Jones, Moses Johnson, Jim and John Packer, none of them twenty-five years of age, upon this conclusion, were taken from jail, hanged, shot, and burned while yet alive the night of Oct. 12. The same report says Mr. Johnson was on the best of terms with his Negro tenants.

The race thus outraged must find out the facts of this awful hurling of men into eternity on supposition, and give them to the indifferent and apathetic country. We feel this to be a garbled report, but how can we prove it?

Near Vicksburg, Miss., a murder was committed by a gang of burglars. Of course it must have been done by Negroes, and Negroes were arrested for it. It is believed that two men, Smith Tooley and John Adams belonged to a gang controlled by white men and, fearing exposure, on the night of July 4, they were hanged in the Court House yard by those interested in silencing them. Robberies since committed in the same vicinity have been known to be by white men who had their faces blackened. We strongly believe in the innocence of these murdered men, but we have no proof. No other news goes out to the world save that which stamps us as a race of cutthroats, robbers and lustful wild beasts. So great is Southern hate and prejudice, they legally(?) hung poor little thirteen-year-old Mildrey Brown at Columbia, S.C., Oct. 7, on the circumstantial evidence that she poisoned a white infant. If her guilt had been proven unmistakably, had she been white, Mildrey Brown would never have been hung.

The country would have been aroused and South Carolina disgraced forever for such a crime. The Afro-American himself did not know as he should have known as his journals should be in a position to have him know and act.

Nothing is more definitely settled than he must act for himself. I have shown how he may employ the boycott, emigration and the press, and I feel that by a combination of all these agencies can be effectually stamped out lynch law, that last relic of barbarism and slavery. "The gods help those who help themselves."

Questions for Discussion and Journaling

1. What is Ida B. Wells-Barnett's main argument in this essay? How does she support it? Be specific and provide three examples from the text to support your answer.

2. Consider this quote: "It is also a remarkable and discouraging fact that the majority of such scoundrels are Negros who have received educational advantages at the hands of the white taxpayers. They have got just enough of learning to make them realize how hopelessly their race is behind the other in everything that makes a great people, and they attempt to 'get even' by insolence, which is ever the resentment of inferiors." In this quote, Wells-Barnett uses a pathetic appeal, showing how frustrating it is to be caught in a cycle of systematic oppression. What other rhetorical moves can you identify? Find at least three and reflect on how they work to persuade her audience.

3. Wells-Barnett does an excellent job of refuting claims from the white presses, for example: "This same press service printed that the Negro who was lynched at Indianola, Miss., in May, had outraged the sheriff's eight-year-old daughter. The girl was more than eighteen years old, and was found by her father in this man's room, who was a servant on the place." Using what you learned in Chapter 3, "Analyzing Arguments," find another example of refutation. Using that example, write a 250–500 word essay explaining how Wells-Barnett uses refutation to strengthen her argument.

NEW AMERICANS IN MEMPHIS

Latino Memphis and New American Economy

"New Americans in Memphis: A Snapshot of the Demographic and Economic Contributions of Immigrants in the Metro Area" was composed by New American Economy (NAE), "a bipartisan research and advocacy organization fighting for smart federal, state, and local immigration policies that help grow our economy and create jobs for all Americans" in partnership with Latino Memphis, an organization "[assisting] Latinos in the Greater Memphis area by connecting, collaborating, and advocating for health, education, and justice." The report is different from the other readings in this textbook; it presents information via an infographic and, as a result, is full of graphs, statistics, and limited alphabetic text. As you read through the report, consider the strengths and weaknesses of this format. Do you see a clear argument in the report even though there is no explicit thesis? What is the rhetorical impact of summarizing their findings in an infographic format rather than a text-heavy article?

New Americans in Memphis

A Snapshot of the Demographic and Economic Contributions of Immigrants in the Metro Area[1]

POPULATION GROWTH

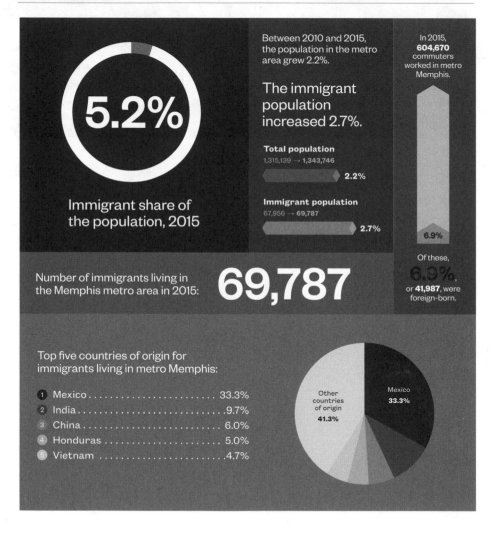

5.2%

Immigrant share of the population, 2015

Between 2010 and 2015, the population in the metro area grew 2.2%.

The immigrant population increased 2.7%.

Total population
1,315,139 → **1,343,746**

2.2%

Immigrant population
67,956 → **69,787**

2.7%

In 2015, **604,670** commuters worked in metro Memphis.

6.9%

Of these, **6.9%**, or **41,987**, were foreign-born.

Number of immigrants living in the Memphis metro area in 2015: **69,787**

Top five countries of origin for immigrants living in metro Memphis:

1. Mexico 33.3%
2. India 9.7%
3. China 6.0%
4. Honduras 5.0%
5. Vietnam 4.7%

Other countries of origin **41.3%**

Mexico **33.3%**

New Americans in Memphis

SPENDING POWER & TAX CONTRIBUTIONS

In 2015, foreign-born residents in metro Memphis contributed
$4.2B to the metro area's GDP.[2]

Given their income, immigrants contributed significantly to state and local taxes,
including property, sales, and excise taxes levied by state or municipal governments.

Amount earned by
immigrant households
in 2015:

$372.1M went to federal taxes.[3]

$109.7M went to state and local taxes.[4]

Leaving them with

$1.1B
in spending power.[5]

$1.6B

This means that foreign-born
households held **5.4%** of all
spending power in the Memphis
metro area, slightly more than
their share of the area's
overall population.

Immigrants also support federal social
programs. In 2015, they contributed
$191.0M to Social Security and **$46.9M**
to Medicare.

Share of spending power

5.4%

Share of population

5.2%

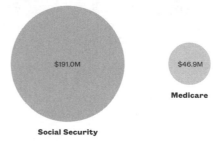

$191.0M

$46.9M

Medicare

Social Security

New Americans in Memphis

LABOR FORCE GROWTH

Although the foreign-born made up **5.2%** of the metro area's overall population, they represented **6.7%** of its working-age* population, **7.1%** of its employed labor force, and **14.4%** of its STEM workers in 2015.

Immigrant shares of the...

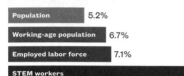

Population	5.2%
Working-age population	6.7%
Employed labor force	7.1%
STEM workers	14.4%

* Working-age refers to people ages 16-64 years old.

Immigrants are significantly overrepresented in several **key industries** in the metro area. This includes:

Construction
24.5%

Share of workers in the industry who were foreign-born, 2015

General Services[6] 9.8%

Transportation & Warehousing 7.9%

Wholesale Trade 7.1%

Retail Trade 7.0%

5.2%
Share of population

Nancy Aguila
Editor, *La Raza*

Nancy Aguila was working in the state cultural department in Jalisco, in west-central Mexico, when her husband received an invitation to work for an air-conditioning business in Memphis. The family has now lived in the city for 10 years.

Aguila, who worked as a journalist in Mexico, has since seen her role shift from one who records history to one who helps shapes it. "This is a challenging time for establishing human rights," she says. "But somebody once said: If you make someone play a musical instrument, they will never use a gun."

The goal may be profound, but Aguila's method is straightforward. By providing in-depth coverage in the Spanish-language media of mainstream cultural events in Memphis, she hopes to encourage participation, strengthen community, and break down prejudice. "Art and culture connects us," she says.

In 2016, she and a colleague started a monthly magazine called *Ruta Memphis,* her most structured attempt yet to promote non-Latino happenings to the Hispanic community. "We didn't want them to know about the events only on a weekly basis, but to prepare for the future, and get them to attend all over," she says. "Sometimes the Hispanic community doesn't feel invited. We wanted to bring the Latino community to everything going on in the city. We felt it made an important example."

A year and a half after its launch, the magazine folded in the face of financial pressure, the latest in a series of media closures that have hit Aguila without once putting a dent in her drive. After arriving in Memphis, she had found work as a freelance writer and columnist for *La Prensa Latina,* which led to an offer to edit the newspaper *El Sol de Memphis.* But funding for that program ended, as well as for two magazines she co-founded, *Ediciones Especiales* and *Ella.*

Aguila is now an editor at *La Raza,* and continues to promote the arts across cultures. "When people enjoy a piece of theater or a piece of music together, they belong to the same community," she says. "Prejudices are broken down."

3

LABOR FORCE GROWTH CONT.

Immigrants tend to concentrate in these **occupations** in the metro area:

1. Construction Workers 6.1%
2. Carpenters. 3.9%
3. Cashiers 3.3%
4. Packers & Packagers. 3.2%
5. Supervisors of Retail Workers . . . 2.6%

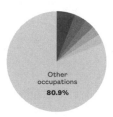

Other occupations
80.9%

Because of the role immigrants play in the workforce helping companies keep jobs on U.S. soil, we estimate that by 2015, immigrants living in the metro area helped create or preserve

3,210

local manufacturing jobs that would have otherwise vanished or moved elsewhere.[7]

ENTREPRENEURSHIP

Despite making up **5.2%** of the overall population, immigrants represented **8.8%** of the entrepreneurs in metro Memphis in 2015.

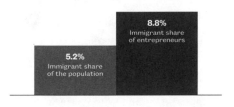

8.8%
Immigrant share of entrepreneurs

5.2%
Immigrant share of the population

This makes the foreign-born **26.7%** more likely than the U.S.-born to be entrepreneurs.

Share of immigrants who are self-employed
8.9%

Share of U.S.-born who are self-employed
7.0%

Memphis Metro Area Businesses, 2012	Sales Revenue, 2012	Number of Paid Employees, 2012[8]
Asian-owned	$2.5B	9,305
African American-owned	$1.6B	9,715
Hispanic-owned	$450M	3,709

4

New Americans in Memphis

SPOTLIGHT ON

Dr. Pedro Velasquez

Founder of LifeDOC

Dr. Pedro Velasquez never intended to emigrate from Venezuela. He had won a prestigious scholarship for a three-year endocrinology fellowship at Harvard University's Joslin Diabetes Center in 1993, and, upon completion, returned home. Then his 5-year-old son was diagnosed with a rare, progressive T-cell leukemia. Harvard colleagues advised him to go to St. Jude Children's Research Hospital.

The boy, Pedro, received four years of weekly treatment and is now a healthy business-school graduate who helps his father run an innovative Memphis health care organization for underprivileged patients with diabetes and other chronic conditions. "The reality is that I want to pay back the community," says Dr. Velasquez, who opted to stay in the city. "I do believe that thanks to Memphis, and thanks to St. Jude's, and thanks to this country, that Pedro was cured."

LifeDOC, which Dr. Velasquez founded in 2005, provides a comprehensive treatment approach for cardio-metabolic conditions. Dr. Velasquez had noticed high rates of childhood obesity and other risk factors for serious, chronic conditions. Yet a lack of treatment among the uninsured led to costlier services, costs often borne by hospitals and government. "And there was not a single clinic that was providing quality of care," Dr. Velasquez says. "By the time these children were adults, they were already sicker. It was work, work, work, get sick and go to the ER. They were affecting also the Memphis health system." By focusing on preventative care, the clinic has been able to reduce the total cost of treating common chronic conditions such as diabetes by an average of 65 percent.

In addition, Dr. Velasquez started a primary-care clinic in a Hispanic neighborhood; he and his sons created LifeDOC Research and Pharmacy, which works with pharmaceutical companies to evaluate and implement therapies for common chronic conditions; and his son Pedro developed Vidaplus, an innovative healthcare membership program that allows the uninsured population to have access to the same quality services their insured patients receive. In total, the organizations employ 60 people.

Dr. Velasquez points out that St. Jude was also created by a child of immigrants. "And I do believe there is something in common with my project and St. Jude, and that is gratitude," he says. "Gratitude to the American community, to the people who gave us the opportunity to do our best, to develop ourselves, to help other people through our jobs, our dreams, our skills."

EDUCATION

Immigrants are more likely to have a **bachelor's degree** or higher.

Share of population over age 25 with an **advanced degree** in 2015:

26.6%
of U.S.-born

29.0%
of Immigrants

Bachelor's Degree

Share of population over age 25 with an **advanced degree** in 2015:

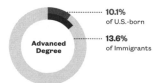

10.1%
of U.S.-born

13.6%
of Immigrants

Advanced Degree

1,079

students who were enrolled in Memphis colleges and universities during the fall of 2015 were temporary residents.[9] International students supported...

377

local jobs and spent...

$28.8M

in the 2016-2017 academic year.[10]

5

New Americans in Memphis

EDUCATION CONT.

Immigrants make up

2.4%

of students under age 18
who attended public schools in
the metro area in 2015.

Memphis Metro Area Immigrants, 2015	Share with a Bachelor's Degree or Higher	Share with an Advanced Degree
Asian	55.6%	27%
Hispanic	6.4%	2%

HOUSING WEALTH

In 2015,

51.3% of
immigrants in the
metro area owned
their own homes.

**Immigrant
households**

■ Homeowners
▢ Other

The total property
value of immigrant
households was

$2.4B.

NATURALIZATION

31.6%
Naturalized

Share of immigrants in metro Memphis
who were naturalized citizens in 2015.

24%
Potentially eligible

Share among those who were not citizens but
potentially eligible for naturalization in 2015.

6

New Americans in Memphis

REFUGEES

6.7%[11]
Likely refugees

Share of immigrants in metro Memphis who were likely refugees in 2015.

8.2%
Likely refugees

Share of immigrants in Tennessee who were likely refugees in 2015.

93.2%[12]
Employed

Share of likely refugees in Tennessee who were employed in 2015.

22.1% .... Share of refugees in Tennessee over age 25 with a bachelor's degree or higher, 2015

7.2% .... Share of refugees in Tennessee over age 25 with an advanced degree, 2015[11]

Between 2011-2015, refugees in Tennessee tended to concentrate in the following industries:

1. Manufacturing 27.1%
2. Retail 15.3%
3. General Services[13] 10.8%

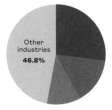

Other industries
46.8%

UNDOCUMENTED IMMIGRANTS

Undocumented immigrants contributed to state and local taxes, including property, sales, and excise taxes levied by state or municipal governments.
Given their income, we estimate that in 2015...

Amount earned by undocumented immigrant households:
$414.8M

$45.0M went to federal taxes.[14]
$16.5M went to state and local taxes.[15]

Leaving them with
$353.2M
in spending power.[16]

New Americans in Memphis

For more city, district, and state-level data,
visit **MapTheImpact.org** and explore our interactive map.

1   We define the Memphis metro area using the Office of Management and Budget definition of the Memphis, TN-MS-AR Metropolitan Statistical Area (MSA). Unless otherwise specified, the data come from 1-year samples of the American Community Survey from 2010 and 2015.

2   These figures are derived from our calculations based on immigrants' share of wage income and self-employment income in the 1-year ACS sample from 2015 and GDP estimates by the Bureau of Economic Analysis, U.S. Department of Commerce.

3   U.S. Congressional Budget Office. 2016. "The Distribution of Household Income and Federal Taxes, 2013."

4   Institute on Taxation and Economic Policy. 2015. "Who Pays? A Distributional Analysis of the Tax Systems in All Fifty States,"

5   Estimates are based on federal tax rates from the U.S. Congressional Budget Office, and from state and local tax incidence rates calculated by the Institute on Taxation and Economic Policy.

6   General services include personal services (e.g. laundry services, barber shops, and repair and maintenance), religious organizations, social services, and labor unions.

7   Vigdor, Jacob. 2013. "Immigration and the Revival of American Cities: From Preserving Manufacturing Jobs to Strengthening the Housing Market." New American Economy.

8   2012 Survey of Business Owners, U.S. Census Bureau

9   Data on total student enrollment is derived from the Integrated Postsecondary Education Data System maintained by the National Center for Education Statistics.

10   Economic data is derived from the International Student Economic Value Tool maintained by NAFSA, the association of international educators.

11   New American Economy. 2017. "From Struggle to Resilience: The Economic Impact of Refugees in America,"

12   The data come from 5-year sample of the American Community Survey from 2015.)

13   General services include personal services (e.g. laundry services, barber shops, and repair and maintenance), religious organizations, social services, and labor unions.

14   U.S. Congressional Budget Office. 2016. "The Distribution of Household Income and Federal Taxes, 2013."

15   Institute on Taxation and Economic Policy. 2015. "Who Pays? A Distributional Analysis of the Tax Systems in All Fifty States."

16   Estimates are based on federal tax rates from the U.S. Congressional Budget Office, and state and local tax rates from the Institute on Taxation and Economic Policy.

Questions for Discussion and Journaling

1. In the section entitled, "Spending Power and Tax Contributions," we learn "that foreign-born households held 5.4% of all spending power in the Memphis metro area, slightly more than their share of the area's overall population," and that immigrants "support federal social programs [by contributing] $191.0M to Social Security and $46.9M to Medicare." What myths about immigrants is the report responding to in this section? Where else does the report respond to misconceptions about immigrants? Was the report successful at challenging myths about immigration and immigrants? Why do you think the report responds to these misconceptions about immigrants without ever explicitly voicing those misconceptions? Was this choice (not to name the misconceptions) rhetorically effective? Using evidence from the report, write a page response to answer these questions.

2. The report includes a number of "Spotlight On" sections that focus on specific immigrants and highlight individual immigration stories as well as immigrant contributions to the Memphis community. Why do you think the report authors decided to include these spotlights? How do these sections contribute to the overall report? What do they provide that the rest of the report is lacking? Why are these spotlights important from a rhetorical standpoint?

3. The report also explains that 31.6% of immigrants in Memphis were naturalized citizens in 2015 and that 24% are potentially eligible for naturalization.[1] What does this mean? If you don't know, do some research. What makes someone eligible for naturalization? Find another section in the report where you need to do research in order to understand a statistic or point the report is making and write a few paragraphs explaining why research was necessary. Use the research you did and information you found to make sense of the numbers provided in the report for an audience unfamiliar with immigration laws in the United States.

4. As you read the report, you may have noticed endnotes (tiny numbers following a sentence or information) following some of the report's claims. Reread each sentence that has an endnote and before going to the next endnote, read the accompanying endnote (found at the end of the report). Did reading the endnotes immediately after reading the information they support or explain change your reading of this report? How do they develop a more rhetorically sound report? How might you use endnotes or footnotes to support a researched argument?

---

1   As you do research on the naturalization process, you will learn that just because someone is not currently eligible for naturalization, they can still be in the United States legally, and they may be eligible for naturalization in the future.

FIRST EVER REPORT OF ECONOMIC CONTRIBUTIONS OF IMMIGRANTS IN MEMPHIS BY NEW AMERICAN ECONOMY

Latino Memphis

This blog by Latino Memphis summarizes the previous chapter ("New Americans in Memphis"). While it isn't investigative journalism, it is included in this section because it is related to the previous chapter. The blog begins by saying, "we often hear... that immigrants are causing more harm than good. However, nationally, the facts say otherwise." Thus, while Latino Memphis helped author the report which did not explicitly discuss misconceptions about immigrants, they chose to address those misconceptions here. As you read, ask yourself why they felt it was appropriate to do that on their blog but not in the report. What about the rhetorical situation was different?

One of the most controversial topics in our country now is immigration. We often hear, especially from the current administration, that immigrants are causing more harm than good. However, nationally, the facts say otherwise. According to the Center for American Progress, immigrants add trillions of dollars to the national GDP, and their contributions are becoming only more significant yearly. However, there was no data on the economic contributions of immigrants locally.

Until now, that is.

On Tuesday, February 20th, Latino Memphis and New American Economy released "New Americans in Memphis: A Snapshot of the Demographic and Economic Contributions of Immigrants in the Metro Area" at a reception with Mayor Jim Strickland celebrating Barrier Free, an art installation honoring diversity, by Yancy Villa.

"Memphis is a city made better by the diversity of its people and the information in this report shows that," said Mayor Jim Strickland.

Immigrants not only contributed $4.2 billion to the area's GDP in 2015 but contributed 481.8M in taxes as well. They also contributed $191.0 million to Social Security and 46.9M to Medicare. Despite only making up 5.2 percent of the area's overall population, immigrants in Memphis represent 7.1 percent of the employed labor force and 14.4 percent of its STEM workers in 2015.

The report by New American Economy also found:

- Immigrants contributed $4.2 billion to the Memphis metro area's GDP in 2015.

- Immigrant households earned $1.6 billion in 2015. Of that, immigrant households contributed $372.1 million in federal taxes and $109.7 million in state and local taxes, leaving them with $1.1 billion in spending power.

- Immigrant households support federal social programs. The foreign-born contributed $191 million to Social Security and $46.9 million to Medicare.

- Immigrants in Memphis are more likely to be entrepreneurs. While just over 5 percent of the population, immigrants make up nearly 9 percent of the metro area's business owners. They are 26.7 percent more likely to be entrepreneurs than people born in the United States.

- Immigrants helped to preserve 3,210 local manufacturing jobs in 2015. Because of the role immigrants play in the workforce helping companies keep jobs local, by 2015 immigrants living in Memphis had helped create or preserve more than 3,210 manufacturing jobs that would have otherwise vanished or moved elsewhere.

- Immigrant households own homes. 51.3 percent of immigrant households are homeowners, making their property value $2.4 billion.

- The undocumented population in Memphis contributed $61.5 million in taxes and held nearly $353.2 million in spending power. In 2015, undocumented immigrant households earned a total of $414.8 million.

"Today, facts matter more than ever, and this report sheds light on the contributions that new and aspiring Americans bring into our local economy. The report also shows some of our opportunities for growth, particularly around education. Memphis needs to consider immigrants, refugees and the US born generations that follow them as part of our smart growth strategy." said Mauricio Calvo, Executive Director at Latino Memphis.

As we commemorate MLK50 in Memphis, his words "injustice anywhere is a threat to justice everywhere...whatever affects one directly, affects all indirectly" ring true today. Immigrants in Memphis and around the country are often seen as an issue to be solved rather than an asset to be valued. I am hopeful that the information in this report will help honor his legacy by helping eradicate the injustices that immigrants are facing.

In this climate of false information and myths, it is important to be purveyors of truth. If the question is whether immigrants, regardless of status, are contributing to our local economy, the answer is a resounding yes.

Questions for Discussion and Journaling

1. Now that you have read both the original report "New Americans in Memphis" and this summary of that report, think about how well this blog summarized the report. Find the summary online (on Latino Memphis's website), figure out who the audience is, and think about why Latino Memphis decided to include some of the findings of the report but not others. Then choose a new / different audience, state who that is, and write your own 200–300 word summary of the report.

2. While the blog is short, there are a number of ways that the authors respond to misconceptions about immigrants. What appeals do you see them using to make their case? Choose two and explain whether or not their use of appeals was successful.

3. The middle of the blog lists some of the key findings of the report, but they only present some of the findings, not all of them. Go through this list and then go back to the report and take note of what they chose not to include. Write a 200–300 word response that considers how the rhetorical situation may have influenced Latino Memphis to include some of the report's findings but not others in their summary of the report.

THE EDUCATION OF DASMINE CATHEY

Brad Wolverton

"The Education of Dasmine Cathey" by Brad Wolverton is an intimate narrative of the trials and tribulations of a former University of Memphis football player. First appearing in *The Chronicle of Higher Education* ("the No. 1 source of news, information, and jobs for college and university faculty members and administrators"), the saga of Dasmine Cathey sheds light on the widespread educational shortcomings of NCAA athletics and the complicated ways such athletes' struggles get brushed under the proverbial carpet. The article is rife with questions of accountability and exploitation and the balance between student and athlete in the 21st century version of the NCAA "student athlete." [The tone of the article is brutally candid yet moving, appealing to the reader's pathos and forcing them to empathize with Cathey's difficult situation. The inclusion of photojournalism also adds a tender touch, making Cathey appear to be a relatable figure that the reader can empathize with as opposed to a faceless name on a piece of paper.] In a sense, this article can be viewed as a case study for the greater failures of the Tennessee public school system as well as an admonishment of institutions everywhere that value what the athlete can do for the institution over what the institution can do for the student. As is the case with many of the articles in this anthology, the argument here is not overt; it is, however, undeniably compelling.

He hid them in a shoebox under his bed. "My own little secret," he said.

Inside the box, he kept 10 thin paperbacks he was given as a child. For years he didn't touch them. But as he reached 19, they became a lifeline.

Each night after dinner, he closed his dorm-room door, reached under his bed, and opened the box. Resting his head against the blanket his grandmother had made him, he pulled out the books: "First Grade, Level 1, Ages 6–7."

Quietly, so none of his teammates would hear, he read aloud, moving his finger across the page.

***

The words are tattooed on his arms: "Family First." But 23-year-old Dasmine Cathey looks after far more people than that. A buddy who just spent four years in jail. A local gang leader looking to join a church. A friend of a friend who had lost a brother. They all remind him a little bit of himself: abandoned at some point by family or friends, too weak to stand up for themselves.

Figure 31-1. Among Dasmine Cathey's tattoos are two prominent words: "Family First." It's a reflection of his many commitments outside college. Courtesy of Lance Murphey.

Most mornings the University of Memphis football player rises just after 5 to drive one of those friends to work. He pushes his 6-foot-4 frame up from the recliner he sleeps in, steps quietly past his brother resting on the couch beside him, and readies himself for the day ahead.

On this day, a cloudy Wednesday in late February, he climbs into a beat-up van parked on the front lawn and drives up the road to fill the tank with just enough gas to make it through the morning. By early afternoon, when his first class of the day meets, the fifth-year senior will have logged more than 50 miles shuttling family members and friends to where they need to be.

Unfortunately for Mr. Cathey, all of that motion has not helped him get where he needs to be. With less than three months until graduation, he hasn't shown up for classes in weeks. Last semester, during his final season of football, he failed three courses. That dropped his

GPA below the 2.0 required to complete a degree, putting extra pressure on this semester's grades.

On paper, three classes are all he has left. But for a guy who could barely read three years ago, every class is a mountain.

***

Growing up, Dasmine Cathey hated everything about school—reading, writing, even the smell of books. To him, school was nothing but a needless burden. Once you learned about your ancestors and your heritage, he figured, what else did you need to know?

He still remembers the day a middle-school teacher asked him to read aloud in class. As he mumbled through, clearing his throat on words he didn't understand, he heard snickers around him. "How can you be so good at sports but so dumb in school?" a classmate asked.

His sixth-grade teacher suggested he enroll in a tutoring program to overcome his reading problems. Mr. Cathey's parents didn't have enough money, so an aunt helped cover the cost. He took classes for two or three months before dropping out. "You need the money more than me," he told his mother.

By high school he still hadn't read a single book. It took him hours to wade through a handful of pages, and by then he'd forgotten most of what he'd read. But outside of class, things were looking up. He was a finalist for Tennessee Lineman of the Year in football and played on a state-champion basketball team at Ridgeway High, in suburban Memphis. And so he got a pass. Few people seemed to care if he was learning.

If not for football, and his hope of one day playing professionally, he never would have set foot in a college classroom. He had offers from other colleges, but he stayed close to home so his mom could watch him play. His first year, there wasn't much to see. His poor high-school grades and test scores forced him to sit out the whole season. Without his sport, he felt lost.

It was the job of Joseph P. Luckey, and the university's eight-person team of academic advisers, to get him eligible to play.

Figure 31-2. Joseph P. Luckey, the U. of Memphis's director of athletic academic services, was surprised by the results of a reading test the university started administering to athletes two years ago: "I was like, 'Holy crud, I can't believe how many kids are reading below a seventh-grade level.'" Courtesy of Lance Murphey.

Mr. Luckey, who is president of the National Association of Academic Advisors for Athletics, says players like Mr. Cathey are the biggest challenge in college sports. While the NCAA says the academic profile of many athletes is improving, big-time programs are identifying an increasing number of players who come to college severely ill-prepared. That puts an extra burden on staffs like his to help athletes whose academic backgrounds look less and less like the rest of the student body.

Until two years ago, when Memphis's athletic department ramped up its screening for learning disabilities and started requiring incoming athletes to take a reading test, Mr. Luckey didn't realize how bad his university's situation was.

"I was like, 'Holy crud, I can't believe how many kids are reading below a seventh-grade level,'" he says. For Mr. Luckey, the question is how many of those students to let in. "What we've all got to decide," he says, "is what's our breaking point?"

***

You can't hide for long in college when you're semiliterate. But somehow Mr. Cathey slipped through his freshman year with just under a C average, taking classes like elementary algebra and music appreciation. Then he saw the syllabus for HIST 2010: U.S. to 1877, his sophomore history class. How would he ever finish five books in four months?

He knew there was only one way: He had to go back to the beginning.

After practice every night, he would close the door to his room in the Carpenter Complex, reach under his bed, and pull out his 10 learn-to-read books. *Twenty minutes*, he thought, looking down at his watch. *I've got to beat 20.*

Over the sound of his roommates goofing around, he practiced the basic skills he had skipped over all those years. His first few sessions, it took him three or four minutes to make it through each book. But week by week he improved, shaving seconds and finally minutes off his times. He was a long way from finishing college-level texts, but it was a start.

Who knows what gives a 19-year-old man the courage to start over? Fear, perhaps? Shame? In Mr. Cathey's case, a sense of urgency seemed to drive him as much as anything. If he didn't do it now, he knew he never would.

As he read the books, he kept his voice low so his roommates—three other football players —wouldn't hear. It was his first season suiting up for the Tigers, and his reading practice was the last thing he wanted spread around the locker room.

Now that he was finally eligible to play, he put his full attention into the sport—or as much as his home life allowed. In his first game, the season opener against Ole Miss, he had three tackles against a team that would finish the year ranked 15th in the country. "You don't see many guys his height who can run a 4.6 forty," says Shannon Morrison, a former Memphis coach, referring to Mr. Cathey's time in the 40-yard dash. "He had all the tools you could ask for."

But off the field that year, his life was starting to unravel. Within weeks, he found out he was going to be a father—not once, but twice, with two different women. His own parents were not around to help. His father was living in Mississippi, providing little financial support. Then his mom announced she was moving to Florida to live with her new boyfriend. Mr. Cathey's three younger siblings stayed with an aunt about a half-hour from campus, and he started chipping in on bills and driving them to school and practice.

With a 40-hour-a-week commitment to football, and all those kids and friends to look after, there was little time left for studies.

***

"Where r u?" pings the text on Mr. Cathey's phone. He is halfway through his senior year, but he hasn't made it to campus in two weeks. Sharyne Connell, the university's head football counselor, knows that if Mr. Cathey is going to get his degree, she still has a lot of work to do.

Figure 31-3. Sharyne Connell, the university's head academic counselor for football: "I just wish Dasmine cared more. You can't make someone care." Courtesy of Lance Murphey.

"Just got done waking up," Mr. Cathey writes back.

"Waking up, it's 12?" Ms. Connell texts. "Omg. Ur class starts at 1."

"Coming trying to get a good car to drive sorry."

Mr. Cathey and Ms. Connell are a study in contrasts. She played soccer at Eastern Illinois University, finishing her degree in three and a half years. She arrives at work by 6:30 most mornings, an hour before the first study hall of the day for athletes, and rarely leaves before 7 at night. In three years at Florida International University, where she worked before, she took off one day—to interview at Memphis.

Mr. Cathey's academic path has been every bit of up and down, and the semester-by-semester grade-point averages on his transcript, which he shared with *The Chronicle*, show it: 2.0, 1.5, 2.3, 2.8, 1.5, 2.1, 1.4, 2.5, 2.8, 1.3, 2.0, 2.9, 0.5, 0.8. "He's like Houdini—he's here, and then he's not," Ms. Connell says. "I just wish Dasmine cared more. You can't make someone care."

He cares a lot about football. But once that ended, Ms. Connell lost her stick. Before, if he skipped class or study hall, his coaches could hold him out of games or put him through extra conditioning. Now, if he doesn't show up, his grades are all that suffers.

A few minutes before 1, Ms. Connell texts one last time: "Mr. Cathey, where r u?"

"Trying to get my ride or some gas $," he writes. "How about you come get me?"

***

Instead of living on the campus, Mr. Cathey has hopped from couch to couch the past few years—moving six times in his senior year alone—so he can pocket the room-and-board money he receives from the university for his family. He's lived in some of the city's most-distressed areas, including South Memphis.

Figure 31-4. Mr. Cathey jokes with his girlfriend on the way to a study hall. Courtesy of Lance Murphey.

Memphis has one of the country's highest violent-crime rates, and the south side of town is among its bleakest spots. The place where Mr. Cathey used to stay sits on a street filled with vacant homes. A neighbor's house is surrounded by yellow tape, and a sign on the board-ed-up front door says, "Property of Memphis Police Department, Organized Crime Unit."

He was evicted from that home after his roommate—a cousin who is his best friend—was arrested for armed robbery. Although Mr. Cathey himself has largely stayed out of trouble—he's been in some bar fights, and has a pile of unpaid parking tickets—he hangs out with a dangerous crowd. Several of his closest friends are in gangs, and almost all have spent time behind bars.

His friend Domaniko (Niko) McCrary, who's 20, just got out of jail for the second time. He joined a gang at 14, and says he's lived in fear ever since. "I've been robbed, shot at, and hit with a pistol," he says. "I wouldn't wish my life on nobody."

The two met through a mutual acquaintance, and bonded after learning they had both lost close friends to gang violence. Mr. Cathey's best friend in high school was killed in a drive-by shooting. Mr. McCrary's older brother was gunned down, too. One took his emotions to the football field; the other to the streets. If Mr. Cathey hadn't been there to help, driving him to work and offering him a spot on his intramural basketball team, Mr. McCrary says, "I probably wouldn't be here today."

Mr. Cathey's tutors and coaches know bits and pieces about his home life, and even that is enough to worry them. One of his coaches was so concerned for his safety that he started sleeping with his cellphone. "I was always nervous my phone would ring at 3 or 4 in the morning and someone would say, 'Daz got shot,'" Mr. Morrison says. "I never got that phone call, but he was the guy I was worried about."

Mr. Morrison and others have urged Mr. Cathey to cut himself off from those friends, but he always resists. In fact, the worse the situation, the more he seems to get involved.

"I hate to see people feel like they're on their own because I always felt like I was on my own," Mr. Cathey says. "I ain't never give up on a friend."

**

"I'm a little scared," Ms. Connell says, knocking on the front door of a weathered ranch house in East Memphis. A few steps away, one of Mr. Cathey's pit bulls sits barking in a parked van, and a Mercedes with tinted windows creeps by.

Figure 31-5. Mr. Cathey, reflected in a mirror at home, has avoided living on the campus, moving six times in his senior year alone so he can use his room-and-board money for his family. Courtesy of Lance Murphey.

In her six years working with athletes, she has never visited a player's house before, but Mr. Cathey is a special case. Memphis's academic-counseling staff, which includes some 20 graduate assistants, interns, and tutors in addition to its full-time counselors, has spent hundreds of hours guiding him through college. All for a guy who wasn't even a regular starter on a team that won just three of 24 games in the past two seasons, one of the worst records in Division I.

The NCAA requires colleges to provide academic support to athletes, and programs can lose scholarships and postseason opportunities if too many of their players fail to graduate. But that's hardly what motivates Ms. Connell.

"I'm here," she says, waiting by the front door, "because I won't give up on him no matter how many times he falls."

Finally, Houdini appears from the side of the house. Wearing flip-flops and black sweats that accentuate his long frame, he moves with a sense of calm. He smiles and invites Ms. Connell inside, where she meets his grandmother and an aunt.

Mr. Cathey takes a seat in the family room, near a table of high-school trophies. The shades are drawn, and a large-screen television flickers from the back of the room, showing images from the NFL Combine.

He and Ms. Connell listen as ESPN's commentators size up Dontari Poe, one of Mr. Cathey's teammates. "Rare size, rare speed. Did a lot of things at Memphis State, fits a lot of defenses. Almost 6-foot-5, runs the 40 in under 5 seconds," says one analyst. "Impressive large athlete."

Mr. Cathey slopes back in his chair. They're not talking about him on the draft show, but he's got his own pro tryout coming up. At best he's a long shot, but he still holds out hope.

He and his counselor sit quietly for a minute, then Ms. Connell looks over at him: "Dasmine, where were you today? I saw like three cars in the driveway."

"Had to pick up my uncle and didn't have no more gas money," he says, staring at the screen. He doesn't mention that his day started before dawn, when he ran a friend to work, then drove his brother to school. Or that it's the end of the month, and his Pell Grant money ran out weeks ago.

"I know you've got to take care of your family," Ms. Connell says. "But if you want to graduate, you need to show up."

***

Actually, that's not always the case. Colleges channel players into all sorts of less-rigorous tracks, some of which require little classroom attendance. One of the popular paths for Memphis athletes—including Mr. Cathey and nearly a third of his football teammates—is an online program designed for working adults and students looking to build their own degrees.

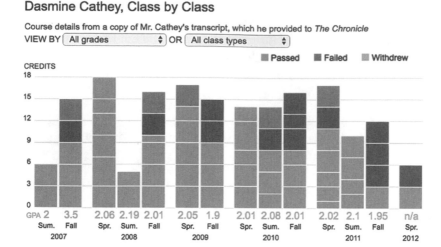

Figure 31-6. Note: GPAs are a running tally, showing a computation of cumulative grades. [Graphic by Brian O'Leary.]

Most semesters he takes a potpourri of courses, hardly building toward any specialization. This year he is enrolled in "Area/Facility Planning" through the School of Leisure Studies, and an online family-communication course. He has also taken "Wellness Concepts," "Introduction to Dance," and a class called "The Developing Adult" (which he failed—twice).

Fortunately for Mr. Cathey, D's count toward graduation in almost all of his classes. And one-third of his credits can come from electives. Over his five years at Memphis, he has gotten credit for 10 phys-ed courses, including yoga, kickboxing, free weights, and beginning tennis (which he aced—twice).

On the whole, Memphis athletes have had a 3.0 grade-point average or better the past three semesters. But many of its football and basketball players come to college underprepared for university-level work. Two years ago, the athletic department started a summertime "bridge" program for transfer students and first-year athletes with academic deficiencies. Of the 50 players who have come through the program, nearly half tested at or below a seventh-grade reading level.

The university recently hired a part-time learning specialist to help those athletes. She is trained to teach basic reading and writing skills, and works with players who have learning disabilities and other academic problems. Across the country, many athletic departments are facing similar challenges. In the past year, nearly one out of every five major-college athletics programs has created a new learning-specialist position.

Even with the help of his academic advisers, Mr. Cathey has still struggled. The university would not provide the names of his professors, saying it didn't want to expose faculty members to scrutiny. But papers from various courses Mr. Cathey has taken—which he provided to *The Chronicle*, in part to illustrate his improvement during college—show a student who has had trouble completing basic assignments. For a developmental-writing class his first year, he submitted a two-page paper, titled "Some Important Womens," in which he was asked to describe common issues or challenges facing characters in several books.

"Fannie Hou Hammer, Irma Muller and Aurthor Mayo-Raggie are important people with struggles, detonations, and failure that surround their environment," he wrote in his introductory paragraph. "Then I give you my points on, 'what I thinks the point that I thought it was making?'"

Joseph Jones, an associate professor of English and director of the university's first-year composition program, says many students with little exposure to analytical writing commit even more "surface" spelling and grammatical errors than they might normally as they try to articulate complicated ideas.

Without commenting on Mr. Cathey, he says instructors are encouraged to evaluate students on a variety of factors, including their improvement.

"On an absolute scale, you might think maybe this student doesn't deserve to pass a class," he says. "But over 15 weeks, if you see a certain improvement and can project a trajectory over the next couple of years that she'll be an adequate college student, you might make a different call."

***

After failing an introductory mass-communication course in his sophomore year, Mr. Cathey signed up for it again two summers later. He showed up the first few days, but then missed much of the next two weeks, recalls Candace Justice, the assistant professor who taught the four-week course.

Figure 31-7. Mr. Cathey cradles his daughter Kassidy while talking to his sister Danielle. Courtesy of Lance Murphey.

When she questioned his absences, Mr. Cathey pulled out his phone to show off pictures of his newborn daughter. "He was like, 'I have a daughter. Oh, she's so beautiful,' and his face just lit up," Ms. Justice says. "I thought, Well, we need more fathers to care about their children in this world."

She allowed Mr. Cathey to make up several assignments, and was impressed that he didn't try to use his status as a football player to get special treatment. "I've had some athletes say they're not going to play football if they don't get a better grade in my class. To his credit, he never mentioned eligibility," she says. "He really tackled whatever I gave him with determination."

For one assignment, he had to look at the covers of 10 magazines he had never read and describe their target markets. "Ladies if you looking for a maganize thats is tagering just you and all about you. Then this one is for you," he said about *Woman's World*. "Telling the ladies how to eat. What diet to be no for your body, and more."

In addition to the grammatical problems, he misspelled "magazine" 13 times, but the professor didn't mark him down for it. In fact, she praised him for his conversational style.

"This is a beginning class where we try to get students to discover the media and start expressing themselves in writing," Ms. Justice says. "If this had been a writing class, I'm sure he wouldn't have passed because spelling and words are so much more important there."

By Mr. Cathey's fifth year, he was still misspelling and misusing words but starting to write complete sentences and tying points together more coherently. Some of his tutors and professors had taught him to write about subjects that he is familiar with, a change that helped him put more voice into his writing.

Lorraine Meiners-Lovel, who teaches his senior-project class, for which he must write a 15-page paper, encouraged him to explore a topic with which he had a personal connection. Initially, he said he wanted to look into communication problems between parents and their children. But after a consultation with his instructor, she figured out what he really meant: parental abandonment.

Figure 31-8. Mr. Cathey (center) is surrounded by family members, friends, and his girlfriend (right) during a surprise visit by his mother, Janice (center rear). Courtesy of Lance Murphey.

A social worker by training, Ms. Meiners-Lovel was excited to help him understand the subject. He had told her how upset it made him when his parents moved away—his mother attended only one game out of nearly 50 his team played over four seasons—and how he had to shoulder responsibility for his siblings.

Mr. Cathey and his instructor met several times to discuss the paper, and a librarian helped him locate journal articles for it. But with less than two months left in the semester, he switched topics. His new subject—should college athletes be paid?—is closer to his field of study, his academic advisers say, and will be easier for him to complete.

Mr. Cathey himself gave another reason: His parents have stepped up lately, reducing the burden on him. His father recently bought a restaurant a few miles from where he and his siblings live, bringing him to town more often. And his mother has taken the bus up from Florida a couple of times this year to be with her children. Maybe abandonment, he says, was too strong a word.

***

"Ok time to go running for a month I need track sprint shoe size 12 or 11.5," Mr. Cathey posted on Facebook in late February. He may cut corners in class, but he never scrimps on football. He needed the shoes to try out for NFL scouts in late March, a last-ditch effort to resurrect a disappointing college career.

Figure 31-9. Mr. Cathey finished his career at Memphis with 67 tackles in 42 games. [Joe Murphey photography.]

Mr. Cathey may have had the height and speed to compete at the highest levels, but his outside distractions prevented him from ever fully committing to the sport, his coaches say. He also never bulked up for the positions his coaches played him at, including defensive end and linebacker. At just 210 pounds, he always had more of a slim basketball body, limiting his playing time.

The football staff gave him anything the NCAA allowed, including weight-gaining supplements. "But the boy just didn't eat," says Mr. Morrison, who now coaches at the University of Cincinnati. "I think he trained his body to survive without food."

Figure 31-10. Strawberry shortcake awaits the attention of Mr. Cathey, a few feet from the recliner where he sleeps at night. Courtesy of Lance Murphey.

Plenty of people tried feeding him. One person says Mr. Cathey came to his house once or twice a week for dinner and always left with granola bars and cans of soup from the cupboard. Others say he often stopped by looking for food for his family. Mr. Cathey says his family has never had much food around, and he probably has a smaller appetite as a result.

Had he gained the weight or made the needed commitments, his story might have a different ending, Mr. Morrison says.

"If he ever could've filled out or 100-percent committed," he says, "there's no telling how big he could've gotten or how good he could've been."

So if not a football player, then, what will Dasmine Cathey become?

***

"Want to pull up your résumé?" asks Kristin Rusboldt, the athletic department's life-skills coordinator. Mr. Cathey is sitting in a bay of cubicles outside Ms. Connell's office, trying to imagine his life after football.

"So what are we doing here?" she asks. "Are you looking for jobs?"

"When I get my car, I'm gonna be looking for jobs," Mr. Cathey says.

But a glance at his résumé makes it clear he hasn't spent much time thinking about what's next.

At the top of the page, his name is centered in small type. A few lines down, in boldface lettering three times larger, he has typed, "University of Memphis."

Figure 31-11. Memphis athletes with GPA's under 3.0 must spend about 10 hours a week in study hall, where academic advisers guide them through their courses. Courtesy of Lance Murphey.

"You need to delete this," Ms. Rusboldt says, pointing at the college's name. "Make the focus be you, not the university."

Near the top, under "Interest and activities," Mr. Cathey has written, "Memphis basketball and because I played high school basketball. Then again I just love sports." He also lists Memphis football and "high school track and because I miss running and I love to run."

She changes the heading to "Leadership and Activities," and asks about any awards he has won. He lists a few from years ago. "Sorry, you can't use anything from high school," she says. "You'll now have a college degree."

She casts about for leadership roles: "Tiger 3.0? Student Athlete Advisory Committee? Athlete of the Week?"

"Yeah, I've been Athlete of the Week," he says.

She plays down the pizza-delivery job and offers advice on the summer warehouse positions he's held. "What you do in a résumé is talk yourself up. Yeah, you worked at Wal-Mart, but you need to show what you learned. Did you have to work with others? Did you work with any computer programs?" she says. "Actually, what was your title there?"

"Stock," Mr. Cathey says.

"That was your title?"

"Yeah."

Ironically, he hasn't played up his football activities, so Ms. Rusboldt encourages him to. "Show Memphis football as a job," she says. "You can talk about teamwork, you can talk about organizational skills, you can talk about memorization of plays. And if you think about it, it was a job. You got paid to come to school, and the work you put in was what you were doing on the field."

Finally, she asks about his degree, which he hasn't listed.

"What's your major?" she asks.

"Sports management."

"Is that a bachelor of science or arts?" she says.

He doesn't know, so he walks a few steps away to ask Ms. Connell.

"Do I have a bachelor of science or arts?" he says.

Ms. Connell comes out of her office and heads toward Ms. Rusboldt. "He has a bachelor of liberal studies in interdisciplinary studies," she says.

Mr. Cathey sits back down, a staff member by each side. He taps out, "Bachelor of Liberal Studies."

"Type 'in Interdisciplinary Studies,'" Ms. Rusboldt says.

"How do you spell that?"

***

After putting himself through a month of twice-a-day workouts, Mr. Cathey decided to ice his NFL dreams. "I'm not gonna go through with it," he said, a few days before scouts were due on the campus. "If I get it, I don't want to be out of the picture with the family."

31

Figure 31-12. Mr. Cathey prepares for a tryout with NFL scouts, in pursuit of his dream of turning pro. Courtesy of Lance Murphey.

He also worried about his friend Niko and the other people who rely on him. "If I'm not there physically," he said, "I know for a fact that ain't enough."

He had always taken better care of people around him than himself, but even this sacrifice seemed extreme. His academic advisers saw it as a sign of maturity. "It sounds like he's actually being more realistic than a lot of guys, and there's a lot of merit to that," said Mr. Luckey, the head of Memphis's academic-services staff. "Daz had a good career here, and physically maybe there's a chance he could go. But maybe he's better off this way."

Then, just two days before tryouts, he changed his mind again, persuaded by his new girlfriend and an old teammate who never took his shot. "Am going in with the east memphis on my back," he wrote on Facebook. "Wish me luck!!!"

He fell short in the tryout, posting slower times and lower marks than he had hoped. But that same week his academic fortunes appeared to be improving. He showed up for study hall three straight days and handed in all his assignments on time. "This week has been awesome," gushed Eileen O'Rourke, one of his mentors. "He's on a roll right now."

And then, in a snap, his world came undone. On his way home from a funeral for an uncle, he was pulled over for speeding. What should have been an ordinary traffic violation turned into something far more complicated, as he was cited for driving on a suspended license with $700 in unpaid parking tickets, and for having failed to show up for a court appearance to defend himself. A police officer handcuffed him and drove him downtown, where he was booked and handed a blue jumpsuit.

He spent the next 12 hours sitting in a jail cell that reeked of feces, thinking about how fast his life was spinning. He said a prayer, asking God for help in understanding what mattered most as he neared the end of his college days. Football was over months ago, but it still ruled his life. His agent had lined up workouts with Canadian and Arena teams, which would leave little time for anything else.

He knew he was treading water academically, with several big tests ahead. He decided to put football on hold—for real this time—while dedicating himself to his classes.

Soon after he was released from jail, he sent Ms. Connell a text: "Dnt u b gvng up on me. Amma gradate," he wrote. "I need u now mre then eva. We gne do dis."

But it was too late. During his court date the next day, he missed a deadline for his family-communication class, and his professor—who had already offered extensions on previous missed assignments—wouldn't let him make it up. A zero out of 100 would be too much to overcome.

Ms. Connell urged Mr. Cathey to devote his full attention to his other two courses. Her advice helped, as he finished with a C-minus in his leisure-studies class. And he got an incomplete on his senior project, giving him an extra 45 days to complete his paper. He plans to return this summer for his final class, with the hope of still completing his degree.

***

A few miles from the Memphis campus, in a neighborhood called Orange Mound, one of the roughest parts of town, Mr. Cathey walks toward the back door of an elementary school.

He is here to work with a fourth-grade student who reads at a first-grade level, a volunteer assignment he picked up this semester.

Inside, he takes a seat at a long table beside a boy with apprehensive eyes.

"Hey, I'm Dasmine," he says, smiling. "What's your name?"

"Darion."

He sizes up the boy, who looks big for his age. Change a few letters in the name, and this child could have been Mr. Cathey a dozen years ago.

"You like reading?" he asks.

"Yeah?" the boy says, his voice rising.

"What do you like about it?" Mr. Cathey says.

"I don't know," the boy answers.

"How do you feel when you start reading?" Mr. Cathey asks.

The boy pauses, looking down at the table.

31

"Nervous?" the boy says. He looks at Mr. Cathey, who nods his head.

"I know how that feels." He pulls his chair forward, inching closer to the student.

Figure 31-13. As his senior year winds down, Mr. Cathey has many ideas about what he'd like to do next. Fixing cars or working at a restaurant are options, but if he had his choice, it would be to work with kids. Courtesy of Lance Murphey.

"When I was your age, you couldn't pay me to read," Mr. Cathey says. "I couldn't read a lick, not a single thing. All I wanted was to race around the playground, be the fastest kid in school."

Darion laughs.

Mr. Cathey puts his arm around the boy's shoulder. Recalling advice he learned not so long ago, he guides the child's finger across the page.

"When you come to a word you don't understand, look at the pictures," he says. "That way, you have a better idea of what you're reading."

After the session ends, Mr. Cathey says he's been thinking more about his career. He's got a lot of ideas. Maybe he'll fix up cars with his uncle, or help out in his dad's soul-food restaurant. But if he had his choice, he'd really love to work with kids.

Then, last month, he took a job delivering beer. Five days a week, he rides around Memphis in a truck, loading and unloading boxes. The hours aren't great, but he says he could see himself staying for a while.

Questions for Discussion and Journaling

[handwritten: more casual more like a story ✗check forewords✗]

1. The tone and diction of this piece varies from other investigative journalism articles in this textbook. How is Wolverton's writing different from other authors in this section? What is the rhetorical impact of crafting his tone in this way?

    [handwritten: less personal, relatable ✗check forewords✗]

2. Images play a huge role in this piece. Lance Murphey's photographs are as poignant as they are revealing, and they seem to tell a story themselves. How might removing the photographs affect your reading of the piece? Do you think that the images dramatically strengthen (or alter) the author's argument? Why or why not?

3. Consider how the piece ends: "Then, last month, he took a job delivering beer. Five days a week, he rides around Memphis in a truck, loading and unloading boxes. The hours aren't great, but he says he could see himself staying for a while." Taken out of context, this conclusion sounds somber or even upsetting. However, within the context of this piece, it feels optimistic. What do you think Wolverton was getting at with his conclusion? Do you think it is more optimistic than pessimistic? Why or why not? *[handwritten: considering the back n arm n lack of commitment, yea optimistic but also not]*

IN THE GAME

Don Wade

Published in the *Memphis Daily News*, "In the Game" by Don Wade takes an inside look at the multi-million-dollar sports industry in our very own city of Memphis, emphasizing the economic impact of landmarks like the FedExForum and the potential for another professional sports franchise to move in. In this article, Wade reinforces the idea that here in "little old Memphis," sports is not only "big business," but a cultural cornerstone that has unfortunately experienced a slight decline in the post-Calipari years. Although Wade's tone is pessimistic at times, his argument is as clear as it is uplifting. While business is typically thought of as measured in dollars and cents, Wade suggests that, at least in Memphis, desire and heart play a role—especially now.

Memphis measures local sports impact in dollars—and desire.

Way back in the 1990s, perhaps before the Grizzlies and FedExForum were even a twinkle in anyone's eye, Chris Wallace came to Memphis and The Pyramid for a preseason NBA game featuring Michael Jordan and the Chicago Bulls.

"A legitimate hard sellout," said Wallace, who became general manager of the Grizzlies prior to the 2007–08 season. "And every time Michael Jordan got the ball there were hundreds of flash bulbs going off. It was not an NBA preseason game; it was a rock concert. A big one, with the Rolling Stones or Beyoncé."

By the time Younger Associates had completed an economic impact analysis of the Memphis Grizzlies and FedExForum for the Greater Memphis Chamber in 2010, basketball and concerts in the same venue—on different dates, of course—had become commonplace.

"In the Game" by Don Wade. From *The Daily News*, January 23, 2016. Reprinted by permission of the publisher.

The Younger Associates study determined that the total annual economic impact on Memphis/Shelby County from events at FedExForum was $223 million. The total number of jobs supported in the Shelby County economy as a result of the economic activity generated by the arena and the Grizzlies was 1,534.

And city and county tax revenues generated as a result of the Grizzlies and FedExForum operations and the related visitor spending was $5.3 million annually.

Fred Jones, founder of the Southern Heritage Classic, which will celebrate its 27th year in 2016, also was part of the NBA Pursuit Team and one of the original stakeholders in the Grizzlies. When he launched the SHC, pitting historically black colleges Tennessee State University and Jackson State University together in an annual football game, he had one major sponsor: Coca-Cola.

For 2015, FedEx was a presenting sponsor, and AutoZone, Allstate and Nike were among the other major sponsors. Malvin Gipson, executive director of the Memphis Sports Council, a division of the Memphis Convention & Visitors Bureau, says the SHC and the AutoZone Liberty Bowl (in town since 1959) each has an annual economic impact north of $15 million and some years as much as $20 million.

Sports is big business. Here, in little old Memphis, Tennessee.

"I was part of two things people didn't think could work," Jones said of the NBA and the Southern Heritage Classic.

In fact, the local sports landscape has come so far that Greater Memphis Chamber president and CEO Phil Trenary is very much future-focused. Worries of the Grizzlies one day up and leaving—St. Louis just lost its second NFL team in 30 years—finally have expired. The local NBA franchise has made five straight playoff appearances, helping to raise the city's profile and embed itself within the fabric of the community.

So if you call yourself a local sports fan but don't know that Marc Gasol is from Memphis, that Tony Allen is The Grindfather, and that Z-Bo is shorthand for Zach Randolph, you've just been lying to yourself.

Meantime, the University of Memphis football team reached new heights and stunned college football experts this past season by cracking the early College Football Playoff rankings and by beating Ole Miss, the only team that defeated eventual national champion Alabama.

Memphis may not have its own NFL team, but soon it will have its own quarterback when some team grabs Paxton Lynch in the first round of next spring's draft.

AutoZone Park, which opened Downtown in 2000, underwent $6.5 million in renovations before last season and again received praise as one of the finest baseball venues in America—major or minor league. In fact, AZP got a new HD video board before Busch Stadium in St. Louis; the Cardinals, who own the Redbirds, will be updating their video board technology this season.

The FedEx St. Jude Golf Classic has been a city staple since 1958 and the Memphis Open Presented by ServiceMaster, the current name of the annual pro tennis tournament, has been around since 1976. Both events have come close to leaving, but that's not the situation now.

"I'm less worried about maintaining what we have," Trenary said, adding that any time a team or an event lands on national television, those sweeping aerial shots of the skyline and the Mississippi River are a recruiting moment.

"Millions of homes are looking at Beale Street," he said. "It's bringing companies, families and jobs. It's very hard to measure the economic impact of that."

BECAUSE THEY CARE

The sports industry is a different animal. Sure, the business side matters. In fact, it matters so much that the NFL, NBA, MLB and NHL all have endured work stoppages because rich players and richer owners couldn't agree on terms.

But consumers and fans are one in the same. Fans unhappy about a team's record are not the threat to a pro team's or college program's well-being. Apathy is. Apathy speaks in a whisper—the emotional calls to sports talk radio that no longer come—and issues ultimatums by its absence: the seats that go unfilled, some of them already paid for.

When Wallace joined the Grizzlies, the first playoff era had ended with the team going 0–12 in three first-round series. The season before Wallace started work, the Grizzlies went 22–60.

Meanwhile, the Tigers under John Calipari would reach the 2007–2008 NCAA national championship game. Perhaps no night in that season was more electric than Saturday, Feb. 23, 2008, when No. 1 Memphis played No. 2 Tennessee and coach Bruce Pearl at FedExForum.

"Tigers basketball was in its glory age with that Derrick Rose team," Wallace recalled. "The great Tennessee game on national TV with College GameDay here and you couldn't get a ticket. I just stood in the tunnel with my pass and hoped they wouldn't throw me out.

"It was obvious this was a great sports town."

Mark Alnutt, who became deputy athletic director at the U of M several months ago, and who had been in athletic administration at Missouri before serving as athletic director at Southeast Missouri State, says he underestimated the passion of the Memphis sports fan.

"You hear it after wins and losses," he said with a laugh. "And that's a good thing."

Memphis Redbirds general manager Craig Unger has been in the market a couple of years now, but he still was taken aback by the stuff flowing through his Twitter feed during the recent national championship game between Alabama and Clemson. He basically noticed two things: One, a lot of people really loved Alabama football. And two, a lot of people really hated Alabama football.

Winning matters. So does presentation and the belief among fans that, to borrow from the Grizzlies' Marc Gasol, the team is playing the right way.

Recently, Tigers senior guard Ricky Tarrant hit game-winning free throws against Temple at FedExForum after a collision with another player left his mouth so bloodied that the officials almost forced him to the sideline. But with an assist from the team's athletic trainer, Tarrant continued. He swallowed his own blood, quickly opened and shut his mouth to show officials he was all right, and then went to the foul line and sank both free throws.

It wasn't the Grizzlies, but does it get more Grit and Grind than that?

"If you put a good product out on the field or the court, then you're going to be successful (financially)," Jones said. "The Grizzlies are going through a transition period, no question about it. I think people will stay with the product even though it's not as good as in the past because it's 'our team.'

"When University of Memphis basketball was on fire, 18,000 was an afterthought. Now it's going through that transition period. But that comes with the territory."

Wallace says during the best of the Calipari years he did not consider the Tigers to be rivals.

"But they were overshadowing us," he said. "They sucked all the oxygen out of the town from that standpoint and we were a distant, distant second to them.

"When I came here in 2007 the bloom had worn off the (NBA) romance, which is bound to happen at some point. Didn't have the playoff success so we had a lot of people jump off the bandwagon back then."

But Memphis is such a strong basketball town, Wallace added, that if you give fans anything at all to latch onto they come back.

"And they've come back in abundance, and the passion fans have had for this team over the last five years in the playoffs has been extremely gratifying," he said. "The team's been here 15 years; there's a lot of young adults between 20 and 30 and they grew up with the Grizzlies and NBA basketball."

WHAT'S NEXT?

Owners will do what owners will do. The St. Louis Rams are moving to the Los Angeles area—from whence they came, ironically enough—because a new state-of-the art stadium and more population add up to more revenue.

The lesson, no matter the city, team or event: Take nothing for granted.

"The U.S. Open Racquetball Tournament was here (but left for Minneapolis several years ago)," Gipson said. "Once those events leave, they don't come back."

Jones recalls that when he started the SHC in 1990, "The term 'sports marketing' was just starting to take shape."

Now a team and a venue are best-served looking for all possible avenues to expand reach, which by extension helps grow that economic impact for the city. The Redbirds and AutoZone Park landed the Gildan Triple-A National Championship Game, a single-game winner-take-all event between the champions of the Pacific Coast and International leagues, to be played on Tuesday, Sept. 20, this year.

"There's a loyal baseball following here, and that's who we want to target," Unger, the Redbirds' GM, said. "There will be some strategic marketing."

It might have to be very strategic given that school will be back in session and SEC football and the NFL will be commanding attention. In the past, the Redbirds and the city have made bids to bring in the SEC's annual postseason baseball tournament in May—that could actually be a tough ticket depending on how things were to play out—and Gipson and Unger say the tourney is up for bid for 2017 through 2021. Gipson believes having the Cardinals and Unger to help with the presentation gives Memphis a better shot.

An NCAA men's basketball regional also is returning to the city in 2017. Again, depending on the year and the draw, previous regionals have had an economic impact of $12 million to $14 million, Gipson says.

Over at the U of M, Alnutt says, a new indoor football practice facility and a new men's basketball practice facility are on track to open during the 2017–18 academic year.

The city also is home to many youth sporting events in baseball, basketball, soccer and volleyball, among others. That's worth millions of dollars, too, Gipson says, as families from out of town turn the destination of their child's big tournament into a family vacation.

Decades ago, Memphis had more than one courtship with the NFL about bringing a team here—the Tennessee Titans stopover doesn't count—but those conversations never led to marriage. Sit down for this, but Trenary doesn't believe it impossible that Memphis could one day support an NBA team and an NFL franchise. Wallace agrees.

But whether that ever happens or not, Trenary is certain that a vibrant local sports market screams "quality of life" to businesses and young professionals considering where to go next.

"It all goes back to growth," Trenary said. "Memphis is a wonderful place to live, work and play.

"To have these (sports) amenities is critically important."

Questions for Discussion and Journaling

1. The timing of this article's publication (January 2016) is notable, both for Memphis and the world of sports. Take, for example, the decline in attendance at University of Memphis basketball games and the noteworthiness of the move by the NFL's Rams from St. Louis to Los Angeles. How did Wade take advantage of the Kairotic moment in this piece?

2. For an investigative journalism article, the argument of this piece is very much overt ("The lesson, no matter the city, team or event: Take nothing for granted."). However, the concluding line is more ambiguous: "To have these (sports) amenities is critically important." Wade could be suggesting that sports are a fundamental institution in the city of Memphis; he could also be implying that, if Memphis were to eventually play host to an NFL franchise, then the city would need to improve its amenities. What do you think Wade is getting at with this concluding line? How does it relate to his argument?

3. Given the amount of data and multitude of opinions put forth in this piece, it could very easily be employed as a launchpad for a greater research project. Brainstorm three potential researched arguments that could be derived from the information and ideas presented in "In the Game." Turn to the "Choosing a Topic" chapter in this textbook and ask yourself the three questions intended to help you choose a topic successfully.

'F' IS FOR FRAUD

Bill Dries

The 2017–2018 school year was a tough one for Shelby County Schools. Embroiled in an academic scandal in which over 1,000 grades were systematically changed at Trezevant High School (including over 300 that were switched from "failing" to "passing"), Tennessee Education Commissioner Candice McQueen had both questions to answer from the press and questions of her own, especially following the school principal's resignation. The numbers she presents are staggering (an overt appeal to logos). Questions of academic honesty and institutional ethics obviously arise (ethos), as do concerns over the well-being of students (pathos), but when you take into consideration that there was no true incentive, financial or otherwise, for administrators to change the student grades, the question on the tip of everyone's tongue amid this scandal was "why?". This piece by Bill Dries, appearing in the *Memphis Daily News*, attempts to make sense of this scandal by probing this complicated question.

Grade-changing scandal rattles Shelby County Schools.

Just before the winter break, Tennessee Education Commissioner Candice McQueen had a lot of questions for the Shelby County Schools system. She had just read a 258-page report from an independent investigation of the school system's grade-changing scandal at Trezevant High School.

McQueen also wanted assurances from SCS superintendent Dorsey Hopson that there would be changes to procedures and more vigilance by the school system.

"Why does SCS leadership think the problem occurred?" McQueen asked in what is the ultimate question.

It's a question Hopson has struggled to answer.

"You don't know whether there could be some financial incentives, which would be criminal," he said. "You don't know whether people were just trying to help people out. But when you have a widespread finding like that with no clear reason for it—it just makes you scratch your head."

More than 1,000 grades were changed over a five-year period by or using the password of Shirley Quinn, a school secretary at Trezevant.

The changes reversed 313 grades from failing to passing. Some but not all of the changes were directed by Trezevant football coach Teli White, who led the school to its first state championship in 2015 and a second state title in 2016.

The grade changes over that five-year period meant 53 ineligible students got diplomas.

The scandal followed the resignation in June of Trezevant principal Ronnie Mackin, who submitted a six-page letter alleging widespread grade changing by White and violations of school policies. Mackin resigned after the school system decided he would not return to lead the high school after a year at the helm. Mackin said he was being made the "scapegoat" for problems he notified SCS of earlier in the school year.

White, meanwhile, was suspended but was to become football coach at Melrose High School last August because only Quinn was implicated in the school system's initial investigation.

When Quinn did a television interview naming White, SCS suspended him again just before he was to start at Melrose.

Hopson had initiated a more comprehensive, independent investigation led by former U.S. Attorney Ed Stanton to determine if similar grade changes were [taking] place at other schools, possibly pointing to a more widespread problem.

When the Stanton report was released in December, Hopson recommended White be fired and the school board voted to start the termination process.

Dixon Hughes Goodman, the CPA firm that was also part of the probe, found seven other SCS schools as well as several charter schools and Arlington High School had percentages at or higher than Trezevant's fail-to-pass ratio of 53 percent. So Hopson has expanded the audit of grade changes to those seven schools.

What happened at Trezevant was different, Hopson said, and in the words of the Stanton report, "systematic."

"What happened at Trezevant was absolutely the most egregious thing you can think about when you talk about changing grades," Hopson said. "Just going in and cheating without any documentation, knowing that it's fraudulent and knowing that it could have an impact forever."

The Stanton report details grade changes for multiple students on the same day at about the same time, as evidenced by computer records.

"Moreover the vast majority of the grade changes were made 18–24 months after the students had completed the class for which the grade was issued," according to the report.

Quinn claimed multiple teachers approached her and she changed grades without any paperwork being required. But the investigators doubted that was the case.

"For Quinn's account to be accurate, multiple teachers had to have decided one or two years later that they gave the wrong grade and all of them had to approach Quinn at the same time in November or in the spring for her to make those changes," the report reads. "For these reasons, little weight should be given to Quinn's contention that all of the changes were specifically requested by teachers."

Initially, Hopson believed the grade changes were all about Trezevant athletics, specifically the football team. That changed once he and the investigators got a closer look at the records.

But there was a different pattern with student-athletes.

"Numerous changes to the athletes' transcripts were made mere minutes apart. It appears that the person using Quinn's credentials would enter a grade and then wait for the computer system to calculate the new GPA," the report reads.

The report, for example, cites an "Athlete #5"—none of the students are identified by name—who received a final grade of 73 in a physical science class in 2013. On Nov. 24, 2015, approximately a year and a half later, the final grade was changed from a 73 to an 82. The audit also shows that Athlete No. 5 took Spanish I in 2013, his freshman year, and received a final grade of 55. On April 25, 2015, at the end of his junior year, a person using Quinn's credentials changed the grade on the transcript from 55 to 86.

'UNCHARTED TERRITORY'

The grade changes at Trezevant did have the effect of upping the school's graduation rate by 12 percent to 13 percent for a 65.2 percent graduation rate in 2015. But Hopson said even that doesn't point to an incentive.

"It was still incredibly low and there was no financial incentive to raise your graduation rate," he said. "There really was no financial incentive to inflate graduation rates, which just makes it even more bizarre."

Hopson calls Trezevant "uncharted territory" but concedes there have been indications of cultural problems even as the school system has stepped up training and oversight as it transitions to online testing, teacher accountability and student achievement, and quick turnarounds of numbers for both.

SCS board member Stephanie Love, whose district includes Trezevant, has urged Hopson to "clean house."

"I know there are people here who knew that something wasn't right and it didn't take this investigation to know that something wasn't right," Love said upon the Stanton report's release.

The school system is retraining administrators and teachers on what is acceptable and what is not in changing grades. It is also examining its procedures as well as oversight beyond the school level.

McQueen has also said the state will audit grade changes in Shelby County Schools for the next three school years.

Hopson's reaction and condemnation of wrongdoing in the grade-changing scandal mirrors what happened at the start of his tenure as superintendent in 2012 when federal prosecutors indicted the first set of defendants in a similar scandal.

In 2009, test proctors for the Praxis exam for certification as a teacher noticed that the same person was taking the exam at two sessions. With that, Clarence Mumford Sr., a former teacher and assistant principal in Memphis City Schools who had worked in other school systems in the region, began burning incriminating paperwork he kept.

When federal prosecutors, led by Stanton, indicted Mumford and others in 2011 it became the largest teacher-exam cheating scandal ever prosecuted in Memphis federal court.

A total of 40 one-time teachers agreed to diversion, including terms in which they gave up their teaching licenses and agreed to not even attempt to try to become teachers again for at least five years.

With the evidence prosecutors and federal and state criminal investigators gathered, they identified about 100 teacher exams taken for at least 50 teachers. Some teachers paid Mumford and others in the fraud ring to take teachers exams for them multiple times.

There is pressure on teachers and administrators to show student achievement growth and that includes graduation rates. If they don't improve, there could be changes. And Trezevant is a high school with a lot of room for improvement even if its football program is the pride of the institution.

Hopson and Stanton's team quickly encountered years of turnover in school leadership and faculty, including three principals in four school years. They are now seeking to reconstruct who was doing what at the school in those years as they pursue the investigation beyond White.

The school has a colorful and controversial history, much of it revolving around football.

In the 2011 Academy Award winning documentary "Undefeated," chronicling the Manassas High School football team, the Trezevant High School football program is featured at a football game in which the down-trodden Manassas High team is taunted on the field by the Trezevant High players. Memphis Police ultimately line up across the football field at the end of the game to stop any direct physical contact between the two teams.

Trezevant became an outpost of the conventional school system in Frayser as the state-run Achievement School District focused on failing schools in Frayser because it has the highest concentration of failing schools of any area in the city.

The ASD targets schools in the bottom 5 percent statewide in terms of student achievement.

It took over seven of the nine conventional non-charter SCS schools in Frayser in its first three school years.

The ASD chose to run directly, without charter schools, Frayser and Corning Elementary and Westside Middle, adding Georgian Hills and Whitney Elementary the next school year also as direct-run takeovers. In the 2014–2015 school year, a local charter founded by the former principal of Westside Middle School—Bobby White—took over Frayser High School for the ASD. Bobby White is also an alumni of Frayser High.

Trezevant High began as an Innovation Zone School—the SCS version of an ASD school—that same school year in 2014–2015 with a new principal, the faculty reapplying for their jobs and an infusion of new teachers making up at least half of the faculty with teacher assistants added. Trezevant boosters were adamant that they didn't want the school's football program shelved as part of the fresh start.

They lobbied school board members for better facilities.

It was more than a dozen years after Trezevant football coach Lynn Lang effectively sold his star player, Albert Means, to an Alabama football booster for $150,000. Lang would later plead guilty to federal charges.

HAMILTON TROUBLES

As McQueen was outlining her questions and next steps in December from Nashville, Hopson's staff was investigating grade changing allegations at Hamilton High School that appear to be connected to the use of grade floors.

Hamilton is not one of the seven other SCS schools with a percentage of fail-to-pass grade changes above the district's average that are being investigated by the school system.

A grade floor is a minimum failing grade a principal and his/her staff can recommend teachers not go below in failing students.

Monekea Smith, in her third year as principal at Hamilton, was suspended without pay after investigators confirmed in December grades were changed there that made failing grades become passing grades. Hopson intends to recommend she be fired by the school board.

"And we are instituting an immediate moratorium on the use of grade floors districtwide," the school system press release announcing Smith's suspension read. "Grade floors were meant to ensure failing grades did not go below a certain level, so our students would have a better chance to improve. They were never intended to allow the changing of grades from failing to passing. … Until we can get a handle on how grade floors are being utilized from school to school, it's in the best interest of our students to discontinue the use of them."

SCS board members were already questioning the consistency of how grade floors are used across the system before the Hamilton revelations.

And grade floors at Trezevant are a topic covered in the Stanton report.

A month into the grade-changing investigation, Keith Williams, executive director of the Memphis-Shelby County Education Association, told school system leaders that teachers at Trezevant were told in writing by the school's vice principal that the school had a grade floor—no grade lower than a 60.

An email exchange between Mackin and Tonye Smith-McBride, the SCS instructional leadership director of Innovation Zone Schools, is a tab in the Stanton report.

Mackin emailed that there is "no policy stating that the common practice of implementing a grade floor of 60 is either in violation or support of Shelby County Schools policy."

"In all actuality, we were not asking them to 'change' students grades because grades had not been entered and verified when the request to consider the grade floor was communicated," Mackin wrote. "This issue has been compared to the 'Trezevant grades debacle' and these are not the same issues."

He also justified a grade floor of 60 saying it "allows students to still be successful in the future and does not cumulatively hold the student in failure for the duration of the school year."

"This is common practice in Shelby County Schools and does not violate any specific policy relating to grades," Mackin wrote, saying the email "encouraged teachers to consider" a grade floor of 60 but did not require it.

Mackin then quoted what is chapter and verse of the grade-floor philosophy.

"When a student receives a grade of 20, there is a mathematical impossibility of scoring high enough to make up the grade in the future," he wrote. "Therefore, creating other situations for the students and teacher, including but not limited to lack of work completion, disruptive behavior, lack of investment in assignments, which can all cause discipline issues with the student for the remainder of the school year."

The distinction appears to be that a school administrator can't order a teacher to abide by a grade floor. But the teacher could still feel pressure to do so along the principal-teacher relationship that comes with some inherent tension.

The bright line on grade floors is that they cannot raise a failing grade to a passing grade.

SCS board chairwoman Shante Knox Avant said after the Stanton report's release that it revealed "a culture that has really not supported our administration and our teachers in the best way."

On grade floors specifically, she added, "We can be very emphatic about what our roles are and how we are going to get there for our kids."

33

Questions for Discussion and Journaling

1. Like much investigative journalism, the argument in this piece is not as explicit as, say, an op-ed. What do you think the primary argument in this piece is and why? What do you think Dries was attempting to accomplish in his writing?

2. Dries mentions Hamilton High School in Nashville as a de facto measuring stick for Trezevant High School regarding the use of grade floors. Obviously, aside from the general rivalry between Memphis and Nashville, there are both racial and economic disparities to consider between these two cities (as well as ones of prestige). Why does Dries make this comparison?

3. Who do you think the primary audience for this piece is? Why do you think so? What beliefs or opinions do you think Dries was attempting to instill within this audience?

4. Reread the last few paragraphs of the article. It ends suddenly, without guiding the readers to a clear conclusion. What do you think the purpose of this terse and understated strategy was? Do you think it was successful?

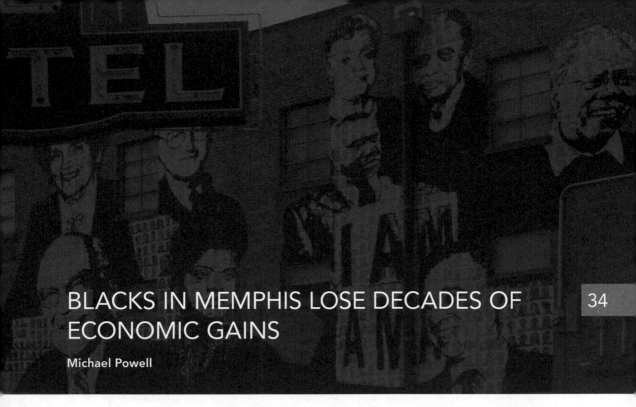

BLACKS IN MEMPHIS LOSE DECADES OF ECONOMIC GAINS

Michael Powell

In the years following the Great Recession (brought on by the Subprime Mortgage Crisis), many of the towns and cities that were hit hardest were predominantly African American and already economically vulnerable (e.g., Memphis). This piece by Michael Powell (first appearing in the *New York Times* in 2010) details the struggles experienced by various African-American Memphians during and following the recession. Primarily focusing on the plight of Tyrone Banks, a single father who had recently lost his job at FedEx and was in danger of losing his home, Powell considers everything from the more general concern of national banks recklessly handing out loans in the early-2000s, and thus leading to the "bubble burst" of 2007, to the more refined focus of how African Americans were singled out and targeted by predatory lending practices.

MEMPHIS—For two decades, Tyrone Banks was one of many African-Americans who saw his economic prospects brightening in this Mississippi River city.

A single father, he worked for FedEx and also as a custodian, built a handsome brick home, had a retirement account and put his eldest daughter through college.

Then the Great Recession rolled in like a fog bank. He refinanced his mortgage at a rate that adjusted sharply upward, and afterward he lost one of his jobs. Now Mr. Banks faces bankruptcy and foreclosure.

"I'm going to tell you the deal, plain-spoken: I'm a black man from the projects and I clean toilets and mop up for a living," said Mr. Banks, a trim man who looks at least a decade younger than his 50 years. "I'm proud of what I've accomplished. But my whole life is backfiring."

Not so long ago, Memphis, a city where a majority of the residents are black, was a symbol of a South where racial history no longer tightly constrained the choices of a rising black working and middle class. Now this city epitomizes something more grim: How rising un-employment and growing foreclosures in the recession have combined to destroy black wealth and income and erase two decades of slow progress.

The median income of black homeowners in Memphis rose steadily until five or six years ago. Now it has receded to a level below that of 1990—and roughly half that of white Memphis homeowners, according to an analysis conducted by Queens College Sociology Department for The New York Times.

Black middle-class neighborhoods are hollowed out, with prices plummeting and homes standing vacant in places like Orange Mound, Whitehaven and Cordova. As job losses mount—black unemployment here, mirroring national trends, has risen to 16.9 percent from 9 percent two years ago; it stands at 5.3 percent for whites—many blacks speak of draining savings and retirement accounts in an effort to hold onto their homes. The overall local foreclosure rate is roughly twice the national average.

The repercussions will be long-lasting, in Memphis and nationwide. The most acute economic divide in America remains the steadily widening gap between the wealth of black and white families, according to a recent study by the Institute on Assets and Social Policy at Brandeis University. For every dollar of wealth owned by a white family, a black or Latino family owns just 16 cents, according to a recent Federal Reserve study.

The Economic Policy Institute's forthcoming "The State of Working America" analyzed the recession-driven drop in wealth. As of December 2009, median white wealth dipped 34 per-cent, to $94,600; median black wealth dropped 77 percent, to $2,100. So the chasm widens, and Memphis is left to deal with the consequences.

"This cancer is metastasizing into an economic crisis for the city," said Mayor A. C. Wharton Jr. in his riverfront office. "It's done more to set us back than anything since the beginning of the civil rights movement."

The mayor and former bank loan officers point a finger of blame at large national banks—in particular, Wells Fargo. During the last decade, they say, these banks singled out blacks in Memphis to sell them risky high-cost mortgages and consumer loans.

The City of Memphis and Shelby County sued Wells Fargo late last year, asserting that the bank's foreclosure rate in predominantly black neighborhoods was nearly seven times that of the foreclosure rate in predominantly white neighborhoods. Other banks, including Citibank and Countrywide, foreclosed in more equal measure.

In a recent regulatory filing, Wells Fargo hinted that its legal troubles could multiply. "Certain government entities are conducting investigations into the mortgage lending practices of various Wells Fargo affiliated entities, including whether borrowers were steered to more costly mortgage products," the bank stated.

Wells Fargo officials are not backing down in the face of the legal attacks. They say the bank made more prime loans and has foreclosed on fewer homes than most banks, and that the worst offenders—those banks that handed out bushels of no-money-down, negative-amortization loans—have gone out of business.

"The mistake Memphis officials made is that they picked the lender who was doing the most lending as opposed to the lender who was doing the worst lending," said Brad Blackwell, executive vice president for Wells Fargo Home Mortgage.

Not every recessionary ill can be heaped upon banks. Some black homeowners contract-ed the buy-a-big-home fever that infected many Americans and took out ill-advised loans. And unemployment has pitched even homeowners who hold conventional mortgages into foreclosure.

Federal and state officials say that high-cost mortgages leave hard-pressed homeowners especially vulnerable and that statistical patterns are inescapable.

"The more segregated a community of color is, the more likely it is that homeowners will face foreclosure because the lenders who peddled the most toxic loans targeted those communities," Thomas E. Perez, the assistant attorney general in charge of the Justice Department's civil rights division, told a Congressional committee.

The reversal of economic fortune in Memphis is particularly grievous for a black profession-al class that has taken root here, a group that includes Mr. Wharton, a lawyer who became mayor in 2009. Demographers forecast that Memphis will soon become the nation's first majority black metropolitan region.

That prospect, noted William Mitchell, a black real estate agent, once augured for a fine future.

"Our home values were up, income up," he said. He pauses, his frustration palpable. "What we see today, it's a new world. And not a good one."

PORCH VIEW

"You don't want to walk up there! That's the wild, wild west," a neighbor shouts. "Nothing on that block but foreclosed homes and squatters."

To roam Soulsville, a neighborhood south of downtown Memphis, is to find a place where bungalows and brick homes stand vacant amid azaleas and dogwoods, where roofs are swaybacked and thieves punch holes through walls to strip the copper piping. The weekly newspaper is swollen with foreclosure notices.

Here and there, homes are burned by arsonists.

Yet just a few years back, Howard Smith felt like a rich man. A 56-year-old African-American engineer with a gray-flecked beard, butter-brown corduroys and red sneakers, he sits with two neighbors on a porch on Richmond Avenue and talks of his miniature real estate empire: He owned a home on this block, another in nearby Whitehaven and another farther out. His job paid well; a pleasant retirement beckoned.

Then he was laid off. He has sent out 60 applications, obtained a dozen interviews and received no calls back. A bank foreclosed on his biggest house. He will be lucky to get $30,000 for his house here, which was assessed at $80,000 two years ago.

"It all disappeared overnight," he says.

"Mmm-mm, yes sir, overnight," says his neighbor, Gwen Ward. In her 50s, she, too, was laid off, from her supervisory job of 15 years, and she moved in with her elderly mother. "It seemed we were headed up and then"—she snaps her fingers—"it all went away."

Mr. Smith nods. "The banks and Wall Street have taken the middle class and shredded us," he says.

For the greater part of the last century, racial discrimination crippled black efforts to buy homes and accumulate wealth. During the post-World War II boom years, banks and real estate agents steered blacks to segregated neighborhoods, where home appreciation lagged far behind that of white neighborhoods.

Blacks only recently began to close the home ownership gap with whites, and thus accumulate wealth—progress that now is being erased. In practical terms, this means black families have less money to pay for college tuition, invest in businesses or sustain them through hard times.

"We're wiping out whatever wealth blacks have accumulated—it assures racial economic inequality for the next generation," said Thomas M. Shapiro, director of the Institute on Assets and Social Policy at Brandeis University.

The African-American renaissance in Memphis was halting. Residential housing patterns remain deeply segregated. While big employers—FedEx and AutoZone—have headquarters here, wage growth is not robust. African-American employment is often serial rather than continuous, and many people lack retirement and health plans.

But the recession presents a crisis of a different magnitude.

Mayor Wharton walks across his office to a picture window and stares at a shimmering Mississippi River. He describes a recent drive through ailing neighborhoods. It is akin, he says, to being a doctor "looking for pulse rates in his patients and finding them near death."

He adds: "I remember riding my bike as a kid through thriving neighborhoods. Now it's like someone bombed my city."

BANKING ON NOTHING

Camille Thomas, a 40-year-old African-American, loved working for Wells Fargo. "I felt like I could help people," she recalled over coffee.

As the subprime market heated up, she said, the bank pressure to move more loans—for autos, for furniture, for houses—edged into mania. "It was all about selling your units and getting your bonus," she said.

34

Ms. Thomas and three other Wells Fargo employees have given affidavits for the city's lawsuit against the bank, and their statements about bank practices reinforce one another.

"Your manager would say, 'Let me see your cold-call list. I want you to concentrate on these ZIP codes,' and you knew those were African-American neighborhoods," she recalled. "We were told, 'Oh, they aren't so savvy.'"

She described tricks of the trade, several of dubious legality. She said supervisors had told employees to white out incomes on loan applications and substitute higher numbers. Agents went "fishing" for customers, mailing live checks to leads. When a homeowner deposited the check, it became a high-interest loan, with a rate of 20 to 29 percent. Then bank agents tried to talk the customer into refinancing, using the house as collateral.

Several state and city regulators have placed Wells Fargo Bank in their cross hairs, and their lawsuits include similar accusations. In Illinois, the state attorney general has accused the bank of marketing high-cost loans to blacks and Latinos while selling lower-cost loans to white borrowers. John P. Relman, the Washington, D.C., lawyer handling the Memphis case, has sued Wells Fargo on behalf of the City of Baltimore, asserting that the bank systematically exploited black borrowers.

A federal judge in Baltimore dismissed that lawsuit, saying it had made overly broad claims about the damage done by Wells Fargo. City lawyers have refiled papers.

"I don't think it's going too far to say that banks are at the core of the disaster here," said Phyllis G. Betts, director of the Center for Community Building and Neighborhood Action at the University of Memphis, which has closely examined bank lending records.

Former employees say Wells Fargo loan officers marketed the most expensive loans to black applicants, even when they should have qualified for prime loans. This practice is known as reverse redlining.

Webb A. Brewer, a Memphis lawyer, recalls poring through piles of loan papers and coming across name after name of blacks with subprime mortgages. "This is money out of their pockets lining the purses of the banks," he said.

For a $150,000 mortgage, a difference of three percentage points—the typical spread between a conventional and subprime loan—tacks on $90,000 in interest payments over its 30-year life.

Wells Fargo officials say they rejected the worst subprime products, and they portray their former employees as disgruntled rogues who subverted bank policies.

"They acknowledged that they knowingly worked to defeat our fair lending policies and controls," said Mr. Blackwell, the bank executive.

Bank officials attribute the surge in black foreclosures in Memphis to the recession. They say that the average credit score in black Census tracts is 108 points lower than in white tracts.

"People who have less are more vulnerable during downturns," said Andrew L. Sandler of Buckley Sandler, a law firm representing Wells Fargo.

Mr. Relman, the lawyer representing Memphis, is unconvinced. "If a bad economy and poor credit explains it, you'd expect to see other banks with the same ratio of foreclosures in the black community," he said. "But you don't. Wells is the outlier."

Whatever the responsibility, individual or corporate, the detritus is plain to see. Within a two-block radius of that porch in Soulsville, Wells Fargo holds mortgages on nearly a dozen foreclosures. That trail of pain extends right out to the suburbs.

BEGGING TO STAY

To turn into Tyrone Banks's subdivision in Hickory Ridge is to find his dream in seeming bloom. Stone lions guard his door, the bushes are trimmed and a freshly waxed sport utility vehicle sits in his driveway.

For years, Mr. Banks was assiduous about paying down his debt: he stayed two months ahead on his mortgage, and he helped pay off his mother's mortgage.

Two years ago, his doorbell rang, and two men from Wells Fargo offered to consolidate his consumer loans into a low-cost mortgage.

"I thought, 'This is great!' " Mr. Banks says. "When you have four kids, college expenses, you look for any savings."

What those men did not tell Mr. Banks, he says (and Ms. Thomas, who studied his case, confirms), is that his new mortgage had an adjustable rate. When it reset last year, his payment jumped to $1,700 from $1,200.

Months later, he ruptured his Achilles tendon playing basketball, hindering his work as a janitor. And he lost his job at FedEx. Now foreclosure looms.

He is by nature an optimistic man; his smile is rueful.

"Man, I should I have stayed 'old school' with my finances," he said. "I sat down my youngest son on the couch and I told him, 'These are rough times.'"

Many neighbors are in similar straits. Foreclosure notices flutter like flags on the doors of two nearby homes, and the lawns there are overgrown and mud fills the gutters.

Wells Fargo says it has modified three mortgages for every foreclosure nationwide—although bank officials declined to provide the data for Memphis. A study by the Neighborhood Economic Development Advocacy Project and six nonprofit groups found that the nation's four largest banks, Wells Fargo, Bank of America, Citigroup and

JPMorgan Chase, had cut their prime mortgage refinancing 33 percent in predominantly minority communities, even as prime refinancing in white neighborhoods rose 32 percent from 2006 to 2008.

For Mr. Banks, it is as if he found the door wide open on his way into debt but closed as he tries to get out.

"Some days it feels like everyone I know in Memphis is in trouble," Mr. Banks says. "We're all just begging to stay in our homes, basically."

Questions for Discussion and Journaling

1. The article ends on a powerful note: "Some days it feels like everyone I know in Memphis is in trouble," Mr. Banks says. "We're all just begging to stay in our homes, basically." What do you think the author was attempting to accomplish by leaving his audience with this statement to contemplate as they finish reading the article? How might this support the implicit argument of the piece?

2. The author relies on pathos throughout the article, but there are strong appeals to both ethos and logos as well. Identify one ethical appeal and one logical appeal. How do these appeals strengthen the author's argument?

3. This article does an excellent job relating the micro (specific anecdotes from real people going through this economic crisis) to the macro (the overarching national concern of our economy in shambles). However, it could be argued that the author is relying on a logical fallacy or two. What fallacies can you identify? Pick one fallacy and explain why it is a logical fallacy. Refer to the section on logical fallacies in the "Analyzing Arguments" chapter in this textbook.

IS MEMPHIS MAKING (ANOTHER) MASSIVE MISTAKE WITH ITS PYRAMID?

35

Kriston Capps

This article (published in *CityLab*) responds to an article in *The New York Times* that announced Memphis's sale of the Pyramid to Bass Pro Shops in 2014. An online news source based out of Washington D.C., *City Lab* is dedicated to writing about urban spaces and creating an supportive environment for those spaces to thrive. The Pyramid, now repurposed as a Bass Pro Shop, was built in 1991 to be a concert venue and home to the Memphis Grizzlies. However, the infrastructure cost the city too much money, and the public considered the Pyramid cursed, since the Grizzlies didn't make the playoffs while playing there. In 2004, the Grizzlies moved to the FedExForum and the pyramid sat empty for over ten years before Bass Pro Shops took over the space. In this article, Kriston Capps tears into the decision-making process of the city and details the financial impact that the Pyramid has had on Memphis by analyzing the impact of big box sport retail stores on city environments. While this article is well researched, the writer makes some deliberate rhetorical moves, which depending on the reader, can either strengthen or alienate their connection with their audience.

A giant Bass Pro Shops outlet is set to move into the infamous landmark. But the city could be on the hook for millions if the deal falls apart.

"Quite frankly, what revenue-producing, tax-producing activities would be well suited to be located in a pyramid?"

Such a churlish question from Memphis Mayor A.C. Wharton, Jr.! Pyramids make excellent seats of administrative power, long-term storage solutions for environmentally hazardous sarcophagi, and transit terminals to other metaphysical dimensions. A pyramid's potential for producing sustainable dark energy alone should never be discounted. Surely, Mayor Wharton and *The New York Times* know this much.

Reuters/Jeff J. Mitchell

Granted, in Memphis, Tennessee, where the Great American Pyramid has sat empty for a decade, the revenue question has been a vexing one. Built in 1991 as a multi-use entertainment venue, it has served as the home of the University of Memphis men's basketball team and the Memphis Grizzlies, both of which decamped to the prism-shaped FedExForum in 2004.

Now, the city is gearing up to re-open the Pyramid as a different kind of entertainment venue, one anchored by a 220,000-square-foot Bass Pro Shop retail outlet. The plan will create 600 jobs for Memphis and pledges to fulfill the Pyramid's potential as a tourist destination, complete with a long-promised observation deck.

Yet what *The New York Times* fails to mention in its writeup about the development—which it describes as "a blessing that brings closure to one of the nation's weirdest urban-development misfires"—is that the deal will cost taxpayers tens of millions of dollars. And if it's anything like other downtown dealings with Bass Pro Shops, it could spell trouble for Memphis. In fact, the Bass Pro Shops plan could be a curse worthy of the Tomb of Doom.

According to the Franklin Center for Government and Public Integrity, Bass Pro Shops has cost American taxpayers $1.3 billion in public deals since the late 1990s. (Its corporate twin and leading rival, Cabela's, has garnered another $551 million in state and local assistance and $400 million from the federal government over the same period.) Government subsidies have enabled Bass Pro Shops to build an empire to rival any pharaoh's.

Many of these deals have failed to materialize, leaving taxpayers stuck with the ticket. The *St. Louis Business Journal* reports that officials in Independence, Missouri, were left in the lurch for a $3.5 million payment on tax-increment financing bonds after a hotel to be built

35

by Bass Pro Shops never materialized and Bass Pro Shops defaulted on its obligations. The deal, which promised some 50 different retail tenants, included an 18-acre lake and waterfall, all built with more than $70 million in taxpayer subsidies.

In a 2012 article for *CityLab*, Scott Reeder detailed how Buda, Texas, taxpayers financed a Cabela's outlet—to the tune of $60 million—complete with "a 30-foot artificial mountain, with taxidermied mountain goats and other wildlife, a 60,000-gallon freshwater aquarium and an exhibit of life-size African game animals." Buda went so far as to establish an economic development corporation that owns 20 percent of the Cabela's store and one-third of the land on which the property stands, rendering much of it null for the purposes of generating taxes.

The Bass Pro Shops deal could give these past morasses a run for their money, in terms of scope and significance. Memphis is a much bigger deal than Buda, Independence, or many of the other towns that have financed the retailer's expansions to their regret. Their number includes Leeds, Alabama, whose former mayor, Eric Patterson, warned Memphis against making a deal with Bass Pro Shops last year.

The libertarian Beacon Center of Tennessee identified the Bass Pro Shops deal in Memphis as one of the state's biggest boondoggles of 2014. City taxpayers are on the hook (so to speak) for $30 million in renovations to convert the Pyramid into a retail store, upscale hotel, underwater-themed bowling alley, and replica Delta cypress swamp. According to that report and a similar one from the Tennessee Watchdog, the public subsidy for Bass Pro Shops amounts to throwing good money after bad: The city has reportedly spent $100 million in various efforts to lure a tenant to the Pyramid.

In fact, the efforts to bring Bass Pro Shops to the Pyramid date back to 2005, just a year after the facility went dark. In a 2007 article, *Memphis* magazine detailed how the city was pursuing negotiations with Bass Pro Shops to the exclusion of other interested developers, including one offer from the Memphis-based Ericson Group. On paper, the Ericson Group deal would have secured not just the financing for renovations—for a plan to turn the Pyramid into an indoor theme park with mixed retail—but also funding to pay off the city's outstanding $12 million public debt for the facility.

But in the years it took to secure the Bass Pro Shops plan, the Ericson Group proposal was never given final consideration from the city, according to reports. From the start, the Ericson Group intended to take the building off Memphis's hands, whereas Bass Pro Shops is only leasing the Pyramid. While the Ericson Group plan might never have materialized (especially given the credit crunch of 2008), Bass Pro Shops has a proven track record of sticking cities with the tabs for failed launches. Now that the opening has been pushed back from this month to May 2015, restaurants in the Pinch are feeling the pinch, with conflicting accounts arising for who's responsible the rent over the interim.

In his *CityLab* article, Reeder speaks with Ball State University economist Michael Hicks, who performed a study of seven Cabela's outlets that opened (with public incentives) between 1998 and 2003 and found no discernible gain in jobs in those communities. Another economist told Reeder that big-box hunting and fishing retailers had the same intoxicating effect on small towns that sports franchises sometimes have on big cities—convincing them to spend millions in public funds for prestige over sound economic interest.

Memphis, a city of just more than 650,000 people, may be unique as a city hit by a development double-whammy. First, Memphis built the Pyramid, which the Division I Tigers occupied for less than 13 years and the Grizzlies called home for all of 3 years: a big-city mistake. A little more than 20 years later, Memphis is paying into a dream of outdoor-sports-retail tourism that has never manifested anywhere: a small-town bumble.

All of this might have been avoided had Memphis officials never removed the mysterious crystal skull that was discovered in the apex of the Pyramid soon after its construction. Perhaps the venture was doomed from the start. But Memphis is only doubling down on the bad juju by investing heavily in the notion that a downtown hunting-and-fishing outlet will bring people from far and wide to the Pyramid.

Questions for Discussion and Journaling

1. Consider the following quote: "Such a churlish question from Memphis Mayor A.C. Wharton, Jr.! Pyramids make excellent seats of administrative power, long-term storage solutions for environmentally hazardous sarcophagi, and transit terminals to other metaphysical dimensions. A pyramid's potential for producing sustainable dark energy alone should never be discounted. Surely, Mayor Wharton and *The New York Times* know this much." How does this opening paragraph set the tone for the article? What does that tone tell you about Capps' opinion? Does this tone help or hurt the author's argument? Explain why.

2. Are the sources cited in this article considered academic? Why or why not?

3. Go to the original platform that this article was shared on:
   https://www.citylab.com/life/2014/12/
   is-memphis-making-another-massive-mistake-with-its-pyramid/383414/

   Reread the article but this time click on the included hyperlinks. Do the choices the author makes change how you read the piece in regard to tone and professionalism? Does it affect the quality of their argument? Explain why or why not.

4. Read the article originally posted by *The New York Times* that this article is attempting to refute:
   https://www.nytimes.com/2014/12/04/us/bass-pro-shops-to-add-a-memphis-pyramid-to-its-business-empire.html?_r=1

   Does reading the NYT's article change your reading of *Is Memphis Making (Another) Massive Mistake with Its Pyramid*? Why or why not? What moves does Capps take to refute the original article? Are these moves successful?

ACADEMIC WRITING

MEMPHIS BURNING

Preston Lauterbach

"Memphis Burning" is a powerful analysis of "the nation's poorest major city" and the segregationist roots that still haunt it today. Author Preston Lauterbach investigates the economic and racial inequality that has afflicted Memphis throughout the 20th century and beyond, using pathos to argue that everything from gun violence to local politics are entangled in a complex web of institutional racism and economic injustice. The pictures included in the article appeal to the reader's sense of empathy, visually highlighting the social strife of the city. Originally published in *Places Journal* in March 2016, "Memphis Burning" provides a potent reminder of the strife that many Memphians still go through on a daily basis and delivers a challenge to its audience: change Memphis's future for the better. According to Lauterbach, "the future begins with destruction."

To understand racial inequality in America, start with housing. Here, in the nation's poorest major city, the segregationist roots go deep.

In the afternoon of February 26, 1953, fire destroyed a landmark in south Memphis, on Lauderdale Street. A stately three-story home, with eighteen rooms and twin gables, burned from its spires down.

Firefighters weren't late to the blaze—in fact, they'd ignited it. The city of Memphis, which was then hosting a convention of fire safety officials from around the country, had authorized the burning of the vacant mansion in order to demonstrate a new, efficient, fog nozzle fire-hose. Thousands stood in the street to watch. For two hours, firemen in black helmets and black slickers fought flames that burst through the roof and out of the windows. After blasting down each fire, they set another part of the home ablaze. Afterwards, the ruins steamed.[1]

"Memphis Burning" by Preston Lauterbach from *Places Journal*, March 2016. Reprinted by permission of the author.

But there was much more to this demonstration than a test of new firefighting equipment. As locals understood, the burning of this particular home was an assertion of power, because of who it had belonged to and what it symbolized. Abandoned, weather-beaten, but still grand, the mansion at 384 South Lauderdale represented the pinnacle of black achievement in the city.

Figure 36-1. R. R. Church family home, 384 South Lauderdale, Memphis, ca. 1899. [Library of Congress]

THE FIRE

A man named Robert Reed Church had built that home seventy years earlier. Church, though born a slave, made a fortune in real estate and was known as the South's first black millionaire. He helped lead the rebuilding of Memphis after yellow fever nearly wiped out the city in the 1870s, and from there he became the key developer of an iconic thoroughfare, presiding over a thriving African-American community on Beale Street. The street is legendary as the home of the blues, but it also nurtured early civil rights activism, notably in the work of crusading journalist Ida B. Wells, and black political power, through Robert Church's son, known in civic circles nationwide as Bob Church.

Bob was born and grew up in the fine house on Lauderdale Street, a half mile from a city park named for his father, in circumstances quite unlike what most African Americans knew. Not only had he come into the world in a mansion, all he could see out its windows were houses like his. Inside those houses lived prosperous whites—the families of U.S. Senator Kenneth McKellar and Supreme Court Justice Abe Fortas—and successful blacks, like city councilman Lymus Wallace and Julia and Charles Hooks, a music teacher and juvenile court judge, respectively, whose grandson Benjamin went on to lead the NAACP.

When Bob was born, in 1885, ten black families lived among whites on three blocks of South Lauderdale. In 1900, there were eleven black households; in 1910, there were ten. The decennial census is a small sample, but it shows a stable, racially mixed neighborhood in the heart of the South, during what were bleak decades for African Americans. And these weren't Negro servants living in backhouse quarters, but a professional class of homeowners. A child growing up on this street would have absorbed a certain sense of equality. These white families tolerated black neighbors, and these black families kept pace with white elites. According to racist doctrine in the post-Reconstruction South, nothing about this was normal.

Figure 36-2. Political kingpin Bob Church, musician W. C. Handy, and civic leader George W. Lee, in front of·Church's office at 392 Beale. [Memphis and Shelby County Room, Memphis Public Library and Information Center]

Robert Church, Sr., groomed his son as his heir in business. He founded a bank and put Bob in charge; built an auditorium and put Bob in charge; and consolidated his real estate holdings, including modest but attractive homes for African-American renters, into the R.R. Church & Son company, making Bob president. But the son yearned for politics. Determined to fight for racial equality, Bob Church saw the greatest opportunity to make a difference at the ballot box.

As a rising Republican star in the early 20th century—at that time the G.O.P. was still the party of Lincoln, and therefore had virtually the entire black vote—the younger Church achieved tremendous victories. He organized and registered black voters, and in 1920 helped win Tennessee for Warren Harding, the first time since 1876 that a former Confederate state had voted Republican. As the chief patronage dispenser in Memphis, Church controlled numerous federally appointed jobs, from postal workers to district attorneys. An admiring foe noted that he had a hotline running from Beale Street to the White House. Memphis blacks revered Church and all he stood for. The house on South Lauderdale symbolized his family's courage, drive, and success, and demonstrated the potential of black power in Memphis. Bob Church strove to make black people "politically alive," in his words.[2]

Meanwhile, a new power was rising in the form of a political machine controlled by Edward Hull "Boss" Crump. The white Democrat had moved to Memphis from Holly Springs, Mississippi, the same town where Robert Church, Sr., was born. Crump was elected mayor in 1909, at age thirty-five, and resigned in 1916. From then until his death in 1954, he ran Memphis as the undisputed boss of a formidable political machine. With his clouds of white hair, bushy eyebrows, and flashy attire, Crump cut an iconic figure, and his sharp wit made him good copy for *Time* and the *Saturday Evening Post*. He characterized one opponent as "the kind of man who' d milk his neighbor's cow through the fence."[3]

Figure 36-3. Boss Crump wields his cane. [Memphis and Shelby County Room, Memphis Public Library and Information Center]

On the surface, Bob Church and Boss Crump, the black Republican and white Democrat, would seem to be natural enemies, yet for a time the two men coexisted and even partnered. In the 1920s, they led a bipartisan, biracial coalition that controlled Memphis politics and elected most of its officials. Crump encouraged the black vote, and in return Church used his sway with Republican presidents to help place friendly officials in federal posts, while protecting the Crump machine from federal investigation. Together, they helmed Memphis through a time of exceptional growth, until the Great Depression hit.

But the period of biracial cooperation would prove short-lived. In the late 1930s, Boss Crump turned on his counterpart. In the span of a few years, the Democratic machine banished Bob Church, seized his property, broke the family fortune, and dismantled his Republican organization, crushing the most vital arm of black enfranchisement in the city.

The betrayal was mostly a matter of political expediency. With Franklin Roosevelt in the Oval Office, Crump no longer needed a Republican ally. As one of his operatives explained, "Pendergast, Daley, Roosevelt, Crump, the one characteristic that they all had in common was the ability, when necessary, to be absolutely and completely ruthless when it came to the organization.... I don't care how close a person was to them, how loyal they'd been, how much they had accomplished, as soon as they felt like they were no longer politically advantageous, out they went."[4] But even by that callous standard, the excommunication of Bob Church was particularly vicious. Crump accused Church of spreading dangerous ideas, and he told the editor of the black *Memphis World*, "You have a bunch of niggers teaching social equality, stirring up racial hatred. I am not going to stand for it. I've dealt with niggers all my life, and I know how to treat them.... This is Memphis."[5]

Smoke in the Memphis sky on that day in February 1953 signaled Crump's complete triumph, as the former Church mansion was burned to the ground. "An act of infamy," the black *Tri-State Defender* called it.[6] Decades later, a black Memphis resident, Lester Lynom, described it as "almost a lynching of the Negroes of Memphis." He added, "It wasn't just the house, it was what the house represented."[7]

Figure 36-4. The Memphis Housing Authority is second oldest in the nation. William H. Foote Homes, a black-only public housing complex, was built in 1941, across the street from the Church family home. [© The Commercial Appeal/Zuma Press]

THE BULLDOZERS

The burning of 384 South Lauderdale was the coda to decades of racist housing policy. When Crump turned on Church in the 1930s, the machine initiated the federally funded "slum clearance" of ten blocks across the street from the Church family home. The problem was that it was no slum at all, but a stable, middle-class, black neighborhood. The clearance area, west of Lauderdale from Vance Avenue to Mississippi Boulevard, featured houses that ranged in size from the Church mansion to the Hooks' single-story, single-family home, and small businesses such as flower shops, groceries, cafes, and funeral parlors. The structures were no more than sixty years old, and the few surviving dwellings from that era attest to their sturdy construction.

Residents beseeched Senator McKellar, their onetime neighbor and a conduit of federal authority, not to "wreck this whole section of the city," as one letter put it. "The home owners are sick and distressed beyond measure."[8] They wrote that that they had toiled for years to pay off their mortgages and fix up their properties, and they'd succeeded in making this the best neighborhood for blacks in Memphis. Their community was more valuable than any relocation funds the city might provide. One of Crump's leading black organizers, the Reverend T.O. Fuller, protested that he'd lose his home, workplace, and church.[9]

Their grievances were ignored. The Memphis Housing Authority—established in the mid-'30s, part of the wave of local authorities begun under Roosevelt's New Deal—leveled a 46-acre area and replaced the single-family homes with a low-rise, 900-unit public housing complex. As justification, the Housing Authority cited statistics showing that the city's black population had doubled in less than thirty years. Densifying an existing black neighborhood was a racist strategy to prevent African Americans from encroaching on predominantly white areas. The complex, known as William H. Foote Homes, opened in 1940—directly across the street from the Robert Church house.

What was left of the city's most prosperous, integrated neighborhood began to deteriorate. Surrounded by dense, low-income housing, the fine Victorian homes were subdivided and turned into cheap rooming houses. The city—which had previously allowed Bob Church to skip paying property taxes—foreclosed on his estate and auctioned off ten properties to pay the tax debt.[10]

Two decades later, the Crump machine finished the job. Another slum clearance program demolished the area east of Lauderdale, including the vacant lot where the Church mansion had stood, and in 1955 the MHA opened the 650-unit Edward O. Cleaborn Homes. Both public housing complexes were designated exclusively for African Americans.

Thus Boss Crump converted one of the black community's greatest strengths into a monument to inequality. No one had ever studied the neighborhood to figure out how it worked, how it had thrived for a half century when social equality failed nearly everywhere else in Memphis, and nearly everywhere throughout the South. Instead, federal funds enabled one group to hold down another, as Boss Crump crushed Bob Church's movement for black political power.

Figure 36-5. Victorian homes in a prosperous, integrated neighborhood on Vance Avenue, east of Lauderdale Street, in 1900. [Memphis and Shelby County Room, Memphis Public Library and Information Center]

THE BOMB

Inequality is *enforced* in Memphis, and it always has been. Indeed, the city was founded on the backs of slaves, as the capital of a cotton empire that stretched across the Mississippi Delta. The great river connected the city to the slave port at New Orleans, while a railroad linked Memphis to another slave port at Charleston, South Carolina. Confederate icon Nathan Bedford Forrest, both a slave trader and an alderman, helped shape the city's identity, investing in the Memphis-Charleston railroad and pushing local ordinances to benefit the business of slavery. Emancipation did little to change his outlook on labor conditions. When asked in 1869 who could solve the shortage of farm workers in west Tennessee, Forrest responded, "Get them from Africa. If you put them in squads of ten, with one experienced leader in each squad, they will soon revive our country." He had already imported one such lot for his Mississippi plantation, boasting, "They were very fond of grasshoppers and bugs, and I taught them to eat cooked meat, and they were as good niggers as I ever had."[11]

Cotton continued to dominate the Memphis economy after the Civil War, with black hands to do the planting, weeding, picking, baling, and the hauling to brokerages and warehouses along the river. Even as the industry declined, the crop defined the city's identity. The annual Cotton Carnival celebrated a "King" and "Queen" who were drawn ceremonially through the streets in a parade of floats carried by shirtless black men in frayed knickers. And the city never totally divested itself of old symbols. To this day, a statue topping the grave of Nathan Bedford Forrest is the centerpiece of a city park. It stood there in 1940, as Boss Crump's machine stripped the Church family name from another park not a mile away.

In 1953, the year of the burning of the old Church home, the Memphis Urban League reported that the median income for black households was $1,348 annually, less than half the white median of $3,085. These figures represent Memphis inequality in the last years of the

Crump era. Roughly 23,000 black families lived in extreme poverty, making less than $1,000 annually, and more black families were grouped in the sub-$500 category than in any other bracket. "Can anyone be amazed when these people appear in large numbers on relief rolls, in juvenile and criminal courts, and as contributors to illegitimacy, delinquency?" observed an official of the Urban League. "Their plight is the result of cheap labor, poor schools, and slums." Inequality was also firmly established at the upper end of the scale. Of the 4,000 Memphis families earning $10,000 or more annually, only 35 were black.[12]

Crump is the master behind the city's narrative, and his legacy lives on. His rule was so absolute, following his destruction of the black Republican organization, that the boss faced no real opposition. He handpicked local officials and candidates who did things the Crump way. According to former machine operative Guy Bates, Crump's reign did lasting damage to the city's long-term development. When the boss died in 1954 he left no heir, and his style of governing allowed no room for competing visions or compromise. No one was ready to take over. "We had generations of office holders and people that literally couldn't think for themselves. He stifled all other political thoughts," Bates said. "Where Houston grew, Dallas grew, and Atlanta grew, Memphis stayed where Mr. Crump wanted it to stay."[13]

Today, the majority-black city ranks first nationally in both overall and child poverty, among large metro areas.[14] A recent study found that 68 percent of the population lives in economic distress, as measured by indices of educational attainment, unemployment, median income, vacant houses, and shuttered businesses.[15] And nearly 80 percent of the poor are black. Elena Delavega at the University of Memphis has reported that black poverty in the city ranks far above state and national averages, while poverty among non-Hispanic whites is below average.[16] Memphis also ranks near the top for murders, aggravated assaults, and robberies per capita.[17]

Figure 36-6. South Memphis. [Andrea Morales for *Places Journal*]

36

Of course, poverty and crime are the symptoms of inequality, not its root causes. To truly understand racial inequality in America, you have to start with housing. In Memphis, inequality between black and white citizens is enforced at the neighborhood level, block by block, house by house.

The burning of the Church family home was far from the last fire in the housing battle. Four months later, on June 28, 1953, an explosion shattered windows at a house two miles away, sending residents of the block running for cover. Integration of that neighborhood had begun peacefully enough—years, in fact, before the integration of city schools, before the desegregation of public washrooms and dining rooms, and before downtown department stores and cafeterias served white and black customers equally. South Memphis could have been the model for an integrated Memphis. The bomb changed all that.

The house that exploded, at 430 East Olive Avenue, had been recently sold to the Williams family, the sixth or seventh black household to move into a neighborhood of small cottages occupied mainly by whites. Apparently, that was one black family too many. Soon after they moved in, white neighbors formed a violent, reactionary mob, shouting epithets at the new residents, patrolling the streets and taking down *For Sale* signs. They threatened to tar and feather homeowners who sold to black buyers. "When they see a house being shown, they round up the mob," said Mrs. L.C. Hauser, a white resident of East Olive. "It's like the Paul Revere signal."[18]

The explosion ignited citywide discussion of "the housing problem," as a rapidly growing black population challenged the status quo of racially segregated neighborhoods. African-American leader Benjamin Hooks—the future NAACP director and FCC commissioner who had grown up on Lauderdale near the Church family—wrote to the mayor: "There is an urgent demand for additional housing facilities for Negroes, which can only be met by natural area expansion...the extension of Negro home ownership into ever-widening areas."[19] This was a clear warning that the clash on Olive Avenue would be repeated, as black families continued their movement into formerly all-white neighborhoods.

Figure 36-7. The 400 block of E. Olive Avenue, photographed in 2016, half a century after a white supremacist mob patrolled the streets. [Andrea Morales for *Places Journal*]

Two months after the bombing, a group of white Olive Avenue residents called on the mayor. They planned to sell their houses, and they wanted the city's protection from the mob. "Mr. Mayor, these Negroes who have moved in there seem to be a fine class of Negroes," remarked one. "They keep up their homes and they look better than when the white people owned them." The group assured the mayor that they didn't object to the presence of blacks: "We object to the whites." But in any case, they were getting out. One owner reported, "My husband says he'll move and let that house sit there empty before he'll stay there. We do not want our children in that situation." Another neatly summarized the theme of the next five decades of Memphis history, telling the mayor, "You have to get out of that neighborhood if you want decent children."[20]

These events took place a year before the U.S. Supreme Court overturned the "separate but equal" doctrine and a year before the death of Boss Crump. But between Brown v. Board and Mr. Edward Hull Crump, it was no contest: the boss would have a much longer afterlife in the city of Memphis.

Today, East Olive Avenue looks as though more than one stick of dynamite went off. Where neat, solid frame houses once stood on tidy little lawns, now derelict buildings are collapsing between overgrown vacant lots. It exemplifies the cycle of fight, flight, and blight that has made Memphis what it is today.

THE GUNSHOT

Fifteen years after the bombing of the house on East Olive, the city's reputation for inequality was reinforced by one of history's greatest tragedies.

In early 1968, city sanitation workers went on strike, appealing for higher wages, better working conditions, and union recognition, following the deaths of two workers who were crushed in a garbage truck. Memphis was now ruled by Mayor Henry Loeb—a staunch segregationist and true successor to Crump. Loeb refused their demands, and the confrontation quickly became not just a labor dispute but a matter of civil rights, attracting national leaders like NAACP head Roy Wilkins and Dr. Martin Luther King, Jr.

King made three trips to Memphis during the strike, first to speak at a rally on March 18, then to lead a demonstration that exploded into a riot on March 28. The riot hurt King's reputation for nonviolence, and his associates organized another event, "the makeup march," to prove that a peaceful demonstration could be held in Memphis. King returned to the city on April 3, and that evening delivered one of his most famous speeches, "I've Been to the Mountaintop":

> Like anybody, I would like to live a long life. Longevity has its place. But I'm not concerned about that now. I just want to do God's will. And He's allowed me to go up to the mountain. And I've looked over. And I've seen the Promised Land. I may not get there with you. But I want you to know tonight, that we, as a people, will get to the promised land! And so I'm happy, tonight. I'm not worried about anything. I'm not fearing any man! Mine eyes have seen the glory of the coming of the Lord!

The next evening, King was fatally shot on the balcony of the Lorraine Motel in downtown Memphis. The assassination stands out not only as a signal moment in American history, but also as a powerful example of the consequences of bad leadership. For in Memphis the persistence of inequality is inextricably bound up with the city's long decline, and Loeb's obstinance seems as crucial to its social psychology as Boss Crump's bulldozers were to its built environment.

Figure 36-8. Dr. King speaks at the Mason Temple in support of the Memphis sanitation workers' strike shortly before his assassination. [Memphis Press-Scimitar via the Civil Rights Digital Library. Reprinted with permission of the Preservation and Special Collections Department, University Libraries, University of Memphis.]

Historian Kenneth T. Jackson of Columbia University is a preeminent scholar of suburbanization and author of *The Crabgrass Frontier*. He's also a Memphian, born and raised during the Crump reign. "Seventy years ago, Memphis, Atlanta, and Dallas were more or less in the same place, size-wise," he said, in an interview last summer. Memphis had the advantage of the Mississippi River as well as rail and interstate highway connections; its economy should have kept pace with, if not surpassed, its southern peers. Instead, Jackson said, it "got obliterated by those other cities."

While Atlanta leadership embraced a racially progressive, pro-business attitude behind Mayor Ivan Allen—adopting the slogan, *The City Too Busy to Hate*—Memphis "got on the wrong side of the civil rights revolution," Jackson said. "I would put a lot of the blame on Henry Loeb." He recalled watching the TV news the day of King's funeral in Atlanta, and seeing the mayor of that city hold an umbrella for Coretta Scott King. "Same night, same news, Henry Loeb was apoplectic, talking about how outside agitators had caused all of this," Jackson said. As the nation mourned, white leaders in Memphis were tragically out of step. *Time* called Memphis a "decaying Mississippi river town," blaming the assassination on "intransigent white mayor Henry Loeb" and his refusal to meet "modest wage and compensation demands."[21]

To this day, many believe that King's death coincided with the death of Memphis, that it marked the beginning of a half century of decline. It's a convenient notion, but it doesn't ring true. The assassination merely punctuated events set in motion decades earlier, when Boss Crump suppressed Bob Church's dream of social equality and economic justice.

THE RETREAT

White flight intensified the geography of disparity. Beginning in the 1950s, working-class whites moved just beyond the city's boundaries, first north to Frayser and south to Whitehaven, and then "out East" to Germantown, Collierville, and Cordova, where they built roads, schools, shopping centers, and hospitals—all the features of a city, spread over small rural communities. The completion of the I-240 freeway loop, in 1984, directed commerce away from the urban core of Memphis and toward the suburbs. Today, the highest concentrations of wealth, educational attainment, and jobs are on the eastern edge.

In an ongoing effort to recapture its lost revenue base, Memphis has annexed this ever-expanding crabgrass frontier so that it can collect property taxes from white flighters. Over time, the city has grown to a sprawling 324 square miles, larger than New York City, Atlanta, or St. Louis, without increasing its population of 650,000. Now the city government is responsible for providing services to that vast area, and yet the county roll shows that a third of the land—95 square miles—is essentially vacant, and much more is sparsely populated. In several cases the city gambled badly, annexing planned developments that never materialized, and now its diminished resources are spread thin across an ever larger territory, much of which generates no revenue.

In modern Memphis there is no figurehead, no Henry Loeb or Boss Crump, to articulate and symbolize the tenets of white supremacy. In fact, one result of white flight and black population growth has been the ascent of African-American political leadership. In 1974, Harold Ford, Sr., won election to the U.S. House of Representatives, becoming the state's first black congressman. In 1991, former school superintendent Dr. Willie Herenton became the city's first African-American mayor, an office he held for five terms. But the election of black leaders has done nothing to end racial division in Memphis—today, white opposition is expressed in continual growth beyond the city. In suburban malls and parks, you hear the loud echo of those nice white ladies in the mayor's office in 1953: "You have to get out of that neighborhood if you want decent children."

The racial prejudice of many suburbanites is revealed by their hostility to integrated public schools. Over the years, proposals to merge the government of surrounding Shelby County with the city government never gained much traction—but when county and city *schools* were finally merged, in 2011, that sparked a new segregationist revolt. Within two years, six suburban municipalities withdrew from the consolidated system and established their own schools (with a huge assist from the state legislature, which changed a law that had prohibited new school districts), and now those suburban districts no longer need to share their resources with the city. Urban residents nonetheless pay both city and county property taxes, benefiting the communities that have withdrawn their resources from Memphis.

The U.S. Census Bureau's 2011 American Community Survey shows the magnitude of disparity between Memphis proper and its suburbs out East. The wealthiest, best-educated households live clustered among the best job opportunities east of the city, while the least educated, most impoverished households live near low-skill, low-wage jobs. The survey found the city's unemployment rate to be double the national average, with black unemployment double that of whites. Median annual household income in Memphis proper was $37,072, compared with $46,102 in Shelby County (including the city) and $51,324 nationally.

THE MONEY

The closest thing modern Memphis has to an era-defining figure is Robert Lipscomb. Quite unlike the audacious Boss Crump, Lipscomb is soft-spoken and nonpolitical. He is also African American, a graduate of storied Booker T. Washington High School in South Memphis. As head of Housing and Community Development from 1992 to 2015, he led many of the signature initiatives of Mayor Herenton and oversaw the transformation of public housing. For a time, he held three high-ranking posts simultaneously, as head of HCD, director of the Memphis Housing Authority, and chief financial officer of the city. That made him the municipal leader most directly engaged with poverty in Memphis, which is to say, with the problems that define the city.

Lipscomb is like Crump in one crucial respect: for many years his actual power transcended his official authority. He outlasted the five-term mayor who appointed him and continued to play a central role in public policy—perhaps *the* central role—through the next two mayoral terms. His reign now appears to be over; in late 2015, he was ousted from power amid allegations of sexual abuse. Yet his legacy will shape Memphis for generations. He had such a profound influence on the built environment that people here compare him to Robert Moses, the powerful midcentury planner of New York City. With that comparison comes the insinuation—sometimes the open accusation—that he wielded too much power.

Figure 36-9. On the west side of Lauderdale Street, William H. Foote Homes, the last of the city's original public housing projects, is slated for demolition this year. [Andrea Morales for *Places Journal*]

Certainly his power is evident in the transformation of public housing that's happened in the past quarter century. When Lipscomb joined the Herenton administration, there were six public housing projects in Memphis. Today, only Foote Homes remains. The rest have been redeveloped under HOPE VI, a Clinton-era initiative that replaces rundown public housing with new, mixed-income developments and turns them over to private management. Lipscomb leveraged tens of millions of federal dollars to demolish the old projects and then partnered with commercial developers to build new affordable housing.

The contrast can be seen clearly on Lauderdale Street, near the former site of the Church family home. On the west side of the street, the squat, brick buildings of Foote Homes glower behind a high black fence. On the east side, the Cleaborn Homes have been torn down and replaced by "Cleaborn Pointe at Heritage Landing," a HOPE VI development of clean pastel townhouses with bright white trim. Likewise, in North Memphis, the Housing Authority under Lipscomb demolished the notorious Hurt Village projects and created the 100-block Uptown redevelopment area, where young professionals live among lower-income residents whose housing is subsidized by federal Section 8 vouchers.

Critics say such efforts don't cure poverty so much as they improve neighborhood appearances and line the pockets of private developers. Steve Lockwood, who runs a community development corporation in Frayser, just north of Uptown, said that his neighborhood now has the highest concentration of Section 8 residents in the city. He associates rising violent crime with an influx of people displaced from Hurt Village.

Housing is not the only sphere in which Lipscomb wielded outsized power. People need jobs as well as shelter, and as it turns out, those pretty pastel redevelopments are located far from the city's best opportunities. Wearing his other hat, as HCD director, Lipscomb was charged with stimulating economic growth in the urban core. Here his legacy is especially controversial. Whereas Housing Boss Lipscomb administered the flow of federal dollars tied to specific projects, Development Boss Lipscomb controlled discretionary funds in the form of Community Development Block Grants. Both funding streams are administered by the federal department of Housing and Urban Development, but the CDBGs come with far fewer restrictions. Which meant that in practice, one man—Robert Lipscomb—could use the community development grants however he liked, within the broad mandate of creating economic growth in impoverished areas. Almost any project could be justified.

With significant federal funds at his discretion, Lipscomb was the point man between the city government and the nonprofit CDCs that operate at a neighborhood scale—and that all across Memphis struggle with the fallout of white flight, with surging crime, failing schools, and blighted properties. The CDCs have scant resources. In contrast, the federal dollars flowing through Housing and Community Development represent the largest pot of money this poverty-stricken city has ever had for alleviating social problems. No private charity or public entity came close to Lipscomb's budget.

Of the dozen or so sources interviewed for this story, all people who are deeply engaged with poverty and inequality in Memphis, none hesitated to bring up Lipscomb by name or to question how "the city"—synonymous with Lipscomb—spends its resources.[22] Two concerns were raised by nearly everyone. First is the disparity between the meager funds spent at the neighborhood level, on CDC programs that assist small businesses and finance home repairs and construction in blighted areas, and the much larger sums of money funneled into big business projects, including for-profit ventures. The second is how the misuse of those federal millions reveals a lack of comprehensive planning.

Attorneys Webb Brewer and Steve Barlow have been engaged in fair housing suits in Memphis for two decades, and in that time they have worked both for and against the city government. In one recent, high-profile case, they represented the city in a predatory lending lawsuit against Wells-Fargo that resulted in a $7.5 million settlement. In fact, it was Lipscomb who alerted Brewer and Barlow to an unusually high number of foreclosures against black homeowners in economically depressed areas.

Despite their professional connections to the city, the attorneys are sharply critical of how funds have been distributed. "If you look at what they were spent for, it's all on macroeconomic development deals," Barlow said. His partner explained how the city has done an end run around federal guidelines that specify that funds must benefit low- and moderate-income people. "What they've gotten away with here forever is saying, 'This is going to provide jobs,'" Brewer said. He cited the widening of Poplar Avenue, the main artery leading out East, as a project funded with community development grants that actually benefited "business people" above all.

Federal money also helped build a new downtown basketball arena and, later, convert the old arena, The Pyramid, into a sporting goods megastore. The Pyramid project was locally notorious: it dragged on for nearly ten years, which did as much to inflame anti-Lipscomb sentiment as the millions of public dollars committed to the conversion of a civic venue (owned and operated by the city of Memphis and Shelby County) into a private business. The Pyramid finally reopened last year, as a Bass Pro Shop that includes a hotel, restaurant, and observation deck overlooking the Mississippi River. As with other projects, the city justified its allocation of HUD funds by promising to create jobs, and federal administrators accepted that at face value.

Yet no matter such promises, it's clear that inequality and poverty haven't statistically improved, despite decades of investment. One specific case seems particularly wasteful: the city's investment in the Peabody Place project, located not a mile from the old Church family home. In 1998, Lipscomb's division gave $1.2 million to Belz Enterprises, the developer of Peabody Place and the nearby Gibson Guitar Factory—the first installment in what would become a steady stream of federal funds that passed through the city to the project. Peabody Place mall opened in 2001, featuring tenants like Gap, Starbucks, and a twenty-screen movieplex; by 2012 it had closed, a casualty of the Great Recession. Over a decade and a half, the city provided more than $26 million in assistance, including $2.7 million in Community Development Block Grants, $14.9 million from a HUD Urban Development Action Grant, and $9.9 million in the form of a Section 108 loan.[23] All those millions amounted to zero long-term job growth, and community activists believe the funds should have gone instead toward tangible improvement at the neighborhood level.

Tom Burns is an urban planning consultant who came to Memphis to work with a local nonprofit focused on neighborhood revitalization. He's been in the field for forty years and has consulted in cities—including Detroit and Baltimore—that also struggle with poverty, blight, and a lack of resources. In Memphis, he interviewed the heads of some twenty HUD-approved community development corporations. It turns out, "they're not getting a lot of city money," Burns said. "Why, given the evident patterns of inequity, [is] there...so little attention and investment in government toward neighborhood revitalization?"

Burns was impressed by Lipscomb's housing achievements, particularly the HOPE VI development in Cleaborn Pointe. And yet, he said, other projects showed that city planners were making no connection between multimillion-dollar municipal investments and the neighborhoods that urgently needed help. "The scale of the problems here is enormous," he said, "but if you're trying to make a big difference, you have to link things up in a way that builds momentum. I don't see the civic leaders connecting the dots." *Connecting the dots*, he said, means linking housing developments to centers of job growth. It means avoiding public-private projects that lack a direct connection to neighborhood concerns. It means avoiding The Pyramid.

The city may no longer have a boss, but nearly a century after it was founded, the Memphis machine is alive and kicking. Here, in the nation's poorest major city, powerful local developers and corporations are siphoning off federal anti-poverty subsidies that should go directly to stimulate the economic progress of poor neighborhoods. That's pretty much the definition of inequality. Boss Lipscomb will be remembered for tearing down the neglected housing projects that symbolized the overt racism of earlier leaders, but he will also be remembered for controlling the purse-strings of a city government that provided a wealthy elite with resources that the poor majority desperately needed.

THE FUTURE

Although Robert Lipscomb had seemed invincible for a generation, his critics now get to see how the city works without its powerbroker. Late last year, in the midst of a heated mayoral campaign, Memphis suddenly found itself at the conclusion of a substantial chapter in its history.

Lipscomb's reign ended with a late-night announcement that the HCD director had stepped down following a criminal complaint that he had engaged in sexual relations with a minor. When reporters rang the bell the next morning, he answered his front door wearing an undershirt. He proclaimed his innocence. Within days, the MHA board suspended Lipscomb from his other job, and as more accusers came forward they cut off his pay.

The timing of the coup, less than six weeks from Election Day, made it seem like a reprise of dirty politics from the Crump era, when physical beatings and character assassination were standard tactics. The allegations came to light as incumbent mayor A.C. Wharton battled a trio of worthy challengers. Opinions flew about whether the city had unburdened itself of a problem or entered a leadership vacuum. Wharton lost in a landslide to Jim Strickland, who became Memphis's first white mayor since 1992. Six months later, no charges have been filed against Lipscomb.

The city now stands on the verge of a new era. Shortly before the election, HUD announced that Memphis would receive a $29.75 million Choice Neighborhood grant to demolish the city's last public housing project, Foote Homes. The feds had declined the city's application for the same project the previous year. Elsewhere, there are signs that the city is ready to turn the page on its racist history. Last summer the city council voted to take down the monument to Confederate hero Nathan Bedford Forrest, although state legislators are trying to block the move.

HCD has a new leader for the first time in nearly 25 years—former sustainable planning director Paul Young—and soon the mayor will appoint a permanent successor at the MHA. The city is working with private developers to replace Foote Homes with 700 market-rate units, and current residents will be displaced starting in April. What happens next in South Memphis is an open question.

Just as Boss Crump shaped the landscape of inequality with the burning of the Church family home, the new regime will have an opportunity to remake the city. What will happen to the poor, mostly black residents who now live in the public housing complex? What kind of community will rise in its place? Will the South Lauderdale neighborhood once again nurture leaders black and white, as it did in the early 20th century? Or will the city continue with policies and practices that have condemned African Americans to live on the wrong side of inequality?

The future begins with destruction.

Questions for Discussion and Journaling

1. How does Lauterbach's essay challenge the American narrative of race and the continual erasure of the black middle class? How does he characterize racial relations in Memphis prior to 1930? After 1930? What is his thesis and purpose?

2. The chapter introduction notes that Lauterbach makes excellent use of pathos; why does he choose to appeal extensively to pathos? Visit the article online at *Places Journal* and note the additional photographs in the full article. How do these images enhance his argument/persuasion? Can images appeal to logos and ethos as well as pathos? How? Where does he further utilize ethos and logos?

3. Lauterbach claims that "The future begins with destruction" (385). What do we need to destroy? What do *you* think will create a less racially segregated and more economically stable Memphis? Develop your ideas as a brief but effective argument (8–10 sentences).

ENDNOTES

1. "Fog Nozzle Spray Shows Speed in Dousing Blaze of Two Houses," *Memphis Commercial Appeal*, February 27, 1953: 1.

2. Walter P. Adkins, "Beale Street Goes to the Polls," M.A. Thesis, Ohio State University, 1935: 88.

3. "Tennessee Primary Politics Shock a Senate Committee," *Life*, August 15, 1938: 17.

4. Guy Bates interviewed by Charles Crawford, February 15, 1977, transcript at the University of Memphis Special Collections.

5. Roger Biles, *Memphis in the Great Depression*, University of Tennessee Press, 1986: 45.

6. "Almost An Act of Infamy," *Tri-State Defender*, March 21, 1953: 9.

7. Lester Lynom interviewed by Charles Crawford, July 6, 1983, transcript at the University of Memphis Special Collections.

8. Letter from Lida and Kate Hewitt to K.D. McKellar, letter, September 27, 1938, in the Watkins Overton Papers, Box Four, Series One, Memphis Room, Memphis Public Library.

9. Letter from T.O. Fuller to Watkins Overton, letter, September 21, 1938, in the Watkins Overton Papers, Box Four, Series One, Memphis Room, Memphis Public Library.

10. "Bob Church Property Will Be Auctioned," *Commercial Appeal*, February 14, 1939: 11.

11. "An Interview with Gen. Forrest: A Talk About the Negro and Railroads," *Memphis Daily Appeal*, March 12, 1869: 4.

12. Statistics are from a Memphis Urban League pamphlet archived with the papers of mayor Frank Tobey, Memphis Room, Memphis Public Library.

13. Bates, op cit.

14. In 2014, Memphis ranked first in overall poverty rate (20.3%) and child poverty rate (30.8%) among the 52 Metropolitan Statistical Areas with populations greater than one million. See Elena Delavega, "2015 Memphis Poverty Fact Sheet" (pdf), data from the American Community Survey.

15. According to an index by the Economic Innovation Group, which uses data from the American Community Survey. See EIG, "Defining Economic Distress" (pdf).

16. Delavega, op cit.

17. 2015 FBI uniform crime report.

18. Quote from an August 26, 1953, meeting in the mayor's office, transcript in the Frank Tobey Papers, "Negro Housing Problem" folder, Memphis Room, Memphis Public Library.

19. Letter from Benjamin Hooks to Frank Tobey, July 16, 1953, in the Frank Tobey Papers, "Negro Housing Problem" folder, Memphis Room, Memphis Public Library.

20. Quote from the August 26, 1953 meeting in the mayor's office, op cit.

21. "The Assassination," *Time*, originally published April 12, 1968.

22. Interviews took place during June and July 2015, prior to the allegations against Lipscomb, which surfaced in August.

23. Memphis Division of Housing and Community Development Consolidated Plan FY 2012, on file at the Memphis Public Library.

36

AFRICAN-AMERICAN ENGLISH: FROM THE HOOD TO THE AMEN CORNER

Geneva Smitherman

This reading was originally a keynote speech presented at the Center for Inter-disciplinary Studies of Writing's 1995 Conference. Written and delivered by Geneva Smitherman, the transcribed speech summarizes her award-winning and field-changing research on the linguistic and rhetorical features of African American English (AAE). The speech uses narrative to amplify her personal experiences and illustrate the rich linguistic and rhetorical features of AAE while also relying on the traditions she introduces to and defines for her audience. Now retired, Smitherman is a distinguished linguist, the author/editor of 5 books and many more academic articles, chapters, and reports, and winner of the Conference on College Composition & Communication's Exemplar Award as well as the rarely given National Council of Teachers of English's James R. Squire Award for "lasting intellectual contribution to English Studies." Before she retired, she was a Distinguished Professor and Founder of the African American and African Studies Program at Michigan State University. Her research also includes a study that found that when Black students employed Black discourse features in their writing, they scored higher on the National Assessment of Educational Progress than Black students who did not and concluded that writing instructors should "capitalize on the strengths of African American cultural discourse; encourage students toward the field dependency style, which enables them to produce more powerful, meaningful, and more highly rated essays; and deemphasize concerns about Black English Vernacular grammar." Her work and research continues to be both foundational to and challenging for writing scholars and teachers and continues to impact educators in fields beyond English.

"African-American English: From the Hood to the Amen Corner" by Geneva Smitherman. Keynote speech presented for the Center for Interdisciplinary Studies of Writing 1995 Conference "Linguistic Diversity and Academic Writing." Reprinted by permission of Dr. Geneva Smitherman.

PREFACE

On May 4 and 5, 1995, the Center for Interdisciplinary Studies of Writing held its sixth annual colloquium, which focused on the theme of "Linguistic Diversity and Academic Writing." The colloquium was designed as a forum for discussions of cultural diversity, multiculturalism, student language, and writing. We invited Geneva Smitherman, University Distinguished Professor of English and Director of the African American Language and Literacy Program at Michigan State University, to deliver the keynote address published here.

As a scholar and as a social reformer, Professor Smitherman has blazed many trails. Her scholarship has been central in the debates, which have legitimized African American vernacular as a rule-governed, richly expressive variant of the English language. Her book *Talkin and Testifyin: The Language of Black America* is the most widely cited source for linguists who have described this dialect. Fifty-two articles and nine books later, her book *Black Talk: Words and Phrases from the Hood to the Amen Corner* continues to illuminate the traditions, evolution, and vitality of African American speech and rhetorical style. No other sociolinguist has established such a distinguished record on such an important topic.

Professor Smitherman's keynote address, "African-American English: From the Hood to the Amen Corner," provides a personal context from Smitherman's own experience for discussions about diverse language practices. It also provides a historical overview of the evolution of African American English and outlines options in the current debate over national language standards.

The colloquium and the publication of Professor Smitherman's speech contributes fresh perspectives that enhance the primary mission of the Center for Interdisciplinary Studies of Writing—improving undergraduate writing at the University of Minnesota. Along with colloquia, conferences, publications, and other outreach activities, the Center annually funds research projects by University of Minnesota faculty who study any of the following topics:

- characteristics of writing across the University's curriculum;
- status reports on students' writing ability and the University;
- the connections between writing and learning in all fields;
- the characteristics of writing beyond the academy;
- the effects of ethnicity, race, class, and gender on writing; and
- curricular reform through writing-intensive instruction.

We are pleased to present Professor Smitherman's keynote address as part of the ongoing discussion about linguistic diversity and the politics of teaching writing. One of the goals of all Center publications is to encourage conversations about writing; we invite you to contact the Center about this publication or other Center publications and activities.

Lillian Bridwell-Bowles, Series Editor
Kim Donehower, Editor
April 1996

AFRICAN-AMERICAN ENGLISH: FROM THE HOOD TO THE AMEN CORNER

I told Professor Bridwell-Bowles that in the Traditional Black Church, which is where my roots are, we have this expression, "Pin the flowers on me now, while I'm living and can smell them." I thank her again for that great introduction, more of these wonderful flowers. She alluded to a speech test that got me started on this road, and I want to amplify on that experience because it really had a profound effect on me. In fact, there was a point in time when I had to learn to talk about it, and my students taught me to talk about it. In fact, it was when I was in one of my first teaching jobs. They said, "You gotta tell that story because it shows what the system can do to people, and it's an inspiration for others." And so I'll tell you a little bit about myself and include that story.

I was born in rural Tennessee where my folks were sharecroppers. I started school in Brownsville, Tennessee, which is about 50 miles from Memphis. My first teacher was Ms. Earline, and as it turned out she ended up being the only African American teacher that I had in all my years of schooling. In those years I was basically monolingual, speaking the African American English of my Traditional Black Church and of my family and also of Ms. Earline. I didn't have any problems in terms of language until we moved to Chicago and Detroit. Living a few years in Chicago and then Detroit, I had my first taste of linguistic attack when my European American teachers criticized my dialect. It was very interesting, too, because in those years they attributed African American English to the South, but no one ever satisfactorily explained why African American people in the North talked the same way as those in the South when they'd never even been South. Because, of course, it wasn't just a Southern type of speech but a form of speech with Africanized roots. Those were the beginning of my days of being non-verbal. I finally managed to finish school, to graduate in fact from a college prep high school in Detroit by just keeping my mouth shut. In college, however, after I decided that I wanted to parlay my Sunday School teaching skills into the teaching of English and Latin, which were my undergraduate majors, I had to try to get a teaching certificate. Teacher training institutions in those years, in about 40 different states, required you to take a speech test—your speech had to be Northern, middle class, Midwestern, White Standard English.

Even though I was writing in the Language of Wider Communication, or Standard English, I hadn't learned to code-switch in speech. So of course I flunked the speech test. If you failed the test, you had to take speech therapy. This was at the height of the Black Liberation Movement, and I figured all this really had something to do with race. So I went into this speech therapy class with a serious attitude. It was a small class, about 15 people. I saw some faces that looked like mine, and I said to myself, "Yeah, just like I figured." And then I saw a couple of brown faces, and I had to stop for a minute, but then I said, "Oh yeah, but they're Hispanic, so they don't like the way they talk either." And then over in the corner I saw two White people. I said, "Now wait a minute, what is dem White folks doing up in here cause I know they done passed the speech test." Well, as it turned out, one of dem White folk was a speaker of what we now in linguistics call "Appalachian English," and the other was from the Bronx.

Now, this speech therapist, she didn't really know what to do with us. She was just this poor little White girl, a Teaching Assistant, trying to get her Ph.D., and here she had this motley crew of 15 people who didn't have aphasia or dyslexia, didn't anybody even stutter! So, she couldn't deal with that because she had been trained to deal with real speech disorders that required therapy. She somehow figured out, back in those days, what we now know through the explosion of knowledge in linguistics, that there was nothing deficient about any of us, that we were all speaking English, we were just speaking different variations of it. We didn't have any delayed language development or any cognitive deficiencies and, in fact, since we were speaking—and had spoken—these variations since infancy, there was no way that we could automatically change our dialects in a matter of 16 weeks. So what she did was she taught us the test. We simply memorized all the lists of words that they had on the test. She set up these little exercises for each of us, depending on which features of the pronunciation system on the test we hadn't mastered. I remember two of my features, which I now understand are carryovers from African languages. One was the so-called post-vocalic r-deletion in a word like "four," which for me is "fo," or "more," which for me is "mo," or "sore," which is "so." I was going around in the 'hood, saying "four," "more," "sore," and all my friends would say, "What's up—that's what you do in college? What is this?" The other feature I really worked on was the "th" sound, the so-called interdental fricative. Initial "th" in words like "then," in my native tongue is "den," or at the end of a word like "mouth," it's "mouf," and "south" is "souf." I was later to learn that in many of the languages of West Africa that my ancestors spoke when they came here in enslavement, there is no "th" sound. So they did what speakers do, they picked the next closest sound and adapted their language patterns to fit the new norm. That speech therapy experience is how I came to switch from a literature major to being a student of the English language.

That experience also taught me something about the misguided attitudes that Americans have toward language. I'm very happy to say that teacher training institutions no longer require a speech test. Because of the work that came out of sociolinguistics, particularly in the late 60s and 70s, those tests have fortunately gone by the wayside. But this shows something about the attitude that people have about what one linguist calls our "national mania for correctness." James Baldwin says that it has to do with the self-consciousness that Europeans in America have about their own language and culture when measured up against the linguistic traditions of Europe. Before we go any further, I think it's important to say that I don't want people to get me wrong, I am not saying that anything goes. Very often those of us in sociolinguistics and linguistics in general are considered permissive—that we say, "Oh, we can talk or write any way." In fact, there are standards.

I am saying that I want us to think about language as a source of power. And if you want to use language as a source of power, you've got to go way beyond basic pronunciations like "fo" vs. "four" and other simplistic notions of correctness. What the great speakers and writers do is use language as power. They try to move mountains. They know that the word, in fact, is power. And it isn't just in the African American tradition. I'm told that in the time of the ancient Greeks, when some orators spoke, the people politely applauded. But when other orators spoke, the people marched. What we want to do with language is to move people, to make them march.

I want to tell you another little story that helps me explain in a quite vivid way this misguided notion of permissiveness, wherein some folks will say, "Well, you know, you can just say any old thing if you're talking Black English. There aren't any standards or conventions." In fact there are definite standards and conventions. A White feminist linguist, a friend of mine, told this little story on herself. She had recently married an African American man who was studying for the ministry. When it came time for him to preach his trial sermon, it was in the Traditional Black Church, the proving ground for Black preachers. The Traditional Black church is the church where the content of the worship is Judeo-Christian, but the style in which people worship is very Africanized. They talk in tongue, they testify, they get the Spirit, they believe in Spirit possession. There's a belief that the way to get the message to the congregation and construct community is for everybody to participate. So you have people talking back to the preacher, and talking back to anybody in the church who stands up to say something. This is the call-response dynamic in African American English. When our novice minister was giving his sermon and he was really getting deep into it, the people over there in the Amen Corner, which is where the cheerleaders of the church sit, started saying, "Ahhhh, watch yosef doc," "Take yo time," "Yeah I hear you," "Come on up now." And so my friend, the preacher's European American wife, started feeling sort of out of it, and she wanted to get into the spirit of things, and so she shouted out, "Now that's a very good point." Wrong response for this audience. She herself laughs about that now. There are definitely standards in African American English as in any other language community—things that you say or don't say, depending on the context.

Let me give a definition of African American English—and I'm talking about it from the Hood to the Amen Corner, which is my way of trying to say there is no rigid division between what happens in the street and the church, that is, between the sacred and the secular. I would define African American English as the mixture of African language patterns with English. This language mixture developed from two different linguistic traditions during enslavement. So we're talking about a language that came out of enslavement. Without enslavement, there would be no African American English, nor for that matter Africanized Dutch, Africanized Portuguese, or Africanized French.

African American English served as a transactional language between the master and the slave or between the master and Africans who sold other Africans into European enslavement. (That's a part of African and African American history that we often don't want to acknowledge, but in fact, that is exactly what happened.) The language mixing is the result of a process when two groups of people come together and they can't speak each other's language. They develop something in between that they use for very limited purposes of communication.

That was one purpose of African American English. But the more important purpose that African American English served in the slave communities was that of a counter language, a bond of solidarity between Africans from different ethnic groups. There was a very conscious attempt on the part of the enslaved to represent an alternative reality through language—through a language which is based on irony, ambiguity, on what Henry Louis Gates calls "double voicedness." In this sense, African American English became the *lingua franca* of those in enslavement communities. This was very interesting because one of the things that the slave masters did was mix Africans from different ethnic groups in the same slave community so as to foil communication. The use of African American English effectively negated that because the enslaved used this new language to talk among themselves—and to talk about massa right in front of his face, using Africanized English with its double meanings. I think it's this function, this tradition of African American English being a counter language, that explains why when a word crosses over into the general White mainstream, it becomes wack—no longer useful, it no longer has linguistic currency in the Black community.

Before going further, it would be useful to review some general principles about language that also apply to speakers of African American English. For one thing, we know that humans are the only members of the so-called "animal kingdom"—I hate saying "animal kingdom"—humans are the only ones who possess a language system in the sense of putting together sentences and statements in novel patterns and new ways of speaking. What the other animals do when they communicate is mimic and imitate, but humans create totally new and different patterns of language use.

It is language, then, that differentiates us from other animal species; it is language that makes us human. In the 17th Century, Descartes said it was thinking that was the essence of humankind. We now know that language is the thing that makes us human. A child comes into the world born to speak. Think about the fact that before you know it, children are going through these steady stages where they coo and they babble and then they'll say one word and then all of a sudden the all-hell-breaks-loose stage of language takes place, at about 18 months or so, and they're just talking all over the place. You don't have to teach children to talk. You send them to school to learn the three R's but you don't have to send them to school to learn speech. They will learn it and pick it up because of this language acquisition device, this microchip in the human brain. They'll learn language, and what they learn will be the dialect version of the language they hear in their speech community. It works the same way for every human being on the planet, regardless of what their race is or their skin color or their gender or whether they grow up in a community with, as Fishman would say, "little languages spoken by little people," or whether they're speaking a dominant, global language.

What we also know about language is that it's a bond of solidarity. It's this sense in which the counter language of African American English developed and exists today, In fact, what you can do is use language to send a message about how loyal you are to a particular cultural group. In my analysis of the Anita Hill/Clarence Thomas phenomenon, I tried to figure out why was it that in all the public opinion polls Anita Hill was not rated very high—she wasn't rated as credible as Clarence Thomas by Black people, not even by Black women. What I looked at, in all the transcripts and all the videotapes we were able to get from the research archives, was the rhetorical style that she used during those hearings in contrast to the style that Clarence Thomas used. Anita Hill used the so-called objective impersonal style, the Language of Wider Communication that she had been trained in at Yale. One thing about that language is that it creates social distance. Thomas, even though he was also trained at Yale, used the discourse style of African American English. That's a style that's hot, it's emotional, it's personalized. You'll remember that he talked about things like the personal effect of all the drama on him, how he hadn't slept in a thousand nights. He used all the hyperbole of Black vernacular, telling us what his mother thought and how she became ill because of the accusations against him. He pimped the tradition. He's not really "black" at all as we can witness in his decisions as a Supreme Court Justice. Unfortunately, Hill, by failing to plug into the Black Verbal Tradition, distanced herself from her audience.

I often say that language is like a marked deck of cards. I think of old-time poker players who hold their cards close to their chests, but there are these little markings that have been put on the back of each card. The player who knows just where to look could tell whether it was a jack or a king. I say language is like that—it's a marked deck of cards if you know what to listen for.

When it comes to Black English, we do know what to listen for now, but this was not always the case. Before the research that was done in the 60s and early 70s, people said things like this: (These are some exact phrases quoted from scholars and writers who talked about the speech of the Negro.) It was "baby talk." Some attributed it to the "jungle tongue" of Africans, their "flat noses," "thick lips," and so on and on, ad nauseam.

So what are the things that we listen for? What are the features of African American English? There are three dimensions: 1) a system of grammar and pronunciation, 2) verbal traditions, and 3) a system of semantics. As an example of the system of grammar, I like this conversation that took place among Black women at the hair braiding shop a couple of weeks ago. One of the women was talking about her new significant other, and she said "The brother be looking good." She was using "be" in the way that many languages of West Africa convey meaning. That is, the verbs don't necessarily have anything to do with past, present or future tense but with the character or essence of something. When she said "The brother be looking good," she didn't mean the brother IS looking good but he BE looking good, which is to say, he looked good yesterday, he looking good today and he gon be looking good tomorrow—cause that's his essence, his nature, he be looking good. Many of the languages of West Africa have this sort of grammatical pattern.

In terms of the pronunciation system, I mentioned my own experience with the "th" sound and the post-vocalic r-deletion. Another interesting feature is the tendency to end syllables with a vowel sound, as for instance, in the Yoruba language. Some people may be familiar with the Hip Hop group, "Soul For Real." I heard them explaining their name on a radio show. One of them said "Well we're soulful and we're for real," and the interviewer said, "Oh, yeah." Of course he didn't get it. I went right out and bought their CD and as I expected, it was "Soul for Real." Since medial and final "l" aren't articulated in Black Talk, this Hip Hop group plays on the identical pronunciation of "so" and "soul" to brand themselves as both "soulful" and "so real."

Another example is the Black Talk pronunciation of the "th" sound. This accounts for the name of the television program, "Def Comedy Jam." Standard English "death" is "def" in African American English and "Def" comes from a phrase dating back to the 1960s, "doing it to def." If you do something to death/def, you do it to the max, to the highest level. So that's how "def" comes to mean something really superb, excellent, great—like "Def Comedy Jam."

I think where the real action lies in Black Talk is in the verbal traditions and in the semantics. That's where you really see the richness of the language. By Black Verbal Traditions, I mean linguistic practices like "The Dozens" (also "Playin The Dozens"). On the East Coast, they call it "snapping." These are ritualized insults where you talk about a person or you talk about their mother. The idea of this kind of game is to say something that is humorous, full of hyperbole and exaggeration. It's a game of back-and-forth verbal play, of one-upmanship. You know, like, "Your mother so ugly, she look like nine miles of bad road with a detour at the end." One of the rules of The Dozens that people forget—I'm saying that these verbal forms have rules just like my feminist friend there in the church—one of the very basic rules of "Playin the Dozens" is that what you say cannot be literally true. That's why it's a game. If you say something that's literally true about a person, or their mother, then it ain't playin no more.

This really came home to me once when I was in graduate school and my son Tony and his friends were into this game of "The Dozens." One of the boys was from a family where his mother had about ten children and she wasn't married. So one of Tony's boyz, when he couldn't think of anything else, said to Ralph, "Yo momma need to take birth control pills." It starts getting heated because the game is no longer play and fantasy, but is now getting into reality and truth. Then Ralph says to Tony, "Don't you say nothing cause least my momma don't buy her furniture from the Goodwill." Now Tony and I had had this big debate about a television table that I had bought for him from the Goodwill. I was a struggling graduate student. I didn't have any money. Ralph's insult was that Tony's momma was "big-time," getting a Ph.D. from college, but she's shopping in the same place as "low-class" Blacks. With the introduction of real life facts from the boys' lives, they were getting fighting mad; it was no longer play. The arrival of truth, which hurts, broke the game up.

Another Black verbal tradition is braggadocio—high talk, fancy talk, boasting, where a person, using exaggerated language, celebrates their accomplishments or the accomplishments of somebody else. It's what you hear in Rap Music and Hip Hop today. My favorite example that I want to share with you is from the first Black female Rapper, at least the first to go public, and it dates back to the 1960s. The Rapper is Nikki Giovanni, a poet. The Rap she performs, which is done to drumming in the background, is her poem "Ego Tripping." What she's doing in "Ego Tripping" is braggadocio, celebrating the female principle of creativity in Africa and in her.

Some lines from Giovanni's Rap poem:

> I was born in the Congo,
>
> I walked to the fertile crescent and built the sphinx.
>
> I designed a pyramid so tough that a star that only glows every 100 years falls into the center giving divine perfect light.
>
> I am bad.
>
> I sowed diamonds in my back yard.
>
> My bowels deliver uranium.

The filings from my fingernails are semiprecious jewels.

On a trip north I caught a cold and blew my nose giving oil to the Arab world.

I am so hip even my errors are correct.

I sailed west to reach east and had to round off the earth as I went.

The hair from my head thinned and gold was laid across three continents. I am so perfect, so divine, so ethereal, so surreal, I cannot be comprehended except by my permission.

I mean I can fly like a bird in the sky.

Another verbal tradition that shows the richness of Black Talk is <u>the Toast</u>. A Toast is a long epic story told in rhymed couplets. It's all about powerful, strong, superbad Africans. The Toast recalls the role of the African griot who was responsible for preserving the legacy and history of their community. To engage in this type of linguistic practice you have to have a phenomenal memory and you have to have a sharp, fluent way with words because if you forget a line, you have to be able to make another one up on the spot.

This was a dying art form until the 90s when Rap artists recovered the Toast tradition. Two Toasts I like are "Signifying Monkey" and "Stagolee" (also "Stagger Lee"). But my all-time favorite is "Shine and the Sinking of the Titanic." As the story goes in the Black Tradition, the fighter Jack Johnson tried to get passage on the Titanic and was refused. A whole long narrative developed around a legendary stoker on the Titanic who didn't actually exist, of course. But the story was that there was one Black person on the ship, a male named "Shine" (appropriately). And he's the only person who survived the sinking of the Titanic.

Shine knows that the ship is sinking, and he run on up to the Captain and he say:

"Captain, Captain, I was down in the hole looking for something to eat

And you know what, the water rose above my feet."

The Captain say, "Shine, Shine, boy have no doubt. We got 99 pumps to pump the water out.

Now boy you get on back down in the hole

And you start shoveling some more coal."

(By the way, people who know versions of this will notice that I've cleaned it up a bit. We use this for a reading series for adolescent readers who are reading below grade level but are too sophisticated for the Dick and Jane readers. So we cleaned this Toast up.)

Shine went on back down in the hole,

He started to shoveling coal and singing,

"Lord, Lord, please have mercy on my soul."

As Shine was singing, "Lord, Lord, please..."

The water, it rose above his knees.

Shine split back up on deck and he say,

"Captain, Captain, I was down in the hole,

I was shoveling coal and singing, 'Lord, Lord, please,' And you know what? The water it rose above my knees."

The Captain told Shine that all was cool.

He say, "Shine, Shine, I done told you to have no doubt, We got 99 pumps to pump that water out.

Now you get on back down in that hole

And you just keep on shoveling coal."

Shine went on back down in the hole,

He kept on shoveling coal,

He stopped to wipe the sweat off his face,

That's when the water rose above his waist.

Shine run back up on deck. He say, "Captain, Captain, I was down in the hole

Just shoveling coal

And when I stopped to wipe the sweat off my face

The water it rose above my waist."

The Captain say "Shine, Shine, boy how many times do I have to tell you to have no doubt

If I done told you once I done told you a hundred times, We got 99 pumps to pump the water out.

Now boy, don't you trust your Captain?

I don't want to see you on deck again, you hear?"

Shine went on back down in the hole.

He kept on shoveling coal.

He stopped to eat a piece of bread.

That's when the water rose above the brother's head.

Shine split back up on deck.

He say, "Captain, Captain, you speak well and your words, they sound true.

But this time Captain your words just ain't going to do.

This here ship is sinking.

Little fishes, big fishes, whales and sharks too, get out my way, cause I'm coming through."

Shine yanked off his clothes in a flash.

He jumped in the water and started to splash.

The Captain saw the water rise out the hole and he started thinking,

"That boy is right. This here ship is sinking."

He called out to Shine, "Shine, Mr. Shine, please save me,

I'll make you master of the sea."

And Shine say, "Master on land, master on sea.

If you want to live, Captain, better jump in here and swim like me."

Then the Captain's wife ran out on deck in her nightgown with her fine, fine self, and she called out to Shine, "Shine, Shine, please save poor me.

I give you more loving than you ever did see."

Shine say, "Loving ain't nothing but hugging and squeezing.

Sometimes it be tiring, sometimes it be pleasing.

I can swim but I ain't no fish.

I like loving but not like this."

Then a old fat banker came up on deck carrying his money bags and he called out to Shine,

"Shine, Shine, please save me.

I'll make you richer than any man could be."

Shine say, "Money's good on land but it's weight in the sea.

If you want to live fatty better jump in here and swim like me."

Shine took one stroke

And shot on off through the water like a motor boat.

And then he met up with this here shark.

And the shark say, "Shine, Shine, you swim so fine

But if you miss one stroke your butt is mine."

Shine say, "I swims the ocean, I swims the sea,

There just ain't no shark that can outswim me."

Shine outswimmed the shark.

After a while Shine met up with this here whale.

And the whale say, "I'm king of the ocean and I'm king of the sea."

And Shine say, "You may be king of the ocean,

And you just may be king of the sea,

But you got to be a swimming sucker to outswim me."

Shine outswimmed the whale.

Now check this out.

When news reached land that the great Titanic had sunk,

Shine was down on a corner halfway drunk.

Semantics is the third dimension of African American English. Contrary to popular notion, these words are not just slang although some are slang in the sense that their life is transitory, that they won't be around for long. But I think you have at root the semantics of a counter language. That is, enduring widespread words and phrases that go across generations and classes, that have been around for a long time and that in fact reflect the reality of the African American Experience. The semantics is what I've tried to capture in my latest book, *Black Talk*. I'm looking at African American English not just as, "What do the words mean," but "What is the cultural situation and the historical background of these words?"

Some terms have their origins in African languages. Think of a word like "bug" from the Wolof word "bugo," which means literally "to annoy." In current Hip Hop talk we have the phrase "buggin out," which means "to act crazy," often in an annoying manner. Think on the term "jazz" from the Mandingo, meaning "to act out of the ordinary," "to act uninhibited." Or think on the good old term "bad," which everybody now knows means "good." But in Mandingo you have a phrase, which means something is "good badly," or "so good that it's bad." This whole idea of taking a term and turning it into its opposite is a feature of many African languages.

There are some words and phrases that come out of the Traditional Black Church, which is a significant social force in the African American Experience. I'm thinking of terms like the "Amen Corner," which James Baldwin used for the title of his play, and which in fact has moved totally out of the church and is used in non-church contexts. I'm also thinking of a term not so complimentary, like "jack leg." A "jack leg" was traditionally an unprofessional or dishonest preacher. By extension the term came to refer to anybody who is trying to be something they aren't. So you can have a jack leg plumber, a jack leg carpenter, jack leg mechanic, whatever; anybody who is claiming to be a professional in a certain area in which they have low-level skills.

Some of the words in Black Semantics have to do with physical characteristics that normally wouldn't make any difference except in a racialist society. In this category, I think of the term "Ann" or "Miss Ann," a negative term for a White woman actually going all the way back to the 19th Century and probably even the 18th. Then there is the term, "color struck," referring to an African American person who thinks that light skin is the very best. Or the term "kitchen," which is not where you cook. In Black Talk, the "kitchen" is the hair at the nape of the neck, which is the most African, the kinkiest part of the hair.

A term that's moved into the public culture, the "N word," (nigga/nigger) has at least six different meanings, only one of them negative. It can mean, for example a Black person who is fearless or rebellious. In this sense NBA player, Charles Barkley, when he was with the 76ers, referred to himself as a "90s nigger." Filmmaker Spike Lee also refers to himself as a "90s nigger"—somebody who goes against the grain. Actually that meaning of "nigger" goes all the way back to the 18th century and the tradition of the "bad nigger," the one who didn't take no shit from nobody, Black or White. The term could also be used to refer generically to any person of African descent. For example, in talking about a party, a Black woman said, "It was wall to wall niggaz there," which just means lots of Black people were at the party. There are at least six different meanings of this controversial word, all of which require you to be steeped in the cultural moment in order to use it correctly.

One of my favorite expressions coming out of the racialist context is the phrase "40 acres and a mule." Spike Lee named his film company "Forty Acres and a Mule," and that phrase has been around in the African American community for generations. If you look up that phrase in a dictionary of Americanisms, it will simply say it is a slogan to inflame the slaves. But "40 acres and a mule" has a whole long history. In *Black Talk*, I give it almost two pages, because it has to do with the promise of land for reparations that came out in an 1866 bill which was passed by both houses of Congress but was vetoed by Andrew Johnson. The concept of "40 acres and a mule" has been around in the African American speech community for generations as "a failed promise," much more significant than a "slogan to inflame the slaves."

Slavery and racism notwithstanding, a lot of Black Talk in the semantic realm has nothing to do with race, but with everyday common experiences that happen to Black people as well as to White people. My favorite expression in this category is "nose open." You can also say, "She got his nose," or, "He got her nose," or, "John got a nose job"—all of which refer to a person being vulnerably in love—so much in love that he or she can be manipulated or exploited. In this context I can't resist telling again what is probably my favorite story. A few years ago when Marion Barry, the Mayor of Washington DC, was having his drug trouble and was being followed by the FBI and wiretapped and videotaped, there was a scene where he was in a hotel room with his ex-girlfriend, Rasheeda Moore. He was admiring this watch she had on, a Rolex, as I recall, and she said that her new boyfriend had given it to her. And he says, "Oh, I guess you got his nose open, huh?" The FBI watching the videotape thought they were talking about snorting cocaine.

Some words in Black Semantics are older terms, which get recycled in a different form. I'm thinking, for example, of the term "homey," which is a variation of the old term "homes"— "down home," "home slice," "home folks"—all of which were used generations ago to refer fondly to Black people. If you hear older Black people talk, you will still hear these same terms. Today your best friend is called "ace cool." It used to be, "ace boon coon," so the new term is just a variation on that older term. Today they talk about "chilling;" that's just a variation on the older form, "cool." Terms like "salty," which means to get angry, or "copacetic," which means something is okay, are terms that are used today that all appeared in the late Cab Calloway's 1938 *Hepster's Dictionary*, which is believed to be the first Black Talk dictionary. At some point in the 1930s, Zora Neale Hurston also published the beginnings of a dictionary which she called the *Dictionary of Harlem Jive*. She also lists terms like "salty," "copacetic," and a favorite of mine, the term "ig," which means to insult somebody by deliberately ignoring them.

One important outcome of the work on African American English that was done in the 60s and 70s is that it clearly demonstrated that this is a language which, because of crossover, has enriched the language of the U.S. mainstream. Words like "hip," "homey," "chill," "bad," "yam," are now part of the common language of all Americans and no longer marginalized as slang. Whites all over the country know about and use the "high five," which is a tradition straight out of Africa. In many West African languages there is a phrase used when you make a statement and you want the person you're talking to to agree with you, you tack a phrase onto your statement that means "put your hand in my hand."

An interesting thing about crossover, though, is that sometimes when words cross over, the meaning changes. A really excellent example of this is the term "rap." In its original Black meaning, rap referred to romantic talk from a man to a woman. It had sexual overtones and was the language of love. When the word "rap" crossed over into the White mainstream, it came to mean any kind of strong talk. The Black speech community added the mainstream meaning to the original Black meaning, reflecting a kind of reverse crossover.

Where am I going with these two decades of work on African American English? Where I would like to go for the 21st century is to a national language policy for this country, one that would emphasize the importance of multilingualism for everybody. There was a time in the 60s and 70s, particularly in the 70s, when the notion was: "If you speak African American English you need also to be able to speak the Language of Wider Communication (or so-called 'Standard English')." One linguist called this the linguistics of white supremacy, arguing that Black people have to learn two languages, but White people only have to learn one.

We've moved beyond bi-dialectalism being for Blacks and People of Color only and have arrived at a point where the whole country needs to be able to speak more than just the standard language. In fact, the National Language Policy of the Conference of College Composition and Communication (CCCC, aka 4 C's) is a policy that would be started in school for kids in elementary school, and it would make them at least tri-lingual by the time they graduate from high school. There are a number of groups now promoting "English Plus," that is, English plus one (or more) languages, for everybody, not just Blacks or People of Color—everybody should be multilingual. Three languages are stipulated in the 4 C's National Language Policy. 4 C's is a very large group of scholar-teachers who teach English and composition and communication in colleges. They're saying everybody needs to be at least tri-lingual. One language would be the Language of Wider Communication, so-called "Standard English." However, CCCC and other language teacher-scholars and their professional organizations are trying to get away from saying "standard," because if there's standard, that means there's non-standard. We like the term linguist Joshua Fishman gave us, "language of wider communication," which is to say, the language that helps people communicate in a broad spectrum outside their own particular speech community. I have this program in Detroit at the Malcolm X Academy, where I deal with seventh and eighth grade young males, you know, they're all strutting, and they're all real nationalistic, and I always have to tell them that I'm saying "wider" communication, not "whiter" communication. That is, *wider communication*, so we can talk outside the 'hood.

The second language that every person needs to become more versatile and more proficient in is whatever their native language or dialect is. For African American English speakers, that would be African American English, giving them the linguistic power to maybe one day produce a narrative like Alice Walker's *Color Purple*, showing their skill in manipulating African American English in creative ways, or at the very least they could become so verbally adept that they wouldn't do what my son and his friends did, when they ran out of metaphors Playing the Dozens and had to resort to truth. In Michigan, there are 90,000 people who speak Polish. Some people in that community are worried that the Polish language is not being passed on to other generations. So the CCCC National Language Policy would be a chance for people in Polish communities to recover their language. The second language, the home language, would, of course, differ according to different communities.

A third language that a person needs is something that for them would be a totally foreign language. At the Malcolm X Academy, the students are studying Swahili and Spanish in addition to the Language of Wider Communication and African American English.

That's where I would like to go with this research and data, this legitimating of African American English. I'd like to make the CCCC National Language Policy the standard in this country.

I want to close out with an example of signifyin, probably the most crucial verbal tradition. I saved the best for last. Signifyin in Black Talk is a verbal insult too, but unlike The Dozens. what you do when you signify is you level a social critique. You use language to comment in a critical way on something somebody said or did that warrants criticism. It requires, as with all other verbal traditions, stunning, clever language. It works because it's indirect and because it has humor. It's a way of using a single statement to communicate on two different levels at the same time.

Signifyin has been recognized in current literary critical theory as a major trope in African American literature. It's what Gates and others talk about when they analyze the "speakerly text." There's a lot of signifyin in African American literature, particularly that by women. So I'm going to let a woman have the last word with a rich, classic example of signifyin, from Zora Neale Hurston's *Their Eyes Were Watching God*. Now Zora Neale, as we know, was both a writer and a linguistic anthropologist. She interviewed real people and studied the language of real people and weaved this into her literary work.

In Hurston's masterpiece novel, *Their Eyes Were Watching God*, there's a scene that marks the beginning of Janie' s empowerment. She's married to Jody, who owns a store in this little small town in the South. It's a gathering place for Black people, they come to Jody's store to sit around and talk stuff—to lie and signify, telling stories and tall tales.

Jody is fussing at Janie because she hasn't cut a plug of tobacco right. He says, "A woman that stay around 'till she get old as Methuselah and still can't cut a little thing like a plug of tobacco...Woman don't stand there rolling your pop eyes at me with your rump hanging nearly to your knees."

Janie says, "Stop mixing up my doings with my looks, Jody. When you get through telling me how to cut a plug of tobacco then you can tell me whether my behind is on straight or not." Jody, of course, is shocked because she's never talked like this. He says, "You must be out your head, talking language like that." And she says "You the one started talking under other people's clothes, not me." Jody says, "Well, what's the matter with you anyhow? You ain't no young girl to be getting all insulted about your looks. You ain't no young courting gal. You an old woman, nearly 40." Janie's reply to Jody's insult is classic, superbad signifyin: "Yea, I'm nearly 40 but you is already 50 and you talk about me looking old, when you pull down yo britches, you look like the change of life."

Questions for Discussion and Journaling

1. In the "What Is Argument?" chapter, you read about the rhetorical triangle and how the rhetor, subject, and audience work together to form an argument. As you read, identify each in the below chart and list all the things you already know or learned about them.

Rhetor	Subject	Audience

Keeping the chart you filled out in mind, return to p. 12 of your textbook, where you read about Discourse Communities. How does the discourse community she wrote this keynote for differ from the audience reading this textbook (you and your classmates)? What can you learn about the discourse community she is engaging with from the textual clues you put in the chart above? How might the fact that you don't belong to her intended audience impact your reading of the piece?

2. What is her thesis or overall argument? Find a sentence or two where she summarizes her argument. Where is this thesis located in the piece? The beginning? The end? Why do you think she decided to present her argument when she did? How did this placement help her make her argument? Does this challenge any of the writing rules you were taught about thesis statements?

3. In other research, Smitherman discusses African American rhetorical traditions such as call and response, signifying, narrative sequencing, and rhythmic communication. You learned about these in "African American Rhetorical Traditions." Identify examples of two of these rhetorical strategies in her piece. Write a 2-page response evaluating how she used these strategies and explaining how her use of African American rhetorical traditions contributed to her argument.

4. As previously noted, Smitherman authored a report that concludes that writing instructors should "capitalize on the strengths of African American cultural discourse; encourage students toward the field dependency style, which enables them to produce more powerful, meaningful, and more highly rated essays; and deemphasize concerns about Black English Vernacular grammar." This research challenged previous research that compared Black students to European American students and misunderstood the fruitful connections between Black

discourse and Black student writing. Indeed, the report concludes that the more a student writer used rhetorical moves typically associated with the African American oral tradition, the higher their writing was scored. Keeping this in mind, write a 2-page informal essay that explains how you think teachers, both in high school and college, can do what Smitherman's report suggests. In your own experiences as a student, did you see her recommendations implemented? If so, then how? If not, then why? Did your teachers do the opposite of what she suggests? What activities did you do or feedback did you get that either supported or contradicted her recommendations for writing teachers?

MAKING NEGROTOWN

Marcus Anthony Hunter and Zandria F. Robinson

"Making Negrotown" is the seventh chapter of sociologists Marcus Anthony Hunter and Zandria F. Robinson's *Chocolate Cities: The Black Map of American Life*, published in 2018 by the University of California Press. In the book's first chapter, "Everywhere Below Canada," the authors explain, "*Chocolate Cities* is built on a simple premise: *our current maps of Black life are wrong*. Instead of the neat if jarring linear progress of movement from the rural South to the urban North, we suggest that the history of Black life in modernity is a boomerang rather than a straight line of progress" (3). The authors base this remapping of Black life in the United States on "two social facts about Black American life": the first being that "Black American social life is best understood as occurring wholly in 'The South' and the second being that Black migrants brought and bring 'The South'—Black regional customs, worldviews, and cultures—with them to their new homes in destinations across urban America" (4). Thus, their book considers life in majority Black cities and villages throughout the United States in order to remap Black life in America into the regions of the "Out South," the "West South," the "Mid South," the "Up South," the "Down South," and the "Deep South." On this Chocolate Map, Memphis is located in the "Deep South," and the "Mid South" begins at the Tennessee–Kentucky Border and includes Oklahoma. In this chapter, we learn about Arthur Lee Robinson's migration to Memphis where he found an existing Black Village that he later contributed to through his labor activism. The authors then turn to a discussion of the final season of *Key and Peele* in order to illustrate that while *Key and Peele*'s Negrotown is an impossibility—the result of a delusion resulting from police brutality—Black communities, such as those found in Memphis, have long created spaces, or what the authors refer to as strong villages, where people like Robinson can be both Black and free.

> The African past lies camouflaged in the collective African American memory, trans-
> formed by the middle passage, sharecropping, industrialization, [and] urbaniza-
> tion.

E. Frances White, "Africa on My Mind," 1990

Despite the relatively short geographic distances between the rural and urban South, internal migration within the South was an equally transformative feat in the making of chocolate maps. Many rural migrants that eventually ended up Out South and Up South were first
urbanized Deep South and Down South, where they stopped off to visit, shop, and sometimes stay for a bit, like when the writer Richard Wright went to Memphis from Natchez,
Mississippi, before heading to other places on the chocolate map in the United States and
beyond. Some people got off the train or the bus where they could or where they had to.
Others intended to stay and see family for a bit and then made the urban South their home.
Still others who left the Deep South and Mid South returned later from their Up South and
Out South lives to tend to the places from whence they came.

As cultural anthropologist Carol Stack reminds us, links between Great Migration destinations and the traditional South endured long after folks left. It was and is common for Black
families to send wayward children to the South to get their behavior and minds right or to
protect them from dangers, perceived and imminent, in their own communities. Funerals,
weddings, and family reunions are the strong cultural incentives pulling Black people back
to the South or across another South. Two popular sources play this social fact out with
great flair.

In his award-winning novel, *Long Division*, scholar Kiese Laymon writes of a young Black
boy's movement between time, dimension, and place, traveling from the civil rights era
to the era of Reaganomics to post-Katrina Mississippi from Chicago, Jackson, and the
Mississippi Delta. One protagonist is sent to the Delta from Jackson, Mississippi, because
of a viral video of an outburst he made on a televised spelling bee. There, in the Delta, a
whipping awaits. But so do profound time-travelling experiences that illustrate where and
how his life is connected to those before and after him. These experiences also make plain
the importance of place making and time making, as the protagonists live a more beautiful
world in a book.

Alongside this novel, we can also look to the popular comedic film *Welcome Home, Roscoe
Jenkins* for evidence of recurrent themes of returning home to the South and sometimes
making a home there in the context of difficulty or the aftermath of a life-changing event.
Though *Long Division* is a speculative novel with time travel as one of its primary devices,
Welcome Home, Roscoe Jenkins features the kind of comedic fantasy that abounds when a
citified Black prodigal son returns to his country family. Starring Black comedian Martin
Lawrence as the titular protagonist, the film centers on the less-than-triumphant return
of Roscoe Jenkins to rural Georgia for his parents' fiftieth wedding anniversary celebration. Jenkins, a middle-aged single dad and host of a syndicated talk show, quickly finds
his Hollywood trappings—a reality TV star girlfriend, a focus on the individual instead of
the collective, veganism—in conflict with the simple life of his small-town Georgia kinfolk.
He learns, sometimes painfully and hilariously, the kinds of lessons about self, family, and
home that are often only possible with a return home.

The story of the Great Migration is often the story of the movement of small-town and farm people from Down South to big cities Up South and Out South, and later reversing course and returning to their Down South origins. We know how they transformed the urban landscape, and we know how they brought Down South customs, mores, and traditions all over the country to make chocolate maps. But what about how they made the places in between? The revival of *The Negro Travelers' Green Book*, a crowd-sourced account of safe places to eat, sleep, and picnic during Jim Crow, evidences that we are now learning more about the process and strategy it took to make a life, to make a place to be free, in an anti-Black country. It is this shared cultural knowledge, now hidden in the spatial organization of Black places, that made a Black world in spaces everywhere below Canada.

This chapter explores these connections between the villages wherein Black people find themselves. Through migration, branches of Black family trees grew across the United States but also provided multiple roots for return. Family events, like reunions, weddings, funerals, or an elder's birthday, can draw even the farthest family member back. While differences abound, it is clear that the village is a central feature of the chocolate city, no matter where Black folks are located on chocolate maps. As we will see, Black villages are not simply a hodgepodge arrangement of locales but instead a purposely created set of places, cultures, and resistive practices that help forge bonds that are able to be sustained across space and time.

Using the adventures of Arthur Lee Robinson and chocolate city imaginings of comedy duo Keegan Michael Key and Jordan Peele's "Negrotown" as bookends, this chapter illustrates how migration, culture, and Black density matter. Villages are not simply small southern towns with Black people. Rather, they are a pervasive practice of Black people getting information. Simply put, there is an art to making Negrotown.

ARTHUR LEE AND THE TALLAHATCHIE

As he rounded the winding highway in the overfull U-Haul, the lights of the city came into view. His daughter, ahead of him in her equally packed car, called him up, trying to hold in her excitement about the sparkling urban sight. "Daddy!" she said. "Look at them lights! You seen anything like that before?" She was teasing, keeping the city mouse–country mouse joke going, which they had always shared. Recognizing the banter, he replied calmly but with a twinkle of excitement peeping through his voice too, "I know something 'bout that." They said their good-byes and hung up, proceeding all the way up Lake Shore to Sheridan to her new apartment in Chicago.

By all accounts Arthur Lee Robinson was a headstrong child, a dangerous attribute anywhere in 1950s America for a Black child, but especially behind the curtain that socially walled off the Mississippi Delta from the rest of the nation. His mother, Celia Mae Robinson, had been widowed in her youth and was raising her children with assistance from her mother, Rosie Robinson, and community support. Celia Mae did whatever was necessary to provide for Arthur Lee and his siblings, striving to protect them from physical, social, and economic death.

Arthur Lee knew Chicago and all spots in between there and the Mississippi Delta. He had a sister in the south suburbs, cousins in Kankakee, a brother in Saint Louis, siblings in Memphis and Clarksdale, and nieces in Starkville, Mississippi. People on both sides of his family were everywhere east of the Mississippi, including all the way Up South in Albany, New York.

In 2016 he had planned a trip to the semiannual Rose family reunion, being held Memorial Day weekend that year in the Catskills, but he died the week before he was to fly out. He was sixty-four, and it would have been his first time in New York and all the way Up South. But Robinson's life and times up and down Highway 61, known as Blues Highway, teach us a great deal about one of the most common movements across chocolate maps: from the Deep South village to the southern city.

Big Mama, as Rosie Robinson was called, knew Arthur Lee was a different kind of child and got after him with her switch as often as possible, striving to compel conformity. He would curse grown folks when he felt slighted and frequently manipulated the White sharecropper boy on the next farm out of his bike, returning it only when he tired of it. When Arthur Lee heard Rosie Robinson's voice echoing and calling for him from her house to his, he sometimes ignored it, knowing full well what the consequences would be. The adults in the community did not know what else to do with this child.

If Arthur Lee had hell in him, perhaps baptism would cure it. All the children of Persimmon Grove Baptist Church in Glendora, Mississippi, in Tallahatchie County were baptized in the Tallahatchie River, plunged into it to be absolved of their sins and to receive eternal life. Neither Glendora or any of the other towns in the Mississippi Delta were a Black utopic Eatonville. So baptism was an important spiritual protection and rite of passage for when, at ages eight or nine or ten, Black children were inevitably and jarringly stripped of their childhoods. The preacher and the Tallahatchie provided the protection of eternal salvation and the blood of Jesus. But not even the blood of the Savior worked on Arthur Lee, nor could it spare him Big Mama Rosie Robinson's whippings.

The Tallahatchie is a rocky river that is not navigable in places for dozens of miles. During Arthur Lee's childhood, it had flowed south with a grave contradiction: it gave eternal life when the preacher plunged one into it but was a violent resting place, temporary and final, when murderous Whites used it to abet and conceal Black death. Arthur Lee was approaching his fourth birthday when the beaten, shot, and burdened body of fourteen-year-old Emmett Till was plunged into the river in the next county south of Tallahatchie, the county of Leflore, by J. W. Milam and Roy Bryant. The Tallahatchie had refused to harbor Till's body for long, and the murder, trial, and subsequent confession of the murderers rocked and rippled across the chocolate map. One of the murderers, Milam, lived in Glendora.

The specter, threat, and reality of death that surrounded Arthur Lee in Glendora in the 1950s and 1960s had sent many families from Mississippi Up South and Out South but also to the relative safety of the urban places Down South and Mid South. Arthur Lee's grandmother, Rosie Robinson, had come west to Glendora to make a life. And so her daughter Celia Mae stayed in Glendora until her children were mostly raised and then moved to the big county,

Coahoma. Celia Mae had made unspeakable and unknowable sacrifices to shield her children from sharecropping, ensure they finished school, and help some of them go to college. They were poor, but, ensconced in the village she and scores of other Black people made, they had a small bit of freedom. For her dedication to them, Celia Mae's children repaid her—to the extent that money can compensate for trauma—by providing for her until her death in 1996.

Rosie Mae Robinson and her daughter Celia Mae Robinson were among the scores of people who stayed in the rural South, making chocolate maps in the village places between the prominent markers on the map. These places are the roots of chocolate maps, places to return and remember and forget, where Black life was lived and forged in the face of palpable and seemingly imminent Black death. Three of Celia Mae's children settled along a familiar route in the middle of the chocolate map: Willie Mae in Chicago, Jesse in Saint Louis, and Arthur Lee in Memphis. Arthur Lee was one of these mapmakers who moved along a path from rural to small town to city in the Deep South.

MR. ROBINSON GOES TO MEMPHIS

Arthur Lee managed to survive Big Mama and White supremacy, finishing West Tallahatchie High School in 1970 and moving to Coahoma County to attend junior college. Clarksdale is one of the Delta's biggest towns and a hub of music, commerce, and culture through which scores of blues musicians traveled on their way to carry the Delta's sound across chocolate maps. They also brought with them what the late geographer Clyde Woods called a "blues epistemology." Woods wrote that the blues emerged

> in a new era of censorship, suppression, and persecution [and] conveyed the sorrow of the individual and collective tragedy that had befallen African Americans. It also operated to instill pride in a people facing daily denigration, as well as channeling folk wisdom, descriptions of life and labor, travelogues, hoodoo, and critiques of individuals and institutions. It is often forgotten that those songs, music, stories, jokes, dances, and other visual and physical practices that raise the spirit of the audience to unimaginable heights also define the blues. The men and women who performed the blues were sociologists, reporters, counselors, advocates, preservers of language and customs, and summoners of life, love, laughter, and much, much more.

It is this epistemology, a blues-informed worldview and interpretative template, that people like Arthur Lee took with them as they moved throughout and beyond the Deep South.

Memphis was not only the nearest big city when Arthur Lee was growing up, but was also where his father, Jack Rose, lived. His brother Jesse had already headed for Saint Louis, where the demand for skilled labor was plentiful. When Arthur Lee finished Coahoma Junior College in 1972 with an engineering degree, he planned to follow Jesse to Saint Louis. There the two children of Celia Mae Robinson and Jack Rose were going to make a life up the Mississippi River. Arthur Lee just wanted to stop in Memphis for a few days and spend time with his Pops and meet his Memphis siblings before heading on to meet Jesse in Saint Louis.

But Arthur Lee never moved to Saint Louis. When he arrived at his father's house in Memphis, around the corner from Stax Records, he was overwhelmed by the warm reception from his Memphis family, including his father's wife, Lula Mae. The Roses convinced him to stay in the city, where the new turn in the soul sound coming from Stax echoed the kind of defiance that characterized his childhood. After the assassination of King, the music from around the corner on 926 East McLemore Avenue had grown ever more resistant.

Black Memphis was still shaken and in mourning, but its will to defy and resist ossified White power made it a perfect fit for Arthur Lee. He channeled the restlessness that made people think he had hell in him in Glendora into the rumbling labor movement in Memphis, which had won significant victories in the aftermath of the sanitation workers' strike. He joined Local 149 of the Bakery, Confectionery, Tobacco Workers, and Grain Millers International Union and labored and advocated for labor for the rest of his life. The 1970s Memphis milieu Arthur Lee entered into had been in the making since Ida B. Wells was on the city's burgeoning lyceum circuit.

Over the nineteenth and twentieth centuries, Black Memphians had survived two yellow fever epidemics, despite being segregated in the north and south sections of the city without sanitation protections. Afterward, in the 1890s, they built their own neighborhood east of South Memphis, on the site of an old plantation. This new neighborhood was the first to be built by and for Black people and was largely populated initially by people from northern Mississippi.

Yellow fever would not be the only epidemic to strike the growing Memphis village. Not long after the fevers passed, a new unknown illness emerged that contributed to an especially high infant-mortality rate for Black babies in the city. Despite Black citizens' protests that something was wrong, White Memphians assumed this high mortality rate could be attributed to Black people's cleanliness or biological inferiority. Yet Black people's folk knowledge would not be so easily dismissed.

In his work on the city, historian Keith Wailoo shows how even before the disease was named and known, Black people were tracking and documenting it in blues music and culture. Although it had been scientifically discovered in the United States in the early twentieth century, little was known about its epidemiology. It was Black folk knowledge and resistance, rooted in the blues, that brought attention to the disease as Black people advocated for better health care and conditions. By the 1950s the disease that had for so long ravaged Black communities across the chocolate map had gained national attention. Within twenty years cases of sickle cell anemia had dramatically decreased.

The city of Memphis had long been a regional medical leader, and sickle cell solidified Memphis's place as a center of Black medical innovation. It was the village in the predominantly Black city, though, that made the city's status possible. On the one hand, the city built its fortunes on the backs of Black pain and disease. On the other, Black people built their lives by making moral and ethical claims that sprung from a blues resistance that had been forged during their movement from rural communities to small towns to the city.

38

Black people in Memphis, then, had been demanding justice and a better life for Black people for generations. They had cared for the sick during the epidemics and demanded to be treated as equal citizens when Whites returned to the city when the proverbial coast was clear. The epidemic had brought Ida B. Wells to Memphis, and she had then spearheaded and galvanized a movement against lynching. Meanwhile, Black people gathered and shared folk knowledge about an illness that was taking their children and kept demanding that someone investigate the health of their communities and treat them with dignity.

When they won recognition, attention, and funding for sickle cell anemia treatment, they pointed to the dangerous work conditions of laborers throughout the city, focusing on its sanitation workers in particular. They survived after the massive spiritual and psychological blow that was King's murder and pressed on with work in their communities. It was into this moment in time on the chocolate map, four years after King's assassination, that Arthur Lee came to Memphis.

The woman who would make Arthur Lee into Mr. Robinson had been born in Grand Junction, Tennessee, twenty days before him. Her family moved to Orange Mound, which was still a thriving Black community in the 1950s, though the ominous hum of urban renewal could be heard from surrounding neighborhoods. She was a teenager when the city began to move with "all deliberate speed" to desegregate schools. She was a sixteen-year-old in Orange Mound when King was killed, and the assassination reflected her mother's cautions about activism. If Arthur Lee was a rambunctious handful as a child, Janice was the opposite. She stayed to herself and played by herself, never troubling anyone.

But Orange Mound, like so many other communities, underwent some significant changes in tandem with the growing movement for labor rights and civil rights. Deindustrialization shuttered some nearby factories that were sources of income in the community. People left as neighborhoods east began to desegregate. In the midst of this neighborhood upheaval, Janice began college in 1970 on the edge of Orange Mound at Memphis State University. Orange Mound had nurtured a quiet upheaval within her too. Her childhood introversion and silent rejection of her mother's admonishment against activism had converged to create a grown city sophisticate with modern ideas about race, womanhood, and partnership and sharp critiques of racism and sexism in the South.

Armed with a journalism baccalaureate and an ingrained awareness, Janice opted to escape the confines of racist and sexist work environments to work as a parent community organizer. She used her post as a substitute teacher to observe conditions and practices in a range of Black schools in the city's public school system, demanding resources for students and conjuring resources from her own funds when the system failed, which happened frequently.

Arthur from Glendora, Mississippi, and Janice from Orange Mound in Memphis, Tennessee, met in 1974, married in 1977, and moved to Whitehaven, known widely as Blackhaven by its now predominantly Black residents. Arthur worked for labor, rallying union members for negotiations and critiquing the changing nature of work brought on by fast deindustrialization. Janice worked for parents in communities, curating and collating information and pressuring school officials, board members, and nonprofit organizations to give Black students what they were entitled to as citizens and taxpayers.

In their Whitehaven home Arthur and Janice used their combined village experiences, which were more similar than they liked to admit, to rear two daughters at the beginning of the millennial generation. Together they gave them, these second-generation city daughters, a multidimensional village sensibility born of the place-making practices of Black people. As they moved, they made a world, bringing with them their previous worlds as the rich soil with which to lay the foundation anew.

In Memphis Arthur Lee became Mr. Robinson, but the blues epistemology of Glendora remained. Memphis was where many country boys grew into misters, as they navigated a changing post–civil rights chocolate city that was different but also sometimes glaringly similar to the rural communities and small towns in which they came of age. Black migrants had been flowing into Memphis since before Emancipation, following the Mississippi to what some people called the Delta's capital. The city's character and spatial arrangements had been shaped by these people's experiences, and Mr. Robinson was among the many who made and expanded the Memphis village.

The notion of the village is an inherently nostalgic concept, and not just because the world has changed significantly. "Village" carries with it an idea of naive simplicity, sameness, and ease that is difficult to imagine in a hypermedia world where anti-Blackness is constant. The increasing visibility of Black death has almost erased this notion of village, even as it persists as an intergenerational set of lived experiences and a spatial fact.

In the Obama era Black artists and intellectuals grappled publicly with two competing representations of the village—that it (1) no longer exists at all or that it (2) could exist if Black people only would return to earlier, supposedly simpler eras of community. They were interested in how protracted anti-Blackness in the United States and beyond fostered Black people's longings for a place insulated from White supremacy. These artists imagined a future, like Arthur and Janice had done, that could be made different through resistance. They also used these possible futures to highlight the failings of the present.

EASE ON DOWN TO NEGROTOWN

Where does the village end and the city begin? We see the village in multiple ways. It is at once a precursor to the places on chocolate maps; a description of existing places, small towns, neighborhoods in big cities, and Black back sides of places on the chocolate maps; and a disposition toward community life that reflects Black people's collective practices of resistance in and through place. Mr. Robinson may have left the village of Glendora and gone to college in the village of Clarksdale, but he brought those villages with him, like so many others did, when he settled in Memphis.

Comedians Keegan Michael Key and Jordan Peele reflect on this movement of Black people, this quest to make place and futures, in the fifth and final season of their acclaimed Comedy Central sketch comedy show, *Key and Peele*. Between sketches Key and Peele are on a long journey through a barren territory. They are headed somewhere on the discursive Black map they have traveled throughout the show's tenure, deftly exploring a multidimensional Black experience in an unequal America. Previous seasons had featured the duo on stage in front of a live audience between sketches; in the final season the men are together in an old beater, driving through the desert headed somewhere for some reason the audience does not know. In the finale we learn their journey throughout the season is a metaphor for the unending search for where Black people can be free.

The sketch begins with an uncomfortable but all-too-familiar scenario. One protagonist, played by Key, is walking alone at night and accosted by a police officer who asks for his identification, pulls a gun on him, handcuffs him, and not-so-accidentally bangs his head on the top of the police car as he is forcing him into the vehicle. Wally, an unhoused man played by Peele who has previously asked Key's character for change, steps in to take over for the officer, who inexplicably removes the handcuffs. Together the two travel through a wardrobe-like portal into a Black Narnia: Negrotown.

Negrotown is sunny and bright and colorful, "a place to be if your skin is brown," one even more magical than Atlanta. It is an actual "utopia for Black people." Wally, now donning a pink three-piece suit, begins what turns out to be a spectacular musical dance number in several ways. An array of Negrotown constituents, clad psychedelically in garb of the past and present, help Wally introduce Key's character to Negrotown. In Negrotown loan applications are always approved, Black people can walk the streets without police harassment; cabs always stop; there is no shortage of Black men for Black women; no cultural appropriation, no racial health disparities, no "trigger-happy cops or scared cashiers" exist; no one is followed while shopping; and no one is murdered for wearing a hoodie. The choreographed number ends with smiles and all fists raised in a Black power salute.

The sketch's perhaps expected ending is that Negrotown is a delusion. There is no village where one can be safe from these everyday experiences of racism in the world. Key's character awakens from a period of unconsciousness caused by the officer's brutality, exclaiming in a state of frightened confusion, "I thought I was going to Negrotown!" The police office responds flippantly, "Oh, you are," as he puts him into the car and drives away. It is a heartbreaking but anticipated ending that answers Solange Knowles's questions with devastating brevity. "Where can we be Black and free?" Key and Peele answer: only in our imaginations.

"Negrotown" reflects a fantastical longing for a place where Black people can be Black and free, gesturing toward what a twenty-first-century Eatonville, a "pure Negro town," might be like. Searching for greener pastures, Black people have always envisioned, and when possible attempted to create, a less complicated freedom, whether in an imagined and generic African past, a Jim Crow southern past in separate cities and on Black back sides, or in the New South Black mecca of Atlanta.

From Emancipation and Reconstruction, to the unrest of the civil rights movement, to the ramifications of the declining urban core, Black people in the United States have moved, shifted, responded, resisted, and created town and neighborhood spaces where they could be both Black and free. As the daily assaults on Black lives continue to play on loop in traditional and social media, Black people's desire for a place to be has become increasingly evident in the ways they imagine alternative Black villages in science fiction, satire, and music. This is not, as political scientist Adolph Reed Jr. has called it, "romancing Jim Crow," or wallowing in nostalgia for a mythical and segregated all-Black past. This is a political imagining and reimagining of the village as a site of past, present, and future resistance. Strong villages became the bricks for chocolate cities, expanding chocolate maps and cementing together the fortunes of Black places with a new kind of blues epistemology: *soul power*.

Questions for Discussion and Journaling

1. Hunter and Robinson explain, "Over the nineteenth and twentieth centuries, Black Memphians had survived two yellow fever epidemics, despite being segregated in the north and south sections of the city without sanitation protections. Afterward, in the 1890s, they built their own neighborhood east of South Memphis, on the site of an old plantation. This new neighborhood was the first to be built by and for Black people and was largely populated initially by people from northern Mississippi" (412). The neighborhood they are referring to here is Orange Mound, and they later explain it was "still a thriving Black community in the 1950s" (413). Write a one-page reflection considering the following questions. What did you know about Orange Mound before reading this chapter? Were you aware of its historical significance? Did you know where it was located? Where and when did you learn about Orange Mound? Now do some research on Orange Mound and see what else you can learn. Does that research and what you learned from this chapter support or conflict with your previous knowledge of Orange Mound? If you had no prior knowledge of Orange Mound, then ask some of your friends who are from Memphis what they know about Orange Mound and then compare that to what you learn when researching the historical significance of the neighborhood.

2. Why do Hunter and Robinson use *Key and Peele* to conclude the chapter? How does their explanation of the season and its conclusion connect back to Robinson's migration to and life in Memphis? How was their use of such compelling and entertaining yet also convincing and appropriate in an academic monograph (book)?

3. Hunter and Robinson use the term Village to describe Black communities, even when they are discussing urban communities that don't reflect traditional understandings of the village. They explain, "The notion of the village is an inherently nostalgic concept, and not just because the world has changed significantly. 'Village' carries with it an idea of naive simplicity, sameness, and ease that is difficult to imagine in a hypermedia world where anti-Blackness is constant" (414). A village is generally defined as "a group of houses and associated buildings, larger than a hamlet and smaller than a town, situated in a rural area." How does the meaning of Village they present in the chapter (which includes more than the quotation above) differ from this definition? Why is redefining what a Village means important to this chapter and their Chocolate Map project more generally? If you were writing a rhetorical analysis of this chapter, how would you analyze and explain this rhetorical redefinition?

THE DYNAMICS OF SECOND-WAVE FEMINIST ACTIVISM IN MEMPHIS, 1971–1982
Rethinking the Liberal/Radical Divide

39

Stephanie Gilmore

In "The Dynamics of Second-Wave Feminist Activism in Memphis, 1971–1982," Stephanie Gilmore focuses on the feminist group Memphis NOW to argue "that location directly affected the ways in which women organized and expressed themselves as feminists." Published in *NWSA Journal* (*The National Women's Studies Association's* Journal), her primary audience is made up of an interdisciplinary group of scholars concerned with women and gender studies. She uses personal interviews, old newspaper stories, and unpublished documents found in the UofM's Special Collections to argue that women's studies scholars need to reconsider the distinction between liberal and radical feminists. By illustrating how Memphis NOW embraced both liberal and radical feminist tactics in their fight for the Equal Rights Amendment and their actions to combat gendered violence, she further claims that scholars should stop assuming activist movements, and particularly feminism, can be generalized by time period because location matters.

This article presents a history of the Memphis chapter of the National Organization for Women (NOW) that challenges traditional analyses of second-wave feminist activism as either liberal or radical. Through examples of feminist activism on behalf of the Equal Rights Amendment, rape and wife-abuse awareness and prevention, and pornography, the author illustrates how one chapter of NOW, which is typically identified as a liberal organization, was simultaneously liberal and radical. In addition, the author calls for more attention to location in order to understand second-wave feminists' tactics, styles, and structures as well as to make more prominent the nuances and complexities of a movement often obscured by the liberal/radical divide.

"The Dynamics of Second-Wave Feminist Activism in Memphis, 1971–1982: Rethinking the Liberal/Radical Divide" by Stephanie Gilmore. *Feminist Formations* 15:1 (2003), 94–117. © 2003 Feminist Formations. Reprinted with permission of Johns Hopkins University Press.

In 1975, feminists in the "rape capital of the nation," as Memphis was known locally, demanded public and political attention to the too-often private issue of rape by marching around the thirteen-block perimeter of Overton Park in midtown Memphis. According to organizer Gail Adkins, "the march was routed through Overton Square because of a recent gang rape in an adjacent parking lot and because one of the bars features topless dancers," asserting the implicit (and radical feminist) connection between rape and the commodification of women ("NOW Members Protest Violence Against Women" 1975). Chanting "Stop Rape Now" and carrying placards bearing such slogans as "Rape Laws are Made for Rapists" and "Dismember Rapists," these feminists further heightened the city's awareness about rape and protested the notion that, according to participant Marion Keisker, "women are only as safe as civilized man allows."

Although the nuances of the story may be different, many feminists in the 1970s could recount similar tales of activism and public protest against rape and violence against women. Taking back the night remains today as a holdover of radical feminism in its heyday. But what is remarkable, and largely unaccounted for in scholarship on the women's movement, is that this group of activists came from the Memphis chapter of NOW (National Organization for Women), an organization that has come to symbolize liberal feminism in opposition to explicitly radical counterparts. In looking at Memphis NOW—a feminist organization that was simultaneously liberal and radical in a "sleepy little river town" (Buring 1997, 17)—I explore the dynamics of feminist activism at the local level and beyond the largest urban centers. Rather than argue against the dichotomy of liberal and radical feminism, I suggest that we turn our attention to the vast space between these concepts and explore how local-level concerns and opportunities shape feminist activism.

As they apply to the literature on feminism and the women's movement, *liberal* and *radical* mark distinctions primarily on the basis of organizational structure and style and refer secondarily to ideology (Freeman 1975; Evans 1979; Echols 1989; Ryan 1989; Whittier 1995; Ferree and Hess 2000). On the one hand, liberal feminist organizations are typically identified by their bureaucratic system of local, state, regional, and national chapters whereas radical groups tend to be recognized by their grassroots, nonhierarchical composition. Liberal organizations operate within the existing political system, often recognizing legislative change as most effective, and value the ability to sway political authorities to their point of view. On (what is considered to be) the other hand, radical groups often find formal political machinations too restrictive and not quick enough to respond to women's concerns. Thus, they pursue more public, "in-your-face" tactics to bring attention to their issues and undermine the system itself.

While all feminists arguably share women's liberation as their ideological objective, methods and goals have separated them historically. By politicizing the personal, radical feminists brought rape and violence against women into public discourse. In order to make the public aware of women's bodies and crimes committed against them, radical feminists often took to the streets, performing zap actions, protests, marches, and demonstrations. Liberal feminists' concern with equity in pay and employment led them to strive for legislative measures. Unlike the issue of rape, pay equity did not generate similar public outcry; likewise, most liberal feminists would not have pursued this or similar measures through radical means (Carden 1974; Freeman 1975; Evans 1979; Hartmann 1980; Ryan 1989; Ferree and Hess 2000). These and other issues, then, have been seen as reflections of ideologies distinguish liberal feminists and radical feminists from one another.

Scholars have acknowledged that liberal feminists and radical feminists borrowed structures, styles, tactics, and ideologies from one another, but they have continued to talk about the two branches as distinct, and their studies neglect the impact that location has played in feminist organizational structures, issues, and tactics.[1] Sociologist Nancy Whittier, for example, identified local NOW chapters with their national affiliation and their emphases on the national political arena, and radical feminists with grassroots organizations in cities and towns (1995). Historian Alice Echols maintained that "liberal feminists remained determinedly individualistic and in this respect their feminism diverged from radical feminism" (1989, 199). Even when scholars have recognized that liberal and radical feminists have merged in significant ways, they have tended to view the influence as unidirectional, with radical feminists influencing liberals but not the other way around.

Liberal and radical, then, were terms feminists used in the heyday of the movement, although NOW members at all levels did not typically identify themselves as liberal. But these concepts clearly have staying power. They have been reified through analyses of the women's movement at the national level (NOW, Women's Equity Action League, and Feminist Majority Foundation are typically defined as liberal organizations) or in large cities, mostly along the East Coast (the most recognized radical feminist groups sprang to life in New York, Boston, and Chicago). The distinctions between liberal and radical feminism are important, lived feminist activism happens somewhere *between* liberal and radical feminist ideology. If their strategies, tactics, goals, and methods are examined, most feminists could be defined as both liberal and radical. Focusing on such dynamic feminism addresses a set of nuanced analytical questions. How do feminists respond to particular local issues and opportunities? How is feminist activism shaped by regional difference?

Regional difference allows us to rethink conventional ways of understanding social movements of the twentieth century. One way to reconsider the past is through a concept historian Susan Freeman calls "the politics of location" (2000). Critical of lesbian and feminist movement scholarship for "elid[ing] geographical nuances, instead constructing an unlinear, national narrative about lesbian feminism," Freeman illustrates how geographical location affected the construction of a lesbian feminist community in Cincinnati, Ohio (140). Because regional affiliation influences identity formation and experience, scholars have examined how the axis of regional identity has shaped people's lives and experiences differently. In particular, scholars have begun to explore how Southern-ness has shaped social movements and institutions such as slavery, civil rights, and gay and lesbian activism and identity (Genovese 1974; Fox-Genovese 1988; White 1999; Carson 1981; Sitkoff 1981; Marable 1984; Weisbrot 1990; Sears 1997; Buring 1997; Duggan 2000). As scholars part what historian Daneel Buring calls the "magnolia curtain," they reveal not only a distinct region of the United States but also a vital facet of identity that facilitates and explains historical change and unsettles traditional historiography (1997).

Looking behind the magnolia curtain to examine the contemporary women's movement, it seems, might yield similar results. What social and political forces brought women together to create a feminist presence? With what success? What issues were most important to Southern women? Of course, there is no single answer to these questions because there is no monolithic South. However, my research on Memphis NOW indicates that location directly affected the ways in which women organized and expressed themselves as feminists.

Forming a feminist organization in Memphis occurred in the wake of the Civil Rights Movement, and sustaining it meant interacting with a less-than-sympathetic political and religious culture. One historian has observed that "Southerners continue to be profoundly conscious of their regional identity" (Grantham 1994, 330). Religious and political conservatism was central to this identity. Memphis's Protestant population, historically composed largely of Baptists, Episcopalians, Methodists, and Presbyterians, provided and perpetuated a worldview and political agenda centered on "'traditional values,' in particular family and gender ethics" as well as race relations (Hill 1983, 1). This religious value system has been buttressed by the equally influential tradition of Southern political conservatism embodied in a distinctive longing for the past and the myth of the Old South. Permeating these religious and political ideologies are chivalrous notions of womanhood and the need to protect Southern women (Hall 1979; Blee 1991; MacLean 1994). This racial, and racist, concept of Southern womanhood exacerbated political disunity among white women and black women. It also explains, at least in part, how some issues, such as rape and domestic violence, were able to garner political support while seemingly more benign concerns of equal rights were hotly contested in Memphis.

Responding to their environment, Memphis NOW members embraced both liberal and radical feminist tactics, structures, and issues. They grappled with such national issues as the Equal Rights Amendment (ERA) as well as community problems of domestic violence and rape. As a result of the myriad concerns addressed, Memphis NOW attracted women from all walks of social and economic life, from housewives to lawyers to telephone repairpersons. Indeed, their socioeconomic backgrounds informed the initial ways women felt about feminism and affected the ways they envisioned their relationship with NOW. While Memphis was home to a branch of the YWCA (Young Women's Christian Association), Planned Parenthood, and a chapter of Federally Employed Women (FEW) in 1970, Memphis NOW was the only explicitly feminist membership-based organization in the city until the early 1980s.[2] There is little doubt that the lack of viable feminist alternatives to NOW affected the ways that women shaped their chapter to fit their needs and definitions of feminism.

CULTIVATING A FEMINIST ORGANIZATION IN MEMPHIS

Understanding the genesis of Memphis NOW demands attention to the cultural milieu in which it emerged. During the 1950s and 1960s, the Civil Rights Movement permeated Memphis. Peaceful demonstrators desegregated lunch counters, bus stations, and public facilities. They also met resistance in the form of white supremacist groups, such as the Ku Klux Klan, and hate-filled individuals. However, throughout Memphis and the South, the movement allowed many people to follow the nonviolent, interracial cooperation that Martin Luther King, Jr. preached, and they worked across racial lines for transcendent goals of equality and justice. By 1968, though, when King went to Memphis to negotiate with city leaders about the local sanitation workers' strike and the apparent racial issues that accompanied this crisis, Memphis was feeling the pressure of more militant groups vying for the recognition of "Black Power" (Beifuss 1990). King and local church officials organized a march not only to bring attention to the plight of the sanitation workers, but also to ameliorate tensions between adherents to passive resistance and the rising militant groups in Memphis.

When King was shot at the Lorraine Motel on 4 April 1968, most African Americans in Memphis felt that "the shooting…was a direct and open attack on the black community itself. He had come to help them and now he was dead" (Beifuss 1990, 401). In the aftermath of the assassination, cities across the nation erupted into violence, and Memphis was no exception. Riots continued in defiance of the police-mandated curfews as many in the city mourned the loss of one of their own. By 7 April, though, Memphians were trying to repair their city and heal themselves by continuing with the march King had planned. A group of people, both black and white, identifying themselves as Memphis Cares, staged gatherings across the city to "express the anguish…many Memphians were feeling" (434). However, African Americans were neither blind nor deaf to the sentiments many whites expressed, especially those that indicated that the real tragedy of the shooting was that it took place in their city and would cause their hometown to be "misjudged" (406).

In the context of a growing discourse about race, discrimination, and equality—and using both legislative means and street protests—Memphians began to form both civil rights and feminist organizations. In some instances, African Americans and white women worked together. For example, an interracial group of women formed the Panel of American Women (PAW) in the aftermath of the shooting to talk freely about racial tensions in Memphis. PAW organized panels with representatives from the Jewish, Catholic, and Protestant faiths, with at least one African American woman among them. One organizer of the local PAW, Jocelyn Wurzburg, was also a founding member of Memphis NOW, demonstrating on a personal level the connection between civil rights and women's equality. Like others across the nation, women in Memphis responded to their tumultuous environment and formed a local chapter of NOW (Evans 1979, 2003; Giddings 1984; Echols 1989; Rosen 2000).

Although such white women as Wurzburg linked their feminist activism directly to the cause of African American civil rights, African American women in Memphis were not necessarily drawn to local feminist organizations. Most focused their political activism on issues of race, and their activities on behalf of women were typically for African American women. Several scholars have highlighted the national tenor of racial divides among feminists (Giddings 1984; Hartmann 1998; Thompson 2002; Springer forthcoming), but it also resonated locally in Memphis and its NOW chapter. In Memphis and across the South, feminist activism was caught in the local political "protection" of Southern womanhood, which was a racialized code for ensuring social and cultural distance between white people and African American people—and demonstrating how the "metalanguage of race" operates (Higginbotham 1992; see also, Hall 1979). Early in the chapter's history, NOW had difficulties attracting African American women because of their overt suspicions of white women. Ruth Spearman, an African American housewife in Memphis, commented that even if the women's movement succeeded in gaining equal treatment for men and women, "I really don't think black women will ever be treated the same as white women are treated" (Gilliam 1971), echoing Toni Morrison's 1970 comment that African American women "look at White women and see the enemy for they know that racism is not confined to white men" (Giddings 1984, 307). Local African American columnist Art Gilliam suggested that, in comparison to being black, the exclusions women face are minor (1971).

Rather than glom onto a feminist agenda that white women in NOW set, African American women created and sustained their own organizations and workshops. For example, Dot Smith and Helen Duncan, directors of the Southwest Mental Health Center, offered a six-week workshop on "Problems of Being Black and Female" in 1978. Both for and by African American women, this workshop addressed African American women's history, family issues, and images of beauty. One group, United Sisters and Associates (USA), formed with the intent of addressing black womanhood in Memphis and nationwide. In attempting to define and legitimate the concept of the African American woman, establish unity among African American women, resist the exploitation that they suffered, and provide an arena for their emotional and spiritual development, USA directed its energies toward black femininity and beauty. To this end, it worked with *Essence* magazine to develop the Miss Essence of Tennessee beauty pageant, bringing "national attention to black women, to the city of Memphis and by example present an image of black womanhood in a manner that renders more respect and appreciation" (USA 1972). Indeed, NOW both locally and nationally could not reconcile its feminist critique of beauty standards for women with such an approach; USA and the NOW chapter could not see eye-to-eye on this issue.

Perhaps more to the point, though, was the fact that some African American women felt that they had little to learn from white feminist consciousness-raising. Although Memphis NOW's minority women's task force leader Merle Smith applauded NOW for its actions on behalf of feminism and women's equality and stayed with the organization "to keep black women visible in the movement," she also understood how many women of color would not be attracted to the chapter. She stated, "you see, we come from a strong matriarchal society and were raised to be feminists, something white women found out about later" ("Old Doubts Deter Feminists" 1973). The Civil Rights Movement clearly affected both white and African American women, but they tended to organize separately and concentrate on different issues. It is quite likely that women forged alliances across racial lines within feminist organizations when local issues demanded them (Hartmann 1998; Naples 1998). Any alliances, however, were plagued with the reality that race had everything to do with capturing the ear of local political leaders. The mostly white membership of Memphis NOW would always have more political voice than black women in Memphis. The dialogue between white and African American women in Memphis, which both mirrors and complicates the national picture other scholars have painted, only reinforces the point that there is no singular narrative of feminist activism.

TOEING THE NATIONAL NOW LINE: THE ERA

The best example of Memphis NOW mirroring the national organization was through its efforts on behalf of the Equal Rights Amendment. This amendment, seeking "equality of rights under the law" for all regardless of sex, represented liberal feminism most directly because it advocated women's equality without directly challenging cultural and social

39

gender roles. In pursuit of the amendment, Memphis NOW utilized the federated structure of the national organization, and its actions on behalf of the ERA reflected liberal feminist tactics. NOW also grappled with supporting this amendment in opposition to anti-ERA women who, acting on behalf of Southern womanhood and traditional Southern identity, insisted that the ERA disrupted traditional gender roles.

In April 1972, Tennessee helped to set the tone of apparent support for the ERA across the nation by becoming one of the first states to ratify the amendment. In fact, within two weeks of congressional passage, the Tennessee House gave the ERA a unanimous vote, and an overwhelming majority in the Senate offered their support (Tennessee House 1972; Tennessee Senate 1972). Like other chapters across the nation, Memphis NOW expressed satisfaction with its apparent success. The chapter sat back and, as a result, watched its success unravel.

In Tennessee and other states around the nation, Phyllis Schlafly's STOPERA campaigns emerged with the goal of blocking the ERA and its perceived violation of the rights of women across the nation (Schlafly 1977; Berry 1986; Mansbridge 1986; Mathews and DeHart 1990). Former Miss America Barbara Walker Hummel led local opposition to the ERA through Memphis-based AWARE (American Women Are Richly Endowed). AWARE women defined themselves as housewives and mothers who supported the notion that men and women were essentially different and who believed that the "equality" granted in the ERA would jeopardize the privilege and protection that women, in their opinion, currently enjoyed. As political activists, AWARE members presented an anti-ERA skit on the floor of the Tennessee House of Representatives. Upon its completion, Representative W.K. "Tag" Weldon, a Republican from Memphis, asked the General Assembly to rescind the amendment's ratification. The debate over whether or not the state could revoke its support of the amendment raged for two years.

Memphis NOW's response to the rescission measure reveals national NOW's early sentiment toward efforts to rescind and the seemingly laughable notion that the ERA would not succeed. Members of Memphis NOW waged a letter writing campaign to their state representatives in support of the ERA and remained sufficiently concerned to orchestrate a blood drive to raise money for the NOW Emergency Fund for the ERA (Willis 1973; "NOW Women Sell Blood to Finance Campaign" 1973). When individual representatives debated the rescission measure in their home communities, Memphis NOW participated in these town meetings, but their contributions did little more than replicate national NOW's attitude that the ERA was a foregone conclusion. In one public forum, for example, NOW women merely carried signs stating "Case by Case Is too slow" and "1776 Was for Women Too" to articulate their support for the amendment ("Women's Rights' Supporters Take Floor" 1974). Memphis NOW wrote letters, organized petition drives, and lobbied—time-honored (and historically identified liberal feminist) strategies—to keep the ERA alive in the Volunteer state (Memphis NOW Newsletters 1971–1982).

In contrast, anti-ERA activists used dramatic tactics to make their points. AWARE presented another skit on 4 December 1973 at the General Assembly of the Shelby County Delegation, a town meeting held periodically for legislators to canvass their constituents' sentiments.

Designed to demonstrate yet again their opposition to the ERA, AWARE presented, among other things, a full rendition of "I Enjoy Being a Girl," complete with piano accompaniment, reinforcing their idea of womanhood through such lyrics as,

I'm strictly a female female

And I hope that my future will be

In the arms of a brave and free male

Who enjoys being a guy having a girl like me.

Through this performance, AWARE reinforced the idea that "equal rights" meant that women had to give up being traditional "girls" (Memphis NOW Newsletters 1971–1982 [January 1974]). At this meeting, NOW representatives Carole Hensen, Linda Ethridge, and Lou Farr had "no designs of speaking on the 'dead issue,'" but offered their arguments in response to the demonstration. The attending members were concerned by the anti-ERA advocates' "apparent success" at the meeting but only encouraged their sisters to write "at least one more letter" in support of their amendment. Rather than respond in kind with pro-ERA demonstrations and a visible presence, Memphis NOW members continued to confine themselves to letter writing.

Following the national group's lead, Memphis NOW also pursued the goal of the amendment to the exclusion of other laws. As a result, AWARE women seemed more willing to work with politicians for piecemeal legislation designed to alleviate specific problems that women faced. For example, Hummel reported that her organization supported two national bills sponsored by Senator Bill Brock (R-TN) that would make it easier for women to obtain credit in their own names. By pursuing the ERA as the only acceptable measure, Memphis NOW seemed rigid, unwilling to endorse this or any other legislation that sidestepped the larger amendment.

In the state legislature, debate over the rescission effort—which was ultimately a debate over womanhood—culminated in Senate Joint Resolution 29 rescinding Tennessee's support of the ERA, finally passed in February 1974 (Tennessee Senate 1974). When the measure came to the House of Representatives, legislators debated the issues of the ERA from restrooms to religion in front of "500 sign-waving and baby-toting women" divided on the measure ("Legislators Vote to Rescind ERA Ratification" 1974). At the end of the deliberation, the house rescinded its ratification by a vote of 56 to 33. That the state attorney general's office ruled that the resolution was unconstitutional became a sidebar to this story in Memphis and nationally. At bottom, Memphis NOW could not compete with the idea of protected traditional womanhood couched in Southern fears of federal encroachment on states' rights, and they did not work very hard to do so.

After this setback, Memphis NOW abandoned the ERA until 1977, when Congress extended the amendment's ratification deadline. At this time, national NOW concluded that the ERA could not be ratified by its 22 March 1979 deadline, and support from all levels of the organization emerged to fight for an extension. In July 1978, 100,000 activists marched on Washington to illustrate continued and renewed support for the ERA. Memphis NOW sent ten members to the march and engaged in yet another letter-writing campaign to their legislators urging their support for House Joint Resolution 638, the measure that would extend the life of the ERA campaign. Their efforts were again countered by anti-ERA forces, many of whom drove from Memphis to Washington to meet with their representatives directly and give them homemade bread, a symbol of woman's appropriate place in the home ("Loaf of Bread, Talk with Senators Aim at Keeping Women in 'Place'" 1978). Pro-ERA forces were able to win what would become a moot victory, though, with the extended date of ratification set at 30 July 1982.

When Eleanor Smeal, president of NOW, rallied the troops with the call that "women should be outraged that there must be a vote to determine whether there will be equality for women," Memphis NOW responded (Memphis NOW Newsletters 1971–1982 [August 1981]). They raised money—specifically, the newly minted Susan B. Anthony dollars—for the ERA through parties and flea markets and pushed for ratification in neighboring Arkansas and Mississippi. Chapter president Betty Sullivan encouraged Memphis NOW members to join the national ERA Message Brigade, a nationwide computer bank service that notified members when a state legislature was scheduled to vote on the ERA. The brigade reinforced the political tactic of letter writing, something Memphis NOW had practiced since the beginning of this debate.

Memphis NOW also took the message of the ERA to the local airwaves. For example, on 30 June 1981, the day signifying one more year to ratify the ERA, Memphis NOW broadcast a series of public service announcements on the necessity of the amendment and held a press conference on the importance of the ERA for women nationwide. In addition, members gave the ERA increasing attention on their radio and public access cable television shows, "Women NOW." Former member Lynda Dolbi recalled one experience on the talk radio show. After speaking for a short time, she fielded questions from the radio audience. One man called into the show, voicing his opinion that supporters of the ERA amounted to "a bunch of lesbians who wanted to go to the bathroom with men." According to Dolbi, this call was the one she was waiting for: "I said, 'you know, what strikes me as odd is that you would even say that. Think about it. Why would a lesbian want to go to the bathroom with a man? Don't you think lesbians would want to go to a women's room?'" Answering this man's challenge was "one of life's high points" for Dolbi (1996).

In many instances, though, high points would be the exception to the rule. As time wore on, women were spurred to increased activity as it became more and more apparent that the ERA was losing ground. In a desire to see the ERA become the law of the land, the Memphis affiliate sent delegates when NOW hosted demonstrations in Illinois and Florida, states with the greatest possibility of ratifying the amendment. In Chicago, "a busload of Memphis women [promised to] bury the image of the helpless, stay-in-your-own-backyard Southern belle." Carrying a banner proclaiming "The South Will Rise and Ratify," thirty-seven women from Memphis NOW joined a sea of thousands of ERA supporters in a lakefront march urging Illinois legislators to ratify the amendment ("Memphians Go to Illinois to Urge ERA Ratification" 1980). Two years later, members of Memphis NOW geared up for the final ERA battle in Tallahassee, Florida. Forty-one members made the overnight trip to the Florida capital for the rally. One member recalled the high emotions and desperate zeal of the participants:

Memphis NOW was one of the last groups to move out marching the "last mile" to the Capitol so we were able to count and feel the fervor and grassroots power behind equality for women. Marching ten abreast, each unit with its gold, purple, and white banner in the lead, the chanting line stretched down the valley and up the hill to the Florida Capitol a mile away. No media report or picture yet has captured the intensity of those women, men, and children. (Memphis NOW Newsletters 1971–1982 [February 1982])

At the height of passion for the ERA, Memphis NOW carried its struggle to the bitter end, but no amount of commitment could save the amendment. Just months before the deadline, Florida, like Illinois, failed to ratify the ERA. Despite the letter writing and late public demonstrations of NOW women at every level, the ERA died on 30 June 1982.

Although their anecdotes provide nuances to the national story of the ERA, these recollections replicate those reported in the literature in many ways. These subtleties illustrate how the Memphis chapter followed national NOW, utilizing the federated structure of the organization to the best of its abilities. However, the story of Memphis NOW also demonstrates how the trope of Southern womanhood shaped the debates about the ERA (Mathews and DeHart 1990). Because AWARE women framed the debate, NOW women in Memphis not only had to defend the amendment but also had to deny categorically associations with their Southern heritage. When Memphis NOW invoked the myth of Southern womanhood, it was to "bury" its image in favor of a Southern woman who supported equal rights. Yet many politicians and citizens in Memphis were uncomfortable with the idea of relinquishing the Southern womanhood that had "protected" them. Though race was a silent factor in public discourse on the ERA in Memphis, it clearly defined the debate and resurrected familiar concerns about equality of all women and all people. As a result, Southern identity not only intersected with the struggle over the ERA, but it also provided a framework for this debate.

ACTING LIKE A RADICAL FEMINIST COLLECTIVE: RAPE AND WIFE ABUSE

Unlike the ERA, rape and wife abuse entered public discourse as a result of feminists' insistence that "the personal is political," and most scholars write about the origins of rape crisis and wife abuse centers as the projects of radical feminists (Echols 1989; Whittier 1995). However, in Memphis, the NOW chapter made the personal political by initiating public debate on rape and wife abuse and generating facilities through the assistance of an umbrella structure of women's organizations, the Women's Resource Center (WRC).

Founded in 1974 by Memphis NOW, the local YWCA, and city chapters of Planned Parenthood, Girls Club, Church Women United, Federally Employed Women, and the League of Women Voters, the WRC dedicated itself to "serv[ing] the varied needs of women in the Greater Memphis Metropolitan area not currently met by existing social service agencies and/or local, State, and Federal Government programs" (*The Wheel* 1974–1982 [March 1974]). Over its eight-year existence, basic funding came from its membership organizations, but other sources of revenue included federal Comprehensive Education and Training Administration (CETA) program funds and a grant from the United Methodist

Church. Throughout its tenure in the Bluff City, WRC offered a laundry list of community services, including assertiveness training, financial educational programs, and other seminars "contributing to a new perspective for women of our area" as well as support groups for women experiencing the emotional trauma of divorce ("Women's Resource Center of Memphis" 1977). It also provided a speaker's bureau, a job bank and training program for women seeking employment outside the home, legal counsel, a library of books on women's history and feminist issues, and programs "designed to focus attention on the changing needs and interests of women as they become more visible and vocal" (*The Wheel* 1974–1982 [October 1982]). Because the WRC was working within the necessary political channels to secure funds for facilities for raped and abused women, NOW women could adopt a more radical approach and actually utilize both liberal feminist and radical feminist tactics. Although members never explicated it in feminist statements, literature, or other extant sources, they were also able to manipulate the well-documented and racialized notions of womanhood and protection of women's bodies.

Rape became a central national issue as well as a local one by the early 1970s. In Washington, DC, NOW announced its commitment to confronting rape as a violation of women's physical bodies as well as a social ill that needed to be alleviated. But in Memphis, the issue of rape took on a personal tone as women confronted their city's reputation as "the rape capital of the nation": in 1973 alone, 534 rapes were reported with victims ranging in age from eighteen months to 84 years. Since contemporary FBI statistics relied upon self-reporting and asserted that only ten percent of rapes were actually reported, the numbers were likely closer to 5000 ("The Comprehensive Rape Crisis Program" n.d.).

Frustrated, angry, and determined to confront women's sense of helplessness in the face of such a crime, Memphis NOW sought to address women's concerns about rape. Rather than limit their efforts to letter writing, they worked with the police department and WRC to initiate a Comprehensive Rape Crisis Program in the city. In concert with local feminist attention to rape as a public issue, the Memphis Police Department created a Sex Crimes Squad. They hired more women to work as counselors, extended their hours into the nighttime, and began using unmarked cars to go to victims' homes in an attempt to protect privacy and anonymity. Hospitals also worked with the police by providing speedier care for rape victims, examining women in private hospital rooms instead of more public emergency rooms, and processing and upgrading physical tests to obtain evidence for the prosecution of criminals (Memphis NOW Newsletters 1971–1982 [1974]). At the same time, Memphis NOW established the city's first rape crisis hotline, staffed with volunteers and managed by the WRC. NOW member Pam Hazen coordinated "People Against Rape" to solicit the larger community's aid in exploding myths about rape and pursuing legislation. In her speeches, Hazen decried Memphis's "badge of infamy" and chastised judges and prosecutors for "totally and unethically ignor[ing] the victim," contending that women were doubly victimized by the perpetrator and the justice system (Adams 1975).

By the end of 1974, the crisis seemed to be escalating: Memphis women reported 607 rapes and attempted rapes. What was most shocking though, was that only fourteen percent of the crimes ended in an indictment, and only nineteen percent of those resulted in a conviction. Not content simply to work within local institutions, NOW women raised the stakes by taking their cause of protection and safety for women to the streets. Commemorating the fifty-fifth anniversary of women's suffrage, approximately thirty-five NOW members protested rape in their city with a "Take Back the Night" type of demonstration. This action, highlighted at the beginning of this article, exemplified their commitment to radical feminist tactics and the philosophy that linked rape to the commodification of women.

Their radical efforts raised political awareness about rape and propelled the Memphis Police Department to form a Comprehensive Rape Crisis Program to complement the Sex Crimes Squad. Perhaps in recognition of Memphis NOW's efforts in bringing rape to the foreground of social consciousness, Mayor Wyeth Chandler appointed chapter president Julia Howell to serve as the director of the city's first Rape Crisis Program. Under Howell's direction, the program shifted from a CETA-funded operation to a component of the city government on 1 July 1978, insuring the longevity of public support for the program. Because the chapter both used radical tactics and took advantage of institutional structures in place, what began as Memphis NOW's grassroots response to a local problem had become "an integral part of the city government" in the space of five years (*The Wheel* 1974–1982 [1978]).

Since violence against women was not limited to rape and sexual assault, Memphis NOW also addressed the problem of wife abuse.[3] While the national organization acknowledged wife abuse as a violent act against women, the impetus for the formation of the local task force did not come from a national directive. Rather, chapter member Angie Russo initiated the effort. In August 1975, she relayed to her fellow chapter members a story of a friend who told her about the latest in what had become a series of fights she had with her husband that, in this instance, resulted in a broken arm, concussion, and black eyes. Devastated and angry that this woman felt she had to stay with her husband out of fear because she had nowhere to go, Russo convinced the chapter to take action against wife abuse and established a public forum to confront the concerns of local women involved in abusive relationships with husbands and boyfriends (Memphis NOW Newsletters 1971–1982 [1975]).

Through the new task force, Russo generated a series of lectures and panels to raise community awareness about wife abuse. Disgusted by the fact that local law enforcement coded wife abuse as regular assault rather than a separate crime, Memphis NOW recognized that women could not turn to the police for help. Operating outside this restrictive situation, the chapter opened the city's first wife abuse hot line in September 1976. The chapter financed the line and volunteers staffed it for three hours daily (Conley 1976). In addition, members from Memphis NOW and WRC-sponsored support groups converged to provide immediate counseling and helped abused women find therapy and temporary shelters (Davis 1976).

As part of their September meeting, Memphis NOW held an open panel discussion for the larger community entitled "Wife Beating: The Crime That Goes Unpunished." Member Edie Sewell told the story of Marie G. Hamlin, shot to death by her husband after years of abuse. Police knew that Millard Hamlin made threats against his wife twice before that month, but they failed to follow up. Sewell then cited FBI statistics to illuminate the seriousness of the crime: in 1974 alone, 1285 wives were murdered by their husbands. Other abuse victims on the panel admitted to losing confidence in themselves, feeling "emotionally shattered" to the point that "the damage that was done...is irreparable" (Conley 1976). Before long, like radical feminists in other cities, the chapter decided that a hot line was not enough and set out to design a shelter for abused and battered wives that would give women relief from dangerous situations and safeguard women during the long legal process.

Under the auspices of the WRC, Memphis NOW organized a Wife Abuse Crisis Service in June 1977. Under Russo's direction, the service opened a temporary shelter in August 1979, the first step en route to a more permanent facility (Memphis NOW Newsletters 1971–1982 [1979]). The shelter offered women safety as well as a separate space to think and discuss options. Moreover, the shelter gave women a community of support and care, things evidently missing from their home life. After 1982, the YWCA adopted the Wife Abuse Crisis Center and funded additional and more permanent shelter space. To celebrate the opening of this new and more secure shelter that was seven years in the making, Memphis NOW hosted "An Evening of Feminist Theater" by bringing the Rhode Island Feminist Theater (RIFT) to town. RIFT presented "Internal Injury," an original play about an abused wife. By embracing feminist theatre, an outgrowth of cultural and radical feminism, Memphis NOW demonstrated that they were not an exclusively liberal organization.

Memphis feminists recognized that abused women often lacked financial resources to enable them to leave, so NOW and WRC established the "Women's Crisis Loan Service of Shelby County" in June 1978. The loan program began with a $2000 contribution from WRC-affiliated organizations, but through donations, it gradually accrued funds to empower eligible women to leave abusive situations and start a new life. So great was the need that the fund quickly suffered serious depletions (The Wheel 1974–1982 [1978]). Memphis NOW raised another $2000 at a fundraiser for the loan service, but funds still fell short (Memphis NOW Newsletters 1971–1982 [November 1978]). It is ironic that so many women utilized this service that the WRC was forced to shut down the loan auxiliary the next year. Still, the program illustrates the understanding that abuse was exacerbated by women's disadvantaged economic situation (The Wheel 1974–1982 [February 1979]).

This service demonstrated how NOW and the umbrella group in Memphis generated alternative institutions at the grassroots level to alleviate women's suffering. Though they could not sustain the loan service, the chapter continued its educational activities, joining with other women's groups to extend awareness of domestic violence to the greater community. In November 1978, NOW along with several other local organizations such as the Democratic Women of Shelby County, WRC, and the National Conference of Christians and Jews, hosted a workshop on "The Problem of Wife Abuse." This two-and-one-half hour assembly illustrated that spouse abuse was not just a domestic problem but rather one of the family and the community. It also spotlighted the shelter for battered women, soliciting financial support and underscoring its importance for Memphis. NOW members also worked to change the current legal system that favored the abuser by placing the entire burden of physical proof on the often reluctant victim without attention to the husband's prior arrest record, previous calls to the police for other instances of wife abuse, or the woman's testimony (Memphis NOW Newsletters 1971–1982 [November 1978]).

At a public hearing of the Judiciary Committee of the Tennessee legislature, Memphis Legal Services attorneys and chapter members Sherry Myers and Bonnie Ragland discussed the dismal situation of legal recourse for abused women. Family violence in the state was considered a misdemeanor; accordingly, police were unable to make an arrest until the victim produced a sworn warrant for the arrest of the abuser. By defining abuse in these narrow terms, most victims were unable to process immediate complaints because the department would only issue warrants on weekdays from 9:00 A.M. to 5:00 P.M. Given that the majority of domestic violence episodes occurred at night or on weekends, most women were forced to wait hours or days to seek any legal recourse, leaving plenty of time for their husbands to apologize or to continue to beat them. Furthermore, police still often refused to intervene because they regarded domestic violence as a "family matter." Myers and Ragland insisted that male judges and police officers often minimized wife abuse and humiliated victims through mockery or scorn after they testified. The Tennessee legislature passed a bill in January 1979 that would alleviate this situation by allowing an arrest without a warrant and by not requiring women to file a formal petition. Nine months after the law went into effect, Myers and Ragland urged the legislature to encourage enforcement of the new laws (Memphis NOW Newsletters 1971–1982 [September 1979]).

Memphis NOW's efforts to combat rape and wife abuse evince its commitment to employ whatever tactics were necessary to effect change. The same was true in the struggle against pornography. When the most egregious example of the genre, *Snuff*, premiered in Memphis in 1977, lurid advertisements boasted that it was "the bloodiest thing that ever happened in front of a camera!! The film that could only be made in South America—where life is CHEAP!" (Findlay and Findlay 1971/1976). The finale of this film was a woman's murder. Members of Memphis NOW attended the movie on its opening night. The next day, several members walked through the rain in front of Towne Cinema, the film's host, with picket signs, protesting "violence against women [and] a film that advocates killing women for entertainment" (Fox 1977). The chapter picketed the theater and circulated a flyer calling for an end to sexual violence in the media:

> Violence for sexual pleasure is portrayed in crime and magazines, TV, police shows, [and] slick publications such as *Playboy* and *Penthouse*. "Snuff" films are the missing link between media violence against women and actual violence that women experience daily. ("Enough SNUFF" n.d.)

NOW members also expressed outrage at the racist attitudes of "a society which says the lives of nonwhite people, particularly women, are less valuable and more available for exploitation than European and American women."

The ensuing controversy over pornography and the degradation of women prodded Towne Cinema owner George Miller to defend the movie as being "no worse than *Texas Chainsaw Massacre* or a lot of other violent films." What seemed to anger him the most was white women demonstrating at his theater, which historically catered to an African American audience: "People see these white women in front of my theater and they just know they don't want to be in the middle of it. I have been harassed from the beginning and now I got white folks picketing me" (Fox 1977). Chapter president Jackie Cash denied that the picketing was racially motivated against him in particular, insisting that the inherent and violent racism and sexism of the movie he chose to show demanded their actions. Although no member ever explicitly stated so, it is likely that the ability to take advantage of racist notions of protections of Southern (white) womanhood figured into their tactics and the ensuing fear that the movie theatre owner faced if he "threatened" white women. Memphis NOW was the only organization that protested this movie; any objection among African American women was not recorded in any of the local newspapers. The chapter's efforts were successful: within days, Towne Cinema pulled the film (Fox 1977).

As the actions to stop violence against women reveal, Memphis NOW was not simply toe-ing the national NOW feminist line or utilizing liberal feminist tactics. Instead, members responded to local situations through whatever means they deemed necessary. Memphis NOW took the lead in bringing rape and wife abuse to the social and cultural forefront be-cause these were issues most pressing to Memphis women. They merged zap actions, such as the protest in response to *Snuff*, with institutionalization and working within the system to create a Comprehensive Rape Crisis Program, highlighting the dynamics of feminism that attention to location reveals.

RADICAL AND LIBERAL FEMINISM

Given that it embraced multiple organizational structures, tactics, and issues, Memphis NOW cannot be described simply as a liberal feminist organization. Women in Memphis NOW were simultaneously liberal and radical. When they worked toward goals defined by the national organization, most specifically the ERA, they operated within formal political channels and adopted more sedate activist tactics. As Memphis NOW confronted violence against women's bodies, however, this same group of women employed radical tactics and rhetoric and embodied radical feminist ideology. Yet as they marched in the streets and po-liticized the personal, they also worked within "the system" to institutionalize local centers to assist physically violated women. In the face of Southern politics, radical feminist tactics combined with liberal ones worked most effectively. When, in 1975, NOW chose as its con-ference theme "Out of the Mainstream, Into the Revolution," they combined and compli-cated feminist rhetoric and activism, focusing on a range of issues from pay equity to rape and wife abuse. What are purported then to be clear divisions between radical and liberal feminism are actually less distinct, suggesting that we must look beyond the constructs of radical and liberal feminist ideology in order to understand feminist activism. Attention to location, perhaps, reveals that nowhere is this dichotomy rigid. Instead, we should look to the dynamics of feminist activism and the context in which it emerges.

Situations unique to or important to women in Memphis may not have been deemed as crit-ical to NOW women in other areas, or vice versa. For example, NOW women in Washington, DC focused their attention on national policy, which is understandable given their location since the mid-1970s in the nation's capitol. Their feminist counterparts in Chicago built upon what they called their "Midwestern practicality" by focusing on such bread and butter issues as daycare, urging local NOW members to work on behalf of all parents and chil-dren. To this end, they conducted door-to-door surveys of homes in two wards to assess the community's needs for child care (Chicago NOW Newsletters [December 1970, September 1971]). NOW members in San Francisco and New York chapters developed coalitions with other feminist organizations to develop cooperative childcare programs; promote wom-en's caucuses in unions, professions, and political parties; and combat insulting images of women in the media (Carden 1974; San Francisco NOW Newsletters [September 1969]). Boston NOW members acted locally through a task force on women in higher education, increasing awareness of gender discrimination at area universities and colleges. They were also instrumental in initiating the Institute of Women's Studies at the seven seminaries of the Boston Theological Institute (Boston NOW Newsletters [April 1970]). While the na-tional organization was concerned with daycare and coalition politics, chapter members demanded attention to other issues. Moreover, members in local chapters pursued such issues as women's studies programs at local seminaries because they mattered to women in the area. Their feminist expressions, like those of Memphis NOW, are situational and do not simply conform to a traditional model of feminist activism. Turning attention to feminist activism that operates between liberal and radical provides a more dynamic way of conceptualizing feminist protest to reveal a more complex women's movement.

While much more work is left to be done on local-level feminist organizations and expressions, I seek to draw some general conclusions here. First, the story of Memphis NOW suggests that local feminist groups, whether affiliated with national organizations or not, may not be either liberal or radical, but are most likely both. Moreover, the issues, goals, and strategies used to garner political attention and change may determine how to locate the group as either radical or liberal. National NOW may fit more neatly into the liberal side of the framework, especially in comparison to radical women's groups of the past. However, local NOW chapters, such as the one in Memphis, reveal how this dichotomous model is not complex enough to capture fully the reality of the women's movement for many of its participants.

Secondly, and related, analyzing the importance of situational politics and feminists' responses allows for a more accurate understanding of feminist expression. What issues compel a group of women to act? How do they interact with and affect the existing cultural and political milieu? While a single narrative will not answer these questions with completeness and certainty, they deserve to be asked. In the case of Memphis NOW, the Civil Rights Movement in their town gave women the impetus to organize, and they responded to the violence in their city. But local political and social conditions offered primary issues for Memphis NOW to contend with and resolve. Rape and domestic violence were not contested in part because these concerns allowed Southern politicians to continue the model of "protection" that "rescued" and "saved" Southern white women while simultaneously addressing and taking seriously feminist issues. Though such racist ideologies were not discussed in the public discourse, it is certainly presumable that Memphis feminists were able to make such quick and impressive gains because the trope of Southern womanhood—with all of its racist baggage—so thoroughly permeated Memphis politics. So when Marion Keisker commented that "women are only as safe as civilized man allows," she was able to fall back—however silently—on racist notions of "civilized man" as well as the seeming need for women to be protected ("NOW Members Protest Violence Against Women" 1975). If this is the case, then it also explains why policy makers, for example, did not openly embrace equal pay as a feminist issue in the march toward equality. Equal pay would, no doubt, threaten the social order of family and gender roles, especially the notion of husband as breadwinner. Equal pay, as a plank of the ERA, then, ultimately buckled under the pressures of those who openly embraced notions of Southern womanhood. When it came to equal rights, womanhood was hotly debated because it was seemingly threatened.

Uncovering such dynamics, then, begs the question of whether feminist activism in the South is exceptional. Southern political and cultural dynamics certainly affected the ways in which feminists grappled with issues, and this case hints at Southern exceptionalism. We will be able to make more certain claims of such exceptionalism when we have more studies of feminist activism in Southern cities. Memphis NOW members chose to work within the system while also working outside of it by taking matters into their own hands. To meet these challenges, Memphis NOW responded to the political and cultural environment of their Southern city while affecting the local political structure, community, and lives of women they touched. Their actions shaped and reshaped their environments in meaningful ways, but issues of race, in particular the racialized trope of womanhood, would be impossible to overturn. Memphis feminists in NOW, however unwittingly, manipulated the notion of protection to their advantage while attacking Southern womanhood openly in contests over equal rights. Location clearly matters when we talk about feminist activism because we have to understand women's day-to-day contexts in order to make sense of how and why women acted and responded in the ways they did to feminist challenges.

Perhaps most important, Memphis NOW demonstrates that it may be more appropriate to think about feminist activism—then and now—in terms of dynamism rather than static labels. While the terms *liberal* and *radical* are clearly important to feminists and scholars, they are not mutually exclusive in terms of feminist activism. Feminists have been, and continue to be, simultaneously liberal and radical. What seems necessary is more research on the dynamic activist tactics, styles, and organizational structures that feminists employ in many different places across the country.

My thanks to Janann Sherman, Leila J. Rupp, Verta Taylor, Susan M. Hartmann, Heather Lee Miller, Susan Kathleen Freeman, Eileen Boris, Anne Collinson, and Elizabeth Kaminski for reading many drafts of this article and offering insights about the many ways to understand feminist activism.

Questions for Discussion and Journaling

1. Rather than begin her article by explaining the distinctions between liberal and radical feminists that she discusses in her third paragraph, Gilmore starts with a story of a specific protest in Memphis. Why do you think she made this rhetorical decision? How does this example illustrate how narrative and story can be useful in academic articles? Would you have been as engaged with her argument if she began with the definitions rather than this story?

2. While her article primarily focuses on Memphis feminists, her final section, "Radical and Liberal Feminism," gives brief examples from Boston, Chicago, San Francisco, and New York. Why did she need to include these other examples? How do they support her argument about the false divide between radical and liberal feminism?

3. Throughout her article, Gilmore references Southern womanhood. Look to the ways she describes womanhood, and consider whether this ideology remains as it was in the 70s or if it has evolved in the years since. Using her words as evidence, write a paragraph summarizing the reasons women's studies scholars such as Gilmore find Southern womanhood problematic.

ENDNOTES

1. Jo Freeman acknowledged that "structure and style of action rather than ideology... more accurately differentiates the various [radical and liberal feminist] groups," and recognized that "even here there has been much borrowing on both sides" (1975, 481). Other scholars also point out that such "borrowing" has taken place, though they are reluctant to provide concrete examples. For example, Ferree and Hess have indicated that "the most marked change [among feminist activists and organizations in the decade between 1973 and 1982] was a muting of the distinctions between the collectivist and bureaucratic strands as they became interwoven into the different strategic forms of associations" (2000, 125). Evans acknowledged how "the radical ideas and cooperative forms of the women's movement were reshaping the more conservative, tightly structured 'women's rights' branch of the movement" (1979, 215). She further described the impact of radical women on liberal ones, noting how, by the early to mid-1970s, national NOW "strengthened its positions on issues like abortion and lesbianism and had considerably changed its style. In several cities NOW became the chief instigator of the new consciousness-raising groups" (215). Whittier also noted that the boundaries between liberal and radical groups became blurry as activists and organizations cooperated across their structural and stylistic differences, but maintained that the distinction between radical and liberal feminists was meaningful to the participants (Whittier 1995, 4–5). Echols dated the merger of radical and liberal feminism to around 1973, when "many liberal feminists came to agree with radical feminists that there was a political dimension to personal life," and she noted specifically how "NOW chapters began to establish consciousness-raising groups for interested women" (1989, 199).

2. Though YWCA, Planned Parenthood, and FEW can be considered feminist organizations, the first two are not membership-based organizations but rather service providers. FEW is a membership group, but their focus was limited to the strictures implied by their name. Thus, while other groups may have a feminist mission and goals, NOW is separated from these groups because of the broad base of issues they addressed and their membership-dependent structure.

3. The term *wife abuse* reflects their concern with battered women within monogamous heterosexual relationships, most typically marriages. This is the term they used and one I have elected to keep in order to reflect their agenda accurately.

REFERENCES

Adams, Alayne Barry. 1975. "Memphis' Badge of Infamy." [Memphis] *Commercial Appeal.* 23 May.

Berry, Mary Frances. 1986. *Why ERA Failed: Politics, Women's Rights, and the Amending Process of the Constitution.* Bloomington: Indiana University Press.

Beifuss, Joan Turner. 1990. *At the River I Stand.* Memphis, TN: St. Luke's Press.

Blee, Kathleen M. 1991. *Women of the Klan: Racism and Gender in the 1920s.* Berkeley: University of California Press.

Boston NOW Newsletter. *Herstory*. Microfilm. Addenda 1A, reel 7.

Buring, Daneel. 1997. *Lesbian and Gay Memphis: Building Communities Behind the Magnolia Curtain*. New York: Garland Press.

Carden, Maren Lockwood. 1974. *The New Feminist Movement*. New York: Russell Sage Foundation.

Carson, Clayborne. 1981. *In Struggle: SNCC and the Black Awakening of the 1960s*. Cambridge, MA: Harvard University Press.

Chicago NOW Newsletters. *Herstory*. Microfilm. Addenda 1A, reel 7.

Conley, Michael. 1976. "Task Force Looks at Wife Beating." *Memphis Press Scimitar*. 8 September.

"The Comprehensive Rape Crisis Program." n.d. Memphis NOW Papers. Special Collections, Ned W. McWherter Library, University of Memphis, Memphis, TN.

Davis, Anna Byrd. 1976. "Memphis Group Offers to Help Wives." *Memphis Press Scimitar*. 2 July.

Dolbi, Lynda. 1996. Personal interview with author. 6 March.

Duggan, Lisa. 2000. *Sapphic Slashers: Sex, Violence, and American Modernity*. Durham, NC: Duke University Press.

Echols, Alice. 1989. *Daring to Be Bad: Radical Feminism in America, 1967–1975*. Minneapolis: University of Minnesota Press.

"Enough 'SNUFF.'" n.d. Memphis NOW Papers. Box 5, folder 25. Special Collections, Ned W. McWherter Library, University of Memphis, Memphis, TN.

Evans, Sara. 1979. *Personal Politics: The Roots of Women's Liberation in the Civil Rights Movement and the New Left*. New York: Knopf.

_____. 2003. *Tidal Wave: How Women Changed America at Century's End*. New York: The Free Press.

Ferree, Myra Marx, and Beth Hess. 2000. *Controversy and Coalition: The New Feminist Movement Across Four Decades of Change*. New York: Twayne Publishers.

Findlay, Michael, and Roberta Findlay, dirs. 1971/1976. *Snuff*, aka *The Slaughter*. USA/Argentina: Michael Findlay/Monarch Releasing Corp.

Fox, Thomas. 1977. "Acting, Fakery in 'Snuff' Should Bring Its Well-Deserved Demise." [Memphis] *Commercial Appeal*. 27 September.

Fox-Genovese, Elizabeth. 1988. *Within the Plantation Household: Black and White Women of the Old South*. Chapel Hill: University of North Carolina Press.

39

Freeman, Jo. 1975. *The Politics of Women's Liberation*. New York: David McKay.

Freeman, Susan Kathleen. 2000. "From the Lesbian Nation to the Cincinnati Lesbian Community: Moving Toward a Politics of Location." *Journal of the History of Sexuality* (January–April):137–74.

Genovese, Eugene. 1974. *Roll Jordan Roll: The World the Slaves Made*. New York: Pantheon.

Giddings, Paula. 1984. *When and Where I Enter: The Impact of Black Women on Race and Sex in America*. New York: Morrow.

Gilliam, Art. 1971. "Few Black Faces in Women's Lib Crowd." [Memphis] *Commercial Appeal*. 7 June.

Grantham, Dewey. 1994. *The South in Modern America: A Region at Odds*. New York: Harper Collins.

Hall, Jacquelyn Dowd. 1979. *Revolt Against Chivalry: Jessie Daniel Ames and the Women's Campaign Against Lynching*. New York: Columbia University Press.

Hartmann, Susan. 1998. *The Other Feminists: Activists in the Liberal Establishment*. New Haven, CT: Yale University Press.

_____.1980. *From Margin to Mainstream: American Women and Politics Since 1960*. New York: Knopf.

Higginbotham, Evelyn Brooks. 1992. "African American Women's History and the Metalanguage of Race." *Signs* 17(2):251–74.

Hill, Samuel S., ed. 1983. *Religion in the Southern States*. Macon, GA: Mercer University Press.

"Legislators Vote to Rescind ERA Ratification." 1974. [Memphis] *Commercial Appeal*. 24 April.

"Loaf of Bread, Talk with Senators Aim at Keeping Women in 'Place.'" 1978. [Memphis] *Commercial Appeal*. 10 August.

MacLean, Nancy. 1994. *Behind the Mask of Chivalry: The Making of the Second Ku Klux Klan*. New York: Oxford University Press.

Mansbridge, Jane. 1986. *Why We Lost the ERA*. Chicago: University of Chicago Press.

Marable, Manning. 1984. *Race, Reform, and Rebellion: The Second Reconstruction in Black America, 1945–1982*. Jackson: University of Mississippi Press.

Mathews, Donald G., and Jane Sherron DeHart. 1990. *Sex, Gender, and the Politics of the ERA: A State and a Nation*. New York: Oxford University Press.

"Memphians Go to Illinois to Urge ERA Ratification." 1980. *Memphis Press Scimitar*. 10 May.

Memphis NOW Newsletters. 1971–1982. Memphis NOW Papers. Special Collections, Ned W. McWherter Library, University of Memphis, Memphis, TN.

Naples, Nancy A., ed. 1998. *Community Activism and Feminist Politics: Organizing Across Race, Class, and Gender.* New York: Routledge.

"NOW Members Protest Violence Against Women." 1975. *Memphis Press Scimitar.* 27 August.

"NOW Women Sell Blood to Finance Campaign." 1973. [Memphis] *Commercial Appeal.* 6 April.

"Old Doubts Deter Feminists." 1973. [Memphis] *Commercial Appeal.* 7 August.

Rosen, Ruth. 2000. *The World Split Open: How the Modern Women's Movement Changed America.* New York: Viking Press.

Ryan, Barbara. 1989. *Feminism and the Women's Movement: Dynamics of Change in Social Movement Ideology and Action.* New York: Routledge.

San Francisco NOW Newsletter. *Herstory.* Microfilm. Addenda 1A, reel 7.

Schlafly, Phyllis. 1977. *The Power of the Positive Woman.* New Rochelle, NY: Arlington House.

Sears, James, ed. 1997. *Lonely Hunters: An Oral History of Lesbian and Gay Southern Life, 1948–1968.* Boulder, CO: Westview Press.

Sitkoff, Howard. 1981. *The Struggle for Black Equality, 1954–1980.* New York: Hill and Wang.

Springer, Kimberly. Forthcoming. *Living for the Revolution: Black Feminist Organizations, 1968–1980.* Durham, NC: Duke University Press.

Tennessee House. 1972. *Tennessee House Journal.* Records for March–April. Bound volumes, government documents, Ned W. McWherter Library, University of Memphis, Memphis, TN.

Tennessee Senate. 1974. *Tennessee Senate Journal.* Records for January–April. Bound volumes, government documents, Ned W. McWherter Library, University of Memphis, Memphis, TN.

_____.1973. *Tennessee Senate Journal.* Records for March–April. Bound volumes, government documents, Ned W. McWherter Library, University of Memphis, Memphis, TN.

_____.1972. *Tennessee Senate Journal.* Records for April. Bound volume, government documents, Ned W. McWherter Library, University of Memphis, Memphis, TN.

Thomson, Becky. 2002. "Multiracial Feminism: Recasting the Chronology of Second Wave Feminism." *Feminist Studies* 28(2):337–55.

United Sisters and Associates. 1972. Press Release. February. Jocelyn M. D. Wurzburg Papers, Special Collections, Ned W. McWherter Library, University of Memphis, Memphis, TN.

Weisbrot, Robert. 1990. *Freedom Bound: A History of America's Civil Rights Movement.* New York: Norton.

The Wheel. 1974–1982. MVC Periodicals. Special Collections, Ned W. McWherter Library, University of Memphis, Memphis, TN.

White, Deborah Gray. 1999. *Ar'n't I a Woman? Female Slaves in the Plantation South.* 2nd ed. New York: Norton.

Whittier, Nancy. 1995. *Feminist Generations: The Persistence of Radical Women's Movement.* Philadelphia: Temple University Press.

Willis, Jim. 1973. "Some Reports Termed False on Equal Rights Amendment." *Memphis Press Scimitar*. 6 March.

"Women's Resource Center of Memphis, Inc." 1977. Jocelyn M. D. Wurzburg Papers, Box 3, folder 15, 14 June. Special Collections, Ned W. McWherter Library, University of Memphis, Memphis, TN.

"Women's Rights' Supporters Take Floor." 1974. *Memphis Press Scimitar*. 9 March.

CULTURE AND RESISTANCE: CIVIL RIGHTS PHOTOGRAPHY: MEMPHIS, 1968

Leila I. Hamdan

"Culture and Resistance" considers a number of photographs (some famous and some never before seen) from Memphis's Civil Rights Era in order to "offer an important counterpart to the written, historical record of the sanitation strike." Published in *Fire!!!* ("a multidisciplinary journal that serves the social sciences, arts, and humanities"), the article uses images to show how a number of important narratives have been left out of the stories surrounding the Sanitation Strike in Memphis. Hamden places the images in historical context to argue for the importance of self-representation, and in doing so, illustrates how the Sanitation Strike was a community effort, rather than a small protest composed only of workers.

For the ones who transcend the romanticism of history and give their bodies, minds, souls to the eternal struggle for Black liberation and human dignity.

ABSTRACT

The struggle in Memphis is most often portrayed through the iconic images of the 1968 sanitation strike and the subsequent death of Dr. Martin Luther King Jr. Local newspapers, primarily the Commercial Appeal *and* Memphis Press-Scimitar, *covered the sanitation strike throughout the duration, but ran stories in support of mayor Henry Loeb's obstructionist stance and against the formation of a union. The visual archive comprised of the photographs taken for local press publication is now housed in various local library, museum, and personal collections. Many of them have never been published. This archive includes well-known iconic images that have come to represent the Civil Rights Movement; less often studied, yet published photographs; and unseen excess photographs that were taken in succession with others during significant events. The images expose a lineage of various African American responses to oppressive forces, along with cultural expressions that emerge and are transformed out of changing social, political, and economic circumstance.*

Figure 40-1. Photographer: William Leaptrott (February 1968). *Special Collections*, University of Memphis.

INTRODUCTION

The modern Civil Rights Movement generated an abundance of photographs documenting the African American fight for economic, political, and social justice and equality. It was a persistent battle against oppressive forces that operated in powerful positions of legal, social, and economic authority. Local and national news outlets employed photography as a tool to visually record events surrounding the African American civil rights struggle. Many photographs have transcended the historic archive to become iconic images that represent a collective memory of the era. The archive, however, extends far beyond the published images well known today.

The struggle in Memphis is most often portrayed through the iconic images of the 1968 sanitation strike and the subsequent death of Dr. Martin Luther King Jr. Local newspapers, primarily the *Commercial Appeal* and *Memphis Press-Scimitar*, covered the sanitation strike throughout the duration, but ran stories in support of mayor Henry Loeb's obstructionist stance against the formation of a union. During the strike, many members of the Black community boycotted the *Commercial Appeal* and *Memphis Press-Scimitar* because of the bias and dishonest reporting.[1] The visual archive comprised of the photographs taken for local press publication is now housed in various local library, museum, and personal collections. This archive includes iconic images that have come to represent the Civil Rights Movement; less often studied, yet published photographs; and unseen excess photographs that were taken in succession with others during significant events. The majority of the photographs have never been published.

The visual archive offers an important counterpart to the written, historical record of the sanitation strike. It calls for re-examination and interpretation by a diversity of scholars including historians, artists, and cultural specialists in order to document the history of a marginalized community, whose experience has been substantially misrepresented or left out of dominant historical narratives. Photographs have the power to expose and create alternative narratives that have the potential to subvert the lacunae within dominant histories. However, photographs should not be used to present fixed monolithic truths.

The photographs I use in this study belong to a long history of civil rights photography.[2] Since the nineteenth century, African Americans have used photography to redefine the meaning of freedom and to help advance a readjustment of racial ideas and identity throughout major social and political shifts.[3] My research is greatly influenced by my studies on early African American photography, including that of Frederick Douglass, Ida B. Wells, W. E. B. Du Bois, Sojourner Truth, Booker T. Washington, and Harriet Jacobs. These six historical figures implemented photography in their fights for justice, equality, agency, and cultural transformation and helped to create and inspire a new type of archive of political expression.

For the purpose of this study, I reviewed over five hundred photographs belonging to the Mississippi Valley Collection in the Ned R. McWherther Library at the University of Memphis. I compiled a set of photographs to examine related to the sanitation strike. However, I suggest alternative ways of interpreting the images by examining them for unexplored issues concerning race, gender, labor, and class, and how they intersect with aspects of activism, agency, and ideology. The images expose a variety of African American responses to oppressive forces, including some aspects of cultural expression that emerged in response to changing social, political, and economic circumstances. In his book *Black Culture and Black Consciousness*, Lawrence W. Levine argues,

> Culture is not a fixed condition but a process: the product of interaction between the past and present. Its toughness and resiliency are determined not by a culture's ability to withstand change, which indeed may be a sign of stagnation not life, but by its ability to react creatively and responsively to the realities of a new situation. The question, as VeVe Clark recently put it, is not one of survivals but one of transformations.[4]

I borrow ideas from Elizabeth Abel, who owes much of her work to concepts articulated by Roland Barthes, to explain how the photographs in this study convey meaning through the medium's inherent iconographic and compositional conventions. Abel suggests that photographs convey "symbolic messaging" through a lexicon of cultural meaning connected to the objects represented in the photographs and through the visual rhetoric of the images. These rhetorical devices include human poses that signify status and character; props that carry specific meanings individually and collectively; lighting that invests or divests certain figures with authority, agency, or spirituality; camera angles that magnify or diminish human subjects; and framing that determines their centrality or marginality.[5]

SANITATION WORKERS AND THE BLACK COMMUNITY

Figure 40-2. Example of the type of automated trucks used in 1968 (August 5, 1981). *Special Collections*, University of Memphis.

On February 12, 1968, a wildcat strike of approximately 1,150 Public Works Department employees began after two sanitation workers, Echol Cole and Robert Walker, were crushed to death while seeking refuge from the rain inside the hull of their faulty garbage truck. The incident happened just one day after twenty-two Black workers from the sewer and drain division were sent home—without pay—due to temporary inclement weather. The tragic deaths of Cole and Walker galvanized sanitation workers already seeking union recognition and concessions from Public Works. City service employees, including those in the Public Works Department, had long been exploited and disrespected by Memphis political and business leaders when Henry Loeb took office as the city's mayor in 1968. Loeb began tightening the already stringent city labor policies and refused to pay overtime while he increased workers' hours and forced workers to operate faulty, obsolete equipment.[6] Many of the sanitation workers qualified for welfare support and received handouts such as clothing and shoes because their pay was drastically insufficient.[7] When the strike began, union organizer T. O. Jones was already in place and leading the workers in a fight to have the city recognize and bargain with their representative union, Local 1733 of the American Federation of State, County, and Municipal Employees (AFSCME).

A photograph by William Leaptrott shows a sea of sanitation workers at a union meeting in February 1968. Hundreds of men are seated and others stand two or three persons deep along the perimeters of the room. The faces of the men in the foreground and middle are tired and worn but serious and determined. Their individual strength increases by their numbers. The camera angle and cropping present the consolidated mass of men as one large power block.

Figure 40-3. Sanitation workers. Photographer: William Leaptrott (February 1968). *Special Collections*, University of Memphis.

The struggle of sanitation workers also galvanized the Black community and reached across poor and middle classes. Within the Black community, there was a great amount of respect for the workers who economically occupied the most menial jobs and received the lowest wages.[8] Stax recording artist Booker T. Jones recalls, "The garbage men were a part of the fabric of the society...My father always taught me to shake their hands and say hello to them. Know who they are. They were closely interwoven into the African-American community. So their fight was everybody's fight."[9]

On February 24, 1968, the day after police attacked peaceful marchers on Main Street with Mace, local Black ministers and community leaders overcame tensions between them and agreed to organize in support of the union. Their new group, Citizens on the Move for Equality (COME), pledged to raise money for the families of the striking sanitation workers and lead an economic boycott of downtown. Within the Black community, the response to the strike was overwhelmingly emotional and brought up long held feelings of frustration. Many people shared common grievances with the sanitation workers such as poverty, poor housing, low-wage jobs, violence and intimidation, police brutality, and legal injustice. As local ministers and community leaders joined forces with the union, the striking public works employees became the symbol of the Black community and their union became their champion. In turn, as long as the union supported the men, the Black community would support the union.[10] The sanitation workers were able to sustain and eventually win their fight due to the strong support of their cause from the Black community.

GENDERING IMAGES

The African American struggle for equality drew substantially upon the intelligence, strength, and power of working class women. African American women's in-depth involvement in the Black church helped to create coalitions within Black communities that were critical to the success of the movement.[11]

During the 1968 sanitation strike, working-class women were vital to the success of the strikers, along with ministers and other community leaders. "Women from the workers' neighborhoods, churches, and other networks became central to the group Concerned Citizens for the Sanitation Workers and their Families."[12] They participated in rallies, marches, and boycotts, collected money and prepared food for strikers and their families. A photograph taken on February 22 shows a group of wives of strikers preparing sandwiches for seven hundred men at city hall. Workers refused to leave the chamber until the council agreed to recognize the union and overrule Loeb's authority. During the sit-in, a local minister called his church for food. Wives of strikers cleared the table where the city's lawyers normally sat, as union supporters brought in a hundred loaves of bread, thirty-five to forty-five pounds of bologna and cheese, and condiments. While the wives prepared sandwiches, ministers preached, and workers sang; the sit-in became a celebration of resistance.[13] The photograph was taken directly behind the ladies from the front of the council chamber. The top of their heads are adorned with hats and their backs are all that can be seen of them, as the women have their heads down diligently working to feed everyone. Strikers fill the seats and stand along the wall in the background. The scale and proportion of the women in comparison to the men places emphasis on the substantial role that women played in creating a sense of unison during the strike.

Figure 40-4. Women prepare sandwiches for strikers at city hall. (February 22, 1968). *Special Collections*, University of Memphis.

Figure 40-5. Women participating in the boycott. (February 26, 1968). *Special Collections,* University of Memphis.

Two days after the formation of COME, daily marches and economic boycotts began. A photograph taken by James R. Reid on February 26 shows three Black females partici- pating in the boycott. The woman in the foreground holds a sign that reads, "DIGNITY AND DECENCY FOR OUR SANITATION WORKERS." Her sign reveals solidarity with the workers and recalls the long history of Black women's collaborative work with Black men in the struggle for racial equality. A trash-filled box from a garment factory in Chase City, Virginia—a town named for Salmon P. Chase, a famous anti-slavery Civil War politician— sits next to the woman in the foreground.

A second woman looks at the camera and smiles, while a tall male protestor stands a few feet behind her holding a sign that reads, "KEEP YOUR MONEY IN YOUR POCKET." Although perhaps not intentional, the light-skinned male figure, sign, and text in juxtapo- sition to the smiling woman highlight the particular difficulties that Black women faced in gaining agency over their own lives and bodies by linking aspects of the civil rights struggle with sexuality. The often silent and veiled struggles they had faced since slavery centered on issues that pertained to dignity and decency. Throughout the twentieth century, the lives of Black women continued to be doubly affected in terms of race and gender due to exploitative labor laws, racial inequality, and sexual stereotypes.

THE HIDDEN TRANSCRIPT: NEIGHBORHOOD RESISTANCE

Figure 40-6. North McNeil Street home of Lyles Caldwell. (February 29, 1968). *Special Collections,* University of Memphis.

The city employed strikebreakers to cross the picket line and operate a fleet of garbage trucks in an effort to clear the increasing amounts of trash. Scab workers threatened to defeat strikers' efforts to unionize. Animosity toward the strikebreakers within the Black community was strong. One worker's home was shot at because he crossed the picket line and another worker's wife left him.[14] Threats and intimidation toward strikebreakers were common.

Lyles Caldwell, of 1430 N. McNeil, reported a brick thrown through a window of his home to police. The brick had a brown paper note wrapped around it that read, "This is a warning. Stay away from work."[15] In the report, Caldwell explained why he continued to work instead of joining the strike. Caldwell's wife had died in 1963. He supported his own children ranging from eight to eighteen years old, and two grandchildren, on the three-hundred-dollar-a-month salary he was paid by the city. Caldwell claimed, "I didn't think it would be right if I went on strike and let my children starve. I just don't know how they would eat if I didn't have any money coming in."[16] His was the second house hit with a brick in two days.

Figure 40-7. Lyles Caldwell of 1430 North McNeil (February 29, 1968). *Special Collections, University of Memphis.*

In other ways, the Black community's opposition to strikebreakers was exhibited through more hidden forms of resistance. The news article "The Newest Memphis Mystery," published on February 24, 1968, reported that in some areas of Memphis garbage was piling up in the streets. "Charles Blackburn, sanitation director, declined to say whether they spilled trash or whether residents backing the union did it in protest of the strikebreakers. Of fifteen residents interviewed, five said their garbage was in their cans, and ten said they just 'didn't know' how trash landed in the street."[17]

Figure 40-8. Saul Brown, The Newest Memphis Mystery, (February 24, 1968). *Special Collections,*
University of Memphis.

A photograph taken by Saul Brown captured a view of Springdale Street between Chelsea
and Jackson Avenue, after it had been littered overnight. The expansiveness of the road is
exaggerated by the cropped framing of the photograph and further abstracted by the large
block of monochromatic grey color. A slight curvature of the sidewalk and the diminishing
scale of refuse offer the only real sense of perspective in three-fourths of the scene. The visual ambiguity illustrates the obscured statements given by neighborhood residents in the
newspaper report. Human figures and automobiles can be seen in the upper quadrant. The
distance between the photographer and unidentifiable residents emphasizes the unspoken
and unseen nature of their response to the strikebreakers.

In his book *Domination and the Arts of Resistance*, James C. Scott states that an act of defiance that is a declared refusal to comply with the normative order of domination can be
interpreted as a symbolic declaration of war. Public and open refusals to comply can be particularly dangerous forms of insubordination.[18] Rather than make a defiant public response
to the city's hiring of strikebreakers, residents of this north Memphis neighborhood swayed
between hidden and public defiance where ambiguity and anonymity were safer modes for
them to voice opposition.

The March 18 *Press-Scimitar* article "Roadblock of Garbage" summarized various
strike-related incidents, including one similar to the "Newest Memphis Mystery."
Hastings Street, between Baby Row and Looney in the Speedway Terrace neighborhood,

was barricaded with garbage in the middle of the night in an apparent strike-support demonstration.[19] A photograph by Tom Barber shows two Black youths walking across the littered street. Less ambiguous than the one taken by Brown, the image shows both sides of the street in sharp focus along with a food store at the end of the road. Two boys walk through the middle ground of the image, unconcerned, with their hands in their pockets and slight smiles on their faces. A well-dressed woman wearing a jacket, skirt, and stockings and carrying a purse walks away from the camera. Her dark suit contrasts against the white houses and accentuates her presence. The photograph suggests the degree to which residents continued to practice this clandestine response nearly one month after the first reported incident.

Figure 40-9. Tom Barber, Roadblock of Garbage, (March 18, 1968). *Special Collections*, University of Memphis.

A HISTORY OF INEQUALITIES AND WHITE-ON-BLACK VIOLENCE

Mrs. Rosilee Ward and her husband Mr. Ward, who was on strike with the sanitation department, were victims of a violent retaliation against their agency and resistance. Unidentified assailants threw a Molotov cocktail made from a quart beer bottle through their kitchen window, which set the room on fire. Mrs. Ward is pictured in her home at 977 Driver Street in the Washington Heights neighborhood of south Memphis, showing the damage to her kitchen. Smoke damage can be seen on the flowery white wallpaper, the four white dry goods canisters set in front of the damaged window, and the white wood-burning stove in the background. Mrs. Ward stands before the broken and patched window holding a large piece of burned housing material. She looks up high at the top of the window with a direct and forthright stare. Mrs. Ward's only adornment is a thin metal watch on her wrist.

Figure 40-10. James R. Reid, Mrs. Ward in her home, (March 18, 1968). *Special Collections*, University of Memphis.

The substandard infrastructure was typical for a sanitation worker's wage. The photograph recalls the conventions of social documentary photography, such as those taken as part of the Farm Security Administration's effort to improve the lifestyles of sharecroppers and migrant workers. However, this photograph was not taken as part of a government initiative to impact the lives of America's poor, but as a part of a local newspaper story documenting White violence against the family of a man involved in the sanitation strike. In a short summary of the incident, published without the image on March 18, Mr. Ward told investigators that his neighbors heard threats from the unidentified men yelling, "We'll get him."[20] Such cowardly acts of violence and retaliation were frequently used by White southerners to intimidate Black working-class communities making attempts at union organizing and other struggles for advancement in the fight for equality.

Title VII of the Civil Rights Act of 1964 prohibited race- and gender-based discrimination that had historically governed southern industry and labor.[21] However, in 1968, inequalities among White and Black workers still existed, and many southern politicians and businessmen remained anti-unionists.[22] Following the sanitation strikers' sit-in at city hall on February 22, city council members agreed to give the workers a raise. They believed that their offer would send the men back to work and end the strike. When City Council President Lewis Donelson presented the council's proposal to the mayor, Loeb refused and demanded that they beat the workers rather than settle with them.[23]

Henry Loeb took mayoral office for the second time in January 1968 after resigning in 1963 to take over his father's business. Loeb was well known for his obstructionist tactics and White supremacist views. He epitomized racist "plantation psychology" by stereotyping African Americans as low-grade social dependents of White men, similar to other paternalistic White Southerners such as E. H. "Boss" Crump who had aggressively controlled Memphis politics from the early twentieth century.[24]

> [Loeb] closely followed the business teachings of his father and his grandfather, who made their family fortune in the notoriously low-wage laundry business, where black women did the great bulk of miserable, hot, steamy work at poverty low wages. Becoming the head of Loeb's Laundry Cleaner Company in 1946, he had successfully resisted efforts by black workers to organize unions, tightly monitored his workforce, and kept his company's wages low in an industry that remained a bastion for highly exploited cheap black labor.[25]

A photograph taken by Jack E. Cantrell shows National Guard troops standing outside of a Loeb's Laundry and Cleaners located at Thomas Street and Firestone Avenue on the edge of the New Chicago neighborhood. It was taken during the four days between March 28 and April 2, 1968, when four thousand National Guardsmen were called in to Memphis following the March 28 riot. The bright glowing lights of the laundry cleaners behind the guardsmen silhouette their bodies as they march past the building armed with rifles with live ammunition and fixed bayonets.

Figure 40-11. Jack E. Cantrell, National Guardsmen Outside of Loeb's Laundry, (April 1968). *Special Collections*, University of Memphis.

The militarization of the city affected Blacks much more dramatically than it did Whites. Excessive force and intimidation used by guardsmen and policemen meant that for many African American citizens, death, injury, arrest, property damage, or at best missed days at work or school were inevitable.[26] The monolithic white block of Loeb's Laundry Cleaners in the center of an otherwise black photograph symbolizes Henry Loeb's obstructive and violent tactics against the Black working-class community as a mayor and his racist, exploitative reputation as a boss and business owner.

On March 28, Dr. King was expected to lead strikers and community supporters in a public demonstration through downtown. Dr. King had come to Memphis to march with the sanitation workers by the request of his friend and collaborator in the nonviolent movement, local minister Reverend James Lawson of Centenary Methodist Church. He planned to lead a nonviolent mass demonstration to enact on a smaller scale what he planned to do in the upcoming Poor People's Campaign. However, shortly after the march began, a riot broke out among demonstrators as police brutally beat, shot, maced, and tear-gassed hundreds of men, women, and children. The violence that began in the morning continued through the night.

One young man was shot and killed. Sixteen-year-old Larry Payne had left Mitchell Road School to march in the demonstration. Payne was seen amid the looting that ensued after the march erupted into chaos. He was seen again later that day at the apartment of his mother, in Fowler Homes, a low-income project just ten blocks south of Beale Street.[27] When policeman Leslie Dean Jones chased a young man carrying a television into the basement of Fowler Homes and demanded that the young man come out, Payne was the only person to emerge. The officer immediately shot Larry Payne at close range with his twelve-gauge shotgun. Jones asserted that Payne had brandished a large butcher knife, but multiple eyewitnesses stated that Payne was unarmed and pleaded for his life with his hands in the air before the officer put the shotgun barrel to his stomach. Police produced a rusty butcher knife that they claimed belonged to the young boy, and Jones was cleared of any criminal charges. According to a *Tri-State Defender* article, Payne's mother, Lizzie, hysterically ran to reach her son after hearing the gunshot and was pushed back by a policeman who yelled at her, "If you don't get back, nigger, I'll kill you."[28]

The family held a public viewing of Payne's open casket at Clayborn Temple on the first two days in April, at the request of local ministers in COME. Thousands of strikers and supporters passed by Payne's casket. During the April 2 memorial service, some five hundred mourners expressed grief and anger and some fainted.[29] Photographer Ken Ross documented the funeral. The downward camera angle from a second-story balcony allows the viewer to look over the subjects. The youthful body of Larry Payne rests in his coffin. A flood of mourners who have come to pay respect surrounds him. The killing was seen by the African American community as an "act of vengeance—an execution committed by one more violent white police officer and covered up by his superiors."[30] Payne's coffin is flanked by two lamps that illuminate his tranquil face and the white fabric lining that encircles his head. He is invested with a sense of innocence in a scene of deep lamentation. His mother is shown with her head thrown back in anguish and her body embraced by the people around her. The mass created by the Black community and church members demonstrates the unifying bond that was felt in the aftermath of such a tragic and unjustifiable show of force by White authority.

ARROW POINTS TO HYSTERICAL MRS PAYNE
youth's mother

Figure 40-12. Ken Ross, Funeral for Larry Payne, (April 2, 1968). *Special Collections*, University of Memphis.

Immediately following Payne's funeral, sanitation workers led a peaceful march through downtown to demonstrate their dedication to nonviolence and honor his death.[31] The death of Larry Payne at the hands of Memphis police officers has never been resolved. When the family of Larry Payne unsuccessfully sued for civil damages in 1971, police chief Henry Lux admitted that Payne's fingerprints had not been found on the knife. He also confessed that police had thrown the knife, shotgun pellets, and Payne's clothing into the Mississippi River and that no evidence of the case remained.

National and local media outlets throughout the modern Civil Rights Movement commonly used images of White-on-Black violence. Martin A. Berger argues in *Seeing Through Race* that "the determined efforts of the white press to frame the civil rights movement as nonthreatening had the collateral result of casting blacks in roles of limited power and consequently limited the extent of social and legislative reform."[32] Despite several written accounts of demonstrators physically fighting back against and shooting at police during sanitation strike events, few if any photographs actually documented these acts of resistance. However, a number of images documented Black citizens employing alternative means of exhibiting agency and power over White authority. A photograph taken by Ken Ross in March recorded strikers walking down a sidewalk with "I AM A MAN" signs hanging around their necks. An armored personnel carrier follows them along the road.

Figure 40-13. Ken Ross, Strikers and military, (March 1968). *Special Collections*, University of Memphis.

Figure 40-14. Marshals at a rally, (April 1968). *Special Collections*, University of Memphis.

Several armed National Guardsmen observe the workers from the top of the carrier. A striker in the foreground looks to the side at the road and keeps his body straight as he continues to walk forward. The excessive use of military force against the strikers as a means to coerce and intimidate was useless in stopping the men from carrying out their actions.

An image that was taken at a downtown strike-related event in April documented youthful strike supporters forming a protective barrier with their outstretched bodies holding hands. Their white armbands designated them as marshals for the event as they testified to their commitment to peaceable resistance in a symbolic role reversal of authority. Over one dozen heavily outfitted Army soldiers stand behind them; one soldier even crosses his arms. On this day, the youthful marshals were the agents of protection for the Black community while the soldiers were observers.

An up-close photograph documented a policeman and a marshal standing side by side in another example of role reversal. The policeman looks at the camera while gripping his shotgun. Although he is in the traditional position of dominance, his furrowed brow and piercing stare translate fear to the viewer. The marshal stands tall with his hands on his hips as he looks away from the camera. The talisman worn around his neck designates him as a Black Power militant, while the armband symbolizes his authority to mobilize people for this event.

Figure 40-15. Marshal and Policeman (April 1968). *Special Collections*, University of Memphis.

Photographs that documented this idea of nonviolent confrontation in action contain alternative narratives to the ones that Berger argues dominated White media. The images visually maximize the bravery exhibited by strikers and strike supporters and the genuine threat that they posed to dominating systems of authority.

DEPICTING BLACK YOUTH IN THE MOVEMENT

Figure 40-16. James R. Reid, Blue-Eye Soul Brother, (February 26, 1968). *Special Collections*, University of Memphis.

A photograph of protesters taken by staff photographer James R. Reid on February 26, 1968, presented a group of young Black men holding up a protest sign that reads, "Sign Contract Blue-Eye Soul Brother." The image offers a response that acts to alleviate fears and the seriousness of their struggle. James C. Scott argues,

> if the anonymity of the messenger is often what makes it possible for the otherwise vulnerable to speak aggressively to power, one might imagine that without anonymity the performance of subordinates would revert to one of compliant deference. The alternative to complete deference, however, is to disguise the message just enough to skirt around retaliation.[33]

Among subordinate groups, euphemisms take on a double meaning when used publically, and are meant to protect and disguise. In this photograph a group of youthful workers make their public statement of rebellion palatable to the viewer. They stand in front of the first Easy Way grocery store, located at 80 North Main Street. Its sign hangs directly above their handwritten one, and mimics the indirect, subversive approach taken by these particular protestors. The request to have their union recognized by the city is offered with an extended gesture of brotherhood. Their working-class struggle crosses racial dividing lines, but this moment is portrayed as a Manichean struggle epitomized by the stark contrast of black and white color in the photograph.[34] Within practices of resistance, issues of dignity and justice become more important than material exploitation.

> But at the level of systemic social doctrine, subordinate groups confront elaborate ideologies that justify inequality, bondage, monarchy, caste, and so on. Resistance to ideological domination requires a counter-ideology—a negation—that will effectively provide a general normative form to the host of resistant practices invented in self-defense by any subordinate group.[35]

These young men provide a counteroffer to Henry Loeb in their message—one of brotherhood—for the purpose of obtaining dignity and justice. One protester's hand even reaches up and points to the word "brother." The young men contrast with the older gentleman whose sign reads, "WE ARE TOGETHER ONCE AND FOR ALL." While the younger men hold a more engaging sign and look directly at the camera, the older gentleman looks toward the sky, with light reflecting from his glasses. In contrast, one of the young men points to the sign and is almost ready to jump in the air. The smiles on the men's faces express an upbeat, resilient attitude that is expressive of the way some young Black males chose to resist during the rise of Black Power culture. William Van Deburg in *Black Camelot* argues that their laughter in the face of adversity could sometimes be seen as an act of courage, not of buffoonery.[36]

The Invaders were a militant Black Power group that worked within impoverished Black communities. Formed in 1967 by Charles Cabbage, Coby Smith, and John Burl Smith, the Invaders was an extension of the Black Organizing Project (BOP), a grassroots organization in Memphis designed to document poverty and organize "young black men living in housing projects and slums, playing in pool halls and hanging out on street corners, students in college and high school, inmates in jail and prisons."[37]

Reverend James Lawson collaborated with several members of the Invaders prior to the formation of BOP and the 1968 strike. Lawson, who was well known for his civil rights activism, headed Memphis Area Project-South (MAP-South), an antipoverty program that was incorporated in 1965. Lawson teamed up with John B. Smith, Charles Cabbage, Coby Smith, and others to address unemployment, job training, and supplemental food distribution;

organize summer youth programs; and coordinate efforts of block clubs, public housing resident associations, and other groups. MAP-South's growing membership reflected its neighborhood roots and the energizing impact of the freedom movement.[38] At a general meeting in 1967, it was reported that membership exceeded eight hundred.

In a defamatory *Press-Scimitar* report from September 1967, Kay Pittman Black accused the Invaders of spreading their Black Power ideologies to the poor communities through their work with MAP-South. Federal investigations and surveillance of the Invaders had called attention to John B. Smith, Coby Smith, and Cabbage's involvement with the federally funded antipoverty program. At the time, John B. Smith worked full-time for the Defense Depot and part-time for MAP-South, which were both considered federal jobs, though only 10 percent of the budget of MAP-South was federally supplied.[39] While working for the program, Smith said his job was to help people organize so they were better able to help themselves economically, socially, and politically. He organized a boys' club in south Memphis for seventy youths aged thirteen to twenty-two and focused his work on the youth, stating, "Nobody has really been able to communicate with them before. I have a different attitude than most social workers."[40] After Smith and Cabbage were both dismissed from their positions following the investigation, they formed the BOP to do work similar to MAP-South.

Members of the Invaders organization can be seen marching with Rev. Lawson during the sanitation strike in a photograph taken in March by William Leaptrott. Invaders were identifiable by the large talismans worn on long cords around their necks. Often the talismans were small sculptures representing shrunken heads or African-styled masks.[41] John B. Smith and Charles Cabbage had both fought in Vietnam. Their participation and training in the war directly influenced their organizing capabilities. In some respects, they had traded their military dog tags for talismans. Immediately following their return home from war, an incident occurred that sparked their decision to organize as the Invaders. Following the war, the two men had felt a stronger sense of their American citizenship, but shortly after returning, they realized that democracy still did not apply to them. One evening, a White man stole Smith's gas cap at a fueling station. Smith called for the police to intervene, but when they arrived, the policemen only spoke to the White man. Smith and Cabbage, who were together at the time, were both arrested. In the photograph, John B. Smith stands behind Rev. Lawson's right shoulder. The sign Rev. Lawson carries reads, "King Henry We Will Not Turn Back."

Figure 40-17. William Leaptrott, Black Power and Civil Rights leaders march together, (March 1968). *Special Collections*, University of Memphis.

Figure 40-18. Tom Barber, John B. Smith and Rev. Bell at City Hall, (March 6, 1968). *Special Collections*, University of Memphis.

A photograph taken by Tom Barber on March 6 captured John B. Smith sitting in the front row at city hall. Smith wears dark sunglasses and a long necklace with a talisman pendant and holds a book. Reverend Ezekiel Bell is pictured with his arm around him. At the time, Bell was the city's only Presbyterian ministers at Parkway Gardens Presbyterian Church; he was also one of the strongest and most militant advocates for the sanitation workers.[42] Another minister sits just a few seats down from them while Reverend Ralph Abernathy earnestly addresses the crowd. Both photographs expose the intersections and collaborations that formed between civil rights and Black Power activists in Memphis for the purpose of achieving their corresponding goals.

Strike supporters, including Reverend Lawson, visited high schools across the city, such as Lester, Northside, Douglass, South Side, and Booker T. Washington, to encourage students to leave and join the March 28 march.[43] An incident occurred at Hamilton High School when a group of boisterous students gathered in front of the school at 1478 Wilson Street in south Memphis during the morning to plan their walk to Clayborn Temple. A small group of students threw bricks at cars with White drivers when a garbage truck operated by strikebreakers and accompanied by a police car passed by. Students hurled stones, bricks, and bottles at the truck.[44] The incident quickly escalated when police arrived on the scene brandishing their batons in an attempt to stop the students from leaving school. A surveillance helicopter arrived on the scene at Hamilton High along with local news outlets. James R. Reid, working for the *Memphis Press-Scimitar*, documented the event through a series of black and white photographs.

Figure 40-19. James R. Reid, Hamilton High School, (March 28, 1968). *Special Collections*, University of Memphis.

Figure 40-20. James R. Reid, Hamilton High School, (March 28, 1968). *Special Collections,* University of Memphis.

Figure 40-21. James R. Reid, Hamilton High School, (March 28, 1968). *Special Collections,* University of Memphis.

Figure 40-22. James R. Reid, *Injured Student at Hamilton High School*, (March 28, 1968). *Special Collections*, University of Memphis.

One young girl was hit in the head by an officer and had to be taken by ambulance to a local hospital to receive multiple stitches for her wound. A rumor quickly spread to the downtown march that a girl had been killed at Hamilton High School. The rumor inflamed tensions in the downtown crowd, especially among student demonstrators. James C. Scott notes that the process of embellishment and exaggeration of rumors is not random, but that as word travels it is altered in a way that reflects the hopes, fears, and wishes of those who hear it and retell it. Scott writes of personal release, satisfaction, pride, and elation as undeniable emotions that oppressed people feel during their first open declaration of resistance. The risk of mortal punishment and retaliation blends fear into the emotional mixture.[45] Police continued to arrive, donning helmets and gas masks, and brandishing their clubs and fists at students. Students moved back and forth to avoid the violence, while some returned rocks for blows. Reid captured the image of a young girl frozen in the act of throwing a rock toward the photographer.

Figure 40-23. James R. Reid, Hamilton High School, (March 28, 1968). *Special Collections,* University of Memphis.

In an openly defiant act, the girl smiles with excitement while students behind her turn in all directions. As dozens of parents came to aid their children and take them away, police tried to form a barrier between them, forcing parents to congregate across the street from Hamilton High School. The distance of the staff photographer from the parents and students visually reinforces the distance that existed between the police as representative arms of White authority and the Black community.

The students' defiant acts of insubordination could not be directly blamed on local militants, though the Invaders were popular among poor Black youths and students whose beliefs aligned with the Black Power principle of self-determination. However, their popularity was hardly positive within the greater Black middle class community. Andrew Young, executive vice president of the Southern Christian Leadership Conference (SCLC), publically blamed the Invaders for instigating the March 28 riot because of their outspoken objection to the march and their public militant views.[46] Leaders of the group insisted that they had protested the march "as an effort to avoid being targeted and personally blamed" for what they knew would become an uncontrollable situation. Invaders had been voicing their concerns to local ministers about the plan to hold a nonviolent march in Memphis.[47] They argued that too many people in the Black community, especially Black youth, were angry and unprepared for a nonviolent strategy.

On April 4, 1968, Charles Cabbage, along with other Invaders, met with Dr. King in his hotel room at the Lorraine Motel to discuss the racial tension and anger within Memphis's poor Black communities. It can be argued that the Invaders and BOP lived in and organized in certain communities and understood their experiences. In discussion of Dr. King's next attempt to march, Cabbage agreed to have the Invaders serve as peacekeeping marshals and spread word to their approximately two thousand members that the march was to remain orderly and nonviolent. "According to Cabbage, Southern Christian Leadership Conference (SCLC) staff wrote the Invaders a check for ten thousand dollars, with the promise of more to come, in exchange for guaranteeing a peaceful march."[48] Moments after the Invaders left the Lorraine Motel, Dr. King was shot while standing on the balcony of his room. As promised, on April 8 the Invaders served as marshals at a rally and march for Dr. King, but this time it was led by his widow Coretta Scott King. On that day, the march remained peaceful and well organized. The Invaders would accept nonviolence as a tactic once more, when they served as marshals and security for the Poor People's Campaign. Following the assassination of Dr. King, several leaders of the group moved or went underground, and the Invaders entered its second phase, this time led by Lance "Sweet Willie Wine" Watson.[49]

CONCLUSION

Some of the most iconic images of the Civil Rights Movement come from the 1963 Birmingham campaign, which was organized by Dr. King and the SCLC to raise awareness of Birmingham's discrimination laws. Images of police dogs attacking demonstrators while others helplessly watch, of demonstrators bracing against and falling from the forceful blasts of water from fire hoses aimed by policemen and others suffering heavy blows to the body by policemen wielding their nightsticks, were widely televised and published by news outlets around the world. The images exposed the abject violence and brutality that dominant forces used to resist civil rights with almost total impunity. The violent images that streamed out of Birmingham were instrumental in creating sympathy for African Americans and mobilizing support for the Civil Rights Act of 1964 in legislation.[50] One the greatest advocates of photography during the Civil Rights Movement was its own iconic leader, Dr. Martin Luther King Jr.

In his 1964 book on the Birmingham struggle, *Why We Can't Wait*, Dr. King declared, "The brutality with which officials would have quelled the black individual became impotent when it could not be pursued with stealth and remain unobserved. It was caught—as a fugitive from a penitentiary is often caught—in gigantic circling spotlights. It was imprisoned in a luminous glare revealing the naked truth to the whole world."[51] Dr. King emphasized to his supporters the power that photography held in capturing the brutality enacted upon Blacks and Whites in the struggle for civil rights. He also stressed photography's potential to display that brutality to the rest of the world through wide-reaching news outlets. Dr. King's testament to the importance of photography in African American life, as a truth-revealing medium, places him within a pantheon of Black freedom fighters that encouraged the use of photography in the struggle. Since the nineteenth century, African American leadership had understood the power of self-representation to counter negative stereotypes and advocate for legislative changes. They also understood the utility of documenting racial violence in the struggle for social, political, and economic advancement. Frederick Douglass, Ida B. Wells, W. E. B. Du Bois, Sojourner Truth, Booker T. Washington, and Harriet Jacobs all implemented photography in their struggles. They are some of history's earliest visual theorists and practitioners of photography, and they were instrumental in creating a new archive of visual culture.

Dr. King promoted a continuation of the building of this archive, to which *The Memphis Press-Scimitar* and its staff photographers contributed. The archive holds pieces to a puzzle of an underwritten and often-skewed history of the Black civil rights experience in American visual culture. By reinvestigating and reinterpreting these photographs, we gain greater insight into the past as well as the ability to counter the dominant historical narratives of oppressed communities and their responses.

Questions for Discussion and Journaling

1. Hamden argues, "Photographs have the power to expose and create alternative narratives that have the potential to subvert lacunae with dominant histories. However, photographs should not be used to present fixed monolithic truths." How does Hamden use images to counter dominant narratives of this time period in Memphis? Why might other narratives have been created in the wake of King's assassination? Why is it important to counter these oversimplified narratives?

2. Hamden's conclusion references Dr. Martin Luther King Jr. and even cites something he wrote. Why did she make this rhetorical decision? How does using Dr. King develop her ethos? As you ponder these questions, consider this journal's publisher, the Association for the Study of African American Life and History.

3. Choose one of the photos from Hamden's article and write a brief rhetorical analysis of that photo. While she analyzes each photograph, your own reading of that photograph may differ. Choose a photo that you see or read differently than Hamden did. What did Hamden miss in the photo? Why do you see it differently than she did? How does this support her point that "photographs should not be used to present fixed monolithic truths"?

ENDNOTES

40

1.   Joan Turner Beifuss, *At the River I Stand* (Memphis: St. Lukas Press, 1990), 131.

2.   For the purpose of this study, I reviewed over five hundred photographs belonging to the Mississippi Valley Collection in the Ned R. McWherther Library at the University of Memphis. I compiled a set of photographs to examine related to the sanitation strike. However, I suggest alternative ways of interpreting the images by examining them for unexplored issues concerning race, gender, labor, and class, and how they intersect with aspects of activism, agency, and ideology.

3.   Maurice O. Wallace and Shawn Michelle Smith, *Pictures and Progress: Early Photography and the Making of African American Identity* (Durham: Duke University Press, 2012), 2.

4.   Lawrence W. Levine, *Black Culture and Black Consciousness: Afro-American Folk Thought From Slavery to Freedom* (Oxford: Oxford University Press, 1977), 5.

5.   Elizabeth Abel, *Signs of the Times: The Visual Politics of Jim Crow* (Berkeley: University of California Press, 2010), 65–66.

6.   Michael Honey, *Going Down Jericho Road: The Memphis Strike, Martin Luther King's Last Campaign* (New York: W. W. Norton, 2007), 99.

7.   David Appleby, Allison Graham, and Steven Ross, directors, *At the River I Stand* (Memphis: California Newsreel, 1993), DVD, 56 min.

8.   Ibid.

9.   Booker T. Jones, interview by Robert Gordon, *Respect Yourself: Stax Records and the Soul Explosion* (New York: Bloomsbury, 2013), 179.

10. Beifuss, *At the River*, 128–29.

11. Civil rights struggles had existed across the United States since slavery, and throughout that time working-class women were leaders in the fight. In Memphis following the Civil War, the majority of the members and leaders of Black women's benevolent societies and social welfare organizations were employed as washerwomen, ironers, and domestic servants. See Bettye Collier-Thomas, *Jesus, Jobs, and Justice: African American Women and Religion* (New York: Alfred A. Knopf, 2010), 86.

12. Lorie B. Green, *Battling the Plantation Mentality: Memphis and the Black Freedom Struggle* (Chapel Hill: University of North Carolina Press, 2007), 281.

13. Honey, *Going Down Jericho Road*, 193–94.

14. Ibid., 105.

15. "Non-striker Tells Police About Threats, Intimidation," *Memphis Press-Scimitar*, February 29, 1968.

16. Ibid.

17. "The Newest Memphis Mystery," *Memphis Press-Scimitar*, February 24, 1968.

18. James C. Scott, *Domination and the Arts of Resistance: Hidden Transcripts* (New Haven: Yale University Press, 1990), 203–5.

19. "Roadblock of Garbage," *Memphis Press-Scimitar*, March 18, 1968.

20. Ibid.

21. Michelle Brattain, *The Politics of Whiteness: Race, Workers, and Culture in the Modern South* (Athens: University of Georgia Press, 2001), 232.

22. Due to the slave economy and the sharecropping economy afterwards, the South was slow in industrial development, which kept trade unionism at bay. At the end of the nineteenth century, southern oligarchs prepared themselves as a class to resist the workers' movement as they began to rebuild the southern economy with industry. White supremacy became a tool used by the southern ruling class to repress workers. Black workers were directly confronted with violence and coercion, while an artificial class separation was created to conceal race and to build unity among White workers by creating race-based job positions and giving White workers certain minuscule privileges.

23. Honey, *Going Down Jericho Road*, 150.

24. Appleby, Graham, and Ross, *At the River*.

25. Honey, *Going Down Jericho Road*, 35.

26. Ibid., 386.

27. Ibid., 359.

28. Ibid., 360.

29. Ibid., 394.

30. Ibid., 359–60.

31. Response to continued police brutality was not always civil. Four days of violence and destruction across the city followed after the death of seventeen-year-old Elton Hayes in 1971. Hayes had been savagely beaten by eight police officers who attempted to cover up the murder. Days of rioting prompted city officials to lead a full investigation and indict all eight officers. However, the trial ended with all eight officers acquitted. See Robert Gordon, *Respect Yourself: Stax Records and the Soul Explosion* (New York: Bloomsbury, 2013), 264–65.

32. Martin A. Berger, *Seeing Through Race: A Reinterpretation of Civil Rights Photography* (Berkeley: University of California Press, 2011), 7.

33. Scott, *Domination and the Arts*, 152.

34. Paul Gilroy, *The Black Atlantic: Modernity and Double Consciousness* (Cambridge: Harvard University Press, 1993), 1.

35. Scott, *Domination and the Arts*, 118.

36. William L. Van Deburg, *Black Camelot: African-American Culture Heroes in Their Times, 1960–1980* (Chicago: University of Chicago Press, 1997), 27.

37. Honey, *Going Down Jericho Road*, 230.

38. Green, *Battling the Plantation Mentality*, 270.

39. Kay Pittman Black, "MAP-South Men Defend Controversial Anti-Poverty Work," *Memphis Press- Scimitar*, September 11, 1967.

40. Ibid.

41. Minister Suhkara A. Yahweh, interview by the author, Memphis, TN, October 7, 2013.

42. Honey, *Going Down Jericho Road*, 115.

43. Ibid., 336.

44. Ibid.

45. Scott, *Domination and the Arts*, 145, 208–9.

46. Kay Pittman Black, "'Bold Concept' for Black Militants Backfires," *Memphis Press-Scimitar*, August 28, 1969.

47. Shirletta Jeanette Kinchen, "*We Want What People Generally Refer to as Black Power*; Youth and Student Activism and the Impact of the Black Power Movement in Memphis, Tennessee, 1965–1975" (PhD diss., University of Memphis, 2011), 234.

48. Ibid., 89.

49. Yahweh, interview by the author.

50. Berger, *Seeing Through Race*, 12.

51. Martin Luther King Jr., *Why We Can't Wait* (New York: Signet Classic, 2000), 25.

BIBLIOGRAPHY

Archival Sources

Mississippi Valley Collection, Ned R. McWherther Library, University of Memphis. Memphis Press-Scimitar Clippings File.

Oral History Interviews

Minister Suhkara A. Yahweh, in discussion with the author, October 7, 2013.

40

Periodicals

Memphis Press-Scimitar (September 11, 1967–August 28, 1969)

Books

Abel, Elizabeth. *Signs of the Times: The Visual Politics of Jim Crow.* Berkeley: University of California Press, 2010.

Beifuss, Joan Turner. *At the River I Stand.* Memphis: St. Lukas Press, 1990.

Berger, Martin A. *Seeing Through Race: A Reinterpretation of Civil Rights Photography.* Berkeley: University of California Press, 2011.

Brattain, Michelle. *The Politics of Whiteness: Race, Workers, and Culture in the Modern South.* Athens: University of Georgia Press, 2001.

Collier-Thomas, Bettye. *Jesus, Jobs, and Justice: African American Women and Religion.* New York: Alfred A. Knopf, 2010.

Du Bois, W. E. B. *The Souls of Black Folk.* New York: Barnes & Noble Classics, 2003.

Gilroy, Paul. *The Black Atlantic: Modernity and Double Consciousness.* Cambridge: Harvard University Press, 1993.

Gordon, Robert. *Respect Yourself: Stax Records and the Soul Explosion.* New York: Bloomsbury, 2013.

Green, Lorie B. *Battling the Plantation Mentality: Memphis and the Black Freedom Struggle.* Chapel Hill: University of North Carolina Press, 2007.

Honey, Michael. *Going Down Jericho Road: The Memphis Strike, Martin Luther King's Last Campaign.* New York: W. W. Norton, 2007.

Kelley, Robin D. G. *Freedom Dreams: The Black Radical Imagination.* Boston: Beacon Press, 2002.

_____.*Race Rebels: Culture, Politics, and the Black Working Class.* New York: Free Press, 1994.

King, Martin Luther, Jr. *Why We Can't Wait.* New York: Signet Classic, 2000.

Levine, Lawrence W. *Black Culture and Black Consciousness: Afro-American Folk Thought From Slavery to Freedom.* Oxford: Oxford University Press, 1977.

McGuire, Danielle L. *At the Dark End of the Street: Black Women, Rape, and Resistance—A New History of the Civil Rights Movement from Rosa Parks to the Rise of Black Power.* New York: Alfred A. Knopf, 2010.

Raiford, Leigh. *Imprisoned in a Luminous Glare: Photography and the African American Freedom Struggle.* Chapel Hill: University of North Carolina Press, 2011.

Scott, James C. *Domination and the Arts of Resistance: Hidden Transcripts.* New Haven: Yale University Press, 1990.

Stott, William. *Documentary Expression and Thirties America.* New York: Oxford University Press, 1973.

Swindall, Lindsey R. *Paul Robeson: A Life of Activism and Art.* United Kingdom: Rowman & Littlefield, 2013.

Van Deburg, William L., *Black Camelot: African-American Culture Heroes in Their Times, 1960–1980.* Chicago: University of Chicago Press, 1997.

Wallace, Maurice O., and Shawn Michelle Smith. *Pictures and Progress: Early Photography and the Making of African American Identity.* Durham: Duke University Press, 2012.

Documentary Film

Appleby, David, Allison Graham, and Steven Ross, directors. *At the River I Stand.* Memphis: California Newsreel, 1993. DVD, 56 min.

40

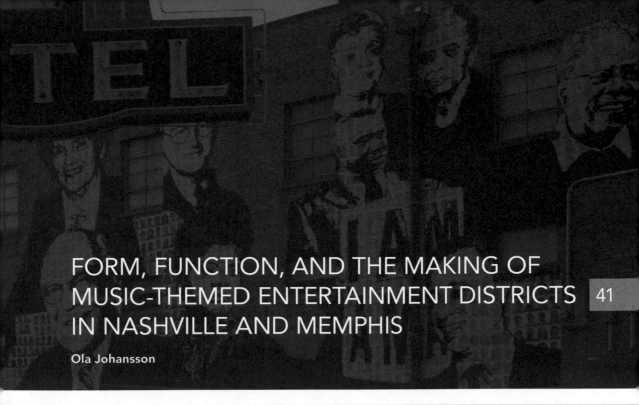

FORM, FUNCTION, AND THE MAKING OF MUSIC-THEMED ENTERTAINMENT DISTRICTS IN NASHVILLE AND MEMPHIS

Ola Johansson

Beale Street is perhaps Memphis' most famous tourism destination. In 2013 it was voted the most famous street in America in a *USA Today* reader poll. Ola Johansson, in her article originally published in the journal *Material Culture*, examines how Beale Street in Memphis and Broadway in Nashville have taken music culture and made it "material" by creating entertainment districts in which music is consumed as a commodity. Johansson examines the way in which these districts have formed and are managed to benefit both cities, determining that there are far more similarities than the differences Tennesseans often focus on. Her argument suggests that the functional businesses and their consumers determine the form of the districts in spite of the attempts to plan such entertainment zones. As you read this article, note the tone of "Form, Function, and the Making of Music-themed Entertainment Districts in Nashville and Memphis."

ABSTRACT

Nashville and Memphis have proceeded along similar paths in creating downtown entertainment districts. During this process, the historic built environment in both places has been transformed (and partly preserved) and themed around its musical heritage. Country music and blues, which are fundamentally non-material cultures, have "materialized" in the urban landscape. This article analyzes the processes by which the districts developed, and their emerging form and function. Land use in Memphis' Beale Street is tightly controlled, as the city owns all properties and uses a private real estate company to manage the district. A more complex, organic process occurred in Nashville's Second Avenue/lower Broadway, where the decisions of multiple actors created an entertainment district. The differences in the built environment

"Form, Function, and the Making of Music-themed Entertainment Districts in Nashville and Memphis" by Ola Johansson. Article and figures were first published in *Material Culture* (2010), Volume 42, Issue 1, pp. 47–69. Reprinted by the permission of Pioneer America Society/APAL and the author.

mean that the districts' form differs, yet they also exhibit strong similarities. The function of the two districts, as measured by the mix of commercial establishments, shows remarkable resemblance despite the fundamental differences in how they were created.

INTRODUCTION

The American downtown has experienced numerous periods of decline and revitalization. Its functionality has also been transformed periodically as society's economy and culture change. Most recently, cities plan for an amenity-rich downtown with an emphasis on public spaces, new forms of retail activities, residential developments, culture, sports, and other entertainment projects. This article will focus on the development of downtown entertainment districts. I have chosen two case studies—downtown Nashville and Memphis—to show how different urban processes underlie the creation of entertainment districts. Both districts are re-created entertainment districts of the past, although the current reincarnations are socially and economically very different places compared to their predecessors.

Connecting to material culture tradition, this paper investigates aspects of the built historic environment. The urban past exists all around us and the city is, therefore, open to analysis as an artifact, a significant aspect of material culture. However, such an analysis should not only include the study of physical structures, but also spaces in the city (Schlereth 1990). The perspective in this paper is contemporary as it emphasizes how historic structures and spaces are used today and how their current form and function have emerged over time. The central theme of both entertainment districts is music—blues in Memphis and country music in Nashville—which as an auditory form of culture does not have an immediate material imprint on the landscape; however, the creation of these two entertainment districts represents a materialization and an embodiment of two distinctly American cultures.

The paper is organized as follows: first, relevant aspects of the history of downtowns are presented, including changing economic conditions and their effects on the built heritage. This is followed by a discussion about the emerging trend of entertainment districts as a component of the contemporary downtown. The two case studies and their historic and architectural characteristics are subsequently discussed. Then, the core sections of the paper analyze (1) the development process and the emerging spatial form of the two entertainment districts, and (2) the functionality of the districts by categorizing existing commercial establishments. The goal is to understand how local conditions—economic, political, social, ethnic—influence the material urban landscape of entertainment districts. The paper concludes with a comparative analysis discussing how differences and similarities between two case studies are evident.

THE HISTORIC BACKGROUND TO DOWNTOWN ENTERTAINMENT DISTRICTS

Downtown policy today is often framed around the idea of revitalization, which implies a need to capture something that has been lost; city centers are in a state of decline and the answer to the problem lies in the past and how downtowns used to function. The late urban geographer Larry Ford (2003) argues that there was no golden age for the American downtown, no specific time or place which embodied everything that was good about traditional urbanism; however, the first two decades of the 20th century is probably as good of a model as any. At that point, the city had overcome some of the worst aspects of the early industrial era. The City Beautiful movement had created impressive buildings and public spaces (Wilson 1994). The electric trolley enabled some suburbanization, but the transportation system reinforced rather than detracted from the dominance of the center (Jackson 1987). Downtown was the undisputed focal point of every city and included multiple activities—business, retail, housing, and so on—that are the foundation for a lively urban environment. It was a city of lights, entertainment, and grand movie palaces. Arcades were built for strolling and shopping where people could see and be seen. This type of public space is rarely found today, or at least that is what we think when we imagine better days and what downtowns ought to be, including their role as an entertainment center. This was before post-World War II automobile-led suburbanization had a profound impact on urban morphology and the fate of downtowns. The policy response to the subsequent center city decline was urban renewal (McDonald 2008). Although urban renewal achieved some of its goals—retaining offices and corporate headquarters downtown—it did so at the expense of all other urban functions that are desirable to have in the center. Urban renewal created "dead" 9–5 downtowns, which reached a low point circa the 1970s. Today, urban renewal is criticized as a flawed approach to city building that probably did more harm than good.

The current planning paradigm aims instead to capitalize on the unique qualities of historic urban spaces. Cities have undergone a post-industrial transformation that fundamentally altered the function of downtowns and some of their surrounding areas. A growth in the advanced service sector has drawn a new demographic, a professional workforce with new preferences and demands on its living environment. They are alternately called yuppies, gentrifiers (Ley 1996), bohemians (Lloyd 2005), or the creative class (Florida 2002), and are preoccupied with nightlife activities and amenities that some central city locations provide.

From a regulatory perspective, the use of historic structures and spaces necessitates some form of preservationist framework. The federal establishment of the National Register of Historic Places in 1966 encouraged the designation of local historic districts (Hamer 1998). The objective of historic districts (and downtown entertainment districts are often considered historic districts) is to protect significant structures and their property values, while also encouraging desirable development (Ligibel, Tyler, and Tyler 2009). The value of a district as a whole commonly exceeds the value of individual structures because of the importance of spaces that are created through the scale of buildings and their internal arrangement, streetscapes, the combination of land uses, and the overall functionality of the place. In practice, a historic district designation is an additional zoning layer that protects against "nonconforming intrusions," although the restrictiveness of such regulations varies from place to place. New buildings are usually allowed, but they should be compatible with their historic surroundings, a.k.a. a "contextualist" approach (Ligibel, Tyler, and Tyler 2009). A certain amount of new construction and adaptive reuse of older structures may even be needed for downtowns to stay useful and relevant. In a best case scenario, contemporary functionality of historic buildings and districts can coexist with preservation, although conflicts between preservation and growth interests are as frequent as cooperation (Collins, Waters, and Dotson 1991).

WHAT IS AN URBAN ENTERTAINMENT DISTRICT?

The downtown revitalization strategy under consideration here is entertainment. The post-industrial city is increasingly a site for consumption, and in this context cities want to be perceived as fun places to live and visit. Terry Nichols Clark (2004) has conceptualized the city as an "entertainment machine." Here, entertainment consists of activities such as restaurants, sports, shopping, tourism and other facets of a visitors' economy (hotels, conventions, and so on), and even cultural attractions. The implication is that these activities are the central driving forces behind urban vitality. In the post-industrial economy quality of life considerations are paramount. Not only are cities with a perceived high quality of life successful, so also are intra-urban spaces that are aesthetically favored. In other words, the eclectic milieu of central cities, rather than suburban conformity, has the capacity to generate entertainment activities.

Ironically, entertainment spaces, when successful, often develop standardized elements, a physical manifestation of the "McDonaldization" of society (Hannigan 1998) with only moderately different configurations from place to place. This familiarity is considered important to attract some consumers, bearing in mind the misgivings suburbanites might have about spending time downtown.

Not surprisingly, such developments have both cheerleaders and critics. A common cultural critique is that these themed urban environments have encroached on the public realm rather than existing in a completely separate sphere (e.g., Disneyland) (Sorkin 1992). The idea behind theming is to create a story, not just an assemblage of buildings, where the value lies in the theme. The quintessential themed destination is Las Vegas, where large developments have been constructed around a particular non-local theme, such as the urbanity of New York City (Gottdiener 2001). But even in the real New York, themed destinations have been developed using some historic feature, such as South Street Seaport, or the entertainment-oriented redevelopment of Times Square (Sagalyn 2001). The theming of entertainment districts based on a specific music genre, as in the two case studies under consideration in this paper, is another approach.

On the other hand, for practitioners of urban redevelopment, such as public officials and real estate interests, entertainment districts are relatively unproblematic projects. For example, the Urban Land Institute, a "think tank" with strong connections to the real estate industry, popularized the planned multipurpose "urban entertainment destination" concept, which includes elements such as entertainment-oriented retailers, high-tech entertainment experiences, themed restaurants, and cinema complexes (Braun 1995). More recently, the Brookings Institution published a 12-step "how-to-do-it" downtown revitalization guide where creating an urban entertainment district is a vital component that spawns further developments in the housing and retail sector (Leinberger 2005).

However, neighborhood interests wonder what, if any, benefits trickle down to inner-city residents from these islands of leisure activity that seem out of place when surrounded by harsher urban realities. Especially in cities that cannot be described as having a lively city center characterized by multi-functionality, new developments have a hard time fitting seamlessly into the urban environment. They often become what Dennis Judd (1999) calls "tourist bubbles." Many entertainment areas are branded to be recognized far beyond the city limits, perhaps even world-wide, with the goal to attract tourists. The historical archetype is arguably the French Quarter in New Orleans (Stanonis 2006). While the French Quarter and its premier event, Mardi Gras, has existed for a long time, it has been commodified, mass marketed, and made into a globally recognized spectacle over the last few decades (Fox Gotham 2002).

Following the lead of New Orleans, entertainment districts have sprouted elsewhere in recent years, although with varying degrees of tourist orientation. For example, Denver's Lower Downtown (LoDo) is a former warehouse district with restaurant, bars, and sports venues (Morley 2006). Similarly, Fourth Street in Austin, Texas is touted as "an entertainment district for grown-ups" (Toering 1996); the 18th Street/Vine entertainment complex in Kansas City ties to the area's jazz and baseball legacy (Gould 1999); and the Gaslamp Quarter is San Diego's dining and entertainment district (Ervin 2007). Authors variously refer to such areas as entertainment zones (Campo and Ryan 2008), urban entertainment destinations (Hannigan 1998), urban entertainment centers (Roost 1998), or urban playscapes (Chatterton and Hollands 2002). However, there is no agreement whether such developments are typically planned (usually through some form of public-private partnership that involves city governments, real estate developers, and entertainment corporations), or whether they are unplanned. Nor does a consistent definition exist of what exactly constitutes such an area, what the activities are, how boundaries can be drawn, and who typically frequents such areas. And finally, some authors view contemporary entertainment areas as standardized and sanitized environments, while others avoid such characterizations.

The only research that first and foremost emphasizes the physical and design qualities of entertainment districts is Campo and Ryan (2008). They view "entertainment zones" as concentrations of nightlife with drinking and dancing as main activities, often located at the margins of downtowns. Campo and Ryan make a distinction between entertainment zones which emerge with little planning or formal administration, and other entertainment areas based on a centralized development scheme. Rather than adopt one conceptualization over another, I will, for the purpose of this paper, use the generic term entertainment district, which implies nothing specifically about the origin of such a place or its "authenticity." By entertainment district, I simply mean a clearly defined space where nightlife-oriented activities, such as bars, music venues, and restaurants are the main ingredients. So while building on Campo and Ryan's "form and function" approach to contemporary entertainment districts, using the following two case studies I will investigate to what degree the planned/themed and the "organically" emerging entertainment districts are entirely separate physical and conceptual entities as sometimes portrayed in the literature.

THE CASE STUDIES

A visit to downtown Nashville or Memphis today is quite a different experience than in the recent past. My first visit to both cities was in the early 1990s, and the impression was one of decay and neglect. The historic built environment that existed immediately surrounding the central business districts exhibited strong signs of disinvestment. As was typical of these peripheral downtown areas—sometimes dubbed the "frame" by urban geographers—properties were unused, underused, or occupied by low-rent commercial establishments that often served a poor central city population (Ford 1994). In the case of Nashville, what is now the center of the entertainment district, peep shows and other adult establishments were commonly intermixed with remnants from Nashville's country music history—honky tonks, record stores, and a few other related activities. On Beale Street in Memphis, an embryo to today's entertainment district existed in the early 1990s, but it was struggling.

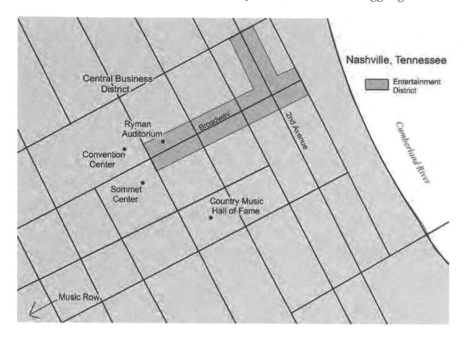

Figure 41-1. Downtown Nashville. Cartography: Michael Inman.

Figure 41-2. Typical Second Avenue buildings, Nashville. Photo: Author.

On the surface, there are some strong similarities between Nashville and Memphis. Both cities rely on entertainment-led revitalization. It is the entertainment districts that largely define respective downtown today and new investment has spread outward from these areas. The developments are sustained by a significant influx of visitors, although city residents may also frequent the areas. The entertainment districts have historically been centers for nightlife and entertainment, so a certain level of functional continuity exists. And finally, the most obvious similarity is that both entertainment districts have a musical focal point—blues and country music respectively. Nashville is the undisputed center of the country music industry, while Memphis can rightfully portray itself as the city where blues and rock'n'roll emerged, although it does not have a significant music industry today. Beale Street is officially acknowledged as the "Home of the Blues" by US Congress decree, and it is also a National Historic Landmark (a designation by the US National Park Service). Both country and blues emerged from Southern folk music traditions. The Mississippi Delta is recognized as the hearth of blues, and as Memphis is located at the northern edge of the Delta, it attracted African-American migrants who brought the blues tradition with them (Davis 1995). Country music originated from Anglo folk music in the Upland South, and while the spatial logic of Nashville as the center of country music is not as immediate as with Memphis and the blues, a concentration of musicians and recording facilities eventually resulted in the city's development as "Music City USA" (Malone 2002).

THE ENTERTAINMENT SPACES

The Nashville entertainment district consists of two streets, Second Avenue and Broadway, which are located perpendicular to each other (FIGURE 41-1). The Second Avenue section is approximately three blocks long and the street has many well-preserved and restored Victorian commercial brick structures, which were erected primarily during the 1870s and 1880s (FIGURE 41-2) (Metropolitan Historic Zoning Commission 2001). As the second street from the riverfront of the Cumberland River, Second Avenue's history is one of commercial prominence; goods were unloaded to the warehouses along First Avenue and then sold in connecting structures on Second Avenue (Metropolitan Historic Zoning Commission 1997). As is typical of commercial architecture of this era, many lot sizes are rectangular in shape but narrow and deep. This layout combined with wall-to-wall properties is efficient use of land, although many buildings lack in natural light and air which makes them less suitable as residential spaces. The design is a so-called "two-part commercial block" (Longstreth 2000), meaning that the function of the first story (e.g., retail) is different than the stories above (e.g., storage, office). The façade of the first story commonly has a large glass window which visually sets it apart from the top section of the building. Mixed ornamentation also exists on the façade, as was typical during the Victorian era, although not to an excessive extent. (This architectural description broadly characterizes both the Nashville and Memphis districts.) Second Avenue is located within the core of the central business district, but its historic structures, for the most part, survived the onslaught of urban renewal in the 1960s and 1970s. Broadway, on the other hand, has a different history and even today the entertainment district is made up of two segments with distinct, separate styles. Broadway is located in the downtown frame of Nashville. It is a major thoroughfare that connects the downtown with outlying urban areas. Broadway was also a commercial street of 19th century origin, although it contained more space consuming businesses, such as furniture, feed stores, hardware, grain trade, and clothing (Metropolitan Historic Zoning Commission 2007). The four block entertainment district portion of Broadway, which in colloquial parlance is called "lower Broad," has an eclectic mix of structures (**FIGURE 41-3**). Small bars and country music venues have also been a long standing tradition on Broadway (Rouda 2004).

Figure 41-3. Lower Broadway, Nashville. Convention Center visible in the background. Photo: Author.

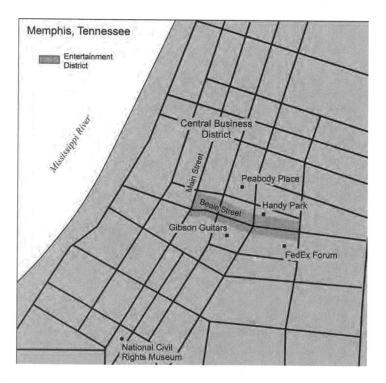

Figure 41-4. Downtown Memphis. Cartography: Michael Inman.

Figure 41-5. Beale Street, Memphis. Note façade preservation on the left side. Photo: Author.

Memphis, compared to Nashville, has a higher proportion of African-Americans. Before the Civil Rights movement and desegregation, an African-American commercial district existed at the southern edge of downtown (FIGURE 41-4). The core of this area is Beale Street, which (partially) was and is an entertainment district. Thus, the entertainment districts in both cities are located in approximately the same space—in the downtown frame where a mix of wholesale, warehousing, entertainment, and retail used to be. Today, Beale Street's entertainment district is only three blocks in length, and thus smaller than the Nashville district (FIGURE 41-5). This current incarnation of Beale Street is also smaller than the original African-American commercial street (Gibson and Connell 2007).

The two districts partially differ in the types of spaces that have been created. Beale Street is relatively narrow which creates an intimate character. The structures are primarily one-to-two story commercial buildings, which provide an appropriate scale for the space. This is reinforced by the decision to block the street from automobile traffic to make it pedestrian. This combination of factors provides the visitor, not coincidentally, with a Bourbon Street-like urban experience. Even curb-side drinks are served so that visitors can freely roam from place to place on the street while enjoying a beverage. The Nashville district does not provide the same coherent space as it consists of two very different streetscapes. Second Avenue has a width similar to Beale Street, but as part of the traditional downtown core, the structures are three-to-four stories, which alter the sense of place. And on one side of Second Avenue, the presence of modern skyscrapers is immediate and visually contrasting. Heavy, but slow moving traffic is also common on Second Avenue. The built environment on Broadway has more in common with Beale Street; the structures tend to be smaller in scale and have not always retained their original architectural qualities. Broadway is imperfect as an entertainment space. It is a four-lane thoroughfare that is hard to traverse for pedestrians who are limited to the sidewalks on either side of the street.

THE DEVELOPMENT PROCESS AND THE EMERGING "FORM" OF ENTERTAINMENT DISTRICTS

NASHVILLE

In the 1980s, for all practical purposes, no entertainment districts existed in Nashville. However, the emerging gentrification trend across the country started to slowly manifest itself on Nashville's Second Avenue, although only modest commercial, office, and residential activity accompanied the reinvestment. So, while the result was an uninspired collection of restaurants and stores, the stage was set for a later take off.

The first main redevelopment project in Nashville was the publicly financed Nashville Convention Center, which was built in 1988 and covers one full city block on Broadway. The locational objective was to create a synergy between convention visitors and restaurants and bars (both existing and envisioned) within walking distance from the Convention Center. At this point, the city also used selective enforcement tactics against non-desirable establishments on Broadway. Minor code violations were enforced against low-end liquor stores and adult entertainment establishments with the goal of "cleaning up" Broadway (Dobie 1989). Anti-loitering regulations were also enforced against the homeless population that frequented the area.

For several years, however, the private sector did not respond with any significant investments on Broadway or Second Avenue. The real starting point of the contemporary Nashville entertainment district was 1993. The first, and arguably most important, catalyst was the announcement in late 1992 by Gaylord Entertainment: the Ryman Auditorium was to be renovated and reused (McCampbell 1993). Gaylord Entertainment is one of the leading corporations in Nashville with an ownership stake in enterprises that span the tourism and country music industries. One of those enterprises is the Ryman Auditorium, which used to be the venue for the musical show the Grand Ole Opry, which played a significant role in the making of Nashville as "Music City USA." The Opry show was moved in 1974 to a new, larger venue in suburban Nashville and the 19th century Ryman Auditorium (originally constructed as a church) was left to deteriorate, only operating as a rather dusty museum for country music fans. The relocation was the equivalent of "white flight," leaving the increasingly poor city behind. Similarly, the return of Ryman as a performance venue coincided with the gentrification of the central city. Now, as a 2,300 seat theater, it is again successfully housing performances by both country music artists and others, on a regular basis. Because of its history, the symbolic importance of the Ryman cannot be overstated. It is situated half a block away from Broadway and only an alleyway separates the Ryman from a few "honky tonks" on the street, the most famous being Tootsie's Orchid Lounge and Robert's Western World. Local mythology has it that Opry performers, during the intermissions of the distinctly family-friendly show, entered the bars for a drink or two via the back alley and subsequently returned to the show. While much of the traditional country music played in many venues in the Nashville district is designed to conform to the expectations of tourists, major artists play at the Ryman in Nashville (similarly to the renovated Daisy Theatre on Beale Street) making the venue an important site, not only because it is historic, but because Ryman exists within a larger functional built environment dedicated to music.

Shortly after the Ryman announcement, plans for a new arena were made public in January 1993. The city's redevelopment authority acquired land covering a city block on Broadway across the street from the Convention Center (Dobie 1994). The city worked with private investors (including Gaylord Entertainment) to successfully lure a professional sports team to the city; NHL's Nashville Predators now play in the 17,000 seat Sommet Center. Both the Convention Center and the Sommet Center are large, space-consuming developments, including large parking lots. However, they are located at the edge of the Nashville entertainment district where they do not disrupt the pedestrian space, and they mark the clear end point of the entertainment district. Surrounding the entertainment district is a zone of parking, which is a common arrangement (Crankshaw 2009). The space and layout of the entertainment district resemble an indoor suburban mall. The Convention Center and the Sommet Center are "anchor developments" that draw large numbers of people, and are located at the edge of the development, much like the department stores at a mall.

After the Ryman and the arena, a series of mid-range and small projects were initiated within a short period of time. The Wildhorse Saloon on Second Avenue started in March 1993 and Hard Rock Café arrived in October 1993 at the strategic intersection of Broadway and Second Avenue. Wildhorse Saloon is Nashville's premier country music dance venue and, again, a Gaylord Entertainment project. Following these announcements in 1993, numerous renovations of neglected structures on Broadway took place and smaller retail and entertainment establishments moved in. The transformation into an entertainment district in downtown Nashville took place during a very short time period. Literally within a year, the area shifted from urban decay to mainstream, middle-class entertainment space.

One exogenous factor played a significant role in the rapid emergence of the Nashville entertainment district. The country music industry experienced a surge in popularity in the early 1990s, with Garth Brooks as the fix star. FIGURE 41-6 shows how country music rose to national prominence parallel to the downtown development. Country music fans always had a propensity to go on "pilgrimages" to Nashville, but now their ranks swelled, and the average country music fan was also more affluent and middle-class than in the past. Consequently, the demand for country music tourism outstripped the limited possibilities that existed at the time. In the past, tourists congregated on Music Row, the near-downtown neighborhood where the music industry is located and where a strip of souvenir stores and the old Country Music Hall of Fame were situated. (A new Hall of Fame was constructed two blocks south of Broadway in 2001.) It was not a foregone conclusion that a new premier entertainment and visitors' space would emerge downtown, nor was it an entirely planned process. The new arena and the various investments of Gaylord Entertainment signaled the economic potential of the area. A socially created "rent gap" had developed, meaning the difference between the realized rent (in essence, profit) of the properties on Broadway and Second Avenue under existing land use and the potential rent that property owners may extract under the "highest and best use" had grown so large that investments in these neglected properties were bound to happen. No single decision to encourage an entertainment district was made; it was a market-based stampede of new rapid investment.

Very soon, preservation minded people in Nashville realized that with the central city's rebirth came a "price of success" (Roberts 1993). On Second Avenue, no historical zoning existed despite the historic nature of the built environment, and only limited regulations were in place on Broadway (the Broadway Historic District was listed on the National Register of Historic Places since 1980). On Second Avenue, to make room for the massive Wildhorse Saloon, two properties were demolished, which disrupted the historic integrity of the street (Shackelford 1993). In contrast, when the chain restaurant Hooters renovated a Second Avenue structure, its design of both the exterior and interior was received favorably among preservationists in Nashville (Roberts 1994b). Ironically, Hooters was hailed as culturally sensitive! In the case of Hard Rock Café, its new presence involved the tearing down of some structures and therefore had a significant impact on the streetscape (Roberts 1994a). Facing Broadway, the entrance of Hard Rock Café is adorned with a large wall music-themed mural and a large free standing guitar. After the quick and not entirely desirable changes at the Hard Rock Café site, the next large national restaurant/entertainment chain that planned for a Nashville location—Planet Hollywood—was subject to more scrutiny. The city's historical commission sparred with Planet Hollywood on the design of its Broadway project, which resulted in minor compromises; the colors on the new façade painting were toned down, but a large globe was attached to the corner of the building despite objections from the historical commission (Thompson 1996). Overall, the local government had to rely on informal cooperation among merchants, property owners, and preservation interests due to the lack of regulatory mechanisms. Planet Hollywood has since disappeared, and after much debate in a city with a southern political culture that does not favor strong public intervention, historic zoning overlay has been implemented (Kreyling 1997). However, new zoning only emerged after the development rush was over, although it has presumably acted as a positive conservation force since. The built environment, especially on Second Avenue in Nashville, became more and more important as an issue of symbolic importance, not just for the directly involved land owners, but for the entire city, which enabled the passage of historic zoning.

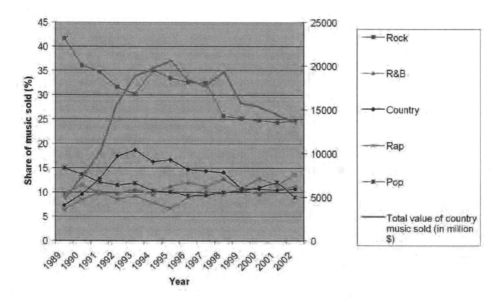

Figure 41-6. Share of Music sold by genre 1989–2002. Chart by author. Data Source: Recording Industry Association of America (1998; 2002).

The zoning requires a design review by the Metropolitan Historic Zoning Commission, which must pre-approve changes following a set of design guidelines. Violations are subject to fines (Metropolitan Historic Zoning Commission, undated). The guidelines, however, only cover the exterior of structures, which is a typical "façadism" approach—a compromise between preservation and the need for adaptive reuse (Ligibel, Tyler, and Tyler 2009).

MEMPHIS

Before the dismantling of legal segregation in the South, African-Americans had limited opportunities for the provision of personal services and entertainment, so distinct African-American commercial districts appeared. Beale Street emerged in this manner as the dominant center for Memphis' African-Americans. It was not exclusively an entertainment district but contained a wide range of commercial and cultural activities. During the 1960s and 1970s, however, Beale Street suffered a serious decline. The decline accelerated following the 1968 riots on Beale Street after MLK's assassination in the city (Gibson and Connell 2007). Not only was Beale Street impacted by the forces of suburbanization, but also by desegregation—a double strike against its raison d'etre. With derelict properties and many significant structures demolished, the City of Memphis took ownership of almost all the properties on Beale Street as an urban renewal project. The city designated a Beale Street Historic District, which was then leased to the Beale Street Development Corporation (BSDC) in 1982, a nonprofit initiative formed with the intent of improving the area. BSDC, which did not have any experience in real estate management, subleased the Beale Street properties the following year to a developer named John Elkington, who now operates Beale Street through his company Performa Entertainment.

Elkington's objective was to revitalize Beale Street by recapturing some of its historic functions as a place of nightclubs and restaurants. A major departure from history, of course, was that the intended market was a general (read: white) middle-class audience rather than explicitly catering to African-Americans. The project had minimal success in the 1980s (Elkington 2008). Obstacles included a lingering image of decay and crime, the perception of Beale Street as an African-American territory, and few other visitor destinations in downtown Memphis. The new Beale Street started to gain some traction in the early 1990s, slightly ahead of its counterpart in Nashville, especially after the BB King's Blues Club opened in 1991. With the blues legend himself as a stakeholder, the original club on Beale Street has now developed into a chain, including one franchise on Second Avenue in Nashville. A critical mass of entertainment spots developed in the 1990s, although not at the explosive pace as in Nashville, and the Beale Street project took off. Over time, infill structures and new businesses were added eastward on the street until the designated historic district was fully occupied (Nobles 1998).

Today, the experiential qualities of Beale Street have much in common with the Nashville district. Two particular forms of Southern music have been made visible in the urban landscape. The districts are ripe with music-themed wall murals and an abundance of commercial signage that invoke music; this is especially powerful during neon-lit evening hours. But it is not only the visual but also auditory experience that has an emotional impact on the visitor. The districts have their own soundscapes with music spilling out from venues into the streets and buskers, adding to the ambience of the public realm. A public space—Handy Park—has been built adjacent to Beale Street, not only for scheduled performances, but also as a space for "planned improvisations" of street musicians. All of this has been received favorably by visitors. Beale Street has overtaken Graceland as the leading tourist attraction in Memphis. It draws approximately 4 million visitors annually (Performa Entertainment 2006).

In the original negotiations, Elkington acquired a 32-year lease on Beale Street. Thus, Performa asserts strong control over Beale Street as its manager, and it will continue to do so for years to come. As the manager, Elkington's ability to select tenants is almost unlimited. He identifies restaurants and night clubs that will work well in the mix of business on Beale Street. Different cuisines and experiences are provided to the visitors so they have a wide selection. A variety of complementary stores, such as souvenir shops, have also been added. In general, Elkington proclaims that Beale Street is an urban oriented district and should not be overly family friendly to avoid a "Disneyfication" (Sitton 1999). Moreover, unique stores and restaurants are supposedly favored over chains.

This operational arrangement has not been entirely smooth. Performa has been in conflict with many interests in Memphis. The City of Memphis, which ultimately owns Beale Street, wants to assert greater control over the affairs of the district at the expense of Performa. The city has, for example, investigated Performa for financing irregularities, a move that was viewed by many as politically motivated (Aaron 1996). The tenants on Beale Street, both existing and prospective, have expressed misgivings about the company's management style. The New Orleans institution Pat O'Brien's, for example, took ten years of acrimonious negotiations with Performa before they agreed to open a "branch" on Beale Street (Nobles 1998). It now operates a Creole-style infill structure on the street. The Beale Street Development Corporation, much like the city, are also interested in ending the lease with Performa. BSDC see themselves as guardians of the African-American experience and how it is represented (Sitton 1999).

Elkington's commitment to neighborhood development, which is the ultimate goal of community development corporations[1] such as BSDC, has been questioned (Aaron 1996). In the commercialization process, charges have been made that the African-American culture of Beale Street has been distorted and exploited. While white tourists are more numerous, Beale Street has, however, become an important node in Memphis' African-American heritage tourism circuit (Gibson and Connell 2007), and Elkington defends his record saying that African-American entrepreneurs own a majority of the establishments on Beale Street (Elkington 2008).

Beale Street has been successful as a catalyst of the surrounding environment. A new NBA basketball arena, the FedEx Forum, was completed in 2004 only a block south of Beale Street. The guitar manufacturer Gibson has a new manufacturing facility (tours are available for visitors) on the south side of Beale Street as well. And a bit further away, but within pedestrian reach from Beale Street, the National Civil Rights Museum is located in the old Lorraine Motel where Martin Luther King Jr. was shot. On the downtown side of Beale Street is a large mixed-use project called Peabody Place which includes many generic retailers and restaurants. Continuous (re)design of Beale Street structures via new doorways, for example, have partially reoriented Beale Street away from its self-contained character, toward further integration with its surroundings (Miller 2001).

THE "FUNCTION" OF ENTERTAINMENT DISTRICTS: AN ANALYSIS OF COMMERCIAL ACTIVITIES

41

The second question this paper attempts to address is not only how the entertainment districts developed, but also their content. To investigate the functionality, I have classified and analyzed existing businesses. The geographic delineation of the districts was based on the principle of continuous, wall-to-wall entertainment-oriented businesses (FIGURE 41-1 and FIGURE 41-4). For the most part, the boundaries were easy to define, as land uses tend to shift abruptly at the districts' edges. As pedestrian spaces, it is street-level commerce that is important and, therefore, only such businesses have been included in the data. Data were compiled by on site field research in 2005. Businesses have been categorized in seven different categories: bars/nightclubs, restaurants, gifts/souvenirs, clothing, office, other, and vacant. The categories were designed after the businesses' activities were recorded to create a comfortable number of internally coherent categories. The categories bars/nightclubs and restaurants are sometimes overlapping, but in most cases the dance and music function clearly dominates the eatery function, or vice versa.

The results are presented in TABLE 41-1. The Nashville entertainment district, as mentioned earlier, is larger than Memphis' Beale Street. In a functional sense, it is more than twice the size with 103 establishments compared to Memphis' 44. Note, however, that nearby developments that emerged after the success of Beale Street have not been included in the Memphis data as they were considered non-contiguous. The two dominant categories in both cases are bars/nightclubs and restaurants, as is expected of an entertainment district. They comprise approximately half of the businesses in the entertainment districts. Memphis has a greater share of bars/nightclubs than Nashville, while Nashville is slightly more skewed towards restaurants. However, the two districts are similar in this regard. Tourists are common in both entertainment districts, and gift and souvenir shops have a similar share in both places: 13 and 16 percent respectively. Clothing retailers is a small category but the share is identical in both Memphis and Nashville, 5 percent of the total. A category that is seemingly out of place in an entertainment district is the office function. Here, a significant difference exists between the two districts. The tightly controlled Beale Street has no street level office space, which is not surprising as Performa makes all the decisions on tenants. In Nashville, on the other hand, seven offices are sprinkled within the district, many of them hold-overs from the pre-take off era. There are numerous other stores which are so diverse that they comprise an "other" category. Examples include psychic readings, museums, art galleries, jewelers, ticket sellers, concert theatres, and a Kinko's. The share of establishments in this diverse category is virtually identical in both districts: 17–18 percent. Finally, there are a number of vacancies in both cases. Nashville has a higher vacancy rate of 14 percent. When the field research was conducted, country music had experienced a few years of slow sales compared to the 1990s peak, which also meant fewer tourists. Defunct chains, such as Planet Hollywood and Nascar Café, left temporary holes on Nashville's Broadway, although new businesses have moved in since. At 9 percent, the vacancy rate in Memphis is lower. This is a modest vacancy rate and probably due to the "normal" transition from one tenant to the next. These vacancy rates are similar to downtown real estate in general (Collier International 2009).

Table 41-1. Commercial activities.

	Nashville		Memphis	
	Number of establishments	Percent of total	Number of establishments	Percent of total
Bars/Nightclubs	23	22%	14	32%
Restaurants	24	23%	9	20%
Gifts/Souvenirs	13	13%	7	16%
Clothing	5	5%	2	5%
Office	7	7%	0	0%
Other	17	17%	8	18%
Vacant	14	14%	4	9%
Total	103	100%	44	100%

Two other functions that the data can offer some insight into are how tourist-oriented the two districts are and whether chain businesses dominate. The idea of social mixing is important in urban design and redevelopment, so a blend between local and tourist visitors to the districts is important to counteract a "tourist bubble" effect and the perception of inauthenticity. An abundance of well known chains might give a visitor the impression that the place is not "real" and that it lacks unique qualities on which historic downtowns thrive. First, I have classified some establishments as directly tourist-related. This includes the aforementioned souvenir shops, but also some other stores that logically are located in the districts because of the high level of tourist foot traffic. These would include establishments such as a Nashville boot store and a music record store that sells classic country vinyl. This is not to say that many restaurants and other establishments are not frequented by tourists; in all likelihood they are, but they cannot be assumed to be "tourist businesses" per se. The number of establishments deemed to cater exclusively to tourists is 19 in Nashville (18 percent of all establishments) and nine in Memphis (20 percent of all establishments). Again, the similarities between the two districts are strong.

Secondly, I determined how many stores are non-local establishments (chains, franchises, and so on). I used the Internet to determine the origin of businesses, and with the caveat that a small error may exist, 9 percent of the establishments were non-local in Nashville, while in Memphis 11 percent were non-local. Examples include Hooters, Hard Rock Café, the Melting Pot, and BB King's (classified as non-local in Nashville only). These numbers underestimate the importance of chain establishments as they generally occupy more square footage and have larger sales than other places. Assuming that tourists are the target audience for chain establishments (if locals intends to frequent a chain restaurant they probably select a suburban location rather than go downtown for that purpose) the tourist orientation of both districts are at very similar and relatively high levels, if both directly tourist-related business and chain categories are considered. (Tourist officials in both Nashville and Memphis can estimate the total number of tourists to their cities, but data on the ratio of tourists vs. locals in the districts does not exist.)

41

At the same time, developments around the entertainment districts have increased the potential for locals to visit the districts in three different ways. In Memphis, an arena for an NBA team is located in proximity to Beale Street, and Nashville has a NHL team. The advantages of these professional sports are that over 500,000 spectators travel downtown during a long 40 home game season[2]. From the entertainment district perspective, many games are played at non-peak times in the middle of the week and during the winter half of the year. While winters in Memphis and Nashville are cool, it is often pleasant enough to frequent public spaces. Only a fraction of the sports spectators have to venture to the entertainment district for the location of the arenas to exhibit synergy with the districts. Sports fans often establish informal spaces to gather before and after games. In Nashville, for example, the bar Wolfy's is such a place and dubs itself the "hockey tonk." Summers, on the other hand, are prime tourist season and an abundance of out-of-town visitors can carry the districts then. Secondly, local youth is attracted downtown by nearby developments, such as Memphis' Peabody Place which had a Tower Records open in evenings, and a cinema complex (both are recently closed, however). Over 21 clubs and bars near Broadway in Nashville attract local young adults. Thirdly, residential downtown developments have mushroomed in both cities since the establishment of the districts in the 1990s. Such "neighborhood" population has been attracted by growing amenities at a walkable distance.

CONCLUSIONS

The contemporary functionality of the historic built environment is important to all who are interested in material culture as usefulness results, at least partially, in preservation. This comparative study has shown many similarities between the development of two entertainment districts in Nashville and Memphis. Both are located in what used to be somewhat peripheral parts of downtown, but where the historic built environment enabled revitalization and functional continuation with traditional land uses. The de facto centers of the downtowns of Nashville and Memphis have shifted toward the entertainment districts, which have spurred further developments. The districts have also become better integrated with their surroundings over time. The experiential qualities of both districts are also very similar as two particular forms of Southern music have been made visible and audible in the urban landscape and soundscape. Both districts equally commodify a folk culture, although turning a cultural expression into a visitor attraction is more contentious in Memphis considering its racially divided history.

The process by which the entertainment districts emerged is very different. The Nashville district developed during an extremely short time period, primarily due to the explosive nature of real estate market forces. Beale Street's take off was slower as major investments in multiple properties had to be made. For this, market forces were not enough; rather, a top-down interventionist strategy was used instead. Two distinct development paradigms are represented here: the "organic" process with multiple actors and decision-makers in Nashville, and the single-entity manager approach in Memphis, which was initially enabled by the decrepit state of Beale Street that led to the purchase of all properties by the City of Memphis. This has left Nashville's district less planned, and, some might say less "user friendly" (i.e., less pedestrian, more non-entertainment spaces such as offices and vacancies), while others may consider it, in a positive way, less "groomed" than Beale Street. The renewed functional usefulness of both districts means the historic buildings that do exist are not threatened today, in part due to the extension of historic zoning, although some structures have been altered or demolished in the recent past.

Perhaps the most striking aspect of the two districts is that in a functional sense, they are near identical. To generalize, the categories within the two entertainment districts are approximately 50 percent nightlife business, 15 percent directly tourist related businesses, 25 percent other businesses, and 10 percent vacant real estate space. Big chain establishments have been part of the development of visitor-oriented downtowns in both Memphis and Nashville. Even if only a moderate amount of national brands exist, they do represent larger investments than many smaller retail enterprises and the overall level of tourist-orientation is palpable. On the other hand, both districts have "anchors" (i.e., arenas, convention centers) and adjacent real estate developments that draw both visitors and locals, creating some social mixing and reducing the tourism bubble effect.

The final conclusion must be that it apparently does not matter whether market forces are predominantly at work or a centralized entity plans the entertainment district in great detail, the end result is nevertheless highly similar. Both paths lead to, perhaps not the same place, but at least to the formation of spaces that are very much alike in a functional sense. This calls into question the idea in the literature that highly planned entertainment districts are always different than bottom-up developments. Further case studies are needed to investigate if this conclusion is generalizable for other downtown entertainment districts across the United States, and if so, under what conditions and circumstances.

Questions for Discussion and Journaling

1. How and why did the entertainment districts in Memphis and Nashville form differently? What impact did the history of each city have on its entertainment district?

2. Compare and contrast the tone of Johansson's article with that of "Entrepreneurship and Crime: The Case of New Restaurant Location Decisions" by Sloan, Caudill, and Mixon. Note the tonal shifts and differences in word choices. For example, Johansson uses the familiar "I" and her anecdotal, personal experience. What effect does this have on her credibility? Why? What does this tell us about each writer's audience?

3. Note the structure of Johansson's article. Does she seem to rely on any one rhetorical appeal or does she make good use of multiple appeals? What effect does this have on her persuasion?

41

ENDNOTES

1. Community development corporations are non-profits that provide poor neighborhoods with programs and services in housing, real estate development, education, and other areas with the intent to promote economic development.

2. This is based on the 2008–2009 season attendance figures from Nashville Predators and Memphis Grizzlies.

REFERENCES

Aaron, C. 1996. "At the Crossroads: While Developers Celebrate the Future of a Booming Beale Street, Critics Complain That The Thrill Is Gone." *The Memphis Flyer*, Dec. 5–11, 1996. http://www.memphisflyer.com/backissues/issue407/cvrstory407.htm. Last accessed: August 5, 2009.

Braun, R. 1995. "Exploring the Urban Entertainment Center Universe." *Urban Land* (supplement). Vol. 54 (8): 11–17.

Campo, D. and Ryan, B. 2008. "The Entertainment Zone: Unplanned Nightlife and the Revitalization of the American Downtown." *Journal of Urban Design*. Vol. 13 (3): 291–315.

Chatterton P. and Hollands R. 2002. "Theorising Urban Playscapes: Producing, Regulating and Consuming Youthful Nightlife City Spaces." *Urban Studies*. Vol. 39 (1): 95–116.

Clark, T.N., ed. 2004. *The City as an Entertainment Machine*. Oxford: Elsevier.

Collier International 2009. *2009 U.S. Real Estate Review*. http://www.colliers.com/Content/Repositories/Base/Corporate/English/Market_Report_Corporate/PDFs/CUSRER2009.pdf. Last accessed August 19, 2009.

Collins, R., Waters, E., and Dotson, B. 1991. *America's Downtown: Growth Politics and Preservation*. Washington, DC: The Preservation Press.

Crankshaw, N. 2009. *Creating Vibrant Public Spaces: Streetscape Design in Commercial and Historic Districts*. Washington DC: Island Press.

Davis, F. 1995. *The History of the Blues: The Roots, the Music, the People*. New York: Hyperion.

Dobie, B. 1989. "Harassing the Honky-Tonks on Lower Broad." *Nashville Scene*. Vol. 7 (39): 5.

_____. 1994. "Playing Ball." *Nashville Scene*. 7 (April 7): 12.

Elkington, J. 2008. *Beale Street: Resurrecting the Home of the Blues*. Charleston, SC: The History Press.

Ervin, J. 2007. "Reinventing Downtown San Diego: A Spatial and Cultural Analysis of the Gaslamp Quarter." *Journal of San Diego History*. Vol. 53 (4): 188–217.

Florida, R. 2002. *The Rise of the Creative Class*. New York: Basic Books.

Ford, L. 1994. *Cities and Buildings: Skyscrapers, Skid Rows, and Suburbs*. Baltimore: Johns Hopkins University Press.

_____. 2003. *America's New Downtown: Revitalization or Reinvention*. Baltimore: Johns Hopkins Press.

Fox Gotham, K. 2002. "Marketing Mardi Gras: Commodification, Spectacle and the Political Economy of Tourism in New Orleans." *Urban Studies*. Vol. 39 (10): 1735–1756.

Gibson, C. and Connell, J. 2007. "Music, Tourism, and the Transformation of Memphis." *Tourism Geographies*. Vol. 9 (2): 160–190.

Gottdiener, M. 2001. *The Theming of America: Dreams, Media Fantasies, and Themed Environments*. Second edition. Boulder, CO: Westwood.

Gould, K. 1999. "Kansas City Jazz." *Urban Land*. Vol. 58 (2): 62–67.

Hamer, D. 1998. *History in Urban Places: The Historic Districts of the United States*. Columbus: Ohio State University Press.

Hannigan, J. 1998. *Fantasy City: Pleasure and Profit in the Postmodern Metropolis*. London: Routledge.

Jackson, K. 1985. *Crabgrass Frontier: The Suburbanization of the United States*. New York: Oxford University Press.

Judd, D. 1999. "Constructing the Tourist Bubble." In D. Judd and S. Feinstein (eds) *The Tourist City*. New Haven, CT: Yale University Press.

Kreyling, C. 1997. "Re-making History: The Fight Against a Rezoned Second Avenue." *Nashville Scene*. Jan 23, 1997. http://www.nashvillescene.com. Last accessed: June 11, 2002.

Leinberger, C. 2005. *Turning Around Downtown: Twelve Steps to Revitalization*. Research Brief. Washington DC: The Brookings Institution.

Ley, D. 1996. *The New Middle Class and the Remaking of the Central City*. New York: Oxford University Press.

Ligibel, T., Tyler, I., and Tyler, N. 2009. *Historic Preservation: An Introduction to Its History, Principles, and Practice*. Second Edition. New York: Norton.

Lloyd, R. 2005. *Neo-Bohemia: Art and Commerce in the Postindustrial City*. New York: Routledge.

Longstreth, R. 2000. *The Buildings of Main Street: A Guide to Commercial Architecture*. Walnut Creek, CA: AltaMira Press.

Malone, B. 2002. *Country Music, U.S.A.* 2nd edition. Austin: University of Texas Press.

Metropolitan Historic Zoning Commission. 1997. *Second Avenue Design Guidelines*. Nashville: Metropolitan Government of Nashville and Davidson County.

_____. 2001. *Nashville Footnotes: A Walking Tour of Downtown History and Architecture*. Nashville: Metropolitan Government of Nashville and Davidson County.

_____. 2007. *Broadway Historic Preservation District: Design guidelines*. Nashville: Metropolitan Government of Nashville and Davidson County.

_____. Undated. *Historic Zoning*. Nashville: Metropolitan Government of Nashville and Davidson County.

McCampbell, C. 1993. "Ryman to Ring with Music Again." *The Tennessean*. March 23, p. 1.

McDonald, J. 2008. *Urban America: Growth, Crisis, and Rebirth*. Armonk, NY: M.E. Sharpe.

Miller, K. 2001. "Beale Street Seeks Revenue Increase in New Five-Year Plan." *Memphis Business Journal*. December 7, 2001. http://www.bizjournals.com/memphis/stories/2001/12/10/story6.html. Last accessed: August 5, 2009.

Morley, J.M. 2006. *Historic Preservation and the Imagined West*. Lawrence: University Press of Kansas.

Nobles, B. 1998. "Investors Line Up for Pat O'Brien's As Change Marches Down Beale." *Memphis Business Journal*. May 22, 1998. http://memphis.bizjournals.com/memphis/stories/1998/05/25/story2.html. Last accessed: August 5, 2009.

Performa Entertainment 2006. "Beale Street." http://www.performaentertainment.com/bealestreet.htm. Last accessed: August 12, 2009.

Recording Industry Association of America 1998. "1998 Consumer Profile." www.riaa.com Last accessed: August 15, 2003.

_____. 2002. "2002 Consumer Profile." www.riaa.com Last accessed: August 15, 2003.

Roberts, T. 1993. "Second Avenue May See Protection: Push for Redevelopment District Inclusion." *Nashville Business Journal*. September 27, p. 1.

Roberts, T. 1994a. "Second Avenue's Commercial Metamorphosis Raising Concerns." *Nashville Business Journal*. April 11, p. 1.

Roberts, T. 1994b. "Hooters Plans Historically Sensitive Eatery." *Nashville Business Journal*. May 16, p. 23.

Roost, F. 1998. "Recreating the City as Entertainment Center: The Media Industry's Role in Transforming Potsdamer Platz and Times Square." *Journal of Urban Technology*. Vol. 5 (3):1–21.

Rouda, B. 2004. *Nashville's Lower Broad: The Street That Music Made*. Washington DC: Smithsonian.

Sagalyn, L. 2001. *Times Square Roulette: Remaking the City Icon.* Cambridge, MA: MIT Press.

Schlereth, T. 1990. *Cultural History and Material Culture: Everyday Life, Landscapes, Museums.* Charlottesville: The University Press of Virginia.

Shackelford, J. 1993. "History at Risk with Economic Progress." *Nashville Business Journal.* August 9, p. 1.

Sitton, Ron 1999. "Beale Street Culture Blues." *The Southerner.* Vol. 1 (4). http://www.southerner.net/v1n4_99/soculture4.html. Last accessed: August 5, 2009.

Sorkin, M., ed. 1992. *Variations on a Theme Park: The New American City and the End of Public Space.* New York: Hill and Wang.

Stanonis, A. 2006. *Creating the Big Easy: New Orleans and the Emergence of Modern Tourism, 1918–1945.* Athens: University of Georgia Press.

Thompson, K. 1996. "Planet Hollywood, Historic Group Reach Accord." *Nashville Business Journal.* June 3, p. 14.

Toering, A. 1996. "Positively Fourth Street: An Entertainment District for Grown-Ups Blossoms in Austin." *Metropolis.* Vol. 16 (5): 15–19.

Wilson, W. 1994. *The City Beautiful Movement.* Baltimore: The Johns Hopkins University Press.

ENTREPRENEURSHIP AND CRIME
The Case of New Restaurant Location Decisions

CarlyWill Sloan[a], Steven B. Caudill[b], and Franklin G. Mixon Jr.[c*]

Originally published in the *Journal of Business Venturing Insights*, "Entrepreneurship and Crime: The Case of New Restaurant Location Decisions" is a well-constructed statistical analysis arguing that restaurants often open in areas with higher crime rates. Relying heavily on logical appeals, Sloan, Caudill, and Mixon use Memphis as the site of their study, finding that assaults and burglaries have the greatest correlation to new restaurant location openings. They reiterate the "hot spot effect" theory that heavy pedestrian traffic is a draw for both restaurant entrepreneurs and criminals. As you read, note their discussion of research methods as well as the structure of the reported findings.

ABSTRACT

This paper examines the impact of various violent crimes on restaurant location decisions in a single city, Memphis, TN. Using location information on crimes and newly opened restaurants, we are able to match crimes and restaurants in parcels we construct. We examine the impact of the number of burglaries, assaults, rapes and murders in each of 400 to up to 1,000,000 parcels occurring from 2009–2013 on the number of restaurants opening in 2014 in models including dummy variables capturing neighborhood effects. Regression results indicate that each crime is positively related to the number of new restaurants in a parcel. This suggests that even with the crime problem, these locations provide sufficient benefits, perhaps population density which make them attractive to restaurant entrepreneurs.

a   Department of Economics, Texas A&M University, College Station, TX, USA

b   Department of Economics, Florida Atlantic University, Boca Raton, FL, USA

c   Center for Economic Education, Columbus State University, Columbus, GA, USA

*   The authors wish to thank an anonymous referee and Dimo Dimov for providing helpful comments on an earlier version, and both the Shelby County Clerk and the Memphis Police Department for making available the data used in this study.

"'Nobody ever robs restaurants,' Tim Roth's lowlife stick-up man famously wonders in the opening of [the movie] *Pulp Fiction*, citing the lack of security, disinterested and/or undocumented employees reluctant to play hero, and the sheer novelty of the prospect. 'Why not?... A lot of people come to restaurants.' And, moments later, he puts his new-found plan into action."   **Moyer, 2015**

1. INTRODUCTION

On the evening of August, 20, 2015, restaurant diners and staff members of the upscale New Orleans restaurant, Patois, were held at gunpoint and robbed by three men dressed in hoodies and wearing skull caps (Wells, 2015). The armed robbers forced the 15 patrons and five staff members, including the restaurant's owner, to lie on the floor, while each person's wallet or purse was collected and the money in the cash register was stolen. Unfortunately for the citizens of New Orleans and individuals who value the city as a tourist destination, the late summer scene at Patois appears to be the beginning of a trend, as another upscale restaurant, Atchafalaya Restaurant, was robbed on September 24, 2015, by two masked gunmen who appear to have repeated the scene one month earlier at Patois, which is less than three miles away (Moyer, 2015).[1] Four nights later, on September 28, 2015, the masked gunmen struck for a third time, robbing patrons and staff at Monkey Hill Bar, which is located only three blocks from the original target, Patois (Moyer, 2015).[2]

Episodes such as those described above serve to illustrate the point that crime often occurs in the vicinity of restaurants and in restaurant districts in American cities. Swann (2015), for example, reports on the September 2015 stabbing of four individuals outside of a pizza parlor in Syracuse, New York, while the sexual assault of a 10-year-old girl near a Palmdale, California, restaurant in January of 2014 continues to haunt city officials, who recently renewed authorization of a $20,000 reward for information leading to an arrest (City News Service, 2015).[3] These episodes also highlight the sentiment in the epigraph above regarding actor Tim Roth's portrayal of a criminal in *Pulp Fiction*, depicting restaurants and their surroundings as hot spots for criminal activity. In that light, the present study examines the relationship between restaurant openings and crime in a single city—Memphis, Tennessee—from 2009 to 2014, using information on the locations of violent crimes (e.g., murders, rapes, burglaries and aggravated assaults) and the locations of newly-opened restaurants. Our statistical results suggest that new restaurants tend to open in parcels with historically higher crime, with elasticity estimates of the responsiveness of the number of new restaurant openings to past crime ranging, in one specification of our empirical model, from a low of about 0.01 for murder to a high of about 0.76 for burglary.

---

1   These robberies are somewhat similar to one that targeted Crema, an upscale restaurant in the Flatiron District of New York in September of 2014 (Parascandola and Sit, 2014).

2   Monkey Hill Bar is described as upscale (Moyer, 2015), making it a target similar to those posed by Patois and Atchafalaya Restaurant.

3   The suspect in the sexual assault case is believed to be a local panhandler (City News Service, 2015).

2. PRIOR LITERATURE: A BRIEF REVIEW

42

The impact of crime on property values and flight to the suburbs has been the subject of a great deal of academic research, including work by Cullen and Levitt (1999), Glaeser and Sacerdote (1999), Burnham et al. (2004), Gibbons (2004), Linden and Rockoff (2008), Pope (2008), Ihlanfeldt and Mayock (2010), Bishop and Murphy (2011), Pope and Pope (2012), Congdon-Hohman (2013) and Caudill et al. (2015). In contrast, very little has been written about the impact of crime on business. Notable exceptions are the studies by Schwartz et al. (2003), Burnham et al. (2004), Greenbaum and Tita (2004), Abadie and Dermisi (2008) and Rosenthal and Ross (2010).

Using repeat sales and hedonic regression models on New York City data from 1988 to 1998, Schwartz et al. (2003) determine the extent to which lower crime rates led to the 1994 real estate boom. They find that about one-third of the post-1994 property price increase was due to falling crime rates. Similarly, using data on 318 U.S. counties from 1982 to 1997, Burnham et al. (2004) find that violent crime has a negative effect on economic growth in nearby suburbs, and a negative, but smaller effect on more distant suburbs. Greenbaum and Tita (2004) use zip code level data for five U.S. cities (from 1987 to 1994) to examine the impact of increases in crime on the creation, destruction and growth of business establishments. They find that increases in violence have the greatest impact on service-related establishments in low crime areas. Lastly, using building-level data from Chicago, Abadie and Dermisi (2008) investigate whether terrorism caused a decline in agglomeration economies in the post-9/11 period. They find a post-9/11 increase in vacancy rates in three of Chicago's largest buildings.

A more recent paper by Rosenthal and Ross (2010) examines the relationship between violent crime and business activity and, in particular, restaurant activity. In conducting their investigation of restaurant activity, these authors distinguish between high-end and low-end restaurants in order to learn more about how the relative share of business activity, measured as either employment share or number-of-establishments share, is affected by violent crime. To do so, Rosenthal and Ross (2010) construct data sets that capture monthly census tract crime statistics for Atlanta (over the period 2004–2008), Chicago (over the period 2007–2008), Houston (over the period 2005–2008), Indianapolis (over the period 2006–2008) and Seattle (over the period 2003–2007). These statistics are matched with zip code-level information on business activity for the third quarter of 2007 to form a single, pooled data set.

Rosenthal and Ross (2010) treat crime and business activity as endogenous, where business activity is affected by crime, while crime is influenced by the level of business activity. More specifically, Rosenthal and Ross (2010) point out that retail and high-end restaurants not only react to crime, they also contribute to local crime by presenting criminals with attractive targets, even in the presence of an enhanced police presence in retail and restaurants districts. They find that both low- and high-end restaurants are all more active in areas with higher local rates of violent crime, a result that could be due to the idea that violent crime is attracted to urban restaurant districts, which describes the *hot spot effect* that is discussed elsewhere in the criminology literature (e.g., Sherman et al., 1989; Weisburd and Mazerolle, 2000; Braga and Bond, 2008; Braga and Weisburd, 2010; Sherman et al., 2014). Given that restaurant patrons are more likely to be potential victims of crime, particularly at night, there may be *hot spots* for individual crimes created by traffic around restaurant locations. The finding that both low- and high-end restaurants are all more active in areas with higher local rates of violent crime could also be due to the notion that other sectors of the economy (e.g., residential) outbid low- and high-end restaurant entrepreneurs for safer locations in the urban environment (Rosenthal and Ross, 2010).

The work of Rosenthal and Ross (2010) is consistent with earlier work by Bull and Winter (1991), which points out that in some cases the published literature relating to business location supports the theory that business locations are selected to minimize costs, while in other cases it supports the theory that entrepreneurs select certain locations because of personal preferences. These authors find a negative correlation of two entrepreneurship measures to environmental factors that are usually considered to be desirable, including low crime (Bull and Winter, 1991). Relatedly, in an examination of crime and small and medium-sized enterprises (SMEs), Masurel (2004) finds that one-third of the entrepreneurs do not feel particularly safe at their current location. This sense, however, does not lead to any significant differences in the levels of investment in security measures, as the general investment in security is only about one percent of a firm's sales.[4] More recently, Lee and Cowling (2013) add that there is little evidence that firms in deprived areas actually perceive different problems than those that are perceived in more affluent places. Using a sample of SMEs in England, they find that firms in deprived areas perceive a lack of access to finance as the only significant barrier to success (Lee and Cowling, 2013). Lastly, taking the analysis a step further, Bullough et al. (2014) examine the effects of perceived danger, entrepreneurial self-efficacy and resilience on entrepreneurial intentions in wartime Afghanistan. They find that although perceived danger is negatively related to an individual's entrepreneurial intentions, it is less so for highly resilient individuals and for those who believe in their entrepreneurial abilities (Bullough et al., 2014).

Building upon the research by Rosenthal and Ross (2010) and other recent studies, the present study examines the relationship between restaurant openings and crime in a single city—Memphis, Tennessee—from 2009 to 2014, using information on the location of murders, rapes, burglaries and aggravated assaults, as well as that of newly-opened restaurants. This location-based information allows us to divide Memphis into parcels of any size we choose, and to count both the number of crimes and the number of new restaurants in each parcel during a given time period. Additionally, our approach limits the impact of the endogeneity issue present in Rosenthal and Ross (2010) by examining the impact of *past* crimes on *current* restaurant location choices. The details of our sample and empirical approach are provided in the next section of the study.

2.1. DATA AND MODEL

Our crime information is based on the Memphis Metropolitan Statistical Area (MSA), and is obtained from the Memphis Police Department's (MPD) Crime Report Map (Memphis Daily News 2015).[5] Through the Crime Report Map (CRM), we collected data on the time

---

4   Interestingly, using data from Belgian SMEs Janssen (2009) finds that a firm's environmental characteristics have very little influence on the growth of SMEs.

5   This Map can be found on the *Memphis Daily News'* website (see Memphis Daily News, 2015).

and location of several types of crimes, including murder, rape, burglary and aggravated assault, from 2009 to early 2015.[6] The data set used in this study also includes information on business licenses for new restaurants that were granted between January of 2010 and January of 2015.[7] This information includes the proposed location of the new restaurant. From the location information on crimes and restaurant openings, we construct parcels. We control the size and, hence, the number of these parcels. To develop of grid for the county, we determined the most northerly, southerly, easterly, and westerly crime in the data set. Based on the locations of these crimes we determined the size of the geographic area that would include all these crimes (and thus all crimes in our data set). We then choose the number of parcels to be constructed.[8] In one specification we construct 1,000,000 parcels based on a 1000 by 1000 grid covering the entire geographic area. The width of each parcel is approximately one thousandth of the distance between the most westerly crime and the most easterly crime in Shelby County. The length of each parcel is about one thousandth the distance between the most northerly crime and the most southerly crime in Shelby County. As Shelby County is approximately a 30 mile by 30 mile square, these parcels are about 160 feet by 160 feet. For each of these 1,000,000 constructed parcels we determine the total number of each of our four crime types per year and the total number of new restaurants opened each year. Lastly, given that our parcels are constructed and thus artificial, no other information on each parcel is available. In an effort to include some "neighborhood" fixed effects, we constructed "neighborhoods" by grouping each 100 by 100 group of parcels into constructed "neighborhoods" resulting in a set of one hundred neighborhood dummy variables. Including this set of dummy variables should help to average out differences in characteristics like population density, income, and education across neighborhoods.

Other specifications are also tested in this study, each employing a unique construction of parcel size. For example, we also construct 10,000 parcels based on a 100 by 100 grid covering the entire geographic area. The width of each parcel in this case is approximately one hundredth of the distance between the most westerly crime and the most easterly crime in Shelby County. The length of each parcel is about one hundredth the distance between the most northerly crime and the most southerly crime in Shelby County.[9] Two other specifications tested here construct 2500 and 400 parcels, respectively, based on 50 by 50 and 20 by 20 grids, respectively. The width of each of these parcels in is approximately one fiftieth and one twentieth the distance, respectively, between the most westerly crime and the most easterly crime in Shelby County. The length of each of these parcels is about one fiftieth and one twentieth the distance, respectively, between the most northerly crime and the most southerly crime in Shelby County.[10]

---

6   The MPD's rape counts include both statutory and forcible rape. Additionally, burglary includes all business burglary, while aggravated assault refers to a particularly severe assault, as defined by the MPD.

7   These data were provided by Shelby County Clerk officials. Shelby County is approximately a 30 mile by 30 mile square.

8   In our statistical exploration discussed below, we found that changing the parcel size had little impact on our empirical results.

9   As Shelby County is approximately a 30 mile by 30 mile square, these parcels are about 1600 feet by 1600 feet.

10   As Shelby County is approximately a 30 mile by 30 mile square, the parcels in these two cases are about 3200 feet by 3200 feet and about 7900 feet by 7900 feet.

Table 42-1. Summary statistics, OLS results, and elasticities: 1000 × 1000 grid

Variable	Summary Statistics	OLS models				
	Mean [Std Dev]	(1)	(2)	(3)	(4)	(5)
nassault	0.0109 [0.024]	3.224e−3* (15.58)	8.781e−3* (49.20) [0.127]			
nburglary	0.0067 [0.21]	0.019* (88.23)		0.020* (99.73) [0.178]		
nrape	0.0012 [0.04]	−0.001 (−1.12)			0.021* (19.91) [0.033]	
nmurder	0.00028 [0.02]	3.580e − 4 (0.15)				0.035* (14.91) [0.013]
nopenings	0.00075 [0.04]					
nobs		1,000,000	1,000,000	1,000,000	1,000,000	1,000,000
R^2		0.011	0.003	0.010	0.001	0.001

Notes: the numbers in parentheses beneath the negative binomial marginal effects are t-ratios, where * denotes .01 level of significance or better. The numbers in brackets under the marginal effects are elasticities calculated at the sample means.

Two features of these constructed data sets are important to note. First, we are able to control the size of the parcels constructed. Second, we examine the impact of past crime on restaurant location decisions. That is, we examine (1) restaurant location decisions in 2010 as a function of crimes in 2009, (2) restaurant location decisions in 2011 as a function of crimes over the 2009–2010 period, with this process carrying forward over time to an examination of (3) restaurant location decisions in 2014 modeled as a function of criminal activity in the area over the 2009–2013 period. Our empirical approach is similar to that in previous work by Rosenthal and Ross (2010). Our full model is given by,

$$nopenings = \beta_0 + \beta_1 nmurder + \beta_2 nrape + \beta_3 nburglary + \beta_4 nassault + \varepsilon, \qquad (1)$$

where nopenings represents the number of restaurant openings in a particular parcel in Memphis in a particular year. As indicated in (1) above, we estimated the regression model including the number of crimes by each crime type on the right-hand side. To explore the presence of multicollinearity in this unrestricted version, we also estimated versions of the model with each crime variable as the sole regressor.

3. ESTIMATION RESULTS

Summary statistics and estimation results for the 1000 by 1000 grid specification are given in TABLE 42-1. Column two of TABLE 42-1 presents the means and standard deviations for our sample. Unsurprisingly, the more violent crimes of rape and murder occur less frequently on average than assault and burglary.[11] Next, our empirical results are based on OLS estimates with models including a full set of neighborhood dummies. A preliminary OLS investigation, shown in column three of TABLE 42-1 wherein only the numbers of assaults and burglaries are significantly related to the number of restaurant openings, indicates that there is likely multicollinearity among our four crime types. Some empirical studies solve this problem by summing over crime types, which eliminates multicollinearity but yields an uninterpretable coefficient estimate. We have elected, instead, to focus on some parsimonious regression models.

The first simple regression model we consider contains *nassault* as the sole independent variable. These estimation results are given in the fourth column in TABLE 42-1. In this case, the R^2 is 0.003, which is about one third of that from the full model just discussed. The parameter estimate for *nassault* is positive (i.e., 8.781e − 3) and significant at the 99% level of confidence. The positive sign indicates that prior assaults are directly associated with new restaurant openings in a given parcel. In this case, the elasticity estimate of 0.127 suggests that a 10% increase in past assaults is associated with a 1.27% increase in restaurant openings in the current year.

The fifth column in TABLE 42-1 reports the results for a model containing only *nburglary* on the right-hand side. The R^2 is, at 0.010, approximately as large in this case and that from the unrestricted model in column three. The positive coefficient attached to *nburglary* (i.e., 0.020) is also significant at the 99% level of confidence. In this case, the elasticity estimate, 0.178, indicates that a 10% increase in past burglaries in a parcel is associated with a 1.78% increase in the number of new restaurants locating in the parcel in the current year.

The sixth column in TABLE 42-1 presents results for a restricted model containing only the number of rapes in a parcel, *nrape*, on the right-hand side. The R^2 (i.e., 0.001) is relatively small in this case, although the estimated coefficient for *nrape* is, unlike in the unrestricted model, both positive (i.e., 0.021) and significant (at the 99% level of confidence). The elasticity estimate (i.e., 0.033) indicates that a 10% increase in past rapes in a parcel results in only a 0.33% increase in the number of new restaurants opening in the current year. Lastly, the seventh column in TABLE 42-1 presents results for a simple regression model containing only the number of murders, *nmurder*, on the right-hand side. This model produces an R^2 of 0.001, while the coefficient estimate for *nmurder* is both positive (i.e., 0.035) and highly statistically significant. The elasticity estimate is 0.013, indicating that a 10% increase in the number of past murders in a parcel leads to a 0.13% increase in new restaurant openings in the next year.

---

11   It is also possible that crimes are vastly underreported. Our data set can only account for the crimes reported to or recorded by the Memphis Police Department.

Table 42-2. Summary statistics, OLS results, and elasticities: 100 × 100 grid

Variable	Summary Statistics	OLS models				
	Mean [Std Dev]	(1)	(2)	(3)	(4)	(5)
nassault	1.093 [3.26]	0.007* (3.60)	0.018* (10.81) [0.261]			
nburglary	0.666 [2.43]	0.046* (20.44)		0.048* (22.99) [0.424]		
nrape	0.125 [0.47]	0.008 (0.66)			0.072* (6.58) [0.119]	
nmurder	0.029 [0.19]	−0.085* (−3.14)				0.027 (1.05) [0.010]
nopenings	0.075 [0.50]					
nobs		10,000	10,000	10,000	10,000	10,000
R^2		0.085	0.045	0.082	0.038	0.034

Notes: the numbers in parentheses beneath the negative binomial marginal effects are t-ratios, where * denotes .01 level of significance or better. The numbers in brackets under the marginal effects are elasticities calculated at the sample means.

Summary statistics and estimation results for the 100 by 100 grid specification are given in TABLE 42-2. Column two of TABLE 42-2 presents the means and standard deviations for this sample. A preliminary OLS investigation, shown in column three of TABLE 42-2 wherein the numbers of assaults and burglaries are positively and significantly related to the number of restaurant openings, while the number of murders is *negatively* and significantly related to the number of restaurant openings, again indicates that there is likely multicollinearity among our four crime types. As with the 1000 by 1000 grid, we have elected to focus on some parsimonious regression models.

The first simple regression model we consider contains *nassault* as the sole independent variable. These estimation results are given in the fourth column in TABLE 42-2. The parameter estimate for *nassault* is again positive (i.e., 0.018) and significant at the 99% level of confidence. In this case, the elasticity estimate of 0.261 suggests that a 10% increase in past assaults is associated with a 2.61% increase in restaurant openings in the current year. The fifth column in TABLE 42-2 reports the results for a model containing only *nburglary* on the right-hand side. The positive coefficient attached to *nburglary* (i.e., 0.048) is also significant at the 99% level of confidence. In this case, the elasticity estimate, 0.424, indicates that a 10% increase in past burglaries in a parcel is associated with a 4.24% increase in the number of new restaurants locating in the parcel in the current year.

Next, the sixth column in TABLE 42-2 presents results for a restricted model containing only the number of rapes in a parcel, *nrape*, on the right-hand side. The estimated coefficient for *nrape* is, unlike in the unrestricted model, both positive (i.e., 0.072) and significant (at the 99% level of confidence). The elasticity estimate (i.e., 0.119) indicates that a 10% increase in past rapes in a parcel results in a 1.19% increase in the number of new restaurants opening in the current year. Lastly, the seventh column in TABLE 42-2 presents results for a simple regression model containing only the number of murders, *nmurder*, on the right-hand side. The coefficient estimate for *nmurder* is, unlike in the unrestricted model, positive (i.e., 0.027) yet statistically insignificant.[12]

Table 42-3. Summary statistics, OLS results, and elasticities: 50 × 50 grid

Variable	Summary Statistics	OLS models				
	Mean [Std Dev]	(1)	(2)	(3)	(4)	(5)
nassault	4.373 [9.58]	0.005 (1.30)	0.022* (7.85) [0.319]			
nburglary	2.663 [6.30]	0.069* (16.50)		0.071* (18.49) [0.627]		
nrape	0.498 [1.17]	−0.005 (−0.19)			0.115* (5.35) [0.190]	
nmurder	0.115 [0.45]	−0.071 (−1.27)				0.121† (2.32) [0.046]
nopenings	0.302 [1.11]					
nobs		2500	2500	2500	2500	2500
R^2		0.219	0.129	0.218	0.117	0.109

Notes: the numbers in parentheses beneath the negative binomial marginal effects are *t*-ratios, where *(†) denotes .01(.05) level of significance or better. The numbers in brackets under the marginal effects are elasticities calculated at the sample means.

---

12   The elasticity estimate is 0.010, indicating that a 10% increase in the number of past murders in a parcel leads to a 0.10% increase in new restaurant openings in the next year.

Summary statistics and estimation results for the 50 by 50 grid specification are given in TABLE 42-3. Column two of TABLE 42-3 presents the means and standard deviations for this sample. A preliminary OLS investigation, shown in column three of TABLE 42-3 wherein only the number of burglaries is positively and significantly related to the number of restaurant openings, again indicates that there is likely multicollinearity among our four crime types. As with the 1000 by 1000 grid, we have elected to focus on some parsimonious regression models. The first simple regression model we consider contains *nassault* as the sole independent variable. These estimation results are given in the fourth column in TABLE 42-3. The parameter estimate for *nassault* is, unlike in the unrestricted model, positive (i.e., 0.022) and significant at the 99% level of confidence. In this case, the elasticity estimate of 0.319 suggests that a 10% increase in past assaults is associated with a 3.19% increase in restaurant openings in the current year.

The fifth column in TABLE 42-3 reports the results for a model containing only *nburglary* on the right-hand side. The positive coefficient attached to *nburglary* (i.e., 0.071) is again significant at the 99% level of confidence. In this case, the elasticity estimate, 0.627, indicates that a 10% increase in past burglaries in a parcel is associated with a 6.27% increase in the number of new restaurants locating in the parcel in the current year. The sixth column in TABLE 42-3 presents results for a restricted model containing only the number of rapes in a parcel, *nrape*, on the right-hand side. The estimated coefficient for *nrape* is, unlike in the unrestricted model, both positive (i.e., 0.115) and significant (at the 99% level of confidence). The elasticity estimate (i.e., 0.190) indicates that a 10% increase in past rapes in a parcel results in a 1.90% increase in the number of new restaurants opening in the current year. Lastly, the seventh column in TABLE 42-3 presents results for a simple regression model containing only the number of murders, *nmurder*, on the right-hand side. The coefficient estimate for *nmurder* is, unlike in the unrestricted model, both positive (i.e., 0.121) and significant (at the 95% level of confidence). The elasticity estimate (i.e., 0.046) indicates that a 10% increase in past murders in a parcel results in a 0.46% increase in the number of new restaurants opening in the current year.

Table 42-4. Summary statistics, OLS results, and elasticities: 20 × 20 grid

Variable	Summary Statistics	OLS models				
	Mean [Std Dev]	(1)	(2)	(3)	(4)	(5)
nassault	27.333 [45.58]	−4.651e − 3 (−0.41)	0.018* (2.95) [0.261]			
nburglary	16.645 [26.17]	0.093* (7.77)		0.086* (8.57) [0.759]		
nrape	3.113 [4.93]	0.021 (0.25)			0.149* (2.84) [0.246]	

Variable	Summary Statistics	OLS models				
nmurder	0.718 [1.60]	−0.224 (−1.31)				0.013 (0.09) [0.005]
nopenings	1.885 [3.63]					
nobs		400	400	400	400	400
R^2		0.517	0.408	0.511	0.406	0.390

Notes: the numbers in parentheses beneath the negative binomial marginal effects are t-ratios, where * denotes .01 level of significance or better. The numbers in brackets under the marginal effects are elasticities calculated at the sample means.

Summary statistics and estimation results for the 20 by 20 grid specification are given in TABLE 42-4. Column two of TABLE 42-4 presents the means and standard deviations for this sample. A preliminary OLS investigation, shown in column three of TABLE 42-4 wherein only the number of burglaries is positively and significantly related to the number of restaurant openings, again indicates that there is likely multicollinearity among our four crime types. As with the 1000 by 1000 grid, we have again elected to focus on some parsimonious regression models. The first simple regression model we consider contains *nassault* as the sole independent variable. These estimation results are given in the fourth column in TABLE 42-4. The parameter estimate for *nassault* is, unlike in the unrestricted model, both positive (i.e., 0.018) and significant at the 99% level of confidence. In this case, the elasticity estimate of 0.261 suggests that a 10% increase in past assaults is associated with a 2.61% increase in restaurant openings in the current year.

The fifth column in TABLE 42-4 reports the results for a model containing only *nburglary* on the right-hand side. The positive coefficient attached to *nburglary* (i.e., 0.086) is again significant at the 99% level of confidence. In this case, the elasticity estimate, 0.759, indicates that a 10% increase in past burglaries in a parcel is associated with a 7.59% increase in the number of new restaurants locating in the parcel in the current year. Next, the sixth column in TABLE 42-4 presents results for a restricted model containing only the number of rapes in a parcel, *nrape*, on the right-hand side. The estimated coefficient for *nrape* is, unlike in the unrestricted model, positive (i.e., 0.149) and significant (at the 99% level of confidence). The elasticity estimate (i.e., 0.246) indicates that a 10% increase in past rapes in a parcel results in a 2.46% increase in the number of new restaurants opening in the current year. Lastly, the seventh column in TABLE 42-4 presents results for a simple regression model containing only the number of murders, *nmurder*, on the right-hand side. The coefficient estimate for *nmurder* is, unlike in the unrestricted model, both positive (i.e., 0.013) and significant (at the 95% level of confidence). The elasticity estimate (i.e., 0.005) indicates that a 10% increase in past murders in a parcel results in a 0.05% increase in the number of new restaurants opening in the current year.

As in the study by Rosenthal and Ross (2010), the results in TABLE 42-1 through TABLE 42-4 indicate a tendency to establish new restaurants in areas with higher local rates of violent crime, regardless of the type of violent crime. This result is supportive of the *hot spot effect* discussed in the criminology literature, in that restaurant districts are attractive targets for both restaurants and criminal activity, as customers and employees move to and from these locations both in large numbers and at night. The observed tendency is also consistent with Rosenthal and Ross' (2010) conclusion that residential and perhaps other sectors of the economy tend to outbid restaurant entrepreneurs in the market for relatively safe locations in the urban environment, as well as with earlier studies by Bull and Winter (1991) and Masurel (2004) regarding the inverse relationship between low crime and business location. As such, the empirical analysis in this study supports the conclusion in Rosenthal and Ross (2010) and earlier studies that community efforts to redevelop distressed portions of cities must first ensure that such areas are safe for both the workforce and potential consumers.

4. CONCLUSION

This paper fills a gap in research on business location and, in particular, restaurant location by estimating the impact of various violent crimes on restaurant location decisions in a single city, Memphis, Tennessee. Using location information on crimes and newly opened restaurants, we are able to match crimes and restaurants in parcels of any size. Consistent with previous literature, we limit the impact of the endogeneity problem of crime location/ business location by examining the number of new restaurants opening in a parcel in a year as a function of the number of *past* crimes in the parcel. In simple regression models, we examine the impact of the number of burglaries, assaults, rapes, and murders in each parcel of Memphis occurring from 2009–2013 on the number of restaurants opening in 2014. The results from various regression models indicate that each is positively related to the number of new restaurants in a parcel. This indicates that even with the crime problem, these locations provide sufficient benefits to make them attractive to restaurant entrepreneurs.

Questions for Discussion and Journaling

1. What are the economic conditions of Memphis that make the city a likely location for the analysis that Sloan, Caudill, and Mixon conduct? Are we a community of entrepreneurs? Why? How do the conditions that promote entrepreneurship also encourage crime?

2. What discourse community are Sloan, Caudill, and Mixon writing for? Determine a number of the conventions of the discourse community. Why might this community reject pathetic appeals?

3. Notice the document design and structure. What is the relationship between the charts and the discussion of the information presented in prose? What appeals do these make and why are both necessary?

REFERENCES

Abadie, A., Dermisi, S., 2008. Is terrorism eroding agglomeration economies in central business districts? Lessons from the Office Real Estate Market in Downtown Chicago. *J. Urban Econ.* 64, 451–463.

Bishop, K., Murphy, A., 2011. Estimating the willingness to pay to avoid violent crime: a dynamic approach. *Am. Econ. Rev.* 101, 625–629.

Braga, A.A., Bond, B.J., 2008. Policing crime and disorder hot spots: a randomized controlled trial. *Criminology* 46, 577–608.

Braga, A.A., Weisburd, D.L., 2010. Policing problem places: crime hot spots and effective prevention. *Oxford University Press*, Oxford, U.K.

Bull, I., Winter, F., 1991. Community differences in business births and business growths. *J. Bus. Ventur.* 6, 29–43.

Bullough, A., Renko, M., Myatt, T., 2014. Danger zone entrepreneurs: the importance of resilience and self-efficacy for entrepreneurial intentions. *Entrep.: Theory Pract.* 38, 473–499.

Burnham, R., Feinberg, R., Husted, T., 2004. Central city crime and suburban economic growth. *Appl. Econ.* 36, 917–922.

Caudill, S.B., Affuso, E., Yang, M., 2015. Registered sex offenders and house prices: an hedonic analysis. *Urban Stud.* 52, 2425–2440.

City News Service, 2015. $20,000 Reward Renewed to Find Palmdale Panhandler Wanted for Child Molestation. *Los Angeles Daily News.* 29 September. (www.dailynews.com/general-news/20150929/20000-reward-renewed-to-find-palmdale-panhandler-wanted-for-child-molestation).

Congdon-Hohman, J., 2013. The lasting effects of crime: the relationship of discovered methamphetamine laboratories and home values. *Reg. Sci. Urban Econ.* 43, 31–41.

Cullen, J., Levitt, S., 1999. Crime, urban flight, and the consequences for cities. *Rev. Econ. Stat.* 81, 159–169.

Gibbons, S., 2004. The costs of urban property crime. *Econ. J.* 114, 441–463.

Glaeser, E., Sacerdote, B., 1999. Why is there more crime in cities? *J. Polit. Econ.* 107, 225–258.

Greenbaum, R., Tita, G., 2004. The impact of violence surges on neighbourhood business activity. *Urban Stud.* 41, 2495–2514.

Ihlanfeldt, K., Mayock, T., 2010. Panel data estimates of the effects of different types of crime on housing prices. *Reg. Sci. Urban Econ.* 40, 161–172.

Janssen, F., 2009. Does the environment influence the employment growth of SMEs? *J. Small Bus. Entrep.* 22, 311–325.

Lee, N., Cowling, M., 2013. Place, sorting effects and barriers to enterprise in deprived areas: different problems or different firms? *Int. Small Bus. J.* 31, 914–937.

Linden, L., Rockoff., J., 2008. Estimates of the Impact of crime risk on property values from Megan's law. *Am. Econ. Rev.* 98, 1103–1127.

Masurel, E., 2004. SMEs and crime: evidence from the Netherlands. *Int. Small Bus. J.* 22, 197–205.

Memphis Daily News, 2015. Memphis Daily New Crime Report Map. February 20.

Moyer, J.W., 2015. Foodies Watch Out: Masked Men are Robbing Upscale New Orleans Restaurants. *The Washington Post.* 30 September 2015. (www.washingtonpost.com/news/morning-mix/wp/2015/09/30/foodies-watch-out-masked-men-are-robbing-upscale-new-orleans-restaurants/).

Parascandola, R., Sit, R., 2014. Three Masked Men Rob Upscale Restaurant in Flatiron District, Brandish Machete. *New York Daily News.* 13 September 2014. (www.nydailynews.com/new-york/nyc-crime/masked-men-rob-upscale-restaurant-flatiron-district-brandish-machete-article-1.1938349).

Pope, D., Pope, J., 2012. Crime and property values: evidence from the 1990s crime drop. *Reg. Sci. Urban Econ.* 42, 177–188.

Pope, J., 2008. Fear of crime and housing prices: household reactions to sex offender registries. *J. Urban Econ.* 64, 601–614.

Rosenthal, S., Ross, A., 2010. Violent crime, entrepreneurship, and cities. *J. Urban Econ.* 67, 135–149.

Schwartz, A.E., Susin, S., Voicu, I., 2003. Has falling crime driven New York City's real estate boom? *J. Hous. Res.* 14, 101–135.

Sherman, L.W., Gartin, P.R., Buerger, M.E., 1989. Hot spots of predatory crime: routine activities and the criminology of place. *Criminology* 27, 27–56.

Sherman, L.W., Williams, S., Ariel, B., Strang, L.R., Wain, N., Slothower, M., Norton, A., 2014. An integrated theory of hot spots patrol strategy: implementing prevention by scaling up and feeding back. *Criminol. Penol.* 30, 95–122.

Swann, S., 2015. Acropolis Manager Discusses Criminal Activity near Restaurant. *The Daily Orange.* 8 2015.September. (http://sports.dailyorange.com/2015/09/acropolis-manager-discusses-criminal-activity-near-store/).

Weisburd, D., Mazerolle, L.G., 2000. Crime and disorder in drug hot spots: implications for theory and practice in policing. *Police Q,* 3, 331–349.

Wells, C.K., 2015. Uptown Restaurant Patois, Customers Robbed at Gunpoint during Dinner. *The Times-Picayune.* 21 August 2015. (www.nola.com/crime/index.ssf/2015/08/patois_robbed_gunpoint_uptown.html).